Critical Practice from Voltaire to Foucault, Eagleton, and Beyond

Studies in Critical Social Sciences Book Series

Haymarket Books is proud to be working with Brill Academic Publishers (www.brill.nl) to republish the *Studies in Critical Social Sciences* book series in paperback editions. This peer-reviewed book series offers insights into our current reality by exploring the content and consequences of power relationships under capitalism, and by considering the spaces of opposition and resistance to these changes that have been defining our new age. Our full catalog of *SCSS* volumes can be viewed at www.haymarketbooks.org/category/scss-series.

Critical Practice from Voltaire to Foucault, Eagleton, and Beyond

Contested Perspectives

John E. O'Brien

Haymarket Books
Chicago, IL

First published in 2014 by Brill Academic Publishers, The Netherlands.

Published in paperback in 2014 by
Haymarket Books
P.O. Box 180165
Chicago, IL 60618
773-583-7884
www.haymarketbooks.org

ISBN: 978-1-60846-421-0

Trade distribution:
In the U.S. through Consortium Book Sales, www.cbsd.com
In the UK, Turnaround Publisher Services, www.turnaround-psl.com
In all other countries by Publishers Group Worldwide, www.pgw.com

Cover design by Ragina Johnson.

This book was published with the generous support of Lannan Foundation and the Wallace Action Fund.

Printed in Canada by union labor.

10 9 8 7 6 5 4 3 2 1

Library of Congress Cataloging-in-Publication Data is available.

CONTENTS

ACKNOWLEDGMENTS

Given the intricate nature of the project, I must express my appreciation to the editor of *Critical Sociology* and this book series *Studies in Critical Social Sciences*, David Fasenfest, for his encouragement and support during the two years needed to finish the research and draft this manuscript.

It is also with considerable gratitude that I acknowledge the publishers of the works from which citations are taken to illustrate the critical position of those featured in the case studies; publishers who continue to put before the public writings of this kind so as to keep the critical spirit alive.

From well before the plan for this study was finalized, through to its end, I much appreciated both the moral backing and the technical suggestions from Dennis Broe, who was always willing to interrupt his own reading and writing to offer me council.

Throughout, without the support of my wife, Josiane Martin O'Brien, there would have been no way to assure the balance needed to ride the fine edge on the frontier between outrage and acceptance that is the necessary dialectic fuel of engaged social philosophy.

Finally, I must thank Lesley Kenny for invaluable suggestions and expert help in preparing the manuscript.

Other than the material attached in the Appendix, none of this text has been previously presented in any form.

PREFACE

This study of critical practice is placed under the figure of ambiguity: ambiguity defines the lives of the six fascinating individuals at the center of my in-depth case material—Voltaire, Friedrich Schiller, Michel Foucault, Jean Baudrillard, Terry Eagleton and Hayden White—as well as the content to be drawn from their diverse and influential writings and the method of research used to investigate the soundness and direction of the result. This palpable presence of the nebulous and ambivalent closes all doors to exactitude, precludes positive determinism, excises the casually precise from the range of possibility. Like the role of the indeterminate dark matter for the physical universe, without ambiguity as background there would be nothing for critics to study, no openings toward other futures to propose. As with the formless voice of the Greek chorus for its theater, by imposing a presence of form on the shifting contours of experience it is the mysterious that makes possible the presentation and appreciation of the actual.

A double dance of ambiguity enters into cultural criticism as objective, and the historical-materialist method as mode of investigation. Since exploring this objective with that method is the purpose of this study, waves of ambiguity can be expected to splash about these pages with no intrinsic strain toward modulation.

Criticism involves selecting an historical object of interest, then describing its sources of generation, presence in society and future tendencies; selectively considered in reference to some valuing criteria according to which a judgment is drawn about its justice, necessity and possibility for change. Historical objects of major public interest (a political regime, economic mode of production, religious institution, educational structure, etc.) are always of vague contours, which is why their identity remains ambiguous no matter what the effort at precision. The same hesitant quality pertains to the valuing criteria used to assess institutional quality and potential. Since judgments of the desirability of social conditions, such as general well-being or the best interests of humanity, are inherently subjective, the outcome of critique is always open to further critique.

This investigation of the critical project in general, via the historical-materialist (H-M) method in particular, will display the seemingly occult, often attacking, occasionally condemning, nature of censorship against public leaders and actions, which occurs frequently when a determined critic speaks out. Reliance on the force of conviction by critics in action is evidence of the inherently proximate, iterative workings of cultural criticism, which forces the critic to deal with history twice and each time ambiguously: first with the history of the present, looking at the layering and contemporary contextuality of the social practice or ordering under scrutiny; and second, with history as—well, something about the past, intruding in the present as a call for future direction, which fuels or activates social action as society.

As if further complexity were needed, this is a meta-critical examination of the cases under study. Deploying the H-M method to study the critical work of others requires that I, as author, apply my own standards of judgment, which only opens the door to further perplexity.

To keep the work anchored as much as possible in givens that predate my writing, these case studies focus, with particular acuity, on those subjects as real human beings, engaged with determined conviction in their local conditions and times. Each is framed, however, by a formally argued commentary, intended to draw out the general lines of critique as passion and product, as well as the workings of the historical-materialist method as research technique.

In keeping with the uniqueness of such work by high quality critics, each of the six central chapters is composed as a free-standing narrative—telling a story all its own. To the extent that this project is successful, in spite of the often emotionally agitating aspects of the critiques leveled at the way the West now lives, the effect of the whole is neither comic nor tragic, but aesthetic in nature; an intensively human exercise, demonstrating the degree to which critical practice is a work of art.

While using copious citations to assure that the critics to be studied have plenty of opportunity to speak for themselves, and while attempting to approach this very serious problem with a certain lightness, many notes and references are nonetheless attached, to show the historical material that lies behind their work and that which informs ours. Consequently, as attested to by the extensive bibliography of works cited and notes attached to this text, one might almost believe that the entire wealth of the past two-and-one-half centuries of intellectual activity contributes to the foundation of western critical practice as we conceive of it; which, in a way, it does.

Regarding my own historical roots, I would like to acknowledge appreciation for the librarian in the small town where I was raised, who, in spite of my being under-age at the beginning (ten years old), allowed me access to the adult section anyway, providing me with my first experience of freedom. With unsupervised access to all those books, I learned the first truth of the library: the frontiers of learning are undefined.

Finally, while being respected by the specialists is always important to an author, a certain priority in this writing has been given to potential readers who are not necessarily specialists. In 1936, Edmund Husserl wrote a text focusing on the cultural crisis of that time, which he identified, effectively, as due to the exhaustion of the mode of consciousness and action which characterized what he labeled with the generic reference, 'European Man'. The problem that he then detected implicitly is the explicit point of our critique now: the need for a new condition of general consciousness and action on the part of those who might one day lead the West out of its self-imposed limitations, based on a reconfigured optic of truth, being and interests.

At the moment—and even if often only at the intellectual margins, there is being produced in Europe, the U.S. and elsewhere, a crop of individuals who hold the potential for carrying forward a transition into a different future, as re-foundation for western civilization. Without organization or unitary identification, these individuals are characterized by common experience: they are multi-lingual, have studied and been educated in more than one country, are well traveled, have been exposed to variation in ways of life, religion and basis of belief; are conscious of the limitations of conventional politics, of unbounded religiosity, of unrestrained capitalism, of mindless consumerism; of a society where aggressivity is mistaken for competence, and feigned indifference used as cover for bigotry. Refusing complicity with the powers that are, yet far from revolutionaries with dynamite in their backpacks, they are sprinkled around the world from New York to New Delhi, from Paris to Tokyo. As inspiration for the potential energy of this new category of global individual, ready to work for a way beyond the current crisis of unchecked authority and unrealized community, it is for this group that this book is intended, as it concerns the future for which they will be responsible.

OVERVIEW

This is not a history of criticism but a methodological reading of its practice, constituted around in-depth case studies of six individuals who found themselves in that role. Selected because of the timing and method of their work and the reach of their influence, in order of appearance here, they are: François-Marie Arouet Voltaire (1694–1778); Friedrich Schiller (1759–1805); Michel Foucault (1926–1984); Jean Baudrillard (1929–2007); Terry Eagleton (1943–); and Hayden White (1928-).

Constituting the core of this volume, each of the case studies concerns an individual in a particular historical situation, working with the material at hand, confronting social order and culture with the available tools of his times, then putting the result out as literature. There will be very little comparison between them until the end (Chapter Eight), when I speculate on the essential qualities of the object and method of critical practice and their relation to social-political change.

In addition to demonstrating their different styles of attack, I chose my subjects both to highlight the importance of a major shift in method during the 19th century and to deepen discussion of the factors associated with how the choice of object and method of attack mediates the political impact of critique. That modification in the methodological strategy of critique will be particularly evident when comparing the work between the first and second pairs of critics in our study. Additionally, the last two cases were chosen to provide the basis for assessment of the current state of critique at the opening of the 21st century, allowing speculation as to the future for this vital intellectual undertaking.

Providing counsel for those who would dare to be critically engaged, this case material is also developed around a pedagogical objective: to demonstrate the relentless, disciplined, highly personal determination needed by anyone who undertakes serious cultural criticism.

The Method of Critique

Although not formally harbored within any academic discipline, this study will nonetheless provide readers with practical examples of what C. Wright Mills labeled "the sociological imagination" in action (Mills 1959); or what Michael Burawoy refers to as "public sociology" in practice

(Burawoy 2005a). In keeping with their vision of engaged scholarship, the case studies at the heart of this book provide a set of lessons in the conduct of critical study of society exemplified by the situated history, biography and critical work of those six fascinating individuals.[1]

Beginning the case studies with personalities from the eighteenth century, it is evident that this project is not offered as test, or in support of any particular contemporary social theorist or commentator. Rather, the same socio-political circumstances that occasioned the work of others such as Mills and Burawoy, largely explains the intellectual intention behind this volume. That is not to say that this study is without stimulation from the work of others and I have a responsibility to make that known.

Historical Roots of this Study

This study is situated in the wake of the project initiated by Max Horkheimer in the 1930s in Germany, which gave rise to what has been informally labeled since the 1950s as the Frankfurt School (FS) of critical theory. Like thousands of others I was taken by his insightful 1937 essay, *Critical and Traditional Theory*, and what came to be treated as its elaboration, the *Dialectic of Enlightenment* (2001/1944), which he composed in collaboration with Theodor Adorno. This was followed over the years by many other contributions associated with or influenced by that movement, including those by Walter Benjamin (Benjamin 1934; 1936; 1940), Herbert Marcuse (Marcuse 1991/1964), and, though somewhat indirectly, but no less influentially, Georg Lukács (Lukács 2010/1911; 1968/1916; 1990/1919). From there, the field of reading opened widely.[2]

Of the original group drawn into that movement by Horkheimer, the most fascinating for me continues to be Theodor Adorno; the Adorno

---

[1] C. Wright Mills: *The Sociological Imagination*, (1959), following by a few years, *The Power Elite*, 1956. For a discussion of the recent intensification of interest in this project see, Stanley Aronowitz, "A Mills Revival?" (2003). In his 2005 Presidential Address before the American Sociological Society, Michael Burawoy urged his colleagues to make more space for the serious pursuit of Public Sociology, contrasted with the ivory tower form of social research that is habitually favored. The importance of Mills as inspiration was attested to some years earlier by Burawoy in his 1991 work: *Ethnography Unbound*.

[2] Throughout this book, in my citations, I have indicated first the date of the publication to which I refer, and after the diagonal, the year of original publication. While this may make for a more cumbersome citation, the accuracy of listing only the more recent publication date can serve to (unintentionally) mask the historical place of the text and thus where it sits chronologically in conversation with the other texts. Unless otherwise indicated, all translations from French are mine.

whose devastating dialectical churnings provide the counterpoint resonance to the virtuosity of Horkheimer's social philosophy; the Adorno who delivered the devastating, if apparently well intended critique, of the early plan for Benjamin's Paris oriented Arcades Project (Adorno 1935); the Adorno—lover of music, who delivered an outrageously irreverent critique of Jazz (in *Prisms* 1995a/1955); the incensed Adorno who directed the revealing study of the *Authoritarian Personality* (1950); the Adorno as author of the short collection of dialectically diabolic cultural critical aphorisms, *Minima and Moralia: Reflections from Damaged Life* (1951); and finally, the Adorno who died trying to specify an *Aesthetic Theory* (1995b/1970), as demonstration that society might hang together due to the intrinsic harmonies of humanity, in spite of the technical discords and exhausted rationality of modernity.

After some years of attention to questions stimulated by the Frankfurt School movement and the Marx-Engels project that initially charged its batteries, I began to wonder just why there was so little apparent political effect in the West from those very determined writings of the likes of Marx and Horkheimer, or others stretching from Nietzsche and Sartre, to Bourdieu and Barthes. Beyond furnishing a rather dark form of ironic humor, it was as if social criticism was without consequence. Adorno's restlessness about this possibility took a truly ominous form. As he put it, in a 1951 essay, "Cultural Criticism and Society":

> Cultural Criticism shares the blindness of its object. It is incapable of allowing the recognition of its frailty to arise, a frailty set in the division of mental and physical work. No society which contradicts its very notion—that of humankind—can have full consciousness of itself. (1995a/1955: 27)

Was this a sign that we had witnessed the disestablishment of cultural critique? Is it possible that Fukuyama (1992) was right: that we have come to the *End of History*? With global hegemonic capitalism in action, supported by the many user-unfriendly domestic institutions needed to assure it, is the current heteroclite assemblage of unmanageable western nations now leading the charge, the best that might be for humankind?

Institutional History and Cultural Criticism

Of course there have been changes over the years. For centuries before the French Revolution, western people were trapped by ecclesiastic-aristocratic-feudalism. Then, following a phase of intense critical activity during the mid-1700s (some of which I examine in the first two case studies), a revolutionary rupture occurred in European governance. However, by the mid-1800s, the West proved capable of preserving its elitist fundamentals. By changing only the costume of the aristocratic oligarchs, the momentary vacancy at the top of the western social structure, created by revolutionary enthusiasm, was rapidly filled by a new genre of elite consisting mostly of the money-centered bourgeoisie. This was accompanied by new institutions even more diverse and subtle in their manner of extending, reinforcing and sustaining widespread domination in favor of privilege for just a few. How are we to explain this seemingly eternal return in the enlightenment west to a society of façades, sold to the people as if just, equal and sincere?

Not everyone was pleased with those post-revolutionary developments, most famously, Marx. More than a century and a half ago, he confected the intellectual armament for a new frontal attack on the institutionally unacceptable: not directly placing in his sights the structures of western government as mode of societal organization, but focusing rather on the power of capital as economic motor for the technical production of society. While his work stirred up a certain amount of additional revolutionary fervor elsewhere, it yielded little modification in the core of the West.

Some generations later, in the 1930s, breathing new life into the Marx project, the critical theory movement was put into action under the impetus of Horkheimer in Frankfurt. Based on momentum gained during the next two decades, a new wave of critical ambition surfaced, such that by the second half of the 20th century, the flurry of critics and critical works in Europe reached a veritable crescendo.

So much critical effort, so little change: why? Rather than continuing to raise questions about the *bien-fondé* of the Marx project because of the failure of the capital powered system to implode due to its internal contradictions, perhaps the problem had shifted; that something unintended about the playing out of the cultural criticism movement itself had fostered stasis, indifference and complacency rather than mobilization and political foment.

To better explain the limited effect of critical work, attention was then shifted from the content of critique by this or that specialist to the method used for its conduct. Perhaps what occurred was less mysterious than might at first appear. Under the royalist regimes and through the mid-nineteenth century, power was housed in individuals; to shift the power, one might attempt to dislodge key actors. Next, following a hesitant form of political compromise, western regimes moved to parliamentary structures, thus deconcentrating power, at least in principle, in the name of representative democracy. Yet the basic problem continued: the few benefited handsomely from the effort of the many that benefited little.

Under those changed conditions, the critical challenge had become much more complicated. A practical expression of this new form of liberal, democratic regime was the generation of a sophisticated lattice of state institutions. While this was sold to westerners as if for popular advantage, what occurred in crucial sectors of public activity, particularly economic, was promulgation of an elaborate institutional shield behind which the power-dominating interests might hide.

Since social injustice continued, given that new institutional environment, it was necessary to develop a new method by which to penetrate this institutional shell so as to expose the underlying forces at work that could explain the persistence, power and self-propelling quality of institutionally embedded social processes. It was this very service that was rendered by the Marx project, based, in my judgment, on the core of his innovation, which was the development of the historical-materialist method of critical study.

As we will see from the first two case studies, during the eighteenth century, under conditions that were propitious for confronting the ancient royalist regime, a 'name calling' form of critical strategy proved effective. Then after the revolutionary decades, with the shift to new, more institutionally complex regimes, a new method, more sophisticated, more trenchant and historically sensitive was needed; this was provided during the nineteenth century thanks to Marx. And then, early in the twentieth century—well, there was Horkheimer, the Frankfurt School and the rest, whose work aimed to resuscitate this method which had already gone a bit moribund.

Yet something went wrong: twentieth century critics seemed appropriately armed to take on the institutional apparatus that gave rise to the injustice and ineffectiveness which plague western societies, and busy they were. Yet the result was political apathy. Had the critics lost track of the essential problem, becoming sidetracked with what amounts to secondary issues? Might the following common-place adage capture metaphorically the problem of cultural criticism after WWII: when up to one's ears in alligators, it is difficult to recall that the problem is to drain the swamp?

So, what about the swamp?

Critical Theory in Question

The above chain of reasoning, partly appreciated in advance, fully understood only in hindsight, guided this study. To capture those dynamics of method, timing and effect of critique, the cases were chosen by selecting three pairs of subjects who worked under three different socio-historical conditions. First, backing up to the pre-revolutionary age of the eighteenth century when modern critical activity was born, Voltaire and Schiller were selected as case-study candidates. Next, in order to study the result of the shift in method of criticism during the nineteenth century as fueled by the Marx project and reenergized by the Frankfurt School moment, I jumped ahead to the mid-twentieth century, and drew in Foucault and Baudrillard.

Finally, I identified the last two cases, Terry Eagleton and Hayden White, whose energetic and productive critical work, while also demonstrating the use of the H-M method, comes toward the end of what Hobsbawm (1994) ironically labeled, "the short 20th century." This last pair represents critique less influenced by the reactionary straight-jacket that had rendered hesitant even the more daring critics during the middle years of the querulous last century. By including the work of these two still-living intellectuals, it was hoped that the debate about alternative possible futures for the West might be intensified.[3]

Once having set to work on these studies, it became clear that even if the methodological mainspring for contemporary critique proved sufficiently robust, the process was being somehow misapplied. This brought me to the matter of content and suddenly I found myself formulating a critique of the critical theory itself. Was it possible that the Frankfurt School movement had lost its rudder, swamped by some form of over-rational determination?

Midway through this writing, fortune would have it that I spotted a small and unrecognized volume by Horkheimer in a Paris bookstore: a 1930 French translation, of *Origins of The Bourgeois Philosophy of History,* which had been available in Paris for a generation. While the book is charged with vital insights, I was amazed to discover that nearly everyone who dealt with critical theory seemed to have overlooked it to such an

[3] Contemporary historian Eric Hobsbawm was unrelentingly and thus controversially faithful to the socialist possibility; the last book in his remarkably long list of publications, published just before he died (2012) was: *How to Change the World: Tales of Marx and Marxism* (2011).

extent that it suffered the ultimate shame of authorship: it had never been translated into English.

Thus, the problematic broadened to include not just the question of method of critique, but in a certain way, returned to the problem of the object of critique. As I will develop in Chapter One, I conclude that the social-change potential of the historical-materialist digging recommended by Horkheimer in his universally recognized 1937 text (*Traditional and Critical Theory*) has been under-realized because of a misapprehension of the importance of the object of critique (*The Bourgeois Philosophy of History*) as he identified in this overlooked 1930 essay.

Consistent with the epistemological claim that the {method and object}[4] of research are related dialectically, I advance the hypothesis that by misappropriating its object, the method of critique lost much of its character, as critical attention drifted in the direction of alienation as displaced consciousness or rationality, thereby sapping the political acumen needed to formulate and mobilize support favoring more activist institutional alternatives for deranged social practices.

Historical-Materialist Method

Independent of its particular target or the value attached to the findings, as the case studies will reveal, the power of cultural criticism is now due largely to the widespread application of the historical-materialist method; the exceptional utility of which owes to the way that its deployment transforms questions about the history of social forms from interpretive curiosity into practical actual force. Developed by Marx in the nineteenth century, and assuming the target is well chosen, the broad use of that method harbors revolutionary consequences both intellectually and politically (Marx 1867, 1885, 1894, 1975; Marx and Engels 1845).

The advantage of this method is that its use provides an original way to appreciate the force of the past in forming structures of action in the present, as guide for the future. Being decidedly dialectic, with its use, rather than as a reactionary anchor, history arrives as a constituent of the living expression of the present. This demonstrates how the realism of historical

[4] Bracketed terms indicate what are treated in this text as dialectic conceptual couplets.

idealism incubates the contemporary actualization of the material relations, bound together, but not unchangeably, as a culture system.[5]

Using accounts of the past as a trampoline into the present, to anticipate future movement, the method forecloses the necessity of rigid historical determinism and thus leaves open the possibility of radical rupture.[6] With it, history is seen to enter twice into social practices: as a state-variable for a cultural system, implicated in its present as oriented by a past and as orientation toward a certain future; and as a trace of the movement of that system, as a set of collateral and multilayer events, on a world-line through time.

Critical practice directs attention to that dual dialectic of living systems, of which a society is the most significant form, exploring what might be otherwise about the historical object of interest and with what potential effects; exposing the forces beneath cultural history as ensconced in and exuded by the collective effort of a people, generating channels and pathways, as constraint and possibility.

Who Are Critical Practitioners?

Critical practice evades generic description. As opposition to everyday politics, it dates from Socrates. More recently, but still five hundred years ago, in the aftermath of the Italian Renaissance, outspoken consternation about the royalist ecclesiastic order that imposed a life without liberty on the general population took on particular importance.[7] Due to a new view of humanity, evaluation of social practices shifted. Based on ideas concerning individual potential and the common good, this pushed to the

[5] Time binding was first described in a paper by the individual who later established the Institute of General Semantics (Korzybski 1924). The notion was picked and used in a modified manner by a number of others including E.T. Hall (1959), and Gregory Bateson (1972).

[6] Avoiding historicism is not easy in this form of study. I accept the commonplace view that while history does not plot, people do; still, the flow of events can not be simply reduced to expression of human will, because the human plot is shaped or conditioned by circumstances, including historical frames and possibilities. For a solid examination of the way that history is treated in the West, see Charles Tilly's "Three Visions of History and Theory," (2007).

[7] A precursor to contemporary cultural criticism was Thomas More with his *Utopia* (1988). Even if only a mythic allegory, the work put him at odds with his former close fiend, Henry VIII concerning civic justice; More's portrayal of a socialist alternative to the then dominant despotic royalist regime proved too much for the Monarch, who signaled his displeasure by having More beheaded.

forefront the need to amplify the critical call for general liberation from institutional repression.[8]

By that shift toward liberation in the interests of justice and freedom, the expression of modern cultural criticism arose hand in hand with that of political freedom. Liberation as continuous consequence of democracy seems automatic, but it is not. This study is aimed at better understanding the resistance to that tandem expression and the means for its achievement.

If our concern is with the politics of criticism, this is not to suggest that all criticism has politics as its objective. Most genre criticism (of art, literature, music, cinema, etc.) is aimed at decoration of the status quo and not its transformation. Nonetheless, every critical project undertaken in public carries political potential. Each is an engagement based on the expression of judgment regarding immediate conditions, putting in question some aspect of social convention.

Even if this methodological study is not directly associated with a particular school of thought, I must still use someone's language or else no one will understand what follows. For that I fall back on European social sciences. Since, in the ears of Anglo-Americans, that foreign idiom comes across as social-philosophy, a brief explanation is in order about its usage.

Social philosophy identifies a conjoint interest in the truth of the concept (usually liberty in the largest sense) and the means of putting that into practice. Classic names associated with this include: Jean-Jacques Rousseau, Karl Marx and John Dewey. In France, since the frontiers between history, sociology and philosophy are not well defined, this label might well pertain to an enormous share of all work in the social sciences and humanities. While of the above named three only Dewey ever formally annexed this label to his work, significantly for our purpose, at the University of Frankfurt in 1927, Max Horkheimer was named to fill the first chair in social-philosophy ever created in Germany.

---

8 On the Renaissance, see Jacob Burckhardt (1818–1897), *The Civilization of the Renaissance in Italy*, (1990/1860). Beyond only politics, stressing the value of art as aesthetic entry into history, Burckhardt was the first to propose a cultural history, to explain social dynamics by focusing on a particular conjunction of time, place and people. With that new appreciation of the power of ideas came the development of ideologies, including such enduring 'isms' as republicanism, communitarianism, liberalism and Machiavellianism. An additional 'ism' of note which developed then and continues to explain the enduring force of the Renaissance as culture image in Europe, is civic humanism, as ideological opposition to liberalism or rationalized acquisitive individualism which today can be seen as a defining tension of late modernity. For more on this theme see Athanasios Moulakis, "Civic Humanism," *Stanford Encyclopedia of Philosophy* (Winter 2011).

As for that content, since social action is ever evolving, its intimate connection with 'truth' as cultural production, fits well with the observation by Einstein, that understanding what new theories mean (of the sort he proposed) often requires accepting that 'concepts can change.'[9] This is because the truth of social action, of which new ideas are a form, is both historically conditioned and a constituent of those conditions. This raises problems of a dialectical nature which explains why the optimum approach for cultural criticism as social-philosophical project is the historical-materialist method.

One practical aspect of Horkheimer's intellectual strategy (in its own way as revolutionary as was Einstein's) was his insistence on the interdisciplinary nature of critical research. Discussing that in connection with what he takes to be the core of critical theory, which "very much designates a certain *type* of theory and not *a* particular theory," the French philosophy professor Durand-Gasselin observes that a crucial quality of critical theory has been its "character at once postmetaphysic, interdisciplinary and articulated in empirical research." Such study is based not just on the logical relations among concepts, but on persistent study of social conditions from an interdisciplinary angle, which, citing Horkheimer, "can only be actualized by constructions that refuse at least to a certain degree the treating of this or that knowledge base or theory as sacred, as is the case in association with 'traditional theories'" (Durand-Gasselin 2012: 8).[10]

Even if not overtly campaigning for the elimination of disciplinary identities in the social sciences, as a recognized leader in U.S. sociology, Michael Burawoy expresses a remarkably similar continental intellectual attitude about critical studies. But then he ought to, having started life in Europe, passed his early studies in England (still his current citizenship), before migrating to the U.S. where he earned his advanced degrees before landing his professorship at Berkeley. Along the way, he worked and conducted research in Europe and Africa, capping his career when elected

---

[9] Einstein developed this position concerning conceptual relativity in response to the incessant questions he received about what it meant to say that the maximum velocity of radiation (light) is fixed, and that the contours of any position of space are defined flexibly by what occurs within it. For a sample of his non-technical writings, see Albert Einstein: *Physique, Philosophie Politique* (2002).

[10] Jean-Marc Durand-Gasselin's newly published history of the *L'École de Francfort* (2012), which does include passing attention to Horkheimer's 1930 text, is based on a somewhat different reading of that movement than provided in the current standard reference by Jay (1996): *The Dialectical Imagination: A History of the Frankfurt School and the Institute of Social Research, 1923–1950.*

President of the American Sociological Association (ASA) in 2004, and from there to the post he currently fills as President of the International Sociological Association.

Burawoy generated a bit of a stir when he used the occasion of his Presidential Address for the ASA to promote "Public Sociology" as an important yet generally undervalued domain of intellectual practice. While some critics came forward to disqualify that proposition in favor of traditional theoretical forms of academic study, others questioned whether Burawoy's project was radical enough. A striking example in the latter category was Stanley Aronowitz, from the Graduate Center, City University of New York, who took Burawoy to task for failing to champion a more elaborated core of philosophical writings and more historically anchored conceptual issues.[11]

Writing in *Critical Sociology*, Aronowitz (2005) expressed a position that fits amazingly well with what Durand-Gasselin identified as Horkheimer's ambitions concerning critical theory as social-philosophical project. The way he put this was:

> My main concern with Burawoy's call [for a Public Sociology] is that I believe the human sciences need desperately to blur, if not abandon their disciplinary boundaries; [becoming] willing to examine the shifting sands under their feet... In fact, intellectually the main problem with American sociology is that it has abandoned philosophy... . (Aronowitz 2005: 336)[12]

On the European side of the Atlantic, I call attention to another individual who shares with Burawoy and Aronowitz this same sense of transdisciplinary urgency: the French intellectual, Philippe Corcuff, who identifies himself variously as sociologist, political sociologist and social-philosopher. Strongly influenced by Pierre Bourdieu, Michel Foucault and Ludwig Wittgenstein, Corcuff also holds in high esteem his former

---

11 Burawoy's intellectual project is tightly woven with his history, and his times. He went out of his way to reveal the details of this in a truly anomalous intellectual autobiography, "Antinomian Marxist," (Burawoy 2005b). Composed just as he was being elected President of the American Sociological Association, there he not only deals in a forthright fashion with the particular brand of neo-Marxism that he favors, but describes the difficulty of maintaining a non-dogmatic position in the critical social sciences, when all the time aware of the horrid contradictions of, and necessity for, fundamental modification in current social conditions. His 2004 Presidential Address, "For Public Sociology," was published the following year in the *American Sociological Review*, (2005c). His remarks in the debate with Aronowitz were published as, "The Critical Turn to Public Sociology," (2005a).

12 See Stanley Aronowitz, "Comments on Michael Burawoy's 'The Critical Turn to Public Sociology'" (2005). More original in inspiration and directly related to our study of critical method is his essay, "A Mills Revival?" (2003).

teacher, Luc Boltanski, whose work is discussed at some length in Chapter One. Corcuff is interested in social action as language-game, demonstrating his sympathies for American-style ethnomethodology. In a recent book about critical intellectual work in France, drawing principally on work previously published over the last twenty years, Corcuff (2012) provides a careful assessment of the social criticism and its potential.[13]

In keeping with the European tradition of history of sociological thought, the interrogations of Burawoy, Corcuff and Aronowitz exemplify the study of social practices as if viewed through an intellectual kaleidoscope in which the shifting constituents of its objective consist of concepts drawn from the spectrum of disciplines in the social sciences and the humanities. While surely not pleasing everyone, this tendency in the direction of eclecticism is needed to address the range of factors associated with the human condition, from action to consciousness, from individual autonomy to collective restraint, from freedom to responsibility.

Historical-Materialist Invasion

In the wake of the nineteenth century work by Marx, the historical-materialist method gradually invaded studies in the social sciences and humanities to such an extent that today, even critics who are offended by the political end that Marx drew from his work are dependent on him. They are implicitly obliged to adopt his method in order to conduct the research with which to oppose the conclusions he reached while developing it.[14]

I believe that it is not only possible but now customary to disconnect the method from the evaluative content of the Marx project. This book is

---

[13] Corcuff is a participant in the contemporary French intellectual movement labeled pragmatic sociology which expresses an ambition very similar, but not identical to that of public sociology advocated by Burawoy. In addition to the recent volume cited above, (*Où est passé la Critique Sociale?*), his long term project is described in a pair of parallel volumes: *Les Nouvelles Sociologies: Constructions de la réalité sociale* (1995) and *Les Nouvelles Sociologies: Entre le collectif et l'individuel* (2007).

[14] The most ambitious long-term effort to use the H-M method to gather evidence for why Marx was wrong has been under way for some years by Deirdre N. McCloskey, attested to by the title of her latest book, *Bourgeois Dignity: Why Economics can't Explain the Modern World*, (2010). This work follows an earlier book in the series, *The Bourgeois Virtues: Ethics for an Age of Commerce* (2006). Her affirmative enthusiasm for the bourgeois philosophy of history is boundless and her skill at using history to vilify the Marx Project, of rare quality, based on an unblemished orthodoxy developed while still studying at Harvard, when she was recruited by the arch-conservative economist, Milton Friedman to the University of Chicago (in economic history) for a post she occupied for twelve years.

a certain demonstration of that procedure. That is not to denigrate the substantive conclusion by Marx, but only to put in suspension the validity of that judgment so as to leave the field cleared for concentration on the question of method which is at the center of this study.

As the specialists know, to speak of that distinction between the method of Marx and his judgment about the political ramifications of his study, suggests a repeat of the position articulated by Georg Lukács in his famous 1912 (Lukács 1919) essay, "What is Orthodox Marxism?" Since he used that text to open the book that made his fame among radical intellectuals a century ago, *History and Class Consciousness* (1990/1919), the essay is among the most referenced ever written on the Marx question in the twentieth century. His infamous claim, against which 'true believers' rebelled, while hardly uncontestable, is clear:

> Orthodox Marxism, therefore, does not imply the uncritical acceptance of the results of Marx's investigations. It is not the 'belief' in this or that thesis, nor the exegesis of a 'sacred book'. On the contrary, orthodoxy refers exclusively to *method*. (Lukács 1990/1919: 1)

While I agree with the claim, the direction I take following from it is far more methodologically robust than supposed possible by Lukács. After all, he was neither historian nor philosopher, but a *littéraire*, who, at the time of that writing, had just 'discovered' Marx. Lukács read Marx as 'literature,' which he should have, since Lukács' prior writings, *Soul and Form* (2010/1911), and *Theory of the Novel* (1968/1916) contain unduplicated insights concerning the problem of twentieth century literature. While a reading of that nature may well reveal the methodological skeleton beneath (or perhaps frame around) the 'narrative' of capital, cultural critical texts, of which Marx supplied major early examples, can not be appreciated from within their own bounds.

At least as concerns the work of Marx, the reason for this 'limits of the literary' quality of critique as literature, is indicated, if unknowingly, by Lukács himself within his most famous essay. To begin with, in reference to Marx the determined dialectician, Lukács says, "dialectics insists on the concrete unity of the whole" (1990/1919: 6). Furthermore, according to Marx, "The concrete is concrete... because it is a synthesis of many particular determinants, i.e., a unity of diverse elements."[15] Thus Lukács' conclusion:

[15] Lukács takes this citation from Marx: *A Contribution to the Critique of Political Economy* (1859).

> Marx's Dictum: "the relations of production of every society form a whole" is the methodological point of departure and the key to the historical understanding of social relations. (1990/1919: 9)[16]

This stress on 'totality' cannot be underestimated, which, as shown by the schematic appended to this book, I take very seriously. As concerns method, it is capital, since, as Lukács adds:

> It is perfectly possible for someone to describe the essential of an historical event and yet be in the dark about the real nature of that event and of its function in the historical totality, i.e., without understanding it as part of a unified historical process. (1990/1919: 12)

The problem is to avoid being caught (to play a bit with Hegel) in the ruse of 'thinking' as if 'thinking' were the cause of doing and being rather than its result. As Lukács puts it, citing a signature sample of Marx's dialectic:

> Idealism succumbs here to the delusion of confusing the intellectual reproduction of reality with the actual structure of reality itself. In thought, reality appears as the process of synthesis, not as starting-point, but as outcome, although it is the real starting-point and hence the starting-point for perception and ideas. (1990/1919: 9)

Beyond Lukács I searched for additional corroboration for my emphasis on the broad testability of Marx's method as research template. This eventually led to a well-crafted, if somewhat obscure, text by W.H. Walsh: *An Introduction to the Philosophy of History*. First published in 1951, this book contains an exploration of the subject of its title, impeccably written by that professor of logic and metaphysics from the University of Edinburgh.

It is important to note that rather than a Marxist, Walsh was an avowed philosophical idealist, opposed to every form of materialism, including most certainly, anything connected with the discipline of sociology. His distrust of the notion is so patently powerful that in a very brief discussion of August Comte, who gave sociology (as "science of society") to the world, Walsh was not even able to use the word. His hesitancy to elevate the issue of material history to consciousness, which includes, after all, questions of class relations and human liberation, is demonstrated by the way he finished his historical review with Hegel. Apparently then noting that such a halt was a bit short in temporal reach, he attempted to deal with Comte

16 Lukács takes this cite from Marx: *The Poverty of Philosophy: Answer to the Philosophy of Poverty by M. Proudhon* (1847).

and Marx anyway (along with Toynbee) by adding a brief final chapter, laconically titled, "Some Further Writers."

Passing over Comte and his positivism as having served little useful purpose other than to tarnish a bit the discourse of Marx, Walsh revealed, probably unintentionally, his fundamental accord with what is asserted here to be the general utility of the Marx method, distinct from the evaluative substance of the Marx critique of productive relations under capital.

Not hesitating to belittle the "unsystematic character of Marx's writings," and the way, "Marx adopted Hegel's conclusions without accepting his premises," (Walsh 1968/1951: 159), Walsh was obliged nonetheless to notice a valuable derivative from the Marx project. Deciding that indeed there is something about Marx that is not identical to Hegel, and perhaps even a bit admirable at that, Walsh arrived at the following observation:

> These considerations suggest another way of looking at Marx's theory of history. Instead of regarding it as yet another philosophy of the speculative type, in which an attempt is made to find unity and intelligibility in the historical process as a whole, we can treat it rather as a theory of historical interpretation, concerned with the elucidation of particular situations. On this view it can be represented as recommending to historians a way of dealing with any events they may be called on to explain. (p.161)

While it is evident that Walsh (like Lukács) was not particularly versed in the language of method, what he said here is that the Marx historical-materialist method is of all-purpose utility for research undertaken in the interests of what he referred to elsewhere in his volume as a "critical philosophy of history." Beyond that, he was evidently faced with the perplexing popularity around him of the Marxist perspective among what he labeled "working historians." Thus, almost in spite of himself, he continued by noting:

> It may be added that the interest shown in Marxism by working historians is also to be connected with the theory's serving as a guide to the interpretation of particular historical situations, a sort of recipe for producing empirical hypotheses. (Walsh 1968/1951: 162)

It would seem that by this reference, Walsh denied being a member of the class, 'working historians' which is a strange admission for a well recompensed Scottish philosophical historian. However, avoiding praise for a cause that he would rather not recognize, following the above affirmative observations as to the utility of Marx's method, he went on to criticize the logical underpinnings of historical-materialism as a theory of history.

Rather than with that controversy, the import question here is that this confusion on the part of Walsh helps make my point: his inability to keep straight the distinction in the Marx Project between its content (which he rejects) and its method (which he applauds with muffled hands) sharpens the lines which distinguish them.

Recovering from that oscillation on his part resulted in a final affirmation that summarizes the issue:

> Yet it remains true that whatever damage philosophical criticism can do to the Marxist theory, it cannot overthrow it altogether. The reason for this should not be difficult to see. The theory (at least on our interpretation of it) recommends to historians a procedure for dealing with empirical situations; and the ultimate test of it must be whether it is in fact a fruitful procedure. This is something on which no *a priori* pronouncement can be made: it can be decided only by actually following the recommendation and seeing what happens. (Walsh 1968/1951: 163)

I couldn't agree more and pursuing such a test is the very task for which this small study of critical practice was designed.

CHAPTER ONE

WHAT IS CRITICAL PRACTICE?

Modes of Critical Practice

Cultural criticism is conventionally partitioned according to a critique of social practices and a critique of literature and the other arts. The former is habitually pursued by studies in the critical social sciences, the other by cultural critics in the humanities. Thereafter, the carrying power of the result is largely dependent on the art of its packaging by the critic. In order to get their work out so that it might have influence, each must produce some form of literature (essays, theatre, poetry, plastic art, etc.), which requires approaching the political with the eye of an aesthete. Once achieved, whatever the form, such work provides an opening for an additional mode of critical activity: the meta-critique, or the critical study of the process and impact of critical projects in general. This chapter is of that third nature, with the focus principally on critical method.

In order to frame the main case studies that fill the following six chapters, here I will discuss each of those three modes of critical occupation (i.e., critique in the social sciences, in the humanities, and meta-critique) by focusing on the work of three authors. I begin by considering a recent book by the French sociologist, Luc Boltanski: *On Critique: A Sociology of Emancipation* (2011), which exemplifies H-M oriented research in the critical social sciences. A discussion of H-M oriented critical work in the humanities follows, demonstrated by a short study of a recent volume by the American Professor, Teresa Ebert: *The Task of Cultural Critique* (2009).

This chapter closes with a study of a 1930 essay by Max Horkheimer (*The Origins of Bourgeois Philosophy*), on the basis of which he subsequently composed in 1937 what is generally considered the archetype of meta-critical work (*Traditional and Critical Theory*). As the initial announcement for the critical theory project of the Frankfurt School, these essays by Horkheimer provide the orientating perspective that has largely dominated western cultural criticism up to the time of this writing.

Because of the role played by Horkheimer in setting the stage for critical practice across the 20th century, my analysis of his meta-critical writing generates a double-distancing historical-materialist study of the critical theory movement itself. As will be developed, this occurs because we locate the historical-object of critical theory as identified by Horkheimer in his 1930 text, rather than in his 1937 text, as is typically the case. If my judgment is valid, the true object of critique lying at the base of Horkheimer's project is the "Bourgeois Philosophy of History," as he developed it in 1930. However, this text has been largely unnoticed by other cultural critics, and therefore it has not been cited in the more popular writings on the subject. If the material in the 1930 essay carries the importance that I attribute to it, the fact that it was somehow allowed to slip from view, has allowed his methodological piece of 1937 to be treated as if it is the source of the cultural figures that most deserve to be the target of cultural criticism, with unfortunate consequence in the political arena.

As I will try to show, this oversight or what might be called an 'error of praxis,' led to a gradually expanded insistence on the importance of a critique of western rationality. Accordingly, individuated human activity is placed in the center of the critical picture, displacing the culture structure of society which more properly ought to occupy that place. This facilitated a drift back into the idealist terrain from which the Marx project was intended to rescue the West and about which Horkheimer attempted to sound the alarm in 1930.[1]

Offering the above observation only as a hypothesis, I approach the political consequences of critical practice in a fashion somewhat compatible with the position of Gramsci. In his famous *Prison Notebooks* (1971), he attempted to detail the lack of generalized diffusion of socialist ambitions to more countries in the world during the early 20th century. He was particularly concerned with the way most members of the oppressed classes and even the disenchanted members of the bourgeois classes remained faithful to a system of production and politics that had manifestly unjust and unequal effects for citizens. Beyond only trying to understand this

---

[1] Dematerialized Rationality. As I will touch on briefly in Chapter Eight, the drift in critical attention away from structural matters, to favor a critique of rationality itself, accelerated as the direction of the Institution for Social Research in Frankfurt passed successively from the hands of Max Horkheimer to Theodor Adorno, to Jürgen Habermas, and now, to Axel Honneth. This is explainable in part by the way Horkheimer defined the form of rationality he condemned: what he called technical-rationality, which is the transformation not only of reason into a tool of technical accomplishment, but the transformation of the reasoning human-being into such a tool as well. This thread was not completely overlooked; it was picked up by another member of the original Frankfurt School participants, Herbert Marcuse, whose 1964 essay, *One Dimensional Man*, became a cult-read for the New Left movement during the late 1960s in the U.S.

paradox, in keeping with the logic of social-philosophy, he was interested in what might be done to rectify it.

Using deceptively simple language he expressed an important insight about the practical problem of societal revolution. For instance, when a progressive movement confronts a reactionary one, there is the "war of maneuver," as frontal attack, or out-and-out confrontation by the mobilized population against the repressive regime, which, in turn uses every means to remain in power and continue with its advantages. Simultaneously, as Gramsci put it, there is the "war of position" between the factions, stimulated partly by progressive intellectuals who work to shift the world view of a people away from support of the political position associated with the current regime. This is necessary if one is to sincerely reject unjust social conditions such as continuing privilege for the elites, the sanctity of the ruling classes to effectively run a country without real opposition, or the convention of treating the underclasses as if they are responsible for their own exploitation and marginal life style.

As Gramsci wisely saw, even if a political revolution, non violent or otherwise, is carried out, unless a substantial share of the civil society is aware of the progressive possibilities of a change in regime and committed to that pursuit, once the overt struggle is over, there will be, invariably, a counter revolution from above, as occurred famously after the French Revolution with Napoleon. This will restore the structures of power and practices of exploitation against which the revolutionary opposition had arisen in the first place, because of the sense of legitimacy attributed by the majority of politically active members of the society to the prior form of societal organization, in spite of its abuses, inequities and unsustainability. Unfortunately, under conditions of intense political ambiguity, people tend to assume a reactionary posture. This explains the effectiveness of terror and fear tactics as the major tool of conservative regimes.

It would appear that the sense of rightness of the social practices associated with the bourgeois philosophy of history as articulated by Horkheimer in his 1930 essay, has so colonized the common consciousness of westerners that only an elaborate form of war of position, of the sort spoken of by Gramsci, might set the stage for needed radical societal change. If so, then the appropriate object of critical practice in the West should not be limited to the economic machinery of capital as system of production (which is of course the main material expression of the problem), or to focus exclusively on the charade of popular participation and responsiveness associated with western style presidential electoral democracy. Rather, the direct object of cultural critique ought to be the bourgeois philosophy of history that sustains those archaic and unjust practices, including the political regimes, economic forms and structures of social ordering needed to assure their realization.

As we move through this book, it will become evident that various facets of that philosophy of history have been the target of critique for centuries. But this was approached, particularly in the last half of the 20th century, principally as if the issue was lodged in the minds of public leaders or intellectual elites. However, this ignored raising the level of critique to that of the bourgeois philosophy of history itself, and I propose that be changed.[2]

Luc Boltanski: Social Science Critique

The French sociologist, Luc Boltanski (1940–), exemplifies with his work a contemporary derivative of the critical theory movement. Expressing his own flavor of that by layering it on an intellectual heritage strongly marked by the French culture and intellectual climate, I introduce him to help position the current study in the flow of the critical social sciences.

From the opening line of a major recent book, *On Critique: A Sociology of Emancipation* (2011), Boltanski's determination is clear:[3]

> I shall approach critical sociologies starting from the concept of social domination, a polemical notion if ever there was one, because it has been a major axis of critical theories which having often been rejected by other currents in sociology, at least when the term domination is used not only to refer to different ways of placing power in the service of politics, whatever it might be—as is more or less the case with 'modes of domination' in Max Weber—but also serves to identify and condemn manifestations of power deemed extreme and abusive. (Boltanski 2011: 1)

Even if liberation is his objective, the tone of his writing is more that of a detached researcher than of an advocate or change agent, suggesting a political passivity that is all too common among intellectuals today in

[2] Among those who resisted this tendency in the direction of the dematerialization of critique, in France, was Louis Althusser.

[3] This volume by Boltanski was stimulated in part by the invitation he received in 2008 from Axel Honneth to deliver a series of conferences at the Institution for Social Research, University of Frankfurt, Germany, the site of the launching of the Critical Theory movement by Horkheimer in 1930s and still active today. The published text is an elaborate discussion of the position he described twenty years earlier in a paper, "Sociologie Critique et Sociologie de la Critique" (Boltanski 1990).

Europe. While I would prefer a greater charge of militancy on his part, Boltanski seems resolute in his position. In a recent interview on a French radio station about this very issue, he announced:

> Even when it is of critical intention, sociology ought not to be accusative. … [in spite of] cases where this is difficult [to avoid], for example, concerning the misuse of webs of power. (Boltanski 2012)[4]

Boltanski trained in Paris under Pierre Bourdieu (1930–2002), who was renowned for his attention to the impenetrability of systematically reproduced class barriers and the consequences of that for the perpetuation of structures of social injustice. Bourdieu advanced a form of structuralism oriented by the notion of habitus: this involved a decidedly French and thus strongly symbolic explanation of social class dynamics, structured by family and workgroup socialization of lower classes, so embedded by necessity in structures of labor and other routines of survival as to be unable to see any way out.[5]

---

4 Critique without Accusation. Boltanski reiterated this position, which he had assumed for years, during an interview on the radio program, "La Suite dans les idées," Radio France Internationale, 18 fév 2012a, when he was interviewed about another book that came out while this text was being composed: *Énigmes et Complots: Une enquête à propos d'enquêtes* (2012b).

His is a very complex argument: that in order to be effective, cultural critics should deliver their views not with a wink but with an authentic smile of acceptance of the object of their negative judgment. My case studies do not demonstrate the viability of that strategy, assuming that social change is the motive of critique. Still, this position is not unique to Boltanski; it was also assumed by Raymond Williams in England. Williams was the mentor of Terry Eagleton who we will study in Chapter Six.

5 Reproduction of Inequality. The influential career of Pierre Bourdieu was marked by his early studies of the way that higher education, as a system for the assignment of social status to its graduates, reinforces the trans-generational continuity of the social class structure and thereby of social and economic equality, in spite of the fact that the avowed mission of a national educational system is exactly the opposite. See his: *Les héritiers: les étudiants et la culture* (with Jean-Claude Passeron, 1964); *La noblesse d'État: grandes écoles et esprit de corp.* (1989), and *La reproduction Éléments d'une théorie du système d'enseignement* (1970).

Bourdieu was a structuralist. He argued that interaction is determined by macro-structures; this placed him in a position in France a bit parallel with that of Talcott Parsons in the U.S. During the 1970s, for a complex set of reasons, Western intellectuals (exemplified in particular in France by Foucault) turned against the structuralist position with considerable vehemence. It became fashionable to favor some form of individualist negotiationalism according to which each person, in any social situation, is free to negotiate or act, with individual expression in interaction determining the shape of social relations, rather than some pre-formed force of social structure.

Bourdieu developed this position in, *La distinction : critique sociale du jugement* (1979) [Distinction: a Social Critique of the Jugement of Taste, 1984] and *Sur l'État: Cours au Collège de France 1989–1992* (2012).

Always concerned with the selective attribution of privilege and the curiously passive acceptance of that on the part of the oppressed, and thus committed to the liberation theme, after finishing his studies, Boltanski nonetheless distanced himself from the position of his mentor. Faulting Bourdieu for being both excessively normative and structuralist, he decided that it was not useful to overemphasize that portion of variance in social behavior that is determined in advance of actual human encounters by historical forces developed in family, neighborhood or workplace. Boltanski considered that there was more possibility for the development of models of social reform if one concentrated rather on the way everyday social action is negotiated in situations of uncertainty. This set him on a path favoring a particular view of symbolic interactionism, which he formalized progressively over the years as 'pragmatic sociology'.

His fascination with more dynamic, individual-initiative oriented models of social behavior arose as he began to consider models of action as the constitution of social structure, rather than models of structure as foundation for social interaction. This prompted a move in the direction of experimental social psychology, aimed at getting to the truth about the determinants of interaction, inductively, by the laboratory study of interpersonal behavior requiring cooperation and concession. While woven from a perspective of symbolic interaction, rather than structural determinism, increased the humanist appeal of his writings, Boltanski's studies come across as largely descriptive and explanatory at the micro-level of social action, resting noticeably silent about the defense or advancement of community dynamics.

The sociologies that Boltanski discusses in his writings (and in this he follows Foucault, who, as we will see, always discussed knowledges in the plural) and the forms of sociological practice that Boltanski favors, occupy conceptual space with ethno-methodology, inclining toward dramaturgy. Unfortunately, due to the formal properties of the unit of analysis of that mode of research (human dyads, triads, and small groups), it is difficult to bridge the gap from the research setting to the political arena, where the unit of concern shifts, to focus on an entire population, a major institution and/or an all-embracing historically anchored world view for a people. However, to the chagrin of those favoring the big picture on social action, the alternative can easily transform the liberation theme into a platform issue, without clear acreage in empirical work. To get around that impasse, Boltanski fell back on the Neo-Kantian tactic: when intellectually blocked, one possible solution is to reconceptionalize one's strategy, then move onward.

Spying on the World from the Library

A major problem with action-oriented social research is how to make the jump from understanding, through evaluation, to action: from findings to recommendations for mobilization; or, as Foucault might have put it, from knowledge to power. Boltanski attempts to deal with this by slicing critical practice in two, distinguishing the investigation phase from the policy evaluative phase. The way he approaches this helps sharpen the central debate that occupies us here.

The transition from the is-to-ought of research is a high stakes undertaking. In order to advocate change one must first be solidly informed about the object of interest. This need not involve quantitative field study or laboratory designs, often depending on (some claim better facilitated by) direct exposure to the situations of collective action: in factories, in political campaigns, in the corridors of economic power, or simply from living among the elite or the oppressed for extended periods of time. Second, whatever their form, once the data are in or the observations secured, an evaluative stance must be assumed, advocating a value position about the findings in reference to some claimed advantage, presumably for humanity, concerning some contingent aspect of the current conditions that not only might be, but ought to be, different.

As concerns his discipline, whatever the data-gathering details, Boltanski considers all first-stage data-generating research as deployment of a critical sociology. Thereafter, if one chooses (which need not be the case), one can use the results from the first stage of research, as the basis for a second, evaluative phase: extruding from one's empirical findings justification or recommendations for political action or social change. This second stage of the process he labels a pragmatic sociology of critique.

Having thus differentiated critical practice, at least for sociologists, into two phases, he speculates on the qualities that distinguish them. If we follow his lead, the first stage of the process, the everyday sort of canonic undertaking, is aimed at deepening and broadening understanding of the constituents, causes and consequences of the systems and structures of society. Even this implies an initial value judgment that some aspect of the current social practices is poorly understood or perhaps otherwise sufficiently questionable to merit deeper investigation. On that basis, he boldly announces, every sociology is socio-critical by nature, which is why he labels all stage-one studies as the pursuit of a critical sociology.

If extended to all the social sciences, this suggests that while all first stage research is inherently critical, this is only in reference to the internal definition of the discipline, profession or interest area of the researcher, without any inherently larger practical reach. If this is so, then first level social science research is another, generally more abstract, form of what I identify elsewhere as genre criticism: as when film specialists conduct critical film studies principally for other specialists about film; sociologists do similarly for other sociologists; economists about economics for other economists, etc. To the extent to which this is valid, it explains why problems often arise when findings from first stage studies are announced as if directly policy relevant for some community issue, since their design often precludes that direct leap into practice.

Boltanski's use of the label 'pragmatic sociology of critique' for the second stage of the process exposes the philosophical dimension of his European sociological training. French pragmatism is far less formally developed in terms of purely philosophical justification than is the case in the U.S.A.[6] As I see it, what Boltanski proposes for second stage critical studies is equivalent to the application of the famous "pragmatic rule" announced by the American social-philosopher John Dewey about a century ago: the truth value (as extracted by second-stage critical research) of current knowledge (as developed from stage-one studies) is in its practical consequences. While Boltanski does not cite Dewey on this point, I will. As Dewey put it a century ago:

> Let us follow the pragmatic rule, and in order to discover the meaning of the idea ask for its consequences. ... A moral situation is one in which judgment and choice are required antecedently to overt action. The practical meaning of the situation—that is to say the action needed to satisfy it—is not self-evident. It has to be searched for. ... What is needed is to find the right course of action, the right good. (Dewey 1950/1920: 133)[7]

---

[6] Brutal pragmatism implies the morally unjustified instrumentalisation of theoretically justifiable motives. A usual example is Nazi fascism where, in the interests of 'internal national coherence,' those of differing blood or national fidelity were exterminated. Boltanski is very aware of the risk of opening this issue in Europe, as evidenced by his attempt to deal with it in his book (with Laurent Thévenot): *De la justification. Les économies de la grandeur* (1991).

[7] The referenced book is based on lectures delivered by John Dewey in Japan in 1919, on the theme, "Moral Reconstruction," as the attempt to justify the importance of a moral guide for human action, in the direction of the good, the right and the just. In addition to providing a statement of his famous "pragmatic rule," this small text of Dewey's is one of the few where he expressly labels his project "social philosophy," or a pragmatic philosophy aimed at human liberation from any form of oppression, whether intellectual, ideological or political; see his Chapter Eight, "Reconstruction as Affecting Social Philosophy." There he also addressed the danger of unreflective teleology, which can be the result of the vulgar application of the pragmatic rule in social affairs, when reduced to a crass Machiavellian logic of ends justifying means, particularly because of the technical-instrumental potential of its application.

Following Dewey, antecedent to "overt action," passing from research to political engagement, there must be a phase of moral judgment by the critic as to the ethical, aesthetic and/or civic consequences of the intended intervention. This implies a pragmatic interpretation of the results of critical research: their meaning, as implications for action, is assessed for the community of reference existentially and socio-behaviorally rather than only rhetorically, conceptually or theoretically.

This opens the issue of the source of the moral criteria which are appropriate for application in a critical social science, a challenge that does not escape Boltanski's notice. He deals with this definitionally, proposing that laying the framework for some moral mission is inherent to the conduct of critical social research in the first place. Still, by not confronting directly the problem of the source of the moral criteria of judgment, he opens himself to attack for begging an essential question of critique. Far from blind about that charge, he raised it forcefully in reference to the liberation problem of social class studies. He concluded that others in the field lack clarity about the valuing criteria used to orient their projects and judge their product, with the result that:

> ... critical sociology is most often consecrated to the critique of inequalities without explicitly constructing the norm of justice permitting the justification of the critique. That is done in the name of a division between judgments of reality and judgments of values, often applied under the authority of Max Weber; without a doubt constituting one of the least questioned dogmas of the practical epistemology of sociology. (Boltanski 1990: 130)

Aside from his evident uncertainty about the justice of the Weberian framework and a certain form of positivism, Boltanski believes that critical thinking is not a gift selectively attributed to intellectuals, but a general human disposition, which may be more or less refined in practice. He thus denies the untested assertion of a fundamental asymmetry between researchers and social actors. He calls for study of the critical processes as deployed naively, automatically, yet necessarily, as the organizing force that shapes everyday life. The researcher is thereby warned against imposing theoretical interpretations on data drawn from observation, with particular proscription against models drawn from what "classic sociologists" commonly call the social structure (Boltanski 1990: 125).

The oscillation implied by him between the detached objectivity of the researcher and the subjective commitment of the social advocate imposes a serious balancing act. Since that very oscillation is the life-dynamic of critique, in spite of certain lack of clarity in his treatment, Boltanski's dealing with it in a particularly forthright fashion explains our choice to include him here.

While a *critic* is one who undertakes a *critique*, it is apparent that in this line of work, there is no way to separate the investigator from the investigation. In spite of that apparent subjective dimension of such practice, when well done, there is a manifest objectivity to the outcome. As will become strikingly evident from the in-depth case studies, this constancy of the critical process in spite of the personalization of its execution is one of the great mysteries at the center of this book.

Liberation

Resisting the vulgar label of institutional theorist and preferring the language of symbolic interaction, engaged sociologist Boltanski must nonetheless deal with the issue of social class. He chastises 'classical sociologists' who apply one or another of the accepted standard models to social life, generating findings that may conform to the chosen prototype while indifferent to the life and minds of real individuals in concrete situations. According to him, such sociologists proceed as if most individuals live in the illusion of autonomy, freedom, and choice, while they are actually dominated by institutional constraints, oppressed by frontiers of every sort, facing options that are largely defined by markets and hierarchies. It is not so much that he denies the content of that alleged populist illusion, arguing, rather, that classic strategies of social research tend to be artificial and thus incapable of getting to the truth:

> The opposition between reality and illusion, the ideal according to which social actors are [supposedly] dominated by their illusions and the conception of a social order resting on a sustained illusion, are central for the architecture of sociology such as it was constituted in the 19th-century... . (Boltanski 1990: 126)

From his own work and that of the collaborators in the research center he directs in Paris, he confronts this issue a bit on the oblique, stressing what he labels the "language of normativity," used in daily life. Accordingly, he says that ordinary people approach the class issue mostly by questioning why it is that 'always the same' individuals pass or fail major competitive examinations, secure or are rejected for important jobs, receive or are denied loans, etc.[8] He judges this as evidence that most citizens perceive and experience class-based discrimination or advantage, but for lack of

[8] Always the Same. This is Boltanski's way of acknowledging the social class problem, the systematic production and reproduction of inequalities in supposedly free and open societies. For a further discussion of this issue in a section headed by the cited phrase see Boltanski 2011, p. 37.

broad-spectrum language, are incapable of generalizing this awareness in a fashion that compels political response. This suggests an important role for cultural critics in the raising of consciousness and the stimulation of communities of common concern about issues of domination and exploitation (Boltanski 1990: 37).

In a mild display of categorical turn-about then, Boltanski ultimately admits that by "adopting the standpoint of the totality" and thereby giving minimum voice to ordinary actors, "despite everything... overarching critical sociologies" are able, "to generate a critical power superior to that of pragmatic sociologies of critique." Yet he is hesitant to fully embrace this position, offering arguments intended to tone down the apparent superior pragmatic effectiveness of the work of "classical sociologies of critique" (Boltanski 1990: 44). I evaluate this as evidence of the dialectical nature of the form of critical practice he admires, which, by resisting straightforward Kantian conceptualization, frustrates Boltanski's efforts to explain it as the simple expression of linear rationality.

Elimination of all Social Differentiation?

Finally, we must call attention to a key meta-ethical issue that he identified from his studies. Since a principal problem that motivated 20th century critical practice was domination of some category of people by another, is it the case that every observable asymmetry in society is a sign of oppression? Do all distinctions based on some general quality such as class, caste, gender, ethnicity, religion, sexual preference, etc., merit equal critical attention? Is the objective of liberation to eliminate all differential social treatment or interaction patterns based on such social asymmetries? If so, the result would be what Boltanski discusses (in the wake of Marcuse, 2006/1955) as "surplus repression" (Boltanski 2011: 47).

It seems folly to proscribe the notion of justice as equality of opportunity in society and under the law, as if blind to absolutely every general vector of personal identity. Rather than exclusive concern with the gross categorical problems of society as structures of differentiation and integration, should not the point of critical practice be to focus on the less visible but no less institutionally embedded issues related to the hidden nexus of power and its pernicious ambition? This might draw attention to issues such as how natural categorical differences among members of a society are treated as selection attributes by marketing specialist in hopes of more efficiently identifying, and manipulating, commercial and political niche-markets.

Boltanski stresses the "necessity of critique" as, "the only bulwark against the domination liable to be practiced by institutions." But by virtue of their "bodiless being," institutions are elusive targets, forcing critics to attack institutional proxies, which is to say, "their embodiment in spokespersons" (Boltanski 1990: 83–84). This implies that critical tactics such as skewering the fictive justice of pseudo-democracy by lambasting a president or other political leader is easier than to attack a faceless institution like the banking or television industry. Yet, to target public personalities with strong invective attacks is more likely to lead to condemnation of the critic for libel, than to a ground swell of revolutionary fervor demanding reform of institutions.

Even when not trapped by the problem of "disembodiment," institutional critics (which in the end, at least moderately, Boltanski seems to be) face a formidable challenge due to the tripartite nature of institutions which are at once semantic systems, social organizations, and technical administrations (Boltanski 1990: 94).[9] As huge logical-meaningful apparatuses, the integrity of which is contingent on the mutual accommodation of the whole, it is very difficult to modify a particular element without jeopardizing the survival or continuity of the assemblage. Although Boltanski does not prolong this line of his thinking, if cultural critics are to deliver meaningful indictments against major institutions of society, rather than only focusing on issues related to misguided leadership, the objective for change must also include the normative structures that supply the driving energy for the production and reproduction of social relations.

Detective Work as Critical Social Science

Before turning to the next section, on critical practice in the humanities, I would like to bring to attention a new essay by Boltanski that appeared in the French bookstores after this chapter was largely finished. It will serve my purposes both by presenting a study based on a temporal architecture similar to the one I am using in this book and by setting in motion an argument about how the seductive attraction of literary criticism can sidetrack attention from the object of criticism that ought to motivate it.

---

[9] The lack of precision in Boltanski's somewhat lyrical reference to the social-system construct exemplifies a shortcoming for which the social-ecology systems model {PETOS} contained in the Technical Appendix of this text is intended to help resolve.

The title of his latest book is *Enigmas and Conspiracies: An Inquiry into the Problem of Inquiry* (Boltanski 2012).[10] With it, Boltanski surprised his customary readers by shifting somewhat his conceptual attention from its usual zone in the social sciences to the direction of a different corridor of academe—that of the humanities. The result is a socio-historical study of the late 20th century political climate, aimed at explaining the contorted nature of contemporary democracy, based on a reading of police novels.

Boltanski constructed this highly applauded analysis of the crisis in contemporary democracy, principally by drawing on writings from the Sherlock Holmes series by Arthur Conan Doyle (1859–1930) and from the detective series by the Franco-Belgium author George Simenon (1903–1989), whose investigative hero is named Commissaire Maigret.[11] The decades separating the writings by Doyle on Holmes (principally between 1880 and 1914) from those of Simenon on Maigret (this fictional character first appeared in 1930), supply the markers needed for Boltanski to identify what he takes to have been a shift from the nineteenth to the 20th century in the way that democracy under-delivers on its promise due to a serious deficiency in critical acumen.

As I will illustrate in this chapter, Boltanski's use of literature as window to social issues is common for cultural criticism in the humanities. It is justified contingent on the validity of the aesthetic claim that life is mirrored in art; if so, then art constitutes an important material content that under proper scrutiny, allows a critic to expose otherwise hidden surfaces of cultural processes.[12]

---

10 Detective Research. *Énigmes et Complots: Une enquête à propos d'enquêtes* (Boltanski 2012a). Due in part to its paradoxical title, this book drew instant attention from Paris journalists. It is a critical literary study of detective fiction, as a data mine on which to base a number of generalizations about the impact of institutional uncertainty, often manipulated by politics and economics, on the state of common consciousness. Basing his interpretation on a rather quiet Marxist reading of class tension and domination, Boltanski judges that a principle effect of life in the West, given current state practices, is not just alienation but paranoia, touching not only the masses, but also the elites and government leaders as well. For a critique of this book, see Jean Birnbaum's "Boltanski, détective critique," in *Le Monde des Livres* (2012).

11 For most readers, English author Arthur Conan Doyle's Sherlock Holmes needs no introduction. His yield of detective adventures was four novels and 56 short stories. The Belgian-Francophone author George Simenon (1903–1989) is less well known. Compared with Doyle, or for that matter, with the widely read contemporary British author, Agatha Christie (1890–1976), he was remarkably productive. Christie's yield was 66 novels and 14 short-story collections; Simenon published about 200 novels and 150 novellas, of which 75 novels and 28 short stories featured Commissaire Maigret. For a very informative Simenon—Maigret Web-site, see: http://www.trussel.com/f_maig.htm.

12 This postulate explains how genre criticism can be the basis for serious cultural criticism, although to carry it out requires considerable skill and breadth of knowledge.

While I have no argument about either that postulate or strategy, after examining Boltanski's new book, the question instantly arose: is the result of his exploration of the culture-sleuth as socio-political detective, an exercise of critical social science, of literary criticism, or of farce? Other readers, or in this case listeners,[13] raised the same concern, arguing that by tangling his sociological agenda with the playful literary irony of Homes and George Simenon, Boltanski effectively disqualified this work as of legitimate critical value.

Demonstrating a curious dynamic of late capitalism by which uncertainly concerning its value often drives the market demand for a commodity higher, the stir generated in Paris by this book quickly transformed the work into an event.[14] Not only did Boltanski make the rounds in February, 2012, of radio, television and press hawking this book, but within a few months, a new literary prize had been constructed, sized remarkably well to fit his profile. Thereafter he was named first ever recipient of the new French literary prize, "Le Prix Pétrarque de l'essai France Culture-Le Monde."[15]

Apparently, through the years Boltanski sought relief from the reality of teaching and research by reading crime and detective stories where crime does not pay because most of the time the sleuth gets the culprit.[16] What is unusual is how this late-work seems to expose Boltanski's

---

[13] Radio Interview, "La figure de Sherlock Holmes aujourd'hui," (20 Feb., 2012c). A twenty-five minute round table discussion (in French) of Boltanski's book, by Antonio Casilli, Hervé Le Tellier and Philippe Tretiack. http://www.franceculture.fr/emission-la-grande-table-la-figure-de-sherlock-holmes-aujourd-hui-retour-sur-l-oeuvre-de-paul-strand.

[14] Boltanski's media sweep about his new book was concentrated during the week 13–19 February, 2012. Contrary to the Andy Warhol formula of fifteen minutes of fame, in Paris, a top outing of this sort is managed to cover all media outlets, goes on for about seven days, and then dies.

[15] Boltanski's prize was presented (16 July, 2012) at the 27th "Rencontres Pétrarque," a five day meeting, held in Montpellier, France, under joint sponsorship of *Le Monde* (the Paris newspaper of reference), and *France Culture* (the high-brow culture chain of Radio France). Boltanski delivered the Inaugural Lesson for the five day Conference, addressing the theme of, "*Notre avenir est-il démocratique*?" ("Is our future destined to be Democratic?").

The Italian, Pétrarque (1304–74), is considered by some as the father of humanism. His having spent most of his early years in France, including studies at the University of Montpellier, explains both the topic of this conference and its location. One might judge it a bit grandiose to connect Boltanski's work with the image of Pétrarque; but this also indicates the high level of prestige often enjoyed by French intellectuals.

[16] The extent of Boltanski's exposure to this form of literature is demonstrated by the 40 pages of Notes appended to the paragraphs of this book, which includes citations to dozens of volumes of stories, not just limited to Holmes (Ch. 2: "The Investigation of a London Detective"), or to Simenon (Ch. 3: "The Investigation of a Parisian Policeman"), but drawing on many others including Poe, R.L. Stevenson and Agatha Christie.

biography: having labored for decades in the canonic social sciences, all the while dipping into detective stories for distraction, he now undertakes a more forthright confrontation with the world of real politics, fueled by a residual appreciation of fiction, convinced at the age of seventy years that the hollow drama of contemporary politico-economic action is equivalent to the sort of conspiratorial subterfuge that animates detective stories. And that critical sociology is primarily in the business not unlike that of a police investigator, trying to tease the 'real' of reality out of the way it is presented in everyday life. Unfortunately, the story never ends in everyday life: not for lack of deserving conspiratorial culprits, but for lack of an effective critical political process with which to catch them, rebuke them and move on to better things.

It is said that the validity of an accusation is justified in proportion to the vigor with which its attribution is denied; little explains this better than the conspiratorial tendencies that lurk behind the visible quagmire of geopolitical strife and the work of sociological detectives to get to the bottom of it. Thus for Boltanski to focus on manipulated collective paranoia as mass deception to shield conspiracy—as the unexpressed but real source of political theater as public spectacle, seems justified. However, the extent to which he succeeds in establishing this as a metacritical view of research in the social sciences, based on metaphorical inspiration from his research on the unwinding of crime in detective novels, is far less certain.[17]

While his intention is clear, the sinuous flow of its causal logic and the lack of material anchorage either at the beginning or the end of his thought-trail, raises serious questions as to whether Boltanski carried this historical-materialist detective exercise through to its ends. Unfortunately, the result fails to provide a promising point of departure for political engagement toward change.[18]

What might explain the allure of this book in Paris is the sophisticated way Boltanski approached the crisis of democracy: not by proposing a

---

[17] Political Theater. Boltanski defends his anti-structuralist position claiming, that it makes no difference if one can not make global announcements about social class, community or some other macro-structural entity based on local, primary researches, for the simple reason that such entities (units of analysis) are the invention of intellectuals and not actually experienced in the reality of everyday life. Yet it is clear even to him that this makes it very difficult to deal with political issues.

[18] Boltanski's treatment of detective literature exemplifies a problem addressed by Teresa Ebert (see following section). Literary critics can become so overtaken with the drama of the stories they read and the fascinating response this generates, that they lose sight of the need to tie critical readings back into political practice.

solution for it, but by raising its question. In the French world, since at least Montaigne (1533–1592), the importance of any discourse (of which Boltanski's book is an example) is measured against the question that it attempts to confront. Propelled by a logic of interrogation, this is often frustrating for Anglo-Saxons who, on confronting those of French style, find their question responded to with another question.

According to the abstract prepared in advance of Boltanski's inaugural lesson at the Pétrarque Conference, with this study of police novels he addressed the following four-element historicist postulate *cum* rhetorical question:

> Why with the move from the 19th to 20th centuries, do we observe in turn: the development of the police novel, of which the heart is the investigation, and of the espionage novel, that has as subject the conspiracy; the invention, by psychiatry, of paranoia, of which one of the principle symptoms is the tendency to undertake endless investigations, prolonged to the state of delirium; the new orientation of political science that, taken by the problem of paranoia, displaces it from the psychic plain to the social plain so as to take as object the explanation of historic events by the 'conspiracy theory'; finally, to sociology, that is gifted with specific forms of causality–said to be social–, for determining the entities, individual or collective, to which can be attributed the events that punctuate the lives of persons, of groups or even of the course of history?[19]

What this tells us about Boltanski's underlying thesis is that during the period either side of 1900, detective novelists, psychiatry, political science and sociology contributed effectively and conjointly, though be it unknowingly, to the sinister cycle of circumstances behind the breakdown of contemporary democracy. It is difficult to judge whether this suggests an intellectualist exercise in the generation of a conspiracy theory or only publicity for pulp-fiction.[20]

Judgments about projects of this nature depend on how they are read. Fortunately for the good name of Boltanski, the internationally reputed

[19] Audio archive of Boltanski's inaugural lesson, "Critique et démocratie: la cause de la critique," is available at: <http://www.franceculture.fr/emission-les-rencontres-de-petrarque>.

[20] History as Conspiracy. Locating the historical roots for some contemporary problem by backtracking until finding some discipline or profession to accuse, was, as we will see in Chapter Five, the artistic signature of Michel Foucault. Having been educated in an atmosphere of heavy Foucauldian influence, probably explains the nature of this deduction by Boltanski. However, where Foucault was generally content to find fault with the origin of one single discipline at a time, in achieving an analogous critical conclusion, Boltanski found the occasion to weave together four of them at once; the conspiratorial ring of which, given the topic, I can not resist pointing out.

French sociologist, Bruno Latour, stepped in to defend the critical intellectual soundness of this study against those who argued for its disqualification in that regard. Writing in a popular French philosophy monthly, Latour salved the situation with an interesting dose of rhetorical ointment, contending that Boltanski's latest production was "very much a book of criticism, but not of literary criticism; the critique which it is about, is the paralysis of the critical spirit" (Latour 2012). This suggests that critical social scientists have become ill fated detectives; whatever the finding, their subject of inquiry usually evades the common regard because the faculties of critical judgment have been progressively deactivated among the general western population.[21]

In anticipation of the argument I will develop at the close of this chapter, based on the early work of Horkheimer, I interpret this tragic malaise hinted at by Boltanski in that recent book (deactivated faculties for judgment) as symptom of the conquest of the common conscience of westerners by the bourgeois philosophy of history. Before getting to that, it is time to discuss criticism in the humanities, as a second leg in this chapter on the object and tactics of critical practice.

Teresa Ebert: Humanities Critique

Teresa Ebert is a literature professor at the State University of New York, Albany, specializing in cultural studies and criticism. Calling for nothing less than a "transformative materialist cultural critique" (Ebert 2009:xvi), her work exemplifies how the historical-materialist method has found a place in the humanities, for studies based on data drawn from literary studies rather than from the direct analysis of social interaction. A Marxist (romantic) like Luc Boltanski, the differences in their approach concerning domination and liberation help clarify both the sense of those concepts and the distinctions between critical research in the humanities versus in the social sciences.[22]

---

21 While I agree that, as suggested by Latour, some form of 'critical paralysis' has denatured cultural criticism, and without doubt Boltanski shares that view, the real issue is what might rectify that lacuna. As I see it, the problem is less one of style than of institutional follow-through, less a matter of what mode is used (literature or social science) than the way the critic follows her work to its material ends.

22 Revolutionary Romantics: It takes no genius to see how out of control speculative capitalism, as a machine for endlessly intensified concentration of the means of production i.e., Capital, will necessarily break the back of any society, which is what draws Marxists Romantics (no violence intended) in common cause whatever the details of their differences.

Based on scrutiny of literature, television or cinema, no matter what their theoretical acumen, humanities professors are often accused of being mere genre-critics, positing results about social structural matters based on subjective readings of media or texts, ignoring the standards of objectivity and measurement as applied in the social sciences. Reciprocally, humanities professors decry what they consider the pseudo-empirical critical studies done in anthropology or sociology, yielding texts that are dry as dust and so detached from human experience that few might identify with them.

Neither Ebert nor Boltanski suffer from this intra-critical blindness. In fact, during the composition of this book, both of them were producing new work of their own, with results which certify this point. In the previous section, I discussed Boltanski's latest work, based on a close reading of detective fiction. Although perhaps less famously so, Ebert has been equally busy, preparing her next book for publication, *Marxism and the Task of the (Post)Humanities;* written in collaboration with Mas'ud Zavarzadeh, with whom she works regularly. Although pre-publication announcements can be misleading, here is what the book intends to say:

> In the wake of the "theory" revolution, the humanities have changed radically, but the most important transformation is in their interpretive logic, namely the assumptions, discourses, and reading strategies by which they made sense of cultural texts – from novels and poetry to films, videos, cultural events (e.g. sports) and social moments (e.g. Katrina, war). Understanding these changes is necessary because they have great significance in shaping the cultural consciousness and interpretive unconscious of people in their everyday lives. This volume argues that as a result of these changes, humanities have been reduced to teaching communication and the digital and affective skills which are necessary for the contemporary cyber work-force. Consequently the role of humanities, which is to produce critical understanding of cultural meanings and social values in a democratic society, has been diminished. The book proposes a new mode of teaching humanities based on critique and a materialist understanding of language.[23]

Carrying a manifestly Marxist title, it is unlikely that this volume will make the same splash in the U.S. that Boltanski's achieved in Paris. However, the significance of its theme must not be overlooked. As Ebert calls for a shift on the part of the humanities teaching corps in the direction of social sciences, in his volume comparing critical sociologists with police

[23] Transformative Humanities. See the Macmillan Palgrave Web-Site regarding Ebert's 2012 book: http://www.palgrave.com/products/title.aspx?pid=490065.

detectives, Boltanski criticizes his own discipline's inertia, by encouraging greater openness among sociologists to inspiration from popular literature. From this it should be clear that critical practice knows few disciplinary bounds.

Blame it on Dilthey

Wilhelm Dilthey (1833–1911), was a German historian who inspired not only Max Weber and by that the ensuing development of sociology, but also helped clarify the uniqueness of the humanities. Thanks to that common intellectual parentage, the tense inseparability between the now artificially divided social sciences and humanities is as understandable as is the endless contest between them for higher moral ground.[24]

Until the time of Dilthey, or Marx and Nietzsche for that matter, the humanities were present in fact but not really as disciplines. For instance, as will be elaborated in Chapter Six when discussing the work of Eagleton, English as a discipline was invented at Oxford during the Victorian epoch for reasons that were as much political as intellectual. And according to White (see Chapter Seven) the discipline of history was birthed at about the same time and also for social-political reasons. That time-frame pertains as well to the founding of sociology, highlighted by Auguste Comte's (1798–1857) project to apply systematic, objective methods to the study of society.

Unlike the disciplines of English or History that today constitute the core of the humanities, a distinction of Comte's sociology was his attempt to link the methods of natural science to the study of society as historic object. At the time this seemed reasonable because of the then still vague distinctions between the yet non-formalized disciplines of history and sociology.

Positivism in the social sciences implies insistence to stick with rational social facts, remaining value neutral, distant, objective and abstract when studying society. Perhaps for contemplating the solar system that is

---

24 The crucial introductory portion of the work where Dilthey laid out his project, *Introduction to the Human Sciences* (1991/1883), is available online. A readable anthology, which includes important translated portions (into English) of Dilthey texts, is: Marcello Truzzi: *Verstehen: Subjective Understanding in the Social Sciences*, Boston, Addison-Wesley, 1974. The Truzzi volume is the source of the material quoted in these paragraphs. For an overview of Dilthey's project from the perspective of the philosophy of history see Rudolf Makkreel, "Wilhelm Dilthey," *The Stanford Encyclopedia of Philosophy*, Ed. Edward N. Zalta, (Summer 2012). http://plato.stanford.edu/archives/sum2012/entries/dilthey/.

reasonable, but far less so for study of the web of human meanings which give life to society as a system of ever evolving collective action. Still, the issue of empirical exactitude cannot be avoided, requiring considerable training in positive methods, in order to conduct good quality evaluative, normative studies in the social domains. While hardly extreme about this, Comte was among the first to argue in favor of positivism. This is largely the reason for the ambiguity associated with his enduring reputation.

Attacking the question of subjective understanding in social life (*Verstehen*) and in opposition to the analytics of Comte, Dilthey proposed an anti-positivist correction for the social sciences and a strengthening for the humanities. He insisted on the inherent inseparability for understanding of the {empirically logical and the symbolically meaningful}. Concerning the human condition, based on the "mind-body unity of life itself," he decided that the academic distinction of {fact—and—value} is vacuous; rather, understanding is an interpretative act based on empathetic appreciation of some by others, given the local community as context.

The result of Dilthey's work was less to fold the humanities (or "humanist studies") into the social sciences than to expand the scope of the former to englobe the latter; the point being to try to understand "how human states are consciously lived". As a result:

> A study belongs to the human studies only if its object becomes accessible to us through the attitude which is founded on the relation between life, expression and understanding. From this common nature ... follow all the peculiarities which have been emphasized in discussions on the human studies, of cultural studies, of history, as constituting their nature. Thus the peculiar relation in which the unique, singular individual stands here to universal regularities [and] then the combination which takes place here of statements of fact, judgment of value, and ideas of purpose. (in Truzzi 1974: 16–17)

Debate continues as to whether such understanding is constitutive of general truth for the social sciences, pertinent beyond the situation of its origin, or whether the incisive study of social action is so dependent on the subjective engagement of the researcher, as to seriously limit the wider generalization of results no matter what the procedure.

Perhaps the output from criticism is only literature in the mundane sense. If so, then the same would pertain to writings in all the sciences. Assuming there is something of quality to be found within it, the real question concerns less the accuracy of that possibility than whether there is a way to work from the texture of literature back into the material force of social life.[25]

Ebert's treatment of texts demonstrates that, independent of origin, a well read critic from the humanities can use literary material of every nature as a convincing window of entry into tough-minded cultural analysis.

Is All Literature Criticism?

To set the stage for a discussion of the particularities of critical research in the humanities, of which Ebert's is a fine example, I will turn briefly to *The Norton Anthology of Theory and Criticism* (Leitch 2001). As evident by its 2,600 rice-paper pages on which is assembled a carefully compiled history of literature and criticism of western civilization, the reach of critical activity in the humanities is enormous. Working with five collaborators, the editor, Vincent Leitch, called on another hundred specialists to identify and describe the intellectual context and work of the one-hundred-and-forty greatest names in western literature and criticism, over the last 2,500 years.

As for the six intellectuals discussed later in my in-depth case studies, only one (Voltaire) is absent from that *Anthology*. While that is probably a serious oversight, considered as a whole, this huge compilation of writings and references demonstrates the extent to which the history of critical practice is blurred, owing in no small part to the uncertain frontier between the social sciences and the humanities.

Theory as Method in Humanities

Less universally so in the social sciences, the method of critical study in the humanities is considered as the active expression of 'theory'. That is not quite to say that the distinction between theory and method is denied

---

25 Art as Truth. If there is a legitimate intimacy between {literature and life}, then Hans Georg Gadamer was right in arguing that there is truth in art. The hermeneutic challenge is to draw that truth out from the mere art-form which supports it. See his *Truth and Method*, 2006. This is also consistent with Lukács (2010/1911).

Still a question remains: how is one to explain the truth-content of or 'in' literature? Maurice Merleau-Ponty offered a proposal, arguing in a critique of the first novel by Simone de Beauvoir that the essential quality of truthfulness in a work, which is immediately perceivable or appreciable by readers, is 'there' in so far as the author has implanted a metaphysical element at the center of the work, which resonates as its 'truth' and is picked up as such by readers or audiences of art-works in general. Maurice Merleau-Ponty, "Metaphysics and the Novel," in *Sense and Non-sense* (1996/1945).

in the humanities, but only to say that theory in the humanities is principally considered as an epistemological ambition, driven by the search for general principles from particular cases. To the extent that this is so, unlike much other 'non-critical' work in the humanities, critical research in these disciplines is conducted with less attention to the uniqueness of this or that text or event, treating the object under study as expression of some socio-cultural force more general than only its authorship.

According to the editors of the *Norton Anthology*, the notion of theory can be "descriptively termed" as "cultural critique"; less concerned today about Kantian questions of the way we humans arrange our mind-set to accord with experience, than, "with investigating and criticizing values, practices, categories, and representations embedded in cultural texts and surrounding institutions" (Leitch 2001:xxxiii). This results from a more fundamental movement: at the beginning of the 20th century, "the history of criticism was part of the history of literature"; in the course of the century that was altered, such that, "now the history of literature is part of the history of criticism" (Leitch 2001: 1).[26] If so, literature is now treated — at least by cultural scholars, as the critical expression of some larger principle by the author or artist; and its study is thus meta-critical by design.[27]

The editors of the *Anthology* acknowledge the radical feature of this paradigmatic shift within the humanities, carrying with it a major movement from the exclusively figurative, in the direction of the practical; from a "disinterested, objective inquiry into poetics and the history of literature," toward "advocacy" — sponsorship, promotion, protection, endorsement. This shift in priorities is a "revealing fault line" between "traditionalists" and "contemporary theorists" (Leitch 2001:xxxiv).

Interpretive Impasse

Teresa Ebert is not among the one-hundred-and-forty names in the *Norton Anthology*, much less identified there as a canonic icon of literary-critical work. Nonetheless, in her study, *The Task of Cultural Critique* (Ebert 2009), her determined bringing to bear of theory as method and the search for general conclusions based on reading particular texts, is remarkable.

[26] Literature as Sign. Editor Vincent Leitch of the Norton Anthology cites Jonathan Culler (1988), as the source of this insight. For a collection of Culler's writings on the future of literature, see Culler, 2007.

[27] Meta-Readings. This view of meta-criticism is consistent with the position of Boltanski, as discussed earlier in this chapter, where he contends that the ordinary individual has as much direct access to the truth of social life as does the professional researcher; but not the same capacity to express that truth.

In that book she argues that, "contemporary cultural critique has been reduced to the interpretation of representation, thereby translating the social world into culture and equating culture to meaning." This is to deny the materiality of culture as phenomenalized, as dialectically transposed from meanings into life, palpably evident as the systems and structures of society. Invariably, the interpretive view, "obscures the underlying structures of material social relations such as class and instead focuses on the technologies of signs and their concrete surfaces," rendering it "impossible to understand social injustice, class differences, and the violent rule of capital as objective historical reality" (Ebert 2009:vi).[28]

Referring to this distortion of material history, she observes that reducing the social-real to little more than the way the story is told signals the force and danger of the "canonic critique." No longer is exploitation wrong or right, since that sort of judgment is rejected as dogmatic closed- mindedness; rather, asks the canonic apologists, why not consider this differently, as if 'consideration' as inside job by thought, modifies reality as external fact of society.

Submerging Truth in Layers of Linguistic Foam

Ebert assails the dominant critical mode in forcefully proscriptive terms. Ironically dignified by use of always new and more englobing language, the popular solution for each social problem is to dissolve it in waves of discourse, analytically constituting what Richard Rorty labeled, a "higher nominalism."[29]

This is achieved not by arguing about the objective standards of truth, but by denying they exist. To the extent that existence is treated as if in "a world without an outside," stripped of all possibility of a regulative principle larger than the paragraph used to describe it, any given situation can be respun as best fits the desire of those who control the loom.

---

[28] The brief Preface Ebert composed to introduce this book (2009) is an important essay all its own, on: "The Critique of Interpretive Reason."

[29] Nominal Superiority. Formally trained in philosophy, working at the border of the humanities and literature, Richard Rorty (1931–2007) was one of the more appreciated U.S. intellectuals of the second half of the twentieth century. He decided, not exactly that the lie is the truth, but that surely the joke about truth is on us, because Western savants, as disciplined ironists, use convenient, or at least academically acceptable, "contingent vocabularies" to interpret life in ways that fit with the pragmatic requirements of various disciplines, even if often holding little identifiable relation with truth. His best known books are *Philosophy and the Mirror of Nature* (1979) and *Contingency, Irony, and Solidarity* (1989). As will become apparent, his work fits with the position of both Michel Foucault (Chapter Four) and Hayden White (Chapter Eight).

To counter this distortion, Ebert undertakes to "critique this interpretative logic," with its "displacing of materialism by materiality, the substitution of the concrete for the abstract." Considering Marx as source of more than just polemic literature, she recommends we "begin to understand culture in materialist terms as an extension of the social relations of production" (2009:xii).

The alternative she favors to interpretation is explanation, cutting short the critique as play with words, by undertaking "an analytics of cause and effect." Capital interests find that dangerous because, "explanation is a foundationalist analysis that understands the everyday by appealing to Truth." Interpretation, on the contrary, "is represented as a reading that is free from the metaphysics of essence (Truth)" (2009:xiii).

Re-centering criticism on the productive truth of social relations is the objective that motorizes Ebert's book. She goes at it by examining various zones of critical engagement, including feminist critique, postcolonial critique, queer theory, and the romance novel movement (particularly its latest incarnation, "Chic-Lit"). Rather than targeting her chapters on conceptual issues of social sciences, she weaves in her strongly held critical views about social dynamics pretty much everywhere along the way.

The scope of her concern about the denial of external referents is not a worry about the insipid consequences for students in humanities classes, but for political spokespersons that use this logic to justify as reasoned interpretation the spread of deception as truth. While those who confuse interpretative critique with culture critique are surely not liars, by default the result verges on complicity.

Her heavy hand fingers a number of intellectual icons of the last half-century: in one sole paragraph in her Preface, she tars with the same brush, Richard Rorty, Susan Butler, Clifford Geertz, Jacques Derrida, Martin Heidegger, Eve Kosofsky Sedgwick and Michel Foucault. Throughout the book she returns to their texts to buttress that negative assessment. She judges them all as having been seduced into propagating one or another "version of the Kantian immanent critique in which the outside is collapsed into the inside," such that being is reduced to a state of mind, and the truth, as that which is consistent with itself, conflates certainty with self-obsession" (Ebert 2009:xiv).

Ebert calls for a "transformative cultural critique (that) ineluctably involves class analysis." It must "go beyond textual analysis, which... gives pleasure to the reader," so as "to produce knowledge of actual material conditions, which are always matters of class." This would be achieved, she argues, "by writing materialism and class back into cultural critique" (2009:xv). Thus, her theme:

> The task of a transformative materialist cultural critique is to provide, by explanation, critique-al knowledges that can be deployed not only to fight cultural oppression but also to struggle for freedom from necessity. (2009:xvi)

Marx and Critique

The middle pages of Ebert's book focus on how alienation as the crisis of labor is linked to structural issues, the denial of which is the political ploy of mundane critical activity. To demonstrate how this is done she focuses much of her study on the un-critical style of most critics, many of whom are very well known, and, if still among us, probably find her position disconcerting.

The biggest dead-name in literary criticism she challenges is Paul de Man (d. 1983). He is responsible for the widespread use of the trope 'reading,' which is found salting various pages of countless contemporary books, even this one. The biggest living-name she targets is Judith Butler, who gives us another popular trope, 'performativity' (which I tend to avoid). Ebert is particularly aghast at the way such terms are assembled, generating talk such as, 'a performative reading of social texts.' While the result is lyrically fascinating, in terms of critical practice, it goes nowhere.[30]

She is lucid in her position, which makes clear the connection she sees between the Marx critique in particular and literary criticism in general. What she says is:

> Today the Marxist roots of cultural critique are largely obscured by the 'linguistic turn' that has instituted topological reading as the canonic protocol of reading. [because] ... Contemporary readings are shaped ... by two contesting analytics: the topological and the materialist. Topological reading is antimimetic and grounded in its questioning of the correspondence between language and reality. It situates what is traditionally called the 'meaning' of the text in the text itself. [Alternatively]... the materialist theory of reading understands meaning primarily as a social relation. (Ebert 2009: 173–74)

---

30 Dematerialized Texts. Paul de Man's most attended collection of essays is: *Blindness and Insight: Essays in the Rhetoric of Contemporary Criticism* (2006/1983). Although she has written a great deal since, particularly on feminism, Judith Butler's career rests largely on the reworking of her doctoral dissertation: *Subjects of Desire: Hegelian Reflections in Twentieth-Century France* (2012/1984).

She develops this position in an incisive argumentative style, using the historical-materialist strategy in such a manner that effectively embodies that method as text. This is achieved by maneuvering between claims by critics that rest internal to their writings, linked with referents in the larger reality which they ignore and establishing in the process not exactly an error of logic in ordinary criticism but a general fault of misplaced consequentiality. While that approach comes across as a form of critical pragmatism, unlike what is suggested by Boltanski, Ebert's approach is manifestly dialectic and materialist and thus more penetrating and less easily irrefutable.

By tragic necessity, truth implies untruth. Yet irony (as tool of conventional critique) breaks the connection between signifier and referent, such that the truth announced by the adjectives attached to the one does not pertain to the referent as commonly understood. Like the grinning flame that leaps voraciously from the fireplace and singes Cinderella's dancing slippers, irony is neither denial nor falsehood but easily turns into malicious deception, with a smirk.

Teresa Ebert eschews irony; yet singe she does. She rolls through her text like a rail-checker on a handcar, constantly assessing what is beneath the wheels causing the bumps and grinds of the ride. The truth of the adventure is in the unseen material forces, even if the glamour of the trip is in the open sky above.

Probing the Historicity of Material Reality

In an important chapter in her study, "Reading Ideology: Marx, de Man, and Critique," Ebert demonstrates the justice of the historical-materialist method for literary criticism.

The problem as she sees it (in agreement with the view of Hayden White in Chapter Seven) is that, "normal contemporary cultural critique—meaning 'normal' as in 'normal science'—is tropological."[31] A trope is a term like Big Mac, which supposedly nourishes its meaning via self-consumption. Like a Gibralteresque Rock, there on its own, the result is

---

[31] Revolutionary Science. Ebert cites Thomas Kuhn (1962) here, in reference to the 'normal science' notion, which in terms of her text is a meta-trope, explaining how one or another such figure of thought colonizes and dominates every academic discipline until displaced by a "paradigm shift" as epistemological revolution. For the record, it is possible that inspiration for this observation, which makes the fame of Kuhn, actually lay with the work of Michael Polanyi, whose work has yet to be fully appreciated for its originality. See Michael Polanyi, *Personal Knowledge: Toward a Post-Critical Philosophy* (2007), based on his Gifford Lectures, Scotland, University of Aberdeen: 1951–52.

unarguable; it simply is, and by that says it all. For lack of depth within, as well avoiding concern for any standard of taste for comparison from beyond, tropes stifle reflection; beyond their immediate and ephemeral inhalation, there is nothing to think about. (In spite of the millions sold annually, who has ever contemplated deeply while eating a Big Mac?).

Whatever they help recall by ingestion, tropes leave few memory traces; not only crimes without victims, but as if without criminals. The only justice to be sought is self-inflicted capital consumption for having been bitten by the same tropic bug again.[32]

The tropist is like a fellow on a train with his smart-phone, absorbed in the magical production of the last picture he shot, wrapped up in the process with such fascination, that he not only misses the view but fails to notice when the trestle over the canyon on which his car is passing begins to collapse. If, as a result, "reading is an account of a text's self-difference," focused on an expression's playing with itself, then casting a determined gaze on a trope as if true is about as satisfying as peaking through a keyhole to observe someone captured by bodily self-obsession. From there back to thought: who can disagree that, for a tropist, "[ordinary] philosophy is a form of reading as writing," with the image of mental masturbation that this conjures up (Ebert 2009: 169–70).

Ebert anchors her proposed alternative to the tropist whirl-pool of normal critique, in the *German Ideology* text of Marx and Engel (1845). Along the way she clarifies the boundaries, ideal-typically, between normal or canonic cultural criticism and historical-materialist alternative.[33]

If we return to the train ride and the rock-'n-roll carriage, with our average hyper-modern humanoid there with her ever-flashing smart-phone; what normal critique shows is that the ride is simply lovely. But what a historical-materialist critique reveals is that the smooth sailing of the engine on that glistening ribbon of track rests on the backs of Chinese and Irish immigrants, many of whom died on the job, historically enabled by the power of capital to indenture if not actually enslave the thousands of men and women needed to level mountains and traverse ravines, using that very human muscle to assure the durable material of that transport structure:

---

32 Tropic Strides. In Chapter Seven, we will see that Hayden White bases his *Metahistory* study of the evolution in the way academic history was written during the nineteenth century, on the movement over time from one dominant trope to another.

33 Playing Favorites. Although unambiguous about those she disapproves of, it takes very careful reading to determine which major critical figures Ebert admires. In her favored category it is difficult to extend the list beyond Roland Barthes and Jean-Paul Sartre.

> Dominant cultural critique marginalizes the idea of reading as a materialist practice whose trajectories of interpretation are determined not by the desire of the reader or by the tropics of the text itself but by class relations. (Ebert 2009: 170)

This process of marginalization is political all the way down. If it is not swept away as subterfuge, the danger is apparent because "a materialist reading... [invariably] shows how the logic of the social relations of production determine both critical and uncritical readings of cultural texts" (Ebert 2009: 171).

Ebert's alternative is unambiguous:

> Materialist reading is a casual analysis of the way things are and why they are that way, which ultimately is a question of the relationship of the forces and relations of production. Its reading is always global in its reach and explanations which involve analysis of the structures of class relations and indicate that there is no such thing as a 'cultural logic'—that all cultural writings, affects, and interpretations have one and only one logic, which is the logic of production. (2009: 171)

Chick-Lit and Capitalist Domination

I close this section by drawing on one of the many cogent observations raised by Ebert concerning the architecture of domination under capitalism, which is the target for her study of contemporary literature. To set the stage, we return to a line from the *Norton Anthology*: at the beginning of the 20th century, the history of criticism was considered part of the history of literature. By its end, there had been complete reversal, such that the history of literature is now seen to be part of the history of criticism. I wish to emphasize the dramatic nature of that category shift.

As that which carries a message of meaning from one to the other of us, even if not transformed into a free standing text or art form, every human action that leaves durable effects in the collective world is literature. Following Marx, world transforming, meaning investing action, is work; and the product of labor is value added depending on how it is subsequently used, which is to say 'read,' and its meaning ingested and applied. If the result is indigestion rather than progression, there is more work to be done, more meaning to be disposed, more labor needed to repair the littered humanized landscape, and so the cycle continues, of which each loop is critical practice in its most elementary form. Institutionally, the result is political steering, economic management, educational professing. The personal equivalent is the cycle of micro-critical activity, of arranging and negotiating in the flow of everyday life.

Under capitalism, alienation is the name for the decrepit existential state when conditions go badly for the work force. Being fed the illusion that one day it will pay off, a majority of people labor to scratch out a life, principally to maximize the private gain of a few nameless others. The result is lethargy, illness, unemployment, truancy, delinquency, fraud, apathy, hostility, nameless fears, suicide, violence, alcoholism, drug addiction, unplanned pregnancy, incest, corruption. The list of 'symptoms' of estrangement from the products of one's own labor is so long as to be meaningless, which, paradoxically, is a main argument against alienation as justification for social change.

Exposing the illusion of betterment, as denial of always the same, is but a step in the process. As Ebert notes, "to critique these illusions is, at the same time, to call for building a true reality that does not need illusions to make it livable" (2009: 97).

Ebert does not dwell on the story of alienation as social process but on the truly bizarre way that western society attempts to compensate for this enormous distortion in the fabric of life. Whereas Boltanski appears to seek refuge from the trials and tribulations of being a radical critic in a reactionary conservative world by reading detective books, Ebert says she reads romance novels, which explains the practical content of the final portion of her critical work.

What she determines from her study of romance is that with life reduced to literature in the commodity sense of the market, the output is love reduced to property; whatever the domain, under capitalism that principle is universally valid. Alienation is experienced when mere being as doing is manipulated into an exchange on the cheap, stripping universal experiences of the meaning they merit. Which is why, as she reads it, in the final analysis, Chick-Lit is always about a property relation, and, "property with a wink is still property" (Ebert 2009: 108).

In advertising and the mass media, while everyone knows that most particular advertisements are misleading, as Roland Barthes pointed out, the cascading power of the total process produces widespread trust in media advertising as a process.[34] This exemplifies the ideological impact of much collective experience, explaining why, with concerted effort, virtually any illogical view can be diffused as if beyond debate. Ideology overwhelms resistance and is the primary vector by which modern economic organization (money plus power plus communication) gains and

34 Studying Barthes on the media can begin with his *Mythologies* (2012/1957), *L'Empire des Signes* (2007/1970), and *Image-Music-Text* (2005/1977).

maintains the upper hand, even if all the time dependent on the willing labor of a human work force that is systematically denatured as a result.

Of course a spoonful of sugar is needed to keep the rebellion down, and that is delivered by consumption: assured today as the overcoming of disaffection by loaning people the money to buy something. No matter how hard one works at it, consumption as fulltime job does not pay off, yielding in fact only a second layer of alienation to the one associated with the job, assuming one is fortunate enough to have one.

Ebert's question: given that, "Chick-Lit is Not Your Mother's Romance Novels," what is it and why is the market not only huge but growing? Strangely, the love-story bazaar is expanding in the same way as is that for cocaine: it sells itself. Why so? Without going into the plot action of the contemporary romance, focusing rather on the marketing game under advanced capitalism, Ebert delivers the message strong and clear: women must seek a dose of aesthetic promise in fantasy, and "Love is the cure for alienated labor" (2009: 107).

Of course the truth of life exposes the empty hope of cheap romance: soon after the uplift benefit from reading the last page of one of these books, the downer of depression returns, for which the only fix is another dose of Chick-Lit.

Ideology spreads a single grand interpretation of all lesser interpretations: You are either with me or you are a terrorist; America, like it or leave it; In God we trust — printed on the dollar. Ideology is a mode of declaration that accepts no response, refuses clarification, short-circuits criticism. It denies the existence of sub-strata forces, principally economic, that drive the action of domination of real life, principally class-based. Thus, Ebert concludes, rather than search for another ineffective fix for the alienation produced under the illusion of capital, the critical challenge is to propose a redesign of society so as to eliminate the need for illusion to render existence tolerable.

If current practices in the social sciences and the humanities identify the field of inquiry for cultural criticism, and if the historical-materialist method specifies the preferred instrument for the undertaking, a final question to be addressed is: just what is the source of the illusion that sustains the legitimacy of the capital mechanism, while turning aside the forms of liberty and participation announced by democracy? That is, what explains the western paradox of plenty that yields inequality and oppression for the many, and confusion of identity for all? For my judgment as to the historical-object which accounts for all that, and which thus ought to be generic target for critical practice, I will wrap up this chapter by reviewing, in the next section, a generally overlooked early work by the German social-philosopher, Max Horkheimer.

Max Horkheimer: Meta-Critique

Critical practice is aimed at human liberation from conditions that frustrate justice and creativity, and from repression, domination and exploitation, which render existence less than might be, under reasonable standards of fairness and equality. In this final section of the introduction, I turn to the third mode of cultural-critical activity, the meta-critique, the use of the critical work of others as data for the study the question of critique in general. While every high quality critical project eventually forces its initiator to confront the meta-critical problem, as demonstrated by the early work of Horkheimer, or mine, here, some studies are manifestly that from the start.

By way of review, in the first two sections of this chapter, the work of Boltanski and Ebert demonstrated differences and commonalities of cultural criticism in the social sciences versus the humanities. Critics of Ebert's type begin by focusing on some literary or other artistic genre, to explore what the work expresses about the historical forces of culture, the underlying, collateral and antecedent influences that predispose the production and give general meaning to literature and the arts. Artistic products are thus treated as a special form of social work; the nature of that work is not just a sign of deeper historical influences, but a direct expression of the cultural forces that drive the society in which the work is conducted.

The challenge for a critique from the humanities is to apply a credible form of aesthetic interpretation to the object of study, a task about which the final word is yet to be said. Nonetheless, after analyzing (i.e., interpreting) the forms of expression and contradictions in the cultural object of interest (some form of literature in the largest sense), if the result is judged as potentially misleading or simply mind-numbing for its intended audience, and if it indicates dehumanizing structural propagations at large in society, the obligation of the critic is to extend the analysis: to consider what structuring forces are represented by the work, and what might that signal about a point of intervention or change. While this strategy might be aimed at any form of aesthetic creation, such as paintings or sculpture for example (think of a Picasso or a Rodin), the advantage of using novels, theater or cinema (think of a John Steinbeck, Virginia Woolf or Fritz Lang), is that the metaphysical content is more directly evident, providing a logical basis for putting in question the deeper cultural-historical influences exposed by the work.

From Boltanski we saw how critical work can be directed at primary forms of social action, most often using observations and other findings from social research as data for a socio-political critique, which, by deployment of a historical-materialist method, seeks a further degree of cultural-meaningful penetration; intended to identify the forces and factors that contribute to the problem put in evidence by the first-phase of a social research study.

As pointed out by him, while virtually all social science research harbors the potential for critical analysis and political advocacy, these are further, fully optional steps, requiring a form of interpretation that is far from universally applied by all researchers. Indeed the purists in the social sciences often deny the rightness of that additional process, contending that to enter directly from social research into the political realm demands special expertise for which ordinary social science practitioners are unequipped.

Now, in this section, drawing heavily on the early work by Max Horkheimer, I will discuss the third mode of cultural criticism, that of the meta-critique. In a meta-critique, the object of study is not some product of culture, such as particular patterns of social action or particular forms of creative expression, but the structuring forces of the culture itself. But, due to the massive fact of culture, from within one, to avoid simply affirming its principles in some more or less decorative fashion, incisive critique demands use of exceptional research strategy. As Horkheimer put this, if western critics wish to take on the western culture of which they are a product and participant, then *traditional* theory must be forsaken in favor of a new *critical* theory. While on the surface that seems straightforward enough, by this announcement, Horkheimer opened a veritable intellectual conundrum, equivalent to attempting to determine the nature, potential and direction of movement and contents of a fully dynamic, windowless barrel, while locked within it. In this case, the barrel is the western cultural system, of which its various societies are its material realization, concretized as nation-states, sustained and reproduced by the social action of the people in diverse national groups, who collectively compose the subjects of that culture system, and who perpetuate it, literally, by their life's work.

Horkheimer proposed a solution to this problem in two moments. First, he advocated use of the historical-materialist method as most suited for the conduct of cultural criticism, which he acknowledged, is the method developed by Marx. However, in order to understand the reason why traditional methods would now suffice and why this alternative critical method was needed, Horkheimer had to take in hand the problem of specifying the nature of the mysterious cultural barrel in which we western people are contained and which constitutes the dynamic frontier that frames and informs our collective fate. From there it is apparent that if there are fundamental problems affecting the conditions of general well being, if those problems persist no matter what interior minor adjustments are attempted, then only a renovation of the containing barrel itself will do if the true objective of amelioration of the human condition is to be achieved.

This awareness shifts attention, away from the lesser levels of interaction to the global or macro-level of cultural reproduction. It becomes necessary to specify the parameters of culture that explain its force for shaping local collective behavior and how they might be reconfigured so as to fit better with the society and people contained within that culture system, and at the same time fit better with the operating environment through which this magic barrel called the western civilization is sailing on its world line.

Treatment of a culture system as if a moving and volatile container for national societies and peoples, also draws attention to the ambiguous nature of the steering mechanism and the motor force of culture. Consider everyday examples of ordinary dynamic conveyances: bicycles, automobiles, ships, airplanes, submarines, space ships. While the operating environment, to borrow a term from the world of computers, establishes the parameters, the motor force of the conveyance must fit with the other structures and sub-systems of conveyance, with the whole configured so that the human passengers can use it, steering and controlling sufficiently to assure that it meets their objectives to some minimal extent.

The difficulty with applying this form of analysis to historical, cultural, or 'humanized' systems, is that rather than concrete like a bicycle, the container is symbolic (constituted as allegoric packages values, attitudes and normative patterns); yet it is eminently real. Identifying the cultural configuration of, in this case, western civilization, in some detail, so as to specify its dynamic qualities and their consequences, is an essential step in diagnosing the strengths and weaknesses of the whole, which is the point of cultural critique. Perhaps Horkheimer's greatest contribution was in specifying the bundle of symbolic qualities of the cultural container for the West, which he labeled the bourgeois philosophy of history. For a yet-to-be-specified reason, once initially laid out, Horkheimer did not place further stress on this important aspect of his work. Perhaps he assumed it to be such evident groundwork for cultural critique as not to need further emphasis. Or he may have forgotten that anything worth saying is worth repeating. I consider the text where he developed that position as of paramount importance, which is why it occupies an important place in this book.

Stalking Western Civilization

If Horkheimer was right, the core issue about which cultural critics should be concerned, appears to be nothing less than the philosophy of history that has driven political, economic and social practices in western countries for the past five-hundred years. If he was correct, then the content of the common-consciousness and collective practices adhered to by westerners are the valid expression of that philosophy, materialized in everyday social action. Given the resistance to change over the centuries, if fundamental conditions of social justice and liberation from necessity are to be attained, nothing less than a major reworking of that philosophy of history will do. For those under its charm, this claim may appear counter intuitive. They argue that the West owes its greatness to this world view, demanding not the need for its revolutionary reform but rather for its extension and reinforcement on a worldwide basis. I propose something quite different: that this long denied foundational issue be confronted, repudiated, dispatched and replaced.

This position is based on the rarely cited early text by Max Horkheimer (1895–1973), written in 1930, *Les Débuts de la Philosophie Bourgeoise de l'Histoire*.[35] There he provided an outline of the underpinnings of this world view, the pervasiveness of which probably explains better than anything else why the diverse critical work over the past centuries of the type addressed by the cases we study, has had very little fundamental effect on the everyday socio-political activity.[36]

---

[35] The seminal text for this section by Marx Horkheimer is, *Les Débuts de la philosophie bourgeoise de l'histoire suivi de Hegel et le problème de la métaphysique* (2006/1930). This translation is from the German version (1970), available in France since 1974. For mysterious reasons it is not yet available in English translation (2012). Attached to the main text is a shorter one by Horkheimer concerning Hegel, dated 1932, which I am not directly addressing at this time.

[36] Mentality. The idea of a culture-force expressed as mentality or national character is at least as old as Herder; its often contested existence implies an aesthetic *a priori* to

Through time, reinforcement of the world view that materializes this philosophy of history has sustained the growth of a western way of life that is now seriously out of fit with contemporary conditions. Through the generations, even if the operating environment, technical infrastructure and the position of the West in the world has shifted considerably, the guiding principles, particularly concerning how society is steered politically, and how it is powered economically, have not adapted as needed. Instead, the economy and political apparatus have become locked in a reactionary grip. Relations of production and distribution comply with forms that are seriously dated. The market economy has developed its own sources of rigidity that limit equality, misallocate burden, deny the worth and dignity of the individual, and payoff handsomely, but only for very few. Unabated for centuries, the protracted nature of these problems has generated unacceptable distortions between the promise of western modernity and its material realization.

While the tandem of practices both active and ideological associated with that world view is the basis of western hegemony, serious questions are now being raised within and beyond the West regarding not just its effectiveness but the possibility of its continued perpetuation, raising the question: will the West fall? It appears that this particular philosophy of history is the guilty party against which the call for liberation is justified and thus ought to be the primary target for cultural criticism.[37]

---

rational thought, which is the way I intend it here, as carrier at the cultural level of the bourgeois philosophy of history. See Johann Gottfried Herder, *Histoire et Cultures* (2000/1774), including Herder's "Une Autre Philosophie de L'Histoire" (see p. 71 for his reference to the "charatère des nations"), with selected extracts appended from Herder's, "Idées pour la philosophie de l'histoire de l'humanité."

37 Philosophy of History. A philosophical project constitutes a global postulate, proposing a model of humankind and of society, suggesting a particular logical mapping of the one onto the other; as if given the opportunity, individuals of that nature could construct or at least choose to inhabit a world based on such a model of society. With varying degrees of formality and completeness, all great philosophers (e.g., Plato, Descartes, Kant, Hegel), advanced that sort of proposition, furnishing major philosophical templates that mark the history of philosophy.

Academic philosophies are not equivalent with the world view that constitutes the social-philosophical terrain of common consciousness for an entire society, establishing frontiers on the possibilities for being and knowing as understood and put into life through collective action. Rather, the contours of a philosophy of history make themselves evident (as dialectical constructs) in direct proportion to the energy with which critics internal to the societies they support put in question its moral boundaries. For a discussion (not entirely consistent with mine) of this difficult subject see W.W. Walsh, *An Introduction to the Philosophy of History* (1992/1951).

What Historical Origins for Critical Theory?

By this strong reading of the largely underplayed 1930 essay by Horkheimer, I am going beyond what is conventionally used to date the origins of critical theory. Paradoxically, that conventional dating is also derived from the writings of Horkheimer, but from the somewhat later and very well known work, his 1937 manifesto, "Traditional and Critical Theory." It seems reasonable to argue that in the first of those essays, he formulated an understanding of the proper object of critical studies, namely, the bourgeois philosophy of history. Then, in his 1937 essay, he argued for a particular application of the historical-materialist method as appropriate mode of investigation, if that historical-object was to be effectively taken to task. Curiously, the 1930 text is very little known, not yet translated into English nor even cited by Horkheimer in his own widely read and highly applauded 1937 methodological essay.[38]

Having arisen to inform western civilization many generations ago, what Horkheimer identifies as the bourgeois philosophy of history now constitutes the ground rules for the relations of production in the West. The effects of this have agitated cultural critics for centuries. Yet, over that period resistance to fundamental modification of the western way of

[38] Textual Disconnection. The personal crisis faced by Horkheimer between 1930 and 1937 (chased from his job in Germany, migrating ultimately to the U.S.) undoubtedly had an inestimable impact on his aesthetic orientation, of which the disconnection between his first and second text is probably only a minor sign. A remarkable new study of the Frankfurt School movement just out in France by Jean-Marc Durand-Gasselin (*L'École de Frankfurt*, 2012) includes only brief attention to the 1930 text by Horkheimer.

When explaining the lineage of critical theory, Durand-Gasselin is clear as to his priorities: "We privilege here the texts of Horkheimer and principally that of 1937 for three reasons: the central institutional position of Horkheimer; the date of this text (at the beginning of his stay in the USA before any evolution in his position, during the classic period of interdisciplinary work); and, the fact that is it the text of reference by Habermas and Honneth when they set out to relaunch the enterprise on new theoretical bases" (Durand-Gasselin 2012, Note 143: 473). By this announcement it is evident that he largely bypasses the 1930 text.

Durand-Gasselin is a very well-read Germanist and historian of philosophical thought. This book, his first, is very well researched. The product of years of work, it is anchored with 85 pages of notes. He insists on the importance of the influence of Lukács in the constitution of critical theory in Frankfurt; due to the complexity of the career of Lukács, that opens a number of issues which I will not deal with in detail. However, Lukács definitely participated in the early meetings called by Horkheimer's predecessor in Frankfurt, Karl Grünberg, who was able to raise the money to get the Institute off the ground, literally, in a new building constructed for it in Frankfurt in 1924. By that time, all three of the major early works of Lukács, *Soul and Form* (1911), *Theory of the Novel* (1916) and *History and Class Consciousness* (1923), were in circulation and surely provided him with considerable leverage of expression.

societal organization has been striking. While initially somewhat different in form and effect, by the 20th century, no matter what the method or celebrity of the critic, in the end, the western way always seems to right itself, and like a kayak in a torrent, indifferent to the jeopardy of its human cargo, roar onward.

The implications seem clear: either cultural criticism will continue to achieve little more than planting petunias on the dangerous machinery of western modernity that dehumanizes existence as it transforms social relations into commodities, or the philosophy of history that determines the self-righting capacity of the West will be challenged directly and changed.[39]

Horkheimer's Bourgeois Philosophy

Horkheimer's text (2010/1930) on the bourgeois philosophy of history demonstrates the critical acuity that opened the way for his legendary career. Following completion of his studies in 1925, and after a brief period in the role of professor, he assumed the role of Director of the Institute of Social Research at the University of Frankfurt Germany (1930), and initiated the Institute journal, *Studies in Philosophy and Social Science*. He also recruited most of those who contributed to the development of what came to be known as the Frankfurt School of Critical Theory. Having only begun, he was soon evicted from his post by the Nazis (1933). With the subsequent closing of the Institute, he moved to New York City (by way of Switzerland and France), where he composed the text that is considered the *methodological* manifesto of the critical theory movement, *Traditional and Critical Theory* (1937). As a sort of sequel, before returning to Germany he collaborated with Theodor Adorno in writing *The Dialectic of Enlightenment* (Adorno and Horkheimer 2001/1944), which continues to excite interest in that intellectual movement.[40]

---

39 Post-Modernity. On the basis of the current crisis of the West, we endorse the validity of the postmodern possibility as what Alain Badiou might label a contemporary event: meaning, in this case, the eruption of the possibility of the deinstitutionalization of the bourgeois philosophy of history and its replacement with something different, which by definition would mark the dissolution of the modern age. See Alain Badiou, *L'Être et l'Événement*, 1988 [*Being and Event*, 2002].

My view of a postmodern condition does not imply the 'end of truth' but only of its refoundation, leading to a reconstitution of the {Symbolic—Organizational—Technical} domains of Western Society (See Technical Appendix).

40 Intellectual Nomad. The main elements of the text, *Dialectic of Enlightenment*, were composed in 1940, although the text was not published until 1944, when Horkheimer returned to Germany. Given the problems he faced personally and historically between

While his 1930 essay constituted the silent background, in his 1937 text, Horkheimer provided a historical and conceptual justification for critical theory as mode of engaged research by placing in question the unreasonable pursuit of the ambition of western enlightenment as underwritten by its philosophy of history. The result was far from innocent, demanding that cultural critics undertake rational-evaluative study of the workings of western society, linked with propositions about what might be done for its betterment in the interests of humanity.[41]

Given Horkheimer's lack of subsequent direct attention to it, there is some risk that my assertion as to the protean importance of that 1930 text is unfounded.[42] Still we must note that, though enigmatically, he provides evidence in support of this case. The issue concerns philosophy of history itself and he admits as much in his Preface to that book. While acknowledging that "these studies were drawn by the author in view of his own edification," he was convinced that it was important because, "current reflection on history is also located at the center of history of which the roots plunge well in advance of the present," (Horkheimer 2010/1930: Preface 9).

That mystifying reflection is a wonderful summary of the dialectics of history: both as philosophy and as realization of the way the actual history of a culture group constitutes a preconditioning force from its past, carried forward as world view about the ideality of some particular future condition. A formative force is then exerted on social production in the present, mobilized as collective action that favors movement

---

1930 and 1947, it is remarkable that Horkheimer maintained not just a certain intellectual consistency, but even the capacity to work at all. There was his own personal experience with the penetration of political forces into the university milieu, the eviction of Jews from Europe, the destruction of his homeland by war, the strange misunderstanding of all that by the U.S. population, the aftermath truth about the Holocaust, the guilt issue of having been one of the few to get out alive, and finally, his return to Germany, under destitute conditions.

41 Subjective Understanding. As discussed briefly in this chapter, centered in the {fact versus value} debate, the distinction between natural science research and studies of the effects of human action in the world, was the topic of interest more than a century ago for Dilthey. See his, *Introduction to the Human Sciences* (1991/1883).

42 Object and Method. Analogous with the work by Descartes long before him, Horkheimer treated his cultural critical project in two moments: the first, in 1930, identifying the object of his concern, the second, in 1937, specifying the method for its critical study.

In Descartes' case, the first moment was specification of his method (*Discours de la méthode* 1637), the second was a metaphysical justification for its use (*Discourse on the Method* 1641). Because of formal differences, this analogy concerning their method of procedure must not be pushed beyond its explanatory utility.

toward a favored range of possible futures, as if predetermined 'naturally' in advance.[43]

Putting into action the critical project identified by Horkheimer implies use of the historical-materialist method as the only way to go after the culture system as such. However, that method is itself historical material, which came into being thanks to earlier work by Karl Marx. Not specially because of Marx, Horkheimer, or that movement, but because of the proven analytic-synthetic power of that method, to undertake cultural criticism today is to perceive society as constituted via patterns of human relations and modes of production; woven together (synchronically and diachronically) by symbolic constructs that inform the common consciousness, exhibiting tensions, contradictions and possibilities that demand critical attention if human well-being is to be assured by their product. Today this method has expanded its reach and now effectively defines the operative mode of critical social science.[44]

As for this philosophy of history, Horkheimer was its discoverer and not its perpetrator. No one can say how an overarching philosophy develops as the figurative domain of the material constitution for a society. As it occurs, it imposes itself as conventional understanding in action, establishing the contours by which current historic conditions are lived into reality as the structuration of collection action for a culture group. It furnishes key elements of both description and justification for a recognized collective history and future destiny, mobilizing a particular range of coordinated action and belief, in opposition to that judged as impossible or dangerous, yielding a package of advantages and constraints for a population vis-à-vis their real circumstance.

---

43 Historicism. The material from Horkheimer's Preface demonstrates the strong historicist vector beneath his writings, a vector I accept and explain in action as capturable in its manifestation via application of the historical-materialist method. The murky, in fact dangerous nature of the question of historicism during the 1930s in the context of the then rising German nationalism, probably also contributed to his *Bourgeois Philosophy* text.

44 Totality. Horkheimer's 1930 essay predates the release of the early Marx writings so his attachment to Marx was probably mostly associated with Marx's later writings, where Marx elaborated his view of scientific materialism and the class-issue in his study of capital. This perspective was reinforced by the work of Georg Lukács on *Orthodox Marxism* (in his volume on Hist*ory and Class Consciousness,* 1919), which came out just as Horkheimer was beginning his career.

Lukács stressed the notion of totality, in the sense that, "Only in [a] context which sees the isolated facts of social life as aspects of the historical process and integrates them in a totality, can knowledge of the facts hope to become knowledge of reality" (Lukács 1990/1919: 8). Collaterally, as I noted earlier, the language Lukács cites from Marx (synthesis of determinants and unity of elements for society as a whole), indicates that not just Horkheimer and Lukács, but Marx also was a general-systemist well before the hour.

As the operating environment shifts both within and beyond a society, the overarching and guiding philosophy of history becomes a source of contradictions, requiring structural response. As the disparity between the ideal and real increase and corrective measures become more imposing, the logic behind the current societal order is called into question. Sectorial conflicts develop, the social fabric becomes seriously strained and problems of governance mount. At the limit, the result is a cultural crisis. Fortunately, as products of history, the determinant practices associated with such a philosophy can change, and with that the world view of philosophy in its ensemble. However, resistance to a basic rupture is intense.

In his 1930 text, Horkheimer presented a description of the emergence, in Europe, about five-hundred years earlier, of this philosophy of history which drew into itself a highly selective vision of reality as portrayed by a few key intellectuals. As guide for western national action, this appears to explain the peculiar mix of advances and restriction that has characterized western civilization ever since, including the progressive intensification of contradictions that now place the West in crisis.

He undertook his study resulting in that text just as he assumed Directorship of the Institute in Frankfurt (1930). Although the details are unknown, his treatment of this issue was surely conditioned by political events centered in Germany. By then, the radical right-wing swing toward Fascism was accelerating and the institutional dehumanization and war-making energy generated by that was evident to astute observers. Economic conditions were horrid as Europe confronted the loss of its world leadership to the U.S., and the Germans were in a resentful mood of counterattack against what were widely considered to have been the unreasonable terms imposed on their country by the Armistice that arrested the shooting in WWI.[45]

---

[45] Modern Tragedy. The 1930 essay by Horkheimer followed a long build-up of the Nazi movement. *Mein Kampf* was mostly composed by Hitler in 1923/24 while he was in prison for preaching sedition linked to an anti-Semitic theme. There were major political rallies in Germany by 1928, and in the elections of 1930, the Nazis took 18% of the vote, leading to 107 seats in the German Parliament.

Horkheimer's agitation about these developments is hardly surprising. Some interpreters view his immediate response to this as unnaturally dark and desperate and by that, somehow less than fully reasoned. I disagree, and do not think that he set the thesis of this book aside, as if some less revolutionary potential for repair might be identified by conscientious culture critics, so as to save modernity (and its philosophy of history) from destitution. This issue is also dealt with by Durand-Gasselin in the final chapter of his 2012 book.

Horkheimer was pressed to explain how, after centuries of technical progress associated with the spread of democratic processes, Europe could give rise to this fascist political menace. He set out to explore this question, and after scanning back over the late modern epoch to is origins in the Italian Renaissance, this is what he said in opening his text:

> What is common about the historic problems treated in his book, is not only their contemporary significance, but also the fact that, in the primitive form that they are presented, they too have their origin in the same historical condition: the bourgeois society [which five centuries earlier was] in the process of liberating itself from the feudal system. Thus present realities are directly tied to the determining needs, desires, necessities and contradictions of that society. Such as they are, they are characterized here as problems of the *Bourgeois Philosophy of History*. (2010/1930: Preface 11)

His intent was clear: to explore the broad contours of this world view, which continues, to this day, to exercise the ambition not just to explain political truth and how it is known, but to propose a justification concerning how the history of the future ought to proceed for western people, following certain principles that ought to guide historical movement, and the end state toward which the West as culture group ought to be moving if it is acting in its own best interests.

A philosophy of history is thus a statement of oughts, a moral evaluative position, a secular theology, if you will. To the extent that it informs the organization of the state as steering and protection apparatus, it motivates an institutional single-mindedness as captured in law, about the rightness of particular forms for the civic constitution to be exercised by citizens in good standing. When widely subscribed to and mobilized in action, it seeds the diffusion of powerful, invasive ideology, ingested as an integral world view, usually centered on the rightness of a particular image of society and politics, unquestionably defended against any alternative, and diffused in connection with a spectrum of collective practices—economic, political and civic.[46]

---

[46] Philosophical Underpinnings. Max Horkheimer was very widely studied, rendering the philosophical side of his work an eclectic air, the foundations of which he never specified. In my view, his work shows traces of the projects of the four philosophers: of Plato (interpretive reading of cultural signs as project toward truth); Descartes (recognizing the force and limits on thought and the supremacy of judgment over the otherwise terminal split between mind and body); Kant (considering critical reflection, of ideas back on themselves, as a fruitful humanism); and Hegel (acknowledging the importance of History as societal project, yet not as if history is a force even if institutionalized-consciousness, which as necessarily heavily historic, is).

While any philosophy of history tends to underwrite imposing social practices, during late modernity in the West this has been coupled with development of an advanced techno-administrative structure, leading to enforced application of the logic of instrumental rationality, not just for the material means of production, but for the organization of work and the structure of social relations associated with consumption. This has reached such an extreme that the western mode of societal organization exhibits dangerous fascist tendencies under the best of circumstances.[47]

Machiavelli + Hobbes + Vico = Bourgeois Dystopia

Horkheimer's study of the formation of bourgeois philosophy of history is both edifying and frightening. He identified this process of socio-cultural emergence as resting on three legs: one constructed following the figure of politics first painted by Niccoló Machiavelli (1469–1527); a second fashioned in keeping with the dark figure of humanity as laid out by Thomas Hobbes (1588–1679); and a third based on the determined evasion of the utopist lesson of an ideal society exemplified primarily by Thomas More (1478–1535) and Thommaso Campanella (1568–1639). Horkheimer tied the parts together in a neo-mythic reading of western culture as elaborated by Giambattista Vico (1688–1744): of human history as the cyclic and invariably tragic struggle of humankind to realize its higher potential by repetitively deficient attempts at the establishment of durable and effective civilized states.[48]

Linked with the work of that handful of key intellectuals but surely not planned by them, Horkheimer traces this development as the result of the spontaneous accretion of effects carried forward by self-reinforcing

---

[47] Fascism. Fascism is a mode of radical corporatist organization, most notably evident these days in some large, Western, multi-national economic enterprises and government security agencies. In reference to twentieth century industrial history, fascism is the strategy labeled Taylorism pushed to its limit. The fact that this same logic infested the political sector in Germany during the 1930s indicates the extent of its menace. Independent of the horrid circumstances for the Jews, those events exemplify the tragic danger of elevating productive rationality as measured by technical efficiency to the absolute standard of judgment for the institutional organization of a society.

[48] History Covers a Long Time. In the final case study of this book, I feature the critical historian, Hayden White who delivers a major critique of the notion of philosophy of history, based on an historical analysis beginning with the work of Vico. In other words, White's work starts where this small study by Horkheimer ends. If Horkheimer was right, then White started his career more or less mired in the snare of the bourgeois philosophy of history. It is not certain that he was able to sufficiently detach from that attitude to clearly grasp the critical forces with which his study of 19th century historians was concerned (see White's *Metahistory*, 1973).

state practices. His text is a loose narrative description of the cumulative realization of that conjuncture of motives as action, during the 16th and 17th centuries, emphasizing the articulation of those key outlooks about politics, economics, social order and humankind. It culminates in the interlaced diffusion, reinforcement, and, as needed, adaptation to circumstances of the unstoppable imminent progress of that philosophy of history, defined as its own realization in action, that has dominated western society ever since.[49]

Horkheimer treats society as a multi-polar dialectic system, emphasizing the relationship between the {idea-structure and normative practices} of culture, fused and concretized as what in fact is perpetually destabilized collective action, rendering at any point in time a certain shimmering equilibrium to communities, politics, economy and the rest.[50] Accordingly, he outlines the historical-materialist oscillations between society as {matrix of social action, and culture as web of images and meanings}, as society traces a world line through history. The tensions occasioned by the necessity of a minimum synchronicity among diverse sites and forms of social action and ideas, as associated with movement along the world line between the past and future, generate a further dialectic which must be mediated in the present. This two-fold dialectic nexus is the object of study for the historical-materialist method, applied in this case to the bourgeois philosophy of history as macro-social, symbolically-materialized fact.

The substantive conclusion that we draw from Horkheimer's study is as follows: first, *à la* Machiavelli, to the extent that it realizes as practice the principles of bourgeois philosophy of history, western society is characterized by instrumental action at the level of the state system oriented by the vulgar pragmatism (anything goes) of doing whatever is necessary to assure maximum opportunity for achievement of the bourgeois dream of

---

49 Psycho-Cultural Analysis. There is a strong parallel between Horkheimer's 1930 historico-cultural analysis of western culture, and the study by Sigmund Freud of the psycho-analytic contradictions generated by western civilization. See Freud's *Totem and Taboo* (1998/1913) and *Civilization and its Discontent* (2010b/1930). However, Horkheimer based his study on a detailed review of some very complex historical texts, lending the result an air of empirical robustness that is somewhat absent from the more mythic renderings by Freud. Horkheimer is concerned about his findings in reference to state building and organization, rather with personal psychic organization and disorders as concerned Feud.

50 Ideas and Practices. The evident parallel between the historical view of this problem by Horkheimer in 1930, with that developed at about the same time by Gramsci (*Prison Notebooks:* 1929–1935) is remarkable.

wealth building and concentration by the elite classes within any nation. Second, *à la* Hobbes, since the world is supposed populated by nasty and brutish humans, with everyone implicitly at war with everyone both within and between countries, for bourgeois advantage, it is necessary that there be diffusion of an ideological smog, which, like a drug, lulls the masses into accepting the cruelty, exploitation, domination, inequalities and other hindrances to general well-being; thus assuring a minimum of needed social integration at the community level and, above all, legitimating the regime that governs.

Third, given the practical negation of the progressivist optimism at the hands of Vico's mythic reading of history as real-politic, and given that bourgeois society consists of a bundle of explosive contradictions, it is impossible to suppose that the type of utopia imagined by Thomas More (or Campanella) might actually be achieved. Only a Machiavellian political regime can maintain the needed order in a Hobbesian jungle of nasty and brutish people, rolling forward from crisis — to recovery — to crisis. Along the way, the bourgeoisie must always benefit most, not just because of birthright or even necessarily because of superior competence, hard work, cunning or stamina. The bourgeoisie must benefit most, because if not, their various classes will withdraw support for the political regime, resulting in collapse of the general order and ruin for all. In practical terms this means that as goes bourgeois well-being, so goes the state and the human future.

Over time, and technically progressive as it is (*à la* Vico), due to economic struggle and war, general uncertainty and the rest, bourgeois society will inevitably blossom and decline. In any given country, political regimes of variable moral character, sometimes cruel, sometimes less so, will succeed one another. Through it all, thanks to the promise expressed in its founding philosophy of history, bourgeois society will advance nevertheless, ever increasing the wealth of the elites, who, in turn, will support the governing regime whatever its form which, as both Machiavelli and Hobbes considered it, while surely not utopia on earth (which is taboo to discuss anyway), will be at least (and well before Leibniz, 1969/1710, 1968/1714) the best of all possible worlds.

In evidence of this summary of Horkheimer's investigation of the *Débuts of Bourgeois Philosophy of History*, I will briefly review some of the language he used to explain the contribution of Machiavelli in this unfolding drama.[51]

---

[51] Nationalism within Universalism. Even if the overarching world view described by Horkheimer is a valid explanation for a certain communality among nations in the West,

Machiavelli's Vision

Machiavelli composed two important texts: *The Prince* (~1513, 1532), and the *Discourses on the First Decade of Titus Livy* (1517). *The Prince* focuses on strategic issues of politics and stresses pragmatic solutions for immediate problems of stability for leadership. This work establishes Machiavelli's contemporary reputation. *The Discourses*, on the other hand, dealing more with political philosophy, was originally considered the text of reference, but today is largely overlooked.

Thanks to his ability to conceptualize what he observed while working as a state bureaucrat and political advisor, Machiavelli effectively established what is known today as the discipline of political science. An unfortunate aspect of this heritage is the predominant attention given to his text, *The Prince*, extolling the pragmatic virtues of cunning, dark, manipulative, aggressive, publicly misleading state Leadership, and the concomitant lack of attention to the more balanced approach to issues of political governance that he demonstrated in his *Discourses*. However, that long-term misreading or biased interpretation of Machiavelli's view of governance as work of art is clearly in keeping with the ideological supremacy of the bourgeois philosophy of history that its deployment helped construct. The point is to assure the well-being of the bourgeoisie, as crucial for assuring in turn the reign of the Prince: all other considerations are secondary.

As concerns the human condition, Machiavelli was impressed by the Renaissance preoccupation with uniformity as general concept: uniformity of human beings, of problems, of virtues, of vices, of state formation, of qualities of leaders, of power in its various expressions. As he put it in reference to humans, "all men are born, live and die in following always the same laws" (cited in Horkheimer 2010/1930: 18). For their part, state forms were considered uniformly, inevitably cyclic. Thus, societies and governments:

> ...go successively from good to bad and bad to good. Virtue gives rise to resting about, rest to laziness, laziness to disorder, and disorder to the ruin of states; and then just before ruin is reached, the order is reborn [via strong Monarchy], order gives rise to virtue and virtue begets glory and prosperity of the state. (Horkheimer 2010/1930: 21)

---

this is not to deny the existence of sub-Western, cultural particularities that lend a nationalist character to different peoples in the Western group. Although never reducible to a single theme, such qualities of national character or mentality are marked by powerful affirmations that standout boldly: examples include Manifest Destiny for the USA; Divine Right of Nobility for England; Infallibility for Rome; Europe as Community for Western Europe; Chosen People for Israel.

Machiavelli was concerned with government only as means to an end. The point was to "promote the power, grandeur and solidification of the bourgeois state," by eliminating all blocks to development of commerce and enterprise, so as to maximize the "free play of economic forces," promoting the well-being and ambition of "Entrepreneurs, Merchants, Shippers and Bankers" (Horkheimer 2010/1930: 27).

A False Good Idea?

There are competing interpretations of the bourgeois state: some focus on this movement as having been necessary for putting an end to the domination and rigidity associated with Feudalism; perhaps it was. Accordingly, many argue that the call of bourgeois philosophy of history has resulted in a much expanded range of personal liberties, a greater general voice in government, more dynamic and creative work in technology and trade, and links to vastly expanded fluidity in the disposition of economic resources; cumulatively yielding a general increase in personal well-being and level of life style for westerners.

The alternative reading is less flattering. As Horkheimer points out, while this movement toward bourgeois domination of Europe may have been needed to break the grip of Feudalism, other than for the elite classes and their agents, the effect was to transfer the domination of the ordinary classes of westerners from the chains that formerly bound them to feudal serfdom on landed estates, to new chains of market driven necessity that now tie them to urban centers of capital. While over the centuries this has contributed to an average per capita improvement in economic well-being, the spread of benefits among the lower classes has always been both limited and at the pleasure of the elite classes.[52]

Along the way, the stress on technique as aid to human work, rapidly turned into impersonal domination of workers by machines and forced common people to migrate into centers of population concentration, establishing marginal communities that are recurrently fractured by crisis of one form or another. As for representative government, there is little

[52] The position of Horkheimer concerning the transient utility of the cultural transformation out of Feudalism was expressed in remarkably similar language at about the same time by John Dewey, in lectures given in Japan (1919), where he observed: "The reforming zeal was shown in criticism of the evils inherited from the class system of feudalism, evils economic, legal and political. But the new economic order of capitalism that was superseding feudalism brought its own social evils with it, and some of these ills utilitarianism tended to cover up or defend. The emphasis upon acquisition and possession of enjoyments took on an untoward color in connection with the contemporary enormous desire for wealth and the enjoyment it makes possible" (Dewey 1950/1920: 144).

more voice shared with the people than can be conveniently purchased by resources under elite control. Finally, internal stability and durability of domestic economies under bourgeois capitalism exacerbates geo-political tension, resulting in cycles of exploitation of foreign populations by political or economic colonization, and, as needed, bloody warfare that over time becomes more wicked because it is more impersonal.

Horkheimer explained this malaise as the result of transforming a historically situated, once assumedly progressive solution for a particular problem (putting an end to Feudalism), into a commanding world view, seeding diffusion of a nest of ideological elements that treat a once useful strategy of limited reach, as if remedy for every subsequent human condition. The fallacy is not to deny that compared to the blockage posed by Royalist Feudalism, the embourgeoisement that occurred in Europe during the 16th and 17th centuries resulted in improvement of the structures of governance more in keeping with the interests of humanity. The misconception lies rather in assuming that this particular solution (Machiavellian state-form working for bourgeois interests) for that historically specific problem (ending feudal despotism) should be the all purpose elixir for the human condition ever after.[53]

Treating that bourgeois project as both a universal and eternal cure, while continuing the Machiavellian logic of political regimes to manipulate the (supposedly) rebellious potential of a population of rabid social animals, the effect has been to transform actual communities into the equivalent of high-tech prison exercise-yards, with citizens on work-release status: under constant surveillance, fearful and anxious. This domination is steered by a rigid, non-progressive, and now extremely reactionary state system in service to bourgeois interests, shackling the majority of people not just in the West but everywhere in the world, in a lattice of dehumanizing alienation.[54]

---

53 Temporary Tyranny. It could be argued that Machiavellian governance is only a softer form of tyranny, perhaps useful in the short run for the management of a country under siege, but fatal for a society if it endures too long. In Rome, this was considered politically legitimate; under military threat, the power of governance would be granted to one individual (the Tyrant), and accepted as temporary necessity in order to assure consistency in content and expediency in execution of central orders at critical moments. In principle, after the war ended or the threat subsided, the Tyrant was to abdicate and a democratic form of government restored. Often, the Tyrant enjoyed the power and refused to abdicate; a famous example of this was Nero.

54 Constitutional Reformation. The intransigence against fundamental change is attested to by the U.S. as hegemonic global empire, guided by a badly dated constitution, which fit the operating environment for a heteroclite population of immigrants under frontier conditions in 1776, but which is of questionable fit with current conditions in 2013.

As Horkheimer reports, Machiavelli:

> ...demanded the submission of all scruples to what appeared to him as the supreme objective: realization and maintenance of a durable strong centralized State as condition for bourgeois prosperity. (Horkheimer 2010/1930: 27)

Machiavelli proposed his project in keeping with what was occurring five centuries before our time, during the growth of the bourgeois society in Italy. For this, he was inspired by his study of Roman history, dating from fifteen centuries before his time, and what that might suggest about how to enhance the prosperity and stability of 16th century Italian city-states. Unfortunately, once having developed it, he then promoted his program with messianic enthusiasm, effectively proposing that his view of state organization and leadership be treated as, "an Eternal Law of human history" (Horkheimer 2010/1930: 29).

Apparently Machiavelli was a social realist as well as a political one. He believed that even if the only true virtue is "bourgeois freedom," achieving this would be at the cost of "battles among social classes": the bourgeois against the aristocrats, the common people against the bourgeoisie, and everyone against state authority. This would not be a problem, he believed, since conflict of that nature would surely toughen up society without threatening its form (Horkheimer 2010/1930: 31–34).

As for state leadership, there was the issue of the Prince. Building a very non-human view of humankind into the mainstream of bourgeois philosophy, Machiavelli believed that, as is the case for every category of being, political leaders are all of a kind. That decrepit denial of the value and uniqueness of individuals at the center of this project explains the cynicism about the noble potential of human beings in contemporary Europe and America, justifying treatment of everyone as an object or commodity, including other bourgeois by any given category of them.

As now seen retrospectively and for historical and not personal reasons, the fallacy is that Machiavelli was blind to the truth of historical materialism: applying a dogmatic reading about the quality of leadership because he could not see, "that the psychic and physical elements of society determine the constitution of human nature as an integral part of historic reality." Once the "absolutism" encouraged by Machiavelli had "accomplished its historic function, the overturning of feudalism, and instauration of the necessary State centralism," what justification or need was there to continue to endorse absolutist regimes that spread deception as the truth, use force as substitute for negotiation and treat their citizens as if incapable of wise judgment, needing social control under the law rather than opportunity protected by justice (Horkheimer 2010/1930: 42–3)?

Horkheimer was adamant in his rejection of the medieval principle of uniformity as applicable in a free republic: when social conditions shift radically to alter relations and priorities among all sectors and classes, change occurs:

> ... not only in practical institutions, forms of government, the laws but also human nature. The foundations of human rapports, that is to say, the manner by which men procure their means of existence, is submitted to change, and this movement is the origin of transformation in the spiritual domain: sciences, arts, metaphysics, and religion. It is false to affirm that, the times change, yet the nature of man rests the same. (Horkheimer 2010/1930: 44)

Horkheimer insisted, however, that one must avoid "historical agnosticism," as if there is no constancy in human being, rendering historical comprehension futile. The fact that there have always been dominated classes, submitting to the whims of dominant classes, proves nothing about other possibilities. Rather than taking the history in Rome with the slaves and at a time of crisis at that, for example, (or the 19th century U.S. with slaves also, and in crisis also) as proof that certain categories of people are born to lead and others to grovel; to do so attests to the grim fact that there is yet to be a society organized and governed with encouragement of the world community, in a manner that facilitates movement away from a structure based on differentiation between self-reproducing dominating versus dominated classes that such societies systematically reproduce. From there it is clear that:

> Society has its own laws, and without study of those laws it is as impossible to understand men as to understand society without individuals and the latter without understanding the exterior world. (Horkheimer 2010/1930: 50)

Summary

I am not going to belabor the reader further with a description of the profile of effects from Horkheimer's work, or of the other major currents of the package of cultural (mis)shaping practices that he describes: of how the heritage of Hobbes contributes still to a decidedly less than fully humanized view of the nature of humanity; of how continuing enchantment with the mythic view of Vico about the ironic cyclic struggle of the human species to save itself from the extremes of those who assume power distracts westerners about the possibility of fundamental social change; of the anti-Utopian position used to justify negationism as response to every proposal for progressive social change, based on the outrageous argument that nothing better than continued realization of the bourgeois philosophy of history is possible, feasible or desirable.

During the generations since its inception, other than the galloping potential of its global hegemony, there has been little change in the societal form driven by that philosophy of history, except perhaps a deepening of the trench dug by the capital machine, separating the categories and classes of elite from those of the general populations associated with the profound political cynicism that pervades the active community.

With critical work still to be done and given the, until now, insurmountable power of the structures and systems issue of that philosophy of history, I offer the following in-depth case studies; providing insight into the strategic methods of critical practice in the spirit of encouragement for those who suppose the possibility of a different future for the West and are willing to work toward that.

CHAPTER TWO

VOLTAIRE: SETTING THE ROLE OF PUBLIC INTELLECTUAL

On Vigilance

My first in-depth case study is of the life, times and works of the 18th century French historian-philosopher who published under the name of Voltaire. He generated radical criticism, aimed at the core institutions of his age: hereditary monarchy, elite nobility, an archaic righteous religion, and abused, exploited and neglected masses of under-classes. Before getting to him in detail, I will summarize my approach to his work, thereby exemplifying the general strategy used with all six case studies.

With special attention to his methods of procedure, I will attend not just to his writings and biography, but to the historical dynamics that set the stage for his work. Since my substantive concern is with issues related to domination, alienation and liberation from necessity, I will mostly attend to the political and economic tensions at the time he worked, focusing on how he dealt with what he judged to be the seriously misaligned determinants of the organization of society and what he proposed in terms of reform or revolutionary change.

With Voltaire, as with the others, I will show how history is woven into criticism by virtue of the critic who practices it, how subjective individuality mediates the expression of history, rendering manifest the dialectic tension between conservatism and change. This will shed light on the ambiguities of critical method, its vitality, necessity and contradictions in application.

Critical Judgment

Critical practice is the expression of judgment: situations and events are evaluated this way or that, not by a committee or impersonal government, but by a given individual. The evaluation is drawn from some sense of community as politics, rendering generalizable a judgment that might otherwise be only subjective. Political life in a modern community requires that everyone of good standing devote some energy to this sort of critical activity. However, most ordinary individuals are too involved in daily problems to be greatly concerned, content to defer to the guidance of others, those considered leaders or specialists of one sort or another.

For mysterious reasons, every age produces a few precocious and well read individuals, who, with special access to marker-experiences, transform the common capacity for critical judgment into an intellectual specialty of a spectacular nature. Working more like artists than technicians, they gain notoriety in the role of public intellectual, presenting their judgments and recommendations on cultural conditions as if speaking for the general well-being.

Like the other five major figures in these in-depth case studies, Voltaire demonstrated one variation of this special way of life. However, unlike the others, because he worked before this role was consciously considered as it today, he helped establish its contours.

Beyond issues of timing and style, historical moment and willingness, and fortuitous access to revelation and information, cultural criticism depends on a sense of good judgment against which current practices are qualitatively evaluated. In this regard, Voltaire was outstanding. Intellectually curious and personally disciplined, he was a trend-setter for an outrageous form of intellectual work, displaying the power of surprise based on an acute intuition about social forces, processes and events, linked with an exceptional capacity to describe what he saw in a poem, a story, essay or theater piece.

Although Voltaire worked in an exceptionally individualized fashion, and while remaining formally undefined, the evaluative criterion that guided his work is remarkably similar to that which was operative with the other five cases in this study: as if oriented by a postulated standard of humanity, violation of which is inexcusable because it would cause oppression or alienation, and on that basis, merited rectification. This unstated humanist principle is linked to the western enlightenment as cultural movement, concerning individual freedom and equality as progress on the one hand, and collective organization and stability on the other. Since those two hands of enlightenment are related but different in their expression, the result is dialectic. Critical practice addresses that dialectic, accounting at once for its opacity and importance.

Critical practice depends on not just viewing social dynamics from a lay-moral perspective, but the additional requirement of willingness to recommend negation, intervention, reform, even revolution when that standard is violated. This requires an extreme political engagement, straining, as we will see, toward the dangerous and desperate, if not the courageous and heroic. Yet, exercise of moral judgment is always as contestable from beyond as it is uncertain from within. Thus the fascination with the role of critical practitioner over the centuries, explaining the choice of the individuals who are highlighted in this book.

Here is Voltaire

Voltaire, born François-Marie Arouet (1694–1778), is among the most remembered, if often misunderstood participants, in the text-driven battle for free expression that marked the 18th century.[1] His was an age of despots, indifferent hereditary monarchs, pompously pristine prelates and greed-mongering entrepreneurs, under whose influence ordinary life was rude when not desperate. On behalf of the common good, his erudite insolence against what he considered the degenerate opulence of aristocrats and the arrogant abuse of power on the part of both royalist and ecclesiastic authority, exposed him to constant pursuit by censor and judge.

Although it is not possible to establish a causal link between his work and the ensuing U.S. and French revolutions (1776, 1789), along with others, including Montesquieu, Jean-Jacques Rousseau and John Locke, he helped clear the way toward a sea-change in social-political practices that has yet to be completely achieved. Beyond its political force and volatility, and as recognized through the years by virtually every major literary specialist since Goethe (1749–1832), Voltaire's writings also show exceptional literary form: during his life, even his political detractors attended his plays and read most everything he wrote.[2]

---

[1] For a brief biography of Voltaire see Ben Ray Redman's "Editor's Introduction" to *The Portable Voltaire* (1977). For the full story of his life see René Pomeau (1988), *Voltaire en son Temps*, Voltaire Foundation, Oxford. Tome 1: *D'Arouet à Voltaire* (1694–1734); Tome 2: *Avec Madame du Châtelet* (1734–1749); Tome 3: *De la Cour au Jardin* (1750–1759); Tome 4: *Écraser l'Infâme* (1759–1770); Tome 5: *On a voulu l'enterrer* (1770–1778).

[2] While Voltaire (1694–1778) read and was influenced by many others, his was a special relation, often contested, and historically much discussed, with Jean-Jacques Rousseau (1712–1778). Rousseau appealed to his readers at the level of emotion and sentiment in a fashion quite different from Voltaire, with his incisive intellectually sharp texts. The work of the two played an amazingly parallel role in supplying critical ammunition for the French Revolution (1789). Not choosing to detail those issues here, I am obliged to mention Rousseau's most read text, *The Social Contract: or Principles of Political Law* (1762), which followed up on a problem he explored earlier in his *Discourse on Inequality* (1754), where he raised the famous rhetorical question of, 'why if born free, are humans everywhere in chains of oppression,' and then theorized (1762) on the integration of otherwise self-driven individuals into society based on the dynamic expression of a 'general will.'

His first brush with the law due to his critical position was in 1716, when he was briefly exiled from Paris for putting in circulation a satirical poem concerning the hypocritical maneuvering intended to disguise the incestuous marriage of the ever-so-Christian Duke d'Orleans.[3] Returning to Paris after that first exile, he persisted in his derision, by composing two additional short poems, further ridiculing the pseudo-sanctity of the French royal family. He naively admitted authorship of those clandestinely circulating poems to an informer for the court, and at the age of twenty-two years, was sentenced to nine months in the prison of Bastille. Jail-time hardened his resolve against unjust authority and gave him a chance to develop practical wisdom as well: admit nothing to strangers, and when warrants are issued with your name on them, it is wise to run.[4]

During one of his later and more reputed exiles from Paris (1726–1729), he spent three years in London. There he came to appreciate the political advantages of the parliamentary reforms already underway in England. Still a young man of thirty-years, he evaluated the climate in London as more favorable for liberty and progress, in comparison to what he considered as the heavy handed, restrictive, reactionary structure of the authoritative hereditary-monarchy that at the time still ruled over the French and the rest of mainland Europe. Once having left England, over the years, he became less convinced about benefit for general freedom of the parliamentary-royalist form of government. Yet as a life-long reformist rather than revolutionary, in spite of such judgments, he was never ready to preach open rebellion.[5]

His vast knowledge and elegance with the quill-pen was so remarkable that, when not threatened by arrest, he was treated as court favorite wherever he went. He stayed with Richelieu in 1720, was invited to the wedding of Louis XV in 1725, was admitted to the French Academy, spent time in

---

[3] Voltaire was sent to the Bastille by Philippe II, Duke Philippe d'Orléans (1674–1723) who, at the time, was French Regent (1715 to 1723), occupying the role of formal authority of French Monarch, from the death of Louis XIV until Louis XV came of age.

[4] Since European monarchs occupied their post by divine right, to ridicule their moral behavior was the highest of crimes. Two of these condemned poems (in French) bore the same title, "*Sur Monsieur Le Duc D'Orléans et Madame de Berri*," the first (1716) of six lines, the other (1717) of eight lines. The third poem, of thirteen lines, was in Latin: "*Regnante Puero*" (1717). See Macé, 2010.

[5] Voltaire, *Letters Concerning the English Nation* (*Lettres Philosophiques sur les Anglais*), composed 1722–1734, first published in English, in 1734. When later published in France this text soon was soon banned. At the time of that writing in England, Voltaire was still relatively optimistic for humanity and while not overwhelmed with England, was decidedly negative about France—and for good reason, since he was under sentence of legal exile from Paris.

the court of Louis XV, and relocated for a time to Potsdam, Germany, where, on personal invitation from Frederick the Great, he was received into the Prussian court.

Voltaire was shrewd in business affairs and benefited personally from the opportunities for rapid gain on the capital he accumulated. However, unlike most in the European upper strata that profited from those times, he used his resources to support the production and publication of audacious and well-reasoned criticism against injustice, intolerance and political insolence. Thus the contradiction: between exile and time in some Royalist bourgeois circumstance, he circulated in Europe as the house guest of aristocrats. But wherever he went, he would continue to write, and with salacious results; suddenly he would find himself once again on the run, often leaving behind the smoke from his burning manuscripts. The Roman Catholic Index of Banned Books was regularly expanded to include his latest musings, and much of what is today his most remembered work was at the time either published clandestinely or remained inaccessible until after the French Revolution.

Voltaire's spirit of youthful daring turned into a lifelong determination to expose the truth, which for political reasons forced him to live far from Paris during the last years of his rather long life. Specifically, on leaving the court of Frederick of Prussia under bad circumstances (after three years, in 1753), he was threatened with arrest in Frankfurt for criticizing the closed-mindedness of the head of the Berlin Academy of Sciences. Crossing the border into Switzerland, then discovering that he was again going to be refused reentry into France, he decided to stay in Geneva, maintaining a main residence in Lausanne.

Soon after, 'someone' secretly released the latest and one of his more scandalous plays: *The Maid of Orleans*, a bawdy politicized rendering of the myth of Joan of Arc, exposing a much less pristine saintliness and a great deal more coarse worldliness than is usually associated with the story told of this hazy historical figure. Released under the noses of the then-dominant Calvinist religious reactionaries that controlled Geneva, this play generated considerable uproar and Voltaire found himself unwelcome even in Switzerland.[6]

Leaving Geneva under duress, in the interests of peace and personal security, he acquired a domain near the village of Ferney, on the border

---

[6] In French, the title is *La Pucelle d'Orléans*, with Voltaire's Joan of Arc presenting an image little in keeping with the self-sacrificing, heroic, faith defending, vestal virgin legend associated with the Christian story of his day.

between France and Switzerland, to which he moved and where he remained in voluntary exile from Paris until the end of his days. The advantage of the location was that he could step across the border one way or the other, whenever a sheriff appeared. He lived there off his investments and built a huge château and grounds, to which he regularly welcomed guests for extensive stays at his expense. Critical of the European elite for the way their social practices fed into royalist insolence, he was nonetheless courteous, personally, toward those from the elegant reaches of the French society that he repeatedly mocked with his writings.

Those last twenty years in Ferney were highly productive, not just in theater pieces (of which he composed about sixty) and essays (which fill dozens of volumes), but in correspondence as well. Voltaire's archives contain nearly 15,000 letters, composed and sent daily, to the more literate members of that strangely contradictory French society which, as it turned out, marked the decadent end of the royalist domination of Europe. In 1777, at the age of 83 years, he composed his last two plays, one of which was selected to be staged in Paris. He decided to risk a personal return visit, to oversee the staging of his new show. The event was a triumph in every detail save one.

Arriving in Paris, February 10, 1778, for his first extended visit in more than twenty years, while his work with the play (titled *Irène*) went famously, along the way he caught a bad cold. Due to the long term deterioration of his health, associated with a pulmonary condition dating from childhood, his recuperative capacity was limited, and for lack of available treatment, he died, May 30, 1778.

Until suddenly stricken with that last fatal condition, during those last months he was treated in Paris as the greatest of returning dignitaries; those of importance sought his audience, including the then first U.S. Ambassador to France, Benjamin Franklin. Nonetheless, when he died, given his recurrent tendency for church bashing, he was denied right of sanctified burial, which at the time was the only option in Paris. This official reticence on the part of the church and state to treat his death with respect led his collaborators to smuggle his body out of Paris and bury it clandestinely.

After the French Revolution, his coffin was returned to Paris, and placed in the Pantheon, directly across from the spot into which was eventually placed the tome of his critical-antagonist, Jean-Jacques Rousseau. On the day of his posthumous move into that post-revolutionary sanctuary of republican honor, the passage of Voltaire's casket through the streets of Paris (July 11, 1791) was marked by an enormous throng of applauding, cheering onlookers, estimated to have included one million individuals.

Is Voltaire a Category Error?

Some readers may wonder as to the choice, not just of starting my in-depth case studies with Voltaire, but having included him at all. It might be argued that he was over accommodating about monarchy and the ancient nobility, and, as a reformist rather than revolutionary, insufficiently dedicated to social equity at any cost. While it is true that, during his early life, he believed that the way to save humanity was via the installation of enlightened monarchs in its kingdoms and principalities, after three years at the court of the then most enlightened European leader, Fredrick the Great, Voltaire left that hope aside as empty illusion.

Others rebuke him for his anti-religious views; not for being mislead about the repeated misuse of position among Christian church leaders, but for having discredited the business practices among some members of the Jewish business community. Thus, his ideological even-handedness is questioned, in spite of the distinction he made between the rightness of each to believe as he or she might and his relentless call for religious tolerance; or his outspoken condemnation of economic and political manipulation of religious identity and institutions, no matter what the spiritual belief.

Then there is the issue of gender and racial equality. As an early advocate of free speech and other civil liberties, and against summary imprisonment for political outrage, Voltaire's critical position is often discounted because he was not militant against slavery, or decisive on the question of the genetic equivalence of the different human races, or about women's role in public life.

Most importantly, the contested view about his critical stance can not be properly adjudicated without attention to his position concerning the corrosive potential of wealth and ambition. Voltaire was a shrewd businessman, made a great deal of money and used his funds to live comfortably, either as guest with others of high-stature, or in his own stately demure, surrounded with well-to-do house guests. Is it possible for someone who pursues a cloistered intellectual life in a *châteaux, made possible from the profits on capital,* to seriously address questions of social justice and the exploitive means used to drain the surplus value from the productive labor of the lesser classes—in order to assure the revenue on which he lives?

Voltaire was one of the first to distinguish between the possession of wealth and the social indifference and economic exploitation that may or may not accompany it. He exemplified the difference between the bourgeois-attitude of privileged entitlement, and the gain and use of funds for an ethically responsible life-style and public causes. For him, the issue of wealth concerned less its existence than how it is accumulated and used, and by whom. He abhorred the ease with which excessive funds can reduce their holder to cronyism and barbarism, disguised as the finest fabric of society.

While it is easy to judge his position regarding brute-wealth as duplicitous, without resources, given his times how else might he have gained the education and exposure necessary for cultural criticism? Only after one has access behind the veil of apparent decorum is it possible to accurately evaluate the social and political extremism which often infects the salons of the economically and politically prominent. Without the means necessary to gain general respect, there is rarely the power of position necessary to assure that one's critical position is well informed, much less taken seriously.

Critical Perspective at the Margin

The relation between a cultural critic and the elite structure of society is necessarily tangled. Whether by education or otherwise, it is necessary to somehow accede to a certain legitimate status as a point of entry for critical observation. However, having this access guaranteed via some special case of advancement, whether by cultural or economic heritage, generally has a dampening effect on one's social engagement. Although the late work of the English intellectual, Bertrand Russell, is a prominent example of how a strong critical position can develop for an individual in spite of advantageous birthright, and although there have been a number of others like him through the centuries, most of those born with a maximum of social advantage lack perspective on how society might be organized differently.[7]

As I move through this study, it will become evident that, all six of the case-study figures somehow arrived in a position of strategic observation

---

[7] Bertrand Russell spent six months in prison (1918) for lecturing against the request of the King (George V) for entry of the U.S. into WWI on the side of England. For earlier pacifist activities he had already been dismissed (1916) from his post at Trinity College after being convicted under the Defense of the Realm Act. Born to a family of grand status in the royalist bourgeoisie of England, of gifted genius and refined education, after doing prison time for challenging the judgment of the King about war, and developing a reputation as the first famous anti-war hero, he became a progressively militant critic of autocratic political authority and power, gradually shifting in the direction of socialism, with a decidedly anti-capitalist, anti-elitist commitment. For a sample from among his hundreds of volumes of writings see *Let the People Think* (2003/1941).

based on a comfortable life-style, as a necessary condition for their opportunity to work. In each case, that exposure had conflicting effects, the upshot of which was a fierce choice of criticism rather than complacency.

From a social-anthropological perspective, each of those selected for the in-depth case studies was in a liminal position relative to the social order: on the cusp between class, cast and authority categories, neither fully within nor fully beyond the effete zone of status and influence. Yet, owing to pragmatic education and precocious intellect, each became inexorably committed to exposing the truth no matter where that led. Put differently, a striking feature of this handful of critical practitioners is the evident possession of what in the U.S. is called horse-sense. Certainly that quality characterized Voltaire, on which basis alone he merits a place along with the others, in this book.

Battle Against Fanaticism

Voltaire demonstrated the dramatic power of critical practice, not only thanks to personal attributes and local circumstances, but because he was there at a moment of history in European society when it became possible and necessary to challenge the legitimacy and functioning of the social order and government. While he alone was responsible for the many small steps that led him to mount upon it, the hand of history constructed the stage and arranged the scene for his work.

Surely a complex and gifted individual, Voltaire surfaced on the streets of Paris at a time of transition, in a western world until then stabilized, if not ossified, by monarchy, nobility and religious hierarchy; a Europe about to break into a new political and social order, neither strategically planned nor intellectually anticipated. Once on the move, following what must have been his shocking introduction to domination as real-politic, his work shows the acumen essential to critical practice: willingness to put one's reputation, livelihood, even personal freedom on the line in support of human well-being and social justice.

To explore how he expressed that commitment as action, I will briefly overview a sample of his decades of writings. This is not easy because of the horrid treatment he and his works received during his lifetime; unauthorized, pirated and incomplete versions of his works circulated in numerous languages, often after destruction of the original drafts in regal grandeur by fire, before a would-be executioner. Associated with his incessant relocations, it is still difficult two and one-half centuries later to gather all his material together and in one language, for clear reading. It is doubtful that the last word will ever be said about him.

In spite of, or perhaps because of the recurrent effort to censure him, Voltaire was incredibly popular during his lifetime, which meant that many of his widely read texts necessarily circulating illegally. From the mid-1700s onward, for nearly a century he was the most read author in Europe. By mid-19th century, popular liberty was again being restricted, principally in the interests of assuring that socialisms did not get a toehold in the bourgeois capitalist west. Voltaire's theater was still attracting attention, but by then, only the less controversial pieces and thus largely as pleasant distraction. Although he was read in the 20th century, those years were too turbulent on the military front in Europe for there to be much attention to the serious limitations on individual liberty and freedom under western representative democracy. Now, in the 21st century, liberation movements are again on the rise; so too, is the currency of Voltaire's writing.

To show his critical method, I will focus on a couple of his better documented texts. I consider them exemplary, even if, when it comes to Voltaire, the selection process can be deceptive. Trained as an attorney rather than a philosopher, he was concerned with the applied consequences of ideas in law rather than on the definition and meaning of the key notions implied by those ideas or laws. Voltaire composed literature as if in argument before a jury, pleading a case by sinuous revelation of commonly known events and occurrences, which could serve as precedents for accepting the justice of his position. Yet, behind that lawyerly-mode of discourse, often woven with an air of well-evidenced sophism, relying on what might be called the entertaining side of the tragic, sparkled his famous ironic aspect: calling as testimony profoundly serious issues, usually with a wink, if not with a very bold grin.

For a first look at the dangerous expression for which he was condemned legally and loved popularly, I turn to Voltaire's famous *Philosophical Dictionary*. He began this project in 1752, during the three years he spent in the Prussian royal court near Berlin, as personal guest of Prince Frederick II. He worked on this document for a decade, publishing the major part of it for the first time in 1764. Laid out like a short-form encyclopedia, the entries for each key term or notion are arranged alphabetically, followed by a usually mocking exploration of the way the idea or notion was actually put into practice, as counter point to the way it was commonly admired and revered. With those pages, Voltaire exposed the manipulative contradiction between what was said and what was done in reference to the most central and sacred rights and processes of his day.

Summarized in a line, Voltaire's project was, a battle against fanaticism (Macé 2010: 7).[8] The strategy used in his *Dictionary* was to link the indexed notions to some category of social actor, royalist, military, ecclesiastic, or other, and expose with words how the concepts or ideas were pushed to the extreme of expression, usually to turn back upon, then subvert—if not completely invalidate—the motive or cause that the notions implied.

To minimize legal exposure, the *Dictionary* entries included only masked references to the particular individuals of high stature whom he speared. This amplified the prurient intrigue for his readers, by only hinting, though very strongly, at the strain toward hypocrisy on the part of those he featured, most of whom were well known personalities of the day. Despite the veiled details, the result was almost immediate censure by the monarchy and church, amid jubilant reception by those educated enough to read him.

Encyclopedic Demystifications

His *Dictionary* is considered the most philosophic of Voltaire's works. His point was to elaborate each notion or concept with an eye to unveiling its true meaning. The content differs from ordinary works of this sort because it steps beyond the neutral zone of etymological usage to expose the practical, political exercise of individuals who put these notions and concepts into real life. In this set of short pleadings, his point was not just to define in a phrase the headlined content for each entry, but to expose its truth value, which was usually in subtle contradiction with its value in mis-use.[9]

The legendary Voltarian irony took a special double-expositional form. Rather than used only as a humorous literary tactic via a play with words, as might comics or satirists in the popular press, he applied his journalist method for the study of duplicitous confusion between public

---

8 As noted by Laurence Macé (2010) in the introduction to her collection of *Voltaire: Textes Interdits* [*Voltaire's Banned Texts*], '*Écraser l'Infâme*' as, "slogan-idea of the 1760s… [against] superstition, fanaticism, all forms of despotism and intolerance, is found everywhere in the works of Voltaire."

9 Having begun his *Dictionary* project while with Frederic in Potsdam, Voltaire did most of its work after moving to Ferney. It began as a series of journal entries, not unlike a well regarded exercise of a similar vein entitled, *Minima Moralia*, (1951) composed by Theodor Adorno while in exile in America during World War II.

presentation and hidden intention, between words and deeds, which he judged to be unnecessarily common in the respectable circles of his day. With his expository writing, he unveiled and put before his public the contradictions, between *être et aparaître*, true-being and fabricated appearance, as manipulation and put-on among the prominent and elite of his day.

In France during those same years, as serious counter-point for Voltaire's *Dictionary*, Denis Diderot and Jean le Rond d'Alembert were directing the construction of the immense French *Encyclopédie*. The Diederot-d'Alembert project was intended to collate, in one set of volumes, a detailed record of knowledge covering all sectors of achievement in then-modern Europe. Particular attention was paid to the contributions made in France, summarizing the technical accomplishment of the enlightenment project in that country, for (supposedly) transforming the world for the benefit of humanity.[10]

Even though he made a modest contribution to that enormous project (twenty-six entries concerning literature, history and philosophy), Voltaire was struck by the ethical inadequacy of its editorial direction. Not that he thought there was a conscious dissimulation of the truth about the entries that were included, or a refusal to solicit contributions by those best informed on those topics. Rather, he was critical of the basis of choice of the entries in the first place as well as the editorial slant of the content.

In deference to the censors, the editors of *L'Encyclopédie* restricted attention as much as possible to what we would today refer to as the politically correct. This allowed endless discussion of technical notions and apparatuses, while bypassing moral and ethical issues. Specialists analyzed all manner of machine, but no facts of slavery to get the work done; entries discussed all manner of productivity, but no mention of the concentration of the profits thereof in the purse of a few; entries presented multidimensional views of factories and mines, but no indication of the pestilence and malnutrition of the miners and factory workers, linked symbolically to the mechanism or mallet by chains of necessity.

[10] Jean Le Round d'Alembert and Denis Diderot, (Eds.), *L'Encyclopédie ou Dictionnaire Raisonné Des Sciences, Des Arts et Des Métiers*, (1751–1765). Published over twenty years (1762–1772) it is comprised of twenty-one volumes of text and eleven volumes of diagrams and illustration. It contains more than 70,000 entries, composed by 140 collaborators, measuring more than 20,000,000,000 words, and includes 18,000 pages of text, and ~2,500 illustrations, with an initial print-run of 4,250 copies, at a time when virtually nothing was printed in more than runs of 1,500 copies.

With his *Philosophical Dictionary* (2006/1764), Voltaire set out to achieve quite the opposite effect. He focused on the moral and ethical aspects of current beliefs and practices, highlighting the real-politic consequences of their understanding and use. He believed that truth is never value-neutral, and that even if only in some vague way, a standard of humanity and its well-being must serve as legislative basis for sound judgment.

The extent to which Voltaire was a self-aware critic is demonstrated by the lucid yet bitingly ironic way he addressed his readers in the "Preface" of his *Encyclopedia*:

> This book does not demand continuous reading; but at whatever place one opens it, one will find matter for reflection. The most useful books are those of which readers themselves compose half; they extend the thoughts of which the germ is presented to them; they correct what seems defective to them, and they fortify by their reflections what seems to be weak.
>
> It is only really by enlightened people that this book can be read; the ordinary man is not made for such knowledge; philosophy will never be his lot. Those who say that there are truths which must be hidden from the people, need not be alarmed; the people do not read; they work six days of the week, and on the seventh go to the inn. In a word, philosophical works are made only for philosophers, and every honest man must try to be a philosopher, without pluming himself on being one. (2006/1764: 5)

Following is a sample of entries from his *Dictionary*, including the critical sense, though here seriously abridged, of their content.

On *Adultery:*

> Allowed by the church to permanently separate from an adulterous wife but never to remarry nor to find intimate solace in another women unless he wants to end up in Hell, left by his wife for another lover, a wronged man is obligated by his religion (Roman Catholic) to suffer the pain of sexual abstinence, as if in earthly purgatory for the rest of his life for the sins of a former wife who chose to runoff with another man in the first place. (2006/1764: 11)

On *Authority*:

> A covey of cardinals who knew little beyond the pleasure of the pope condemned Galileo to die unless he would renounce as false his valid observation that the earth turns about the sun. (2006/1764: 46)

On *Arts*:

> Man and the other animals can exist very well without organizations of bakers, novelists, and theologians, witness the whole of America, witness three quarters of Europe of 1770, still, members of these trade specialties attempt to establish a monopoly lock on everyday life, impose the prices

they wish, according to their own standards with little concern for public service. (2006/1764: 27)

On *Authors*:

Ridiculing the then, and still common practice of rejecting publication of truly original texts that announce contra-normative truths, he railed against the endless enthusiasm and resources made available to publish and circulate volumes of empty headed negative attacks on truly good creative works, in tacit support of unrestricted license for the uncritical self-satisfaction of the elite. (2006/1764: 48)

On *Bankruptcy*:

Because bankers are the inevitable beneficiaries thereof, the principal agents responsible for bankruptcies are not faulty debtors but the bankers who hold title to the loans. Yet, who goes to debtor's prison due to bankruptcy, always the debtor and never the banker. (2006/1764: 51)

On *Bishops*:

This post is a silly late-church invention, a sort of superfluous ecclesiastic middle management, useful for flattering the families of those thus installed, leading to a horrid waste of money and the building of local religious-political dynasties that erode rather than improve the earthy well-being of the Ordinary. (2006/1764: 55)

On *Books*:

Those who govern are from among the elites or their agents, all of whom are generally literate, yet those very classes include a majority of members who detest reading and books. Why so, because "thought is regarded largely as an object of commerce," of utility as long as it economically benefits printers and bookseller, with little commercial benefits for authors. Why so, because to take the creation of books as important suggests that those who do not compose are but literate buffoons or market opportunists. What is the result, the circulation and reading of large volumes of marketable junk, empty of meaning and thought, the reprinting of old news as novelty, the fabrication of dictionaries based on other dictionaries, that in the end, abrogate or disqualify deeper reflection, which is what quality books should express and inspire. (2006/1764: 57)

On *Concatenation of Events*:

While it may be true that, "*the present is pregnant with the future*," the worldly future in society is open, undetermined, not fixed in advance; fatal necessity as advanced by Leibniz is evidently false, rendering his sufficient-reason argument largely deficient; there is more to reality than predetermined, "*cog, pulley, cord, spring*," as if existence is but a vast machine. Even if Newton

> was partly accurate, the chains of causation are plural and branching, such that while, "*every being has a father, every being does not have children.*" (2006/1764: 80)

On *False Minds*:

> While the greatest geniuses can have false judgment about a principle they have accepted without examination, all that certain tyrants of the soul desire is that the men they teach shall have false judgment. (2006/1764: 128)

On *Mohammedans*:

> The European Christian community demonizes the Arabs for their religion based on unsupported claims. While Christian monks, priests and abbots pursue a licentious life-style at the expense of the people, they enthusiastically condemn Mohammedans as voluptuous and sensual. Even if by western standards, the latter tend to deprecate somewhat the status of women and of art, unlike in the west where it is rampant, moral degradation among Muslims is hardly the tendency. (2006/1764: 220)

On *Nakedness*:

> Why the extravagance and superstition against nakedness? The Christian churches are full of statues and paintings of naked gods and saints, the issue of nakedness being not just accepted but often discussed as necessary ritual for full spiritual attainment in the bible. Clothing is clearly a cultural add-on that under many circumstances, depending on local climate, is fully optional. So how is this prejudice against nakedness justifiable? (2006/1764: 222)

On *Free-Will*:

> Like beauty, goodness and justice, the words liberty and free-will are abstract general words. These terms do not state that all men are always beautiful, good and just, similarly, they are not always free. (2006/1764: 142)

On *French*:

> The genius of this language is order and clarity, for each language has its genius, and this one consists in the facility which the language gives for expressing oneself more or less happily, for using or rejecting the familiar twists of other languages. French having no declensions and being always subject to the article, cannot adopt Greek and Latin inversions; it obliges words to arrange themselves in the natural order of ideas. (2006/1764: 146)

On *Tolerance*:

> Tolerance is the consequence of humanity, formed of frailty and error, we ought pardon reciprocally each other's folly—"that is the first law of nature." (2006/1764: 302)

Voltaire closed his *Dictionary* with a long list of 'why' questions, including:

- "Why does one hardly ever do the tenth part of the good one might do?"
- "Why is the great number of hard-working, innocent men who till the land that we may eat all its fruits, "scorned, vilified, oppressed, robbed"; and why is it that the useless and often very wicked man who lives only by their work, and who is rich only through their poverty, is on the contrary "respected, courted, highly considered?"
- "Why, since we complain ceaselessly of our ills, do we spend all our time in increasing them?" (2006/1764: 313)

Dangers of a Progressive Position

A hallmark of Voltaire's *Dictionary* was mockery: of western false modesty, of its lip-service toward tolerance, of the chronic manipulation of the call to freedom; mockery of scientific arrogance, of the ideological masking of political truth, of Islamophobia, of papal Christian political interference. Mockery of royal censors, of corrupt bankers, of self-serving publishers, or mockery of venal tradesmen and about peasant-class exploitation. Given his critical bluster, virtually all those of superior status in 18th century European society had something to dread in Voltaire. Yet, the sophistication of his renderings drew even those who feared him to read his work.

According to the contributors to a 2008 issue of the French monthly, *Magazine Littéraire*, devoted to Voltaire, his popularity is again on the upswing. The extent of this resurgence in his recognition, more than two centuries after his death, is signaled by the editorial decision to announce this issue (No 478) of the magazine with a front page title, "Voltaire: our new philosopher."

Assembled in a special section of the magazine under the title, "Voltaire, Here and Now," specialists from around Europe were invited to contribute short essays on his work.[11] All of the contributors described in their own way the particular relation between Voltaire's personal history and the rapidly altering social, political and economic context of those times. The comprehensiveness and power of his critique owes much of its vitality to that dialectic.

[11] "*Voltaire, Ici et Maintenant.*" Coordinated by François Aubel and Michel Delon.

Even if clandestinely, Voltaire was widely read up to and through the early years of the French Revolution (1789). Thereafter, his fame spread remarkably, only to fall, once more, as the revolutionary movement toward general liberty was largely silenced with the restoration of a royalist aristocratic regime in France.

The shunning of his work by the middle of the 19th century was not an exclusively right-wing, reactionary political response. The development of the European socialist political movement also dates from the post-Revolutionary period, taking speed after the 1850s due to the work of Karl Marx. While many left-leaning intellectuals admired the oppositional posture of some of Voltaire's writings, others attacked him for his lack of political fortitude, as if a bit of an intellectual imposture, or the pseudo-critic of the bourgeois lifestyle that he himself lived, and secretly seemed to admire.

Not only do the articles about him in the French monthly magazine underline his contemporary stature in France, but in 2008, his *Philosophical Dictionary* was on the reading list for the famous French national school examination, called "*L'Aggrégation*," the scores from which are used to rank top level university graduates, on the basis of which future careers depend.

Writing in *Magazine Littéraire*, the French philosophy professor, Élaine Martin-Hagg, discussed what she considered to be Voltaire's determination to be "Reasonable." In that regard, his role in the expansion of the European enlightenment project was considerable, projecting a rationalist attitude that did not please everyone. One of the more notable consequences is that, while French intellectuals often questioned Voltaire's vision, the British continue to love him unconditionally. The explanation is direct: exiled from Paris early in life following a prison term for slander, after his three years in London, Voltaire announced that, "reason was born during this 18th century in England."[12] For having rendered such a compliment, it is hardly surprising that the French Voltaire is still treated today as an English cultural hero.

Although admiring the somewhat greater general justice attributed at the time by British royalists to the bourgeois elite, Voltaire never actively voiced a preference for the English culture. As for language, which for him was the ultimate organ of culture, he considered the French language a

---

12 *Letters Concerning the English Nation* (*Lettres Philosophiques sur les Anglais*), composed in English between 1722 & 1734. [V-English on-line at: <http://www.gutenberg.org/files/2445/2445-h/2445-h.htm>].

vastly superior means of expression compared with English.[13] Also, while in England, he was quite aware that economic oppression of the under-classes was the order of the day.

Concerning the scientific attitude, Voltaire respected the use of empirical methods as the basis of strategic action, which was then more prevalent in England than in France. The alternative is deductive logic, at the time the more decidedly French preference, orienting action by grand doctrines or theories. In political life, the latter often leads to misapplication in particular cases of general principles, because of the imposition of ideological requirements based more on prejudice or momentary desire on the part of the powerful, than on well reasoned arguments.

Voltaire's appreciation for physical, material, empirical data and inductive reasoning, rather than metaphysical speculation, contributed to his famous condemnation of the rationalist-idealist philosophy of Leibniz. However, his differences in this case arose as much due to religion as to philosophy. He resented the recurrent invasion of civil society by augments based on dogmatic Christian orthodoxy, and judged Leibniz's view as tacit justification for what he saw as the poorly founded political side of that religious position.

At the time Voltaire matured, the idealizing world view of Gottfried Leibniz (1646–1716) was widely accepted among European intellectuals. Voltaire differed with Leibniz principally on one fundamental issue. Expressed overtly in his *Théodiciee* of 1710, Leibniz considered the world to be the handiwork of the gods, and us humans part of that creation-determined totality. Whatever human evidence there may be suggesting the contrary, Leibniz argued that the gods assure that our operative reality describes, both theoretically and practically, the best of all possible worlds. Voltaire refused that position; he saw too many forms of social abuse, military cruelty and natural catastrophe to allow him to suppose that the hidden hand of the gods was assuring the best for humankind at all times, or that political arrangements in Europe were beyond basic reform for the better.

By favoring rationalism of this political nature, Voltaire implicitly sided with the English against a certain aspect of what is known today as

13 One view of language is as the power of expression of culture, where linguistic capacity varies directly with cultural force. This may explain the association between the global diffusion of the English language and the hegemony of the now U.S. lead western imperialism. In Brussels, the 'universal' use of English as a way around the linguist variations of the European community is said to come from the application of language developed by Singapore Bankers, referred to as 'Singlish.'

continental thought.[14] Still, his fascination with the English utilitarian, pragmatic manner concerned less science, properly speaking, than the vast question of humanity as expression of freedom. He differentiated the physical world from the moral or ethical one, and judged that the second defies precision via the usual empirical methods because of the singularity of social-human experience. Every society is in a state of flux, between cycles of dissolution and fluid renewal, such that historical precedents for establishing determinant future predictions are informative but never definitive.

Another effect of the time he spent in England and Germany was that it provided Voltaire with practical experience concerning what we now identify as cultural anthropology. Of course, in the 18th century that discipline did not exist, but the appreciative equivalent did, at least for the better informed and widely traveled, including most certainly the unusually intuitive and perceptive Voltaire. Although hardly rock-solid, the comparative attention he devoted to national-cultural distinctions among the different European peoples of his time continues to feed debate.

Intellectual Acumen

Whether as expression of chauvinism or sound judgment, to believe the contributors to the collection of essays about him in that 2008 *Magazine Littéraire*, Voltaire's work so incarnated the Enlightenment that one might almost believe that to be fully modern is to be manifestly, if not enthusiastically, a Voltarian.

One of the articles in this vein was by Spanish philosophy professor, Fernando Savater. He judged that while forthrightly confronting the violence associated with social, nationalistic, religious and economic conflict, Voltaire avoided the morose or melodramatic by stressing the

[14] For reasons somewhat different than those of Voltaire, 18th century English empiricists (as opposed to those from Germany) were also skeptical about the contribution of Leibniz, partly because of his metaphysical bent and partly because they deprecated his originality by comparison to his contemporary, and their fellow countryman, Isaac Newton. If Leibniz was accurate, then the best of worlds is attained by eliminating human freedom to block its achievement. If all is determined in advance, then the idea of individual freedom is vacuous. Yet to deny that society as collectivity can and does override individual freedom as possibility is absurd. British-American analytical philosophy avoids this issue somewhat by focusing on empirical problems. This leads into the quagmire of supposing that a scientific method assures a value-free valid basis for knowing about and guiding practical human action.

positive potential of a better future. Even when the subject was dark and dangerous, Voltaire considered well-expressed *savoir-faire* to be a joy rather than a burden.

Reaching beyond the frontiers of his own country, France, Voltaire brought to bear a trans-European, cross-cultural perspective on the problems of society and humankind, seeing Europe as a nation of nations, putting into words innovative insights, establishing a new form of cosmopolitan criticism. All in all, Voltaire not only promoted the then newly emerging concept of Europe, but as Savater puts it, "invented the figure of the intellectual" (2008: 70).

In another essay in the collection, "The Acknowledged Ambiguities of the Philosopher from Fernery," Pierre Milza, a French political historian, discussed the difficulty of nailing down the position of Voltaire concerning the enormous range of hot topics that he confronted. While always amidst a crowd of important and/or informed others, Voltaire worked alone intellectually, with no evident effort to mobilize political support for his views. Yet, when his works surfaced in public, the resulting texts, poetry and plays had a mobilizing impact, as if the genie came from the literature rather than from the man.

This nearly messianic quality of Voltaire's works, distinct from his person, was probably facilitated by the fact that, being always on the run, the only way he could express his true judgments was by de-intellectualizing the content, then hyper-personalizing the mode of expression of each text. The result was the subtle capacity to be a force of mobilization via the workings of ideas linked with judgments, put forward thematically, as in musical compositions, without need to mount on a tribune or lead a political manifestation. On this basis, Milza also concluded that, from a historic perspective, Voltaire was the "first of the (public) intellectuals."

The Enlightenment Quagmire

Whatever global compliments he enjoys, conceptual arguments about 'what Voltaire really meant,' seem endless. As much as a problem about his perspective and style, this was, and continues to be, associated with the inherent ambiguity of the Enlightenment itself.[15] As that innovative

[15] As discussed in Chapter One, the most recognized 20th century critical study of the contradictions of the enlightenment was by Adorno and Horkheimer: *The Dialectic of*

vision of human potential spread about Europe, it occasioned development of new ideas about the state and its government, about economic processes, about science and about individual knowledge and consciousness. This stimulated innovative forms of intellectual activity, evidenced by the composition of a set of basic texts that are still largely unsurpassed concerning how humankind and the world are understood by westerners. The litany of famous names responsible for these works include Bacon, Machiavelli, Hobbes, Bentham, Smith, Mill, Descartes and Kant.

In no particular order, following a logic of convenience largely defined by bourgeois interests, the enlightenment world view announced a set of totalizing postulates, widely accepted with little debate: that nature is rationally organized, that humanity is part of that, and thus naturally organized as well, except for one thing: that the mysteriously, magnificent human mind, and particularly the bourgeois mind, escapes from that anchorage.

In this unstable sea of material and metaphysical convulsions, Voltaire demonstrated a key quality of critical practice. He would dip within the status quo to take its temperature, then retreat a bit to describe it and put it into life. In the end, however, he was obliged to language his critique so that the bourgeois of the day might understand it, and that necessitated a form of verbal complaisance with his object of criticism. This defined the high art of dramatic irony that is associated with his name, used by him, not with the intention of deception, but rather with that of analysis and explication for revealing the truth.

Banished Realism

For a more decidedly contested look at Voltaire, I next call on a small book, recently published in France (Macé 2010), of a selection of his infamous *Banned Texts*. The possibility of such an anthology is not difficult to imagine, given what I have already said about his work. Since he wrote every day, and almost always with political edge, then was chased by legal authorities when the result appeared in public, the challenge for the

---

Enlightenment (1944). By cutting loose western humanity from the bonds of a naturalist-theological determinism, the new individual freedom occasioned by the enlightenment movement allowed greater openness to the future, which is to say, favored creativity. The bad news is that this fractured the ties of human beings from the social bonds of community, gradually imprisoning each in an individual consciousness, without vectors of commonness needed to support and solidify personal identity through social ties.

French philosophy professor who drew up this anthology of censured writings was how to limit its size.[16]

Professor Macé's book contains one hundred and fifty pages of extracts taken from Voltaire's prohibited essays, poems, theater pieces and journal entries. Composed by Voltaire over a sixty year period, each text had been condemned by authorities representing a sitting French King or Pope, for: the salacious impertinence used to describe the royalty and churchmen of his day; for his true telling of the unnecessary, cruel warfare; of the endless financial manipulations; and the non-stop sexual dallying on the part of the secular and ecclesiastic elites who then dominated France, Europe and western civilization. Whatever the nature of the world as given by the gods, he judged that most of the misery we humans face is due to the profligate ignorance, incompetence and self-serving ambition among the portentous leaders who could easily do better.

The slices of material in this anthology of banned writings provide endless evidence of Voltaire's resolve to speak up, and the determined response on the part of civil and ecclesiastic authority to shut him up. As the first in this long series, one fine example is the poetry that sent him to prison in the Bastille for the first time, and in a way, set his confrontational role for a lifetime.

Voltaire's condemnation to prison was based on three very short satiric poems. The first, published in 1716, cost him six months of banishment from Paris. Upon his return, in 1717, he composed two more of the same allegedly slanderous nature. Thanks to fourteen lines in two French poems and thirteen lines in the third poem in Latin, he went straight to prison. Born in 1694, Voltaire was an outlaw by twenty-one years of age, sentenced not by judge but by personal order of the Regent of France, one Philippe II, Duke d'Orléans (1674–1723), who, as nephew of former French King, Louis XIV, was serving as temporary Monarch until Louis XV came of age.[17]

As royalist power holders go, Philippe II d'Órléans was generally no worse than most. He enjoyed a lavish life style, considered war-making as more entertaining than fox hunting and enjoyed being flattered by

---

16 Laurence Macé's volume of *Voltaire's Textes Interdits* (2010), was included at newsstands as a bonus for those who bought one of the weekly editions of the French news magazine, *L'Express*.

17 The French version of these poems is available online: Volume I of *Voltaire's Complete Works* produced between 1877 and 1883 by *la Maison d'Edition Garnier* at <http://fr.wikisource.org/wiki/Livre:Voltaire_-_%C5%92uvres_compl%C3%A8tes_Garnier_tome1.djvu>).

architects who erected monuments in his name. Philippe II was also a precocious and persistent womanizer. When at the age of eighteen years (1692) it was decided that he should marry, he was ordered by his uncle, the sitting French King Louis XIV, to marry a cousin. While thus keeping the patrimony all in the family, the resulting marriage was formally incestuous, which was not then exceptional among aristocrats. However, despite having eight children together, Philippe and his cousin-bride detested one another. Beyond that, as if his legitimate offspring were not sufficiently numerous, Philippe supplemented his list of progeny with at least three other legitimatized-illegitimate children, plus an unknown number of others, never recognized.

Evidently there had been a tragic explanation for Philippe's difficulties, for his tormented sentimental life and his unpleasant corporate marriage. In his youth, while still single, Philippe had been love-struck by a beautiful girl who had herself been the illegitimate child of an aristocrat, but subsequently granted legitimate status, which at the time was rather common practice among the nobility. Nonetheless, because of her thus defined vulgar status, he was refused the right of marriage with his true love. Philippe's response turned into a Freudian nightmare, as he was forced to marry instead a woman whom he later referred to as "Madame Lucifer," or the Devil Lady. He worked through his tortured sentiments as best he could, attempting to resolve his agonized complex of love-lost, by using the Petit Palais (built by Cardinal Richelieu), across from the Palace of the Louvre (now the museum) in the center of Paris, for dinner parties, routinely transformed in sex orgies.

While gossip about the bombastic and bawdy lifestyle of Philippe II d'Orléans circulated widely, not having been born an aristocrat, it is unlikely that Voltaire was ever invited to the party. Whether motivated by youthful revolt or perhaps a bit of envy for not being on the guest list, Voltaire wrote those three poems, mocking the incestuous, licentious truth, about Philippe. They are short limericks, of the type which comics still use to lampoon celebrities. However, Philippe II did not take the joke well. After the first poem hit the streets, Voltaire was exiled from Paris. On returning, he secretly composed and anonymously circulated the second two; unfortunately, he unknowingly admitted his authorship to a spy for the Regent, which cost him eleven months of hard-time in the Bastille.

When he went into prison, Voltaire was still known only by his christened name, Francois-Marie Arouet. On exiting from prison, just before leaving for a three year exile in England, he changed his name, first to "De

Voltaire," eventually modified to Voltaire. In France, the '*de*' is the indicative-nominative that formally identifies an aristocratic family. By tradition, only kings or princes can attribute such rank to elevate a commoner to noble status, usually to reward complicity or minimize subversion.

Although not really of course, by thus changing his own name, Voltaire ennobled himself. Right from the start his critical practice involved not just his literature, but his identity. Mocking false privilege of status just by announcing himself noble, he transformed his existence into irony by lifestyle.

The Danger of Being Earnest

Speaking of jail as reward for calling out the elite, Oscar Wilde's most famous story comes to mind, as does the man, Wilde himself. Conjointly, he and Voltaire exemplify an additional aesthetic dimension of critical practice. In order to be aware of the misfit nature of the social and political order, the critic necessarily must have been born just right. The good news is that this worldly education opens windows of awareness about class and necessity that remain fogged over for most others. Providing as this does the grist for critical appreciation, it can also impose a prejudicial stance which negatively colors the critical positions thus assumed. The result is an inner contest without drawn swords, between aristocrat-bourgeois true believers and the critique, in which questions of prurient deception often play a part, with shifting moral consequences depending on who is up to what.[18]

As concerns Oscar Wilde (1854–1900): having been born and raised in the finest 19th century bourgeois style, his artistic nature and homosexuality made it impossible for him to live comfortably on the terms that life provided. His theater bore a prickly edge, both formally and actually, linked, it would appear, to the tragic tensions of his uncertain personal identity. Wilde died in Paris, of disease contracted while imprisoned for two years at hard labor in England. He was sent there thanks to a criminal conviction for his homosexuality based on the virtuous vengeance of a righteous reactionary royalist, the 9th Marquess of Queensberry, one John Sholto Douglas (1844–1900), driven to the extreme of reprisal because his

[18] The full title of the famous 1895 play by Oscar Wilde is, *The Importance of Being Earnest, a Trivial Comedy for Serious People*. His other most remembered work is, *The Picture of Dorian Gray* (1890).

third son, Lord Alfred Douglas (1870–1945) had become Wilde's intimate male companion.

In terms of historical predisposition (but not sexual preference), Voltaire's socio-historical background proved similarly dangerous as later did that of Wilde's, though fortunately for Voltaire, not fatally so. In order to criticize the twisted effects of royalist ecclesiastic domination of Europe, Voltaire had to come of age not just proximate to the milieu of that domination, but he then had to work his way high enough up the pyramid to appreciate the self-serving vehicle that carries privilege to the elites. This existential proximity to the social crime under criticism probably explains a certain lack of revolutionary determination in Voltaire's critical announcements, often coming across more in cartoon fashion, not as damning by faint praise, but rather as lauding by weak condemnation. While both of those are ironic forms, the latter is the more enticing, almost delicious, since it can raise laughter more than anger on the part of most everybody other than those who are its precise critical target.

Assertively Modern

The more Voltaire wrote and the more he was chased by the sheriff, the more also was he admired by the *lettrés* of his day, virtually all of whom were from the elite classes and thus heavily invested in the institutions that he criticized. The biting wit of Voltaire's writings, like those of Wilde's plays was based on the parody of being insightful in a world of institutional denial, and insisting on breaking the silence. Unfortunately, it is hardly a recent phenomenon that intellectual good-faith on the part of critics in a world of bad-conscious is usually more decorative than dangerous in consequences.

In light of the tragically shortened life of Wilde, Voltaire's survival long into old age is astonishing. His was an existence of contradictions: one part enemy of the hypocrisy linked with unjustified privilege, and one part *arrivist* bourgeois who enjoyed elegant living among European Aristocrats; one part seeker of wealth who used early capitalism to his personal profit, and one part critic of social injustice fed by luxury demands of the elites; one part modern version of Greek tragic poet incapable of going beyond the tension of effort and the frustration of accomplishment, and one part modern satirist who expressed evident joy in his reflections even when touching on horrid real-life subjects. That makes a lot of parts, such that no one has yet figured out just what does the name Voltaire say.

Voltaire's modernism opened a frontal attack against what is classically referred to as the *Noble Lie*.[19] This dates from Plato, who, as a closet elitist, expressed little confidence in the good judgment of ordinary people. Like a medical doctor with a smooth bedside manner, many among the elite tend to believe that common limitation justifies diffusion of half-truths by the leaders they choose, in order to allow the lumpy burdens of citizenship to be more easily swallowed by average people. In our modern times, the equivalent tendency on the part of political and economic leaders and their agents is referred to as Machiavellianism, which is but the noble lie in polysyllables.

Today we see this recurrently, the diffusion of misleading if not patently false messages as justification for regressive taxation, for launching of needless wars, and for manipulation of economic processes to the detriment of all interests other than those of capital and its main profiteers. This form of universally acknowledged public lie is perhaps the most rot-hastening aspect of contemporary societal relations and against this, Voltaire was one of the first to speak out.

To accept that only the elite should know the whole truth, and that leaders must deceive to keep the ordinary people passive and orderly, is an insult to humanity that Voltaire was determined to expose. The retaliation that this stimulated on the part of the religious, political and social elites of his day attests to the justification for his criticism, as well as of its necessity.

More Than Just Digging Up Dirt

Compared with the many popular-culture critics who today turn insight into literature, Voltaire went deeper than simply to surf on the backs of the personalities and the trivial front-page incidents associated with celebrity, to expose issues related to the distorted effects of social status and economic power. For comparison, consider the case, in New York of the 1960s, when Truman Capote (1924–1984) prowled the after-hour streets of Manhattan, sneaking past doormen to crash the parties of the

[19] Plato's Noble Lie. Described in the *Republic*, this is a strategy attributed by him to Socrates as an explanation and justification for the conscious use of myth or untruth by the leaders of the city to promote social harmony, devotion to the community and support for the law. See Catalin Partenie, "Plato's Myths," *The Stanford Encyclopedia of Philosophy* (Fall 2011 Edition), Edward N. Zalta (ed.), <http://plato.stanford.edu/archives/fall2011/entries/plato-myths/>.

New York penthouse crowd, in search of two things: free booze and a bit of gossip around which to base his next day's writings.

Capote became a successful and much discussed author whose most recalled works are two. First, a novella, *Breakfast at Tiffany's* (1958), which, when transformed by Hollywood into durable celluloid (1961), turned actress Audrey Hepburn into a household icon of naive beauty, revealed in technicolor, in the devil-may-care world of superficial glitz which was at the time, New York uptown café society. The result charmed the critics who nonetheless recognized that Hepburn possessed all the Hollywood talent necessary for success except that of acting, so they issued the film a sort of workman like booby prize, awarding the music men (Mancini and Mercer) who composed its sound track, an academy award for best song. The good news for Capote was that this assured him a life beyond financial burden; the bad news is that this played into his pronounced proclivity for a marginal lifestyle that eventually put an end to his work and his life.

Horrifying rather than beautiful, unless one is sufficiently morbid to consider the horrifying as the pinnacle of beauty, his other great work was, *In Cold Blood* (1966), still his most read work . Although more recently the Cohen Bothers tried, with *Fargo* (1996), to achieve a more aesthetically admirable version of this morality saga, the dramatized telling by Capote of the excitement and horror of desperate fellows in search of non-existent loot, cruelly murdering a Midwest farm family of four, raised enough goose bumps on the popular conscience to make an even more enormous fortune for its author. Almost immediately, this too was turned into a film (1967), about which the critics were mixed. As nominee for a number of Oscars, it was washed out in the finals, probably for an excess of earnestness: it was the first major studio film in U.S. history to use the word, 'Shit'! That is America to this day: celebrate murder in cold blood but not with dirty words.

The tie between Voltaire and Capote is not a matter of personal habits or writing style, it is how they worked, in constant movement between the scene of the crime called high culture, twisted in service to high society, and then to retreat from that, to write it into literature. Like Voltaire, Capote based his scenarios on the antics of the real people whom he met as he foraged about the Manhattan rooftop gardens of the powerful and rich of his day. Voltaire's words took many forms: poetry, journaling, and novellas. In his day, the best way to assure that the results were seen by the public was to write scripts for theater pieces, then see to their production. The books and movie renditions of Capote's stories gripped audiences from the silver screens of the U.S. of the 1960s, much as had the works of Voltaire, in circulated texts and live on stage, in Europe, centered in Paris, two centuries earlier.

As concerns literature, Capote's famous murderous mystery was based on personal interviews with the two killers in a Kansas prison, on death row. Since this was a very widely publicized crime, more than only concerning its literary merits, investigative critics were able to study the factual accuracy of his story telling. In the interests of dramatic effect, he had fiddled just a bit at the margins with his facts. Nonetheless it was decided that he had brought to life a new literary form, that of the Non-Fiction or True-Crime genre of novel. This is now generalized as documentary-fiction, yielding such delicious television distraction as the over-dramatized, heavily narrated telling of the last days of Ann Boleyn, the opportunist second wife of the English King Henry VIII. The documentary ends with her ho-hum beheading under the ax, duly witnessed by a bevy of Lords and Bishops, arranged to occur while the lecherous king, who paid the executioner for that service, went hunting quail with his cronies.

The weaving of fictional stories around real historic figures and events was also a literary specialty of Voltaire in the 1750s. Generally avoiding gratuitous gossip and ego mongering, his writings demonstrate unusual intellectual acumen linked with a finely honed sensitivity to the dark undercurrents of human affairs.

Not disposed to escapades of wanton voyeurism, later told in a manner to capitalize on its stock value, Voltaire seems to have entered the Paris salons and country châteaux of the wealthy and famous in good faith, expecting to find the honorable and admirable among the brambles of pretense and ambition. He was too often disappointed not just with what he saw but with its gratuitous justification: the perennial mouthing of the ultimate non-sequitur, that against the evidence, all is wonderful in our best of all possible worlds.

That view, lifted from the texts of Leibniz, particularly offended him. It was used by the elites to excuse every happening, no matter how costly or gruesome the consequences: war, pestilence, witch hunting, unbridled injustice in the name of higher justice, immorality and cultural defamation in the name of religion and spiritual calling. To each such event was attached the 'hold harmless' claim: all is as well as might be. The notion of personal benefit was profligate, but that of personal responsibility, nonexistent.[20]

---

[20] "The Best of all Possible Worlds" is found in the only work published by Leibniz in his lifetime: composed in French, *Essais de Théodicée sur la bonté de Dieu, la liberté de l'homme*

Best of all Possible Worlds: Not Lisbon

Against the hollow song of irresponsible optimism and official blindness as substitute for good judgment, Voltaire's compassionate realism is famously evident in a long text he composed in the aftermath of the earthquake and tidal wave which, in 1755, reduced the center of Lisbon to rubble and decimated its population.[21] At the age of sixty-one years, he seemed to have decided that life is hell, and then we die, although it had not always been that way with him.

This Portugal disaster poem stretches for two-hundred-and-thirty-eight lines, written in a classic French that, without considerable accompanying commentary, is difficult to read even for most of today's French university graduates. When translated into English, it loses some of its punch and most of its nuance. Still, it is apparent how vigorously Voltaire condemned the lamentable misreading of reality, on the part of not only royalists and the religious, but many philosophers and scientists.

Europeans were shocked by the disaster that devastated the capital of Portugal, the oldest integral country in Europe. In a city which was at the time perhaps the most affluent capital in the world, ruin and death were the rule. Still, the righteous ecclesiastics reasoned differently: that the gods are good, justice is done, evil is only of man's doing and deserved when it occurs, no matter what the local crisis and we live in the best of all possible worlds.

Under the full title, "Poem on the Lisbon Disaster: or an examination of he axiom, 'All is Well'," (1756) Voltaire lashed out in all directions at what he judged to be the strange attitude of human irresponsibility when dealing with disasters, linked with a bizarre messianic view that such events are entirely the expression of the will of the gods.

---

et l'origine du mal (1710). This claim ("*Le meilleur des mondes possibles*"), was a key view in the Leibniz strategy to develop an optimistic solution to the problem of evil, effectively, that evil is only a passing issue, that in the end, given what he assumed to be our self-righting world, evil action will be overcome by what amounts to the effect of positive social momentum. The brief and most commonly read summary by him of his general philosophical project is found in *La Monologie*, composed in 1714, first published in Latin, in Leipzig Germany, in 1721. The French original version was not published in France until 1840.

21 While in Potsdam, Voltaire composed *Micromégas* (1752), which, along with another of his satiric imaginary works, *Plato's Dream* (1756a), has a place in the history of literature as an early contribution to the development of the science fiction genre. As concerns critical method, *Micromégas* was also a pioneer effort in the use of an outsider viewpoint as a perspective to generate a critique of western culture. His most regarded exercise in frontal literary criticism is extensive, *Commentaire sur Corneille*, (~1761), which fills 1128 pages (Volumes 53–55) in the Oxford University Edition of his Complete Works.

He opened with a calling-out of pollyannaish philosophers:[22]

> Come, ye philosophers, who cry, "All's well,
> And contemplate this ruin of a world. ...
> Ask of the dying in that house, of grief,
> Whether 'tis pride that calls on heaven for help
> And pity for the sufferings of men.
> "All's well," ye say, "and all is necessary."
> Think ye this universe had been the worse
> Without this hellish gulf in Portugal? (1911/1756: e-book, p.134)

Beyond god as questionable practical guardian, he favored humanism:

> God I respect, yet love the universe.
> Not pride, alas, it is, but love of man.
> Confess it freely – evil stalks the land
> Its secret principle unknown to us.
> But how conceive a God supremely good,
> Who heaps his favors on the sons he loves
> Yet scatters evil with as large a hand? (1911/1756: e-book, p.135)

Against the mystical-idealism of Leibniz, he said:

> From Leibniz learn we not by what unseen
> Bonds, in this best of all imagined worlds,
> Endless disorder, chaos of distress,
> Must mix our little pleasures thus with pain:
> Nor why the guiltless suffer all this woe
> In common with the most abhorrent guilt.
> 'Tis mockery to tell me all is well. (1911/1756: e-book, p.137)

On Humankind, and far from optimistically, also...

> Man is a stranger to his own research;
> He knows not whence he comes, nor whither goes.
> Tormented atoms in a bed of mud,
> Devoured by death, a mockery of fate. ...

---

22 *Poème sur le désastre de Lisbonne* (1756b). All citations taken from: *F. M. A. de Voltaire, Poèmes sur le Dèsastre de Lisbonne et sur La Loi Naturelle avec des Prefaces, des Notes etc.*, Genève, n.d. Reprinted from *Selected Works of Voltaire*, edited and translated by Joseph McCabe, Watts and Co., London, 1911; reprinted in the Thinkers Library, 1935.; online at as an E-Book at: <http://files.libertyfund.org/files/349/Voltaire_0029_EBk_v6.0.pdf>.

This text by Voltaire ignited a critical response from Rousseau who viewed this disaster differently, and played into their famous conflict concerning the essence of social responsibility and human rectitude. Then Kant got on the problem, and decided that the message from this event was technical: why not build buildings of better structural qualities. The global study of earthquakes dates from that event.

For a recent review of international political impact of that tragic event (80% of Lisbon buildings destroyed, ~15,000 killed), see Araújo, 2006.

> This world, this theater of pride and wrong,
> Swarms with sick fools who talk of happiness.
> With plaints and groans they follow up the quest,
> To die reluctant, or be born again. (1911/1756: e-book, p.138)

He closed the poem with what comes across as a late-style existential prayer, concerning lines of fatigue on the face of an age:[23]

> Once did I sing, in less lugubrious tone,
> The sunny ways of pleasure's genial rule;
> The times have changed, and, taught by growing age,
> And sharing of the frailty of mankind,
> Seeking a light amid the deepening gloom,
> I can but suffer, and will not repine.
> A Caliph once, when his last hour had come,
> This prayer addressed to him he reverenced:
> "To thee, sole and all-powerful king, I bear
> What thou dost lack in thy immensity—
> Evil and ignorance, distress and sin. (1911/1756: e-book, p.138)

He might have added one thing further to that final list: hope.

As woefully acknowledged here, by the age of sixty, Voltaire had lost much of his youthful optimism. For decades, even after being condemned twice to prison for his proclivity for politically irreverent poetry, having also been banished numerous times from Paris for failing to respect the tested adage—say what you wish, but be careful what you write—Voltaire

[23] As developed later in this chapter, the late-style aesthetic of creative insight based on historical distancing is particularly well explored in Edward Saïd's study of virtuosity in his *On Late Style: Music and Literature Against the Grain* (2007). Edward W. Saïd also drew attention to the importance of the development of critical perspective, of the critic's personal-historical relation vis-à-vis the spheres of power and influence of society, near to, but not embedded in, on the margins of influence but sufficiently detached to avoid domination. In the keynote essay which opens his *Late Style* book ("Timeliness and Lateness," based on a lecture given in London in 1993), Saïd turns his study of 'late style,' which he acknowledges is a notion developed by Theodor Adorno in an 1938 essay on Beethoven, back on Adorno's career of critical practice. As Saïd judges it, the essence of 'late style' is a sort of dialectic mix, playing at the margins with the soul of a social form, participating in its movement but always to a different drummer. Saïd associates Adorno's critical perspicacity to, on the one hand, "his elitist predilections (as) function of his (superior) class background," and, on the other, of his "defection from these ranks," while preserving a liking for the "ease and luxury" of the status, which allowed "continuous familiarity with great works, great masters, and great ideas, not as subjects of professional discipline but rather as practices indulged in by a frequent habitué at a club" (Saïd 2007: 21). Exemplified by Adorno's career, Saïd observes that, "to be late meant therefore to be late for (and refuse) many of the rewards offered by being comfortable inside society," since in the end, "late style is *in*, but oddly *apart* from the present" (2007: 22). While this issue is too important to pass over in a line, it is my judgment that late-style as Adorno intended that and Saïd discussed it, is critical-practice as I intend it here.

continued to believe that humankind held the potential for good and that, with a bit of prodding, the powers-that-be would modify their shabby manner. As evidenced by the tone of this poem, that was no longer the case.

Voltaire's naturalist humanism took a perilous form when he worked it into his plays and lyric poetry. He linked a decidedly secular philosophy to a particular critical content, that of the heartless and opportunist behavior of the elites of his time. With the passing of the years, the core of these protestations became more severe. With this double edged mode of critical posturing, being both intellectually sophisticated and practically vulgar, his insistence on ridiculing not only those occupying official seats of power, but widely held and cherished beliefs as well, put him on the run for much of his life.

Critical Value of the Systematically Absent

Voltaire's contribution must be assessed not only by how he handled the objects of his criticism, but how he dealt with his times. During the 18th century, royalist and ecclesiastic authority, reinforced by the self-serving opportunism of the elite classes, was so unyielding that, as an ironic Marxist might put it, the impossibility of general political liberty was overdetermined by limitless official commitment to a well-ordered state.

Yet quality critical work requires exceptional originality, which is principally the expression of free-thinking. This is achieved by viewing one's critical object from beyond itself. This supposes a major exercise of mental acrobatics, entailing not only an exceptional capacity for clear thinking, linked with willingness and access to the cathedrals of power, but also the capacity to take the enormous leap of consciousness needed to allow appreciation of what the situation is, as if from beyond its own frontiers.

As a contemporary example, I draw attention to an unusual feature of critical study by Edward Saïd (1935–2003) of the work of the Canadian pianist, Glenn Gould.[24] Gould (1932–1982) was a remarkable music composer and performer. While he played Bach perhaps better than any who tried in the 20th century, he was particularly innovative in his method of composition. Rather than turning his back on tradition to concoct a new form, he drew on the existent, which in a way he decomposed and

---

[24] See "The Virtuoso as Intellectual" in Saïd, 2007, where he elaborates on the critical value of the systematically absent.

recomposed for a traditional performance. Topologically, this is equivalent to commencing on-stage, 'within the system', to orient one's art by drawing on what is there, then migrating symbolically backstage to assume a posture of negation and then returning to present the work on stage, within the system once more.

While we are formalizing the argument, it is on this basis that Saïd affirmed that Gould's work, "places him in a particular intellectual critical tradition," with results, "radically at odds" with usual performative music (Saïd 2007: 121). Quality music is necessarily critical to the degree that the current performer finds an original manner to present a musical exercise drawn from preexisting compositions. Gould went further to create new musical *forms* by drawing on the given to rework its form, often while in the act of performing it, and that is not common at all.[25]

As for the system and its negation as crucial for critical practice, as Saïd reports, in 1964 Gould gave an address to the graduating class of the University of Toronto where he elaborated on how this comes about. Music, he said, "is hewn from the negation" of what surrounds it, which is why all music is a "purely artificial construction of systematic thought." The key to "invention," to generalize the concept, is arrived at by "a cautious dipping into the negation that lies outside the system from a position firmly ensconced in the system" (Gould, in Saïd 2007: 123).

While the architecture of Gould's critical process is direct enough to describe, the ambiguity is in its execution. A system (musical or otherwise) is defined by the finite content that it envelops; beyond its frontier, however, there is an infinite amount of excluded noise. Creativity of Gould's sort, which in a way was characteristic of not just Voltaire but the other five of the cases I will study, requires exploring the negation of the current system, that which is left out, on the basis of which, by original importation of previously excluded forms, the system as such might be reconfigured. The challenge is to identify from the excluded residue just what to import, generating agreeable novel effects, without destroying the imaginative attractiveness of system as origin. Demonstrating the required sensitivity needed to identify what is pertinent from that 'mass of the absent' is the true secret of virtuosity. This requires special deployment of aesthetic consciousness, the full use of which seems to be rare.

---

25 This view of art as the affirmative denial of the evident, fits with Adorno's *Aesthetic Theory*, as elaborated by Frederic Jameson in his study of that text, in Part III of *Late Marxism* (2007/1990).

In 20th century social sciences, this process of paying attention to the 'off' to better grasp the 'on,' central to the sociology of everyday life, is identified with the notion of dramaturgy as articulated by, among others, Erving Goffman (1959; 1974). To understand the dynamics of social role enactment, it is insightful to study behavior arising in situations of diffuse role definition. One might, for instance, follow the executive or banker to her sports club to find out what really drives her professional motor. The difficulty of doing so is related to its necessity, since evasiveness is part of the requirements of the role of executive and banker.

The amusing theater piece by Frank Loesser (1910–1969), *How to Succeed in Business without Really Trying* (1961), bears witness to certain parodied expression of this truth. In order for the new fellow with an entry-level job in the mail-room to advance quickly in the corporation, he decided to get discovered by the chief executive. From his low-status vantage point, the young fellow determined, among other things, that when puzzled, the boss would take to his rocking chair and, like a grandmother with a shawl, knit mittens. So, positioned and timed just right, he set himself up in a chair with shawl and knitting, so as to be 'discovered by accident' by the boss when he left after-hours for the corporate garage. This exemplifies a certain practical enactment of the critical art: seizing upon back-stage information for front-stage purposes.[26]

Creative Value of Negativity

Following the essential leap beyond the given that true criticism requires, there is still the problem of expressing novelty. Voltaire oscillated, one minute playing the role of participant in the masquerade of complaisant despotism and the next, escaping the shackles of authoritative repression to write it up with style. Since language and reference are within the bounds of culture, how does one find words from beyond culture with which to criticize that constitution and the historical event that it objectifies? The critic must impose a new aesthetic on the existent, to reveal its backsides without prejudice. Getting to that is no simple process, which is

[26] Frank Loesser: during a rather short life he was enormously productive in stage, screen and musical creativity. *How to Succeed in Business Without Really Trying* ran for 1400 performances and won the 1962 Pulitzer Prize for Drama The best known of his many other Broadway productions was *Guys and Dolls*, (both won Tony Awards), He also won the 1949 Academy Award for Best Music, original song. For a review of the latest (2011) Broadway revival of *How to Succeed...* see Ben Brantley, 2011.

why Voltaire was so busy, in so many ways, simply trying to express himself.

Voltaire's many compositions were intended as: orientations, hypothetical replies, as affirmations, declarations, negations, and reconstitutions. He was like a baker for whom the existential situation was the grist for his mill, the yield from which he transformed a thousand forms of always flat-bread. His message was evident: the crushing overhang of self-serving authority that characterized France in those days, precluded from the start the lightness of being, not to mention the practical productivity, for which the full reach of human potential is intended.

For all his productivity, two-and-one-half centuries later, it is evident that the best Voltaire could offer was a descriptive mode of cultural criticism. Prior to the 19th century, there was no clear distinction between personal attributes and institutional forces. In fact, there continues to be considerable confusion on this point, which explains, in part, the ineffectiveness of not only most affirmative cultural movements, but also the powerlessness of westerners, in spite of their considerable levels of education, to establish progressive modes of governance. Humanity thrives in a progressive climate, which conservative reactionary forces attempt to thwart at every turn.

Higher-grade cultural criticism is more than the expression of existential pain aimed to reveal unjust civic power as the demon to be vanquished. To realize its full ambition, cultural criticism must open a path for reform and revolution, which is only possible if one can identify a means to modify the underlying energy that motorizes institutional power. Until the mechanism for the production and reproduction of social power is specified, and until a critic of the status quo weaves that awareness into his or her work, the full reach of cultural criticism remains unachieved.

In setting the stage for modern cultural criticism, Voltaire's judgment was neither god-like nor uniform in application. More able to connect the distortion of ideas and leader behavior with the conditions of general well-being than most of the well known cultural critics who preceded him (Boethius, Thomas More or René Descartes, for example[27]), he was able to

---

[27] To recall the details: soon after the Ostrogoth conquest of Rome, while in prison waiting to be executed, Boethius (480–524), composed his still much admired *Consolation of Philosophy* (524). A millennium later, Thomas More (1478–1535) composed his *Utopia* (1516) as a satirical dystrophic story, of a humanist society, socialist in form, aimed at harmony and equality—for which he was beheaded. Shortly after that, René Descartes

discern that the source of injustice, tyranny and domination of individual liberty which he witnessed and felt, was in the workings of government and religion; that, more than this particular king or prince, or that particular pope or bishop, the source of the hurt was in the role rather than the person, in the institution rather than the discrete act. Still, he was unable to further advance his argument in favor of change since he arrived in the world before anyone had formulated a language of institution and role. No one had yet recognized that the motor force of history is not a personal matter, that changing heads or even chopping them off will not modify the status quo unless the underpinnings of social order, the productive sub-structure of society is demounted and replaced by another order for being.

It is my view that until Karl Marx conducted his epoch-defining study of which the text, *Capital*, is the centerpiece, the full reach of cultural criticism was impossible. Since Voltaire worked nearly a century before Marx, it is hardly a personal deficiency to recognize that his critical perspective remained partial. It is thus understandable that his work be located in liminal conceptual space, half-way between the classical critical mode of ancient Greek tragedy and what we now accept as a progressive critique according to the contemporary critical formula.[28]

Theater of Opposition

Even if of vast education, reading and experience, it is important to underline that Voltaire was not a social philosopher in the contemporary sense.[29] He did not adopt or propose an integral model of human being

(1596–1650) composed his *Metaphysical Meditations* (1641) with the intention of demonstrating why it is possible, via good judgment based on careful thinking, for human beings to get to the truth without first clearing the content with either king or cardinal. His books were banned at the Sorbonne for a century.

[28] Liminal: in Cultural Anthropology, this terms is used in reference to life-course transitions, such as from adolescence to adulthood or from single to married, where there is a period, more or less formally defined, when the transients occupy a temporary role: 'betwixt and between' the stable ends of the transition. In the sciences, liminality refers to the cusp between dark and light, which occurs for brief, passing periods, during a lunar eclipse. See Victor Witter Turner, 1969 and 1974. For a discussion of this as a three-step process of status movement, see Arnold van Gennep (1977: 21).

[29] Social-Philosophy. As discussed in Chapter One, Horkheimer was the first individual in Germany to occupy a university chair in Social-Philosophy. It is a domain of study concerned with how to *use* the products of abstract research for social intervention aimed at betterment of the human condition. Formally considered, Voltaire's contemporary, Jean-Jacques Rousseau was more of a social-philosopher. In the 19th century, the critical project by Karl

and the world, and the ties between them, to use as a telling guide for his critical practice. It is not that Voltaire's work was unprincipled, but only that its guidance was implicitly linked to a conventional 18th century enlightenment view of humanity, with the potential for virtue and dignity supposedly motivating creative and disciplined rational movement against want and suffering. His concern was with the recurrent violation of that higher principle, not as the result of natural events such as floods or shipwrecks, but due to the diabolical and self-serving tendencies of the wealthy, the churchmen, and the aristocracy. Since such injustice and cruelty was ever-present in those times, he apparently felt little need to assemble documented proof about the societal problems that were evident around him. Instead, he operated on intuition linked to active appreciation of contradictions, against choices disguised as god-given or entitlement disguised as justifiably earned.

There is no necessary connection between engaging literature to explore social issues, and the mobilization of political movements which might better the general well-being. Whatever the skills of authorship, transforming criticism into high-quality productions assures no real change in the misuse of opportunity by bourgeois-royalists elites, greed driven business leaders or religious manipulators. Voltaire apparently understood this very well, explaining the care with which he attempted to package and diffuse his writings, with just the touch needed to attain the desired effect. The theater piece to be studied next is a fine example of this determination.

Candide as Tragicomedy

As a final example of his method of practice, it is time to examine Voltaire's most recognized work, *Candide*.[30] This book-length tale (169 pages) is

Marx provided what is considered the case-model for this double edged and difficult specialty. At the close of his famous *Theses on Feuerbach*, Marx wrote: "The philosophers have only *interpreted* the world, in various ways, the point is to *change it*" (1992a/1845: Thesis 11). That line is the most succinct statement to date of the mission of this discipline. A certain social-philosophical position is necessarily implicated in the critical practice of all six figures featured in the in-depth case studies.

For a brief textbook discussion of it, oriented around the question of the tension between {liberty and constraint} at the core of society see Joel Feinberg, *Social Philosophy* (1973, now in its 22nd printing).

30 Voltaire, *Candide*, 1759. The original Front Page of the book, first published in French, says, "translated from the German by Mr. Dr. Ralph." In fact, that was a pseudonym

divided among thirty short chapters. Plotted as a world spanning road-chase drama, given the times, it includes movement by horse and ship.

All begins in an idyllic Bavarian castle where commoner boy (Candide) meets aristocratic girl (Cunégonde); it is a love at first sight affair, which, when detected by her father, is dissolved by ejecting Candide from the château. This cruel separation motivates the hero to go to any lengths to reunite with Cunégonde in the anticipated bliss of love.

After a subsequent attack on the castle by merciless brigands, with villainous disregard for her fragility or nobility, the girl is spirited off to pass the following chapters bouncing from one dangerous circumstance to another. Candide sets out on the chase, tracking her along a sinuous route around Europe, confronting endless hazards. Along the way he is tortured personally or as witness, by vile wrongdoers, financial scams, physical intimidation, enslavement, thievery, sexual abuse, starvation, even a near-death experience via botched executions.

From the title of the first chapter of this allegoric saga ("How Candide was Brought Up in a Magnificent Castle, and How He was Expelled Hence"), it is clear that we are about to witness a beastly story, at the center of which is an enthralling fellow.

Of charming innocence, a posture that he never sacrifices in spite of the unthinkable adventure that unfolds, here is how we meet the star of the show in the first line of Voltaire's most read and discussed drama:

> In a castle of Westphalia, belonging to the Baron of Thunder-ten-Tronckh, lived a youth, whom nature had endowed with the most gentle manners. His countenance was a true picture of his soul. He combined a true judgment with simplicity of spirit, which was the reason, I apprehend, of his being called Candide. (Chapter 1).[31]

Once on the road in quest of the girl, our male-lead frequently became separated from his spiritual beacon, a blindly optimistic teacher-philosopher, Doctor Pangloss, who is a Leibnizian to the core, but with no practical sensibility for the pain that earthly struggle can impose on real human beings. As the drama unfolds, along the way, by land and sea, with him

(one of many) used by Voltaire to disguise responsibility for importing the printed text into Paris. The continuing contested nature of this work, two-hundred-and-fifty years later, is demonstrated by the fact that, among other places, it is available for download from the Ralph Nader Web-Library, along with many of the most radical and socially critical texts ever produced in (or translated into) the English Language. <http://www.naderlibrary.com/index.htm>.

[31] The following quotations from *Candide* are taken from the website version at <http://www.naderlibrary.com/index.htm>.

and other companions of lesser status, Candide trudges on optimistically toward an unspecified destiny.

As literature, the work displays a certain Woody Allen double-story structure: the perturbed love interest assures movement to the plot, constantly frustrated due to the unjust and gratuitous opportunism of connivers from every station in life. The plot carries on its back, as it were, the true aesthetic tension, concerning the contradiction Voltaire lived personally: between sincere intellectual potential as means for human betterment and the nasty blockage to authentic expression of that, due to the oppressive effect of closed-minded, simple thinking, platitudinous pseudo-intellectualism, of the 18th century. This way of thinking was epitomized by an idea derived from a vulgar understanding of what Leibniz intended, with that tension vocalized principally in the carefully timed meta-dialogue between the naively optimistic Candide and intellectually diffident Pangloss, which runs throughout the play.

On and on with the chase: at each tormented turn, while the insatiable allure embodied in his lady-fair remained beyond reach, Candide was inspired in his optimism by the message of Pangloss, who knows nothing in particular, save for one blind belief, expressed no matter how bloody and violent the scene:

> Pangloss was professor of metaphysico-theologico-cosmolo-nigology. He proved admirably that there is no effect without a cause; ... 'It is demonstrable, said he, that things cannot be otherwise than as they are; for all being created for an end, all is necessarily for the best end'. (Chapter 1)

Motivated throughout by our hero's attempt to link up once again with the girl, always rumored to be in the next town on the map, onward they rolled or floated or walked, across western Europe: Bulgaria, France, England, Italy, Bordeaux, Lisbon, Venice, Constantinople. There is even a brief passage in a utopia, named El Dorado of course, vaguely located in the Americas, the land of the Aztecs, where for lack of excitement they did not stay long. For the ironist Voltaire, nothing might be more boring than the elimination of necessity.

For Candide, each stop contains the promise of reunion with his lady, which is always frustrated. Rather than realized joy via reconciliation, about which Voltaire continues to feed the hope of his readers, the inevitable end of each chapter is not just disappointment but usually features some violent act of wanton aggression, expressing the demented will or idle pleasure of someone in authority against defenseless others of decent motive. Given the trail of wreckage, muggings, hangings, rape, slavery, physical disfigurement, gruesome torture, even if told with a bit of tongue-in cheek, toward the end, the major question is 'how much worse can this get?'

No matter what occurs, the smooth-talking Doctor Pangloss continues to chant the Leibnitzian metaphysical mantra: all is well, in our best of all possible worlds. In the end of course, the lovers are united although the original pristine beauty of our fair lady (Cunégonde), is by then extremely shop worn. As for the philosopher, he got through with not much more than his life, having been seriously disfigured by losing an eye, the tip of his nose, an ear, with a limp tossed in to boot; but, much as with Alfred E. Newman of *Mad Magazine* fame, through to the end Pangloss' attitude remained: 'what, me worry'?

Revolutionary Praxis with a Hoe

As the tale unfolds and the characters are tested in an almost indescribable manner, the ability of Pangloss to put a shine on adversity remains unshakeable. Near the end, after being unexpectedly reunited once again, Candide admits to Pangloss that during their last time together, the situation of Pangloss had appeared hopeless. Still the question remained:

> Well, my dear Pangloss, said Candide to him: when you had been hanged, dissected, whipped, and were tugging at the oar [of a galley-slave boat], did you always think that everything happens for the best?
>
> I am still of my first opinion, answered Pangloss, for I am a philosopher and I cannot retract, especially as Leibniz could never be wrong and besides, the preestablished harmony is the finest thing in the world... (Chapter XXVIII)

Biography Trumping History?

Sensing that enough is enough, Voltaire set the stage for the denouement: the group happens across Cunégonde, owned-in-service, better known as slavery, under a Transylvanian prince. She is old, weakened, wrinkled, and above all, sun-tanned, with the latter a condition beneath mention for the European elite of that era. At first glance of recognition, "seized with horror," Candide's immediate response is to "recoil three paces." Fortunately, "good manners" toke the upper hand and out of common courtesy they exchanged a kiss on each cheek. That touchy formality having been surmounted, all embrace all, and then thanks to a fast capitalist business transaction, Candide demonstrates suitable responsibility by buying her and "the old woman" she's with out of bondage.

Yet the lingering question: would they marry? Candide was still technically disqualified, because, although I forgot to mention it at the beginning, he was the illegitimate child of an aristocrat, which is why he was chased by the old Baron from the castle in the first place: to protect his daughter from contamination not just by a commoner, but by a bastard at that.

This touches an issue from Voltaire's own youth: before the age of twenty, while in Belgium, he met a flaming beauty of aristocratic status. Since he was of lower social status than she, that first-love was thwarted for social-class reasons, and he was hustled back to Paris. It is interesting that he returned to this autobiographical incident in his theater, nearly fifty years later, as dramatic motive for his most popular work.

At last, there on the outskirts of Constantinople, in this thicket of love, tangled among the thorns of social convention, Voltaire drew the story to its flash point: would his incompatible non-blue-blood stature continue to disqualify Candide from marriage to a princess as 'lovely' as Cunégonde?

The issue of marriage had to be settled, about which no woman of class might in those days decide for herself. A negotiation was begun between Candide and Cunégonde's brother, the young Baron, who as son and now successor in authority to his (and her) father, was alone capable of exercising the necessary authority concerning the matrimonial potential of his sister. Resting faithful to his aristocratic responsibility, the young Baron had little choice but to refuse Candide's marriage proposition. There on the farm, the tension mounted:

> Cunégonde did not know she had grown ugly, for nobody had told her of it, and she reminded Candide of his promise in so positive a tone that the good man durst not refuse her. He therefore intimated to the baron that he intended marrying his sister.
>
> I will not suffer," said the Baron, "such meanness on her part, and such insolence on yours. I will never be reproached with this scandalous thing; my sister's children would never be able to enter the church in Germany. No, my sister shall only marry a baron of the empire. (Chapter XXIX)

From there: the action is deadlocked. What will they do?

In 18th century Europe, independent of the wanton indifference about the life of ordinary people, since the pretentious resistance to daily reality among the elite knew few limits, the worry about 'what those in the next pew might think,' about a down-class marriage, was more fundamental than the woes of Job. We discover here also another irritant of aristocratic misdirection that bothered Voltaire: the Princess did not know that she had grown ugly, because no one would tell her of it. That was apparently one of the more devastating aspects of elite life style: even physical beauty was manipulated in the interests of class, status and power?

Decency Flashes in a Dehumanized World

The 18th century European situation in which Voltaire staged his Candide adventure, was self-serving, barbarous and duplicitous. Beginning in already heavily compromised circumstances, through its many brief chapters, the characters found themselves in ever more grotesque danger. Having clearly reached a maximum of bas-fortissimo decibels, the remaining challenge of authorship for Voltaire was how to get the troupe off stage.

Bereft of messianic inclination, he was surely not about to propose salvation by an archangel with flaming sword, nor could he allow the diabolic alternative, with the entire cast exterminated, perhaps crucified as with the legend of the Apostle Peter, on the outskirts of Constantinople. However, given the atmosphere of the piece, had it been ended by parlor-game lottery, the second of those choices would surely have been the guess for most of the audience.

Voltaire decided to sprinkle the last scene with just enough romanticist dust to maintain the loyalty of the faint hearted, and with just enough exotic spirituality to allow a minimum degree of humanist reconciliation. Since this formula dates from Greek tragedy, and is now unabashedly overused for mundane soap operas, that choice of closure by Voltaire continues to provide the purists at Yale theater school with a target for condemnation. But as Voltaire said in correspondence with friends about his difficulties with censorship, "in order to burn my books, they first have to buy them!"[32]

Since she was now old and ugly, "at the bottom of his heart Candide had no wish to marry Cunégonde." He went forward anyway, "determined to conclude the match" as proof of the unfoundedness of the young Baron's interference. Doing so required getting him out-of-the-way, and deciding how required a consensual agreement of the troupe: "Martin was for

[32] For the exact language of that ironic observation see the Introduction by Macé (2010: 8), where she cites a letter from Voltaire, dated 24 July, 1756.

throwing the Baron into the sea," but that was rejected as too light a sentence. The decision was more severe: without telling Cunégonde, who might have objected to such a cruel treatment, they decided to use the last of their remaining funds to pay the captain of a galley boat to haul her brother the Baron to Rome and turn him over to the "Father General of the Holy Order;" to the head of the force of order for the Vatican, somewhat equivalent to today's Swiss Guards, known in the 18th century for their skill at doing God's work in a torture chamber.

The adventure ends with the whole troupe on a farm near Constantinople, in the equivalent of little house on the prairie; Candide, Pangloss, Cunégonde and the others were road-weary, aged, physically battered but nonetheless content. They divided up the chores according to natural aptitudes and dispositions, thus turning themselves into a self-sustaining micro-community. How very modern.

Moral Rectitude in an Immoral World

Together at last, and only a few pages from the end, the commentator speculates that one might have supposed that with "Candide married and living with the philosopher Pangloss" and the others, he "must have led a very happy life." That was only marginally so since, among other things, they were without funds. As for Cunégonde, she "became uglier very day, more peevish and unsupportable," while, "Pangloss was in despair at not shinning at some German university."

Still, should a large issue come up on the farm, it was dealt with via a neo-Buddhist response which has turned this story by Voltaire into a still living legend, by confronting his audience with a layperson version of the ultimate moral question. Voltaire laid this out in three stages, with the opening coming from an "old woman" who one day inquired whether it is worse to be ravished, bullied, whipped, hanged and dissected; "or to stay here (on the farm) with nothing to do?" Candide decided that was, "a great question" which "gave rise to new reflections." This necessarily motivated the transcendental quest for resolution of the question of resistance, to be completed in about two pages, indicating the shallow sincerity with which Voltaire considered the redemptive illusion.

Second step: someone recalled that living nearby was "a very famous Dervish, esteemed the best philosopher in all Turkey." Sought out by the troupe, when asked, "why so strange an animal as man was made," the Dervish replied laconically that it makes no difference, and it is best to "hold your tongue." His response was not judged to be particularly helpful.

Third step: on the way back to the farm, they encounter a "good old man," sunning himself near an orange tree. Approached about their existential distress his response was immanently practical: "I presume in general, he said, that they who meddle with the administration of public affairs die, sometimes miserably." Thus, rather than getting politically agitated, which was evidently dangerous at best, the "old man" claimed that he contented himself by working his little farm. Whereupon the light went on, as, "on his way home, Candide made profound reflections on the old man's conversation."

Thus, twenty lines from the end the key insight is announced when the wisdom falls from Candide's lips: "I know... we must cultivate our garden."

Whereupon they all concur, each in his or her way, sanctioning that truly enlightened choice as the wisest alternative. Pangloss takes one last opportunity to retrace the sufficient reason that drove the adventure, "in this best of all possible worlds": if Candide had not been ejected from the castle, with all the pain and suffering which followed, then he "would not be here [on the farm] eating preserved citrons and pistachio-nuts."

"Very well," answered Candide, then repeating, "but let us cultivate our garden."

With that, the curtain fell, and the still-continuing debate erupted about how to interpret his ironic closing.

Soft on Politics?

The full title of that work was "Candide: or Optimism." Carried on the surface by satire, the deeper message is ironic. Satire suggests a put-on, the serious overplayed, the negative exaggerated, pretense puffed to the bursting point. Irony means that the story as told is not in the truth of the telling, implying less error or willful deceit than intentional distortion of the human resonance of the issue as presented, so that the response thus generated in the audience is in contradiction with the manifest claim of the story.

On first reading, this adventure has surely a satirical tone. But, whatever the smile generated by this or that incident, a bit like late 19th century realism well before Stendhal, the cumulative horror of what is depicted cannot be hidden beneath a snicker.[33] While some might consider his

---

[33] Stendhal was the pen name of Marie-Henri Beyle (1783–1842), a 19th century French writer. His early form of psychology-exploring drama brought realism to the novel. Two of

main device to have been ridicule, the stronger and more apt term is mockery. Voltaire leveled it with both barrels, at theologians, philosophies, religion, armies, churchmen, aristocrats, merchants and scientists. His chief target, the vulgar optimism attributed to Leibnitz's theocratic world, concerned the insurmountable force of material determinism, misapplied in his day to justify continuing current practices as if not just the better policy, but the only feasible one, in this best of possible worlds.

With its blasphemous references to the Church, its seditious implications for politics, and its general insult of the sciences and philosophy, after being published clandestinely (and simultaneously in three different places), the book, *Candide,* was immediately banned in France. This occurred just as Voltaire was deciding to seek refuge in Ferney, where he remained for the next twenty-years. Still, with *Candide,* many critics judge that Voltaire was soft on politics: where is the formal appeal for manifestation, rebellion, taking arms against the aristocrats and bourgeois capitalists? Clearly absent.

The literary critical disaccord about this piece is how to read the 'tend your garden' closing metaphor. According to the surface reading, in the face of injustice or political and economic indifference, in the short run it is best to let go of the major issues such as politics, war and religion, being content in fundamental service to self and others in the immediate circumstances of life. Given, for example, that this was the strategy of most of the bourgeoisie who remained in Europe during WWII under a German Nazi regime, it strikes me as highly improbable that something equivalent was Voltaire's intention. Thus we read this line as the ironic face of a call for open resistance or other action—when the time is right.

Yet as literary form, rather than ironizing in the void, as, 'oh well, we need only tend our garden,' do our own thing, take care of ourselves and let others do the same; would it have been more aesthetically forthright of Voltaire to have had Candide lead a charge on the local garrison, with the troupe butchered like stray dogs on market day? While some centuries later Albert Camus delivered a much more open 'vote with your life' political message of that sort, did not Voltaire achieve an equivalent effect, but ironically?[34]

---

his most studied works are *Le Rouge et le Noir* (*The Red and the Black,* 1830) and *La Chartreuse de Parme* (*The Charterhouse of Parma,* 1839).

[34] The writings of Albert Camus (1913–1960). Since 2013 marks the 100th anniversary of his birth, the French Minister of Culture is devoting funds to a special year-long tribute to his project, with activities centered in a museum in Aix en Provence. An interesting aspect

Considered across the sixty years of work that he produced, the last thing Voltaire appears to have had in mind was passive acceptance of the politically or ideologically unacceptable. The aesthetic of submissive resignation, adopting the attitude of 'happy Christians' in early ancient Rome, in chains outside a Coliseum, waiting, perhaps to become lion lunch, is not the natural *aboutissement*, the artistically unavoidable point of *Candide*. The reclusive calm with which this adventure ended was only a resting point; the next cycle of movement aimed not at the illusion of cloistered fulfillment, but at the fact of political confrontation. As appreciated by audiences ever since, the truth of the work is ironically passive, which means not really; the political pertinence of the piece is demonstrated historically by the contribution made by Voltaire's work to the mobilization that ultimately removed the French King, Louis XIV, from his throne, and the head from his shoulders.

What of the 'spiritualist' side to the final motivation in *Candide*: was this a sign that, under it all, Voltaire was a closet churchman, as if with secret ambition to be named cardinal? Indeed, he had Candide consult a Dervish, but the advice received was politically impractical. As for the old woman's moral question, and the old man's real-political response: neither can be read as other than ironic recognition that there is more to rationality than the workings of linear thought.

If Candide was to find a bit of serenity, it was necessary to listen as much to his soul, in the lay sense of the terms, as to his mind, all the time balancing advice from Pangloss as rigid intellectual advisor with that of an anonymous spiritual guru. This implies a 'limits to rationality' thesis, the acceptance that, while the hope of enlightenment is not to be rejected, following its call in exclusively intellectual terms is inherently limiting.

Disillusioned Utopian?

This study of Voltaire sets the stage for my project. Through the 18th century, even if direct when not outright inflammatory, critical practice was

---

of this celebration, which ties it in with Voltaire in particular and critical practice in general, is that there was a major political battle over who should direct the production of the tribute, on what grounds, in what interests. The political right wanted its share of the action since Camus was a high profile commercial product. The political left wanted its share since he was an outrageous critic of complacency in the face of injustice. But he was also involved in mixed manner with the Algerian Issue as well as the Stalin Issue, such that it is almost impossible for anyone to find a way to position him that is 'politically correct.' Thus the conflict, demonstrating that even in death, high level cultural critique is a contested perspective.

rudimentary by contemporary (21st century) standards, and lacked appreciation of the multi-layered structure and dynamic movement of social-historical action. Criticism was blocked at the surface of experience, not that the result was necessarily inaccurate but only less compelling for lack of penetration concerning root issues. Voltaire wrote toward the end of what in France is known as the Classic Period, before the shift away from the detached formalism of the last days of royalist domination in Europe, which, in spite of his remarkable discipline, explains a certain lack of consistency in, and effectiveness from, his writings.[35]

After he died, with the agitation accompanying the French Revolution, the earlier, rather flat-land view of European society was reexamined, and the multidimensionality of political-economic organization discovered. During the ensuing century, it became evident that the foundation of society is a social magma, a pulsing web of collective action, the stability of which depends on how history is woven into the present as motor force toward the future. Historicity renders society dynamic, stretching it beyond its own spatial and temporal frontiers. Due to that meta-materialist energy, it is as if the human condition propels itself toward greater levels of complexity, lifting itself, as it were, by its own bootstraps.

By the 20th century, a new mode of critical practice was possible and necessary. While not invalidating use of the older rudimentary form, it shifted the way westerners account for experience. Whatever the limitations in its practice, the principle of democratic society depends on the production of some form of social criticism to assure a minimum guidance for what occurs. Consequently, critics were invited into the corridors of power, to provide assistance in the steering of society. Vastly enhancing the legitimacy of critical practice, it has become apparent that the undertaking can be easily subverted from a force of correction against the predilections of self-serving power, into a tool for expression of that power. The fact that the latter occurs so frequently is evidence of the continuing force of the Machiavellian logic.

35 The Classic Period in European history is usually said to cover the time from about Columbus, the discovery of America, through to the French Revolution; thereafter the West entered its current, Late Modern period. The shift was most evidenced in Europe, less so in the U.S. because there was little historical reference prior to that time for America. Historians from every branch of knowledge and action, political, technological, institutional, have attempted to unravel this mysterious shift, including three of the figures who we will deal with later in this book: Foucault, Eagleton, and White.

Now in the 21st century, there are well-funded formally established institutions called Think Tanks, some well intended, others aimed principally at the deception of, or at least the insulation of, the public concerning critical truths about the sitting power of state and economy. When the latter predominate, renegade critical action like that exerted by Voltaire is perhaps the only form possible for overcoming resistance, for awakening the common consciousness, to paraphrase Marx, from the slumber induced by the washing-machine discharge of disintegrating information in which contemporary life is now bathed.

It is difficult to summarize Voltaire's project with a concept. According to Husserl, every philosopher travels with her god in her pocket: to understand anyone's critical work it helps to determine the theoretical master or ideology that inspires that work. Applying this principle to Voltaire is hazardous since his foundational inspirations are not clear. He was a social critic who produced literature, while working directly on the world without the literature of others as mediation. As evidenced by the most famous of his quotes, even his position on the divine is shrouded in ambiguity: "If God hadn't existed, it would have been necessary to invent Him"[36] (Voltaire 1768: 405).

By his life, Voltaire established the role of European intellectual; more than a simple peripatetic, a document dabbler, an intellectual dilettante, without sacrificing his ethical standards he lived the ongoing struggle on life's terms. His perspective was sharp, his admonitions forced, but not for a minute did he act as if his conscience ought to be anyone's guide but his own. He promoted individual liberty as good judgment, while all the time questioning its application.[37]

---

[36] Voltaire was probably more agnostic than atheist. He derided manipulative deific justification for inhuman and oppressive political action and military violence. The reference quoted here is from a letter he composed, in poetic form, where he challenged the work of other authors (see *Épître à l'Auteur du Livre des Trois Imposteurs* [*Letter to the Author of The Book of Three Impostors*] 1770). This text is available at the University of Chicago Web-Site: "*Voltaire électronique: Bibliography of Works by Voltaire.*" See http://www.lib.uchicago.edu/efts/VOLTAIRE/restricted/VOLTAIRE.bib.html, which presents the late 19th century Paris Edition, in French, of this work, of Voltaire [1768], *Epître à l' auteur du livre des Trois imposteurs* (*Oeuvres complètes de Voltaire*, ed. Louis Moland, 1877–1885, Tome 10: 402–405).

[37] What audience for critique? This raises the important issue of the communicative strategy associated with cultural criticism. One function of critical practice is 'consciousness raising,' bringing to light contradictions so that those who ought be most concerned might break their denial, and then act. Voltaire sensed that until the bourgeois elite were convinced of the moral and political danger of their ways, there would be no change; thus he aimed his messages at the superior status categories. By contrast, Rousseau considered

Without specified political foundations and thus bereft of a clear call for action, the critical determination of Voltaire exuded nonetheless an important social energy. More than only personal discontent with scandal, by voicing a formative, reformative, nearly revolutionary call, his works promoted acceptance among western elites of the justice of critical practice and the need to put their own ways in question. This is proof of the extend to which the persistence of his work and the breadth and variety of his exaltations drew practical attention to the structural impasse which gripped the West in the 18th century.

On the other hand, Voltaire's indecisiveness concerning what to do about the ecclesiastic-royalist situation that so incensed him was the result of his not having the tools to express the possibility of institutional renewal. He was unknowingly blocked at the level of personal expression, conditioned by political atmosphere of his time. Thus he oscillated between {complacency vs. condemnation} of the elites and their life mission, between {giddy optimism vs. black pessimism} about humankind, between {faith laden hope vs. forlorn desperation} about God, and between {trusting in the possibility of a better way vs. laconic indifference} about the function of the state. In spite of a certain appalling response to his stories, his sophisticated expression of this lack of finality in the human condition undoubtedly explains the universal and continuing appeal of his work.

it vital to direct his critical appeal to what in Marxist terms is called the proletariat, those who suffer most from civil injustice. As concerns the intention of critique, debate concerning this difference between the strategies of Voltaire versus Rousseau is unresolved.

CHAPTER THREE

SCHILLER: REFORM CONSCIOUSNESS TO CHANGE THE WORLD

Here is Schiller

Johann Christoph Friedrich Von Schiller (1759–1805) spent all his life in what is now Germany. This somewhat restricted home-range was the result of financial limitations in his youth, coupled with an early dissident determination to live outside the feudal economy. That marginal existence led to his contracting tuberculosis, crippling his lifestyle with progressive severity, leading to the grave at the age of forty-five years. This relative immobility did, however, provide ample opportunity to pursue his first passion: authorship. The result is an enormous collection of writings, filling row upon row of shelves in German libraries.

Schiller was a sparkling example of the capacity to 'live locally, think globally.' This animated his critical perspective and allowed him to focus in very real terms on his immediate condition, considered always in reference to a global standard of the infinite promise of the moral and intellectual human potential that defined European enlightenment.

The shortcoming of pressing too intensively on that nearly eschatological vision of enlightenment is that, in socio-political terms, local reality is invariably disappointing. Like Voltaire before him, Schiller was aghast with an acute sense of injustice for what he considered the rampant violation of the noble human potential that he endorsed as uncontestable principle. Rather than retreating into passive intellectualist cynicism, spiritual retreatism, or 'going over to the enemy,' by deciding to profit as much as possible from the inequality of the situation, he held to his intellectualist ethical position and set down what he saw, as literature.

Going a step further took him out of his personal space and into the political; building that into his writings, his work generated furious backlash and as with Voltaire before him, Schiller found himself in agitated turmoil wherever he went. However, unlike Voltaire, Schiller was unable to keep his emotional distance from the critical issues which he explored. If there is place for psychological autopsy in this book, it is probably just to assert that this essential difference in personal style, of engaged-detachment by Voltaire, of nearly hyperventilating-engagement by Schiller, may well explain why the one lived twice as long as the other.

University Politics

The tension generated by Schiller's rarely inactive critical judgment was demonstrated in remarkable terms when, in 1789, he accepted an invitation to join the faculty of the German university in Jena. The fact that this was also the year of the French Revolution was but a coincidence, yet the explosive effect of that series of events in France was mirrored in a small way for him personally as he assumed the post of professor.

By the time he arrived at Jena, Schiller had already demonstrated his extremely serious edge, his capacity for sober historical scholarship and his ability to write; in other words, he was qualified for an entry-level professorial post. But there were issues, particularly his having spent time in prison for insulting the local political authority with his first theater piece, *The Robbers*, which he composed while still in military school, and which continues to be staged, with particular popularity among students, two-hundred and fifty years later. The fellow whose recommendation got him that first appointment was none other than Goethe, by reputation the greatest German intellectual that the language has ever known. Goethe was caught between admiration for Schiller's potential, and the problem he had restraining himself, which is why that first, and last, teaching post was unpaid, obligating Schiller to attract paying students to his seminars if he hoped to earn a living, which he never achieved.

In keeping with custom in German universities, on joining that faculty Schiller was expected to introduce himself by delivering a public lecture. While the result turned the student-packed amphitheater into an uproar of adoration, it surely did nothing to improve his standing with the other professors. The theme for his Inaugural Lesson was "Universal History" (1972/1789). A perspective central to the enlightenment, this theme involves the supposition that the force of humanity as inner essence has propelled the gradual movement or progress of humankind, from savage natural conditions, up to culture and civilization. The fact that this was an ethnocentric, European-centered world view was not recognized in the 18th century, allowing for a certain mysticism concerning humanity on the part of not just Schiller, but many others, including Jean-Jacques Rousseau.

Given the circumstances, universal history was a grandiose theme to tackle for someone less than thirty years of age. Further, Schiller approached the issue by addressing himself exclusively to students, seemingly indifferent to what he was saying to other professors who were also in the audience.

He opened by announcing his enthusiasm for youth, arguing that studying history is the way for them to "keep that enthusiasm for truth... without it being dissipated on fraud and deception." Since, "the realm of history is fertile and comprehensive; it embraces the whole moral world"; and, "it is just to men that it speaks." This suggested that history can be understood by anyone, without mediation or interpretation of expert historians, a view that by the mid-19th century was underwritten in an unexpected fashion by Marx; not because of denial of the possibility of universal history (within any given cultural group), or the impenetrability of its content by the common mind, but because of the lack of universality of perspective of most expert historians (1972/1789: 322).

As he proceeded with his introductory remarks on the subject, Schiller devoted roughly the first third of his speaking time to deride the work of ordinary scholarship and professional practices, undercutting the very profile of professorial activity that probably characterized most of the permanent faculty at the university that he was joining, many of whom were in the audience.[1]

Already experienced in theater composition, his language for this presumably solemn occasion probably came across as too colorful, rhetorical and direct for classical German scholarship. He took off on what he called the difference between "the bread-and-butter scholar and the philosopher." The former is the disagreeable sort of faculty person, working at universities, not for love of higher learning and teaching, but only, "to improve his material position and to gratify his petty craving for recognition," attending not to the needs of students, but exclusively to his "profession," with "all his diligence focused on the demand made of him by the future master of his fate," concerned principally "to show off his accumulated pearls of wisdom" (1972/1789: 322). Thus coining the 'pearls of wisdom' metaphor that endures to this day, Schiller delivered this line as a severe slap to many of those whom he was supposedly in the process of joining as a colleague.

He went on to disqualify the "bread-and-butter" types as reactionary and conservative professors, "impeding the progress of salutary revolution in the realm of learning," because, "in defending the academic system they are fighting for their lives." Along the way, while "no one complains more about the thanklessness of his work than the bread-and-butter scholar; he

[1] Questioning Historians. Schiller's questioning the justice of production by ordinary historians, as seconded by Marx, but on somewhat other grounds, is also central to the critical analytic of Hayden White (see Chapter Seven).

expects his reward not in currency of ideas but in reputation, in preferment, and in tenure" (1972/1789: 323).

Then, with clear reference to his own situation (being obliged to fill his classes with paying students), Schiller went on to lament the plight of the young scholar who takes a first post at a university, obliged to work as a "day laborer," with "the soul of the slave," such that, "soon enough his specialty will disgust him as piecework... and his talent will mutiny against his vocation."

He then swung to consider the idealized alternative, judging, "how entirely differently does the philosopher conduct himself" whose sincere thirst for comprehensive knowledge is constantly frustrated due to the artificial distinctions between disciplines, struggling for "restoring" the unity of understanding, by breaking the grip on learning by abstractly defined academic disciplines.[2]

Schiller's summary of the notion of universal history was stimulating, insightful and clear; that by "no longer dissipating his powers uselessly in wretched self-defense," the civilized and cultured individual had "won the precious privilege to freely direct his own potential and to follow the call of their genius" (1972/1789: 327). While eventually demonstrating his insight and grasp of historical issues, having gone on for the first third of the lecture in an open attack against the academic institution, it is little wonder that Schiller got on badly as professor and was soon counting his days in Jena, waiting to escape the university forever.

Whatever the misshapen results for his emotional well-being or paid professional career, his university appointment was a valuable step in Schiller's career; not the least of which was that it provided him the opportunity to cement the relationship with Goethe that ultimately assured his fame.

As demonstrated by this first scholarly outing, determined to expose institutional and political misalignments that were negative for human creativity and general well-being, Schiller had difficulty going beyond the initial negative phase of criticism. In spite of his humanistic faith, his optimism was frustrated by history: from the sidelines he watched the early hopes of revolutionary progress in France (1789) dissipate due to ideological infighting and opportunism. Thereafter, the question became: how might one envision, not the just the necessity of fundamental change

---

[2] Schiller's attack on the disciplinary balkanization of knowledge and learning in universities clearly anticipated, if not actively inspired, the famous Power/Knowledge perspective developed by Michel Foucault (see Chapter Four).

but the material conditions for successful revolution; otherwise, what chance remained for realizing the liberation movement that ignited that intention?

Once beyond the university walls, the more alarmed Schiller became about the unpromising autocracy of Germanic centered Europe. The incongruity between actual social practices and his idealist disposition weighed heavily on his spirit. His was an existence in search of the full promise of humankind, with the pain of frustrated experience inevitably outdistancing those aspirations. The emotional tension this generated in him is a signature quality of Schiller's critical practice, palpably evident in his writings at every stage of his brief life.

Nonetheless, his work is a marvelous example of the personal use of one's self as instrument of inquiry, of standard for comparison, as basis of knowing and judgment. Whatever the limits in his philosophical sophistication or his excesses of theatrical-poetic flair, his work constitutes a landmark in European thought, of critical practice in action.

Critical Production

In the twenty-seven years between his first writings and death, Schiller covered an enormous amount of cultural ground. His collected works (published plays, poems, historical studies and philosophical writings) fill twenty Britannica-sized volumes; his correspondence, ancillary writings and various versions of final or unfinished works, plus material done jointly with Goethe, add nearly thirty volumes more.[3] His dramatic theater alone, which continues to be staged regularly around the world two-hundred years later is of such a lasting stature as to justify labeling him the German Shakespeare.[4] His most often produced work, the famous stage rendering of the Swiss legend, *William Tell*, is well enough known to be treated as if timeless folklore without real authorship.

---

[3] Schiller's Volumes. All his material is publicly available in the open stacks of the library of the University Technique, in Berlin, to which anyone has a right of access on a day-use basis.

[4] Speaking of Schiller. "The German Shakespeare," is the title of review in the *Guardian* of London by Michael Billington (2005) of Schiller's play *Don Carlos*, which was then about to open at the Gielgud Theatre, London. One of Schiller's many great dramas, on stage for the first time in 1787, this was later transformed into an opera by Giuseppe Verdi (1813–1901), originally in French with a Paris debut in 1867. As a sign of the difficult durability of Schiller's work outside Germany, the subtitle of this London review is telling: "Schiller used to be box-office poison. Why are his plays suddenly back in favour, asks Michael Billington."

While his works are often assessed as melodramatic displays of imaginary mystical calling, right from the start, Schiller was a determined social-political critic. His lifelong concern was with freedom, both physical and spiritual, severely obstructed at the time by dictatorial practices and unjustified entitlements on the part of the various elite classes which then dominated Germany's many independent principalities.

Little attests more to his skill and boldness in capturing the restrictive and frustrating tenor of his times than his first theater piece, *The Robbers* (1781). He started writing this at the age of nineteen; produced shortly thereafter, it was viewed as such a seditionist threat for the local aristocratic regime that he was jailed for two weeks for having gone to see it on stage. Thereafter, he was ordered to permanently cease producing literature of any nature. As evidenced by the thousands of pages that eventually flowed from his pen, his resolute resistance to censure was total. This dissidence was not without personal costs, contributing to the decline of his health that ultimately cost him his life.

Like Voltaire before him, Schiller died with an aristocratic title (*Von* Schiller), with which he had not been born. Unlike Voltaire, who early in life and after his first spell in prison ennobled his own name as a curious act of mocking self-affirmation, Schiller was entitled by legitimate aristocratic authority (1802), due to the recommendation of Goethe and in recognition of the significance of his literature.

The reach of Schiller's work was enhanced enormously by his intimate working relationship Goethe (1749–1832). The jury is still out as to exactly which of these men was most influential for the other, Goethe being the imperturbable, stately figure of classical European literary taste and Schiller setting the role of hyper-intelligent, emotionally charged, politically dissident author.

A Man of Three Seasons

Schiller's brief professional life can be divided into three periods: an exuberant, revolutionary-liberation phase of youthful theatrical productivity; a historical-aesthetic phase exploring diverse themes touching on culture and civilization, beauty and art, human action and the question of freedom; and, a return-to-literature phase, during the years of association with Goethe. It was during this last period that he produced what the specialists consider his most solid theater pieces, central among which are the *Wallenstein Trilogy* (1798–1799) and the aforementioned *William Tell* (1804), his final and most popular work. However, *Tell* is as much the expression of revolutionary engagement as it is decorative high theater, demonstrating that until the day he died, he never renounced the humanist call for justice beyond repression.

The son of a military doctor, Schiller's upbringing was far from aristocratic; during his youth, his father moved about frequently, with the family ultimately settling in the vicinity of Stuttgart, at the time under peremptory authority of the Duke of Würtemberg. Young Schiller's intellectual verve attracted attention, and he was chosen as a candidate for the Duke's elite military school.

In keeping with feudal tradition, he was directed to follow his father's vocation and assigned to medical education. He detested the mechanical, technical, uncreative imposition of such a formation, yet went through to a degree (1780) for lack of alternative. By the end of those studies, his impertinence in the face of authority was evident. More interested in poetry and social issues than military maneuvers and strategy, while yet in the academy, he began work on his first play, *The Robbers* (1781), a dramatic critical piece exposing the dangerous and stifling aristocratic rule that then characterized the regimes in the German principalities.

Schiller expressed his existential distress not just in radical literature, but in frequent personal correspondence, most of which has been preserved. Examining this material opens a view on an unusually bright young man, not only passionate and determined in the pursuit of his art but informed and reflexive regarding the forces and limitations that he and the world faced. For instance, at the end of his military school studies, he lamented having been subsequently, "obliged to take a title as medical doctor" and that it bothered him greatly to have to subvert his "inclination for the theater," in order to spend at least six months writing a medical thesis (Letter 01 April, 1782).[5]

His writings at the margins of his theater are equally informative about the uncommon and complex nature of his learning and experience. In the original *Preface*[6] to the first version of *The Robbers*, Schiller drew

---

[5] In his, *Friedrich Schiller: Autoportrait*, Hugo von Hofmannsthal (2004/1926) assembled a fascinating collection of preface material from Schiller's theater and extracts from Schiller's correspondence, where Schiller displayed in an 'off-stage' way, his personal situation, intention and emotion. Of particular interest for most readers in this short volume is the material from his correspondence with Goethe. All "Letters" and "Preface" material referenced in the section are from this volume, with English quotations translated by me from the French.

[6] Robbers. Schiller put out a series of versions of *The Robbers* with minor variations in the body of the play, and usually attaching a new Preface; for the one referenced here see Hofmannsthal (2004/1926).

attention to the existential contradictions depicted in the key characters as developed in John Milton's (1608–1674) *Paradise Lost* (1667; 1674), Shakespeare's (1564–1616) *Richard* II (~1595), and Miguel de Cervantes' (1547–1616) *Don Quixote* (1605 & 1615). Beyond acknowledging inspiration from this triad of luminaries, and demonstrating a precocious capacity for comparative analysis concerning the messages and meanings in literature, just having read these three authors was unusual for a fellow only twenty-two years old, who had studied not at a university but in a military academy.

On leaving school, with this first theater piece finished, Schiller was assigned to a post he detested, as medical officer in a local regiment. What actually concerned him was how to get his first play staged. Facing the uncertainties of the *débutant* author in search of an outlet for his first work, it is evident he felt insecure. Since the piece mounted a piercing attack on the lifestyle and official practices of the local nobility, he was concerned that his approach might be taken by the audience as excessively brutal (Letter: 06 Oct., 1781). Apparently with that concern in mind, after rereading this first play, he rewrote it a bit, trying to soften the dialogue with less offensive language. He also composed a new "Preface," assuring his intended audience that with the unfolding of the "remarkable catastrophe" which the play portrays, "vice would know the results which it deserves," and in the end, "virtue would carry the day" (Hofmannsthal 2004/1926: 12).

To his delight, in the neighboring principality of Mannheim, a theater director decided to stage *Robbers*. When it opened in 1782, the play was a popular hit, but not with the Duke of Stuttgart. Due to the way the play depicted the corrosive social-political structures under autocratic authority, the tension mounted in his principality. The Duke's people judged this romanticized drama as a veiled call to revolution. To make matters worse, Schiller violated regiment rules by slipping across the principality border from Stuttgart to Mannheim to see the show on stage. This cost him two-weeks in the brig for negligence of duty, coupled with a cease and desist order against further writing.

On his release from jail, banned from writing, Schiller responded in a fashion reasonable for a fiery and spirited lad. Deserting the army and fleeing his home country by night, he headed for Mannheim. Rebuffing the authority that he abhorred, he decided to commit his life to writing and to assure his survival exclusively by the revenue generated by that work.

Whatever the romantic justification for that existential choice, the practical result was to make his daily life very difficult. While at the time, fleeing one principality for another was like changing countries and thus assured protection from legal pursuit, the problem was how to support oneself after one arrived. Due to the institutional overburden of German principalities, not just one's life, but the quality of one's survival was a feudal prerogative. To leave one's homeland would cut one off from access to a livelihood, without guarantee of its reestablishment at the destination of one's migration.

Leaving Stuttgart for Mannheim, Schiller hoped to receive assistance from the director of the theater, one Baron Von Dalberg, who had staged the premiere of his *Robbers*. At first Dalberg distanced himself from this fugitive on-the-run. After nearly a year living as a barely surviving vagabond, Schiller was awarded a contract with the Mannheim National Theater to compose three plays.

The first of his three Mannheim dramas, *Fiesco; or, the Genoese Conspiracy* (1783), is considered among the less successful of Schiller's plays. Still, it bears his unmistakable critical imprint: tragic drama built around a ruthlessly ambitious Genoese nobleman, Fiesco di Lavagna, who instigates a successful rebellion against the Genoan Prince, Andrea Doria, only to reveal himself, after the successful coups d'état, to be an even more power-driven and dangerous tyrant than the one whom he replaced. The unsurprising denouement is Fiesco's assassination.

Fiesco's too obvious plot formula (even the powerful must abide by the standards of humanity, less the hand of destiny put an end to their show) was apparently forced. And the thinly veiled call of sedition, hidden within this theatrical exploration of heavy-handed Machiavellian manipulation and unjustified elitist privilege, undoubtedly reduced the work's general appeal among bourgeois critics. And what other sort might be able to read the text?

If that first work by Schiller in Mannheim was a study of the seductive force of power and ambition, his next one, *Intrigue and Love* (1784), centered on social criticism. This is the first time Schiller launched a frontal attack against social class injustice, doing so well before the notion of class had been formally developed. Accordingly, the male-lead, Ferdinand von Walter, falls in love with Luise Miller, the daughter of the local music instructor. Their marriage is thwarted by aristocrat-commoner differences and poisoned by bourgeois ambitions and ruthless family intrigues, which infest the scene to a degree that only tragedy might terminate. Recalling the tested Shakespearian formula, *Romeo and Juliet*, the end comes by death all around, contributing nothing by its price to any limitations on the viperous poison of righteous elite hypocrisy that then infested the courts of Europe.[7]

His third work at Mannheim, *Don Carlos* (1787), was a historical drama, which turned into a lengthy research project. Not intended to be accurate on the details, Schiller was nonetheless obligated to carefully study the events on which that fictional story was based, set in Spain at the end of the 16th century.[8]

It must have been a pleasure to create Carlos, the crown prince, in line to eventually succeed his father on the Spanish throne, who is:

> ... consumed by melancholy... crushed by this claustrophobic world, his father's bitterness towards him, his hatred for his father and the terrible guilt he harbors regarding his secret, unrequited love... . (Stevens 2004)

Carlos' difficulty with love is easy to understand: the love-object of his childhood fantasy, the exotic Elizabeth, was stolen away as a delectable marriage partner by none other than his father, Phillip II of Spain: transforming his mystical ingénue into Carlos' step-mother! Then, as only Schiller could cook the plot, not just Carlos but Lady Elizabeth, had "... contracted the same terrible disease: humanity. And humanity you know is very contagious."[9]

The individual moral tension of this work is the quest for liberation from personal domination by bourgeois civilization, in the form of family and class repression of personal choice. As usual in Schiller's theater, there was also a parallel geopolitical tension, in this case involving the effort of the Dutch to liberate themselves from Spanish domination, with the whole story centered in the psychic-social contradiction experienced by Don Carlos due to the burden of his elite cultural heritage. As Schiller judged it, while the route to political freedom is difficult but open, personal liberation from the encumbrance of birth generally rests tragically blocked for a lifetime.

---

[7] *Intrigue and Love* (1784). The plot line from this stage drama shows more than coincidental resemblance to the actual marital situation of one of Schiller's closest friends, and eventual benefactor, Christian Gottfried Körner, whose marriage to a 'commoner' was held back until the death of Körner's father, who vociferously opposed the marriage.

[8] *Don Carlos* (1787). While Schiller's play centered on the Spanish end of this conflict, the battle started when the Dutch revolted against Spanish control in the 1560s, ultimately gaining political autonomy in 1648 (The Peace of Westphalia). This set the Netherlands on the path to their rather brief moment of World Empire.

[9] For an informative review of a 2004 London revival of this play see; "Schiller's *Don Carlos*: the light and warmth of a timeless play," by Robert Stevens. *World Socialist Web Site*: wsws.org, 12 November 2004. http://www.wsws.org/articles/2004/nov2004/schi-n12.shtml.

Having arrived in Mannheim as a fugitive, the grant to Schiller was for a one year writer's pension, in anticipation that he would compose three plays for that theater company. Given the rebellious posture of his compositions, it is easy to understand why he never saw a second year of financial support. With *Don Carlos* still unfinished, he was once again without work and sponsorship, in evident financial need, with no appetite for ordinary occupations, no steady revenue from his writing and nowhere to go. Schiller was by then seriously fed-up:

> I can not stay in Mannheim. I have spent twelve days with that thought in my heart, and it is like a decision to leave the world. The people, relations, general conditions both earthly and spiritual are horrid. (Letter: 22 Feb., 1785)

He went on to report that while Mannheim felt like a prison, "Leipzig appeared in his dreams and anticipations like a morning rose on a wooded hillside." As revealed in his correspondence but evident implicitly throughout his work, Schiller was at once plagued and energized by affective oscillations. In his theatrical writing he was like a heartless surgeon with a culture-critical scalpel, ready to remove infected organs from the social-political body; but on the personal front, in addition to being an early intellectual romantic, he was in a constant state of emotional turbulence. The contradiction he felt personally between the critical intellect versus sensitive soul explains the dramatic tension evident in character development for his theater. While the result continues to captivate audiences two centuries later, the personal effect for Schiller was far less healthy.

With a manifestly mystical side, he took seriously the idea of destiny, supporting a form of nearly blind self-confidence that was recurrently validated by the way fate seemed to rescue him from desperate situations. While languishing in Mannheim with nowhere else to go, as if in response to some resonant celestial chord but aided surely by a growing reputation for quality work, his financial distress was unexpectedly abated thanks to an offer of assistance from an acquaintance, the Dresden jurist Christian Gottfried Körner (1756–1831). That was in 1785, necessitating a move to Leipzig, with considerable time also spent with Körner, in Dresden. During this period he was able to complete *Don Carlos* (1787) as well as other works of lesser importance.

Schiller was profoundly touched by this unexpected gift from Körner; after its announcement, he wrote the stunning ode, *Ode to Joy* (1785). This piece continues to enchant listeners the world over, since it served as inspiration for the final, Choral Movement of Ludwig von Beethoven's remarkable, *Ninth Symphony*, among the most widely appreciated classical orchestrations ever produced.

The aesthetics of the result are stunning, hope spawned of tragedy as not just the heart of the work but in the being of the compositional team: music written by a deaf musical composer, Beethoven, around a libretto driven in part by the spontaneous expression of gratitude of a most remembered German classical playwright, Schiller; who, while himself a thinly veiled anarchist, was faced with the contradiction that violence never facilitates social harmony and only generosity and compassion can open the path to a better world.

Revolutionary Theater

Although often disappointed in practice, the idea of liberty is now associated with a particular view of political democracy. Quite differently, in the 17th- and 18th centuries, without yet even the pretense of general freedoms, under the feudal system, economic prominence and political leadership were determined by birthright, military despotism, and belligerence among and within elite families. Not always tyrannical and cruel, sometimes the result was a certain human capacity and vision on the part of the elites chosen to lead; more often, the result was mistreatment of those of lesser classes at the hands of reigning nobility suffering from no fault more basic than self-centered blindness to the condition of others. While the usual effect was repression and exploitation of the many by the few, when calling for greater human treatment and justice, virtually no one took seriously the possibility of putting an end to monarchy as governmental form.

Schiller reduced the issue of freedom to simple formulas: not elimination of law but equality before the law; not elimination of social control in the interests of public order, but fair handedness in the application of civil authority; not elimination of profit or gain but the just distribution of the fruits of labor, starting with those who do the laboring. Freedom thus exercised would assure, he believed, a public atmosphere of equal concern and respect, which is the view of the good life that he endorsed philosophically.[10] What renders this outstanding is less his view of this condition

[10] The debate in political philosophy concerning the value hierarchy that ought to guide public action is unrelenting. As I will get to later in this chapter, the proximate influence for Schiller concerning political ethics came from his contemporary, Immanuel Kant. For a 21st century point of reference, Schiller's political philosophical position fits closely

than the passionate capacity he displayed for transforming that insight into theater pieces with galvanizing effects on his audience. The way he achieved this in his very first piece is worth a bit further study.

Setting the Scene for 'The Robbers'

The Robbers is a skillfully plotted morality story, where the contradictions of the run-away practical madness that colonizes the elite of every age, degenerates in a modus operandi common among the frustrated bourgeoisie: betrayal. Featuring two brothers of noble family who, by their way of being, pursue to the death the unsustainable duplicity of power acquisition at any cost, or at least as its own reward, with the plot softened a bit along the way by faint expression of a vacuous sense of higher calling that provides the distant grandeur of the elites, and now and then allows one of them to show compassion for the fate of humanity. The story pits younger brother, Francis, the power seeker and sniveling opportunist, against older brother, Charles, purveying the aristocratic spirit of noble responsibility, which by its lack of practical applicability, leads to disaster in the name of the general good.

As staged, the fraternal antagonists are supported by three other archetypal personages: in reference to Charles (who anchors the intrigue), they are Girl-Friend, Father, and Underclass Buddy. As heavenly-beauty incarnate, the Girl sets an irreproachable and unapproachable standard for moral rectitude; on the other hand, Father is a diffident Baron, dangerous because at once powerful and anesthetized by his royalist-bourgeois comforts; the Underclass-Buddy demonstrates the adventurous contradiction of self-driven youth, of thoughtless indifference concerning the means used toward questionable ends.

By the dénouement, the moral beacon of love proves too fragile to show a path of reconciliation; in a chain of tragic events set in motion by the manipulative younger brother, the potentially Salvationist climax goes ballistic, setting the stage for the sublimity of love, the consummation of which is achieved not in bed but by the sword: his in her. Duke Von Moor is the melodramatically misshapen father of the contesting sons (Charles and Francis), in his eighties, in his castle, beyond autonomous action. Too long dependent on his status and house staff, he has been transformed into an icon of aloof

---

with that of Ronald Dworkin (1931–), of which his study of *Law's Empire* (1986) is the foundational text.

nobility, righteous to the end, demonstrating how abstract virtue without practical anchorage disqualifies itself.

Then there is the gang of thieves that prowls the Black Forest, led by the black-bearded personality, Spiegelberg, Charles' underclass buddy. Along the way, having become the shabby inspiration of Charles, "Spigel" proves to be a fully despicable, villainous character of the darkest nature: scarred on the exterior, armored on the interior, decidedly not the sort of person one would hope to encounter while strolling down a dark forest lane on a summer day.

It is a folk drama of noble intensity, including: brotherly betrayal, parental *dépassement*, love thwarted by steel penetration. The sole happy folks, and then only occasionally, are the nasty gang of thieves. The aesthetic apex of the balance beam for this plot is fratricide: indifference to the equal humanity of others, foreclosing solidarity and compassion, beyond trust and cooperation, with tension perpetuated by royalist political domination, oriented by a chase for values that don't exist in reality even among aristocrats. The conundrum of consciousness is global: most are aware that an autocratic world is a machine for domination, alienation and social instability. Yet, under that very same form of unitary authority, every legitimate avenue for change seems foreclosed. As anticipation for entry into a revolutionary age, Schiller's *Robbers* hit the nail on the head.

While it is never possible to know the intention of authorship, Schiller himself provided some commentary about this piece, in the form of *Preface* material and *Notices*, some of which I have already referenced. Part of this was expository and part was defensive. Given its horrifying and scabrous nature, after finishing the original version, he felt obliged to soften some of the dialogue. In the 1770s, as is still the case today, most theater goers were from elite classes, among whom decorum defines the beautiful. Schiller's story line was not pretty: justice betrayed, love violated, and family integrity dishonored. He was worried that the play might close for a lack of draw, simply because of the bourgeois necessity in every age to feel vindicated rather than threatened by art.

The Curtain Falls

Leaving the action to the reader to do with as she wished, it is telling to see how Schiller chose to announce his moral position for that first play. In the original *Preface*, (1781) he sounds like a criminology professor, proposing a theory about the virtuous benefit of the study of vice:

> It is… not so much the bulk of my play as its contents which may banish it from the stage. Its scheme and economy require that several characters should appear who would offend the finer feelings of virtue and shock the delicacy of our manners. … It is the course of mortal things that the good should be shadowed by the bad, and virtue shine the brightest when contrasted with vice. Whoever proposes to discourage vice and to vindicate religion, morality, and social order against their enemies, must unveil crime in all its deformity, and place it before the eyes of men in its colossal magnitude; he must diligently explore its dark mazes, and make himself familiar with sentiments at the wickedness of which his soul revolts. Vice is here exposed in its innermost workings.[11] (Preface 1781)

Schiller went on to prefigure the central tension of the plot. Focusing first on younger brother Francis, malicious, calculating, self-interest driven to the limits of the inhuman, Schiller says of him:

> I have endeavored to sketch a striking and lifelike portrait, to hold up to abhorrence all the machinery of his scheme of vice, and to test its strength by contrasting it with truth. (Preface 1781)

Roughly translated, this indicates that second son Francis found a way to advance around his older brother's place in the line of succession for the family title without quite resorting to arsenic.[12]

By contrast, older brother Charles, originally an ethical idealist and naive political realist, is victimized by existence and fate. He is:

> A remarkable and important personage… [for whom] erroneous notions of activity and power, an exuberance of strength which bursts through all the barriers of law, must of necessity conflict with the rules of social life. (Preface 1781)

In other words, Charles becomes an anarchistic highwayman, but only for good causes.

From there, it is a short step to generalize and justify in artistic terms, the aesthetic violence of tragedy. Thus, says Schiller:

> A certain strength of mind is required both on the part of the poet and the reader; in the former that he may not disguise vice, in the latter that he may not suffer brilliant qualities to beguile him into admiration of what is essentially detestable. … In consequence of the remarkable catastrophe which ends my play, I may justly claim for it a place among books of morality, for

[11] Preface 1781 citations from online edition.

[12] During the high age of aristocracy in Europe, which went on for centuries, plots and murder were so common among elite family members as a way of succeeding to title, authority and wealth, that arsenic, the poison, was ironically referred to as the 'potion of succession.'

> crime meets at last with the punishment it deserves; the lost one enters again within the pale of the law, and virtue is triumphant. (Preface 1781)

In another *Advertisement* for this work issued in 1782, Schiller promised that the piece would expose, "the interior economy of vice," and, in the end, deliver the ultimate lesson of Greek tragedy, namely:

> ...that the invisible hand of Providence makes even villains the instruments of its designs and judgments, and can marvelously unravel the most intricate perplexities of fate. (Hofmannsthal 2004/1926: 9)

In those writings attendant to his first play, Schiller revealed a great deal about his personal aesthetic underpinnings, the expression of which marked his literary-critical work for the rest of his life. Oblivious to institutional dynamics, he focused on humanity as evidenced by individual behavior, for better or worse, emphasizing the states of consciousness according to which he assumed individuals chose to act. He harbored a particular enlightenment view of humankind, of which the following line is a rather succinct declaration:

> Every man, even the most depraved, bears in some degree the impress of the Almighty's image, and perhaps the greatest villain is not farther removed from the most upright man than the petty offender; for the moral forces keep even pace with the powers of the mind, and the greater the capacity bestowed on man, the greater and more enormous becomes his misapplication of it; the more responsible is he for his errors. (Preface 1781)

From Theater to Philosophy

After 1785, Schiller's attention gradually shifted away from theater as he became preoccupied with the study of history. Drawn into it innocently, as a secondary factor to his theater interests, he was soon back at his writing table composing serious historical texts. This had a curious effect for him personally, leading to his nomination by Goethe for the faculty post in history at the University of Jena, for which (as discussed earlier) he proved to be remarkably miscast. As he lamented in his correspondence, once on the faculty, he discovered that nothing interferes with intellectual creativity like the necessity of delivering amphitheater courses for distracted and often disinterested students, usually with so many under foot, as to block pedagogically useful interaction.[13]

---

[13] Letter of 28 May, 1789.

It was in Leipzig after leaving Jena, under sponsorship of his friend, Kröner, that he found a good library and the time needed to plunge into the study of European history. That interest had been developing as he undertook composition of his *Don Carlos*, when he decided to anchor that drama in the facts of 16th century Spain. By then he lived in northern Germany, which had been the scene of centuries of war, and he became intrigued with the strange way the country was cut-up into a patchwork of principalities, with somber political tension persisting among them.

As with most intellectuals, it was impossible for Schiller not to write about what he read. Before long, he had launched into the composition of two major historical studies, the first, a *History of the Netherlands*, was published in 1788, and the second, even more massive and important, a *History of the Thirty-Years War*, came out in 1789–1791. It was the first of these works that attracted the attention of Goethe.[14]

Only ten years older than Schiller, by the time he nominated him for Jena in 1788, Goethe already played an important role in the German intellectual world. At the time, university appointments followed from feudal nomination, which in turn depended on the recommendation of an influential figure such as Goethe. At first Schiller found the history post absolutely ravishing, and it was during that exuberant phase in Jena that he met and married his wife, Charlotte, with whom he had four children. As expressed often in his correspondence, he had great difficulty with close personal relationships, particularly with women. He had decided early that if he remained unmarried until the age of thirty, he would be a lifetime bachelor. Charlotte arrived just in the nick of time; they married three months after his thirtieth birthday.

As his emotional exuberance alternated with cycles of despondency, Schiller's periods of intellectual pessimism alternated with unrealistic grandiosity. Nowhere was this more evident than during his 'history

---

[14] History. Schiller's Europe had been shaken by two distinct 'thirty-year-wars,' both fought principally in what is now Modern Germany. The first, about which Schiller wrote the history, was the 17th century one, in which, among others, Descartes did a bit of soldiering; due to its religious undercurrents, it was particularly ruthless, ending with the Peace of Westphalia (1648).

The second series of wars occurred between 1733 and 1763, divided among three long incidents, of which the third had international consequences, and is known in the U.S. as the *French and Indian War*. The Prussian, Frederick the Great (with whom Voltaire spent three years) was a major instigator in these conflicts, with the result having little effect on European land treaties, but out of which the Prussian reputation for unrelenting warmaking was established. Schiller's father was involved in the last Seven Years War segment of these events, which undoubtedly had some influence also on Schiller's early critical motivation.

period.' He began reading history to fill out his theater and was soon swimming in archives like a fish in the sea: "Every day I love history more," he announced, adding that nothing would please him more than to, "study only history, ten years nonstop" (Letter: 15 April, 1786).

Soon he was writing it up with grand erudition. Within a few years, not only did he report to a friend that he considered it possible to become Germany's number-one historian, but that he was working with such intensity as to, "nourish the idea of being a German Plutarch" (Letter: 26 Nov., 1790), comparing himself to the Grecian-Roman (46–120 AD) who wrote into life the emperors from antiquity that had proceeded his epoch. Plutarch followed this with a series of historical biographies, where he often contrasted pairs of major historical personages, attempting to show how the moral dispositions of leaders, better or worse, played themselves out in life, to determine the fate of major events.[15]

By this work, Plutarch established the biography-based style of historical narrative, oriented by the postulate that human moral principles, often decidedly a-moral in content, drive practical political strategy. It is not clear if Schiller was a naive believer in the truth-value of the great-person centered, historical narrative; certainly in his theater pieces he was determinedly critical of abuses of power, cruelty and social injustice, and held leaders responsible when justice was violated. However, acknowledging that leaders can abuse power is not to deny the importance of leadership, not as autocratic dictator, but as facilitator, without which no community is able to assure the best interests of its people.

As demonstrated by his aesthetic writings and the sub-surface message of his theater, Schiller believed that human well-being was sufficient motive to overcome individual resistance to the collective action needed to construct a better world. Yet he evidently recognized the practical

---

15 Being anecdotal by contemporary standards, no one is sure as to the factual details of *Plutarch's Lives*. Still, his writings provide what is taken to be the most authoritative personal information on that crucial period of history, during which the center of gravity in the West shifted from Greece to Rome. For a sample of his writings in English, see *Plutarch: Makers of Rome*, translated and with an introduction by Ian Scott-Kilvert (1965). Plutarch exposed two of what are taken as having been major qualities explaining the expansion and stability of the Roman Empire: courage and persistence in foreign warfare, and skill and willingness for domestic compromise, between the elites and popular classes, that is, between patrician and plebeian. The timeless necessity of war making and state craft is explained by the persistence of cross-national jealousy and misunderstanding, and domestic inequality. Schiller based his cautious political optimism on the possibility of an end to international tensions and internal disparities of the sort that Plutarch considered unavoidable.

limits to that optimism. This is why his plays displayed a decidedly classical tragic face, according to which destiny writes the script, fate drives the action, and in the long run, things turn out in keeping with the call of humanity.

His determinant fatalism was nowhere more evident than in his decision to reject the practice of French tragic theater then current in Europe, by reinstating the chorus in some of his stage pieces. This was a daring move, since even in German cultural circles, the 18th century, as the *Century of Louis XIV* (the title of a major text by Voltaire), was admittedly, if grudgingly, said to be centered in France. While Racine and others rejected it as a formalist intrusion, Schiller insisted that the voice of the chorus in theater constituted a vital framing principle, exuding a moral atmosphere that contributes to the humanistic pertinence and soul-searching power of classic Greek drama; that the then contemporary choice in Paris to eliminate the chorus was done at a price and that restoration of this theatrical element was essential for assuring the critical mass of tragedy.

Narrative Arc Defined

Schiller was an inveterate discursive thinker. He read and observed a great deal, wrote about what he read and observed, reflected consciously about what he wrote, and put the results into further writing, as stimulation for further study and observation. Nowhere is this more evident than when he described in a letter what has come to be known as the narrative arc, a way of framing a novel, treatise or play that continues to be a common standard for composition. This has furnished subsequent generations of editors with a tool for assisting authors to assure a certain coherence of text. This exercise of formalization necessitated not only that Schiller engage in the process but become sufficiently conscious of it to describe it in words.

Authorship requires turning inspiration into a project and the project into a text. As he put that in a letter, as enthusiasm and ideals give rise to a project, it is like throwing a ball into the air, out in front of where one stands: before falling eventually back to earth, "the ball makes a circular arc as its violence is broken in the air." But at the moment of the crystallization of the project, under the spell of passion and energy, we do not consider this inevitable "trajectory of reality." He went on to draw out the significance of "this allegory" of the arc as figure, which:

> ...prefigures the destiny of all human projects like a symbol... All of them rise and aim at the zenith like rockets, but all human projects trace that arc and fall once again to mother earth. But considering this process, this circular arc; my how beautiful it is. (Letter: 05 Oct., 1785: 25)

Schiller's life displayed that magic trajectory: living, then learning, then writing the truth of existence back into life. In a way he was a classic poet. But as a fully modern fellow also, his journey took him to the library, where the longer he stayed, the more he extended his intellectual reach. Still, there was the evident problem of practical politics, which he aggressively confronted in his theater but which he avoided facing on a daily basis by staying close to his reading and writing table.

As established by early correspondence, he had developed this practice very early on. In the spring of 1887, when still only twenty-eight years old, he read Voltaire, including his more famous historical works *The Century of Louis XIV* (1739) and a historical novel on the Swedish King, *Charles XII* (1968a/1731). Contrary to received opinion, he judged the latter as more captivating than the former for its superior realism as against a certain distant grandiosity in the other (Letter: 25 April, 1787). But he also complimented the skill with which Voltaire expressed his individuality, "joining the interest of a robinsonade to that of a philosophical spirit."[16]

By the following year, he was in frenzy: "I work harder every day... I write a great deal and am on the path in danger of literary death, due to an excess of writing" (Letter: 18 Jan., 1788). Soon he was into the Greek classics. He started with *Homer* in German translation, studying it until he had "learned it by heart"; next he went to the Greek version, working that through, repeatedly, both to learn the Greek language and to be sure he grasped its sense (Letter: 20 Aug., 1788). By the time he got to the theater of Euripides, the master of the attic comedy, he reported having become bogged down; not content to only read Euripides in Greek, he decided to produce an authoritative German translation. As a

---

16 "Robinsonade" is a trope drawn from Daniel Defoe's, *Robinson Crusoe* (1719). The book circulated widely in Europe soon after its publication, inspiring a genre of lost-adventure images that continue to stimulate the literary imagination. The term itself, robinsonade, was coined by a German novelist, Johann Gottfried Schnabel, in the Preface to a book composed in 1731 that had been inspired by his reading Defoe (a lost-adventure novel, *The Island of Felsenbourg*). Use of this trope demonstrates Schiller's evident fascination with Voltaire's individualist temperament which, linked to his intellectual engagement with current human events, allowed the deployment of an acute critical perspective. Even if it is a role charged with contradiction and danger in a desolate world of economic savagery and civic danger, Schiller probably hoped to engage similarly, in a way emulating Voltaire.

perfectionist, he voiced concern that he was forcing the translation before "studying the text deeply enough" to get its full meaning (Letter: 20 Oct., 1788).

The further he progressed in these studies, the less time there was for creative writing. He reported that he was working on history because it "pays off," even if there was a risk that this would transform him into only a journalist rather than poet, more of a "Montesquieu than Sophocles" (Letter: 12 Feb., 1788).

Social-Philosophy with Feeling

Following his history spell, he went off on a more social-philosophical path. Having come to see that understanding is mostly based on history, he was puzzled to explain the interface between intellectual activity and the immediate experience and appreciation of life. Continuing to compose shorter poetic works, it was in the half-dozen years following Jena that he finished the two philosophical-ethics essays which established his aesthetic authority. The first to come out, *Grace and Dignity* (1793), served as a prelude for the second, his *On the Aesthetic Education of Man* (1795), which was a didactic exploration of the crisis of moral consciousness in the West, including a call for reform based on the aesthetic education of the European population.

A year later he completed a third essay in this series, *On Narrative and Reflective Poetry* (1796). In about one hundred pages, he crafted what is judged as one of the most influential critical essays ever written in the German language (Reed 2002: 103). This included exploring the cause of major cultural shifts from antiquity to modernity, with particular attention to changes in literary forms and genres. Before examining those three texts more carefully, there is more to be said about Schiller's personal story, particularly his relationship with Goethe.

Goethe

When he was discovered by Goethe in 1788, Schiller was working on his *Netherlands History* project, as opening move in his historical-aesthetic turn. In spite of the way the Goethe-Schiller reputations are connected in the popular consciousness, their relationship took time to develop and along the way had to surmount a certain resistance. It was not until six years after their first meeting (1794) that their collaboration in writing had begun,[17] requiring another five years until Schiller moved for good to Weimar (1799), to live and work within reach of Goethe. That final, much discussed proximity, was in fact quite brief, since only six years after arriving in Weimar, Schiller died (1805). While the theater pieces which he did during those last years in Weimar are stunning, much of the writing on which Schiller's reputation is based was done independently of Goethe.

It is often assumed that first impressions are determinant for personal relationships; if that were universally valid, the arrangement between these two men would never have deepened. Schiller's early response to Goethe was hesitant. Having just met him and then only on professional terms, Schiller doubted that, they "would ever find themselves becoming close to one another" (Hofmannsthal 2004/1926: 32). He did not denounce Goethe's work, which had inspired him for years; but after meeting him, he judged that Goethe had already passed through stages of development and interest that he had yet to complete. Schiller also identified what he took as signs of a major difference in aesthetic motive between the two of them:

> ...his [Goethe's] entire being is disposed from the start as different from mine, his world is not mine, our modes of representation appear essentially different. However one can not conclude anything with certainty from a first encounter of that sort. Time will tell. (Letter: 12 Sept., 1788)

Within six months of that first meeting, and thanks to intervention of Goethe, it was clear that Schiller would be moving to Jena as a history professor. Considering his difficulties with personal finances, one might suppose that this would have very much pleased him. In fact, the entire affair was charged with apprehension. In a New Year's Day letter of 1789,

---

[17] In 1794, seeing the need to enhance popular judgment and general understanding, Schiller decided to start a new literary journal, *The Hours* (*Die Horen*). Faced with much competition from other journals, he did this with the manifest intention of raising German literary standards, a mission of grandiose ambition. By seductive correspondence, he drew Goethe into the project. Before long, all other collaborators were left behind, with Schiller and Goethe filling a majority of the pages. Because of Schiller's editorial determination, the journal stirred up criticism from German traditionalists who began to call into question not just Schiller but Goethe. Goethe was not a passive fellow in the face of criticism; in response, he and Schiller set out on an elaborate project of what for the time was politically challenging writing. By this, Schiller drew out Goethe's critical perspective to a certain extent, in a way that otherwise would probably never been fully expressed. This short-lived yet intense journal exercise was a crucible of mutual information between Schiller and Goethe. By it, Goethe was set on a path of generating literature of higher moral ambition, while Schiller learned to better deal with his polemic energy in the interest of greater literary elegance (see Reed 2002).

before he'd actually begun the job, and with no prior professorial experience, Schiller lamented the idea of university teaching: would his creative capacity survive the load?

> ...my life as citizen of the world which I have pursued up to now will be ended, as this year I enter into the useless servitude to the State. ... It is a heroic act of renouncement of all joy during the next three years... (Letter: 01 Jan., 1789)

After his entry into the faculty, Goethe came to Jena quite often. As with benefactors throughout history, Goethe seems to have been fascinated not just with his talent but with Schiller's person as well. Expected to express his gratitude to Goethe by being readily available, Schiller found his artistic and intellectual sensitivities being encroached upon. His response was as respectful as it was unflattering:

> It would make me unhappy to be any more often in the entourage of Goethe. Even in regard to his closest friends, there is never the least moment of equanimity with him; he never lets up. In fact I think that he is an egoist to an inhabitual degree. ... He freely reveals his existence to others, but only like a god, without giving himself at all. ... That is what leads me to detest him, even if I love his spirit with all my heart, and gives me a grand image of him. A totally singular mélange of hate and love, that is what he awakens in me... I could kill his esprit and love him again with all my heart. ... I attach a very great importance to his judgment. (Letter: 02 Feb., 1789)

Schiller's oscillation between attraction and repulsion for Goethe touched issues of both style and quality of work. In the end, productive substance took the higher ground and his view of Goethe was gradually resolved in a positive direction. Within a month of writing the above-cited reproach against Goethe, Schiller was again in correspondence with his friend in Dresden, Körner, but this time exuberantly praising Goethe's work. Speaking of theater and in reference to Goethe, his position was now unmistakably complimentary:

> ... when he wishes to employ all his force, I do not measure up to Goethe. He surely has more genius capacity than I, richer in knowledge and sensibility; other than that, he has a bright and refined artistic sense that can be expressed in every species of art; something I miss to a degree that approaches total ignorance. (Letter: 25 Feb., 1789)

The question arose as to the range of issue which might be broached in conversation with Goethe; rather quickly, Schiller discovered that personal matters were not part of the package:

> … I don't like to discuss things with him which closely concern me. He is entirely bereft of the cordiality necessary for sharing anything of a personal nature. For him, the entirety of philosophy is subjective, and as for conviction or further discussion, that is the end of it. As for his philosophy, I do not really like it. It places too much emphasis on the sensual world, while as for me I put all emphasis on the soul of being. (Letter: 01 Nov., 1790)

However defined, the working relationship between the two marked an irreversible shift in the literary-intellectual landscape of Europe.[18] It is difficult to decide the extent to which the times or epochal conditions were responsible for that change in literature and thought, versus the role played personally by the Schiller-Goethe team. Some argue (*à la* Plutarch) that turning-point events are the work of great individuals at propitious moments; others contend that such ruptures are the surface expression of alternations in underlying forces of cultural production, that particular individuals serve as signposts regarding the direction and velocity of cultural change, rather than as causal forces for such change. The jury is out, whether life follows art in the largest sense of the term, or if art, including the art of political leadership, is merely the dramatic revealing of the inner

---

[18] *Sturm und Drang*. Schiller and Goethe play central roles in two important German literary movements, with the first spilling into the second.

The "*Sturm und Drang*" movement was short lived (~1765–1785); its meaning in English is 'storm and urge,' usually translated as 'storm and stress.' This was a proto Romantic Movement, i.e., a movement against the intensely rational, formal German classical style associated with the early 18th century and Immanuel Kant. Rather than blocking, rejecting, denying the emotional basis of action, this movement stressed the free expression of emotional extremes and personal subjectivity. As built into theater, such as with Schiller's *Robbers*, this implies a frightening aspect of shock aimed at the audience, not just because of the violence of action, but because the heroes are motivated not only by some high noble calling, but are simultaneously driven by downright desperate intention, of greed, revenge, jealousy, etc. In the present case, one of the enduring results was that by his play *The Robbers*, Schiller reintroduced the melodrama into Western literature, a theatrical form which had been somewhat dormant since Euripides.

Weimar Classicism was also brief, starting ~1770, but concentrated in the period 1788–1805, from the time Schiller started to work with Goethe, until his death. Here the mission was more complex: to bridge or integrate questions of {feeling and thought} or {mind and body}, which again, under Kant, had been transcended by a pure idealist synthesis. The Weimar work was aimed at achieving that synthesis in more down to earth, one might say, materialist terms, but without denying the idealist reality. The point was to portray cultural or societal totality, as a strain toward harmony, much as was depicted in the classic Greek theater of Sophocles. The object was continual historical renewal, stressing the pedagogical value of aesthetic practices, of education via art, of art as joyfulness deployed, of artistic production as play, of its product as play-filled. Even if after affiliating with Goethe, Schiller's working style lost a bit of its edge and even if he did discuss the value of 'play' in his aesthetic writings, right to the end, as we sill see with his *William Tell* play, while less overtly violent in stagecraft, he remained actively committed to revolutionary movement in the name of human liberation.

societal tensions, of the dialectic contradictions, of the forces in opposition, which, through time, drive life and society.

Given their divergent aesthetic and emotional disposition, the relationship between Schiller and Goethe was ambivalent; but then so was that between Rogers and Hammerstein or Laurel and Hardy. Ambivalence at the level of consciousness is tension expressed in the world; without a strong dose of ambivalence also at the human level, any creative partnership can go stale and lose its life.

Schiller left a generous correspondence attesting to his cycles of inner torment and external pique. Goethe's similarly ample letter writing provides a remarkably direct description of how he responded to their encounters.

In Goethe's long and complex professional career, the event of greatest self-reported impact was 09 May, 1805: the death of Schiller. In a letter written shortly thereafter, Goethe claimed the effect was as if, "I am losing half my existence. He later added, "who will reach out his hand to me as I sink in the real." As Goethe indicated in a letter, 10 January, 1829, the persistence of this sense of loss went on to his last days: "I really do not know what would have happened to me without Schiller's stimulus" (Reed 2002: 103, 114).

Subsequently, Goethe tried unsuccessfully to fill the painful gap in his creative life by finding a collaborative replacement for Schiller; this never worked out. Alone and alienated from the by-then dominant German romantics, after finishing his famous *Faust I* (1808), he was unable to set his sights on further external missions. Goethe occupied the last twenty years of his life with autobiographic self-exploration, aimed not just at "intimate self-insight," but at the study of himself as subject, engaged in his objective context (Nicholas 2002: 35–36). As for the effects in the long run, of the significance of Schiller for him, he reported in a letter many years later, "I really don't know what would have become of me without Schiller's stimulus" (in Reed 2002: 114).

From their professional work together, backed by their correspondence, most believe their relationship to have assumed a symbiotic dimension; not everyone agrees. Nietzsche, in particular, was uncertain that Schiller lived up to the grandeur of Goethe, and in his *Twilight of the Idols: or How to Philosophize with a Hammer*, went so far as to disavow use of the word 'and' to speak of them in the same breath, as if doing so were an unjustified confabulation.[19]

[19] Nietzsche compiled the elements of his *Le Crépuscule des Idoles ou Comment on Philosophe au Marteau*, in 1888 (2005a) and it was published the following year. The

Whatever the personal drama or trauma of working together, Goethe and Schiller sounded a charge which opened the door toward a new view of being human in the world; they inspired both the romantic literature of the artist's novel and the realists approach, the novel of education.

The revolutionary dimension which continually surfaced in Schiller's writings is largely absent from the work of his older and more formally respected collaborator. Speaking only of Schiller, by going beyond the then dominant alternatives, he contributed to a process that eventually nudged the critical community out of the stasis of classical idealism (Kant), forward, then traversing structural idealism (Hegel), arriving finally at a practical realism (Marx). However, the core of his work was a two-edged mixture of consciously appreciated and politically enacted optimism, a brief discussion of which is next.

Critical Tension: Materialist and Idealist

Comparing Schiller's critical optic with that of Voltaire's, puts in relief a major ambiguity about the enlightenment. While freedom was a central theme, was the mission mostly about liberating human energy and initiative to allow for material progress, or mostly concerned with the full blossoming of human consciousness, breadth of understanding and existential well-being? The two dispositions, {materialist—idealist} are dialectically linked: the question of priority has fueled debate in the West for five-hundred years.[20]

contents are really a set of notes, assembled in rough thematic sections, generating the aphoristic style for which he is well known. It is possible to read these notes on their own terms, since they represent his research during the phase of composition of his famous *La Volonté de puissance*, which he had just renounced to release formally. This resulted in a continuing battle among specialists about the authenticity of that famous work, which necessarily came out posthumously and which, nonetheless, is why he decided to publish these notes on their own. So in a way, much of this volume might be read as the real subtext for the virtual *Volonté de Puissance*. In any event, in Paragraph-16, Section "*Flâneries d'un inactuel*" (in contemporary English, meaning "Strollings about of a Contemporary Trivializer"), Nietzsche is hammering away at what he ironically refers to as *l'esprit allemand*, which results from going to school in Germany and reading the assigned literature. The literary targets of his critique of "*médiocratie*" were limitless, including Dante, Kant, Victor Hugo, Zola; but he seemed to admire Ralph Waldo Emerson. The short paragraph of Section 16 targets Schiller and Goethe: the latter admired, the former not respected at all, justifying in his eyes the observation: "that which I can not stand to hear either is the 'and'... [when] the Germans say 'Goethe and Schiller'—I even fear that they will [soon be saying] Schiller and Goethe" (Nietzsche 2005a/1888).

20 This dialectic designation of {materialism—idealism} is descriptive and exemplary, not formal or derivative; it is applied here in the sociological sense, intended to highlight

On initial reading, both Schiller and Voltaire were aghast in response to royalist-aristocratic-bourgeois domination. They opposed the quest for notoriety, transient pleasure or simple distraction, justifying a life for the elite based on oppression of ordinary people and cruel warfare when wanted. They deplored such conditions and set out to warn the world about them, perhaps mobilizing the courage of their audiences to change. Thereby comparable in ultimate goal, they differed in their mode of critical expression: Voltaire was more of the materialist, and Schiller decidedly more idealist.

Voltaire worked as if mounted on a critical steamroller; no matter whom or what he encountered, at the sign of injustice or vulgar abuse of position, he rose to the occasion and called foul. Bypassing state-of-mind issues, he focused on the material-behavioral aspects of political injustice, economic exploitation, and social class abuse. Often deploying his cry of alarm as if screaming *FIRE* on stage in an Italian Comic Opera, no one missed the point. However, to identify Voltaire as a materialist is not to say that he considered human-beings to be trapped in a frame, predetermined by material circumstances; he believed that humanizing progress was possible, if, for instance, philosopher-kings replaced the ordinary despotic sort. As discussed in Chapter Two, after three years in Potsdam with Frederick the Great, he saw the fault in that optimistic belief.

Schiller approached the problem of freedom and liberation differently; rather than focus primarily on the material restrictions resulting from domination and exploitation, he was particularly sensitive to the impact of ethical subjugation on the state of mind and consciousness of human beings. Oppression at the hands of indifferent government leadership or socio-economic elites not only imposes a life of necessity, poverty and physical suffering on exploited individuals, but existential pain as well: it hurts to be poor, to confront unjustified elitist privilege, to witness others indentured, imprisoned or even executed without clear accusation or due process. For his theater, strongly felt existential trauma was the practical factum behind Schiller's political call.

This distinction between Voltaire and Schiller is linked to their different personal histories. Voltaire matured in a France under the sway of a meta-Newtonian, material deterministic world view; by the time (and in a

how these two conceptions of reality influence social practices, and in particular, the critical practice of Voltaire and Schiller. The same dialectic polarity is still alive in the West two-centuries later, driving arguments about the main competing currents of political economy and the critical practice which that debate occasions.

different country) Schiller came into maturity, German Idealism, exemplified particularly by the program of Leibniz, was sweeping Europe. Schiller not only absorbed the effects of this movement, as it was intensified by Kant, but made his own contribution to it.

Leaving Voltaire aside, describing the shift in the aesthetic climate that affected Schiller's critical practice requires attending to his special relationship with the work of Immanuel Kant (1724–1804), with whom he was contemporary and by whom he was strongly influenced.

Freedom as Judgment

After accepting the post as professor at Jena (a role for which he proved to be horribly miscast), Schiller received a grant (1791) from the Danish Court, which gave him time to begin to study philosophy. He was particularly interested in Kant and focused principally on his then most recent writings. Although twenty-five years younger than Kant, the two were contemporaries during their most productive years; the importance of the study of Kant by Schiller is well established, how Schiller might have influenced Kant is undetermined.

Schiller found Kant's works very difficult, particularly the first of his two famous Critiques, of *Pure Reason* (1968/1781 and 1787) and of *Practical Reason* (2007a/1788), which seemed as murky as they were revealing. He was motivated nonetheless to continue studying Kant in preparation for a university seminar he was planning for the following winter (Letter: 31 March, 1791). Whether by well-tempered intuition or wise advice, he found himself drawn to, then focusing on, the just-then available third major Kantian work, the *Critique of Judgment* (2008/1790).

Starting his reading of Kant's *Critique of Judgment* almost immediately after its publication, Schiller's was one of the first studies ever to be undertaken of this historically significant work. While the aesthetic question is central in that final great Kantian text, the issue was also evident in Schiller's writings before he came to Kant. Further back still, after many centuries of neglect, the term, *aesthetic*, resurfaced in 1735 as the title of a text by another German, Alexander Baumgarten (1714–1762).[21]

---

[21] Although, *Aesthetics* is the title of an important work attributed to Aristotle, the modern bringing back to life of the figure is attributed to Alexander Baumgarten (1714–1762); he first used the term in 1735, eventually composing a two volume work on the subject, *Aesthetics*, which came out in 1750 and 1758. He used the term in reference to the sensuous capacity of humans to directly appreciate worldly experience, independent of higher

Although Baumgarten used it in a more limited sense, aesthetics is now said to concern the massive issue of evaluation or fit (as harmony, beauty, rightness or correctness) of particular actions or elements in reference to some larger event or system of which they are constituents. Commonly reduced to the exercise of good-judgment, the aesthetic debate is complex: is good-judgment possible? If so, how and with results of what degree of universal appeal?

Schiller got to aesthetics from its political dimension: if life should be beautiful and harmonious, how is it possible to explain a stable society given the oppressive action against the general welfare by the elite? Are the dominant classes aware of the negative effect of their action on the dominated? If so, how is it possible for them not to judge this as in violation of the standards of humanity; and if they do, how is it possible in good faith for the elites to continue to exercise exploitive leadership?[22]

While neither of them coined the term aesthetics, nor did Schiller wait to explore the issue until arriving at Kant,[23] it was largely by their work that the dialectic sense of the notion of aesthetics expanded to its level of contemporary usage: referring both to the appreciation of harmony, beauty and integrity of the social action or 'art' as encountered in the world, and to the expression into the world of the human creative action

---

rationality; this he considered as not mediated by the work of the mind, and on that basis judged such sensual appreciation as a less than fully human act. By comparison, Schiller considered the aesthetic moment to be one of higher human elevation, or what I consider as the expression of the fully conscious condition of being. The shift from the Baumgarten view to that of Schiller is a telling indicator of the force behind German Romanticism, a movement which in its turn was ultimately considered a form of degraded expression.

22 By the 20th century, aesthetics had taken a manifestly political turn: once imagined to concern effete issues of beauty as décor, it is now seen to reach much deeper to the core of moral, ethical and civic action as the basis for social-political harmony. Hannah Arendt debated this famously in her study of the "banality of evil," raising the question of how is it possible for a society to rest intact when a condition such as the Holocaust is active within it (Arendt 1951 and 1963). Pierre Bourdieu raised the issue differently than had Schiller, in reference not to the elite but to the oppressed: how to explain the more or less pacific perpetuation of Western societies with such manifest internal social inequality, other than as the result of a socialized, internalized twisted sense of aesthetic judgment (Bourdieu 1979).

23 By the time (1790) Kant wrote his third critique of aesthetic judgment, usage of the notion had evolved considerably away from the Baumgarten view, by then connoting aesthetic appreciation as a higher, more nuanced human disposition. This distinction lay the grounds for various subsequent movements referred to as 'romantic,' which place superior emphasis on aesthetic, intuitive or otherwise direct appreciative capacities, as the more certain guide to life than is the intellectual-conceptual analysis. Today, in the fine arts, aesthetics supposes not only a way of appreciating the world, but a just manner of self-exposition, for leaving an artistic, symbolic imprint on the world; we might consider as examples the aesthetic of Picasso, Proust or Beethoven.

as production of common meaning for a community.[24] Beyond sharpening his own view, by reading and writing about Kant on judgment, Schiller helped build the interpretive bridge by which this third element in the Kantian project, on *Judgment*, was transported for application during subsequent centuries.[25]

Schiller was also familiar with other Kant's writings, of which the famous *Groundwork of the Metaphysic of Morals* (1785) had just come out; in follow up to that, he was among the first to question the moral standard at the center of the Kantian project. Kant had proposed that judgment is guided by intuitive application of a universally self-evident principle of aesthetic harmony, with everyone intending to act as if following a standard accepted by all of humanity, without concern for personal need or desire.[26] While it is clear that universal compliance with that imperative would assure a well-ordered and just society, Schiller saw too much practical evidence of its violation. Thus he questioned not the desirability but the actuality of Kant's now famous Moral Imperative.

What concerned him was not so much the difficulty, in real situations, of appreciating what would constitute the ideal mode of action, so as to

---

Following Baumgarten, Schiller stressed the practical moral force of aesthetic work: not just that art follows life, but that art can itself be a source of moral transformation, not just of the artist, but of society. However, the agreeableness of powerful aesthetic profiles is variable. For a lead into this topic see "Alexander Gottlieb Baumgarten," Encyclopedia Britannica Online. <http://www.britannica.com/EBchecked/topic/56478/Alexander-Gottlieb-Baumgarten>.

24 Neither Kant nor Schiller discussed the dialectic quality of the two edged {appreciative—expressive} dynamic that I believe animates the aesthetic moment. While the aesthetic of Hegel formally inclined in that direction, it was not concretized until emergence of the Marx aesthetic.

25 Kant's writings represented a working through of a set of problems related to the nature and experience of knowing, and of knowing what is; in spite of his determination, his resolution of that was incomplete and tentative. Those difficulties, as encountered in particular when Kant composed his *Critique of Judgment* (2008/1790), supplied the point of entry for Schiller into the Kantian debate. For one brief and readable study of Kant, see Hartnack, 1967.

26 Schiller's divergence from Kant on the moral issue touched on the question of human nature. Kant's approach to every question was an appeal to pure-practical reason as the basis for generating a categorical rule, which in this case, would cover moral (i.e., ethical) behavior, as if all human beings were categorically similar by practical-reasonable disposition, and thus prone to respond almost mechanically to high moral calling. The result was his famous categorical imperative. Since the wording varies across his writings, what I propose in my text is a heuristic reading of it, aimed at displaying the aesthetic sense of his moral argument. His imperative focused not on actual moral behavior but rather on moral intention, which is to say, the general guiding intentionality that he believed characterized every actual human being. Schiller had problems with this position as have many since him, including Theodor Adorno.

represent the best possible intention on behalf of all humankind.[27] Nor was it a matter of the likely unwillingness of most individuals to act-as-if there were no personal interests at stake. No, the issue for Schiller concerned the separation that Kant insisted on between the natural dispositions of humans and their higher, reasonable, humanized nature, as if setting aside ordinary needs and wants was natural among 'enlightened' human beings.[28]

Schiller considered such a separation as descriptive rather than factual. He argued that, "man is not destined to accomplish particular moral actions but to be a moral being" (Schiller 1998: 38). He offered the alternative argument that higher moral being is based not on denial of necessity associated with natural needs and wants (such as to eat or escape a menace), but by consciously overcoming domination by such necessity, via or as expression of freedom and how to respond to it, given the circumstances when it arises. For Schiller, extending beyond passive appreciation or immediate conditions, freedom pursued through political action in a community is the penultimate moment of personal liberty: or, both personally and collectively for a society, freedom in action is the overcoming of domination by necessity in the interests of the right.[29]

The originality of that content is masked a bit by the strong Kantian inspiration of its form. Appreciating Schiller's novelty here will be aided by a further look at some of his other writings.

Revolution as Change in Consciousness

Not formally trained in philosophy and working in advance of contemporary psychology, Schiller was nonetheless plowing the path of what might

---

[27] In his seminars on *Moral Philosophy*, Theodor Adorno voiced many of the reservations expressed by Schiller about Kant's moral position; see his *Problems of Moral Philosophy* (2000/1963).

[28] Finding a third-way between the classic Kantian modes of experience {sensual—intellectual}, resulted in Schiller's development of the concept of "play" (as a state of dynamic equilibrium, animated by the tension between the two Kantian alternatives, inclined into the world and thus toward the future, of the individual as aesthetic being) which I will touch on further in the closing section of this chapter.

[29] The lucidity of Schiller's reading of Kant has been questioned. Some assert it to be a distortion. For one example of how Schiller dealt with Kant, see his *Grace and Dignity* (1998: 38–40). All citations in English from that work are my translations from the French.

The difference between Schiller and Kant concerning the real versus philosophical separation between {natural-nature and humanized-nature} is similar to the argument about the justice of the Cartesian distinction of the 1650s concerning {material-body—thinking-soul}. These relations are dialectical, a form of dynamic expression that was as poorly be considered a 'concretized' form of philosophical idealism. He assumed that life is a matter of ideas in action, where those actions are evaluated by further activity of the mind, leading, at least potentially, to change based on sound judgment. He did not discuss the distinction between conscious and unconscious motivations, remaining relatively silent about conceptual-intellectual faculties and the inner structure and hidden workings of the soul.

Schiller seemed plagued by the inner struggle of two minds. He believed that the human experience in good-will and harmony is the natural state of being in the world; yet, often as not, this or that particular individual is a horrid and dangerous creature who must be shackled and silenced if general harmony and well-being are to be assured. Manichean is the label often associated with that two-minded dilemma (humankind as naturally good yet many individuals are manifestly dangerous) which tormented Schiller, and which, while animating his poetic creativity in ways that are rarely surpassed, fractured his persona in ways that may have contributed to his early death.

Schiller spoke of consciousness rather than the mind, as the soft-shell of inner life, the seat of judgments, emotions, sentiments, motives, aspirations, fears and the like; consciousness as symbolic mainspring of being, which to the extent that the word applies, bears witness not just to one's being but is morally responsible for it. Of course, people also behave physically, acting this way or that for practical, material reasons, with variable consequences for the rest of us. Still, for a philosophical idealist, priority is on the mind or, in the case of Schiller, consciousness, constituting the idealist search-light for material being, which, endlessly on the move, follows necessarily the existential path thus illuminated.

The precision of Schiller's idealist perspective was modified (in a positive way as I see it), by a recognizable dose of materialist realism. He knew that the vicissitudes of one's life and times endlessly alter the point of one's movement long before its destination is attained. Since life is a journey and not a destination, the objective for the good life is to live as expression of an affirmative state of consciousness, as a first step in modification of one's situation.

He believed that a moral and principled life issues from good consciousness; the problem is to explain its content, amplitude, plenitude and how it might be altered, recharged, revolutionized. Everyone assumes that the

appreciated during the scholastic period, at the end of which Descartes worked, as it was still in the 1750s and after, when Schiller was active.

guidance furnished by one's own consciousness is justified; even a bank robber considers his calling about as noble as any other. If each consciousness is its own legislature, would not its expression, under conditions of radical liberty, yield freedom's anarchy? Political libertarians endorse this line of argument; but is it defensible?

While the call to freedom was his dictum, Schiller was no libertarian; he eschewed radical individualism, seeing in that a grave danger. Still, at the beginning of his career, he considered freedom the greatest need which meant somehow putting an end to domination by interests of class, religion and aristocracy. The practical result was proto-revolutionary; at the end of the last play which he composed, *William Tell*, the people rally and overthrow the prince. At the end of the first one, *The Robbers*, the two brothers whom he created to incarnate the misdirected tensions of class and status, religion and state, both perish ignominiously.

When he began writing, Schiller seems to have been convinced (as had been Voltaire before him) that just changing the regime enough to let the ordinary masses become free would assure the establishment of the just society. Unfortunately, during his lifetime there was a stunning example of that very possibility and the results were discouraging to say the least.

As he was maturing, Europe was theater for the French Revolution (1789) and what a sign of hope that was until it turned nasty, not in overthrowing the monarchy or burning a few châteaux, but in the violence with which the representatives of the people in Paris attempted to enforce a new order on that disorderly world. It was as if the only choice was either chaos or autocracy. A vulgar form of dictatorship of the people temporarily replaced the royalist aristocratic dictatorship which the revolution had been mobilized to combat; suddenly this new regime showed signs of vengeance and war mongering nearly equal to that of the royalist regime that the revolutionaries had set out to replace. Schiller was horrified. What had gone wrong? Why was it that, once freed from external political constraint, the people were unable to establish a just society, with stable form, using peaceful means?

The answer seemed clear to him: the content of the popular consciousness was faulty, and until this was altered for the better, there was no hope that a sound society based on equality and compassion might see the day. This new awareness led Schiller to back away a bit from theater and poetry, which had occupied him during his early years, shifting his attention to the question of consciousness, its internal contradictions and its potential reform.

He decided that the people needed to undergo a giant pedagogical treatment, promulgating what he described in his most elaborate intellectual work, as the *Aesthetic Education for Man* (1795). If the general conscious is badly informed, the solution, he thought, might be to reform it with more substantially balanced moral material. Were that to be achieved, the otherwise silent majority of individuals might be stirred, diffusing a life-world of justice and meaning, based on commitment to the call of humanity; demanding equanimity and forthrightness as mission of any government which they endorse. Still, this is difficult to achieve since, regardless of moral content, consciousness is inherently self-serving, in the sense of self-preserving.

Schiller believed in the potentially 'good' majority, presumed to be disposed to live harmoniously in communities where the well-being of all would be reflected in the constancy of each. While his was not a formally utopian vision, he did endorse the general validity of the self-fulfilling prophecy; if most members of society believe that existence is a brutal battle for supremacy at any cost, then existence will mirror in action that prophecy of spirit. So, were there to be an aesthetic re-education of westerners, oriented by the humanist call of compassion and equanimity, tolerance and negotiation, then the structures of consciousness would be progressively reshaped, and the practical expression of that as life in society would in turn be reshaped as well and for the better.

Beyond Beauty

Given his complex sensibilities, eclectic education, rebellious political inclinations and identity insecurities, the texts Schiller produced are a recurrent source of surprise. The piece he wrote on *Grace and Dignity* exemplifies this. An admittedly fast worker, and intensive as well (he could not sleep through the night due to his tuberculosis), this essay came out in 1793, almost immediately after he started studying Kant.

Approaching the human condition from what is referred to as a god's eye view, Kant's was among the first major examples of pure intellectual criticism, of 'Mind's working on Mind's work,' offering a remarkably coherent, practical solution for the mapping problem between worldly experience and human consciousness. But, what Kant did not do in his three large Critiques and many years of work, Schiller accomplished with less than one hundred pages, in just a few months: he brought the categorical conceptual apparatus, as detailed by Kant, out of the stratosphere of intellectual abstraction and showed its pertinence for grasping the real stress and strain of the individual human condition. In practical terms, Schiller exposed the meaning of Kant for you and me, which is to say, 'in history'.[30]

As were most major 18th century critics (famously including both Voltaire and Rousseau), Kant was perplexed by the issue of freedom. In the preceding centuries it had become evident that humans warrant being free, that the world would be better if they were but that the western system is neither freedom-based, nor freedom-producing; it is domination based and highly restrictive.

Until near the end of his life when he addressed it directly in his essay, *Perpetual Peace* (1795), Kant dealt with the freedom issue not as practical guide for external action but on the basis of rationality. While the result impressed Schiller, the more compelling need as he saw it was to apply this critique of freedom, less in regard to the use by consciousness of freedom as self-justification for its rationality, than in regard to the inner being of human consciousness as the original font of freedom in the first place.[31]

Schiller shifted the critical problematic away from exclusive concern with appreciative-judgment, as in the attainment of rational understanding about being and the world, toward freedom as expressed to the world as principles, and by that, as a power for making and remaking the world by one's being as consciousness. More than only concerned with the rightness or accuracy with which the facts of life and worldly-being are assessed, freedom is a mode of expression by which the nature of one's being and of one's world is established, maintained and transformed.

Defining full expression of aesthetic judgment as freedom beyond domination, yields a strange reversal of common opinion. While those who suffer from physical domination under external constraint experience a degraded state of material-freedom, those responsible for structuring a society of domination demonstrate a more pernicious lack of liberty

---

30 Kant was not interested in history as determinate force, much less in the possibility that his concepts were 'historicized' and thus somehow mirrored phenomenally in reality. This is immediately given in his effort to develop a transcendental analytic. Yet, when he got to the end of his life and dealt with war by writing on *Perpetual Peace* (2009/1795), it was clear that history mattered a great deal.

31 While I argue that Schiller read Kant on aesthetic judgment, then proposed an ameliorative modification (more decidedly political in consequence), others contend that Schiller only puttied-over a Kantian antinomy, without really moving beyond it. Paul de Man famously made that countervailing argument, a study of which is provided by Terada, 2005.

because of the necessity of imposing on themselves a way-of-being in violation of the higher principles of humanity. Under Schiller's reworking of Kant, aesthetic judgment is thus transmuted into a fundamental political vector of the human condition, such that, slave-masters or the dominating class members are no more free than the slaves or those they dominate.[32]

Freedom Beyond Necessity as Grace

Schiller conceptualized the human aesthetic condition by three notions, which he considered related in a special manner: beauty, grace and dignity. In sum, thanks to possession of this package of virtuous assets, individuals disposed of full aesthetic potential will behave in the world (politically) with justice as mode of expression.

The notion of serenity as silent presence might be used to describe personal experience constituted of that triadic complex of qualities, beauty, grace and dignity. Yet Schiller was not stoic; rather than passivity in the face of difficulties, he considered these qualities to be achievements that result from certain modes of self-exposition or self-expression into the world. To the extent that one's socially-engaged behavior is good, just and civically responsible, then one will actualize that harmonious inner state. This is to posit that fully expressed freedom as action via the good life by anyone will diffuse an aura promoting extension of equivalent freedom for all. Were that to be generalized, then everyone would be so disposed and acting as such; resistance against constraint would dissolve, because oppression and domination would no longer define the structure of society.

Schiller's modified philosophical idealism led him to slip a bit uncritically into in the direction of a certain version of moral idealism. This is a common problem when beginning with state-of-mind qualities as if determinant of state-of society: even if the body is in chains, the mind is believed able to think itself free. He avoided the extreme of this position by asserting that there is a progressive interactive step from inner state to social action, which assures a minimum of material validity for otherwise detached virtue.

---

32 Schiller's work represented a moment in the transition toward a more historically anchored and engaged political aesthetics, but surely not its attainment. While anticipating and influencing both Hegel and Marx, Schiller's position was far less abstractly idealist than was that later proposed by Hegel, and far less coupled with the social material of history than Marx achieved in the following century.

The first step in his argument is that *beauty* is a universal-given as expression of the nature of human-being as such. Thus considered, beauty is not an accidental personal quality that varies in response to individual action but rather is an inevitable reflection of necessity. Being humanely alive in the world, is both *beauty* incarnated and *beauty* defined: thus according to Schiller, as state of being, life is beautiful.

Grace, on the other hand is a yield from action, linked with the manner of personal choice as expression of freedom. While beauty is a gift, intrinsic to human-being, grace is the issue of personal merit. In the face of pressing forces of necessity (such as hunger, or an itch on the nose) the meritorious act, exposing good judgment, would be expressed as the intention to act gracefully; so as not to eat like a hungry tiger or scratch one's nose like a monkey. Thus, *grace* is a movement of being which requires a decision in the face of necessity; it is never spontaneous or given in advance, but has to be demonstrated as the occasion arises. Even if a natural potential, grace can not be forced by conscious willful determination because imposing control on action is not free but simply submission to a higher necessity, which is why (think of a dancer) graceful action always appears effortlessly beyond discipline (1998/1793: 14–27).

Being graceful implies a higher-grade expression of human being, engaging spontaneously to intervene in response to the force of necessity. This is what Schiller defines as humanize action, different quite evidently from what he considered to be the more automatic or instinctive behavior of animals which might be beautiful, but nothing more (1998/1793: 30).

The political-moral question is how to satisfy the sensory, physical demands of necessity, such as hunger and thirst, in a way which will not only address the immediate need or desire, but which by its deployment contributes to the general well-being, gracefully (1998/1793: 33).

Schiller established the moral grounding of the aesthetic issue as if it were the spontaneous movement of human life: as if the experiencing of personal satisfaction, without willful forcing, by acting gracefully, is inclined by nature to be consistent with inner intention (to satisfy personal desire) toward the general well-being of all. Since one's personal aesthetic is initially the issue of an inner state of consciousness, it can be restrained personally or externally; but it can not be granted or shaped by external authority (Thomas More went to Henry VIII's chopping block, gracefully).

The essence of personal freedom is thus a gift, beyond earthly determination. For that to hold requires the postulate that moral action is not conduct that conforms to the law (formal or informal); but rather a state of inner spirit that rests on principle of unconditional duty (1998/1793: 38). Following from that combination of general intention and practical action, Schiller closed the loop with the position of Kant, arriving at the base of the latter's famous categorical imperative, of action always guided by the principle of general well being.

Achieving a graceful existence implies that the human capacities to know, evaluate, judge and choose are in balance with the sensual forces of material necessity. The mediator here is identified by Schiller as 'reason'; before action, one makes a reasoned appeal to general-reason, asking: 'How would the well-reasoned individual act in this situation?' The key action is not the content of the resulting choice but the delay in the face of necessity long enough to appeal to higher reason. If this two step, iterative process holds, (i.e., beautiful predisposition actualized as graceful response to necessity), according to Schiller, the result is a *Bell Âme*, a Beautiful Soul, appreciated by its graceful way of being. Schiller summarizes this with the following formula:

> It is thus a Bell Âme where sensibility and reason, obligation and inclination are harmoniously aligned, and Grace is its expression in the phenomenon of worldly action. (1998/1793: 41)

Dignity as Freedom's Higher Calling

Concerning *dignity*, as the highest aesthetic expression: Schiller admits that in certain situations, for instance when faced with the necessity to escape from a burning house, to debate the moral question may prove fatal. What if there is another potential victim, injured, needing help; run or aid, the choice is there. When struck by the need or desire to satisfy a powerful necessary calling, no matter what, doing so reasonably is *grace* in action; but doing so with a sublime state of mind, is *dignity*! Thus the formula: "The domination of impulsive action by the moral faculty constitutes the freedom of mind, and dignity is its expression in the phenomenon of worldly action" (1998/1793: 47). Elaborating a bit, he argues that, grace is evident in difficult action while dignity is evident in silent (long) suffering; in classical terms, the former is evidenced as *ethos*, the latter as *pathos*. Consistent with his general view of the holistic nature of individual being, Schiller stresses that even if distinct as expression, both grace and dignity are present in the same individual; the two are entwined, such that dignity assures the value of gracefulness and grace assures the authenticity of dignity (1998/1793: 52).

From the way he closed this text, it is clear that his professorial duties disturbed his concentration for writing; the result is ironic:

> If it is true that one has the occasion to observe grace affected in the theater or Ball Rooms, one can often study false dignity in the offices of Governmental ministers or in the studious offices of scholars (notably around universities). (1998/1793: 57)

Alas, by his own admission, Schiller was regularly unable to live by the principles of grace and dignity that he supported. He nevertheless considered this moral lesson-for-life as the proper pedagogical program for all humankind. How he proposed to achieve that is the subject of the next section.

Aesthetic Education: Revolution as an Inside Job

Perceptive and engaged for the interests of human kind, determined to voice a call for reform, Schiller was nonetheless caught in a classic critical dilemma: blessed by an acute awareness of human nature, he was insensitive as to the structural determinants of political life. While it is true that what humans are determines what they do, it is equally important and this time extrinsically, to accept that what humans do collectively determines what they are; and what they do is heavily constrained by their material circumstances, forcefully shaping their practical consciousness. This dialectic relation explains the indeterminate outcome of rupture and revolution as the effect of both material circumstances and consciousness: simultaneously, identically, or compatibly.

Schiller was sure that the key to political change must start with innerpersonal reform. He was a God-fearing fellow who did not consider the possibility of human organic remaking, focusing instead on what he considered to be the inherent fluidity of consciousness and the ability to act freely. Although the explanation for the process of being in the state of freedom remains mysterious, it seems correct to assert that consciousness does generate images: of tranquility or terror, confidence or panic, generosity or menace. It seems further evident that terrorized, panicky, threatened individuals often generate an infectious aura, which can propel events so as to realize as fact, a dangerous, fear stricken world.

Might not the fluidity of consciousness also allow for progressive movement to re-inform individuals at the level of consciousness, more in keeping with a humanist calling and thereby intensifying general awareness that a happy life is beautiful, generous, just, good and civically responsible? Were that achieved, might not the general societal aura be transformed for the better; might not such a community of being assure a politic of greater equity and general well-being, minimizing domination and exploitation, cruelty and vengeance, opportunism and deception? Schiller believed this to be the case, in defense thereof he composed his *Letters on the Aesthetic Education of Man* (1795).[33]

His announced theme was clear: to, "plead the cause of the beautiful," of which the most attractive state of all is liberty. Although as a self-avowedly if moderately reformist Kantian, he was skeptical about the limits of intellectual-conceptual activity, contending that, "philosophy finds synthesis only by analysis," his ambition was to get to the true nature of man through art (1795:I). However his view of art was cosmic: "The most perfect of all works of art… [are a product of] the establishment and structure of true political freedom." This might only be achieved by shifting control from, "the law of the stronger," to the "calm judgment of reason" (1795:II).

How is humankind to be released from determination as physical necessity, to allow for freedom expressed as the moral law (1795:III)? Schiller judged that the 18th century social-political order was nasty and brutish, dominating and exploitative, as a residue of the long centuries of ferocious battling for survival on the part of European peoples. He believed that the days of wicked necessity were over, thus ending also the necessity of brutality of rule. This provided an opening for a shift of consciousness, in the direction of humanity as higher calling, of morality as expression of that calling, and of well-ordered, content society as material result.

Particularly during the 20th century, the question was posed as to the possibility of external forces imposing major modification on the state of consciousness of individuals; and if possible, of the justice of setting out to do so. The danger in this possibility concerns brain-washing, the manipulation of the inherently pliable human consciousness, taking it hostage and thus partially mechanizing human action; by that, instrumentalizing behavior, transforming individuals into commodities in the service of ideological interests. In this view, ideology is like a coat of plaster layered on consciousness, producing an atrophy of good judgment, such that individuals become confused as to their welfare. The result, patently, is 'false' consciousness.

---

33 Schiller's, *On the Aesthetic Education of Man in a Series of Letters* (1794), and other writings touching the same theme are available at the Gutenberg Public Domain Web site. See *Aesthetical and Philosophical Essays, by Frederick Schiller*: <http://www.gutenberg.org/files/6798/6798-h/6798-h.htm>.

Schiller considered only the potentially ameliorative aspect of this possibility and not the sinister potential of ideological manipulation. If certain events can subvert expression of the humanist ideal, other events might liberate it, and this was the anticipated result of the aesthetic education that he proposed. For lack of ability to logically confirm this possibility, Schiller appealed to a demonstrative metaphor of the sculptor, who attacks a stone to impose on it his artistic intentions; the "artist of political education" must transform what man is, but not destroy it in the process (1795:IV).

The evident difficulty with this form of argument is its circularity. How might we specify what is the human-essence to be preserved, deepened and expressed as and by freedom; to be liberated from the persistently stubborn, human remainder that continues unmodified, until the noble aspect of personal constitution is beautified—in the political sense, via aesthetic education?

Following Schiller's lead, I offer my own descriptive image. The traditional Alaskan Inuit artist regards a section of mastodon tusk and meditates that the gods liberate that which is there, inside; once this is achieved, the artist is duly inspired, and forthwith carves a seal or a salmon, or whatever it is that was within the object to be drawn forth, not by chipping away the distorting crust from the exterior, but by freeing the full internal content. Schiller was confident of an equivalent possibility, thus proposing a human liberation movement, from within consciousness. Even if doubting his confidence that reform of the general consciousness is the first step to structural change, it is difficult to deny the beauty of this ambition.[34]

Simply as literature, more than just a statement of a program for action, a remarkable feature of his *Aesthetic Letters*, is the rhetorical force of his argument. Exploring in words how humans deploy their character into life, Schiller was a constructive phenomenologist well before the concept. Speaking always collectively, with the attitude of humankind, he asserted that "man [sic] paints himself in his actions"; that unfortunately, "egoism has founded its system in the very bosom" of otherwise "refined society." Since the result was an "age of evil," secular salvation would depend on freeing the noble expression of humanity. When this occurs, change would follow, since, "what is the nobler is the more revolting in its destructions" (1795:V).

---

[34] This interplay between modified general consciousness as awareness and mobilized political action is captured by the dual image of War of Position and War of Maneuver as discussed one hundred fifty years later by Gramsci (1971) in his *Prison Notebooks*.

As concerns imminent evil, Schiller was equally direct: the community or state "measures man by his function," transforming humans into "fragments of the whole," "chained down," as part of the "perpetually revolving wheel;" nothing counts but qualities related to "honor and profit." The state is therefore a "stranger to its citizens," and public affairs, a "monotonous circle of objects." Concomitantly, culture is a matrix of contrasts, a conflict resolving system, within which intellectual work has a particular role to play: rather than only serving as "arms against error," philosophy must turn to the "poetic," so as to "reform by superior art" what a lesser art has "destroyed" (1795:VI).

Play

For a further look at how he approached the issue of consciousness-raising in his *Aesthetic Letters*, I will briefly examine the somewhat counter-intuitive introduction by him of the notion of "play" as a proposed resolution for one of the major ambiguities in the program of Immanuel Kant.

In dealing with this face of Schiller's project, we will confront a much more philosophical form of discourse. His use of this mode of interrogation distinguishes him from Voltaire, who rested in the zone of critical description of the politically real, without venturing into a meta-discourse on humanity as justification for critical practice. Schiller conveyed both a powerful critical sensitivity and, even if not formally anchored, a distinctive if not entirely original intellectual reading of the problem for which critique is the intended remedy. In doing so, he displayed a sharp skill with abstract analysis amidst his expository writings; requiring a certain degree of double-reading to appreciate.

On the surface, the proposal sounds outrageous: one is to get beyond the celebrated antinomies of Kant, which plagued Kant to his death, by putting life into "play" as full expression of human vitality. This is not to be confused with the Shakespearean image of 'life as stage,' on which all of us are actors; for Schiller, play was not the issue of fun and games, much less a masquerade or pose.

As raised by Kant, the challenge is to explain the unity of experience in spite of the apparent incompatibility between {the animal-instinctive aspect and the rational-reasoning aspect} of human nature. Kant concluded that on existential grounds (that is, phenomenally), this was impossible. Schiller thought differently, requiring a counter-intuitive proposal as the only way out of the excessively-intuitive cul-de-sac into which the Kantian project might terminate.

Elaborating the way Schiller developed this argument will allow me to raise the issue of political-aesthetics, which is another major vector of his influence for cultural criticism; as well as to more clearly chart the evolution in the method of critical practice that interests us here.

Woven almost surreptitiously into his *Aesthetic Letters*, Schiller's attempted correction of Kant was a bold move. He judged the Kantian antinomy in the dualism between the {formal and sensual} aspects of human being as a sign not of an insurmountable problem (as had Kant), but rather as signaling need for further work.

Approaching this conundrum of reason from a radically non-Kantian angle, Schiller's proposal is plausible. By ceasing the internal pirouette of consciousness, no longer obsessing about the reasonable determinants of understanding and living instead as a present exercise (but surely not thoughtlessly), would render a healthy, aesthetically appealing life possible: through political engagement in the world, achieved as existence with other, by putting one's life authentically into "play". In other words this suggests the spontaneous expression, without anterior manipulation, of a form of innocent being, in the world. While the harmony of the result, were that to be generally applied by everyone in a community, would be marvelous, the danger linked to such a state of non-calculating defenselessness is evident.[35]

Schiller introduced this complex issue in his *Aesthetic Letters*, intended for a general readership. Rather than deconstructing Kant, then theorizing about his own proposition (as an academician might), he simply wrote about it, using the word "play" in a variety of ways, in association with an equally varied expression of the Kantian antinomy, impressing on the reader the power of his position by the diversity of its applications.

The practical issue that distinguished Kant and Schiller concerned freedoms as expression of civic authority. When Kant dealt with this, he decided that either the animal-sensual side of man drives human action or the reasonable-rational side is in charge. Due to the furtive quality of the former and the need for a more universally transcendent authority, he decided that only higher human reason might be one's guide. This

---

35 Play. This postulate is premised on the assumption that humans really are disposed of the admirable qualities of beauty, grace and dignity, as previously discussed in this chapter. With that profile, Schiller stipulated the model of humanness at the base of his critical program.

supposes, as practice, that if a population is properly educated about the facts as determined by reasoned research and argument, then there automatically will be better quality of guidance, both personally and collectively.[36]

Schiller insisted on two points: first, he refused to discount the rightness of the voice of material necessity or sensual desire as a legitimate, though not exclusive source of personal authority. Second, based on his own observation, he judged as futile the hope of improving the moral, ethical, civic quality in society simply through technical, rational education.

He proposed an alternative explanation of authority (or freedom) for both collective and personal experience, which he considered anterior to the *a priori* duo {rational wish and maternal need} identified by Kant. As alternative to the bifurcated state of human being proposed by Kant, he drew attention to the human subject in its integral being. By the nature of its expression, life thus reconceptualized is intrinsically harmony-in-being, displaying fitness not only with nature, but with self as construction and with others in society through time. If that integrity is shattered, only then is life (*à la* Hobbes) nasty, brutish and short.

Schiller did not consider the bio-material drive as a foreign or dangerous force, which might somehow intrude on the legitimate authority of higher-reason. Rather, he reversed the equation, starting with the 'play drive' as existential vital force, which, by its deployment of being in the world sets in motion the necessary tension between the {"sensual drive" and the "formal drive"}. Rather than (*à la* Kant) the binary opposition of the latter pair of drives frustrating logically and terminally the unity of human being, Schiller proposed to begin with the unity of being, expressed as the play of being in the world, which, while never in stasis due to the tension of the other two drives, allows the governance of existence in a

36 Schiller's view of the central role of popular education as precondition for general freedom has been widely echoed through recent centuries. From before him, by Voltaire, through John Dewey who set the scene for the philosophy of education in the U.S. for the 20th century. The deeper issue, however, as Marx pointed out, is 'who teaches the teachers'? As it has gone, there are two streams in the educational movement: public education is pitched to accord with the ideology of the state that funds it, which (in the modern western countries) if we are to believe Horkheimer (from my Introduction), will inevitably endorse the bourgeois philosophy of history, with all its negative consequences, the more devastating of which is the exploitation of the many to benefit the few. The other stream is private education, which depends on the generosity of the elite, which again will assure that no content of education subverts that same world view. Rather than continuing the impossible struggle of 'improving' it by calling on a more authentically compassionate humanism, the more fundamental issue concerns the possibility of freeing education altogether from domination by the bourgeois philosophy of history.

fashion that assures at least a minimum of authenticity in a society of harmony.[37]

In his *Aesthetic Letter-XIV*, Schiller reduced this claim to a formula:

> The sensuous impulsion excludes from its subject all autonomy and freedom; the formal impulsion excludes all dependence and passivity. But the exclusion of freedom is physical necessity; the exclusion of passivity is moral necessity. Thus the two impulsions subdue the mind: the former to the laws of nature, the latter to the laws of reason. It results from this that the instinct of play, which unites the double action of the two other instincts, will content the mind at once morally and physically. Hence, as it suppresses all that is contingent, it will also suppress all coercion, and will set man free physically and morally. (1795:XIV)[38]

Then, in *Aesthetic Letter-XV*, he provided an operational definition of "play":

> The object of the play instinct, represented in a general statement, may therefore bear the name of living form; a term that serves to describe all aesthetic qualities of phenomena, and what people describe, in the widest sense, as beauty.

Further along, in *Aesthetic Letter-XXVII*, he restated this postulate as follows:

> In the midst of the formidable realm of forces, and of the sacred empire of laws, the aesthetic impulse of form creates by degrees a third and joyous

[37] Harmony. For Kant, life is a 'construction' of mind that somehow allows a modicum of balanced expression of what one considers to be one's material state in counterpoint to ones mental, intellectualist state. For Schiller, life is the 'initial given,' and as it 'plays itself out,' its practical dynamics are constitutive of what is taken to be one's material state in counter point to one's state of consciousness.

While Schiller was not a dialectician, he contributed groundwork for that movement. In this instance it is not really the case that the play-drive as he proposes it is the synthesis of the {thesis—antithesis} relation of {formal-drive and sensuous-drive}; rather, to borrow an image from late Adorno, play is the negative dialectic of that binary tension.

To use the above 'simplification' as the basis for another: it might be argued that Hegel followed the lead of Kant, and went from the antinomies of mind to the idea as ultimate synthesis; Marx, on the other hand, started in the world as actual experience and explored (particularly in his early work) the social conditions of material necessity.

[38] As concerns the conciliatory capacity of the "play" instinct to override the Kantian antimonies as discussed in AL-XIV, the cited phase deals with one of the four sources of authority over action that Schiller attended to: in addition to "exclusion," he also dealt with the parameters of temporally, determination, and control. In so doing, Schiller's proposed correction of Kant focused on the parameters associated with sources of authority derived from the four-causes of Aristotle: material, efficient, formal and final. It must be underlined that Kant was not concerned with the authority to furnish regulative principals for practical action in the world, as was Schiller, but with the source of authority which justifies confidence in human understanding as issue of reason.

> realm, that of play and of the appearance, where she emancipates man from fetters, in all his relations, and from all that is named constraint, whether physical or moral.

Schiller's basis for judgment is aesthetic-consciousness; for Kant it is rational-consciousness. If Kant was right, then life is a struggle to make reasonable sense of our being-as-understanding in spite of our place in an irrational sensual world. If Schiller was right, then the authority for human being is the way of living humanly: the exciting, dynamic, innovative, surprising, fascinating playing out of life itself, for which the tension between our formal and sensual dispositions provides the spice.

Political Aesthetics

Viewed from a distance, this face-off between Schiller and Kant demonstrates a fundamental difference between the workings of a cultural critic and an intellectualist critic, which, in most general terms, distinguishes social-philosophy from canonic-philosophy.

Rather than starting, as does Kant, with the problem of the nature of reality and how we know that for what it is, as demonstrated by Schiller and the others in my case studies, the critical practitioner starts from the standpoint of the world as work done and explores the degree to which the unrolling of that fits the sensibilities of individuals as humanized beings. The critic thus examines the fit between a certain model of humanness and a certain model of the social organization. This is often carried out either by importing a model developed by others or by a rather casual exercise of original construction. For traditional theorists, the result may appear shaky even if the pragmatic yield of the undertaking seems strikingly on target. This vulnerability explains why it is easy for intellectualist counter-critics to discount a practical-critical position on formal grounds, thus eliminating the necessity of debating its substantive content.

For a canonic-philosopher (such as Kant), the question of fit, in moral or ethical terms, of humans with their world, is not the first concern; but this is to deny primary space to history, leaving the focus abstract, aimed at gaining conceptual clarity about human-being and/or the world—in theory but not as reality. The result of this search for transcendental models—independent of time, space and culture, is to paint a cold picture (*nature morte*) of a dehumanized existence in a dehistoricized world.

The universal appeal of a vulgar evolutionary theory is easy to understand; stripped of its humanization and historicity, existence is reduced to a mechanical system of mutual accommodations, with everything working out as 'well' as might be. Accordingly (as with not just Kant, but Leibniz before him and Hegel after him) moral issues are relegated to religion, ethical issues are filed by lawyers, and aesthetic issues deposed in museums. By that, practical experience is taken as a given of material history, with ethics, civic issues and aesthetics considered as of only local political interest, thus denying those virtues their place among the universal forces that are assumed to drive collective life.

Politics as social-action thus reveals itself as how public action imposes on and/or constrains collective life, creating some strain or influence for the general order. Yet from family to nation-state, since endowed with some apparatus for conflict definition and resolution, every social system is political before it is anything else. Still, canonic-philosophy reduces the problem of social organization to that of a minor political maneuver and the rest of what interests a cultural critic (i.e., aesthetics in the large sense) is treated as only décor.

Unexpectedly perhaps, if one reverses the order of construction, as did Schiller, when working from politics as liberation back into the universe of human understanding, the aesthetic moment assumes universal significance.

As function, aesthetics is concerned with harmony or fit of elements and systems. Disharmony, or poor fitness, indicates tension or conflict. Accordingly, when aesthetic issues grate on the common consciousness, this is not because they cause problems but rather that they signal the need for conflict resolution as political action.[39] When a solution is affected, even if couched in technical terms, the result is ultimately tested against aesthetic (or moral) criteria. Aesthetic judgment is then seen to be the standard for evaluating political resolution, which is why aesthetics is

---

[39] Art is known by its discordant insistence on recognition; imposing thus on the status quo, this is another face of the politics of aesthetic works. For Schiller, human life is a work of art, the original aesthetic product, defining beauty by its very being. Putting life into society is thus an aesthetic imposition, inherently political in nature both as generative force and sustenance of being. However, ordinary high-culture art of any kind, literature of any genre, is also an aesthetic item, which when put into the public has political effects and ramifications.

This second, more limited high-culture focus on the politics of art-works is the center of attention of one of the most active contemporary commentators on the issue of political-aesthetics, Jacques Rancière. See for example his *The Politics of Aesthetics: The Distribution of the Sensible* (2004), and "The Aesthetic Revolution and its outcomes: Emplotments of Autonomy and Heteronomy" (2002), and one sample commentary by Katharine Wolfe: "From Aesthetics to Politics: Rancière, Kant and Deleuze" (2006). Rancière's project seems to neglect Schiller somewhat, probably ill advisedly.

always concerned with community as political arena and politics is always concerned with judgment guiding action via aesthetic criteria, as harmony or fit. On that basis, to treat aesthetic problems as 'only secondary' is to dismiss the importance of community as crucible for political experience; a dismissal refused by serious cultural critics.

For Schiller, the aesthetic basis of judgment was integral harmony of human-being as such, where life is beautiful to the degree it is free, open to opportunity and choice, and associated with a reasonable mix of risks and benefits. Unfortunately, as a universal standard, that principle weakens under the pressure of individual interests. As routine position for any social organization, sitting authority is self-affirming, judging the realization of its responsibility as beautiful, rejecting accusations of domination, exploitation or oppression as other than occasional and necessary. On that basis how might cultural criticism stake its claim, other than decoratively?[40]

As shown by Schiller's portfolio, rather than ornamentally, aesthetics marks the end of the trail of thought's work. Along the way its expression is dialectic—sometimes negatively, which is why it can be mistaken as truth's camouflage. While knowing aesthetics for what it is occurs at the end of the train of reasoned practical experience, were one bereft of the capacity for aesthetic judgment in the first place, then the initial step down the road of intellectual-conceptual discovery would be blocked. Aesthetic judgment is prerequisite for appreciating truth, for recognizing the right next step from the misstep. Then as its end, aesthetics is called upon once again to make sense of the details of the movements of being, to render possible their meaning in expression, and by that, a beautiful life. Without it, the pursuit of coherent action, much less its exercise as a politic in action, is senseless; rendering the category of rationality (which is the centerpiece of Kant's program) unexpectedly empty as well.

Late Drama

After finishing his *Aesthetic Letters* in 1795, the friendship with Goethe continued to deepen until, in 1799, Schiller moved to Weimar for good. With increasing regularity and drawing on what would become almost

40 As discussed in Chapter Two, the bourgeois philosophy of history reduces the issue of harmony to what fits in the immediate, with bourgeois appetite and desire; one distortion from that form of short-term means-end pragmatism, is that it ignores the cumulative effect of means thus used, and the shortsightedness of the result for long-terms ends.

daily contact with Goethe, he turned once again to theater and poetry. Although he probably did not know it, his days were numbered. While providing moral support that aided Goethe to return to his writing, Schiller continued to compose at a feverish pitch, contributing to his legacy what are considered two of his best theater pieces: the *Wallenstein Trilogy* and *William Tell*.[41]

Wallenstein came out first (1798), comprising three volumes of open-verse dialog and setting instructions, which fill nearly fifteen-hundred pages in the contemporary German library edition. The historical-fictional plot traces the tragic flight of a treacherous military commander, Albrecht Von Wallenstein, battling in Bohemia, when his country was embroiled in the (first) Thirty-Years War (1618–1648). That was a particularly brutal conflict which over the course of three decades dragged pretty much every European principality into a pitiless bloodbath of pillage and destruction.

The length of the work by Schiller is explainable by the fact that he had earlier studied then composed an actual history of this war; stuffed to the brim with its central facts and images, the flow of the writing was probably self-propelling. This is not to understate the spectacular quality of his authorship. It is rare that anyone can carry out the research and compositional labor for such a large factual historical study, then draw out its dramatic content so as to capture its aesthetic realism for the stage. Scholarly historical writing and artistic theatrical composition seldom flow from the same pen.

The politics of Wallenstein's war were secondary to the force which drove it, explaining why the devastation was so horrible; rather than only a matter of jealousy and greed among feudal neighbors, the impetus for the conflict was religious ideology. Most of the fighting occurred in what is now Germany, and by the end, the population of the German principalities was reduced by an estimated forty percent.[42]

---

[41] Goethe's literary image is most associated with a theatrical character he created in the piece by the same name, *Faust*; *Part I* (1808) is most read by students, with its Prologue set in Heaven, as the Devil (Mephistopheles) lays a bet with God for the soul of the scholar Faust. It was completed three years after Schiller died. Although influence of this sort is difficult to assess, it appears that when Schiller moved to Weimar, it was in part to offer moral support to Goethe, who at the time (1799) was suffering from a slump in his reputation and loss of creative energy. It is unlikely that this work would have ever been finished had Schiller not arrived on the scene. As for *Faust, Part II* (1832), this was finished nearly a generation later, just as Goethe was about to die. It is very complex and much less commonly read.

[42] In a remarkable study of 16th century Europe, social historian Donald R. Kelly (1981) argues that the emergence of 'ideology' as mode of domination in the West was generated

Hitting the Arrow on the Head

William Tell, also a well researched documentary-fictional piece, was Schiller's swan song; under the personal direction of Goethe, it premiered in Weimar, March 17, 1804. He had little time to appreciate the further acclaim which this yielded, since he died the following year.

There is no mincing words: the work is an open call on the part of people everywhere, for a liberation movement through overt revolution should their national autonomy be encroached upon by autocratic power. However, this revolutionary call and its defense are housed in a realist drama set in a timeless nether-land which maximizes the personal identification of ordinary individuals with the strains and dangers of life under tyranny. Since most readers are familiar with the outcome, I will not be spoiling anything if I elaborate just a bit how Schiller arrived at those ends.

William Tell, the hero, is a manifestly honorable fellow of ordinary birth, a family man, widely appreciated for his work as a huntsman and willing to play his part in the larger plan of community. In the end, he must shoot an apple off the head of his son, Walter, whom the megalomaniac Hapsburg Governor Gessler has tied to a nearby fruit tree. As well as demonstrating his marksmanship, by saving his son, due to further complications, he must also send his second arrow through the heart of that tyrant bully. Since Judgment Day among Christians is not generally a pleasant affair for those who kill others, in the course of the play, with, as we know, the notions of grace and dignity as sub-text, Schiller's Tell was obliged to somehow rationalize the violence of that final deadly act against Gessler, exemplifying in the process the aesthetic effect known as the sublime.[43]

Given its immediate impact on the viewing public, there have been times and places over the past two hundred years where this piece could be staged, and others where it was censored. Without surprise, Hitler

---

by the wars of religion, during the century preceding the period that concerned Schiller; since then, the battle for domination in the West is always for control of the content of the dominant ideology, which, to believe Horkheimer, was eventually reoccupied by ideological grounds resting on the bourgeois philosophy of history.

43 *On the Sublime* (1801) is Schiller's most referenced essay on the subject. According to available information from the Schiller Institute it is not certain when he wrote this, but that it "...reflects Schiller's mature thinking on Kant, who devoted the better part of his Critique of Judgment to the question of the sublime, and Schiller's superseding of Kant's system." Two other essays on the same theme, done about ten years earlier are, *Of the Sublime,* and *On the Pathetic.* <http://www.schillerinstitute.org/transl/trans_on_sublime .html.

found it disagreeable. The reception in the U.S. is unsurprising also, but in a quite different sense: there is a popular joy in the U.S. with the William Tell story, as long as it is presented politically uncritically, or at least only about what ought to be done for other peoples, in other countries.[44]

Beyond Schiller's genius, the continuing reputation of *William Tell* is also owing to Gioachino Rossini (1792–1868), who, in 1829, produced an operatic version of this play. He staged the French original in Paris, with an Italian version coming later. The show has always been treated with some hesitation in Italy, because its message is obviously out of fit with the Machiavellian soul of that country. Due to its enduring popularity, like *Romeo and Juliet* (~1595) or *Don Quixote* (1605; 1615), *William Tell* has effectively become its own allegory, serving as the meditative base for further artistic creation.

In the U.S., most quiz-show contestants can recall the essential of the *Tell* drama: the handsome mountain fellow, the hat with the feather, the leather shorts with suspenders, the hobnail woodsman's boots, the crossbow, the loving son, the arrow and the lemon tree, and above all, the apple on the head. While most in America are familiar with its dramatic basis, the revolutionary point of the work has been washed from the common consciousness. As for Rossini's opera, the most that might be appreciated is the cavalry-charge fourth-movement, with orchestra a-gallop amid thundering sound of horns and trumpets; yes, the same theme music for *The Loan Ranger*! The U.S. has transformed the *Tell* allegory into a profitable western folk hero.

Revolution as Determined Political Action

Redressing the crisis of political vindictiveness against popular liberty fueled the plot of *William Tell*. The demonic despot is named Gessler, for whom there are no sex issues, no food issues, no drug issues, just an out-of-control, dehumanized sense of political authority, the right to impose order as he wished, with thou-shalt-do or thou-shalt-die power over those who must comply.

---

[44] As an example of its U.S. popularity, The William Tell Festival in New Glarus, Wisconsin, celebrated its 75th anniversary in 2012. Schiller's play was the centerpiece, first presented many years ago exclusively in German, then with performances also in English; until 2012, when the German original was set aside for lack of Germanophile attendees, in favor of English-only.

Set in the Swiss Alps of about 1330 and based on historical facts of those times, this is a down-to-earth version of a morality play about salvation from hell: of political deliverance, aimed at general freedom from diabolic political repression. While it necessarily features a central heroic figure, Tell, it is a tragedy of collective determination to go to any lengths, open rebellion if necessary, to achieve what would otherwise be denied: the elimination of hollow elitism in service of arrogant leadership, in violation of the enlightenment principle of the equivalent worth and dignity of each individual.

With each centered in a mountain valley around a village, at the time the Swiss Cantons were under the control of the Hapsburg monarchy. A governor was assigned to the area, whose job was to maintain the general order, promote workman-like discipline, and harvest the rewards of such labor for the aristocratic and ecclesiastic elites. Gessler, the governor or Viceroy, was given a free hand in administration, with life and death determination over everyone within reach. Taking his duties seriously, he proceeded as only a tyrant might: the villages were flooded with police and spies, ready to jail anyone who took an unjustified privilege or spoke out against the system.

The Swiss are depicted as sincere and caring, with a natural tendency to trust leadership and do as they are told. Yet with general well-being stifled in a country of natural abundance and prisons being filled and new ones constructed, the evident injustice of the circumstances propelled even this naturally calm people to the brink of desperation. Expressing the sad fact of worker exploitation, Tell laments: "The land is fair and bountiful as Heaven; But they who till it may never enjoy the fruits of what they sow."[45] As the people became more reticent and vocal against their circumstances, Gessler retaliated with ever more imposing measures. Tell continues: "The fields are all the bishop's or kings; The game is all the monarch's—birds and beast; Stream, lake, and sea, all to the king belong."

The ultimate step, which sets the stage for the apple and arrow scene, was Gessler's decision to build a new fortress for himself, in front of which he ordered hung his royal cape on a pole. Located in the village square that all must cross, he further commanded that as a sign of fidelity to his authority, every passing person must bow before the royal cape.

Determined in the extreme by freedom, Tell came by, failed to bow, was caught in the act and Gessler decided to extract retribution. The way this

---

[45] Citations in this section from The Project Gutenberg EBook of *Wilhelm Tell* by Friedrich Schiller: http://www.gutenberg.org/files/6788/6788-h/6788-h.htm.

was done is a bit Shakespearean: rather than extort a pound of flesh as in the *Merchant of Venice*, Gessler orders Tell to shoot the apple off the head of his son Walter, backed up against the lemon tree there in the square.

> Gessler: "Thou art to shoot an apple from his head! I do desire—command it so." Then pointing to the boy, Gessler continues, "Bind him yonder to the [lemon] tree!"

As we know, Tell uses his cross-bow with expertise, and gets the apple rather than his son. But, as he prepared to shoot, he took two bolts (special cross-bow arrows), one of which he placed in his belt as reserve. When afterwards Gessler questions him about this second bolt, Tell admits, "If that first had struck my darling child, this second arrow I would have aimed at you, and, be assured, I should not then have miss'd."

Hardly amused, Gessler sentenced Tell to the dungeon for life. After further drama on the way to the prison, Tell cleverly escapes. With that one remaining bolt for his cross-bow at the ready, he posts himself on a mountain pass that Gessler is expected to cross. As if his own Greek Chorus, we hear Tell's inner thoughts: "For every road conducts to the world's end. They all push onwards—every man intent on his own several businesses—mine is murder!"

Representing high human dignity nonetheless, Schiller's Tell is obliged to justify setting out to kill another human in cold blood. From the depths of his sacred soul, he points to political tyranny as being not just beyond the law, but beyond defense. Since the cause of liberty must have its day, he lays responsibility for this deadly passion for vengeances on Gessler: "The milk of human kindness thou has turn'd to ranking poison in my breast; and made appalling deeds familiar to my soul."

Eventually Gessler arrives on horseback; he is met by a poor lady with many children who pleads for release of her husband from prison. To the last, Gessler reinforces the popular view of the nasty inhumanity of autocrats:

> Say what you will: I am the Emperor's liege... He did not send me here to fawn and cringe, and coax these boors into good humor. No! Obedience he must have. The struggle's this: Is king or peasant to be sovereign here? ... I will subdue this stubborn mood of theirs, this braggart spirit of freedom I will crush, I will proclaim a new law through the land; I will... .

Cut off in mid sentence by a bolt in the heart from Tell's cross-bow, those are Gessler's last words.

From there, popular rebellion ignites; prisons are razed and royalist-aristocrats are faced with the choice: either resign all titles and join the common people in good faith, or flee the country. Along the way, the Hapsburg King is assassinated by his nephew; not in pursuit of general freedom but, as with elite families everywhere, the young Prince kills his uncle King because of an unsettled claim over shares of inheritance. The resulting disorder in the Hapsburg monarchy opens the way for general political liberty, in the form of returned local control to the Swiss Cantons.

The play closes in Tell's mountain cottage, with wife and sons, soon surrounded by an entire community of joyous mountain folk. Tell is complimented by his loving wife, Hedwin, who, addressing the sons, lauds the marvelous services of her husband: "My own dear boys! Your father comes to-day; He lives, is free, and we and all are free; the country owes its liberty to him."

Outside the dancing, singing throng echoes this appeal, as altogether, they herald, "Long live brave Tell, our shield, our savior!" With a last word from a former aristocrat who has gone over to the side of the common people. Joining, as it were, the proletariat, he announces, "And from this moment all my serfs are free!"

Who might ask for more? Power to the people, not granted, but won, because of heroic collective action, catalyzed, mobilized by the courageous leadership from one of their kind.

Closing on Form

It is difficult to evaluate the practical consequences of Schiller's critical work. Since his stature was not established until after tying in with Goethe in the 1790s, he contributed little as incitation for the French Revolution of 1789. Further along, under Bismarck during the 19th century, there was the formation of the German mixed royalist-parliamentary democracy, which modified at the margins the autocratic potential of the German royal house; whether Schiller's work had residual effects on this is not established. However, one clear political influence of Schiller's late work is with the Swiss, who, to this day, dress in the mountains like Schiller's Tell and keep a rifle over the hearth in case some foreign power threatens their freedom.

More than only remarkably enduring theater, Schiller's writings have also had a major impact on literary theory. His elaboration of the aesthetic distinction between form versus content, and the significance of the relationship between the two, continues to have repercussions. The derivative observation, that the power of what is said is heavily determined by how it is expressed is, one might say, the grounding, albeit highly contested postulate, not just of contemporary literary theory, but of the communicative philosophy of culture that now dominates the western world view.[46]

Whatever the power of theatrical delivery associated with Schiller's revolutionary rhetoric from *The Robbers* to *William Tell*, it had very little real effect. This attests to the capacity of real-world oligarchies to persist, no matter how violently they are called-out by sensitive critics. The same was the case in regard to Voltaire's blunt political criticism. The facility of sinister interests to undergo clever metamorphoses in a chameleon like fashion, so as to continue in control while changing only the costume, is truly remarkable. Sensing that structural intransigence may explain at least in part why Schiller focused more on revolution of consciousness than on institutional overthrow. He seemed to have recognized that it is possible to reach at least some of the people, some of the time, with a message of social justice wrapped in literature, even if official organs of the state and economy remain unmoved.

As with Voltaire before him, Schiller lived before the conceptual work had been done needed to furnish a language for the analysis of social institutions. This precluded the formulation of proposals about fundamental societal modification. This began to change with the French Revolution due to the tensions and contradictions among interests, classes and social castes (between the various Estates as it was put in those days) which forced social structural issues to begin to assume a place alongside psychological or personal ones. While that forced into the open the true nature of social movements and of the part played by social agents and agencies in the organization of society, this was not understood conceptually until it was unambiguously announced by the research of Karl Marx in the 19th century. This new awareness of society as a social construction constituted a major watershed in the method of critical practice, evidence of which will be apparent from the in-depth case studies in the two succeeding chapters.

---

[46] Early in his career, George Lukács picked up the lead opened by Schiller, both in his first published work, *Soul and Form* (1910), and in a subsequent study, *The Theory of the Novel* (1916). Coupled with the writings of Mikhail Bakhtin (1895–1975), associated with the view first offered by Schiller, this work has inspired a century of discussion in the humanities related to literary theory and the theory of the novel.

Bakhtin's most important texts are assembled in an anthology, *The Dialogic Imagination: Four Essays* (1981).

The prescience of Schiller's critical eye was remarkable. He anticipated 20th century phenomenology concerning the immediate expression and appreciation of being in the world. He explored the limits of intellectual-conceptual analytics, proposed a novel form of renewal of aesthetic consciousness, and linked this all to a creative view of political progress. As he put it, "to arrive at a solution even in the political problem, the road of aesthetics must be pursued; ... which will lessen the dynamic influence of feeling and passion, [and] place them in harmony with rational ideas, ... by taking from the laws of reason their moral constraint" (1795:II, XVI). Thus bringing to light the danger of the excess instrumentalization of existence for yielding the hideous estrangement of humans, as alienated from the community of their own making, Schiller also anticipated the 19th century critical development of historical materialism.

CHAPTER FOUR

FOUCAULT: THE END OF EVASION

Foucault Uncorked

It is difficult to decide how to start with Foucault (1926–1984). Disposed of vast intellectual interests encompassing not only history, philosophy and society, but psychology, politics and literature, from a distance he appears as a typical 20th century French scholar of high accomplishment. Having been well born and properly raised, he had access to preparatory school, then an elite university, where he worked with the ranking professors, struggling just enough to fully deserve a fine career. He repaid his debt to society for that refined education by busying himself about France, Europe and elsewhere, publishing numerous major books and articles, giving a non-stop stream of lectures and interviews, along the way returning regularly to the library to verify his sources. Finally, finding time to champion a few radical causes, he demonstrated the political sincerity at the base of his being, which, particularly in France, is part of the professional package. While all this is a certain truth about Foucault, it is a distortion nonetheless.

This is not to suggest that Foucault failed to cover those standard steps in what is known in France as the Royal Way to success and prominence, because he did. He was born to a family of medical doctors; after initial studies in the town of his birth, Poitiers, he moved to Paris. After a year of preparatory studies at the exclusive *lycée*, St. Stanislaus near Montparnasse, he passed the examination for entry into the École Nationale Supérieur (ENS) which, in the humanities, marks a top rung for France, if not the world. Along the way, he attracted the interest and aid from a number of the major French intellectuals of the day, including Jean Hyppolite (1907–1968), Maurice Merleau-Ponty (1908–1961) and Louis Althusser (1918–1990); so far, so good. However, those generalities hide the ragged truth of his struggle to find a place in society.

To begin with, laying the groundwork for a lifelong authority problem which he took to the grave, he did not get along with his father. On finishing at the *lycée* (high school), he failed the examination for direct entrance into ENS, and was required to spend an additional year in preparatory school. Once there, he was not well socially integrated or particularly adept for the work. Commenting on classic texts, penning paragraphs by hand as if written by a typewriter, avoiding commentary, accepting the passive absorption of professorial performances in lecture halls was not Foucault's style. He was so disinclined along those lines and so poorly equipped to work this out otherwise that while at the university he was led to express the ultimate cry for salvation, or was it, in his case, the definitive announcement of bad-faith, by attempting suicide—twice.

On finishing at ENS, there was another major hurdle, a test called the *aggrégation*; he failed it the first time and had to remain an extra year to deepen his capacities, before a successful second try. He was regularly complimented for his precocious grasp of complex questions but when the tension mounted, he seemed unable to deliver a superior performance.

During his university years he acknowledged, at least to himself, that he was gay. If this shamed him or his father and whether it turned him away from his classmates or assignments, it is difficult to say how this private fact played out in his public life, other than, ultimately, to help cut it short.[1] Foucault died of AIDS, which, due to confusion and institutional denial, killed hundreds of thousands before it was taken seriously enough for epidemiological study. That was the end, in 1984, of "Michel" Foucault, since he had long ago truncated the Paul from his original Paul-Michel, which had been added at christening as a sign that he was the son of a father named Dr. Paul Foucault.

It is rare for someone with such professional notoriety while still living and an even more enormous posthumous stature, to have died in ignominy; but effectively that was Foucault's lot. In the early 1980s, AIDS was denied as a general condition. Considered then as exclusively limited to gay men and due to the politically conservative and religiously fundamentalist sentiment against them, the condition was largely ignored by the legitimate medical establishment. When he finally weakened enough to have to be hospitalized, doctors avoided being direct with anyone about his condition; as he was shamefully shuffled between hospitals as if a danger for respectable folks of good faith and necessarily also, of 'normal' health.[2]

---

[1] Homosexuality. For a controversial but very well documented biography of Foucault (where, among other issues, the nature of Foucault's sexual behavior is decrypted as a sign of issues related to his scholarship) see James Miller, *The Passion of Michel Foucault* (1994).

[2] Foucault's intimate companion for twenty years prior to his death, Daniel Defert, while initially refusing commentary regarding Foucault's personal life, ultimately

The paradox for Foucault is enormous. He was born into a medical family that he disappointed by refusing to follow in that career. Then, during a very secret private life, he transformed this experience of misapprehended authority into a relentless determination to expose the dangers of blind institutional power, of mindless domination by repressive normativity, generated by entities such as police forces and medical practice. This very anti-institutional, hyper-rational view that became his intellectual signature for more than thirty years developed as an unintended yet pernicious residual effect of the depersonalized instrumentality of modernity gone wild, against which he lectured and wrote until that vicious disease ultimately finished him off, rapidly and at the time as a matter of general indifference.

Gunning Away From the Intellectual Stratosphere

Constantly on the move intellectually, psychologically and physically, Foucault advanced through life at break-neck speed. Reading his words shows a storm of interrogation, to this side or that of some manifest problem, suddenly returning to re-plow old grounds, sometimes for clarification, other times for rectification, occasionally for complete rejection of what he had formerly said.

Since the difficulty is both conceptual and temporal, no one is quite sure just what he intended or what meaning to assign to the result. He took his studies in psychology and philosophy, with the latter being more deeply pursued than the former; so was he a philosopher? He seems to have thought not, preferring to identify himself as an historian, interested in the history of knowing, which, within the usual frame of academic study, implies the history of ideas. He was uneasy about that as well.

The mark of a philosopher is conceptual clarity: key concepts or notions are identified, defined and elaborated, with the search for the truth of their expression being the object of study. To identify the link between such terms and worldly experience requires some orienting (theoretical) framework, based on opening postulates about the nature of humankind and the world, then applied in research following a systematic method. Foucault refused to accept the force and stability of concepts and notions; this prevented him from following with fidelity the chains of association

---

acquiesced to give an interview, "*Les Derniers Jours*," for the Paris Newspaper *Libération*, (19 June 2004), which provides details on the events leading to Foucault's death.

by which conceptual clarity might eventually replace general ambiguity. The result is not exactly confusion but a decided lack of consistency in his use of vocabulary, which in spite of personal inventiveness, led many in the philosophical community to abrogate his work.

Still, there is history. To the extent that he ever said anything with force, it was that he was out to investigate the history of the events by which meaningful conjunctures arise in a society; such that in the hands of particular classes of social actors, a package of ideas and know-how can take on the power not just to inform, aid or protect the members of a population but to exert a real force over their existence that is negative for personal liberty.

Here is an example. We all now live with the 21st century worry called global terrorism, as justification for the so-called war on terror. While some observers take the menace seriously, as a domestic strategy of social control, the result has objectively preposterous consequences for the civil population. Yet the terrorist threat is now so generally accepted that there is little outcry against the dehumanizing existential effects and horrible costs of this outrageous encroachment on individual freedom, left to the furtive handiwork of the U.S.'s newly christened mega-ministry, the Homeland Security Agency. Given that, a decade ago, it was nonexistent, how is this strange assemblage of power linked with knowledge, housed in institutions staffed by thousands, to be explained?

Foucault died before terrorism was transformed from exotic risk to ever-present menace. Still, the case exemplifies the sort of problem of historic emergence of modes of societal domination that interested him. He wanted to explore the convergence of circumstances, cultural, technical, political, economic, psychological, material, natural, ecological, or other, which explain the coming into being of this sort of nexus of "power/knowledge." In this particular example, this nexus puts seven-hundred million ordinary westerners firmly in its grip via a profusion of means that generate an inescapable vice of ideological domination through the definition and then the imposition of normative control based on a politically motivated vision of deviance, put in place, perpetuated and profited from handsomely by a particular class of agents, professions and disciplines.[3]

[3] Power/Knowledge. This is perhaps the best known figure in Foucault's narrative, seeding many of his texts, essays and interviews. In English translation, a highly informative set of essays where he explored this theme is collected in the anthology, *Power/Knowledge* (1980), edited by Colin Gordon.

Given his particular historical orientation and interest in how events during the 18th century classic age had enduring structural effects for 20th century western society, Foucault might have focused his studies on macro-cultural distortions associated with misshapen democracy, capitalism and/or Christianity. For autobiographical reasons, he targeted instead a number of then (1950s and 1960s) less commonly considered but still undeniably important issues, which we might label niche-issues: social-problems such as mental illness, criminality, sexual and gender identity.

A social problem is a condition that is felt as painful by individuals, of which the source is collective or societal. Such problems can be treated only with palliative means at the level of the affected individuals, but might be redressed by structural change at the institutional level. The classic examples are racial discrimination and poverty: individuals suffer from these but are individually incapable of their rectification. Although he never used the term social problem, Foucault focused on such problems, and thus his critical practice was historically anchored in the sociology of deviance.

Rather than siding with the establishment in its struggle to contain certain categories of allegedly dangerous or disruptive behavior as is the case for many specialists in social deviance, Foucault took the side of those whom he considered the innocent victims of the western system of illogically rational societal management: those who are unjustly labeled as deviant and subject to invasive treatment. At the same time, he was interested in how it came to be that the 'normal' or general population went along with this process, since, while affecting directly those who are labeled as deviant, it is a mode of social control that has pernicious effects for everyone.[4]

The spectrum of issues facing individuals on the margins that interested him is doubly related to Foucault's personal trajectory, constituting both the conceptual boundaries of the object of his critique, and the practical boundaries of his personal history from within which he exercised his criticism. He studied: mental illness, or madness, as he referred to it;[5] criminality, as the system of general standards for defining right versus

---

[4] Victimized by social control. The daily life effects of excessive deviance control are now everywhere evident: in airports, for instance, everyone is assumed to be a potential terrorist until proven otherwise.

[5] Mental Illness as labeling. He first dealt with this in research for his doctoral dissertation: see, *Folie et Déraison: Histoire de la Folie à l'âge classique* [*Madness and Civilization*] (1961).

wrong behavior as enforced by police-officers, judges and above all, prisons;[6] academic professions and disciplines such as those that colonize universities; and sexuality, with particular attention on the proscriptive factors according to which certain natures of sexual performance are judged legitimate and others as taboo. Foucault wrote about how these lead to a world of domination on the part of the state by diffusing a cloud of "governmentality" deployed via "biopolitics," based on the biological characteristics and needs of people.[7, 8, 9]

Critical Particulars

Foucault leveled audacious attacks against the deployment of expertise-based power in post-enlightenment democratic society, which, purportedly in the interests of general well being, safety and security, victimizes particular categories of individuals by stripping them of their freedom of lifestyle, while imposing the vague worry on all citizens that they will be next. He bypassed the global question of institutional justice to arrive at the personal face of this issue: that of individual liberty in day to day life.

He was convinced that freedom of choice in the West was woefully overstated. Not only is personal behavior, such as sexuality, regimented in an irrational fashion, but so also is the very organization of expertise and knowledge (such as university disciplines and professional specialties) on the basis of which westerners differentiate the rational from the irrational. The result of this is such that arguments about behavior framed in the language of right vs. wrong, truth vs. falsehood or effective vs. dangerous, are often little more than manufactured conventions, with the specifics being accidents of circumstances. As a sort of social disaster chaser, he

---

[6] Criminality. See *Surveiller et punir: Naissance de la prison* [*Discipline and Punish: the Birth of the Prison*] (1975).

[7] Sexuality. Interest in this theme, as with his study of *Madness*, has a powerful autobiographical air: see *Histoire de la sexualité*, in three volumes, 1976, 1984a and 1984b.

It was in the first volume of this work (1976), following on a position announced in *Discipline and Punish* (1975), that Foucault most developed his critique against the state and its tools of "governmentality," as unjustified intrusion against individual liberty.

[8] Biopolitics. Foucault dealt with this topic at length in his lectures at the College of France in 1978–79: see his *Naissance de la biopolitique* (2004).

[9] Foucault did not exactly consider the members of university disciplines or liberal professions as 'deviants,' but he did treat them as if members of a cartel, controlling a knowledge resource and exercising its deployment as power to dominate social action: see *Les Mots et les Choses*, [*The Order of Things: an Archaeology of the Human Sciences*], 1966.

spent his life attempting to explain the cause of such socio-cultural accidents of history.

Foucault leaned decidedly in the libertarian direction, according to which macro-societal problems of fairness and equality dissolve to the extent that personal liberty is free from constraint. Rather than social discrimination, environmental protection or international peace, he focused his research on particular institutions aimed at social deviance, demonstrating how, due to them, and in spite of whatever is achieved in controlling truly undesirable action, in the end ordinary citizens pay a huge price in loss of general freedom. By this tactical shift to the politics of the every day, he justified his view that the problem of depleted personal liberty as an identity issue associated with how one is labeled and classed, should take priority over impersonal categorical concerns and institutional reform.[10]

What then of general societal change as critical intention? When Foucault studied at ENS, the intellectual climate was dominated by the political left, for whom socialism was their moderate ambition and communism the legitimately discussable, if more politically extreme alternative. Although never personally active, Foucault was a member of the French communist political party from 1949–1952.

After leaving the school and The Party, he became disenamored with the version of Marxism that then circulated in France. This went hand in hand with his expanding libertarian inclination, rejecting every form of centrally-ordered state-system, including both the capital dominated versions as well as the political alternatives offered by socialism.[11] The more his dogmatic insistence on the unacceptability of central state ideology grew, the more vocal became his anti-Marxism; even while distanced from capitalism, his inclination toward a libertarian extreme increased. In the

---

[10] Radical Liberty. Foucault seemed to assume that all social problems affecting disadvantaged minorities might be resolved by a single extreme treatment: the elimination of all formal institutional constraint on personal action.

[11] Most libertarians oppose the state categorically, asserting that excepting police and soldiers, government is an obstruction to freedom, endorsing instead the principle of 'freedom from ...' restraint. Paradoxically, Foucault comes across as a libertarian of the Left, since he was also very concerned with 'freedom in order to...' be admittedly homosexual, for instance. Reading him about rights and justice resonates with the position of Isaiah Berlin (2002), but is quite different from Montesquieu (1748). We also see his position in harmony with how the American political-philosopher, John Rawls, decided to interpret (in *Political Liberalism*, 1993) his famous *Theory of Justice* (1971).

The U.S. legal philosopher, Ronald Dworkin, would differ, stressing equal care and concern under the law as the true expression of liberal democracy (*Law's Empire*, 1986). If he is accurate, then responsibility is the goal of freedom, with community as its ideal.

end, though neither a political reactionary nor radical conservative, his position was easily co-opted by the conservative political right. Thus his writings proved to be more acceptable in bourgeois circles on either side of the Atlantic, than was the case, for example, with the work of the outspoken and famously Marxist, Jean-Paul Sartre.[12]

Over the years, Foucault's anti-Marxism undoubtedly facilitated diffusion of his writings. But by leaving aside the categorical conditions that produce and reproduce the forms of obstruction to personal liberty which he criticized, he drained much of the political clout from his program. Still, through a particular mingling of private life and public outspokenness, he delivered his message with a manifest energy, clearly linked to his biographical trajectory, demonstrating by that, as is the case with the others featured in this book, that critical practice is the expression of a nearly single-minded agency of unflinching confrontation and candid presence, of the autonomous critic in a real historic situation.

Sawing off the Limb on Which He Stood?

Foucault eventually assumed the role set by Voltaire, as public intellectual, with the important difference being that while Voltaire had worked as free-agent, Foucault enjoyed full institutional support.[13] Given the 1960s climate in which he got his start, it was appropriately anti-establishment of him to decry as dead-end the study of canonic philosophy and criticize typical history as little more than romantic storytelling. Still, that fuzzy identity cut both ways: what was the public to make of a fellow, who

---

[12] Marxist or Bourgeois? In a review of the book that first brought Foucault to prominence in France (*Les Mots et les Choses:* 1966; *The Order of Things*: 1970), Sartre accused Foucault of being a bourgeois apologist disguised as an activist. The truth is difficult to sift from the rhetoric: over his career, Foucault gradually drifted away from Karl Marx, 20th century western European Marxism and socialism; but then so did most European intellectuals (not including Sartre).

We could say that he was a Marxist without class; he applied what appears to have been a derivative of the historical materialist method developed by Marx, but did not consider the social class issue as fundamental, nor place importance on capital as the underlying structuring force of society. The ambiguity of the results of his work demonstrates one of the limitations with any effort to unknowingly shear the Marx-method from the content of the study where it was developed. A recent volume by Isabelle Garo includes a fascinating and detailed study of Foucault vis-à-vis the Marx-question (see her: *Foucault, Deleuze, Althusser & Marx*, 2011).

[13] Public Intellectuals. Unlike other moments in history where they tend to arrive one at a time, the post-WWII period was the incubating ground for a veritable covey of them, including, in France, Jean-Paul Sartre, Roland Barthes, Claude Levi-Strauss, Jacques Lacan and Maurice-Merleau Ponty.

sometimes referred to himself as a Nietzschean and other times as historian of modernity?

Foucault was snared in a self-imposed double bind: philosophy as search for truth in ideas, was denied by him, yet, that very philosophy justified the critical study of the rational movement that defines modernity as progressivism. Realization of progress depends on thought's work in action; or at least, that is the common understanding of modernity of which, supposedly, Foucault was a historian. By rejecting the validity of that unfolding ideational force, did not Foucault thereby alienate himself from the historical object that interested him?

He might have decided that he was 'against modernity,' a historian of the 'end of modernity,' proposing a postmodernity as working base. But he was too much of a Kantian (of the first two *Critiques*) to imagine beyond modernity. If thus remaining fully modern, there was another possibility: he might have turned to a less abstract, more engaged sociological method, which since its origin has served also as a critical tool of modern institutions; but he didn't.[14]

Unless going to the extreme of a nearly mechanical form of positivism, it is difficult to both reject the historical materialism of Karl Marx and still endorse the sociological postulate: that institutions are doubly real, informing and reinforcing both human behavior and structuration of society as a whole; with that movement carried via the interplay of the logical-meaningful structures and systems of society as they are commonly understood and enacted by the members of a human community.[15]

---

[14] The claim that he used the tools of enlightenment to attack the legitimacy of the modern age, without supposing any form of historically-conditioned successor for that, is a generally common criticism of Foucault, advanced famously by, among others, Jürgen Habermas. As I will return to in Chapter Eight, after his status had risen, Habermas himself imposed a major correction on critical theory and by that against the base on which the reputation of the Frankfurt School rested. Ill-advisedly or not, Habermas helped cleanse critical theory of its Marxist underpinnings, as if Marx was not the exemplar for the critique of Modernity that Horkheimer put forth as grounding for that movement.

Most 20th century European intellectuals were neo-Kantians, in constant argument about the limits of Kantian idealism. They were mostly, also, historical-materialists, arguing with their publics about the tarnished revolutionary image that this carries with it due to its association with Marx.

[15] Scientific Positivism. Auguste Comte was accused of going too far in his effort to apply the positivist logic from the physical sciences to the study of society; he elaborated this position, more nuanced than generally recognized, in a series of public lectures given in Paris between 1830 and 1842, published under the title (in five volumes) *The Course in Positive Philosophy.* It was at the end of the series (lessons 47–51) where he proposed that sociology, or the "science of society," necessarily identified the most comprehensive discipline (Comte 1999/1851–54). He reasoned that since all other studies are pursued 'within'

Unfortunately there is a certain risk in refusing to acknowledge the wholeness or unity of society, as a meaningful demonstration of human-being as work done in the world. While surely disqualifying the classic leftist argument associated with the political program of Marx, in the same sweep this position invalidates arguments about the underlying economic dynamics of bourgeois capitalism. That step, in turn, marginalizes the critical study of the production and reproduction of the liberty-limiting institutions dealing with sex, criminality, medicine, disciplines and professions, and the general strategies of "governmentality," which so incensed Foucault.

Having decided that Marx was substantively wrong, as was sociology, canonic philosophy and history, Foucault advanced nonetheless with an air of near messianic rightness. He was determined to justify his critical view of the misshapen settings of social practice by surveying the tortured public space, to explain, historically, how the disaster had occurred. He used the words *archaeology* and *genealogy* to describe this probing; we might suggest calling the result an autopsy of modernity. However, that would be to admit that modernity had in fact already died, another conclusion that Foucault rejected.

Ten Years Stalking a Doctorate

Stripped of customary methodological armature, and abhorring theory, Foucault traveled the world, writing texts and giving lectures, always of a critical nature. Could there be a result beyond intellectual agitation, based on a rationalist world-view that negated its own position? Of course there might, if, like Foucault, one assumes that the be-all and end-all of the human condition is *discourse*.

After finally passing the *aggrégation* out of ENS in Paris in 1951, he accepted an entry-level teaching post in a *lycée* in rural France. With a doctorate as his goal, which he eventually achieved, the trajectory he followed was both atypical and difficult, requiring ten years to complete.

During the High School teaching period (1952–55), he published his first book, *Mental Illness and Personality*, later revised and then retitled, *Mental Illness and Psychology* (1954). It is often said that an author's first novel is a thinly disguised exercise in autobiography. Given Foucault's

---

the structure of a society, understanding society as a system would be revealing for understanding the basic principles on which all understanding rests, regardless of discipline.

earlier personal struggle for psychological stability, including suicide attempts and psychiatric treatment, it is difficult not to discern a strong personal motive in opening his career with a study of mental illness. Once published, even after some rewriting, he chose to disavow that first work, placing its continued reprinting on hold. While perhaps defensible, such auto-critique transformed into auto-censorship seems a sharp contradiction on the part of one of the most outspoken libertarian intellectuals of the second half of the 20th century.[16]

With that first research, Foucault attempted to describe the historical emergence of mental illness as a collective concern in Europe, and how that eventually played into the development of a particular psychological model of human being, which, under scrutiny, includes many highly arguable elements and at the same time, the empowerment of a set of new professional specialists with uncontested authority. That work exemplified what proved to be his central interest: the historical analysis of the concretization of the modern world view in the form of particular, well-encapsulated fields of science, scholarship and professional practice, and how this allowed modern western society to hold its supposedly free citizenry within an inescapable ideological grip.

While not denying the importance of the substantive issue at the core of that first study, he decided that there had been a methodological glitch in its conduct, the nature of which points out an important postulate of his critical method. The idea that there is any social force of expression, be it physical, mental, symbolic, or institutional, which emanates from the event of its constitution, enduring long enough thereafter and in such a general way as to shape and constrain what subsequently happens for humanity, was an unacceptable postulate for Foucault. By logical extension, that rejection of conceptual constants with a force larger than the moment of an event, led to the practical disavowal of social systems in general and with that, historical-time as a social force.

Not every cultural historian denies so radically the vector of time as having continuous significance. To study the construction of a powerful, knowledge-based social form such as mental illness usually requires

---

[16] Auto-critique, auto-censor. Foucault was hardly the first major critic to repudiate his own earlier work. György (Georg) Lukács did this also, in reference to his most influential book, *History and Class Consciousness* (1923). After establishing a strong reputation among cultural critics based on this and two other early texts [a collection of essays published in, *Soul and Form* (1910); and a monograph, The *Theory of the Novel* (1920)], Lukács used a reissue of his *Class Consciousness* book (in French, 1960) to attach a Postface, where he largely repudiated his earlier position about the nature of "orthodox Marxism."

accepting the justice of institutional history as an at least partially self-propelling temporal force; Foucault would have none of this.[17] Yet in his first book, he based his analysis on a rather standard foundational view about historical time as cultural unfolding: that commonly held ideas (historical consciousness implanted as social action via enduing social institutions) exert an undeniable forward propelling energy.[18]

It was a related aspect of the Marx thesis that led Foucault to turn against the content of historical materialism. Paradoxically, he could only expose this form of what he considered a shortcoming in conventional historical studies, against the postulate of institutional continuity as self-reinforcing power, by applying a historical-materialist method as developed by Marx. That separation of the Marx method from his materialist conception of history, then use of the former to disqualify the latter is a common even if not consciously recognized strategy among anti-Marx critics.

Following his high school experience as literature professor in France, Foucault took a position teaching French language and culture at the University of Uppsala, Sweden (1955–58). While there, he submitted (1957) a doctoral thesis proposal to a professor at the Swedish University based on a study of the history of psychiatry, which after reworking became his *Folie et Déraison* (*Madness and Civilisation*) text; that draft was rejected for want of a more 'positivist' strategy (i.e., more empirical and less openly

---

17 Unlike Foucault, both Henri Bergson and William James asserted that the temporal passage of history, comprised of blocks of relations in series, is an immediately given fact to human consciousness. If you are conscious, then you have such time-passing experience as a continuous consequence of your being alive. Does that mean that time is there in some material sense, like an apple tree, which grows or extends, with consequences for those who might nap beneath one? Kant said that time is that which does not change.

Foucault did not argue about metaphysical or mystical issues, favoring a heavily materialist 'mode of discourse.' Accordingly, only people express anything, and never abstract or inert cosmic properties such as 'time'. If so, then it is invalid to study a social event as if it is a product of history, in the sense that its own history is part of the explanation for its continuing expression; this leads to rejection of the system perspective as I advance it in this book, explaining in part the decision to include the Technical Appendix on General Systems.

As for the first mentioned specialists in this note, although their positions on this issue were somewhat different, both considered society as totality in which temporality plays a vital part; James and Bergson were acquainted with, and appreciative of, one another's work. See Bergson, 2011/1889, 2010/1896 and 1981/1907; James, 1877, 1996a/1909 and 1996b/1911.

18 Historicism. The 20th century champion of the often contested view, that 'history is on the move and going places,' understanding history, of course as the record of human activity within a culture group, is R.G. Collingwood, whose most important text was a collection of his lectures published posthumously as: *The Idea of History* (1993/1946).

narrative). Leaving Sweden and still hesitant about returning to France, he spent one year as Director of the French Institute at the University of Warsaw, Poland (1958); while there, after some reworking, he sent a copy of his *Folie* text to Professor Georges Canguilhem in Paris, who responded, "Don't change anything; it's a thesis."[19] Canguilhem, a major figure in the history of sciences in France, eventually served as his director of doctoral studies.

Soon thereafter, Foucault moved for a year to a similar post in Hamburg, Germany (1959). While in Germany, inspired with confidence for finding a path toward a doctorate in Paris, he prepared the required complementary thesis, initially titled, *Genèse et Structure de l'Anthropologie de Kant*, based on an original translation into French of Kant's *Anthropology from a Pragmatic Point of View*, which was attached as an Appendix.

Modern Rationality as Institutional Abuse

After five years out of the country, Foucault returned to France, accepting a first level university teaching position in a city south of Paris. Thereafter, with Georges Canguilhem as his director of studies, in combination with the complementary thesis, *Introduction à l'Anthropologie de Kant* (an obligatory and more formal theoretical text) (1961b), he submitted and defended the study, *History of Madness in the Classic Age* on the basis of which he was awarded a Doctorate in *Lettres Modernes* in 1961.

While his *History of Madness* and his translation of *Kant's Anthropology From a Pragmatic Point of View*, were both soon published, after depositing them in the Sorbonne university library, Foucault decided not to release his "Introduction" to Kant's Anthropology. By terms of his will, he requested there be no posthumous publications; nonetheless, forty years later, this mysterious "Introduction" was finally translated into English (Bove 2004) and put on-line as a public domain text.[20]

There is considerable ambiguity about Foucault's view of the Kant project. He may have judged as heavy-handed academic proceduralism the requirement that he compose that second text for his thesis, with a

---

[19] See *Foucault Chronologie* by Daniel Defert, in *Dits et Écrits*, v. I: 24 (2001a).

[20] Foucault's translation of *Kant's Anthropology* was published in Paris, in 1964. An online English version of his "Introduction" to Kant's Anthropology was provided by Arianna Bove, who attached that original translation by her as Appendix to her Doctoral Thesis at the University of Sussex, England in 2004: *A critical ontology of the present*. (<http://www.generation-online.org/p/fpfoucault8.htm>; <http://www.generation-online.org/p/fpfoucault1.htm>.)

resentment motivating the decision never to look at the Kant study again. Yet for the rest of his life, he conducted his work as if Kant was the intellectual genie in his pocket, now seen as inspiration, now denied.[21]

Foucault later acknowledged that it was during his study for *Madness and Civilization* (1961a), that he refined the critical target for his subsequent work. These writings aimed at exposing not just the substance of certain social problems, movements or disciplines, but the spectacular way that by such developments, knowledge as power had become the illogical expression of the western enlightenment as unbridled rationality.[22]

Whatever the technical gain from modern logical rationality, one dehumanizing result has been to impose offensive forms of definition and regulation on civic life. While this is due to the way modern society is organized, rather than focusing on structural solutions, the priority for Foucault was on the unacceptable personal consequences of this for ordinary life.

In his first study, Foucault concerned himself with madness, defined and adjudicated in service to the needs of modern mental-health disciplines and professions. More than only receiving patients for treatment, and aside from body mechanical issues such as a broken leg, are not most

21 Double Dissertation. By Sorbonne tradition dating from the 17th century of Descartes, until rather recently, the doctoral thesis in France consisted of a pair of free-standing texts, one more theoretical, linked to past authority, the other a report on the original research of the candidate. Although he abhorred such traditional obligation, Foucault complied with it in a perfunctory fashion. Nonetheless, from that point onward, his fundamental intellectual argument was with Immanuel Kant, concerning the issues of freedom and critique as modes of human expression.

Unlike Kant (and Descartes before that, but differently), who felt obliged to provide an explanation for the foundation of being and knowledge, Foucault denied the possibility of such a foundation, or at least of our ever knowing what it is. It was for that reason that he qualified himself as Nietzschean. But Foucault kept the 'rest of Kant'; the question then is what does one have if one advances a strong conceptual Kantianism, stripped of foundational, regulative principle? The answer, in brief, is that one is then convinced that the inner-talk generated conceptual organization of the mind is a form of situational knowledge which takes on a vital power by its imposition into the world through a sort of conspiracy of the like-minded. Even if still 'only talk' or "discourse" as Foucault preferred to call it, the result is that not just the meaning of existence, but the very truth of the latter is established by the play of master conventions of culture, managed by professions, disciplines and government agents, which set the limits on the possibilities of well-reasoned talk in the first place.

As discussed earlier, Schiller (Chapter Three) went beyond Kant with his notion of 'play.' Foucault was among the group of intellectuals who went further still, effectively proposing a fourth critique, beyond the three famous ones by Kant. As far as I am concerned, the need is less to revise treatment of enlightenment rationality, than to leave behind the modern historic condition that enables that form of rationality to dominate westerners. For two samples of attention to the possibility of a fourth critique, see Rajchman (2007) and Mitchell (2007).

22 See his *Archaeology of Knowledge*, 1969.

professional social movements substantially responsible for the production via social definition of the human problems that they treat, or the areas of knowledge that they define and investigate? Does not the same pertain for police, judges and jailers in the propagation of the forms of deviance that they subsequently attempt to corral; with similar dynamics explaining the proliferation of exotic intellectual problems, justifying ever more disciplines in universities; or the ever-longer list of exotic diagnostic categories, assuring that new medical specialties and treatments continue to sprout like weeds?

Avoiding (at least overtly) the rhetoric of conspiracy, Foucault's principal institutional targets were the disciplines and professions that relied on innovative ways of talking and arguing, to convince the agents of bourgeois society of the necessity of their action, the legitimacy of their authority and the rightness of the charges they levied. This rationally enlightened activity results less in advances for human well-being, than in the generation of the various feudal domains of power/knowledge which he detested. They create social conduits that channel individuals, by labeling and reinforcing behavior using symbolic modes of social control (mixed coercion and incentive) that are difficult to counter, and depress individual liberty. In all this, the fundamental historical material that Foucault attended to was ideological.[23]

From Literature to Student Upheaval

During the five years immediately following his doctorate (1961–65), while still teaching at a university outside of Paris, Foucault broadened his interests somewhat and published a number of papers on major literary figures; those writings contributed to his popularity among students in the

---

[23] Ideology. In this book I treat the term as, "A distinctive and more or less coherent conglomerate of assumptions, attitudes, sentiments, values, ideals and goals accepted and perhaps acted upon by a more or less organized group of persons" (Kelley 1981: 4). Because of the loaded nature of ideological conflict, in material terms among peoples, and intellectually among scholars, I attempt to treat the issue with great delicacy.

In contemporary usage the meaning of the term owes its origin to an early text published by Marx and Engels, *The German Ideology* of 1845 (1998); it is a postulate (in the wake of the work of Hegel) according to which, "the real world of men has hitherto been dominated and determined by ideas, images, concepts, and that the real world is a product of the world of ideas" (Preface: 30). The Marx critique was that ideology is the product of the work of a people in constructing their world, rather than the independent determinant of the work by which that world is created by a people. Foucault rejected the rightness of any world view, whether determinant or determined, and thus generally avoided discussing it, except negatively.

humanities.[24] During that time he also published a second major historical study in keeping with his primary socio-critical agenda, the *Birth of the Clinic* (1963). This work focused on the late 18th century, at which time the health-clinic movement emerged in Europe, with the new role of clinic doctor, capable of deploying the "medical gaze" to transform virtually anyone into a passive patient, willing to follow doctor's orders, or else.[25]

Like other young men in France of superior educational and professional experience, when the time came he was able to fill his military service obligation by accepting a collateral post with a major French agency in a foreign country. He chose to go to Tunisia, for a form of higher-level diplomatic internship, which he held for eighteen months. Thereafter, he was invited to stay on in the country, as head of the philosophy department at the University of Tunis (1966–68).

This Tunisian experience not only provided Foucault exposure to European post-colonial issues from the receiving end, but established him as a candidate for prestigious university work back in France. Having by then covered the core of the humanities, from literature to social criticism, from history to philosophy, all the time studying social problems as a window on social organization, the diversity of his projects and the personal discipline of his working style laid the foundation for the world-class reputation that he enjoys to this day.

By chance of the calendar, he was not in Paris when the May '68 student movement turned that city into a state of rebellion. That upheaval transformed France almost overnight; from a society characterized by an unspoken certainty of collective mission, principally focused on post-war reconstruction, into a state of personal and institutional indecision concerning the French within their country and the place of France in the world. Even if absent from the turmoil, his writings had already established his intellectual reticence vis-à-vis the institutional status quo, which fit conveniently with the social discontent of the moment.

Being separated physically did not mean he was disinterested intellectually in the social-economic tension building back home in France. Before leaving Tunisia he read Ché Guevara, Fidel Castro's 'spiritual'

[24] Literary Subjects. Although Foucault wrote on many of the great names in French literature, the works he discussed seem to have been chosen with an unusual eye; for one example see *"Postface à Flaubert"* [English publication, 1964; French, 1967.] *Dits et Écrits* v. I (2001a).

[25] The Gaze. The power of doctors to transform individuals into patients is generated by application of what Foucault labeled, the "Medical Gaze": that irresistible regard that falls on anyone who arrives in a medical clinic, transforming a free individual into a passive follower of doctor's orders.

younger brother. In November of that year, he studied the texts of the Black Panthers, the most militant group of U.S. political agitators since the emancipation of slavery movement, which led, as we must recall, to the U.S. Civil War.

It probably appealed to him that the 1960s tumult in Paris took a particularly introspective turn. After a generation of dedication to the demands of rigor needed to assure economic recovery from war, not just the working classes but the young in universities concluded that unbridled capitalist economic development had profoundly anti-humanist consequences, and that forces of technical rationality in service of capital seemed to be squashing the creative freedom and justice-as-equality that French people expected from their country.[26]

In the wake of those events, the most visible effect was a reorganization of the Paris university system. While that choice for change was far from politically innocent, a practical effect was to propel Foucault into political prominence.[27]

University Straitjacket of Conventional Thought?

When Foucault returned to Paris from Tunis in the Fall of 1968, the barricades were off the streets and the ministers of government were trying to save their jobs. Not well publicized around the world, a similarly radical student movement had erupted in Tunisia in March 1968, just before what occurred in Paris. Although he supported the manifestations in Tunis, there in foreign territory under diplomatic sponsorship, Foucault was obliged to act with discretion. This experience increased his willingness to get involved in the events back in Paris, as it also enhanced his stature concerning the student cause.

---

[26] In Paris, the student uprising of the 1960s was only half the battle: there was a parallel mobilization among French workers, reflecting the more fundamental, economic side of this discontent, which was sidetracked when attention became focused on the student movement. Thereafter, the French government was able to avoid dealing with the major problem of social class cleavage generated by the post-war economic boom. That is not to say that the student movement was unjustified, but only that dealing with it was a bit of a smoke-screen on the part of the government agents who then represented French conservative political interests.

[27] University Turmoil of 1968. In the U.S., these events helped explain how Herbert Marcuse was transformed into a student cultural hero when he captured the painful existential tension of bourgeois society caused by irrational instrumental action, in his landmark text, *One Dimensional Man: Studies in the Ideology of Advanced Industrial Society* (1964).

Unlike what occurred at the same time in the U.S., which primarily concerned the anti-war call for retreat from Vietnam, in Paris, the student complaint focused on the organization and content of higher education. Students believed that traditional French higher-education, "*Éducation à la Sorbonne*," was elitist: a factory for the reproduction of superior classes of privilege, as if entitlement by birthright was of greater value than capacity and discipline. It was argued that the pedagogical posture of French scholarship was a century out of date, and for fully French reasons, the focus turned to the study of philosophy in basic education.

On graduation from high school, all French students take a national standard examination, including a major written exercise corrected by philosophy professors, linked to the year-long course on the subject on which all must do well who hope to go on in the French national university system. Members of the student movement were not against the study of philosophy or the examination processes; they were agitated about what was considered the way classic thought was presented, as a non-critical endorsement of the western way of life. Without identifying it as such, what they were effectively rebelling against was the perverse effect in action of what Max Horkheimer described as the bourgeois philosophy of history (see Chapter One) which seemed to be generating social injustice and economic inequality as a necessary aspect of its realization through instrumental progress.[28]

The Minister of Education recognized that some radical or at least visible modification must be implemented concerning teaching-learning in the universities. True to the spirit of hesitant political compromise, the solution was presented as a pilot experiment, to open an innovative new university unit for the study of the humanities, including philosophy.[29] It is not clear if this was done entirely in good faith, or was intended to defuse the tension until the current crop of students graduated. Whatever the case, one argument behind the experimental site was that reformed university training of high school teachers would gradually diffuse its

---

[28] Elite Education. This was a central question in the early critical studies of French Sociologist Pierre Bourdieu (Bourdieu 1989; Bourdieu and Passeron 1964 and 1970).

[29] Fixing University Education. In Paris, following the student revolt, there was another major new Paris university unit established at the same time, consisting of a specialized faculty of the Sorbonne, oriented around issues of management and economy. Through time this evolved into an independent French faculty, with stronger involvement in research, the humanities and social sciences, than is common in ordinary business schools. Now formally known as University of Paris-IX, or University Dauphine, this has evolved into a highly reputed, administratively free-standing institution. The Experimental University of Vincennes enjoyed a far less glorious fate, having been abolished and its buildings razed.

pedagogical effects to the youth of France concerning issues such as social justice, economic equality, the danger of imperialism, etc. Since that possibility necessarily confronts the hidden muscle of the dominant bourgeois philosophy of history, this political ambition in the direction of greater enlightenment via pedagogy is yet to be broadly realized in France.

Experimental University as Spectacle: Thinking Runs Wild

In January, 1969, the experimental university opened in the town of Vincennes, just outside Paris. There would be an innovative structure of departments, better linking the social sciences with literature and philosophy; even a department of psychoanalysis was added, the first ever in the world. As an unusual gesture of political openness, the instructional units were granted extraordinary autonomy in regard to content of study and degree granting, with participative democracy used for curricular decision making, giving an active voice to students.

Driven by a nearly obsessive concern for the dangers of structures of domination, Foucault had already expressed a critical militancy that he assumed characterized universities like everything else; this position was sufficiently provoking to convince the reformists that he was on their side.

In December 1968, after being named professor at the experimental university, he played a major role in recruiting its founding faculty, attracting a number of radical young professors, who, as a group, continue to mark the intellectual landscape in France.[30]

On the Vincennes campus, the new democratic standard for decision-making rapidly transformed the classrooms into tribunes for political debate. A seminar might begin with a hundred students crowding the room; an hour later, they would vote to leave the campus and launch a demonstration in support of better treatment for street-sweepers. Unsurprisingly, this did not go down well with the Ministry of Education.

The issue which brought the government back into action was framed as a question of educational ethics. Among the new faculty attracted by

---

[30] The young faculty who joined Foucault in Vincennes included most of the major figures who marked the field of 20th century Social-Philosophy in France, including: Etienne Balibar, Roland Barthes, Gilles Deleuze, Noam Chomsky, Alain Badiou, Jean-François Lyotard, Jacques Rancière and Tzvetan Todorov. For the record, Louis Althusser, who was for years the most animated Marxist intellectual in Paris, did not engage in the student movement or its aftermath, having judged it as an exercise in 'infantile leftism,' which distracted attention from the social class issue that lay beneath the university crisis.

Foucault was a young woman named Judith Miller, who also happened to be the daughter of Jacques Lacan, a man of enormous professional reputation, who transformed post-war psychoanalytic practice in France.[31] Unlike her father, Ms. Miller was of Maoist sympathies, fully in support of the student movement, ferociously opposed to normative arrangements which favored the elites at the expense of the rest. On the new Vincennes campus, grading standards were highly variable, as were the requirements for entry into advanced level studies. Judith Miller was bold enough to acknowledge this in an interview with a journalist; she was quoted as stating that based on consensual votes by the students, in some "collectives," or academic units, it was decided that grading or, "contrôle des connaissances," would be based on written tests; in other departments a diploma could be awarded to, "any student who thought she should have one" (Miller 2009/1970).[32]

The political response was severe: young professor Miller was ejected from her university post, the degree granting authority in philosophy suspended, thus blacklisting students who took a diploma from that campus from eventually teaching in French high schools. It was judged that, "too many courses were concentrated on politics and Marxism."[33]

The students revolted and immediately occupied the administration building. Foucault sided with the students. The police were called in, the buildings were cleared and he, along with about two-hundred agitators, were rounded up and spent the night in jail.

In spite of a life-long hesitancy to commit to activist political movements, the anti-institutional position of Foucault was definitively announced. Although not quite measuring up to Voltaire who spent six months in prison for what he said in his first poems, or Schiller, who was jailed for two weeks for the seditionist message implanted in his first theater piece, there in Vincennes, in a highly publicized fashion, Foucault earned his radical critical stripes, hauled off by the police to spend a night behind

31 Jacques Lacan (1901–1981) was extraordinarily influential in France, with his ideas developed in an extensive series of seminars that were subsequently put out in print. For one condensed English source of his work, see *Lacan Écrits*, (2006).

32 Cited in the French weekly magazine, *Le Nouvel Observateur*, 13 February 2009; of an interview by Judith Miller given to another French magazine, *l'Express*, in March 1970, where Miller declared: "*Certains collectifs se sont décidés pour un contrôle des connaissances au moyen d'une copie, d'autres ont opté pour l'attribution du diplôme à tout étudiant qui pensait l'avoir.*"

33 See "*Foucault Chronologie*" by Daniel Defert: entry Jan., 1970. In *Dits et Écrits I*, p.47 (Foucault 2001b).

bars for how he behaved after only a few months as head of a university philosophy department.

From Revolution to Promotion

Before the Paris events had occurred, while still back in Tunisia, Foucault had published a third and what turned out for him to be a very important book: *The Order of Things: An Archeology of the Human Sciences* (1966). As if clairvoyant, in that text he had effectively theorized the discontent that the Paris students expressed in action before it had occurred. By the time he went to jail, in spite of its scholarly tone and verbiage, the book had become a French bestseller, tying his personal reputation to that political drama in a curiously fashionable, Parisian manner.

After the incident with the police, in a climate of constant turmoil and thus not without difficulty, Foucault continued in his post at Vincennes. As recalled many years later by Alain Badiou, a now famous former faculty member recruited by Foucault: with Vincennes, the government had created a Frankenstein monster that entirely escaped control.[34] Since external intervention seemed impossible with Foucault still involved, it was decided to create a post elsewhere, tailored to his interests, and by that to assure his voluntary resignation. After the necessary round of occult procedure associated with such appointments in Paris, on April 12, 1970, Foucault was elected to a new chair at the College of France, created to fit him precisely: the History of Systems of Thought.[35]

During the next thirteen years, in addition to delivering his annual seminars in packed amphitheaters in Paris, Foucault traveled the world,

---

[34] Frankenstein Monster. Still very active, Alain Badiou is the most translated French author into English, and thus very well known in the U.S. Some of his recollections about the Experimental Vincennes University, were captured in an interview in the French magazine, Le *Nouvel Observateur* (13–02–09); see "*Vincennes: La nacelle des fous*" [English: "Vincennes: the ship of fools"]. Online at: <http://bibliobs.nouvelobs.com/essais/20090213.BIB2940/vincennes-la-nef-des-fous.html>.

This interview was conducted on the occasion of the publication of a new volume of essays on *Vincennes: Une aventure de la pensée critique*, by Jean-Michel Djian (dir.), 2009.

[35] The College of France was established in 1530. It is a prestigious institution with a worldwide reputation for scholarship. Its lectures are open to the public; there is no connection between it and the granting of diplomas. From all specialties and disciplines, including regular foreign invitees, the faculty members are of the highest calibre. However, there is another very important French intellectual institution, the Academy of Moral and Political Sciences, whose members also cast a vote on proposed candidates to the College of France; although this vote is advisory only, it is worth mentioning that the members of the AMPS voted against Foucault's election to the College of France.

lecturing and writing at a breathtaking rhythm. His political activism gradually subsided, but the power of his discourse not in the least.

As with Voltaire and Schiller, in what follows I will discuss just a few pieces of Foucault's many studies, to exemplify his method of critical practice. I begin with the *Inaugural Address* he gave, December 2, 1970, when he was welcomed into the College of France.

L'Ordre du Discours[36]

From the opening minutes of his first lesson at the College of France, Foucault (1971) exposed his unusual view of humanized being as the continuous expression of intellectual-discursive action played out in a world composed by words. Discounting as occult the conventional belief in human being as freedom of expression, he believed that each speaking event is largely determined by one or another master frame of meaning or *discours*, which sets the rules on this seemingly free, but not really, action. If so, then to be engaged in society is merely to move from one zone of institutionally dominating discourse to another, with very little true liberty of expression.

He wanted to express in his discourse the nature of that limit-setting domination of master discourses, as it affected him that night during his first lecture and as it affects each of us throughout our lives. Therefore, he described his own delivery of that text, from 'within it,' as if a painter before his canvas, yet working only with words, speaking for himself, of his own case as speaker, to be taken by his audience as best they might.

---

36 When this text (Foucault 1971) was translated into English, with Foucault's approval the title was changed to, *The Discourse on Language*. This was necessary since there already was another book in circulation in English carrying the true title of Foucault's address ("The Order of Discourse"). The original title better expresses Foucault's intent.

Foucault enjoyed playing on words, often making it difficult to get at his point; he used the word 'discourse' in two ways: both in the ordinary sense of a 'way of speaking' in fit with immediate circumstances, and as a larger frame by which a given zone of expression is defined and imposed, such as The Discourse of History, or of Criminal Law.

In that first lecture, the "order of discourse" pointed to both the mode of discourse of the College of France, *á la français*, which imposed on him the 'rules' for his presentation that night, and also pointed to the way the particular speech/text that he gave was composed and expressed according to a general intellectual 'code' that further constrained his freedom of expression. Thus, at that very moment when supposedly he, as French Intellectual, was to be establishing the zone of free-expression that would define his work over the coming years, the presentation was under serious institutional constraint of a nature that would always limit his freedom of expression through the coming years.

The result was a very unusual verbal auto-portrait of that event, live and direct, of which his speaking was the central element, in the process of deconstructing discourse, namely his own. He spoke as if a fellow in a boat with no oars, drifting down a river (in the flow of discourse known as College of France), describing the event from his point of view, recognizing that the current and the boat (i.e., the code) were determining the meaning, the outcome of the voyage; the most he might do is throw his weight a bit this way or that. The stream of being in which he found himself and the perspective from which he expressed himself was what he considered the human condition as such: he was talking his way along, participating in the deployment of discourse, as the only way of being-there realistically, as a sort of participant-observer in this heavily pre-formatted speaking event of which he was the centerpiece.

The result was like a novel generated as the narrative flow of the inner voice of the central character. Few have been able to portray lived experience in a more immediate fashion. A close example is from James Joyce (1882–1941), of the stream of consciousness monologue with which he created the central character (Leopold Bloom), for his widely regarded novel, *Ulysses* (1922). However, in that 1970 Paris address, Foucault was dealing with his own real experience in the amphitheater as it occurred; not as if fiction or story telling, not as sign or representation of some larger truth but as a being before and among others, woven into an exercise, of which his particular discourse was but a highly constrained passing moment.

Like a man who had jumped onto a moving escalator going the wrong way, he began with a personal plea; not exactly worried, he was also not in charge:

> In the discourse which I must take up today, as with the others it will be necessary to deliver here, perhaps for many years; I wish I might have slid in surreptitiously. More than to set to speaking, I would have preferred to be enveloped by the talk, and carried by it well beyond all possible beginnings. (1971: 7)[37]

How might one slip unnoticed into a hall, to emerge on center stage, to find oneself already there, delivering a speech? That would require that

[37] The author is responsible for translation of material from the French texts cited in this chapter. There are available English translations of the entire text; see for example, *The Archaeology of Knowledge & The Discourse on Language*, by Michael Foucault, [AK-Translated by A.M. Sheridan Smith; DL-Translated by Rupert Swyer], (1972). Because of the double-passive voice often used by Foucault in his writings, scholars differ as to how to translate him.

the frame-of-the talk, what Foucault calls "the discourse," be there already, flowing before him; that he be less its creator than a participant in its deployment. As if only its human loud-speaker, he continues:

> I would have liked it to be perceived as if well in advance of this moment of speaking, a nameless voice had preceded me: if so, it would have sufficed for me to attach to it, to follow its phrases, to lodge myself in it, without anyone really noticing me; in its interstices, as if the nameless speaking voice, in an instant of pause, of suspense, made a sign of me. (1971: 7)

Foucault's treatment of *discours* strains toward anthropomorphism; as if not just an autonomous dynamic, discourse exudes a meta-life all its own, into which he not only fits and plays a part but which "makes a sign of me". He spoke as if the intellectualist force of the College of France had written the larger text of which his speech was but a small slice of expression. The limit of that image is seen in the next paragraph where he begins to quote that "nameless voice," as if it were an articulate Greek chorus. He elaborates this way:

> I would have liked that there were behind me (as if having taken to talking a long time ago, duplicating in advance what I am going to say); that there were a voice that spoke as follows: 'Continue, I cannot continue, you continue, say those words as they are, say them until they get to me—strange consternation, strange incongruity, continue, it's perhaps already done, they have perhaps already been said to me, they may have perhaps carried me to the limits of my history, in front of the door which opens to my history, it will astonish me if it opens.' (1971: 8)

Foucault's voice gradually shifted, from a position of self-talk, to talk from the other side of self, arriving finally at referential audience-talk; by that identify function, weaving as standpoint the I which is, with the I which was, with the I which must be: together with us, such as we are. So he says:

> There are many, I think, with a similar yearning not to have to begin, a similar longing to find themselves distant from the start of the game, on the other side of the discourse, without having to mull over from the exterior what might have been its singular, fear inducing, perhaps demonic aspects. To this common plea, the institution responds ironically, as it renders these commencements solemn, as it surrounds them in a circle of attention and silence, as it imposes on them, like a distant signal, its ritual forms. (1971: 8)

Consider it yourself: in response to an explicit invitation to speak in a formal circumstance, (at a community meeting or in a university seminar, for instance) on starting to speak, it is often the case that there really is an inner voice that cries out, as if wanting to escape from the confines of that judgment-imposing nest of institutions, from the regulative demands of that field of discourse that determines in advance how you must express yourself and about what. This common anxiety, between the impulse to be yourself and the necessity to play the role, is conventionally labeled stage-fright.

An attorney in a courtroom, a student defending a thesis, a man in a confessional, a woman just whistled down by the traffic officer; each is obliged to enter into a particular form of discourse, institutionally defined in advance, to fit in appropriately with the constraints such as those of the system of justice, school, religion or law, necessary not only to be seen as competent but to have the case appropriately heard. Rather than personal or negotiated, the determinant effect is a product of the ordering force of the depersonalized structure of the discourse itself, which was the point of Foucault's *Inaugural Lesson*.

Foucault knew that the proof of the existence of a force is best demonstrated by the resistance it generates. He had raised here the specter of external institutional constraint, something equivalent to an imposed normative ordering, largely circumventing originality of authorship. The tension, necessarily, is exposed as an argument:

> The inner aspiration cries out, 'I do not want to enter into that risky discourse; I do not want to make a deal with it, concerning what it arbitrates and decides; I want this discourse to be all about me, calmly transparent, profound and infinitely open, where the others respond to my needs and from which, one by one, the truth emerges; I do not want to let myself be carried in it and by it, as if a happy castaway at sea. (1971: 9)

That is hardly the end of the dialogue; the institutional hidden voice must have a last word:

> So the institution responds: 'You have nothing to fear by beginning; we are all here to show you that the discourse is within the lawful order; that one has been attentive to its appearance for a long time; that a place has been made for it, that honors it while making it harmless; and that, should it come to have a certain power, it is very much us, and for us alone, that it applies. (1971: 9)

He continued by pointing out the perplexing nature of this war of the world of words. Is it real? Is there a "material reality" to discourse that can impose itself so forcefully? If not, are we each lost, in terminal confusion, all the time hearing voices without discernible meaning? He wrapped up the opening section of his talk with the hypothetical question:

> But what is there that is so dangerous in the fact that people talk, and that their discourses proliferate infinitely? Where, then, is the danger? (1971: 10)

A Program Without Foundations

In violation of Foucault's disdain for synthetic summations, I will gather, with generalizations, certain methodological basics that drove that inaugural, *Discourse on Language*. His opening reveals a negative foundational argument: there are no universals beneath or beyond the immediate events of existence, which unroll as more or less prescribed conversations, like what we imagine occurs with a particular species of birds on a telephone line. Neither the gods, nor molecules, nor anything in between explains human experience other than participation in the continuous flow of various communities of talk. Since each particular discourse is of transitory immediacy, occasioned by the historically anchored master discourse of which it is an expression, such talk evaporates with the speed of sound.

There is a patina of similarity between Foucault's position here and the negative-dialectic as explored a few years earlier in a book with that title by Theodor Adorno (2001/1966). For Adorno, authentic-being as unity of the subject in action is the negative-dialectical face of non-being in chaos as alienation.[38] In a somewhat similar fashion, according to Foucault, the frontal force of discourse annihilates the residual permanence of any particular effort at creative expression, which if perpetuated would threaten the frame of meaning of the master discourse, the existence of which enables the talk in the first place.

As meaning constrained rule-fullness, a discourse is the negative face of crushing potential against free floating flight-of-mind talk, which would otherwise be bereft of meaning, were it not framed in advance. Yet, in spite of its voice, the meaning allowed is strongly proscribed, almost lifeless. Unlike Adorno, for whom the other, negative side of dialectic is the life giving expression labeled existence, for Foucault as a somewhat overdetermined Nietzschean, by discounting the dialectic, the other-side of any given discourse is at most another one: equally constrained by forces beyond itself.[39]

---

38 *Negative Dialectics* is a 1966 book by Theodor W. Adorno (first translated into English in 1973). For a readable commentary on this very opaque text see Frederic Jameson: *Late Marxism: Adorno or the Persistence of the Dialectic* (2007/1990).

39 Changing the truth by altering the talk. This is not unlike the position of Richard Rorty (see his, *Contingency, Irony, and Solidarity*, 2007/1989), the U.S. Philosopher of neopragmatism, who argued that, rather than truth, late moderns are so bathed in irony as to consider misconception as truth. Accordingly, when faced with conceptual confusion the tendency is to move up the scale of ambiguity, then draw on a more embracing

Foucault never attempted to fill the void resulting from this conceptual negationism with some spatial or temporal architecture. Nonetheless, as he portrayed it, there must be a clear historical continuity of force imposed by *discourse* on discourse, of a seemingly institutional form; were that not so, were discourse as he conceived it not of minimum structural durability, then how might it exert a constraining/facilitating force and by that, affect both the unrolling of speech and the experience of the speaker with others?

There are two common explanations for the systemic continuity of events; either it is assumed that a *form* and its content are generated within the event, enduring longer than the action which it effects, or that simultaneous with the event, some *form* imposes itself from beyond its local frontiers, to shape the content: either the work generates its own frame of meaning by self-reference or that frame of meaning arrives from elsewhere. If discourse is capable of exercising either of these, (deployed diachronically or synchronically), then it or its carrier must exhibit some trans-temporal or extra-spatial quality. This suggests that discourse as Foucault speaks of it possesses a minimum systemic property, more or less general in nature, a conclusion in opposition to other of his pronouncements.

While he professed on the theme of 'systems of thought,' he denied social systems as the institutional frame for such thought, arguing, rather, that thought displays itself as flowing discourse and nothing more. As for discourse as such, although sometimes using the terms in reference to this or that discourse, and other times as if about some genre of discourse in general, by never formalizing that distinction of levels of reference (as we are attempting to do here), he sidestepped the classic debate about particulars versus universals by denying the existence of generic categories. This lack of precision and casual shifting of references lends a poetic air to his work, while making it difficult to track his position.

---

contingent vocabulary, arriving at either complete consternation, or else 'higher nominalism,' meaning, in fact, that meaning is no more or less than what we say it is. As for the possibility of text without constraining discourse, there are various examples that hint in this direction: the Slam, in philosophical cafés, Free-Form poetic verse and impromptu Theater.

As concerns Adorno and jazz: in a number of texts, he argued that rather than free-form, U.S. jazz (at least around WWII when he was in California), was much less free in form than popularly supposed, being simply formatted to give the impression of the rip, which in fact always occurred with rigidly controlled meter. For a sample of that work see *Essays on Music* (2002).

Disciplined Tourbillons

One of the ways Foucault exemplified the emergence of internally self-referential local discourses was with his study of academic disciplines in universities. Rather than based on objective criteria, arguments between professors of physics and psychology, or mathematics and history about what to take seriously, often turn more on academic politics than on empirical fact. Still, purity of discipline is the rule: if not what does the term mean? Justified or not, this is why multi-disciplinary centers and institutes, (like the experimental campus in Vincennes), are often treated with disdain by the university community. In his critique of the emphasis on disciplinary purity, Foucault was atypically universalist: all disciplines were, in his eyes, equally fuzzy zones of nothing but conventions of discourse.

Foucault abhorred the practical consequences of the resulting power/knowledge struggle for domination among university departments. But the battle for domination by discourse is not restricted to schools. Generalizing this issue with studies of criminality, madness and sexuality, he demonstrated how the same problem pertains in other areas of community life. Rather than on objective criteria, according to Foucault, you will be judged or condemned, as mad or criminal, for instance, or granted a diploma for that matter, less based on objective criteria than on how you language yourself, to whom, under what circumstances: how you fit into this or that flow of discourse, of the dominant discipline, profession or practical specialty within which you work.

He did not attempt to defend this critical position with formal logic or rational deduction based on concepts drawn from theory; he believed that there was no force of truth in such logic, concepts or theory. Believing exclusively in the force of words, he wove his repudiations and condemnations via clever syntax and the play of words as he talked, as if narrative were life.

The classic label for rhetorical argumentation is sophism. The term dates from ancient Greece when disputes among citizens were resolved based on open testimony and argument before the community. Long ago it became apparent that under such circumstances, judgment about the rightness of pleadings depended as much on the rhetorical skill of the speaker, as on the truth or technical pertinence of her argument. Considering the Foucauldian position in those terms, on the one hand suggests discourse as work of art and on the other, that talk carries a political edge more in keeping with Machiavelli than Socrates.

In his *Inaugural Address*, Foucault spoke of the Sophists, as if preserving grounds for their condemnation, while attempting to get beyond them. Yet was that exercise by him not an assertion that truth is principally a matter of smooth talk? Foucault contended that "truth as what is said" was invented sometime before Plato, as a means of "ending the domination of Sophists"; generating a new and different discourse, of truth as rationality-expressed, successfully defeating the then prevailing supremacist claim of truth as styled-believability. Yet why should self-certifying, rational-expression trump well styled-believability (1971: 218).

Foucault argued against transcendental truth by what amounts to a dialectical argument, which is a mode of discourse he denied in theory. He said that, "truth freed discourse" from determination by "desire and power," only because desire and power "drive truth seeking" (1971: 219). He believed that this characterizes not just business and politics but universities as well: "Every educational system is a political means for maximizing or modifying the appropriation of discourse, with the knowledge and power it carries with it." On that basis he concluded that the mode of order in university departments turns into a "ritualization of the word" (1971: 227).

The argument that existence is composed of a tissue of speech-acts continues to be central to the work of Jürgen Habermas (1929–), a contemporary of Foucault's. In the 1970s, the two were implicitly in agreement that when a zone of discourse has been "subjugated" to some discipline such as psychology or stellar physics, or by a professional specialty such as law or medicine, the result is to exert control over a major sector of talk. But they disagreed about how this effect is achieved.

Foucault asserted that truth is that form of expression which allows a dominating discipline or profession to maintain its grip on its particular zone of discourse, or for an upstart one to conquer new terrain. If so, rather than concerning content, truth is a dimension of the power of expression on the part of a community of meaning-generating social actors. Unlike Habermas, he denied that the truth-value of the outcome is based on some form of trans-disciplinary, trans-professional validity linked to an inner well of human rationality, because he believed that Platonic argument to be empty (1971: 224).[40]

[40] Truth beyond Talk. Habermas and Foucault agreed on the basics, claiming that control of the truth of expression is effected as different disciplines and professions set the rules for 'how to talk' within their specialties, appropriate to particular situations, such as Foucault did that night, while giving his inaugural speech at the College of France. They

Foucault also questioned, "why is personal authorship important for literature but not for science?" (1971: 221–22). Is it valid to assert that there is a distinction between literary versus scientific statements, that the former are subjective and thus somehow questionable, the latter objective and therefore uncontestable?[41] He believed there is little difference, because even if studies in the different disciplines vary in terms of the evidence on which they are based, the more important issue is the moral responsibility of the author, which should be equal in every case.[42]

If the importance, the solidity, of this or that talk or text is relegated to a secondary position in reference to the frame of discourse of which it is a participating element, then is not the notion of authorship reduced to that of a scribe? Rather than asserting that authorship as subjective moral responsibility is ubiquitous, as if every text is responsible literature or should be, Foucault argued away the foundational status of authorship, as if all is science.[43] He elaborated this view of authorship in other texts, gaining notoriety as this came into conflict with the position of another of his contemporaries, Roland Barthes (1915–1980).[44]

---

differed nonetheless about the truth-value of the communicative exercise beyond the site of its expression, based on quite different foundational postulates about power, ethics and reason in democratic society.

41 Science or Literature? This debate is the cornerstone issue in the program of Hayden White whose work is the focus of Chapter Seven. An early commentary by White on Foucault is still treated as one of the clearest expositions of Foucault ever delivered for English speaking audiences. See White's "Michel Foucault," in the anthology by Sturrock (1979).

42 While often accused of it, Foucault denied that his position amounted to ethical relativism. In practice, such relativism is captured by the argument that allows the hang-man to escape prosecution for 'only following orders of the prince.' To argue differently only makes sense if one accepts a view of higher-humanity that Foucault rejected.

43 Foucault questioned the reality of 'science'; was he right? We say that Newton discovered the law of gravity, not that he invented it, much less cooked-it-up; but no one knows what gravity is. The same with Darwin and evolution (we now know that his announced discovery was highly inexact). As for Einstein, his relativity 'discovery' will surely prove inexact also, since it can not deal with the majority of cosmic reality that consists of 'dark' matter and energy. Yet when discussing Newton, Darwin or Einstein, we use the reference of 'discovered truth,' and never assert that what they composed was only an interesting narrative that fit with the ambiguity of the times. When we get to Freud and the unconscious and so on, rather than discovery, we say that his work is only literature; that in terms of science, he is a bit of a charlatan. The same accusation is leveled at Marx, holding aside a certain aspect of his historical research. Yet the work of Freud and Marx continues to be validated, as if it is 'science' in fact. Is it all science or all literature, or all neither?

44 Author: Dead or Alive? Already well known for his literature, after a trip to Japan where he saw the difference between Asiatic emergent-meaning that arises directly from experience versus the Western mode of meaning-imposed by communicants, Roland Barthes wrote the essay "Death of the Author" (1967). Accordingly, an author presents a

On History as Style

Foucault's oral delivery was decidedly untypical: through the years, each lecture or interview was a verbal sketch of his current project, as if introducing himself and it for the first time. Refusing formalism, he rarely defined concepts, proposed postulates, or laid out models. He simply spoke as a form of self-exposition; not like an author discussing an already written text (which most of them were), but speaking about the text as if he were composing his talk. His paragraphs, like his life, are thus difficult to recount, lest one slip into linear narrative, which he seemed to rely on too heavily in spite of himself, thereby violating his own taboo against determinant history. Yet, how can the flow of his history and biography not be intermingled with determinant force in his writings?

Condensing his "discourses" is like trying to capture the message and meaning from a wall covered by the paintings of Picasso. Foucault portrayed human action as self-projection, forward into existence, following a path illuminated by a sort of intellectual-appreciative searchlight by which to read and respond to the world; yet from a view more intellectual than appreciative, entirely too Kantian for my taste, and for that reason eliminating the possibility of confusing a hypothetical wall of Picasso with the very real display named Foucault.

The world is a crowded place and one's texts must be read by someone; the demand to follow one's own beat must be balanced by calling on some common anthropology, used to frame the commentary with understandable images. Adhering to Kant's analytic heritage, of reason at work, but dispatching with Kant's anthropology as 'only psychology,' as if but a romantic fantasy, Foucault rejected the normative approach to social life with Nietzschean casualness. For a fellow who spoke exclusively with a first-person voice, he thus plowed verbally through experience in an unusually depersonalized fashion, like an icebreaker in the Arctic sea.

---

scene via literature, the meaning of which is drawn out by its reading, which is not under the authority of the author. If that is the case, then authorship is a low-power role, since the potency of a text is in the eye of the reader rather than issue of the author.

In disagreement with Barthes, Foucault formulated his own paradoxical essay on the theme, "What is The Author" (1969), where, rather than saying 'no' to Barthes, he argued implicitly that Barthes' argument missed the essential point: authorness is not what one does in creating literature, but rather what is done to the author based on what critics say of the literature one creates. This touches the notion of labeling-theory as applied to writers, as when the critics decide, even if in vocal opposition to the claims of the writer, that 'she is a feminist author,' or 'he is a Marxist essayist,' or an existentialist, romantic or utopian, etc. Foucault detested labeling in all its forms, seeing it as evidence of the general power/knowledge nexus problem that concerned him.

Foucault unhinged the elements of structural domination by denying the justice of traditional conceptual architectures. This precluded blaming societal problems overtly on institutions such as families, corporations, or government agencies, and of militating to change them in the interests of improved social injustice.

Foucault was convinced that as an entity with a history, 'the West' was little more than a fabricated, flattering object of bourgeois celebration.[45] He was sure that the needed explanatory force was simply not there, neither up from humans as micro-carriers of some magic inner code of humanity, nor down from culture as the diffusing macro-renewal of that code. If the individual force of expression into society is inert and society as collective is empty, what are we to make of the typically taught history of western civilization?

His denial of the validity of the customary social-historical view is based on the idea that it fails to furnish an alternative to explain the emergence and durability of society and its institutional forms. That limitation is characteristic of the nihilist critique, which Foucault favored.

In recognition of this problem, he searched stable middle ground from which to work. Well in advance of his celebrity, he had struggled to explain the appearance and disappearance of social practices. In an effort not to save theory but to renew confidence in the value of history as penetrating description, he undertook a thick-reading of Europe's chronological past.[46]

As groundwork for a comparative study of cultural change, he began by slicing in half the recent four centuries, into the classic period, or 17th and 18th centuries, versus the modern period, or 19th and 20th centuries. But note: it is difficult to justify any historical periodization, and if one does, arguing that such periods are internally unique tends to preclude their further comparison.

A further problem with periodization is that the objects (events, practices, ways of knowing) used for comparison are usually only loosely concordant within temporal periods and rarely sufficiently stable for detailed comparison across periods. If they are rigidly associated with the epoch

---

45 Bourgeois philosophy of history as ultimate Power/Knowledge? In reference to the argument which orients our study, about Horkheimer's early writing, it seems that Foucault was caught too securely in the web of that world view to appreciate its force.

46 Deep Reading. The American, Clifford Geertz was elaborating a method of thick-reading as useful tool for studies in cultural anthropology, just about the time that Foucault was composing his *Les Mots et les Choses: Une archéologie des sciences humaines* [*The Order of Things*], (1970). See Clifford Geertz, "Thick Description: Toward an Interpretive Theory of Culture" in *The Interpretation of Cultures: Selected Essays* (1973: 3–30).

under study, then they are part of the definition of the period, which invalidates their use as comparative analytical constructs. This can be gotten around if one considers history as dialectics, as I do; but that is not the way Foucault chose to work.

Foucault's classic period opens about ~1650, with (among others) Descartes, his *Method* and *Meditations*, then closes about ~1810, when the dust from the French Revolution had been settled after Napoleon Bonaparte's *coup d'état*, which re-instituted the Monarchy and put the people back in their subservience.[47] Foucault's modern period starts somewhere after Napoleon was deposed (~1820), continuing with full force through Foucault's own time, and the late 20th century.

One might argue that Foucault actually differentiated two periods of the modern age: in so far as both fall within the scope of the historical study by Horkheimer (see Chapter One). What he seems to have targeted was the early-modern versus late-modern period. Beyond that, since he treated the future as perpetuation of the present, he rejected post-modernity as period, the postmodern as style, and never seemed to seriously consider the possibility of a new historical condition to replace the modern age, as if that were a discourse of collective madness, which in reference to the modern *épistème*, it appears to be.

Political Ordering: Things and Words

In spite of evident questions about the historical-periodized frame with which he oriented his early studies, after slicing post-renaissance

[47] In the same way that contemporary readers argue about Foucault's text, Foucault argued with his contemporaries about texts that came before him. A famous example of such conflict was between him and his eventually very famous former student, Jacques Derrida, about the *Metaphysical Meditations* of Descartes. The issue, of all things, centers on what to make of the famous episode when, reportedly, Descartes got the essential inspiration for his analytical method, which is today, 400 years later, the method of science in the West. According to the story, Descartes was thus inspired while suffering a fever from a cold, and passing the night in front of a wood stove, charged up to heat like hell; Descartes had a sort of dream in which he intuited his famous 'method,' leading ever since to arguments about what to make of such intuitive inspiration. Are all new ideas flashes of consciousness of that sort? If not, is what is taken as a new idea simply a form of redecorated technology? In his *History of Madness* Foucault discredited such flash-of-consciousness inspiration, and Derrida took issue with that. Later, Foucault delivered a searing counter in the text, "*Mon corps, ce papier, ce feu*," ["My body, this paper, this fire"], paraphrasing Descartes' recounting of the inspirational episode, with this text attached as "Appendix II" when *l'Histoire de la Folie* was re-edited. The original of this counter against Derrida is located in, *Dits et Écrits Vol I* (Foucault 2001a: 1113–1136).

European history into two large chunks, Foucault eventually settled on not one but two terms to denote the quality that establishes the unity of a historical epoch, supplying the integrating texture for a people, which can subsequently dissolve or evaporate, to be replaced by new content, yielding an altered integrating texture for a cultural group. One of these, which we have already discussed is *discourse*, the other was, *épistème*. These terms are necessarily related; yet, given the vast scope of their intended application and Foucault's refusal to rely on canonic definition, each is also vague in meaning.

More than just talk or a way of talking, d*iscourse* implies a way of constituting and inhabiting a world with language. Using a world-religion example, the spiritual discourse of Christianism is different from that of Buddhism, each rendering a world of differences among believers. This position by Foucault implies a semantic postulate: that we experience as meaningful only what we can express with others, and thus our world is a construction contingent on how we 'language it' collectively.

In reference to the sciences, professions and ways of acting via knowing in general, Foucault contended that the classic period differed from the modern, in terms of the *discourse* used to generate sustainable meaning for experience: characterized by particular patterns for how Europeans represented, categorized, compared the details of life in society and, above all, what was considered reputable and believable science. He attempted to demonstrate this claim by his historical case studies: of madness, criminology, medical clinicalization, scientific disciplines and sexuality.

Drawn from the same root as the more common term, *epistemology* (theory of knowing), the other major categorical term Foucault favored, *épistème,* is more difficult to grasp in usage. In keeping with its Greek root, *épistème* (as way of knowing) is differentiated from *techné* (as way of craftsmanship), distinguishing the problem of thinking-the-world, from ways of working-, or doing-life.

As first presented in the mid-1960s, Foucault's *épistème* referred to an even more encompassing cultural frame of possibility for discourses. He might have formalized this to say that the é*pistème* of a historical period frames the master discourses that define the sciences, disciplines and professions of that period, within which individual scientists, academics or professionals script (as *particular discourses*) their professional practice in ways that are considered legitimate. Unfortunately, Foucault did not approach his work with great conceptual precision, resulting in considerable ambiguity for his readers, and occasionally, it seems, for Foucault himself. I will return to this later.[48]

Timeless History

Shrouded in opaque vocabulary and construction and probably troubled by the response from his critics, in the "Introduction" to his *Archaeology* book (2002/1969), Foucault attempted to clarify his position about the study of history. As prelude for proposing an alternative, he leveled a strong critique at the then conventional fashion for historical work. Summarizing what he considered the shortcomings of "traditional history," he proposed a different approach that he labeled, "new history." Due to a certain appeal in his criticism of what he called traditional history, and a certain attractiveness in the sounds of the new alternative, an unintended result was the springing up of a New History movement. As usual, Foucault rebuked this tendency and even if he was considered its originator, he refused to accept the validity of it or any other such movement.[49]

He mocked traditional history as it intended to, "memorialize the monuments of the past and turn them into documents," with historians often treating the results of their studies as if they could speak on their own. If one actually studies the history of ideas, which he did during countless long hours in libraries, the chancy processes of the past, "call into question the themes of convergence and accumulation," and "the progress of consciousness." He insisted on the importance of returning to the study of particular events, to get to, "that type of history peculiar to each one… that cannot be reduced to the general model of consciousness that acquires, progresses and remembers" (2002/1969: 7–8).

---

[48] Framing the Evident. This is not unlike the distinction drawn by Georg Lukács in his early literary essays, collected in, *Soul and Form* (1910). As discussed by Hayden White (see Chapter Eight), terms such as *épistème* and *discours* would be considered among the key tropes used by Foucault for strategic purposes in 'framing' his lectures.

[49] New History. During the 1960s, particularly in England and the U.S., a New Criticism movement was active that encouraged decontextualization of literature (art works), to focus critically on their intrinsic qualities. In France, at about the same time, and as counterpoint, though probably not proposed as such, a Nouvelle Histoire mode of historical research developed, which insisted on the importance of placing the objects of criticism in the historical situation, stressing the relational dynamics of those origins to properly appreciate their qualities. However, due to the complexity of both of those movements, this one-dimensional contrast ought not be overplayed. This is dealt with further in my discussion of Terry Eagleton in Chapter Six.

Foucault asserted that, "one of the most essential features of new history" (2002/1969: 9) is discontinuity as reality. That does not imply rupture in the usual sense, since, as we must constantly recall, he did not believe that there was any underlying socio-historical tissue to be torn. While the notion of historical "event" assumed a looming stature in his texts, his use of the term was atypical, because he rejected conventional attention to the here-and-now, since that implies a time frame of continuity within which particular events are markers. He wanted, rather, to study past events as if unchained from history: as a collection of isolated 'heres,' like so many objects in a museum; as if the events which concerned him from the past were radically situated in a world entirely of their own making, stripped of referents to other worlds of meaning.

In spite of his disdain for pedagogy, Foucault provided a service by specifying the difference between the two forms of historical study. Traditional or total history is based on a sense of "cohesion" around "the same central core... or form," supposing a "system of homogeneous relations," linked in an overall "network of causality," regarding "all events of a well-defined spatial-temporal area" (2002/1969: 9).

New History, by comparison – and it must be said that this was less clearly developed by Foucault than was his fault-finding of traditional history – is a "general theory of discontinuity" (2002/1969: 12), with its "categories of discontinuity and difference, the notion of threshold, rupture and transformations, the description of series and limits." This, he says, (and spearing Kant in the process), constitutes "the eclipse of that form of history that was secretly but entirely related to the synthetic activity of the subject" (2002/1969: 14).

Is Foucault's 'new history' a history beyond linear, unfolding time? This possibility struck many of his readers as counter-intuitive if not manifestly contradictory. To understand how he dealt with this and other of his alleged inconsistencies, I mention again his first book, *Mental Illness and Personality* (1954). That was a historical study of the more conventional narrative form, which he subsequently rejected for that very reason. Even the volume which made his popular reputation, *The Order of Things* (1966), advanced an argument that is difficult to understand without reference to historical time in the conventional sense. Subsequently, with the "Introduction" to his *Archaeology of Knowledge* (1969) text, in a few lines of auto-critique, he attempted not to rectify but to clarify what he considered to have been those erroneous intrusion of time into his earlier historical texts.

A problem with writing is that the writer is implicated in his or her works; to question the legitimacy of one's texts (which he did by refusing further printing of his *Mental Illness and Psychology* volume, later changed into *Mental Illness and Personality*), self-censure, is in a way, to question one's own legitimacy. At one point in another of his much referenced works, *What is an Author* (1969), Foucault tried to define this issue away by contending that authorship in the active sense of engagement as text has no meaning. This seemed a strange position coming from a fellow who was surrounded by an enormous assemblage of his own compositions, virtually none of which could be understood if decontextualized from his very personal biography.

Ordinarily, when someone disavows their own past work, they link it to personal change. Sometimes it is intellectual, as in 'I learned this or that which now sets me straight,' or the revision may be imputed to a fundamental modification of personality due to therapeutic or spiritual experience. Foucault did not believe in personality, much less the trans-temporal possibility of its modification; he did accept learning, but even that idea was difficult for him to consider in its gerund form (as 'learning'), which again supposes the stretching of action—as acquisition and evolution of knowledge and practice across time.

Foucault was severely boxed in by his nihilism. With a dubious rhetorical style, suggesting as much melodrama as self concern, what he said about his own past dallying with historical time, which is to say, about his self-confessed complicity with traditional-history, which he was determined to demolish, was: "It is mortifying that I was unable to avoid these dangers" (2002/1969: 16).

Mortified is a strong term; he did not stop there. He was intuitive enough to recognize that being embarrassed and humiliated by his own works, to which his identity was chained, implied self devastation. Thus he concluded with what, in Greek tragedy, would raise a terminal wail from the chorus: "Do not ask me who I am and do not ask me to remain the same. … I am no doubt not the only one who writes in order not to have a face."[50]

Method as Historical Dig

Whereas the key methodological word for Foucault at the end of the 1960s was *archaeology*, as the 1970s opened he found himself fascinated

[50] *Dits et Écrits*, V. II (Foucault 2002b).

with the notion of *genealogy*. Archaeology is the study of prior events in the constitution of human society, focusing on material culture, as left behind and preserved for reasons often independent of its quality or value. One surveys, excavates and analyzes; most of the residue from such long-past events is buried in sand, deep in the sea or encased in stone; sedimented in place due to chance and circumstance. Such digging is normally aimed at uncovering what occurred prior to written records.

With a rhythm all their own, geological processes preserve artifacts largely indifferent to the human cultural events against which the meaning of past artifacts is evaluated. Even when it can be well-dated historically, there is no way of judging the relative importance of a find, compared to all the other elements of the past event in question that are never discovered. Whatever is said about given artifacts remains speculative, open to reinterpretation based on new material that may be unearthed tomorrow.

Foucault attempted to apply the archaeological process to the study of human history as the material production of ways of talking about existence and the words used to do that. My paragraphs here about his writings are of equivalent stature; I am conducting a sort of light-handed Foucauldian archeologist's study of Foucault's archaeological studies. Usually this sort of exercise is called philology, the study of the emergence and alteration in the use of words and language. Nietzsche, Foucault's symbolic mentor, was trained in that, which may explain Foucault's extension of the practice. (If so, why did he not use the better recognized term, philology?).

Since its deployment by Foucault was more than metaphorical, the practice of archaeology to study events-of-discourse opened a major structural problem. It implied digging beneath the surface, engaging in back-chaining vertical exploration, as if underneath and behind the evident are elements of a material base that play an important part in the structuring of the present and evident. If so, as contemporary expression of underlying, more basic historical processes and forms, then contemporary institutional practices are at least partially determined by historical forces; but not for Foucault.

As pointed out often from Chapter One onward, research exploring the historically-prior underpinnings of current social practices is an application of the historical-materialist method used by Karl Marx. With his archaeology, Foucault applied elements of the Marxist method using a similar social-evolutionary perspective even if his aim was not to focus on the same cultural content. Importantly, Foucault's education in post-war Paris was formally, in fact forcefully oriented by Marxist theory; thus for him to use this method was almost inevitable.

With or without his intention or consent, the success of Foucault's project suggests the justice of the historical-materialist method of Marx: that social superstructure, the everyday organization of life in western society, is driven by some deeper order or force, carried forward as normative action, sustained by continuity in the content of common consciousness which, while not immediately visible, plays a key role in explaining the stability and change in ordinary civic relations. While that might strike a 21st century reader as a fine observation, Foucault himself rejected it formally, because by then he had come to reject the content of the Marxist project.[51]

In the "Introduction" to his *Archaeology*, Foucault specifically spoke against the "anthropology of Marx," and the view of "cultural totality" that he believed Marx to have postulated (2002/1969: 12–13). Foucault disqualified the long term importance of the substance of the research by Marx (about class contradiction as inevitable fatal consequence for capital), arguing that rather than opening a path toward liberation, the political activation of the Marx project (toward some form of socialism) would invariably result in a diminution of freedoms via heavy-handed government. Foucault was inspired in this view by the Stalin period in the USSR; however, that is not to suppose that he was any more pleased with governance in western capitalist societies. For most libertarians, government is always heavy handed.

As underlined by his attention to internal contradiction, while Marx treated society as a system, he did not assert that the result was or ought to be a machine-like society, a rigidly integrated, seamless, "cultural totality." Yet, with considerable originality and using a double-dialectic approach that was vastly more penetrating, Marx did establish the need to study the historical base in order to understand the societal superstructures; that is the essential postulate behind the historical-materialist methodological innovation that allowed him to conduct his world-altering study of *Capital*.

[51] While Marx applied a value judgment to his study of the facts of political-economy under capitalism, Foucault denied the existence of values in the humanist sense; not of the independence of fact—and—value, but that the only value of fact is how it fits into a discourse. For a careful study of the evolution of Foucault about the Marx Project see Garo, *Foucault, Deleuze, Althusser & Marx* (2011).

While in his archeology studies, Foucault used a strategy of historical-vertical research, owing to his proscription against linear narrative history; he could not consider valid the possibility of trans-temporal extensibility of the historic objects that he studied. The danger he saw in the trans-temporal application of the historical materialist method was its misuse as a vehicle for generation of a grand world-historical narrative; Foucault accused Marx of this error on the basis of which he rejected the critique of Marx of the political-economy.

The point in this text is not the dogmatic defense of the content of the Marx critique. Still there is more to be said about what history means in reference to historical-materialism as postulate about the content of social experience, compared to what it means in reference to the historical-materialist method of critical research. The H-M method concerns the generative force of historicized data in reference to the forward movement of a society, with the intention to demonstrate how those data contribute to explaining that movement. However, it is not a historicist postulate about unilateral determination by the past of some inevitable trajectory into the future within a block-universe.

As for H-M as postulate, what Marx said was that his was a "materialist conception of history;" that the cultural material of the present explains the organization of society, particularly its class structure of self-perpetuating categories of economic inequality; that this structure is the material manifestation (incarnation) of anterior historical conditions, with that carry-through supported by ideology. But even that is not a strong historicist statement.

Marx did not say history determines the present or future in this or that unbending fashion; what he said was that the continuing structuring of society based on social class cleavages was generative of contradictions that would eventually destroy the economic motor force of that society. And this destruction would not occur as the blind expression of political history, but due to the vastly overrated hidden hand of the capital market system which, by not taking into account the humanist necessity of well-being, would eventually destroy the social fabric on which the continuing concentration of profits for capital depends. Use of the historical-materialist method thus reveals a contradiction between capital and democracy, between liberty and equality; not because of historical narrative issues but because human existence is a living dialectic and not a machine.

The choices for coping with capitalism are limited. One might manage the capital concentrating process to fit better with the humanist criterion of equality and thus cut into profits on speculation in a way that free-market supporters reject as necessarily resulting in some form of socialism. One might tinker with democracy to make it fit better with capital concentration processes, thus reducing liberty and generating alienation at the expense of humanity, without changing the basics, which is the current practice in the West. Or, one might transform the view of humanity behind the treatment by governments, from that of a living dialectic in a hope-inspired community into that of a rigid machine of depersonalized monads, and thus permanently dissolve good judgment, which is the fascist alternative. Given the three options, Marx backed the socialist possibility.

Disestablishment of Society

With his critical studies, Foucault seemed bent on demonstrating the fallacy of society as a whole. Most cultural critics approach society as if it ought to be saved; that if its major elements (political leadership, economic form, community organization, etc.) are out of balance or constitute a functional menace, then one should propose rectification, addition, perhaps even revolution, such that the justice of society as a whole might be assured in a fashion that fits with some humanitarian value. While arguments abound about the valuing criteria against which to assess deficiencies or proposed alternatives, most critics agree as to that basic objective.

Foucault was preoccupied by the idea of individual liberty; other than as a heteroclite collection of discordant elements that interfered with it, he did not accept the existence of society as a whole. Denying the validity of the notion of general-system, he believed that actual human affairs roll forward as a battle for priority among various collectivities of individuals, coalesced around specific interests, driven by limited sectors of knowledge and know-how. The result pays-off to some extent for limited segments of a population, but not for humanity in general; however, he also seemed to reject humanity as general category.[52]

He focused on the abstract individual as unit of analysis, and then posed questions about what occurs when large numbers are aggregated around a given cause or objective. He concluded that the resulting

[52] Humanity. Unlike Rousseau, Foucault rejected the proposition that humans are noble beings by nature but corrupted and turned against one another by the workings of society. However, while Rousseau seemed confident that there was something worthy about society to be saved, and that this would allow the good of humanity to emerge (*à la* Schiller also), Foucault seemed pessimistic about that to the end.

aggregations (associations, professions, families, government entities, professions, etc.), invariably do more harm than good by using the power that they generate to impose unjustified regimentation against the individual freedom. This implies that society cannot be reformed as a system because it does not exist in that manner, and sub-society units cannot either, because they are always an encumbrance to individual choice. This is the practical expression of Foucault's nihilism.

The interesting question is why did he continue to work as a cultural critic in spite of his socio-cultural nihilism? There is no evident answer for this other than to suppose that, like most human beings, his aesthetic disposition convinced him at some level that society does exist, as do cultures and social groupings, and that the whole with its parts must be attended to if individual well-being is to be fully expressed and protected.

It can be argued that Foucault suffered from a crisis of rationality; he deployed his energies with intellectualist persistence, as if deductions entirely stripped of all relation to immediate perception and appreciation were the only way to certain truth about life. In Nietzschean terms, he was too modern for his own good.

The modern enlightenment rests on two pillars: the abolition of trust in the sacred as guide for life, and the replacement of that by rationality as the drive force for good-consciousness. The difficulty with rationality as a guide for collective action is that it is an inner individual disposition and thus completely subjective in origin. Nonetheless, by long tradition the attempt is made to certify rationality by external material referents, linked to a particular view of historical time. Over recent centuries, this resulted in the preference for empiricism over idealism.

Rather than measured in terms of how an act fits with the present as harmony, or how it fits with the past as continuity, preference is thus given to measuring the rationality of present action in terms of the degree to which it yields future material satisfactions that fit with the present desire of some category of citizen. Conceptually, this suggests a logic of teleological, instrumental pragmatism, with the initial aim guided by pure subjective arousal, which is open to domination by the elite classes. To make matters worse, desire is inherently fleeting, rendering future returns on present instrumental action of dubious value. And vulgar pragmatic teleology in this case suggests a future that can be controlled, which is patently impossible, unless the future is merely an extension of the present, which it is not.

Social institutions are the material expression of the common judgment about how to organize life in society; necessarily anchored in past standards, they are inherently conservative. Whatever positive effects they might generate, they invariably constrain individual choice by frustrating immediate satisfaction of wants; thus a fully rationalist position justifies a negationist condemnation of society and its institutions.

Whether intentionally or not, Foucault effectively applied a logic of the market, where rationality is concerned with current practices only as movement toward future returns. The down-side of this non-critical endorsement of the logic of capitalism is the support it expresses for the transformation of people and social action into market commodities which, even if free in a Brownian-movement sense, achieves this by the denial of individuality. This elimination of subjective sensibility generates alienation: people form the conscious awareness of being treated as impersonal, categorical commodities, as an element in various markets: of labor, consumption, investment, or other.

Foucault apparently did not explore the larger consequences of the logic of social dynamics which his program suggests. Nonetheless, he focused on material evidence of the real, and placed great confidence in his findings. Since he could not establish material proof of the historical continuity of social forms (i.e., what is a family, anyway?), and failed to see empirical evidence of societies across large panoramas of experience, he could not rationally understand why anyone should be asked to sacrifice personal desire in the name of common good to support institutional forms or society as a whole, which rationally he could not understand as existing.

As a human being, Foucault's non-rational, which is to say, aesthetic faculties were sufficiently intact that he could not fail to accept the existence of the truth of society even if there is no positivist manner to establish that existence. That all too common crisis of rationality is the product of its excess: the overplaying of reasoning activity to the determent of other avenues of human awareness, appreciation and action. Those who suffer from it tend to *think* about life too much and *appreciate* life too little.

In so far as rationality entails its self-affirmation as the only legitimate force of human expression and knowledge, while there is more to human consciousness than only rationality, this is denied by rationality itself. Foucault was hardly unique in suffering from this 'rationalist' distortion of self-understanding; it is an endemic disability associated with being born and over-socialized in the modern west. Over the course of the past five centuries, enlightenment determination has elevated {intellectual—conceptual} rationality to allow the human equivalent of providential judgment.

The curious aspect of this history is that the other leg of the enlightenment was belief in promise of secular society, that a well ordered society was possible and necessary for general well-being. Foucault, among others, pushed the individual rationality postulate to an extreme and at the same time rejected the justice of society as real, much less pertinent. What makes Foucault's case interesting is that he took the rationalist tool of modernity and set out to use it to prove that society is merely a word to disguise the disarray of human action, which may distract readers from seeing that there are human ordering principles other than those associated with individual material necessity.

Genealogy

Whether for poetic or analytical reasons, at a certain point Foucault altered the language he used to identify his historical critical method, replacing the word, "archaeology" with "genealogy": this was announced in the often cited paper, *Nietzsche, Genealogy and History* (1971).[53] Because his introduction of the new term was oriented directly around the work of Nietzsche, the shift in vocabulary may have been simply intended to avoid dissonance in the title of the paper. Another possibility was that he used these terms casually, as heuristic literary figures (tropes) intended to intrigue readers more than to inform them. However, since I see that change of vocabulary as at least partial recognition by him of two different ways of working on social history, I will use it as a vehicle to explore a bit more the strengths and limitations of Foucault's method.

In his archaeological writings discussed earlier, he focused principally on the interpretive study of the surface aspects of past events, as expressions of other forces that were simultaneous to those events and played a contextual role in their constitution. The result was to demonstrate how a particular conjuncture of circumstances, under particular historical conditions, led to the emergence of new forms of power/knowledge, vested in

---

53 "Nietzsche, Genealogy, History" (1971), was composed by Foucault shortly after his début at the College of France. If one considers past events to be dialectical in the sense of a bilateral relation between sub-structures and super-structures, and if one considers such events to be dialectically related through time (past events affecting present ones to influence future direction, with the present thus modified to modify in turn how the past is taken in as present influence), and, if one considers both those dialectic actions simultaneously (as double-dialectic, at once vertical-historical and horizontal-historical), then one is formally practicing the historical-materialist method as I speak of it in this book. It appears that Foucault was putting this into practice without formally acknowledging what he was doing. This may explain the circularity of his key vocabulary. To turn Foucault on Foucault, by refusing to deploy a historical-materialist discourse, he ran short of notions and meanings, making it difficult to explain his practice.

particular hands and deployed in a fashion that limited general freedom. He painted verbal pictures of such past events, implying a causative dynamic by association or mutual accommodation, the details of which he rarely elaborated.

For example: as the development of commercial markets for industrial products intensified during the 18th century in Europe, there was need for labor power to assure the productivity of the capital machine, with each worker expected to produce a value of product many times greater than the cost of his or her basic maintenance. Since this was evidently exploitive, how was it possible to assure that, as needed, able-bodied common people would work in exploitive factories? One solution was to treat as criminal anyone who did not work and survived anyway, which was the tactic in England, where work camps were established, to which people were sent who refused to work otherwise.

However there was another venue of social response to this problem which Foucault spotted from his French historical studies, concerning the invention of madness and the opening of asylums. In that country, a few centuries back, there had been a tradition of treating the lost soul, the hapless vagrant, the so-called village idiot with charity, since by human compassion, no one should suffer needlessly. But after emergence of the factory system, if such non-working individuals were cared for, would this not serve as an unacceptable example for members of the exploited working classes, seeing others cared for out of human solidarity rather than obliged to enslave themselves as a labor commodity to some productive machine? The evident solution was to sweep vagabonds off the streets and lock them up in a 'mental' asylum, with inhuman treatment for those who were incarcerated. The circulation of vague general knowledge of what occurred under those horrid conditions helped convince the underclass that being chained to labor in a factory by the force of necessity was the better alternative.

Hand in hand with that dynamic was need for specialists to concoct ways of penning people up and keeping an eye on them, leading to new professional specialties, and institutional containers. This, in turn, led to the development of ever more comprehensive labels for those who ought to be locked up.

The social control pay-of from this was motivated less by concern for those who were put behind bars, than by the strong message sent to those who were free in the community, about what happens to anyone sent to such farms. The message was clear: refusing to work for the interest of capital, no matter under what conditions, could result in an institutional fate worse than death. The study in which Foucault dealt with this general issue, exemplified his use of the archaeological method.

He labeled the other approach to such studies as genealogical: the attempt to explicate present social dynamics by tracing backwards until discovering convincing evidence of the material, ideological and technical factors, which together explain the coming into being of particular social forms, institutions and practices. Investigations of this form allowed Foucault to discuss not only the evolution of particular social practices over recent centuries, but to explore the conceptual question of historical change, including the nature of what is called historical understanding. His approach to those epistemological issues explains in part the continuing interest in many of his essays such as the one dealing with Nietzsche and Genealogy.

In that 1971 essay, Foucault also continued to develop his new-history theme, which he occasionally relabeled as "effective" or "true" history; he contrasted this with what he considered the largely outdistanced methods of traditional-history. He asserted that the world is "a profusion of entangled events," that true history "confirms our existence among countless lost events, without landmark or a point of reference." Accordingly, effective history "encompasses a genealogy of history as the vertical projection of its position" (2001/1971: ¶5).

As indicated earlier, this epistemological contention placed Foucault in methodological difficulty. He continued to argue from a historical-materialist base, while denying systematic links from the material past, carried forward by shared ideas, leading to particular material practices in the present. Associated with his determination to disavow the legitimacy of the Marx position, this left him in a critical quandary.

The Greek root meaning of genealogy is knowledge-of-origins. Foucault was interested in the origin of the generic social form he called the "*épistème*": specifically aimed at identifying the discursive power/knowledge forces that defined and differentiated the classic period vis-à-vis the modern period. However, for him, genealogy was the study of events as beings of origin and not as the origins of beings; it implied continuous generativity without terminating in the synthetic unity of the subject (human being) or the object (worldly content). A discourse of dispersion and fragmentation on his part was the inevitable result (2001/1971: ¶1,3).

Nonetheless, with his case study approach to the origin and deployment of *épistèmes*, over the years he focused on various domains of discourse that contribute to his reputation: including, importantly, the origin of the penal/incarceration system linked to the power/knowledge "nexus" known as criminality, and a similar study of the birth of the medical clinic. A bit less important for most general readers but of vital importance for Foucault, was his historical study of the emergence of the diverse disciplines and related professions in Universities. Finally, there was his last great genealogical study, the *History of Sexuality*, still unfinished at his death. This focused on the colonized consciousness of westerners in reference to sexuality, that ultimate exotic dimension of socio-psychic action, somehow taken control of and twisted in opposition to the manifest objectives of freedom in western democratic society.[54]

"Emergence" was a key theme in his *Genealogy* essay. He wanted to understand how each important *épistémique* signifier emerges amid the "hazardous play of dominations." He believed this "always occurs in the interstice," at the seams between zones of already-claimed competence. In anthropology such zones between the light and dark of day, for example, are labeled, liminal. In reference to social surfaces, those are the zones between moral boundaries, propitious for emergence of deviant orders; or as Foucault put it, the result is "to overcome the rulers through their own rules" (2001/1971: ¶4).

Foucault concluded that chance and not necessity drives the process of the emergence of new disciplines, professions and specialties; that there is no underlying system of social-gravity that propels certain movements, velocities and directions of development, while limiting the likelihood of others. He expressed this with motifs such as separation, dispersion, shattering and disintegration. The result was beyond appeal: "Nothing in man—not even his own body—is sufficiently stable to serve as the basis for self-recognition or for understanding other men" (2001/1971: ¶5).

That is a particularly strong statement of his nihilist position; but then, why not, since a certain homage to Nietzsche was evident by including his name in the title of this essay. As an atypical testimonial from someone who rarely cited anyone, in this text Foucault even quoted his mentor. Summarizing his own view of historical (non)causality, Foucault drew on a line from the text, *Dawn*, where Nietzsche affirmed that events of origin result from, "the iron hand of necessity shaking the dice-box of chance" (Nietzsche 2005b/1881: Aphorism #130).

With that as background, what choice did Foucault have when discussing what he considered true-history, other than to insist on it as parody, as dissociative and sacrificial of old truths? Foucault justified this because,

54 See *History of Sexuality*, 1976 and posthumously.

as he saw life, "all knowledge rests on injustice," "there is no right," the "will to knowledge" is but a "cruel subtlety" (2001/1971: ¶7).

Dispositifs

In 1977, well after leaving Vincennes, having toured the world and produced considerable additional work, Foucault returned to the scene of the crime, so to speak, agreeing to a collective interview with a group of French intellectuals still actively committed to the Vincennes movement. By that time, the Vincennes Experimental University was close to its end.[55]

From the resulting interview, my focus here is principally on the initial volley of questions, aimed at getting Foucault to clarify his vocabulary. With explicit reference to his 1966 text, *Les Mots et les Choses*, then the 1969 follow-up work, *L'archéologie du Savoir*, the group was a bit perplexed with the use of somewhat different terminology in his then latest book, *The History of Sexuality* (1976). He had begun using new terms, perhaps intended to abrogate those which, during the previous decade, had been the basis by which professors and commentators discussed the Foucauldian project. This issue was similar to the one discussed just above concerning the terms *archaeology* vs. *genealogy*, signaling Foucault's testy relationship with the usual standards of semantic consistency.

In the earlier years of his career, while *épistème* and *discours* had been key terms in Foucault's verbal carnival, it appeared to most specialists that the former was proposed as constituting the frame of possibility for the latter during a particular historical period. In the ensuing years, he had begun to use this vocabulary differently, suggesting that rather than somehow epoch-defining in nature, it is possible for more than one *épistème* to exist at the same time; which, among most interpreters, continued to be considered as if he were still discussing 'competing discourses' within a general *épistème*. In this 1977 lecture, he was before a group of philosophers, among whom conceptual vagaries of this sort are unacceptable; the session opened with their attempts to clear that up.

---

55 The resulting text was later printed in the house journal of the Vincennes University, *Ornicar*, which, like the institution, was close to its end; but then so was Foucault. The Experimental University was abolished as a free-standing entity in 1980 and Foucault died in 1984. See interview,"*Le Jeu de Michel Foucault*," in *Ornicar* 10 July 1977, reprinted in English as "Confessions of the Flesh," Chapter 11, in *Power/Knowledge: Selected Interviews and Other Writings*, 1980.

The confusion was intensified by his *History of Sexuality*, when Foucault introduced a third term, "*dispositive*," which is usually translated, into English, curiously, as "apparatus." Seemingly used by Foucault as replacement in usage for *épistème*, his adepts around Vincennes were disoriented by the new term, which, as demonstrated by the following dialogue, was a confusion that Foucault seems to have not only shared, but savored.[56]

> Q: In The Order of Things and The Archaeology of Knowledge, you talked about the épistème, knowledge and discursive formation. Now you are more inclined to talk about 'apparatuses' and 'disciplines'. Are these new concepts intended to replace the previous ones, which you would now want to abandon? ... I am asking this now so that the questions we put to you later will not be at cross purposes with what you are trying to do.
>
> Foucault responds:
>
> But bear in mind that it may be just as well if they are at cross purposes: that would show that my own undertaking is at cross purposes. (1980: 196)
>
> He then went on to say,
>
> What I should like to do is to try and show that what I call an apparatus is a much more general case of the épistème; or rather, that the épistème is a specifically discursive apparatus, whereas the apparatus in its general form is both discursive and non-discursive, its elements being much more heterogeneous. (1980: 197)

From there, he asserted that, "the apparatus is essentially of a *strategic* nature," "always inscribed in a play of power" as "strategies of relations of forces supporting and supported by, types of knowledge," as "elements which participate in a rationality, a given form of coordination" (1980: 196–7).

Apparently sensing continued confusion in his audience, Foucault went on to deliver a key paragraph:

> If you like, I would define épistème retrospectively as the strategic apparatus which permits the separating out from among all the statements which are possible those that will be acceptable within, I won't say a scientific theory, but a field of scientificity, and which it is possible to say are true or false. The épistème is the 'apparatus' which makes the separation, not of the true from

[56] For the English speaking world, 'dispositive' was translated as 'apparatus,' which in the Anglo-American mind, renders a meaning too much in the direction of 'techné,' far more rational-determinant than Foucault considered pertinent. The fact that an English translation of this interview was included in the *Power/Knowledge* anthology is understandable; but as the most widely read collection of Foucault writings in English, this undoubtedly contributes to further confusion about how Foucault is to be read.

> the false, but of what may be, from what may not be characterized as scientific. (1980: 197)

This discussion of the deployment of the "strategic apparatus" is obviously focused on the power that explains why some forms of declaration are allowed in the halls of science for one discipline or another, while other claims are rejected as non-sense. Nonetheless, while power occupied a key position in Foucault's world view, he considered it as more of a passive field property (as with the field of gravity), rather than a point-centered potential in the hands of some social actor, as it is normally treated in the political arena. This justified his claim that, rather than a study of personal circumstances, his new *History of Sexuality* project was an "analytic of power."

If power is a passive field property, it is a ubiquitous aspect of every web of relations, with the web as a whole imposing constraints and facilitating elaboration of potential on its elements that would not otherwise exist. This is to suppose that power is a system-property and system-expression, a field-attribute and not a personal one. But elsewhere Foucault denied the transcendent potential of both social-systems and institutions.

Critic in Kant's Wake

Unlike Voltaire and Schiller, Foucault not only engaged in critical practice, but also wrote about it. By that he provided further insight concerning his methodical disposition, clarifying his use of certain key terms, including archaeology, strategy and genealogy. This better exemplified what he intended when speaking of the "nexus" of "power/knowledge" that supposedly constitutes the event of origin for all fields of science, academic disciplines and professional specialties; i.e., that each field, zoology, maritime law, chemical engineering, etc., is a particular nexus of power/knowledge, explaining the emergence, durability and influence of the members of that discipline or profession (Foucault 2007).[57]

Foucault's critical work on critique had a theoretical anchor, of a negative (dialectical) nature, drawn from the perspective of Immanuel Kant. Kant is not easy to read, much less to make sense of, but by giving the world three major texts, each sporting the word 'critique' in the title, there

---

57 This essay was originally a lecture, "*Qu'est-ce que la critique*," given at the French Society of Philosophy on 27 May 1978, subsequently published in *Bulletin de la Société française de la philosophie* (1990).

was one universal impact of Kant's writings: western intellectuals became irreversibly sensitized to the importance of not just thinking in the mundane passing sense, but of critical reflection: of thinking systematically about thought's work.

Few 20th century intellectuals took Kant's critical rationality to a greater extreme than did Foucault. From his doctoral studies onward, he often turned to Kant, to lay the groundwork for his own philosophizing. His approach differed from, yet at the same time was presented as a sort of methodological extension of the Kantian critical studies. He effectively proposed a post-enlightenment fourth-critique, as follow-up to the three written by Kant two centuries earlier.[58] Given the enormous stature of Kant and the penetration of his analysis, Foucault's hoping to leap beyond him, by effectively turning Kant back on Kant, suggested outlandishly bold ambition.[59]

Kant had proposed that the enlightenment provided, or at least provoked, activation of a new critical tool, that of rationality, as a means of thinking more clearly about the products of thought. Starting from there, Foucault attempted to apply the tool of modern critical rationality as a means of exploring the justice and limitations of the enlightenment project itself. As ambition, it must be noted, this did not differ from a certain aspect of the critical theory project as laid out by Horkheimer (see Chapter One); but rather than using it as insight for an excess to be avoided, much as did Habermas to a certain degree after him, Foucault treated rationality

[58] While the exact intent behind Foucault's possible 'fourth critique' is not known, the fact of its pursuit is generally recognized. In the Introduction to the anthology from which these references to Foucault's "What is Critique," are drawn, the editor of the volume, John Rajchman, offers the following report: "Foucault's lectures on enlightenment (1978–1984) may be read as his search for this new form of critique, this new version of the '4th-critique' he had earlier sought in his archaeological writings" (in Foucault 2007: 23). For another discussion of the '4th-critique' figure, not directly related to Foucault, see Jon P. Mitchell, "A Fourth Critic of the Enlightenment: Michel de Certeau and the Ethnography of Subjectivity," *European Association of Social Anthropologists*, 2007.

[59] Completing Kant. As discussed in Chapter Three, Schiller attempted his own repair of Kant, with the proposal to insert the presence of 'play' as social engagement, in the lacuna between the Kantian antinomies of the drive force of reason against the sensuous drive. That Foucault also wanted to get beyond Kant was by his time almost a tradition among intellectuals. The most successful epistemological effort in that direction to date is represented by a particular thread of the phenomenological movement, of which a certain text by Husserl, late in his career, was initiator (see his, *The Crisis of European Sciences and Transcendental Phenomenology*, 1936), with that thread subsequently advanced by Alfred Schutz (1932, 1966) and also, but somewhat differently, by Maurice Merleau-Ponty (see his, *Structure of Comportement*, 1942; and *Phenomenology of Perception*, 1945).

as not just the better, but as the only tool for advancement of human well-being.

By conventional understanding, it is said that the enlightenment led to an ever increasing precision of critical thinking, opening the way for new disciplines and fields of knowledge of ever advanced content, as guide for the industrial and social progress of western society. In tacit keeping with that assessment, particularly with his first two famous Critiques (of *Pure Reason* and *Pure Practical Reason*), Kant specified how the work of rationality is possible and with what consequences. However, by the end of his life, he came to recognized the limits of rationality thus conceived as sole guide for action and because of that composed his third, *Critique of Aesthetic Judgment*, suggesting that some form of what we would call political-aesthetics was necessary as a standard for judgment of the practical utility of the sort of rational action that he focused on in his two earlier critiques.

Unlike Schiller, as if discounting the importance of Kant's third *Critique*, Foucault took a different approach, choosing to apply an even more intensely rational critique, aimed not at the idea of enlightenment, but at the social-products that are generated by practical pursuit of modern rational progress. His focus was not on material technical progress but on the rationally enlightened specialized fields of knowledge that had emerged over recent centuries, as the driving force for western progress as such.

This explains his study of the various sciences and professions: each the site of some concentrated form of rationality, treated with near religious fervor, with leading scientists and professionals regarded as nearly gods on earth. The cumulative effect of this, as he saw it, was to infest the civil atmosphere with all manner of control, treatment, intervention, mode of organization, way of teaching and learning, etc., which, in the end, rather than service to human kind, reduced individuality to a numb passive state.

By shifting the critical target from the idea of enlightenment to the social practices it gave rise to, Foucault ended up working as a phenomenologist in his critique of historical-material issues. That was not unreasonable or a source of objection, since he had studied with professors such as Maurice Merleau-Ponty who were at the top of the field in this regard. Yet, while on this basis having often been classified as a phenomenologist who used that approach to study issues in a manner analogous to the mode of research of Marx, when questioned on this, he also rejected attaching the phenomenology label to his work.

Critical Truth: "I have no Title"

An important text in his late work where Foucault returned to issues related to Kant and the enlightenment, is *What is Critique* (1978). This is based on a second lecture he gave in Paris for the French Society of Philosophy, seventeen years after having composed his first text on Kant for his doctoral thesis, and ten years after his previous speaking engagement before the same group. Rather than university students, as was typically the case, his audience again consisted mostly of philosophers who were then active in France: both allowing and necessitating greater rigor on Foucault's part, with more attention to issues of substance and somewhat less reliance on metaphor or allusion.

At the earlier occasion before this group (1969), he had delivered another of his much discussed addresses, *What is an Author*.[60] Now, in his 1978 address on *Critique,* before members of the same philosophical society, as an unusually pure example of a Foucauldian undertaking, he attempted to generate a holographic-negative image of the central message from his 1969 text on the *Author.* The result is both informative and self-revealing.

The issue at stake in the earlier essay concerned the status of authorship vis-à-vis a set of writings. If we suppose an author is fully free, then there need be no theoretical or stylistic consistency from one composition to the next. Once a text is finished, would not then the notion of authorship slip to second place with the sense of a text being based exclusively on what it says, without reference to the writer as social agent? If so, in metaphorical terms, this is to announce the *Death of The Author*, which is what Bathes had affirmed a few years earlier before that first talk by Foucault (Barthes 1967).[61]

Often accused of being an inconsistent writer, changing his position radically, seemingly illogically, from one text to the next, this authorship

---

[60] Foucault: *Qu'est-ce qu'un auteur? Dits et Écrits I*, pp. 817–849; original source *Bulletin de la Société française de philosophie*, 63e année, no 3, July-September 1969, pp. 73–104; includes a debate with certain members of the *Société Française de Philosophie*, 22 February, 1969. The following year, 1970, a slightly modified version of this conference was given at the University of Buffalo, New York, published in *Textual Strategies* (1979), and in *The Foucault Reader* (1984). Foucault authorized both versions.

[61] On Authorness. Relative to the substance of Barthes' argument in this famous essay on the death of the author, in this book I assume a moderate historical contextualist position, stressing (but surely not exclusively) the aspect of a text that appears to be derivative of the author's biography and historized voice at the time of composition.

question was a long term, troubling issue for Foucault. In this 1969 address to those philosophers, Foucault set out to bring critical authorship back to life, but in the restricted sense and not as if, in order to read well any given piece of her work, all writings of a given author must be understood as a body. Rather, as an exercise of subjective freedom, authorship appropriately applies in regard to the intentionality behind the production of critical work more than to cold textual products thus generated that later arrive in a library. If so, then even if every important text is an expression of the critical slant of the author at the time of composition, constituting an author-oriented challenge to the culture in which it is generated, there is no logical reason why the subject doing the writing can not shift his or her critical orientation from one time to another. If so, then it is not just likely but reasonable that the texts at different times by the same critic will be in contradiction to some extent. This suggests a historically situated 'relativist' view of truth in judgment, which is not a theme upon which Foucault chose to expand.

The titles of both these lectures (1969; 1978) were a play on words, based on those used by Kant for one of his own essays two centuries earlier, *What is Enlightenment* (2007b/1784). In the 1969 lecture (*What is an Author*), Foucault had provoked a bit of a storm by arguing that as regards literature, authorship as personal control over the evaluative meaning of a work does not exist, because once in circulation such works are too heavily constrained by the fluid interplay of the historical period and dominant ideas at the time of composition compared to knowledge and understanding at the time of a later reading. The point ten years later (*What is Critique*, 1978), was to recover somewhat the primacy of authorship by focusing on the exceptional identity of critique as a particular genre of composition. If he was right, then while literary-authorship, as discussed ten years earlier, is justifiably considered as a less personal than historical realization, by contrast, assuming it is well done, critical-literature is the ultimate in personal expression as a situated encounter at a given moment in time.

After opening this (1978) lecture with brief remarks acknowledging the curious experience of returning to the same audience after so many years, he went on to make a most unusual announcement: "I have no title." He said that the session organizer had offered to make an excuse for him by saying that having just arrived from a trip to Japan, Foucault was pushed for time and had not yet found a title. Displaying again a persistent tendency to slip into categories of discourse the existence of which he formally denied, Foucault's response was: "Truthfully, this would have been a very kind attenuation of the truth." However he confided to his audience that he had been "haunted" by one potential title the use of which he rejected as "indecent." To get the program moving, he recanted a bit, saying that the question for his address would be, *What is Critique*?

Delivering enough content to fill thirty-five pages of text, the bulk of the lecture described his confrontation with the small text by Kant mentioned above, a newspaper article published in Berlin, in 1784: *Answer to the Question: What is Enlightenment*? [62] The issue for him nearly two-hundred years later concerned the opening provided by Kant concerning enlightenment and the continuity or elaboration of that project as Foucault found it around him, during the second half of the 20th century.

He finished the address with the assertion that rather than as expression of descriptive authorship, enlightened intellectual writing is always that of critique. He arrived there by drawing attention to his opening conundrum of choosing a title for this talk, suggesting by that the aesthetic tension fundamental to critical authorship. If we fast-forward to the last of Foucault's words, we can see the fascinating manner by which he drew this issue to a close.

In the final paragraph of his address, using a term with strong psychological implications, Foucault discussed what he called the "critical attitude," a posture which we must suppose he assumed for himself, in order to begin to speak that day. He seemed fascinated by the interplay of that attitude and enlightenment, as well as by the notion of critique as used two-hundred years earlier by Kant to label his three major works; and then as used by him personally there, in 1978, looking back at Kant, who so long ago had assumed the same "attitude" while writing for that Berlin newspaper, about *Aufklärung*.[63]

According to Foucault, the enlightenment set in motion a new awareness, "which swung critical attitude over into the question of critique," amounting in fact to "reassessing the *Aufklärung* enterprise within the critical project." This suggested that the enlightenment constituted the preconditions for the production of Kant's three critical texts, exposing

[62] Immanuel Kant, *Answer to the Question: What is Aufklärung. Berlin Monthly*, 1784. English translation in, *The Politics of Truth* (Kant 2007b: 29–37).

[63] Foucault gave this address in French; the German word, *Aufklärung* translates as '(*les*) *Lumière*(s)' in French, and 'Enlightenment' in English. Due to exceptionally strong cultural conditioning, the similarity of meaning between the three is only approximate. Speaking all three languages, Foucault chose the German version of this notion for this text, and it is preserved here for that reason.

the justice of the claim that the intent of this new critical attitude, "was to allow knowledge to acquire an adequate idea of itself."

From there, in a few sentences before that room full of philosophers, Foucault was able to announce a thesis: that the Enlightenment had birthed the critical attitude, which led to critical practice, which required the internalization of the enlightenment as data, concerning a certain conception of humanness, by which and on which to work itself through. If so, by the 20th century, rather than being framed by the enlightenment as if of a given content, the real challenge for critique was to determine just what was enlightenment, anyway?

Through the centuries then, after "deporting the question of the *Aufklärung* into critique," what had become of the original focus of enlightenment as freedom? Is not the burden of freedom to exist critically?[64] Does this not imply that criticism must turn back against the practical realizations of the enlightenment attitude, against the structures of progress that have been enabled thanks to that attitude? Surely that is the case to the extent that those are structures of domination and not of liberty, justifying a return to the origins of enlightenment, to the "individual and collective attitude" to "get out of one's minority."

This supposes a radical critique of the announced position of Kant, about the promise of freedom, based in part on a reading of Kant's formal critical texts. This implies a particularly irreverent use of Kant, on enlightenment, which is why Foucault felt justified in closing his text by confiding: "You see now why I could not, did not dare, to give a title to my conference since if I had, it would have been—a repetition of the one used by Kant two-hundred years earlier: *What is the Aufklärung*?" (Foucault 2007: 67).

Having done so would have been to announce in advance his intention to impose a major correction on Kant, an announcement which it seems Foucault considered too extreme even for his Parisian audience of philosophers.

Public Reason, Private Reasons

In the debate about freedom and history, Foucault was more overtly radical than Kant had been. While in his 1874 text on enlightenment Kant

64 Freedom's Burden. Sartre thought freedom to be a burden, which is the basis of his admonition that we moderns are, "condemned to be free." First developed in his *Being and Nothingness* (1943), later confirmed in his, *Existentialism is a Humanism* (1945).

endorsed general institutional freedom (no "age" ought "bind" the next generation), as concerns individual political expression, he differentiated "public reason" from "private reason." At Kant saw it, for "scholars before the reading public," intellectual expression as "public reason" aimed at promotion of the general good must be free. By contrast Kant argued that when it comes to "private reason," in the role of the ordinary citizen, the rule of personal restraint pertains for intellectuals like everyone else: one is obligated to act in compliance with the standards of one's society and its institutions, as when a soldier—even with many advanced studies, unquestioningly follows military orders.[65]

Considering the tension to be about freedom-from history rather than about contemporary politics, Foucault did not accept Kant's distinction between public versus private reason, calling for radical freedom in all affairs. While the populist appeal of that is undeniable, given the power of class cleavages and ideological domination in the name of elite interests, most ordinary individuals are probably not well enough informed to express sound critical judgment in any circumstances, either as historical actors or as political ones. This is said not in reference to innate human capacity but as a signal of the stultifying destruction of the basis of good judgment for those who are caught in circumstances of chronic economic necessity.[66]

The debate about freedom that has plagued the West from Kant to Foucault is intellectual quicksand. If critical expression is based exclusively on rationality defined, science-like calculation, in a society dominated by the interests of elite classes, will not the constraints of public order set the standard for rationality, resulting in critical truth being

[65] Authorship Standing. This suggests that the ethical standards of authorship vary depending on the social role. In a public role, to be 'critical' is to follow freely the pursuit of the issue under review without constraint; this is what Kant meant by freedom of authorship. In a private role, however, when the same individual is in the role of ordinary citizen, then the ethical obligation is to comply non-critically, to act in collective situations in fit with the normative order: to follow the 'rules of the road' so to speak. Raising it this way indicates the complexity of the issue of freedom: freedom of open public expression on the one hand and freedom of constrained public social action on the other.

[66] This difference between Kant's consideration of freedom as a contemporary issue related to social order, and Foucault's treating it in reference to the historicity of individuals ensnared in webs of human relations, seems to have been tacitly recognized by Marx well before Foucault. That led Marx to deny individual agency for historical change, stressing collective agency instead, and the class struggle as its instrument. Denying the reality of collectivity, a parallel logic led Foucault to assume a libertarian attitude, as if politics is beyond rectification. Or, in reference to the institutional order, compared to Foucault, Marx was a political optimist.

little more than the expression of the politically correct? But if freedom of expression is left absolutely unconstrained, without any overarching (aesthetic) consideration for social harmony, might not the public space be quickly overrun with the political opportunists, purveying mediatized charlatanry and resulting in populist chaos?[67]

Aware of that fundamental ambiguity, Foucault backed onto safer grounds by discussing the freedom as "critique" in less active terms. As he put it, "critique only exists in relation to something other than itself: it is an instrument" (2007: 42). If so, then the "critical attitude" can be rightly described as a sort of "virtue," a noble stand taken against this or that restraint. For him, any restraint was unjust.

As he considered it, this critical "attitude" developed in the historical context of the 15th and 16th centuries, when the West discovered "how to govern." This applied to experience within families and society but also to self-governance. Generically, government is always a form of restraint on liberty. Thus the primary issue for critique is its opposition not to potentially false "truth," but to "governmentality." Accordingly, critique in a free society is the search for the means of expression of "the art of not being governed quite so much," by calling into question what "authority says" (2007: 45–6).

Foucault contended that critique reveals how enlightened reason as freedom of expression has been captured and instrumentalized as *raison d'état*, then deployed as a logic of internal control, to corral the citizens of western countries in support of the reigning regime. In this way, the successful expression of reason as strategy of government has turned against the expression of the attitude of enlightenment as well-reasoned individual autonomy.

Pursuit of freedom via critique exposes a triangular web of relationships among power, truth and the subject. Accordingly, says Foucault, the power-politics of governmentality is a politics of truth. By rationally deploying Kantian reason for the development of useful or strategic knowledge, "meaning is being solely constituted by systems of constraint characteristic of the signifying machine" (2007: 53). These days, that media-generating machine is the state in service to capital, although similar effects are possible on a lesser scale due to the workings of any major institution such as the family or religion. That process assures that the

[67] This tension explains why free expression is constrained in the West concerning issues such as fascism, religious fanaticism, anti-semitism, racial intolerance and gender equality.

subjects of power, the citizens, remain docile in the face of political (institutional) constraint, accepting as reasoned necessity the following of rules. Foucault was a rebel in this regard, favoring as alternative "de-subjugation" and "autonomy" as opposition to the oppressive "politics of truth."

To believe Foucault, the state develops a reasoned truth about itself, in support of its own agenda, which is then diffused and absorbed by the people; by that, the enlightenment attitude is transmuted into a mechanism of domination against freedom as expression. Critique opposes this self-sustaining power, against that vision of knowledge as the reasonable expression of rightness of governmentality.

Foucault targeted this form of ideological imposition with his famous formulation of "power/knowledge".[68] This, he believed, was the dominant truth of post-enlightenment modernity, against which the claim that the call of humanity is the fundamental urge behind democratic politics, is but a romantic myth.[69]

Philosophizing Without Declarative Sentence

In spite of being remarkably opaque as to detail about the tension between freedom and history that animated his career, the work of Michel Foucault occupies unstinting importance in the critical social sciences and humanities; I will close by letting him speak for himself in a fashion that helps explain the issues of meaning that swirl around that legacy.

On writing (Interview, 1978):

> When I begin a book, not only do I not know what I will think at the end, but I do not know clearly what method I will employ. Each of my books is a manner of [singling] out an object and to forge a method of analysis. (in 2001b: 861)[70]

---

68 Knowledges. *Power/Knowledge: Selected Interviews & Other Writings* (1980). All these papers by Foucault were produced between 1972–1977. In the Foucauldian world view, if power precedes knowledge as its condition of possibility, since there is no one power center, but only a plurality of competing ones, that multitude of powers gives rise to the firmament of earthly knowledges, which is why this word was always treated in the plural by Foucault. Most domains of knowledge are harbored in universities as balkanized disciplines, professions and specialties, which is why he attended particularly to universities.

69 Call of Humanity. Foucault denied its existence (other than talk), Chomsky disagreed vigorously and that is the central issue in their famous debate, "Human Nature: Justice vs. Power" (1971) found with other important texts by each of them in, *The Chomsky-Foucault Debate on Human Nature* (Chomsky 2006/1971).

70 All citations and references in this section are from Volume II of the assembled writings of Foucault, *Dits et Écrits*, (2001b), which together with Volume I (2001a), number 3,400 pages.

On philosophy, (Interview, 1978):

> I do not consider myself a philosopher. What I do is neither to fashion a philosophy, nor to suggest to others what not to do. (in 2001b: 861)

On historical truth (Interview, 1980):

> I am not really an historian. And I am not a novelist. I practice a sort of historic fiction. In a certain manner, I know very well that what I say is not true. An historian might very well say of what I have written, 'that is not the truth'. (in 2001b: 859)

Referring to his early and most popular studies,

> I know very well that what I did, from a historical point of view, is partial, exaggerated; but it has the correct effect "today" that I wished it to have: it expresses "today's truth"; "My hope is that my books assume their truth once they are written and not before." (in 2001b: 859)

On enlightenment and Kant (Seminar, 1983):

> [Since Kant]...the great critical tradition... poses the question of the conditions under which true knowledge is possible; [this is] the analytic of truth. [In contemporary philosophy there is], another type of question, another mode of critical interrogation: ... What is our actuality: what is the current field of possible experience?

Rather than only an 'analytic of truth,' this new orientation is aimed at,

> ...an ontology of the present; ... a critical thought that takes the form of an ontology of ourselves, or an ontology of actuality; it is this form or philosophy that, from Hegel to the Frankfurt School and passing by Nietzsche and Max Weber, founded the form of reflection within which I try to work. (in 2001b: 1506)

On influences (Interview, 1983): Drawing attention to his, *History of Madness*, and acknowledging that this was just after his discovering Nietzsche (~1954), contrary to what others said about it, he quipped, "written in the years 1955–1960, that book is neither Marxist, nor Freudian, nor Structuralist" (in 2001b: 1255).

On the Frankfurt School, he lamented having been uninformed about Horkheimer and the others: "Be assured that when I did my studies, I never heard the least word from any of my professors of the name of the Frankfurt School" (in 2001b: 1258).

But these contents do not include the many books that Foucault published during his lifetime. Before being published in the current assembled form, with master indexes of various sorts, the contents had been available in a series of separate volumes from Gallimard since 1994.

On the moral issue: He was taken by Kant's insight about the "bifurcation" of rationality associated with the Enlightenment, severing "technical reason" from "moral reason." The former took the high ground, the latter was dismissed, explaining the absence of ethical, aesthetic and civic standards from the discourse of the positive sciences, with dangerous consequences, leading to domination in civil society (in Foucault 2001b: 1258).

On power: (Interview, 1983)

> ...in studying the rationality of domination... when I speak of these relations of power, of forms of rationality that can regulate or react to them, this is not in referring to a Power (with a capital P) that dominates the ensemble of the social-body and that imposes on it its rationality; thus I am not at all a theoretician of Power. (in 2001b: 1269–70)

On Marx: (Interview, 1983)

> Questioner: in your, Archaeology of Knowledge, you announced that,
>
> A non falsified Marx would aid in formulating a general theory of the discontinuity... of series, limits, units, orders, etc. Is that to say, Marxism will never be finished? (in 2001b: 1276)
>
> Foucault:
>
> Yes... (elaborating), everything that once figured in a given culture is still present in its interior at least as a virtual object; there in the memory of the culture, it can be reactualized; repetition is always possible, repetition with application, transformation. (in 2001b: 1276)
>
> Foucault continues:
>
> It is certain that even if one admits that Marx is now disappearing, Marx will one day reappear. What I wish... is not really the defalsification, the restitution of a true-Marx, but rather the lightening, the liberation of Marx by rapport to the dogmatism of the Party that at once tied him up, used him and sloganeered him for such a long time.
>
> The phrase 'Marx is dead' can be given a conjunctural meaning, which is to say it is true relative to the moment; but to say that Marx is going to disappear like that... (in 2001b: 1276)

The final and closing question in that 1983 interview is unsurprising, and Foucault's response ironic:

> Questioner: You said in the Archeology of Knowledge that, 'in a certain way Marx operated in your methodology'; is that what you meant to say?
>
> Foucault: Yes, absolutely.
>
> If he relied on Marx: why so few Marx citations?

> I did not do that [make the footnotes], to amuse myself and to jab at those who among the Marxists, had previously jabbed at me precisely about those phrases that I used. That was part of the game. (in 2001b: 1276)

If, as Foucault often suggested, individualized human being is vaporized in a fog of meaningless discourse, might the state assure the missing moral rudder for all citizens? Apparently Foucault thought not. The reason for that probably explains Foucault's contested appeal in the social sciences and humanities.

On the state (Interview, 1984):

> Nothing is more inconsistent than a Political Regime that is indifferent to the truth; but nothing is more dangerous than a political system that pretends to proscribe the truth. (in 2001b: 1497)

Foucauldian Postlude: No Music, No Dancing...

Foucault? It is difficult to qualify his method of practice. Taking his work as a whole, in a fashion which he did not, by weaving the approach he favored with his "archeology" writing in with that of his "genealogy" phase, we see sketched a rather pure form of the historical-materialist method. One searches for an explanation for some social practice, structure or system, by cycles of interrogation, about what lies beneath and collateral to that practice; in alternation with cycles of searching historically behind it, to see what laid the groundwork for its emergence. More than a problem of elegance, when applying that method to a particular social issue, the difficulty is to decide how deeply beneath and how far back historically one must probe in order to exhaust available explanatory power in some meaningful fashion.

Because the historical-materialist method thus involves a doubly-dialectic process (cycling both {beneath and within} and {behind and before} the evident), once set in motion, the track of critical research around a particular social issue knows no natural bounds. Whether as strategy or by oversight, Foucault simplified his work somewhat by using his archeology approach in certain studies and his genealogical approach in others. This resulted in a difficulty due to a lack of integrating language, which he might have resolved by use of a general-systems framework across all his work, but which for him was out of the question.

In spite of his intuition and talent with a pen, the result was a certain open-ended quality to Foucault's undertakings, leaving the question that drove him (about freedom in spite of history) as unresolved at the end as it was at the beginning of his career. Karl Marx, who first developed the H-M method, did better by accepting the existence of society as a system, and then focusing principally on the technical (economic) domain. Even at that, his study of *Capital* remained uncompleted when he died, after twenty-five years work. Adorno found himself in a similar quandary of in his effort to use the H-M method to specify the domain and range of *Aesthetic Theory*; the result was another famous unfinished symphony.

Whatever its power, use of a historical-materialist method as conscious strategy explains a certain inevitable incompleteness inherent to any given cycle of critical research. The calling into question by a historically situated critic of the presence (as force) of history, at the center of which is the historical object of interest, necessarily precludes access to an external position of reference needed to assure, 'once and for all,' a view of the system by which that object draws its meaning. As most critics realize, the resulting ambiguity is less a question of error than of inherent incompleteness. In other words, Gödel was right.[71]

This enigma brought Foucault to a critique of the critical process itself. Having decided that the active instrument of critical practice is historically situated critical rationality, he therefore considered it reasonable that he be manifestly individualist or radically subject-centered in his critical stance or literary voice. Still, there is a Greek Chorus rumble associated with his very personal style of oration, as if a form of universal call against subjectivity, criticizing as total nonsense his rejection of all universality; because if it is exclusively an issue of individuality, such a voice destroys the truth of the subject, which is, after all, the first vector of truth, or at least that seems to be what he believed.[72]

Foucault was a solo player in the carnival of intellectual disciplines and specialties, dancing from one mode of discourse to the next, all the time

---

[71] Boxed in by History. This exemplifies application of Gödel's Incompleteness Theorem to the critical study of social systems. The interactivity of critical research, which must necessarily be done from within the system of concern, and the historical movement of the whole system, locks the investigator within her historical object of interest. According to Kurt Gödel (1967/1931), relying only on parameters internal to a system, there is no way to generate the equations needed to completely explain it. This is different from the more commonly discussed Theorem of Inexactness associated with the Uncertainty Principle of Werner Heisenberg (1983/1927), according to which there is at least a bit of error (of immeasurable magnitude) associated with determining the state of any system, associated with the way a research study modifies the system under study, yielding conclusions that may be only artifacts of the research. See Gödel 1967/1931; Heisenberg 1983/1927.

[72] A final observation concerning the swirling aspect of Foucault's work is that he was a rationalist who took Kant to heart, but without incorporating the aesthetic aspect of

denying the foundational standing of that on which he danced, of the music which animated his rhythms.

He is heralded as the most influential intellectual of the second half of the 20th century, the most cited name for years in the various domains of the humanities. How odd: the definitive skeptical humanist occupying the role of High Priest for the studies of the humanities. No matter what subject, whether history, literature, poetry, film, theater, etc., given the breadth of the problems he discussed, and the volume of work that he generated, when caught in a debate, a Foucauldian announcement will provide a way out. As the ultimate confrontation with problem of enlightenment, as intellectual fulfillment of the bourgeois philosophy of history, nothing beats reading a few chosen pages of Foucault's incisive, profound, yet strangely dissociated certitudes: affirmative propositions often announcing the nonexistence of all certain positions, including his own.

Or, to call back to mind one of his more telling refrains:

> I am not really an historian. And I am not a novelist. I practice a sort of historic fiction. In a certain manner, I know very well that what I say is not true. An historian might very well say of what I have written, 'that is not the truth'." (2001b: 859)

Yet why is he so enticing and convincing nonetheless, for legions of students around the world?

---

critique; promoting Kant without the aesthetic dimension is analogous to advancing a Marxism bereft of social-class. In each case the material anchors of critique elude specification, which dissolves the link between social critique and political inaction.

CHAPTER FIVE

JEAN BAUDRILLARD: CRITICAL PRACTICE AS CORE EXTRACTION

Baudrillard Caged!

Corralling the Baudrillardian critical undertaking in just a few pages is a very tough write. Voltaire, Schiller, even Foucault were intellectual eccentrics of a more typical profile. They were born, formed, then shifted about, encountered the rocks and shoals of their contemporary society, discovered its abusive undercurrents, became taken by those and spent the rest of their lives exploring them, exposing the misshapen structures of domination, the mistaken systems of power in society, driven toward progress at the price of liberty; anticipating not exactly a fast fix, yet at least a bit confident that the future held promise.

Not so for Baudrillard. His was a life beyond continuity; it was impossible for him to contemplate a micro-version of paradise on earth: not by changing regimes or replacing economies; not by shelving religions or altering the way humans talk, share or engage; not by the liberation of judgment or the refounding of appreciative faculties. For Baudrillard, at least from within it, saving the West from itself could not happen.

This bleak prognosis was simple and for that reason as dismal as simplicity usually is: westerners had taken to building a fool-proof society based on the elimination of need via consummate instrumental means; the spirit of desire as higher intention was eliminated in the process, marking the terminal erosion of enlightened humanity. After five centuries of relentlessly rational technical work, the anchor of history was cut, destroying the humanist dynamic of the future. Elsewhere can not be preferable if it does not exist; we are stuck for perpetuity in the status-quo of a consumerist merry-go-round. No longer individuals or even communities at wits' end about out of control structures and systems; we are lost in the manifestations of our own material success, inhabitants not of a sand castle in the sky, but of a monolithic, inanimate, pseudo-culture of discount-satisfaction, where false signs of the real-on-sale have eradicated the real base of being.

One of the most radically critical sociologists yet to walk the roads of the West, Baudrillard believed that something better is beyond hope.

Evil is our end point, the result of out of control material progress, as generative offspring of a run-away rational life-style. A cretin born of what was supposed to have been a noble birth, the West has not just launched a head-heavy model of society on itself, but insistently, irreversibly diffused that on the rest of the world. A lamentable hegemony, a one-world of formless samelessness, one sneaker, tee-shirt, jeans, fits all; meaninglessness for lack of history, bereft of compassion for lack of alternative; without love for lack of other, without self-identity for lack of a legitimacy-conferring mirror.

According to Baudrillard, we confuse the carnival with reality. Lost in the haunted house of distortion, we mill about enclosed spaces with no natural air, without exit; existence as shopping-center, swimming in an industrial food court as if in the ocean of plenty. By comparison, Sartre's Hell as life with others,[1] alienating as that can be, seems like a happy hunting ground. As far as Baudrillard was concerned, put into a contemporary image, as concerns existence, there is no posture more graceful than breakdancing, best appreciated while spinning on one's head.

Ah, To Be Alienated Again!

Baudrillard was gifted with a vivid sociological imagination, allowing him to see the commonplace in stark relief, then pass it by, to get in touch with the undercurrents structuring experience. Although his PhD was in sociology and he acknowledged being influenced by certain of its well known practitioners, the gift of realistic-imagination, of aesthetic appreciation of social dynamics was part of his disposition long before he studied it.[2]

Even today, some sociologists ply their trade with a strong inclination in the direction of Marxist social sciences; however, it was more typical in

---

[1] "Hell... is other people." A famous line from the existentialist theater piece, *No Exit/ Huit Clos* (1944), by Jean Paul Sartre (1905–1980). In Sartre's play set in Hell, existence is shown as under heavy constraint, not due to the devil but because of the others with whom one will henceforth spend every moment for eternity. As we will see later, while perhaps not portrayed as hell on earth, to believe Baudrillard our technical material world has become the ultimate evil.

[2] Imaging the Real. Baudrillard's research constituted a fascinating exercise of the sociological craft, *à la* C.W. Mills (1959), used to explore the integrative symbolic superstructure of the disintegrating inorganic productions of society *à la* Emile Durkheim (1895; 1912). This tying together of a classical continental sociological perspective with an American mode of nearly post-modern sociological destructuring contributes largely to the force and persistence of his critique. For another look at this unusual convergence see Patricia Cormack's *Sociology and Mass Culture: Durkheim, Mills, and Baudrillard* (2002).

Paris during the 1960s, as it was then also at various U.S. university campuses, including Berkley and Wisconsin. Although far from a leftist radical, reading Baudrillard it is apparent that the optic of Marx affected his judgment, intensifying his awareness that a fact of life in the West is that its societies are driven by the motor force of capital. While he accepted the condemnation associated with Marx of the horrid effects of 20th century economic practices, he was without faith that a socialism might work out more effectively. He seems to have believed that the bourgeoisie are as snared by the system as are the masses, providing no vector of initiative by which serious change might be mobilized. Thus, while from early in his career Baudrillard unleashed a penetrating stream of critical studies, he had difficulty formulating positive alternatives.

Arriving at this state of ambiguity took time, study and, above all, practical experience on both sides of the tracks. Jean Baudrillard was born in Reims, France, in 1929, amid capitalism's first great 20th century postindustrial economic crisis. From a rural family of peasants and minor civil servants, a bit like Schiller, whose father was in the military, Baudrillard's father was a village gendarme. Raised in a home headed by a lesser agent of formal authority exposed him to the backside of power, the downside of virtue, the non-said of real-politics. Early recognition of the contradictions between what is said versus what is done, between the normative standard and the deviant event, apparently helped set him up, with about equal probability, to be a police officer, a criminal or a sociologist.[3]

While those vocations differ a bit in remuneration and celebrity, all three depend on a similar key disposition: a heightened sense of presence, as unremittingly intense, conscious observation of the world at hand. Unlike police or criminals, sociologists often go one step further; with oscillating regard, between individual action and collective practice, they theorize marginal social practices, using visible distortions of the ordinary as clues to underlying normativity.

Determined sociological practice is a constant critical take on, if not overtly against, the status quo, glib talk, the masquerade, the put-on, the hollow institutional promise. Put into action vis-à-vis the carrying potential of society and the perforation of its protective moral membrane by ill-intentioned opportunism, Baudrillard's engaged sociology was the generative yeast for perturbing texts, which the powers-that-be often found

---

[3] For a highly informative intellectual biography of Baudrillard, see Douglas Kellner, "Jean Baudrillard" in *The Stanford Encyclopedia of Philosophy* (2009): http://plato.stanford.edu/archives/win2009/entries/baudrillard/.

appalling. Thus his momentum, from the other-side-of-the-tracks, at the margins of France, to world class public intellectual: ignored by the many, understood by a few, indifferent to personal acclaim, he pursued his course non-stop.

Hyperreality as Postmodern Frame

As with Foucault, a certain lack of immediate understandability of what Baudrillard said is an essential aspect of its truth. However, on first reading, the opacity of Baudrillard's position is at least one turn of the screw more obscure. Foucault was a fully contemporary, late 20th century French intellectual, launching a ferocious critique at an excessively modern society, intoxicated by thought's reasoned-irrationality, expressed as mechanisms of domination.[4] Baudrillard, by contrast, penetrated the social fabric of everyday life in the West with such determination that a bit like the *Time Traveler* of H.G. Wells, he ended up in what for contemporary readers is no-man's land: in the hyper-reality called post-modernity.[5]

In order to better comprehend how he came to stage a postmodern critique of modern existence, a bit more detail must be added to the practical portrait of Baudrillard as historical object. But beware: with him as example, anyone who considers economics as the ultimately dismal discipline, has never studied a critical sociology.[6]

---

4 Baudrillard was more successful than was Foucault in evading the 20th century trap that befell those who ignored Nietzsche's warning: that when using the rational {intellectual—conceptual} tools of enlightenment, excessively modern intellectuals cannot effectively criticize the West, which is to say, work from within that system to reveal its deficits and promise. This is linked, unfortunately, to the inherent limitations of those formally modern tools, which is why at the end, for lack of better alternative, Nietzsche encouraged poetry and song, or at least aphorism, as the better (aesthetic) mode of critical discourse. Another solution might be the conscious application of a historical-materialist method for critical study.

5 H.G. Wells. *The Time Machine*, 1895. Wells went further into the sublimity of fantasy with his aesthetic of life in an imaginary future for the West than Baudrillard went into the danger of our actual society as technically realized truth: but not much.

6 Dismal Economics. In his *Past and Present* (1843) Thomas Carlyle (1791–1881), the Scottish Calvinist, satirical essayist and historian, is responsible for labeling economics the "dismal science," an observation that he arrived at based on his morose judgment about 19th century social conditions in England, with its evaporating community values and the surging of unsavory individualist interests, propelled by unchecked capitalism. Known more for his negative assessments of the human condition than for his positive proposals, skeptical of political dogma, he placed his confidence in great persons. One of his chosen historical examples was Frederick the Great (1712–1786), about whom he composed a major study (*History of Friedrich II of Prussia*, 1858), yielding a very positive profile of

Considering his lower class origins and France before WWII, Baudrillard was programmed to finish high-school with a technical vocation, marry the daughter of the local baker and after a tour of compulsory military duty, land a life-time position as mail clerk in the local mayor's office. However, even France has had to face up to the fact that, unlike status entitlement and social ownership, the transmission of native intelligence is not a class thing. Not only is such capacity so abundant among children of elite classes that most of it can be wantonly wasted, but constituting the 'reserve forces' generated under capitalism to assure that the price of labor stays low, the under classes are a source of many very intelligent children, most of whom go unrecognized. When such talent surfaces, and then becomes properly formed, it often becomes a danger for the very system that provides the education. Thus it was with Baudrillard.

One can suppose that, as a youngster in the classroom, for lack of intellectual challenge, he was probably what today would be classified as hyperactive. Fortunately, one of his teachers recognized the precocious potential of young Jean and, as can happen, if too infrequently, he was encouraged to go beyond his social-class station and take his chances at an advanced education in Paris.

Twenty years later, by the end of the 1960s, Baudrillard had become one of the first western intellectuals to take seriously the humanist threat posed by the cybernetic movement, leading as it did to our other-worldly object-dominated, consumer society, marketed by MBAs and diffused by engineer-designed, pre-obsolescent, computeristic gadgets. His first work, constituting his doctoral thesis, was not published until 1968. He was already thirty-nine years old, an age then nearly unthinkable for entry into the realm of serious scholarship in France. The path he'd followed was no ordinary road trip.

After finishing high school (French *Lycée*), Baudrillard was nominated for entry into the distinguished Parisian preparatory school, *Henri-IV*, named after a historically well-remembered, intellectually gifted, and unfortunately assassinated, former French monarch who occupied the throne at the time Descartes was born. This school is one of the two in France most responsible for assuring the entrance qualifications for young people who hope to be received for advanced studies in top French universities and other post-secondary specialized schools of superior

---

Friedrich II (and quite different from that by Voltaire) and by that, of the grandeur of Germanic culture; Carlyle's reputation in Germany has been high ever since.

standing. The going is never easy in those high pressure schools, since even if lucky enough to get into one, the competition is rude.[7]

Given his literary disposition and recognized accomplishment in high school, Baudrillard set out to prepare for the *concours* (the competitive entrance examination) for the French *École Normal Supérieur* (ENS); this is the route taken by most of those of literary disposition who eventually mark the intellectual landscape in France. It was thus for Jean Paul Sartre, Simone de Beauvoir, Jacques Derrida, Maurice Merleau-Ponty, Claude Levi-Strauss, and, as noted in the previous chapter, Foucault. That is not to say that the door to prestige is barred permanently for those who fail to get into that school; for instance, Roland Barthes, who also heavily marked the post WWII French intellectual scene, never attended ENS, but gained a world class reputation nonetheless.

For obscure reasons, perhaps associated with precocious good judgment as to the often empty pretense of the preparatory school environment and the elitist attitude associated with entry into a *French Grande École*, indifferent to the negative effect it might have for his career, Baudrillard abruptly decided against taking the qualifying examination for ENS. Instead he headed for Arles in Southern France, a moderate-sized rural town, made famous a century earlier by the painter Vincent Van Gogh (1853–1890). There he supported himself as a casual farm worker, probably harvesting fruits, then working as a mason's assistant in the off-agricultural season.

After supporting himself by manual labor for five years in Arles, Baudrillard discovered the important distinction between dirty work and clean work. Returning to Paris, he secured ordinary entrance for first-level university studies at the Sorbonne, in modern languages and literature, with a specialty in German. Since the French town of his birth (Reims) is in Northeast France, near to the Rhine, he probably spoke some German in his youth. However, that personal geographical advantage came at a price for the area, since it was the theater for hundreds of years of bloody battling between the two countries over its control. Later, by adding a further qualifying test to his record, and specializing in German, Baudrillard

---

7 Henri IV (1553–1610), was responsible for putting an end to the French War of Religion, tangled with a war of political opportunism that swept much of Europe, decimating about half of the population in the German principalities and leading to the religious stand-off among the multiple Christianities that continue to plague the continent five hundred years later. Henri was cultured and well read, open to a better future; his recompense was, first, assassination by a Catholic extremist, and then to have the finest Paris Preparatory School named in his honor.

was certified to teach modern languages in French high schools and began doing so in 1956.

One of the advantages of working in Paris is that even precocious high-school teachers are often taken seriously by journalists, book editors and the like. This occurred for Baudrillard, who was soon doing editorial reading and taking translation assignments (including the work of Bertolt Brecht) from publishing houses. One of the more important jobs of this sort for him was to translate from German into French the much appreciated work by Karl Marx and Friedrich Engels, *The German Ideology* (1845). Although not the first use of the term, this is the source of the notion of *ideology* as global, mind-conquering symbolic aura, the workings of which often turn diabolically dangerous.[8] That *Ideology* text also contains one statement by Marx of his "materialist conception of history" which was the object at the center of his immense study of *Capital*; in the course of which he developed, via its application, the historical-materialist method that subsequently reshaped western critical practice, and which is at the center of this study.

During the next ten years, supporting himself during the day in the classroom, keeping his mind stimulated at night with translations and editorial readings, Baudrillard gradually became acquainted with a number of already prospering Paris intellectuals, including Roland Barthes, a specialist in the problem of why to write well and how to remain well-intentioned while doing so.

Another individual whom he met was Henri Lefebvre (1901–1991), who was one of the contributors to the establishment of the discipline of sociology in France. Sociology is a very recently recognized academic field in that country. In Paris, until after WWII, the study of social life was largely left in the hands of historians and philosophers; Lefebvre had taken his degree in the latter. Still, he focused on problems exposed by the historical-materialist method: how particular social practices transform into

[8] Karl Marx and Friedrich Engels, *The German Ideology* (1998). Many generations passed between the composition of this text (1845) and its publication in 1932; additional time passed before it was diffused into Western Europe, explaining how it came about that Baudrillard was asked to undertake its translation in France. The English edition also includes other important texts by Marx: his *Theses on Feuerbach*, (composed in 1845, first published 1924), where he formally specified the object of social-philosophy, and the *Introduction to the Critique of Political Economy* (1857), where he delivered a concise statement of his "materialist conception of history." The origin of the term, ideology, is owed to the French enlightenment philosopher Destutt de Tracy (1754–1836). For a study of his work and influence see Kennedy, 1979.

formal institutions, and conversely, how normative institutions impose a moral force on individual behavior, through the passage of historical time.

After beginning with a specialty in rural-sociology, Lefebvre concentrated most of his attention on urban life, which he took to be the most tepid circumstance for the emergence of and, if you will, the battle for supremacy among social classes, practices and institutions. His work was oriented by a humanist postulate, arguing not just that urban life is a fascinating natural laboratory for study, but an essential form of compressing-decompressing context in which the dynamics of civil society generate their own future. An urban social-ecologist before his time, he argued that, as tropical forests preserve the natural environment, the urban scene is essential if humanity is to express its just potential; even if also a minefield for categorical social dissent.

Attracted to Lefebvre and his projects, at the age of thirty-seven, Baudrillard set out to do research for a doctoral degree at a campus of the University of Paris in the suburb of Nanterre. He worked as research assistant for Lefebvre, who served also as his Director of Studies. During that time, Lefebvre published two important books: on urban studies (*The Right to the City* 1968) and on the sociology of everyday life (*Everyday Life in the Modern World*).[9]

The problems raised at the junctures of everyday life in the modern city are powerful: how do primary local practices assure their own sustainability and how can they be enhanced or menaced by practices from external institutions that attempt to colonize the same social space, urban place and society? This eventually constituted the central practical question that drove Baudrillard's research and writing, focusing on how commercial objects as carriers for external institutional power (economic, ideological, political) mediate everyday life in contemporary urban society.[10]

---

9 Lefebvre's work was also associated with the surrealist movement, an aesthetic critique of urban industrial existence as alienation via suppression of the integrality (the dis-integration) of the social; this was the theme of his three-volume, *Critique de la vie Quotidienne* (1947, 1968 and 1981). Throughout, he worked from a highly informed historical materialist perspective; see, for example, his *Introduction aux Morceaux Choisis de Karl Marx* (1934), *Matérialisme Dialectique*, (2009/1940), and, with Norbert Guterman, *Hegel: Morceaux Choisis*, (1939).

10 World as social construction. The influence of U.S. Sociology in France during the 1960s is unclear; however, as Baudrillard was studying under Lefebvre in Paris, the Canadian-born Erving Goffman was active in the U.S., with an evident resonance between their otherwise distinct critical studies.

A concordance of perspectives is particularly evident between Lefebvre and Goffman, with each of them producing an important work in the same year (1974) concerned with a similar theme, the social construction of reality: see Lefebvre's *The Production of Space*,

Baudrillard presented his doctoral thesis before a faculty jury in 1968, with the text published that same year under the title, *The System of Objects*. This is one of the few studies which he wrote in approximate keeping with formal university standards. More than only a litany of analytical details bristling with citations, he demonstrated extraordinary synthetic-interpretive capacities; explicating social practices in association with the findings of positive science, delivered with an unusual literary flair.

Based on fact, yet reading like fiction, that first book drew many readers along as might a historical novel. But not all: he suffered criticism from the purists of every stripe, accused by the Parisian literati of an excess of playfulness in the sand box of metaphor, then rejected by the scientifics for a dearth of tables, charts and, above all, footnotes as homage to the giants on whose shoulders he supposedly stood. Remaining sufficiently tactical to avoid being tripped up by such convention was a key to his originality.

During his two years on the campus in Nanterre, Baudrillard was at the scene of the emergence of the 1968 student movement that transformed the French university world almost in one swipe. As discussed in the last chapter, unlike Foucault, who benefited enormously in career terms from this upheaval, the equivalent was not the case with Baudrillard. By his own admission, he had taken his doctorate in sociology for lack of other practical options and never really considered that he was sufficiently 'pure' in disciplinary terms for a traditional faculty post. Although through the years he was affiliated periodically with CNRS (*Le Centre National de la Recherche Scientifique*) research centers in Paris, he rather rapidly turned into an intellectual nomad, traveling the world, lecturing and writing about the blockages he perceived for human well-being due to the out-of-control success of modern western techno-rational society, warning of the Nietzschean danger of contemporary life, being too modern for our own good.

Imagination and Reality

Baudrillard's work is customarily divided into three chronological segments. In keeping with that convention, I will track his work by focusing

---

1991/1974 (focusing more on formal institutional settings of the city); and Goffman's *Frame Analysis: An Essay on the Organization of Experience* (1974), (concerned more with informal settings of daily life).

With works including, *Asylums* (1961), *The Presentation of Self in Everyday* Life (1959) and *Stigma* (1963), Goffman still ranks among the top five sources of citation in the humanities and the social sciences, on a perch shared by, among others, Anthony Giddens and Jürgen Habermas.

principally on three texts: his doctoral study and first book, *The System of Objects* (1968); his dressing-down of the existential confusion generated by modern western sign-language in, *Simulacra and Simulation* (1981); and his alarming announcement of the assassination of social reality in, *The Perfect Crime* (1995). However, during his last tour of foreign campuses in 2005, he let loose with a final critical calling-out of the modern west as ultimate evil; drawn together, posthumously, as essays, in *The Agony of Power* (2010a), I will review that work to close this study of his critical engagement.

Objects as De-Objectification

In the *Introduction* to this first book, *The System of Objects*, Baudrillard asks: how can we explain the "luxuriant growth of objects," of "gadgets," which spring up among us like mushrooms, spreading rapidly to cover even one another in unrecognizable layers? Were they just there about us, that may be fine; but they are never innocent, and thus the danger: "every object transforms something," most importantly, the person who is possessed by it (1968: 1).

He focused his research on objects that configure everyday western life and by that, our human expectations and opportunities. On a "structural" or "technical plane," the result is a form of communicative impact. Altering how people relate to a world thus materially objectified, there emerges a "system of meaning," orienting patterns of "human behavior and relationships." Remaining largely an "abstraction" or "practically unconscious," there is an elusive presence to the result that forcefully shapes the sense of existence (1968: 2–3).

In 1968, the general-systems movement was still a work in progress and Baudrillard's deployment of its language and principles was more heuristic and analogical than formal and conceptual. Even if the current state (2012) of general-systems analysis is much advanced, the point here is not to propose an upgrade of his view. I would like only to underline his precocious sensitivity to the then nascent appreciation of the systems-dynamics of complex social life in modern western societies, exerting an ever-expanding determinant force in our now largely globalized world.[11]

[11] General Systems. The Technical Note appended to this text includes a visual schematic for a model depicting my conception of a socio-cultural system. Represented by the anagram, {PETOS}, the model concentrates attention on five major domains of general,

Baudrillard focused in an innovative fashion on the clutter of industrially produced objects that impose on our lives, each justified as useful and harmless. This supposes a world configured by we humans, freely choosing what to consume or possess, on the move among ever-expanding racks of available objects; allowing us to maximize our freedom and meet as well as possible the demands of our individual desire, with efficiency of life style and personal happiness thus assured. As products of the economic market, these workings unroll in a fashion that supposedly eliminates danger and risk; with each new add-on object fitting with whatever precedes it. This presumably assures a certain aesthetic harmony, yielding what sounds at first blush like a derivative of the promise from Leibniz: the best of all delivery of technical merchandise in the best of all possible consumer worlds.

Baudrillard argued to the contrary, that the fluid march of technical progress is but a soothing fairy-tale. More than just a menace for this or that element of personal well-being, the cumulative effect of life in a world overdetermined by commercial objects is that it gradually eradicates both the freedom and personal identity that consumption of that sort is said to deliver. As a result, individuality is destroyed as commercial hegemony from without invades to conquer the spirit within.[12]

Baudrillard's originality derives from being one of the first to notice, then describe in detail, this sad feature about our commercially

open-ecological, human historic systems. Applicable independent of complexity and reach, the model pertains for institutional systems such as a nation state, a family, a religious or political organization, a multinational enterprise, etc. The model includes the Population, Environment, Technical, Organizational and Symbolic domains. In addition to providing what I consider to be a useful way to describe the content and strategic relations by which social systems are constituted and function, the model is useful in guiding primary empirical research of actual existing social systems, as well as analyzing the critical research of others. The model is original (O'Brien, 1989), but is of recognized inspiration, thanks to earlier work of a related nature by Otis Dudley Duncan (1964).

[12] According to Gramsci (1971/1929–1935), hegemony, is domination of a people by the ideas and means, which is achieved by attraction rather than by force; diffused via a dogmatic world view (the content of which is assumed to serve the interests of the dominating group). The result is what might be envisioned as a symbolic aura, spread about with such enticing communicative ingenuity that due to its largely non-conscious absorption and thus its largely voluntary adoption, entire populations can be put under its spell and thus behave in ways that are objectively contrary to their own best interests. Gramsci developed this view in regard to the spread and 'voluntary' acceptance of domination by lower classes of the economic exploitation they experience within capitalist societies (Gramsci 1971 [1929–35]). Although it is unlikely that Baudrillard was influenced by Gramsci during his early years, later in his career he became explicit about this, describing one of the ways that a hegemonic force is deployed under bourgeois capitalism: through the seductive marketing of series of technical objects.

objectified world. Once a set of objects, such as those which comprise parts of an automobile or elements of kitchenware are assembled, the object in use generates meanings in practice at the interface between the thing and social action that were not there before. This yields truly emergent or combinatorial effects not just for the product and its companions but for the users and theirs. Further, when a new object is added to an existing set, like a GPS to the dashboard of a car or a microwave to a kitchen, this shifts the systemic contours of the entire assemblage, rearranging meanings and relationships, progressively altering the way human-users experience their lives (temporally, spatially), evaluate their needs and judge their satisfactions.

As this symbolic wrapper emerges, englobing existence in a progressively more complex field of objects, the redefining force of this depersonalized hyper-reality mounts, generating what, in Kantian terms, is not just the reconceptualization of systems, objects and uses of experience, but begins to re-conceptualize human existence, which is to say to reinvent individual identity.

Since human experience is by actual practice technically boundless, there will always be gaps in the market-spread of the available system of objects, ignoring some zones of collective experience, which at least temporally are treated as if of secondary value. Still, under the pressure of Capital, the lattice of "industrial objects" will progressively bridge and cover for that, along the way transforming the "inessential" (through marketing campaigns) so that the overall expression of the system can achieve greater efficiency, shifting the trivial and secondary into the ranks of essentiality (1968: 7–8). As the process continues, we eventually see the emergent influence of even ordinary objects, away from simply a utility or function, as with a coat, watch, automobile, handbag, or telephone as a function: gradually eclipsed by the power of the labels of such objects, as a Dior, Rolex, Jaguar, Hermes or an iPhone.

In closing his *Introduction* to that first book, Baudrillard warned against taking this process to the limit, by supposing that systems of objects assert formal semantic power, imposing lock-step thought and action on humans, beyond individual resistance; his world was not cinema, not even *The Matrix*.[13] Still, on a world-wide wide basis, the production and distribution of such objects, developed and marketed for use

[13] *The Matrix*. To date this film by the Wachowskis (1999) has grossed nearly a half-billion dollars and there is evidence it was inspired by Baudrillard's *Simulacra and Simulation*. However, according to an interview given in June, 2003, with Journalist Aude Lancelin for

within pre-formatted zones of action, generates an ever-expanding "intrusion of a system of practices and consumption," with consciousness re-shaping effects. For that reason, "the description of the system of objects cannot be divorced from a critique of that system's practical ideology" (1968: 9).

To exemplify his claim as to the existential effects of the colonization of existence by objects, Baudrillard drew attention to "Structures of Interior Design," as they implant themselves ubiquitously in private residences.[14] Consider a suburban home, urban townhouse, or loft, with its master bedroom as living room: converted into a multi-media, screen-surfing, keyboard-tapping, telecommand button-punching, smart-phone tweeting, online-gaming, high-definition, digitally-propagated center of—intimate human relations.

The sleeping space in the loft, with whirlpool tub, shower stall of a size once reserved for health clubs, bristling with gadgets serving all imagined acts of body-beautifying, obsessive self-appreciation; and of course, a perched-on-pedestal extra-width king-sized bed, suitable for sex-as-work. As for the cybernetics-room and its system of gadgets, it's all about messages sent and received, occasionally even read; sometimes even thought about. The result is a form of addictive disease: if "hypochondria is an obsession with the circulation of substances," we now deal with the "cybernetician, as a mental hypochondriac, as someone obsessed with the perfect circulation of messages" (1968: 29).

---

the Paris magazine, *Le Nouvel Observateur*, at least from the author's side, there was not and ought not be a link between his view and the film. Their opening exchange went like this:

> *A. Lancelin*: Your reflections on the real and the virtual are one of the references advanced by *The Matrix's* directors. The first episode mentioned you explicitly and one could even notice the cover of *Simulacrum and simulation*, released in 1981. That surprise you?
>
> *J. Baudrillard*: There is a misunderstanding of course; that is the reason why I previously hesitated to talk about *The Matrix*. The Wachowski staff did contact me after the first episode to involve me in the following ones, but that really was not conceivable! (Laugh). What we have here is essentially the same misunderstanding as with the Simulationist artists in New York in the 80s. These people take the hypothesis of the virtual as a fact and carry it over to visible fantasms. But the primary characteristic of this universe lies precisely in the inability to use categories of the real to speak about it.

From *International Journal of Baudrillard Studies*: http://www.ubishops.ca/baudrillard-studies/vol1_2/genosko.htm.

[14] "Structures of Interior Design," is the title of Chapter I of his, *The System of Objects*.

Like rides in a carnival, the objective of these states of affairs is less to stimulate deep, meaningful "movements of the emotions" (1968: 23), than the calculated control of impressions; yielding not a world given in advance to be inhabited, but one which must be constantly recast, "mastered, manipulated, inventoried, controlled" (1968: 28).

Above all, interiors are designed around mirrors, not to accurately reflect people back upon themselves, but to "afford the self-indulgent bourgeois individual the opportunity to exercise his or her privilege—to produce his own image and revel in its possession" (1968: 21). The effect is transformation of human-being, via, "a great anal aggressiveness sublimated into play, discourse, ordering, classifying and placement" (1968: 28). Little wonder that the demand for Zen workshops, yoga classes and psychiatrists constantly expands, almost as rapidly as do bourgeois addictions, from anorexia to crack, or the poor person's alternative, obesity and alcoholism via fast food and beer.

Breathless Atmosphere

Whereas giant amounts of heteroclite objects are rather easily ignored, the insidious power of an organized system thereof is its capacity for self-assertion, independent of the personal will of the people involved. The average garage, or storage locker, and its clutter of miscellaneous contents demonstrates the ease with which mountains of stuff can be treated with indifference; but when computerization turns an automobile into a self-directing plastic cage, no matter what one might wish, it is almost impossible not to buckle up while not moving, not to wipe windows that are nearly dry, not to stop unnecessarily short of the wall when arriving in a parking stall, not to take dissuasive action when the burglar alarm is set off by a passing garbage truck. Once embellished with endless, probably unnecessary technical frills, an automobile, as a system of subsystems of objects, is so compelling that it can take control not just of its own mechanism but of the consciousness of its driver as well.

Still more invasive is the atmosphere which such systems create; a sort of pseudo-emotional aura, exemplified by the annoying mood-music played during the coming-attractions in a movie theater, intended not to quell agitation but to sell pop and corn. Felt emotionally rather than seen or heard, such a mechanically generated atmosphere is the prodigious result of human existence over-implicated in a system of objects. Rather than left to emerge naturally, the intention of the contemporary design for assemblages of objects is largely atmospheric; this reduces the immediate visibility of its effect, rendering them beyond control by ordinary human action.

According to Baudrillard, the point of industrial generated atmosphere is to eliminate "ethical considerations" from overshadowing the "functionality" and "naturalness" of things (1968: 34). The buttons in the car's dashboard twinkle like stars, as if long after sunset it were a heavenly experience to be in desperate need of a toilet while stuck in rush-hour traffic. The ultimate atmospheric filter is "glass," embodying "purity, reliability and objectivity" and above all, the "disavowal of the body" (1968: 41).

The commercial objective takes priority: "atmosphere is always both warmth and distance"; as fully achieved by industrially orchestrated systems, "the sublime ends up as a motivation to buy" (1968: 44). Against all indicators, humans must remain convinced that they personally fill some function of importance: "a system cannot be self-sufficient" (1968: 51). At a minimum, a gesture is demanded on the part of the user to make it work, but not much of one, less there be a moment to reflect on the inanity of such gestures, on the silliness of passing hours clicking keys on a keyboard, zapping among seventy chains of tele-distraction, all the time fondling one's smart-phone as if it were a sex-organ.

A century ago, objects were designed to mediate relations between people and things, or among people themselves. Eyeglasses were useful, as was the telephone, hair dryer or the saddle for one's horse; shoes and boots kept one out of the mud and snow but not in a way that one forgot that life can be harsh, that blisters and wet feet are potential realities, the avoidance of which definitely improves one's day. Now, says Baudrillard, this "mediation between the material to be transformed and the person doing the transforming" is side-stepped, obscuring the fundamental justification of objects and their use. It is as if one were in constant movement, in airplanes, without landing strips: "we have thus moved from the depth of a vertical field to the extension of a horizontal one" (1968: 53).

While some view this as high-grade accomplishment, Baudrillard evaluated it as perpetration of the "functionalist myth... the possibility of a totally functional world of which every present-day technical object is already a sign." This turns systems of objects, "into the actors in a global process in which men and women are merely role players, or spectators" (1968: 58). Forty-years after that writing, the volcanic global financial crisis first announced in 2008, generated in part by autonomous systems of computers, is a striking realization of Baudrillard's astute and worrisome anticipations.

Throw-Away Utility as Universal Form

The unnerving spread of systems of objects generates our out of control problem of junk; since "taste and fashion" are sacrificed in favor of "waste and commercial profiteering," the industrial machine spews out stuff like an erupting volcano (1968: 135). To fit things into tight, imposing, autonomous systems, each element must be refined, specialized in order to be "automated." Unfortunately, automation renders objects more fragile, more single-purposed, less amenable to modification or repair. Rigid systems are difficult to crack open, to replace parts; the more automated its components, the more likely the entire panoply will have to be thrown out when a new element is conceived or an old one breaks down (1968: 118).

Rather than signaling waste, inefficacy or uselessness, the make-believe is extended one further degree; it is not the mechanism which is faulty, or even if it were, it's not that its conception is unjustified. As an excuse, it is said that ordinary people are helpless or uninformed and must be protected from their own limitations by the work of clever engineers.

As Baudrillard put it, "technological society thrives on a tenacious myth, the myth of uninterrupted technical progress accompanied by a continuing moral 'backwardness' of humans relative thereto" (1968: 133). It is this myth that justifies the control of your automobile's functions independent of your personal wishes, and also with the software for your computer that not only fails regularly but limits your freedom to personalize its use; the same with your washing machine, with automated limits on how it functions, in what cycles, how much water it uses, independent of your personal wishes. This feeds the claim that the average westerner is too dense or ill-informed to judge or decide; but if valid, what does that say about the ability to vote or maintain a bank account?

Rather than victims of the system, are we not actually accomplices? To explain our voluntary self-victimization, Baudrillard speculates on the model of human nature which must pertain in order for our world to have been generated in such a way that systems of objects dehumanize it as they do. If there were no pay-off in terms of perceived common need, then this bizarre state of affairs would be modified, would it not?

Baudrillard was unafraid to suppose that practical truth is to be drawn from the theoretical, clinical work of Sigmund Freud: that in spite of conscious proclamations about rationality and logic, we humans are strongly swayed by unconscious compulsions, prone to seek instant gratification at a serious long-term cost.

Discussing "Technics and the Unconscious System" (1968: 138), Baudrillard proposes that there must be something more active here than simply "an absolute and absolutely self-alienating–social agency." If not, how else might we explain the popular refusal to reign in technical manipulation, countering the pronouncements by the agents of the elites, in favor of state regulation? Why validate by passivity the outrageously intrusive, as if endorsing "the bourgeois fiction of 'advanced' technology being held back by moral retardation?" Why go unnoticed, those who call for slow-growth, and those who approve limits on speculative capitalism or favor continental self-sufficiency. Why are those who reject the logic of a throw-away society considered retrogrades rather than progressives? Thus he continues:

> Even if we must assign the lion's share of responsibility to a production system, structurally linked to the social order, which exploits the entire society by means of a system of objects, we still cannot help concluding, in view of the system's permanence and solidarity, that a collusion exists somewhere between the collective order of production and an individual order of needs, albeit an unconscious one;... to put it in the simplest terms, humans demonstrate a profound resistance to imposing rationality upon the purely arbitrary goals of their needs. (1968: 139)

Why do we use our collective talent to generate a self-alienating object-centered existence? Is the noble view of enlightened humanity false; are we driven more by a dark side? Rather than just confused actors, individual or collective, does our putting up with this industrially-created identity "conceal an obsession with our own image, which inclines more toward an increasing dysfunctional world than towards an increasingly functional one?" (1968: 140).

Less Than Entirely Beautiful: America

Exposing the clay feet of the gods is rarely appreciated by their high priests. Like other determined cultural critics, Baudrillard was generally popular with graduate students and intellectual outsiders, but he remained somewhat on the margins of major U.S. university campuses. At the end of his life, a professional journal (*International Journal of Baudrillard Studies*) was launched from Bishops University in Canada, with thematic focus being Baudrillard's project. This supports somewhat the claim that he was more accepted in North America than in France; but even that must be heavily conditioned since south of the 49th Parallel, his popularity was dependent on the extent to which he avoided focusing his sociological eye too intensively on systems of objects made in America. Unfortunately, America as Society represented the extreme expression of the danger about which he wrote. As he saw it:

> America is neither a dream nor reality. It is a hyperreality. It is a hyperreality because it is a utopia which has behaved from the very beginning as though it were already achieved. (1988/1986: 28)[15]

The greater French resistance to his work was probably owing to the fact that his fellow countrymen could immediately understand what he was really saying. His first publication (*System of Objects* 1968) was available in Paris bookstores in 1968; for lack of translation, it was not in U.S. bookstores until nearly twenty years later.

Baudrillard did not accept, any more than did Roland Barthes, taking too seriously the form of an automobile or watch, as long as the cumulative effect of commercial activity was not to snare supposedly free citizens with a net of glitzy gadgets; but it is. He approached this not as an aesthetic issue, as did Barthes, but framed it in a critical, historicized, general-systems perspective. French intellectuals are not prone to endorse the notion of general-systems in reference to French society, much less that France is but one historical-object among others; they are too preoccupied with decorating their systems to be contradicted by the results, even when it is domination.[16]

---

[15] Not all French intellectuals share Baudrillard's critical view of the U.S. In sharp contrast to his position as pointed to by this brief citation, another well known and still active French scholar, Bernard-Henri Lévy, reached a much more romantic critical conclusion. For a well drawn comparison of the work of the two see the 2007 essay by Gerry Coulter: "BHL and JB in America: Review and Virtual Dialogue." This is a crossed critical review of books by the two French intellectuals based on their respective travels in the U.S. The first is by Bernard-Henri Lévy – "BHL" as he is known on Paris television, whose *American Vertigo: Traveling America in the Footsteps of Tocqueville* (2006) provides a vision of America that fits with the ethos of a dispassionate French bourgeois public intellectual, which is a view quite different from that provided by Baudrillard.

[16] Reputation and Legacy. Given his severe treatment of the icons and mystifications of both the U.S. and France, by his last days, it was difficult to decide if his reputation was more tarnished in his home country than in America. For one study of that ponderous issue triggered by the content of the Baudrillard obituaries in the Paris newspapers, see "*Pourquoi y a-t-il Baudrillard Plutôt Que Rien*? The Reception and Perception of Jean Baudrillard in France," by Madelena Gonzalez, (2008). ["Why was there Baudrillard rather

Through the years, while he was invited to speak in seminars organized by progressive professors at selected non-French universities, Baudrillard's intellectual market-value in the U.S. was never fully assured; it turned decidedly lower after the collapse of the New York World Trade Center. Largely ignoring its human-drama aspect, Baudrillard wrote on this deadly happening which, it must be recalled, occurred live and direct on morning television in the U.S.; Baudrillard dealt with this as if a sort of horrid form of Woodstock happening, taken by him as an indicator of the weakened condition of the American monument, seeing in it signs of the inevitable implosion of self-referencing structures, which he asserted that the West in general, and the U.S. in particular, had become (Baudrillard 2001).[17]

Treating it as an irrational institutional form not unlike that of the schizophrenic who thinks that God is on his or her shoulder, Baudrillard's critique of self-referentiality was total. It is generative of only the signs of power and not its reality, expressed as irrational violence, destined to crumple for lack of the necessary interactive, legitimate authority, as sustainability.

Is it possible that the American Empire is largely illusionary: was it possible that the collapse of those Twin Towers as if a house of cards, was but a shocking signal that America is getting the message it deserves from its own echo in the world? By exploring that thesis, Baudrillard's writings on this topic particularly agitated the righteous reactionary element in America. Accepting that dramatic incident as evidencing the Greek tragic potential of out-of-control U.S. hubris, generated by over-reaching empire, was an untenable interpretation on his part and thus an unconscionable insult for those who failed to see the danger of America's being the world's ultimate reference; which, incidentally, confirms Baudrillard's point.

Evident in his earliest studies, even if he struggled to soften his tone, there is ample justification for a certain anti-American reading of Baudrillard's values. Toward the middle of his first book, he had described what he took to be the ideal-type consumer-dominating society, structured by systems of imprisoning, meaning deforming, material objects: arguing further that this scheme incarnated ideally the "American Model."

---

than nothing?" This title was probably inspired by the equivalent rhetorical question used by Baudrillard to orient his *Perfect Crime* (1995: 2)].

[17] He labeled the "9/11" attack as the 'event of all events': the attracting into itself of the disease of cultural decadence by western modernity, triggering collapse. The backlash was severe; as seen from Voltaire and Schiller, those faithful to the bourgeois philosophy of history do not take such critique lightly. Baudrillard's response was to write a book on the same theme, *The Spirit of Terrorism: And Requiem for the Twin Towers* (2002).

Americans tend to be flattered when recognized as 'first' in anything, and so it might be supposed that this observation by Baudrillard showed his willingness to accept that, regarding technical advancement, nowhere outdoes the U.S.

But his commentary about the "American Model" was less than flattering. In practice, this vision suggests that the U.S. plays itself out as a "fragile... compulsive... delusional... exorcism needing... threatening—consumer society." Such terms are not usually associated with the dominant American mind-set, particularly when they are said to result from, "... an irreversible organized attempt to swamp society with objects and integrate it into an indispensable system designed to replace all open interaction between natural forces, needs and techniques" (1968: 143).

Baudrillard wondered if there was a way out of this quagmire. He saw two possibilities: a Marxist one, for the problem of the "the capitalist order of production," which in principle might be "transcended" (i.e., overthrown) by societal revolution, transforming the U.S. and the West into a political economy more like that of India or China (used to be). But, he added, if something deeper is involved than only "the anarchic ends of a production system determined by social exploitation," and remember, the "American Model" is the ideal-type for the content of this line of reflection, then it just might be that the human race is on a suicide course (1968: 143–4).

Thus the evident question:

> Are we contemplating the developmental problems of a society ultimately destined to become the best of all possible worlds, or, alternatively, an organized regression in the face of insoluble problems? Is all this the work of anarchic production relations [of out of control capital's ism], or of the death instinct [thanks to the dark-side of humanity winning out]? What, in short, has made a civilization go wrong in this way? The question is still open. (Baudrillard 1968: 144)

Choice Without Liberty

Baudrillard displayed a rare gift for penetrating social reality. On first cut, his point was to uncover and label the sociologically universal beneath the incidental and evident of collective human experience; to conceptualize the ordinary, as a necessary step for both cross-context, cross-temporal comparison and for theory development and testing. Often, a first-cut generalization is itself a particular example of a still more general conceptualization, if not a more encompassing one that masks a nest of lesser such generalizations; each step of his work thus carrying him further along.

As with Russian nesting dolls, while each more general issue may hide ones smaller, the one at hand may as well be hidden beneath others of still greater reach. In the sort of study of society undertaken by Baudrillard, there is no way to be sure where one has begun in the chain of causes and explanations as social experience. The talent is to follow the threads, explaining how particular aspects of the evident are expressions of other principles and forces, with the process having no necessary terminus.

Baudrillard established to his satisfaction that the West is under the spell of, if not behind bars composed by systems of objects. Since we are nominally free people, this voluntary submission to a state of domination deserves explaining. The key is to identify the points of interplay between that general social practice, namely the industrial production of all that stuff, and the internal state of consciousness of individuals willing to be hoodwinked into playing the role of consumer-dump; sacrificing themselves to a life of work, bound by necessity to assure the profitability of the enterprise-generating capital system that dominates them.

Non-critical analysts accept the myth of the market and its invisible hand; by magic, this brings together freely producing suppliers of objects and freedom expressing consumers. The deal is cut, with smiles all around, certifying the nonexistence of manipulation or domination. The foolishness of that fairy tale should require no exposing, but it does. What is it about the way systems of objects are systematically produced, marketed and consumed that renders the common consciousness immune to resistance?

Baudrillard speculated on the possibility that human beings simply like to be fooled, if not overtly victimized. While that may explain some of the variance, he evidently judged it insufficient, a form of continuous consequent that would inadequately differentiate observed behavior. If indeed most people yearned to be dominated, to work as servants in a vast masquerade for the benefit of elites, there would be no need to mediate oppression as it is now done, at some considerable expense. With nary a whimper, people would behave as docilely as farm animals, without great need of inducements or coercion, providing their labor during a short, dreary life. Elaborate systems of consumer-land objects would thus be superfluous: cows don't have to be given the unrealized illusion that daily life is like Club Med to get them to give milk.

Lacking confidence in psycho-pathology as internal explanation, as well as in the market's dehumanized hidden hand, Baudrillard focused on the special interface that necessarily exists between the objects of the world directly implicated in human experience and the nature of human self-awareness. If there were not a more or less tight fit between our objectified world and how we westerners think of ourselves, then the profligate spread of this arrangement and the tyranny thus imposed would never have reached its present level. He concluded his study by proposing an explanation for the voluntary bondage of otherwise free citizens in a consumer society under the domination of systems of objects.

Debt: Now They Got You, Now You Don't

Baudrillard attempted to explain widespread voluntary compliance under domination by unraveling the "socio-ideological" force of regulated consumption of industrial objects (1968: 145ff). He discussed this seemingly contradictory display of voluntary subservience in reference to the interplay of certain technical material constructions, interrelated with a certain mode of human social organization and with a certain flux of symbolic or ideological content embraced by and transmitted among real human westerners, in everyday life. The result is the generation of a culture as organizing force, driven not by production but by consumption, which he labeled, *La Société de Consommation* (1970).

At the start of his career, he was not precise about the properties of western societies, never spelling out the domains of social action as laid out in the above paragraph; he was a systemist in practice, more than as expression of conscious plan. He simply stressed that once rolling along, an economically developed, high-energy society is both the producer and consumer of that technical, organizational and symbolic material, which emerges out of collective behavior, coming back to motivate and shape its continuity, producing the means of its own reproduction, which is the ubiquitous if potentially dangerous virtue of every general-system.

Systems of this form generate resources and opportunities that would not otherwise exist, at the same time imposing previously absent restraints on action and resource use. As the ever-present manner by which human populations coordinate the exercise of freedom among themselves, this is achieved with a cost: like a high-speed train system, complex chains of machinery amplify the volume of action and opportunity but only by limiting the diversity of routes of expression. Without doubt, Baudrillard was bothered by the way human systems of this sort, once permeated by objects, can become a consciousness-dominating inhuman force. Although I did not go into this in the preceding chapter, Foucault shared this worry; but he was concerned less with collective behavior and focused principally on how such systems of ideational domination might intrude on immediate freedom of personal self-expression.

Baudrillard recognized the interplay of the three domains of intra-societal action as identified above: among technical objects, lifestyle organization and the flux of symbolic meaning. He intuitively appreciated how the interplay among those dialectically interactive domains give rise to emergent properties that forcefully influence both the self-definition and collective well-being of the members of a society. With that as background, it is easier to see the logic of his concern.

The final part of his study of the *System of Objects* covers three themes, divided into chapters dealing with, respectively: Series and Models, Credit, and Advertising. Considered as three steps in a sequence, he offered an explanation for how the consumer society works as a system of social practices, hooking participants into schemes of acquisition and lifestyle, woven of links stimulated and reinforced by advertising practices, amid their personal and shared resources, including work and leisure, expressed collectively as priorities for a political economy.

One begins with objects such as automobiles; the objects are produced as members of series of examples of idealized models, say, of a dream car; as with the surrealist Maserati in the 1989 James Bond movie, "License to Kill," exemplifying the shimmering idealization against which all real cars are assessed. This is the psychological hook, as ultimate model of the do-it-all automobile, or watch, refrigerator, sneaker, urban residence or country home.

Virtually all real examples in any series of objects are far less spectacular than the unattainable ideal model on which the series is based. Still, the ordinary young fellow in a worn-out coupe is led to suppose the aging, rusty car he drives is nearly of rocket ship quality. The game is to get everyone on the ladder of a series—of house, car, watch, portable telephone, starting as far up the scale as the credit office will allow. But the vision associated with this form of virtual scam is always the ultimate model, so that the adolescent in a run-down VW-Beetle will imagine himself driving a Jaguar. Not actually driving one is evident, which then generates the insatiable appetite for more-car, or whatever—bigger, faster, newer, shinier; which justifies any personal sacrifice, including credit victimization and fraud, to junk the current one and replace it with one higher up in the series.

In discussing "the technical deficit of the serial object" (1968: 156), Baudrillard underscored the vital role of "planned obsolescence" in this strangely self-perpetuating cycle of acquisition—elation—depression, based on a built-in "obsolescence of function... of quality... of desirability."[18] Developed and sold as individual objects in a series, the result is flaunted as increased consumer freedom and more particularized meeting of individual desire. On that score, the process acts like a pacemaker, assuring the constancy of the heartthrob of the liberal market-place, beating in the breast of western democratic society. Since this occurs under monopoly organization, the liberating effect is fictitious, imposing in fact a major constriction of freedom. Whether car or home, handbag or watch, hotel or airplane seat, "the most important thing about the fact of choosing is that it assigns you a place in the overall economic order" (1968: 151). In other words it is a class thing, all the way down.

The marvelous "value added benefit" of all those consumer goods turns into "parasitic value" (1968: 153). As with today's smart-phone mania, the process generates not just the obsessive pursuit for ever-more of very-little, but often the willingness to lie, cheat and steal to get it. While the result is a certain degree of personalization, the cumulative, ever mounting cost often attains narcotic proportions.

Due to its class-based foundation, participation in the consumer society generates an atmosphere of personal insufficiency, which might only be overcome by acquiring an object in a new, more elegant series, or one higher up the ladder in one already owned. Since some is never enough, and shopping is costly, the door is open for another great plague of contemporary life: being swept up into the credit system. This is the topic of the second to last chapter with which Baudrillard closes his book (1968).

---

[18] Acquisition of Obsolescence. Although the cross influences are unclear, just before Baudrillard began to work, the 'planned obsolescence' quality of industrial production was first acknowledged by a U.S. industrial design entrepreneur, Brook Stevens (1911–1995), at a 1954 trade conference. According to the documents available from the Wisconsin Historical Society, his remarks "ignited a firestorm in the design community," when he claimed that planned obsolescence was "the central mission of industrial design." http://www.wisconsinhistory.org/topics/stevens/index.asp.

During the first twenty years of Baudrillard's highly active career, the American journalist and social critic, Vance Packard (1914–96), was also busy producing a series of provocative books on related themes, such as his: *The Hidden Persuaders* (1957); *The Status Seekers* (1959); *The Waste Makers* (1960); *The Pyramid Climbers* (1962); *The Naked Society* (1964); *The People Shapers* (1977); and *The Ultra Rich: How Much Is Too Much?* (1989).

Increased debt necessitates increased levels of credit financing, which yields increased personal indebtedness. The cycle is vicious, leading to debt slavery, with multitudes of individuals compelled to work for little gain in response to the supposed moral obligation to pay interest to those who are debt free, as the legal price of their consumer freedom. Since a small percentage of westerners do the loaning and the rest do the borrowing, the effect for the concentration of capital needs no explaining. Issue of false pride, the result is sullen remorse rather than open revolt by the debt slaves.

The final nail in this death-dealing coffin of fictitious opportunity is the use of advertising to wash the common consciousness in such a fashion that commercial pitches are appreciated even for objects which are known to be despicable (consider McDonald's happy-meal ads). This assures that the output from the advertising industry, a system of symbolic-objects in its own right, is considered trustworthy, even if the products thus represented are under performing, causing diseases or simply failing to function.

Baudrillard underlined the emergent quality of this system as a whole. He saw it as a complex arrangement of subsystems, technical, organizational and symbolic, which lock in behavior and by that codify human expression in ways that fit poorly with the call of enlightened humanity on which western civilization is based; even if achieved thanks to technical advancements initially allowed by expression of that very enlightenment.

Dematerialization of Objective Reality

Although the work he did for his doctoral thesis provided the basis for its development, it was not until his second book that Baudrillard landed on the formalization that built his reputation: that of the *Consumer Society* (1970).

Considering the times and context, this elaboration of the material presence of a purely ideational force and its sustaining power as a system of constraint for not just the U.S. but for the entire west, was almost too innovative to be recognized. Perhaps even Baudrillard did not realize just what he had hit upon until he formalized it in that second publication, providing a world readership with what turned into his most regarded essay. Thereafter, elaboration of the *Consumer Society* served as base for his studies over a forty-year career. By a particular application of the historical-materialist method he was able not just to theorize but to demonstrate the emergence and continuity, nearly teleological in expression, of our hyper-modern techno-instrumental society.

He demonstrated in empirical-meaningful terms how, by that process of totalization, consumption replaces production as work and from there via seduction, hooks westerners inescapably, perhaps terminally, in its snare. The fact that he was convincing for his readers is one thing; but it is as if he became so convinced of his own dire conclusions that he decided there truly was, in Sartre's terms, *No Way Out* (*Huis Clos*, play, 1944). Not, however, as with Sartre who decided that 'hell is others' who are always imposing their treatment of us in a way that trumps our own. Rather, for Baudrillard, the hell of it is in the very products of progress that are bought every day, which, disguised as tranquil paths of self expression and self satisfaction, turn against consumers who are transformed into product-slaves. However dreary this proved to be for him, for having so incisively zeroed in on the practical consequences of existence in a society of objects and commodities, which transform consumers into objects and commodities, this second book eventually became his most read and referenced publication.

With those early studies he concretized what turned into "his life-long task of exploring the system of objects and signs which form our everyday life," exploring the shift in the way objects mean, from use-value to sign-value: less what you do with an object, than what it does to you, by the way it announces you as its consumer. Thus the good news: your Rolex watch proclaims your wonder to the world. Yet, too bad: without it, you are nothing, thus signaling the end of individuality, the sacrifice of personal liberty to obligatory participation in the hyper-plenitude of consumption; the more you flash the watch, the more you disappear.

Simulacra and Simulation

During the next ten years, leading to the book I will examine next, *Simulacra and Simulation* (1981), Baudrillard covered a lot of ground; with increased travel, particularly to the U.S. and California, his view of the dominating objects of late modern consumer society that so agitated him underwent a further metamorphoses. What explains the fascinating invasion of everyday life by systems of objects, and the totalizing force of that visceral presence for you and me? Unlike actual physical objects, say a pen or scissors, which interact with me only to the extent that I willfully take them in hand, according to Baudrillard, the power of systems is to directly modify one's state of consciousness as a form of atmospheric effect, largely independent of will or action.

Rather than resulting from personal desire and decision, systemic forces can grip personal being in such a fashion as to override rational choice. This explains the menace against freedom from advertising. Bombarded by properly concocted messages, as 'commercial breaks' during the right sort of atmosphere diffusing television programs like arena sports or blood-emotion pseudo-dramas, given the right pitch, a substantial share of those in the average TV audience will indeed get off the couch, poke around the kitchen, return to their place and nearly poison themselves by the gluttonous consumption of corn chips, soda and ice-cream, or pizza and beer.

Horrid as it is to consider for those who do not profit from such domination, further exploration by Baudrillard of this objective invasion of existence led him to discern an even more insidious step in the process. The original effect of objectified systems was in a way the incidental consequence for citizen-consumers of the cumulative presence of such objects on the commercial market. However, the subsequent recognition of this potential and its conscious amplification by market agents, designers, fabricators, distributors and commercial messengers, has not only vastly accelerated the intrusiveness of objects on life, but added a further layer of manipulative sleight-of-hand to it.

Gradually, the breadth and depth of the falsely objectified commercial atmosphere has become so total that the "sign" is beginning not just to signal the thing, but to constitute it. The image of the real has undergone a transmutation, with make-believe joy becoming pleasurable to the extent of giddiness, and the image of danger becoming treacherous to the extent of panic. Thus the thesis hidden beneath the title of this book: *simulation* is but an intermediary step in the transmutation of representation into pure *simulacra*.

The French term, *simulacra*, is rather wonderfully representative. Exceptionally contextually flexible, its synonyms can include phantom, specter, vampire, illusion, aberration, mirage, fantasy, dream, invention, contra-truth, hypocrisy, dissimulation, and just plan lie. Already fifty-four years old by the time he used this word in that book title, Baudrillard was apparently aware that public indifference to his critical messages would not be overcome by mincing his words.

The key to this nefarious effectivity by objects is their image. In everyday terms, an image is always of-something, of which the thingness thus indicated is the point of expression of the image in the first place. Accordingly, the idea of an image of nothing is logically nonsense. What if it occurs nonetheless that an image be pointed only to itself, yet does so with such conviction that you and I are convinced of its validity: that is *simulacra*.

Referentiality is difficult to exemplify without description; in the old fashion sense, images make reference to something other than themselves, as in: here is a photo-image of my cat or of grandmother's teapot. What Baudrillard argued in this 1981 book was that advertising images were no longer, a "mirror of being and appearances, of the real and its concept." The imaging process had replaced its referential objective so as to become purely operational. By "substituting the signs of the real for the real," the result was the "liquidation of all referentials" (1981: 1).

As sign without meaning other than its own, I draw attention to the 2009 block-buster movie, *Avatar*. The deed matched the word, providing a two-and-a-half hour unfolding image of avatarness: incarnation, reincarnation, alteration, evolution, transformation, renovation, personification, of not just nothing in particular but of nothing at all other than itself: the movie *Avatar* is the rolling image of *Avatar* the movie. In other words, it is authentic *simulacra*.

Once it was supposed (e.g., Barthes 2007/1970) that there was an insistence to representation: it must not just be valid, but provable; it must not just point out something, but point assuredly beyond itself to that of which it is the valid representative compared to other possibilities. This implies a certain faithfulness, of "representations as a dialectic power," which, in "good faith" opposes them to misrepresentation and falsehood. Now, however, as exemplified by the *Avatar* movie or the offerings from TV-commercial-land, unburdened from the obligation of truth, the "whole system becomes weightless... a giant simulacrum... never exchanged for the real, but exchanged for itself" (1981: 5).

Baudrillard goes on to trace the steps in this transition from objects to signs, from images to the rupture of signification, from simulation to pure pretense. He summarizes the process as follows:

> Such would be the successive phases of the image:
> it is the reflection of a profound reality;
> it masks and denatures a profound reality;
> it masks the absence of a profound reality;
> it has no relation to any reality whatsoever:
> it is its own pure simulacrum. (1981: 5)

To buttress his case about the emergence and menace of what he calls the hyperreal, he drew attention to Disneyland, as a giant treatment plant, which "recycles like waste... the dreams... the phantasms... the historical...

fairy-like... legendary imaginary of children and adults... as excrement of a hyperreal civilization" (1981: 10). In an equally irreverent fashion vis-à-vis the dominant mentality in the U.S., he denounced the Watergate scandal as largely a charade, intended to convince citizens about justice, masquerading as a sophisticated system of political domination (1981: 11). As for first-causes, Baudrillard did not beat around the bush. The ultimate culprit is capital:

> ...throughout its history it was capital that first fed on the destructuration of every referential, of every human objective, that shattered every ideal distinction between true and false, good and evil, in order to establish a radical law of equivalence and exchange, the iron law of its power. (1981: 17)

Whatever his criticism of capital and its ism, Baudrillard was far from bullish on socialism. It was not that he opposed social justice, life-chance equality or citizen participation in the affairs of government; on the contrary, his grim judgment against socialism was that the West had become so extreme in its techno-administrative allegiance, so denatured of the humanized dispositions of the good, just and beautiful that the way to socialist reform was blocked.

Of moderate leftist political persuasion, rather than aimed at fundamental societal reconstitution, Baudrillard considered socialism as an agenda for fine tuning the political economy, aimed at overcoming the more dangerous extremes of liberal capitalism. In a way he may have been right: perhaps there is no way to totally reformat the liberal rogue elephant; the only way to assure the liberty of those who share the land with it is to cage the animal. That position would necessitate assuming that there is nothing wrong with using the capital machine to carry out the heavy lifting, as long as softer issues such as human well-being are not sacrificed. Socialisms are in general aimed in that direction, at placing the interests of society over politics rather than the inverse, and the hand of politics over that of the market rather than the inverse. At least in the U.S., this agenda spells revolution, which is why any form of socialism is treated there with contempt before any serious investigation.

No Body, No Murder?

With persistent digging, Baudrillard followed the reciprocating historical-materialist movement, of phenomenally realized material forms as culture formation, through time; and shockingly uncivilized at that: progressively unearthing the deeper sources, material and formal, determinant and teleological, of what might otherwise pass as incidental events of only transient interest.

With biting irony, by his next book, *The Perfect Crime* (1995), he brought before his public a clear view of this merciless, ratchet-like movement: humans concretize their symbolic being, via actual work done in transforming their world; the work is materialized in the production of objects; the objects already produced open the way to more symbolic activity, leading to a further generation of objects; the objects then interact in their meaning as use, at once constraining and facilitating further movement and development. Gradually ensnarling the human community in a giant web of stuff, disguised as a path to liberty, the terminus is existential death.

Considered as successive stages of critical penetration, Baudrillard's books trace a career of ever more unnerving revelations:

1. He assessed how streams of objects and gadgets propel a reconfiguration of culture formats, propagating new history, materialized as systems, which gradually envelop human choice and action: the theme of *System of Objects*.
2. He explored the existential envelope thus constituted as shifting cultural history, propelling further objectified new materialization: the theme of *Simulacra and Simulation*. By this stage in the process, the real is being not just evacuated of meaning, but due to the erosion caused by the flux of signs needed to inoculate existence against that intrusively objectified atmosphere, reality is beginning to be evacuated of content.
3. Finally, he discovered how the momentum of pure signs generates in turn a further meta-historical shift, materialized in a most bizarre, dehumanized form: as Hyper-Reality. Thus *The Perfect Crime:* in Vampire-like fashion, the now autonomous movement of the symbolic force field, under the sway of cultural forces propagated by systems of objects, assassinates the humanized real by draining from existence the last drop of human meaning.
4. The corruption of the hyper-real marks the end, if not of history for the rest of us, at least of Baudrillard's study. Although advancing an epic view that comes across often as a mixture of Friedrich Nietzsche (1844–1900) and Oswald Spengler (1880–1936), he judged the deterioration process as unidirectional, with no likely return at least for the West.[19]

[19] Declinism. Spengler's two volumes (1918; 1923) provide the most cited explanation for the organic development and deterioration that seems to inevitably infect every major

5. In the wake of *The Perfect Crime*, the cultural symbol structure is transformed into a shadowy spectra, a self-perpetuating phantom of the real, which then flows through time in such a fashion that it can only be decorated but no longer fundamentally altered.
6. Like grade-B, *cinema noir*, we thus arrive at the end point in this series of dark steps; at the point of the ultimate of evil, floating as if but a memory from beyond the grave, existing as if forever. Not linked to the ground above with a string attached to a bell so as to sound the alarm in the event that we become conscious of having been buried alive under a mass of systems of objects, no; but now linked instead, in perpetuity, like a chorus of lost angels, with other less than fully human beings, thanks to Facebook, via our smart-phones.

Critical Imaging of the Real Crime

Continuing his publishing and lecturing at a feverish pitch, in 1981, Baudrillard experienced an existential event of major importance: during a visit to Japan he was given a camera. Its use not only transformed him into a dedicated photographer of a certain aesthetic touch, but converted him irreversibly into an appreciator of the force of the image. Convinced that images should never speak for themselves, he quickly recognized that they do so nonetheless.

With his newly acquired camera in hand, he continued to travel and write, with his texts undergoing a gradual modification in style. Perhaps consciously, probably not, he began to compose essays, give interviews and draft chapters for his texts as if he were providing commentaries for photos. The results remained more conceptually grounded than ordinary journalism; he inspired his readers as much as he educated or informed them. While this diminished somewhat his appreciation by the specialists, it allowed him to drive home his points with an ever intensifying lucidity.[20]

---

system of world power, such as the West these days, leading to a form of self-sabotage that destroys it from within. He claimed the life-span for a high culture system was about one thousand years: since, as I see it, the modern west dates philosophically from Abelard (1079–1142) who gave us conceptualism, and institutionally from the Crusades (1095–1270), as the social-political principle of unity among Western leaders in the interests of domestic wealth via foreign military conquest and domination, by that dating, accepting Spengler's hypothesis, although it may be tumultuous, the West has about two hundred years more before its ultimate end. For an overview on Spengler see Keith Stimely, 1998: http://www.ihr.org.

[20] Photography. After once taking a camera in hand (1981), Baudrillard perceived the world from an entirely new angle; no less critically, I must add. In addition to showing his

With his, *The Perfect Crime*, Baudrillard delivered a poignant warning about the frightening state of western society: "the story of a crime—of the murder of reality." How un-modern; there is no one to blame much less convict: "the crime has no motivations and no perpetrators... there is neither murderer nor victim" (1995:xii). Yet, stripped of its vitality, evacuated of its meaning, the decrepit crust of society now drifts like a vacant oyster shell on the sea-bed of existence.[21]

The murder weapon is the materially objectified idea: in a perfected society, achieved as technical-instrumental accomplishment, via production of useful objects by which humans master nature. The success was astounding, too much in fact; nature was tamed, then done in, including human nature a well. Society as the crucible for meaning was transformed into a pressure-cooker, steaming all meaning from its contents: "In the perfect crime it is the perfection itself which is the perfect crime" (1995:xi).

The preconditions for this crime were fully assured: in the post-revolutionary west, the myth of the enlightenment was to be realized by the founding of modern bourgeois society, proffered as sustainable and sustaining reality; but this was only an illusion. Still it was pursued for some centuries; western society proceeded as-if just and progressing, as-if democratic and fair, as-if meeting universal humanized needs. During those as-if years, recognized deficiencies of the real against the ideal opened the way for reformers, guided in the debate by critical consciousness. But no more: inquiring into "the secret vestiges of perfection," Baudrillard takes inspiration from Michel Cassé (2001), and judges that as "heirs both of symmetry and of the breaking of symmetry," we are now present to, "the perfect crime: the destruction of all illusion, saturation by absolute reality" (in Baudrillard 1995: 61).

The initial promise of modernity was to replace ignorance with universal mastery; no gaps in knowledge leading to no limits in doing, with the timetable open, "to be completed at some unknowable date." The instrumental march continued, eliminating all difference, all contrast, yielding the lifeless systemic condition of equalized energy, as universal sameness

photographic work in galleries from Paris to Berlin, one book he dedicated to the subject is *Sur la photographie* (1999a). Additionally, an article in which he sketched what might be labeled his philosophy of the image is, "*La Photographie ou l'Ecriture de la Lumiere: Litteralite de l'Image*," ["Photography, Or The Writing Of Light."] In *L'Echange Impossible* [*The Impossible Exchange*] (1999b). Article online *Ctheory*, 2000: http://www.ctheory.net/text_file.asp?pick=126.

[21] No Corpus of Existence. For a review of this work by Baudrillard, see James Morton, 2003. http://business.timesonline.co.uk/tol/business/law/article1138193.ece.

but in entropic decline; fought against by the negentropic forces of information, the generation of which had become total, but which "contrary to the negentropic illusion of information theory, was itself part of entropic dissipation" (1995: 63).[22]

The technicians of modernity responded in kind; the solution was more intensive study of good-ideas, more fine-grained deductions of elements, more faithfully done digital reproductions. This might help, were it not for the rule of the autopsy: once having cut the thing to death, there is no way of bringing it back to life, of which the residues, "pass into hyperreality, as does any 'material' pursued down to the tiniest detail; all 'scientific' exploration ending up exterminating its real object" (1995: 23).

Relentless reduction of wholes to parts, of parts to digital bites, eliminates the frame of reference of meaning for the result, reducing it to pure facticity; neither more or less than as it is, mathematically speaking, the remainder is zeroed out. Not being a number, zero is also not on the number-line; it is a hole-plugger, occupying vital space with nothing at all:

> The prefect crime is that of an unconditional realization of the world by the actualization of all data, the transformation of all our acts and all events into pure information: in short, the final solution, the resolution of the world ahead of time by the cloning of reality and the extermination of the real by its double. (1995: 27)

---

[22] Entropy: Physical systems consume energy to maintain order; according to the entropy principle, without recharge from beyond their frontiers, the interior energy of a system will dissipate and by that the ordering templates imposed on the real, (which is what every system is about) will deteriorate; gross disorder will result, the frontiers will cease to function and the system will go static if not simply volatize. Entropy is the label for this problem of progressive disorder that is inevitable in a system, unless counteracted; a system which does not thus deteriorate is characterized as negentropic.

The most complex form of general system is the socio-cultural form, of which a society was once considered the closest approximation, with that being supplanted by what some label the world-system (Wallerstein 1974; 1980; 1989; 2011). In such systems (of the sort represented by the schematic in the Technical Appendix of this book), due to the fact that humans are in a way self-propelling constituents, it is argued that since the key to system-organization is 'information' in the largest sense, and since humans can generate information from 'noting' that is external to the boundaries of their existence (as the materialization of mental work or creativity), then via human volitional dynamics, socio-cultural systems might escape the fate of entropy (as internal collapse of the system of order), and in this way assure propagation of the system in perpetuity. Were that possible, such a system would assure its future, rendering it negentropic, in the sense of the term used by Baudrillard in the writings I cite here. For a foundational essay on the subject see Kenneth Boulding, 1956.

Illusion is Better than Nothing at All

When confronted with stress, while any of us may need a crutch, the trick is to minimize the secondary effects of those we choose. This is the first line of defense for those who rely on excesses of alcohol, narcotic drugs, food, sex; for those who lean unnecessarily on a therapist or pass the morning in bed, while wondering why things never get done. Balance is allegedly the key: find just the right dose of solution that is both adjustive and integrative, rendering the tension manageable in keeping more or less with local custom and law.

Formerly, a major source of the existential strain for which such crutches were purportedly palliative, was a life of illusion, mistaking what is as-if it were not what it seems, mistaking what one is as-if one were what one dreams. This implied that there was something real, grounded, solid, behind the facade of botox-lips, cool-kid smiles, muscle-flexing grins; a 'real' you in a 'real' society lurking behind the facade of social experience. For a time in the West, it seemed as if there was something authentic 'behind it all,' justifying hope that one shift or another might better render the local situation in fit with the stable flow of events, reestablishing an authentic way of being in opposition to one of only shallow appearances.

According to Baudrillard, those days are over: fueled by systems of objects, the machine of society has pulverized all anchor-points. Lift the curtain if you will, but be prepared to scream: rather than illusion as signal of reality beneath the shroud, what we now face is terminal disillusion. Were there but some illicit substance to put order in our being, because:

> We labor under the illusion that it is the real we lack the most, but actually reality is at its height. By our technical exploits, we have reached such a degree of reality and objectivity that we might even speak of an excess of reality, which leaves us far more anxious and disconcerted than the lack of it. (1995: 65)

Critique is Dead: Vivre Radical Thought

Rather than being treated as the highest of human faculties, which it is, for a long time, the notion of judgment has been given a bad rap. To believe Baudrillard, those days are now over, not because good judgment has overtaken the West but because its possibility has been obliterated. Exercise of judgment implies a standard of reference: God-given, of human construction, out of nature, or otherwise. If Baudrillard is right, the evacuation of the real from reality eliminates all foundations, rendering judgment itself obsolete. Famously, Kant proposed a different description many years ago. His *Grounding for a Metaphysics of Morals* (1785; 1981), where he explored what is known as the categorical imperative, is still among the most read philosophical texts. The Kantian imperative is now archaic, as is the notion of authority, other than in the sense of situational convention, such as which side of the road to drive.

While surviving moralists may consider preposterous that the rule of the exception is the only remaining central social tendency, those inclined to free-thinking and ludic experience must be overjoyed. However, it is sad to consider that the coming generations of adolescents will have no way of acting out, since the possibility of contra-culture or alternative lifestyle is dissolved. Worse yet, when that generation reaches adulthood, with no authority figure to grouse about, what will there be to say to one's therapist?

Baudrillard deals with this issue extensively in his *Perfect Crime* story, not because of the menace it constitutes for western adolescents, but for the way it effectively demolishes his own specialty: that of critical intellectual. As he saw it, in former times, life as spectacle, "still left room for a critical consciousness"; there were issues to be appreciated or criticized, to be unraveled in detail for amusement if not revolutionary reasons. That, however, was during "the golden age of joyful disillusionment," when deployment of sincere critique was a high-calling. Now, in a "virtual world," freed from the need of "distinguishing true and false, good and evil, etc," we confront what in effect is a new "neurosis": the obligation not just to "reject the privilege of critical consciousness," but to accept the "liquidation of differences, categories and values" (Baudrillard 1995: 28).

Now submerged in a sea of "the simulacrum of thought," we are released from the burden of perpetuating the "dream of critical thought," of "taking in the negative" and turning it to our service. Even for the hesitant, the only choice is to "abandon any critical pretensions" since "against the state of degeneration," classical critical exercise can do "nothing" (Baudrillard 1995: 90). No matter how "one may dream of a happy conjunction of idea and reality, cradled by the enlightenment and modernity, as in the heroic age...," well too bad, since such "critical thought ... is in substance ended" (Baudrillard 1995: 97).

As for affirmative propositions, Baudrillard's offerings are admittedly baroque. On the one hand he announces: "the present world exceeds the grasp of criticism" (1995: 69); on the other hand, he acknowledges: "as for ideas, everyone has them. More than they need. What counts is the poetic singularity of the analysis, not the wretched objectivity of ideas" (1995: 104).

This distinction sheds some light on what he treats as possible antidotes for our pathological societal condition, a mixture of "radical thought" and "irony," put into play by the only self-justifying action that he admires; writing those ideas into text.

Even if his laying it out is less so, the method he recommends is direct: assuming it is other than pure egoistic self-referentiality, to write one must write on something else. The candidate for elsehood is the object before which one stands. That standpoint assures a certain lightness, since, "objects by their very existence, perform an artificial and ironic function" (1995: 75). He's right: is it not tough to muffle a chuckle just thinking seriously about a toaster, or not to snicker a little when contemplating grown men chasing a hockey-puck? So there you have the ironic essence of a contemporary athletic metaphor for the saga of maturity: between family training table and professional ice rink, little Pat becomes a grown up.

Baudrillard was against "playing with truth," which is his indictment against "critical thought" (1995: 97); the trouble is that, "critics, being unhappy by nature, always choose ideas as their battleground."

Fundamentally an exercise in, "the juggling of meaning," the "act of writing" brings one in contact with "language," which is "happy even when referring to a world without illusion and without hope." From there he cautiously specified the engaged posture he admired, proposing a "definition of radical thinking: a happy form of thinking, yet an intelligence without hope" (1995: 104).

Power Begets Agony

Agony of Power (Baudrillard 2010a), is the title of a small book of extracts from material discussed by Baudrillard during a series of conferences given during what turned out to be his last speaking tour of the Americas. That was in 2005; thereafter, on returning to Paris he was surprised with a cancer diagnosis, and did live long enough to personally oversee production of an integrated anthology from these conferences.

These papers exemplify Baudrillard's preferred working style: an expedition to certain foreign campuses, mostly in the U.S. and Canada, giving lectures in which he explored questions partly oriented by current events such as the destruction of the World Trade Center in New York and partly by some aspect of his long term program exposing the modern west as a fully objectified catastrophe; but told with a wink.

More than a subjective examination of his state of mind or a sectarian report on some fully-preformatted research project, the point of his seminars and writings was discovery and consciousness raising. The somewhat enigmatic result illustrates the degree to which, as late-style, Baudrillard's synthetic enthusiasm vastly outreached his patience for analytical detail.

His manner of talking his way into text had both pedagogical and editorial consequences. Exploring and elaborating a view or image of social experience rather than presenting some precise argument fully developed in advance, any single presentation or interview came across ambiguously. Generally dealing with ordinary questions, he worked from such an original angle that the habitual logic of academic presentation was surpassed. Not inclined to formulas, no single phrase definitively captured his view on the issues he considered important; to suppose that would be to impute to his work a formalist intention which he disavowed.

The essays in this last book are related due to the overlapping content of his last round of seminars. However, also added to the volume is a translated (into English) interview, *Les Racines du Mal* (*The Roots of Evil*), published online in 2005, by the French culture magazine, *Critic'art*. In that discussion with two journalists, Baudrillard elaborated an agonizing worry that he confronted during those last years of his life. The stunning success of the western model of object-dominated, commercial society had succeeded too well. On a global level, thanks to that vary uniformity, resulting in the destruction of socio-cultural diversity, the contemporary western Model had itself become the ultimate *Evil*.

This transformation of enlightened good-will into efficient production as social organization and from there to hegemonic globalization as evil incarnate, deserves elaboration. He believed that a one-way world-organizing logic of capital determination had snuffed out the notion of the otherwise—and otherness.[23] Celebrated as if paradise on earth, or at least the next best possible option, there being no debate as to other models, styles or modes of living: the pressured expansion of perfect sameness had absolved humanity from the possible sin of the unaccomplished. To arrive in heaven with no hell as alternative eliminates the moral standard; you can be anything, anywhere, anytime, since unlike the biblical ones, among

---

[23] Extinction of Otherness: For a fascinating discussion of this existentially suicidal tendency see "The Surgical Removal of Otherness" (Chapter 18) in his *The Perfect Crime* (2008/1995).

modern angelic legions, we humans are perfectly equal. What is done personally matters little since the indifference curve of eternity is flat.[24]

Domination and Hegemony

The first essay in that last volume, *From Domination to Hegemony*, sets the tone for his final investigations. The battle for world domination is over; principal actors with a stake in relations within and among nations are now in the fold, committed to the liberal-capital, techno-instrumental political-economy of western origin: depersonalizing societies, denaturing the environment, rapidly erasing the unique marks of culture and even language. Constituted according to objectified principles of material systems, this one-way-logic is applied like plaster to the face of the planet, signaling the daunting consequences, beyond *Atlas-Shrugged*, of liberal-capital's *hegemony-achieved*.[25]

Hegemony as concept is globalization in practice; like gravity, it is a principle all its own, and its own principle. It is voluntary by definition, achieved when others desire to do it 'our way, eliminating many costs of deployment or maintenance. Hegemony is self-asserting, self-propagating as rightness incarnate; it is literally unthinkable to oppose it and lest one does, attention: either do it our way or you are seriously disloyal if not an outright terrorist.

Henceforth, there is but one right way of existence, from food and transportation, to love and marriage, or politics and economics; one way to operate a bank, organize a city, treat garbage, raise crops or animals, build houses, move about, manage a business, secure debt, monitor human action, educate the young, tell a joke, make music, treat disease, etc. The intention is not aesthetic symmetry but absolute similarity.

---

24 Two other essays based on material from his final American tour were published as, *Carnival and Cannibal* (2010b), signaling Baudrillard's ultimate ironic critique of the folly of existence in a hegemonic world structured under the rules of late western modernity, announcing (the hotly contested) entry into a post-modern historical condition. If he was right, today, when people appear to get on well, it is but a show—a carnival; when they differ, it is as battle over privilege, one element of humanity against another, as cannibalism.

25 Reactionary Individualism. Ayn Rand's (1905–1982) allegoric masterpiece, *Atlas Shrugged* (1957), points to illusion of uncritical trust in individual initiative as driving force for the pursuit of interests and as pathway to a good society. The fallacy in her position is with her failure to note that before an interest can be individually pursued, it must first be collectively inspired and its potential satisfactions institutionally defined by an already functioning society.

Rather than by despotic politicians, rabid nationalists or religious fanatics, capital's hegemony as globalization is deployed and reproduced via the impersonal systems of objects and objectified systems that carry the force of the universal liberal market. It spreads and deepens in all countries, for all people, with little time lag. Dissolving the symbolic uniqueness of language, attitudes and values, this announces the devastation of culture as diversity, and as resistance.

The standardization of a world-wide present demands eradication of local history, or at least its rewriting as uniformity rather than exceptionality. The response to the collapse of the New York World Trade Towers was, 'We are all Americans now': true that is, and frighteningly so. As its aftermath demonstrates, there really is no act for redressing to right this wrong. No matter what the call for improvement, all that occurs is to further restrict the liberty of all American free-citizens, and by that, all world-citizens as well, in the interest of hegemonic globalization.[26]

Only one way to act freely announces the progressive destruction of liberty. Under the specter of hegemony, concentrated by free-market communication and consumption, expressions of choice are now ordered according to a single hierarchy of valuing criteria. Initially supported by the elite classes because they believed they might benefit selectively while still escaping its grip, according to Baudrillard, it is now too late: members at one level or another of a silent army of bourgeois co-perpetrators, we are now all accomplices of hegemony.[27]

---

[26] Hegemonic Immorality. As revealed by *Perfect Crime,* in the interest of economic efficiency, the unity of being has been sacrificed by the evacuation of meaning for global affairs; all this is the result of the impersonal power of the objectified systems, without human soul and thus without human moral constraint.

[27] While we discuss general systems in a worry-free fashion, Baudrillard backed away from such talk as if equivalent to using fine words to describe, well—the ultimate evil. This tendency for blanket condemnation (as fact or rhetoric) of social systems (partly for deontological reasons) is unfounded, if one considers (as I do) their internal dynamics to be variable and open to influence by collective action. Justifying that requires a rather elaborate yet clear conceptualization for such systems, which is precisely the objective that inspired the development of the model contained in the Technical Appendix.

In the language of that model, the negative assessment of Baudrillard is fully justified to the extent that the contemporary western system is under the specter of the technical domain, which, unfortunately, it is; however, rather than a given, it is an option. To the degree it is boundless, the technical penetration of the symbolic domain destroys future-determining humanized meaning and locks the common consciousness in a reactionary past of dead history; with unpleasant effects to say the least. In a parallel fashion, excessive technical penetration of the organizational domain destroys group processes (such as family, neighborhoods and unions) and transforms politics into a field of aggression rather than cooperation. The technical penetration of the operating environment destroys

Baudrillard's position about domination and hegemony, is direct: with the logic of the one replacing that of the other, we of the West-driven world have moved from a condition of domination, to one of hegemony. Whether despotic, ecclesiastic, royalist, bureaucratic or other, since the problem of domination dates from forever, no matter what the alternative, leaving domination behind seems appealing. Not so he says: we have moved unfortunately not just from bad to worse, but from bad to evil.

To say that societal conditions are bad implies a continuum, worse in one direction, better in the other. No matter what the particular attribute under scrutiny, according to the rational logic of late modernity, not only is there likely to be movement, perhaps oscillation from good-to-bad, but the possibility is open for systematic action that shifts the momentum either toward the better or toward the worse. This condition is measured routinely, as with the morale of citizens, levels of economic production, business profits, trust of clients for bankers, life expectancy of infants, level of indebtedness of families, the degree of inequality in the distribution of wealth between the elite classes and the lesser classes, etc.

Even when a measured trend shows that conditions are getting worse, the production of statistics is reassuring; mathematizing our existence depersonalizes it, dehumanizes it, transforming it from felt-reality to meta-factual technical detail. Given the contrary rationality of high modernity, to announce scientifically that things are worse in this or that sector implies that with just a bit of effort, the trend can be reversed, for the better. Who might hope for more?

The variability from better to worse is possible due to the existence of good; to measure any collective attribute indicates existence of some civic, aesthetic or ethical pointer marking the top of the scale against which actuality is assessed. This implies a potentially perfect score: the mythic ten-out-of-ten, winner take all, unsurpassed level of attainment. Even if everyone realizes that such ideals are utopian, generation of such measures is a source of consolation; it supplies a seemingly rational basis for the dubious belief that, yes, things are bad, but they surely might be

---

the organic order of relations with nature and among peoples; and finally, as for the population effect, technical excess drives boundless population growth, which can only lead to greater technically destructive dependence, in a cycle of unsustainability. Baudrillard did not word his critique in these terms, but he might have.

worse; and they will probably improve even if perfection is impossible anyway.

In truth, a notion which Baudrillard seriously doubted, such existential measures are largely vacuous; each human existence is a singularity, a natural experiment without replication. Its transformation into a continuum by measurement of attributes, as if the givens of one's life could be placed somewhere along a statistical distribution of possibilities, is nonsense. This justifies the critique of most decontextualized statistics as but a scam; as if Pompeii would have been saved if only its residents had made more frequent sacrifices to the volcano, or cleaned up the graffiti on their toilet walls.

Even if there were significant measures of ideal states of individual or collective life and even if there were justification in statistical comparison of actual with the ideal, even if there were validity to the press-monger trumpeting of the better versus worse of pollster-assessed experience; even if all that were valid, according to Baudrillard, it no longer makes any difference.

The house of cards of statistical goodness has dis-integrated, not for lack of reliability of the measurement process but due to the collapse of the base of existence on which it rests: there can no longer be a claim as to better or worse, because as a result of the exercise of late modern rational determination, the notion of Good has been abolished. This tragic elimination of the possibility of the excellent, due to the over saturation of experience by its attainment, has left the West and its world under perverse sway of the unimaginable specter of evil.

Evil is non quantifiable; it cannot be placed on a continuum, cannot be graded, degraded or coached back to goodness via measured discipline. It is absolute, unrecoverable; beyond beatification, it can only be slain. It is hell, the negative state of no-return. If Baudrillard is accurate, that is precisely where the West finds itself; we have become, as it were, not just our own worst enemies, but our own evil companions at that. Evil cannot be opposed.

Are we lost? Well not quite. To get the better of evil requires casting aside the redemptive logic of eternal progress, of persistent betterment, which has characterized the West for centuries.

The Theory of the Second best

Economists make an interesting argument about improving social practices. Imagine that, faced with some problem, a political agent proposes an ameliorative act. Under questioning, the proposition is defended; if not the best possible choice, so goes the argument, at least it is movement in the right direction. Not necessarily so, says the economist, unless one can identify the first best, the absolute standard of accomplishment that is called for; without that as reference point, there is no way to assure that the actual proposal is better in the least. Billed as second-best, or better than doing nothing, the choice may in fact be disastrously worse; the only way to be sure is to start by identifying the number-one best, the truly good option. Then if one wishes, that may be set aside in favor of a different choice down the line.

Under the magic lamp of modern enlightenment, this is a trap. As terminal perfectionists, the identification of the best alternative for a situation is to condemn anyone who proposes something less; the second-best, thus certified, must be cast aside. If it is known, westerners only go for the best. Thanks to the impossibility of a second-best until the absolute number-one is know, and the impossibility, in general, of specifying what that number-one choice might be, justifies endless analysis, study groups, public monitoring, and then, no action; since for lack of rational justification, inaction is likely to be the least harmful option.

The same cagey economists do not insist on certifying the negative end of the spectrum, the worst possibility. One can propose politically convenient action with impunity, claiming the result will surely not make things worse, without obligation to certify the standard of absolute bad against which to chart the not-so-bad value of the option at hand. This results in the choice of expediency, the pragmatism of popular opinion, the rule of delay, the dispensation of caution, the insurance of folly, all undertaken because in the face of crisis, anything is better than no action at all: but is it?

The history of good and evil practices is rather new for human beings; it began at the dawn of western modernity, with the crusades as its first multi-national expression: aimed at foreign conquest, based on the self-certifying rightness of the destruction of others, with the promised reward being the pillage of war. Kill an Arab for Christ, because the gods wish it so! The standard of good was clear: given the divine calling on earth, if the result was a bit bloody, too bad.

Since the 16th century, the western enlightenment brought the issue down to earth: without calling on the gods, thoughtful humans might know the truth and act accordingly. The transformation of this then newly discovered personal attribute into the art called good-government via free-economy came about with a bit of help from Machiavelli, Hobbes and others.[28] Strategic technique as sound thinking put into action held the promise of endless progress. The key was to tame nature and free human vision, allowing the winds of the market to determine material direction; that which could not be tamed or rendered amenable to market forces was to be destroyed. Success was measured by the number of trees cut to the stump, the number of nature's animals and birds eradicated, the number of rounds of speculative action fired per second. Progress was the result: all westerners might have more and more comfort, assuring that the western elites, no matter what their costume, would have more and more privilege.

After centuries of bloody wars of conquest and technical battles for mastery, the West is saturated by the products of its promised accomplishment and nature is dead. The elites have all the privilege they might carry, and short of resorting to the destruction of wealth in order to assure value for capital that remains, without regular recourse such as foreign warfare as method of deconcentration foreign holdings thanks to the smart-bombs from drones, the process of maximization of capital through exchange of itself has reached a limit.

Children, marriages, sex, jobs, goods, homes, schools, educations, religions: all are available on E-Bay, as are all personal identities on Facebook and all possible information on Google. The technical miracle has been achieved: there is no more reality than the web can certify, which is none; there is no more value than the virtual on-line market can certify, which is virtually none; there is no more legitimacy of leadership than the poll-analysts can fabricate with their algorithms, save the cartoon of power.

We westerners have gotten ourselves into this quagmire of identity confusion by the over production of signals, messages and images; the false presentation of the sign for the fact. The modern western machine of technical-instrumental production has done such a fine job on the naturally given, that it has destroyed it. Since the machine works like a corkscrew, boring into the core of the object to be conquered, like invasion by termites, it destroys from within. Squeezing the life out of the naturally given, the modern miracle has established the preconditions for its own exhaustion. For lack of additional wild frontiers to master, the global societal machine has turned against its own elements; like a giant reptile that eats its own tail when forage is scarce, western modern achievement has

[28] See the Chapter One discussion of Horkheimer's *The Beginnings of Bourgeois Philosophy* of *History*.

turned cannibalistic. By that, says Baudrillard, what was once celebrated as promise of the greatest good has transformed itself into terminal evil.

For lack of an acceptable ethical-aesthetic-civic standard of the good, as good life, good judgment, and the like, the technical instrument behind western progress has turned frantically, then dangerously, and now destructively out of control. It has inhaled the entire world, not as an external force of domination, not Roman-Conquest like, but by invasion from within, by the colonization of the mind, of the spirit of the law *à la* Montaigne, twisted in service of movement as self-possession, then agitation as self-obsession. The result is truly *evil.*

Politics as Despicable Half-Measures

Not only were good and evil of the worldly form discussed by Baudrillard invented since the Renaissance, but those ultimate endpoints for assessing the value of the actual have become its definitive affirmative statement. To be modern is to want the best by avoiding the worst, and to impose on the world whatever is necessary to assure it, in what for westerners are no uncertain terms. This implies a fundamentally occidental ethnocentrism: knowing what good is, and how to advance toward it; a god-like view of the rights and wrongs of the world condition, which, as demonstrated repeatedly since the crusades and the rest, usually proves more than a bit devilish in practice.

First-order evil is easy to track: it's only sin against some standard of good that can be recompensed by appropriate resolve, at a moderate price, in the direction of virtue. Baudrillard's term for this was "relative evil," which "only exists in balance with Good." Not as religious fault, nor by failure of mission, but rather for having over-succeeded as technical-instrumental progress; modernity having assured equality for all, democratic vote for all, some degree of freedom of communication and action in unregulated markets for all; then extension of that as globalization, not as a geographic term but as a metaphysical one, in our hyper-modernity: "Now there is an absolute Evil, a depressive or catastrophic version of this relative evil… that comes from an excess of Good." This limitless *Evil* has arisen in the wake of "an unchecked proliferation of Good, of technological development, of infinite progress, of totalitarian morality, of a radical will to do good without opposition" (2010a: 109).

If Baudrillard was accurate, the utility of purgatory is over; if there will be anything at all, hell is our future. Not so through the ages that gave rise to purgatory. Mortal sinning was too ultimate, the sign of irreversible evil; once in such a state, one might as well live like a devil, because in the end, hell-fire was the inevitable outcome.

The earlier split between Heaven and Hell was obdurate. An intermediate option of moral transgression was called for; the churchmen put their thinking caps on and *voilà*: purgatory was born. You might fall into the most evil of sin, then, via indulgences, buy your way back out: so very modern, that. For some centuries, the West succeeded thanks to adoption of the logic of purgatory. Now in the hyper-reality of a postmodern west, the fall from grace is total, and Evil is our sole immoral companion.[29]

An Aesthetic of Death?

As he approached his drop into the grave, Baudrillard spoke persistently of Evil. In the 2005 *Critique d'Art* interview, with a dying man as we now know, the journalist was a bit perplexed; why this talk of Evil as its "own ideal finality," not contingent on any condition external to its own expression? Why such terminal language, of *Evil* as an "absolute, irreparable, inexorable movement?" Do you suppose that it was a premonition on Baudrillard's part, not of the finitude of the world, but of his own; a fatal psychic self-diagnosis before the fact of the medically announced one that was soon to be his?

Is our desperate historical condition beyond opposition? Following no axis, evil is structurally capricious. For those who take film seriously, it is the *Transformer Syndrome*: modernity as cleaver gadget gone ballistic.

---

[29] Purgatory as Hell on Earth. Considerable work has been done by historians to unravel the timing and dynamics of the various inventions for social control that over the ages have come to characterize the *lebenswelt* of the West. One specialist in such questions is the French historian, Jacques Le Goff, who admittedly uses a form of historical narrative construction that is put in question by Hayden White (to be studied in Chapter Seven).

Le Goff's major study of the struggle for political mastery in the name of souls and salvation was oriented by the life of *St. Louis* (Le Goff 1996); that is, of Louis IX of France, who gave his life while leading a failing effort to win the Crusades, gaining sainthood in the bargain since, when it came to killing infidels, as St. Bernard preached, 'God wishes it!' This followed an earlier study, entitled the *Birth of Purgatory* (Le Goff 1981), in the course of which he determined that the gates of purgatory are located in Ireland of all places.

As discussed by Le Goff, it was during the 13th–14th centuries that the close relationship was announced between the logic of principality, the ideology of corporate Christianity, and the business of bourgeois capitalism. This aspect of his work is elaborated in writings such as: *Marchads et banquiers du Moyen âge* [*Merchants and Bankers of the Middle Ages*], (2011/1956), and "The Usurer and Purgatory," in *The Dawn of Modern Banking*, 1979.

Evil is the formal opposition to life; not as death, but as the refusal of otherwise. It appropriates the force of life as given, transforming itself as counter energy to any move for our salvation.[30]

If Evil of this denatured-nature is real and extra-terrestrial in its way, it is certainly susceptible to be recuperated and exploited in the interests of everyday political domination. Unlike the gods of the Greeks that had clay-feet, the empire of absolute *Evil* rests on solid economic-political foundations. Whatever the implications for the logical integrity of Baudrillard's comments, the point he draws next is well taken.

White Terror

The ambiguity of *Evil* is terrorizing for human consciousness, and that is its signature. The practice of terrorization by the state as with the U.S. War on Terror yields what he labels "White Terror": security measures routinely imposed on honest citizens, surveillance of normal action, no matter where or of what nature. Budgets be damned, no more services in airports, only security officers and spying cameras; no more access into banks, no more tellers at windows, only double safety doors and machines that speak—badly.

The true-story: modern progress as the ultimate good goes to its limit, then critical, finally ballistic; the result is a flip-back as *Evil* beyond repair. The emotion of being in *Evil* is then reinforced politically by declaring a war on it, the War on Terrorism, thus concretizing it, formally institutionalizing it, as the main-mechanism of social control. *White Terror* is the ultimate sign of the skill of the elite classes to turn any menace into an additional tool for domination.

The culprit in this scenario is hegemony as the global totalization of the good: the modern enlightenment dream has been achieved. None might oppose it because we are all accomplices, or almost; there are the disenfranchised, forced to work for the system, those for whom existence continues to be nasty and brutish, who suffer by day and die unnoticed by

30 *The Transformers: The Movie* (1986, Nelson Shin). The movie tagline was "Beyond Good. Beyond Evil. Beyond your wildest imagination." In the movie, the danger for the "Autobot" good-guys comes from the "Decepticons" bad-guys, because the latter have the remarkable ability to re-clone themselves endlessly, to resist destruction no matter how ingenious and determined the attack on behalf of high humanity. Although less anthropomorphic, Baudrillard's treatment of existence under conditions of mechanized commoditization of consumption fits this scenario remarkably well.

night. Statistically, this is the majority, but that makes no difference. There never was the least ambition favoring the majority as enlightenment inspiration.

The principle vector for the spread of hegemony is generalized-exchange; everything is of exchangeable value, open to trade at any time with anyone, known or stranger. Go to E-Bay, the market is universal: sex, marriage, adoption of children, houses, shoes, underwear, false teeth, reading glasses. Thanks to what is now elegantly labeled, the 'social media' revolution, this generalization goes to personhood, so that not just preferences or personal priorities, but also attitudes, sentiments, fears, insecurities, aberrations, perversions, which somehow render a person different; all of this is put on the web for generalized exchange: of a kiss, a hug, a pat on the butt, a one-night stand. Everything is available, on a discount at that, with little meaning beyond the act of its posting: not of its realization, but only of its announcement. As with the contemporary job market, the CV says it all; winning is nothing but a question of addresses, and nothing is easier to fake. The only cost involved is the duration of time for putting the message on the web as for sale, available, dateable, looking to buy, wanting to move, etc.; once on the virtual cloud, there is no further commitment beyond the exchange of tweets.

Given the considerable existential pain hegemony generates, what might be done? As far as Baudrillard could see: very little. Western enlightenment is based on the notion of humanity, of which universality of human being is the core. Achievement of that is supposedly assured by the technically assured generalized exchange described above; nothing is more important or, in that sense, different from anything else, or at least not much.

The discourse of globalization has now become total, internalizing even the notion of the negative; negativity in all its forms, whether cultured interrogation, sentimental complaint, or haphazard rant, all of that is just a different flavor of affirmative expression, another form of flash. This invalidates critical practice, since there is no alternative basis, no differentness against which to compare or contrast the given; everything is achieved. All is now equal, democratic, liberal, free; there are no *a priori* limits, because there is no history.

Not only is the elasticity of the human consciousness limited, but so is the resource world. To function, the capitalist motor must consume ever more energy, keeping the playing field flat, the grass green and trimmed, the lines of play well marked. Due to material limits, once pillaged and drained, much of the globe is left to deteriorate; those who remain behind go with it, into hell on earth. Still the capital machine turns and the limits of the sustainability of the system are further exceeded; the amount of green space is reduced, while the population is allowed to explode.

From Detroit to New Delhi, the effect of globalization is radical discrimination, separating those with a condo on the golf course of life from those in a hovel in an urban wasteland. As the squeeze intensifies for solid ground and the food and water to go with it, all the better-endowed class and ethnic in-groups are growing more hostile toward their out-groups, as if the problem were 'them' rather than 'us': their wanting to play in our park, rather than that the pleasure and comfort provided for the members of every advantaged closed club is too expensive, and not paid for by the members, but rather, imposed as indirect tax on the whole world. There is an unwillingness to accept accountability on the part of those with a superior class of life, who enjoy the privilege of plenty in a world of shortages. Why blame those born on the precarious side of existence, who want a better share of the action, if not the right to migrate to a green-zone of life. The real forest, diverse as it was, open for all, for the good of all, has been slashed and burned for centuries; progressively replaced with the false nature of concrete and sod, in sanitized, securitized, anonymous gated communities.

Bamboozled by Good

In the course of his career, Baudrillard passed from what we might call the fun phase of critical practice to the stage of expressed desperation. Having done so in general good faith and balanced demeanor is a sign of a remarkable stability of character. Neither chaser of fame nor empty polemicist, he ended up a famous public intellectual nonetheless. He focused on the unexpressed element of our collective existence, confronting the ineffably negative with uncompromising critical force. By the end, he judged that intellectual criticism, at least of the 20th century western variety, had outlived its utility, not in terms of personal justification of radical subjectivity as starting point, but in terms of societal change as end point. In a way, he died by announcing the obsolescence of his own way of being.

At a glance, the critical objective wears a Manichean mask: there is good and there is evil, with critique to expose the latter and propose the former. At the start of his career, Baudrillard supposed the world to be thus constructed and his critical mission, even if perhaps impossible, was pursuable; there was a certain truth to it. Also, in the France of his formal education, there was a particular version of right-sized-evil, against which the critical goods were to be marshaled: it was called "domination," opposition to which ought to be aimed at "liberation."

Domination is a political process, expression of the interests of the elite classes at the expense of the majority. There is a bouquet of forms of exploitation, oriented around the imposition of the obligation to work (while not living very well) on some, and the allocation of the privileges generated by that work, to those who do the allocating. When Baudrillard was a young man, one accepted that capital as mechanism was the motor force for social practices; to critique it, one might aim high, at the visible expressions of exploitation and social injustice: how Blacks, Women, Hispanics or Wage Laborers are treated, for instance; or one might aim low, at the economic base, exposing the machinations of capital: at the destabilizing organization of work undertaken in order to more rapidly concentrate the profits from the labor of the working classes to the benefit of the dominating classes. The range of action for critical practice was enormous and intellectual critics were busy as bees.

Like a difficult child maturing into a neurotic over-achieving adult, capital production over-delivered its promise; the opulent land of liberal-plenty has been reached. With freedom of expression and opportunity for all, critical practitioners are watching their role evaporate, or at least their audiences. In a final call for attention, Baudrillard put his finger on how this occurred and with what truly tragic consequences. Then he died.

Cybernetic Vortex

From his first visits to North America, including involvement with the Aspen and Big-Sur groups of avant-garde intellectuals, Baudrillard had become intrigued with the extreme accomplishment of the cybernetics movement which had taken hold in the U.S. following WWII. As it turned out, this was the opening into the computer age.

Cybernetics accelerated an advanced stage of the mechanization of work. Humans have been using machines for thousands of years, to simplify and multiply the physical component of human and animal labor. Initially, the resulting amplification of effort did not include the higher components of work, concerned with planning, decision making and fine-tuning, or the selection of décor, style, fit, for the product of the machine, or its adjustment in mid-stream. Mechanization was initially intended, rather, to assure both a multiplication of muscle power, and increased constancy of value for the products that were ultimately put into use.

With the earlier development of more effective motor forces, wind, water power, steam engines, and the rest, while over the centuries machines progressively took on the heavy-lifting of production, human beings continued to run the machines, controlling their startup, direction, pace, amplitude and intensity of action. But with the transition into the cybernetic age, at least in principle, the result was a world of marvelous mindless machines behind which was a progressively well informed, well-remunerated and capable human labor force. By WWII, increasingly complex webs of mechanized action were established, behind which the human labor force was reduced, as the number of industrial engineers of every specialty, along with administrators, managers and directors expanded exponentially.

Gradually, cybernetics revolutionized the structure of work. The key was the discovery and implementation of a logic of mechanical control for entire systems of functional machines. Rather than simply chaining the work of distinct machines for amplification of effort and efficiency, it was discovered that sensors attached to individual machines for regulative purposes (first stage feedback as single-mechanism control) could be linked into electronic webs of control (second stage feedback as cybernetic-systems management). By this process, the sensors were woven together, yielding a large information web, generating system-wide feedback of the overall state of productive action. This was the crucial step in full-scale automation, later modified by internal sensors for machines, yielding robotics, such as today describes the means of industrial activity for everything, from production of automobiles to the extraction of derivative chemicals from raw petroleum that is pumped out of the ground.

Cybernetics, then, is attention to feedback effects, by which the activity of a machine is monitored by sensors, with the information thus generated partly fed back into the mechanism, so as to alter or sustain, depending on the case, its mode of operation. Secondarily, more importantly, another part of that information is exchanged among machines in such a way that some distant mechanism decides the local activity of this or that mechanical element in the web. In this way, machines have progressively taken on the meta-function of self-control, and then of communication with other machines in a web or system, with a minimum of human mediation.

In industrial production, the human role has been progressively redefined; at first, rather than running them, men and women tended machines. As the process became more elaborate, it was necessary to develop meta-management machines, capable of processing a high volume of retained information, quickly, and then following templates, allocating feedback information to the components. This was achieved by the development of computer technology, with that elaboration now the evident technological aspect of everyday life, in our globalized industrial world.

Cybernetics as concept is the general-system as action. Hard-wired information webs, tying human action into self-governing modules, are today responsible for the most important functions of human experience: stock-markets, bank investing, air traffic control, arming, aiming and firing of aircraft drones, industrial production of food, and of course, the function for which such systems were developed in the first place, the manufacturing and marketing of products for everyday human use, from shoes to espresso machines.

When Baudrillard first arrived in the U.S., the cybernetic revolution was sweeping the industrial world like a fire storm; at first human workers were displaced from doing the most difficult work and they were better paid as a share of the benefits of that productivity. Next they were progressively let go from work, as the machines were found capable of functioning with control from greater and greater distance via technical outsourcing. As the seductive application of this system-logic progressed, the world of work was transformed from a site of physical labor, carried out by millions of workers, to a world under the domination of systems-engineers and business school executives, often miles if not continents away from the scene of activity. This was accompanied by round after round of technical-layoffs, as first, humans were replaced by machines at work, and then, those who held control and decision posts were replaced in turn.

In less than fifty-years, under the demand of global hegemony, the industrial world, in what are called economically advanced societies, has been evacuated of workers, as the needs of life are produced by systems of machines that are even capable of some degree of their own reproduction and improvement. Now in the 21st century, work-life in western societies has lost its rudder: it is not that, "the machines are defective; they are so efficient that there is nothing left to do with this life." At least as concerns work, the end is not just near, but achieved: "the obsolescence of humans has reached its terminal phase" (Baudrillard 2010a: 80).

According to Baudrillard, effectively immune to the traditional tools of critical practice, the human condition under global hegemony is beyond repair. More fluid than the oceans, the working of capital and its market continually concentrate gains from dehumanized production; relying on machines to such an extent that the basic mechanism of the liberal economy, the force of large capital, yields super-structural productivity as goods and services, with little significant intervention by human beings. Like advanced clothes washers, the productive working of capital is now a direct drive mechanism; all humans can do is foul up the timing.

Neither economic nor political in the usual sense, the global market as hegemony marks an "anthropological and metaphysical" revolution; "and it is a final revolution—there is nothing beyond it" (Baudrillard 2010a: 80). The result is well known: industrial cheese, industrial milk, industrial chickens, industrial eggs, industrial feed for industrial cows, etc. The menace is that while the industrial sector now produces only marginally organic products, the 'human interface'—we who eat the eggs, milk, cheese and hamburger—are at least for the moment still fully organic, and thus not necessarily equipped to survive by eating all that industrial stuff. There is no internal cycle of bio-responsive feedback associated with the mechanical material cycling of cybernetics. As bio-glitches are inevitable, the result is now a lethal threat to the well-being of unfortunate consumers.

Markets Make Consumers

Are you more than a niche marker in a capital market? The threat is epitomized by planned obsolescence, which can only succeed to the extent that most of our 'free' consumer desires are produced and reproduced by the same forces that make and sell the products on which we depend. Based on demographic profiling that includes you, a new gadget of some kind, from toothbrush to car, is timed to replace a supposedly less useful or poorly designed current one which those in 'your category' already use and appreciated. Although not conscious for you, but very much so for the market makers, the item is planned to be replaced with something that looks a bit different, performs similarly and is, in its turn, sabotaged by a pre-timed death.

The day the new one arrives on the market, as you feel the first temptation to upgrade, a next one is already being tested, ready to go as high-priced replacement when the planned disintegration of the current one is realized. This is linked to hardware design, aimed also at strategic breakdown, carefully coordinated with production cycles, with you and others in your 'purchasing class' paying the bill.

Delivering in this way ever more superficially spectacular gadgets and fixes, the market has most of us hooked. Discontinuing use of a technical gismo like a touch-sensitive, app-loaded phone, is as difficult as for a crack-addict before his dealer; and the positive effect, the fun-phase of the product is timed to expire quickly, leaving little choice than to return to the trader's den for more if not better, at your cost.

Why do you act? Because of the atmosphere of splendor as force of seduction that surrounds the process: you will be beautiful, powerful, potent, irresistible, listened too, admired. Your desire will be realized, if only you buy it; so you do. Down deep, do you really seek beauty of that sort, or power, potency, seduction, audience or admiration? Probably not; what you desire is to get on well with others and feel good about yourself: yet what commercial product can deliver self-esteem or social contentment? The lotto-ticket advertisement never focuses on serenity as its mega-payoff. Baudrillard refers to this as the, "hyperrealization of desire": death-dealing addiction thanks to an "overexposure to happiness" (2010a: 85).

In our mechanized age, the notion of incomplete is denied; every need shall be met, or else. Because of the open-ended nature of the concept, this invalidates the intention of a fulfilling life as possibility. Machines can not deal with the magical, the mysterious, the authentically enticing. The solution to the empty feeling of loneliness at meal time, alone in the kitchen, is not to change the way one relates to other human beings, but to replace the table with a marble bar or kitchen island. What can be cozier than carry-home stir-fry, eaten out of plastic containers, while sitting alone on a barstool in one's own kitchen? Near a refrigerator charged with beer by the barrel and wine by the box, in front of a supersized screen of non-stop junk images, the final solution is evident: dial-up pizza. Those well-enough endowed to read this paragraph are alone in the equivalent of a sensitivity-sauna of opulence, yet forced to play exclusively with themselves.

Baudrillard inquires: "what are you doing after the orgy?" Evidently, one falls into a "schizophrenic farce" (2010a: 86). The difference between the TV version and the reality of desperate housewives is that real ones are alone, eating lean-cuisine off synthetic marble. The farce is on the television screen, the schizophrenic truth is the kitchen The result is a "symbolic fracture," of which the primary attribute is despair: of having all, yet being nothing and nobody.

Bottoming out this way required serious effort; not just the planned obsolescence of your computer or toaster or microwave, but the exhaustion of the core values of enlightenment humanism. The list is long, rendering the tragedy profound: obsolescence of reason, of history, or work, of desire; of imagination, individuality, otherness, reality. And according to Baudrillard, even of death (2010a: 88).

Rogue Events

We live a crisis not of breakdown or lack but of saturation and plenitude. Like French geese that are fed with a funnel, we are stuffed with enough goods to kill us; in the case of the geese, this assures that before dropping beneath the weight of artificially induced obesity, they develop a bloated, fat-intoxicated liver, which when cut from their guts, will be market as the luxury, *foie gras*. Humans do this voluntarily, at special sites of toxification: shopping centers, where rather than bloated to the bursting point with only food, westerners are transformed into credit-card debt-slaves in the pursuit of consumer happiness.

Who can explain that in the economically developed west, the major form of malnutrition is from over-consumption of calories? Even the elites see this for what it is and yet can only fight it by the even more devastating malediction of anorexia: as a trademark bourgeois disease, driven by the obsession that some is not enough, the solution is to throw up (or have a garage sale) to make room for ever more, of which there will never be enough to fill the hollow of the soul.

Having reduced personal status to market performance, it is no surprise that the reference image for bourgeois kids is the fiberglass dummy in the window of the mall boutique. Were it even that real; now the image is palpably, visibly, digitally manufactured and altered on screen, involving elements of humanoid-features with little more reality than Mr. Potato Head; yet that is the image-setter for the youth of later modernity.

There is nothing to be done from beyond the system; with globalization as hegemonic ideology, there is no outside from which to launch the attack. If change is to arise, it must be from within. Thus the justice in one of Baudrillard's rare affirmative suggestions: beware of *rogue events* (Baudrillard 2010a: 90).

The crumbling of the Twin Towers in 2001 represented metaphorically for him the entropic collapse of the late-modern, "self-referencing" discourse of progress. It also showed the impossibility of revolution in the conventional sense. Pushed to the limit by hubris of good 'n plenty; if there is no vector for change for a mass-world without form or causal logic, the only result of the heart-felt sensation that this really is a sick situation is the transformation of oppositional energy into the ultimate "schizophrenic farce" called terrorism.

Faced with a major dilemma for which no logical response is available, human beings invariably come up with an illogical response. What is labeled terrorism is of that nature. Everything negative in the old sense "has now become parody"; the reality of television invaded a campground in Norway in 2011, and seventy-seven human beings, mostly teenagers and young adults, were murdered in cold blood. Back in the 1960s, when Truman Capote wrote a small scale version of that kind of drama into life, there was a faint glimmer of shock signaling moral rectitude. Now a half century later, incidents of this kind are treated with public moral indignation, that can easily be insincere: what did they do to deserve this, asks the inner voice; who gets the pay off from it asks the twitter voice; who buys the movie-writes asks the trash-magazine reporter.

Without history, rogue events are capricious. They are also the work of the powerless, involving the "turning of the weapons of power against themselves" (Baudrillard 2010a: 90). The lack of sympathy for such events is due to their unreality; "the real only exists to the extent that we can intervene in it" (Baudrillard 2010a: 91). Terrorism is not business as usual; it must be creative: the more ghastly, the better.

Iconizing the World Trade Center implosion, Baudrillard remarked as to the "extreme originality of this symbolic act" (2010a: 93); to capture so much of the heart of the issue of hegemony and then have it shatter, live and direct, on television. Undoubtedly, the other aims that day, directed at Washington DC, were only distraction, the success or failure of which contributed a look of the ordinary to an extraordinary event. "The master-stroke of the terrorists" (2010a: 93) was to pull this off with so few means, prepared for in such an undramatic fashion... with larger than life results.

The issue is not about "spectacular terrorism," concerning, rather, terror as such, "as an infiltration, an internal convulsion, a form of power fighting itself" (2010a: 94). Which is why Baudrillard can assure us: "we know that terrorism will not overthrow the world order"(2010a: 95). The bad news is that being latent and virulent, a sort of cancerous, self-propagating infection, triggered in subtle ways, this leads to deterioration of lesser structures, which undermine major structures. Terror is now as depersonalized as is the hegemony which it combats, such that, paradoxically, as the end of Bin Laden shows, "Terror does not exactly need terrorists now either" (2010a: 95). We are doing it all to ourselves.

Baudrillard's Method

Just what is there to say of Baudrillard's method? According to the title of this chapter, his critical practice is an exercise in core-extraction. Beyond only a literary figure, this metaphor is more realist than not. It fits very well to import an image concerned with drilling beneath the crust of the evident to see what the past history, with its successive layerings and convulsive erosions can tell us about the shaky grounds of our understanding. This implies the study of the present land-forms that establish the contours for the field of being in which the critic is working, achieved by a penetrating unearthing, as cycles of discovery, each deeper than the previous.

If Baudrillard's critical method were only that, then we could say that he effectively borrowed a certain dimension of the Foucauldian archaeological method. But that would leave out history, which, after all, plays an essential role in the historical-materialist method. Returning to the core-extraction process, we know that even if what is extracted is a cross-section plug of the layers of material beneath the ordinary, the meaning of the successive layers is first and foremost that of succession, which signals a history of cumulative effects. This means that the deeper one goes beneath the evident, the further back historically one goes in the process, such that history is a built-in attribute of this form or sub-structural study and on that basis is different by intention, than was the work of Foucault.

Baudrillard worked empirically as a sociologist and thus, for him, history was a parameter of the present. In turn, that historicity of the presently-evident is understood by plunging beneath it with disciplined restraint, to explore the way a set of historical processes accumulate (accrete), then become materialized as a present social form. But, the discussion must begin and end with the evident, even if the middle of a study is concerned with its underlying and historically anterior evidence. On that basis I judge his working method to have been of historical-materialist inspiration, even if the texts (other than the first one associated with his doctoral thesis) were largely expository and narrative in form.

Returning again to the core-extraction image, I must reiterate a point raised earlier: the challenge with the use of the H-M method as an approach to identifying the causal explanation of social forms is to decide how far deep and back to look. This uncertain aspect of the exercise contributes to the inherent ambiguity of critique.

With a brief glance at Foucault, we saw that he died practically in mid-sentence, as he was immersed in the study of the history of sexuality as indicator of what he referred to as 'bio-politics,' indicating as I have also discussed previously, the extent to which use of this method is not an impossible mission to undertake, but only to end. Nonetheless, that final adieu was telling in so far as it demonstrated what he took to be the bedrock on which the various historical accumulations that interested him, lay: the biological condition of human beings, as the basis for a symbolically organized institutional world.

For Foucault, the result was a plenitude of human bodies (now about seven billion of us) ensnared by societal organization, as a jousting contest for supremacy among various power/knowledge disciplines and professions, oriented around the domination of existence: by way of the politics of the human body (and of the natural environment as general bio-form), as those bio-politics drive social action, serving as the basis of norms, setting the limits on moral boundaries, to define deviance in general—with life and death consequences. With his research, he backed this up to the 18th century, the classic age, as he put it, when under the sway of the idea of enlightened progress, via ways of understanding, the logic of disciplines and professions as property, asserting control over ideas and techniques of their application, first formally developed.

Quite differently, the work of Baudrillard achieved an amazingly personal effect by the way he placed it on a bedrock that is immanently collective and normative in nature, linked first to modernity (which I date as having begun about ten centuries back), later filtered by the renaissance (about five centuries back), and then finalized in the wake of the enlightenment (about two and one-half centuries back). In this way, he was clearly expressing in practice Horkheimer's angst as articulated in his study of the bourgeois philosophy of history (see Chapter One).

Baudrillard focused in the present, on technically objectified domination: as conditioned, generated, imposed and sustained by the blinding effect of the false belief in the 'new' and linked with the promise of ever more reassuring progress, thus assuring freedom beyond either necessity or obligation. In this process, while surely accepting that disciplines and professions played a role, he saw this as less a cause of the process than as one of its evident effects.

This brings to light a rather interesting point about the transfer of cultural power, if you will, from modernity, to renaissance, and finally to enlightenment and beyond. Modernity began as a way of organizing international cooperation (for war-making via the crusades, unfortunately, but that was as it was); this demonstrated that warring princes might gain more from pooling their forces than from destructive warfare among them; or at least it was better for domestic populations since the crusader strategy is mostly an exercise in outsourcing brutal violence.

With the enlightenment, the focus shifted to the human individual, then newly recognized as competent to understand and thus judge on her own, without recourse to institutional authority. This thread weakened the monopoly of the collective over the individual, opening the way for a new mode of communal integration to accede to prominence, provided famously by capital market processes. This ultimately returned violence to the internal relations of the West, but shifted its orientation from horizontal to vertical; thus giving rise to the social-class effect as we know it today, which, at least at the beginning, was considered progress over feudalism.

Still, five centuries ago, the early renaissance person was a rather complete creature, a mixture of aesthetic and rational dispositions, a work-of-art that could get work done as well. However, with the ensuing industrialization of enlightenment, the emphasis shifted further, to a very particular form of mechanical determination, placing in brackets, if not in doubt, the justice of believing one's own eyes. This allowed the coming to fruition of the non-utopian dream of the bourgeois philosophy of history: a world of instrumentally rational individuals, indifferent to harmony, beauty and, for that matter, justice; accepting as if given in advance the various levels of entitlement enjoyment, or suffering, depending on who one was. As if entitlement at birth was the real criteria for private property. The deceit-driven Machiavellian aspect of this development was needed to assure stable governance, in a western world henceforth in denial about the nature of the whole person.

And ever after it has been. To now, when under conditions determined according to his own narrative, in the vortex of alienation due to this ultimate evil driven by modern success, Baudrillard dropped from life; not just into a grave, but rather into a state of ambiguity, taking us, his readers, along.[31]

---

31 As we exit this chapter, it is difficult not to consider Baudrillard at the gates of the hereafter, heralded forward not by Gabriel, but rather by the angel of history described allegorically by Walter Benjamin in his famous (9th) *Thesis on the Philosophy of History* (1968), in which he alludes to the Paul Klee painting, *Angelus Novus* (1920); a Benjamin who, without denying the power of history, refused to envision it as progress, because (6th Thesis): "To articulate the past historically does not mean to recognize it 'the way it really was.' It means to seize hold of a memory as it flashes up at a moment of danger" (p. 255). I will discuss his powerful meta-mythic message again in Chapter Seven, on Hayden White.

CHAPTER SIX

EAGLETON: LITERARY CRITIC – LITERATURE OR CRITICISM?

London's Most Loved Literary Critic

Splitting himself three ways, between religious writing, literary criticism and socialist liberation appeals, Terry Eagleton, the "High Priest of Lit-Crit,"[1] is a particularly buoyant Marxist Romantic. While perhaps an existential contradiction, this may also reveal the secret of his highly original critical technique: confessional penance in advance of expressed thought, minimizing the smoke from his militant pitch. His opening the door to revolutionary praxis with the keys to the kingdom of heaven may be intended to assure that he will not be condemned for calling out rebellion.

What does it say if one is forever preaching social ferment to the world, in favor of a crusade of humanist compassion, demanding better treatment of the many as a most generous act of the favored few, with an image of Jesus that practically glows in the dark on one of his shoulders and Karl Marx's bearded face on the other? Marx claimed that religion was the opiate of the masses, and as a self-identified Marxist, few are more indomitable than Eagleton. Yet he has been writing on religion as long as about Marx, as if there is something there from which even a radical leftist apparatchik might profit.[2]

---

[1] "High priest of Lit Crit." Title of article by Nicholas Wroe in *The Guardian*, London (1 February 2002), where he reviewed Eagleton's book, *The Gatekeeper: A Memoir* (2001); introducing Eagleton as, "Britain's best-known academic rebel and literary critic, and as a prominent and unrepentant Marxist revolutionary, Eagleton has a history of placing himself above the parapet and is well used to the abuse that is periodically heaped upon him." http://www.guardian.co.uk/books/2002/feb/02/academicexperts.highereducation.

[2] Throughout his career, Eagleton has fascinated his public by weaving together the holy issue and the revolutionary one. During his student days, he was a member of a Catholic inspired, leftist inclined, political group that put out a short-lived review, *Slant*. Some of the articles he published there were: "Why We Are Still in the Church" (1967); "Language, Reality and the Eucharist" (1968); and "Priesthood and Leninism" (1969). More recent publications include: *Jesus Christ: The Gospels* (*Revolutions*), 2007a; *Reason, Faith, and Revolution: Reflections on the God Debate*, 2009.

If pages published and presumably read by the better-educated English speaking population, count, he is particularly trendy among the London newspaper reading elite. His critical words are legend, his well-articulated thumbnail vignettes in the Sunday editions capable of pinning the most effete authors to the breakfast tables of the finest English manors; all done in a way that complements British humor, "*sans limit*". This is in addition to his carefully narrated, endlessly entertaining book-length studies that appear on university student reading lists everywhere in the English speaking world.

What does all this activity say and more importantly, what movement arrives in its wake? Is Eagleton's critical enterprise more than erudite entertainment, a form of nebulous, bookish boogie by a cross-bearing English equivalent of a dancing Russian unorthodox bear?

According to one of the dozens of web-pages that carry his words or discuss his talks and publications, Eagleton is email adverse; at least until recently, those who cared enough had to deal with him in longhand via the Royal Mail.[3] This was apparently effective, since, whatever else is to be said about what he writes, he shows little sign of input from others, much less overt collaboration. Eagleton is a one-man show who has managed to turn the web-space of some very respectable institutions such as the *Guardian of London* and the *London Review of Books* (LRB) into something equivalent to his personal blog.

In the past twenty years, he has published more than fifty book reviews and critical essays in both the *Guardian* and the *LRB*, which is but the tip of the iceberg; because of the overtly polemic style of his positions, he also generates an enormous volume of rejoinders and idiomatic online response. Assuming that the more brutal comments are censored and that his acrid words stimulate many unconscionable comments, the volume of response to his material must be beyond measure. This plays into the tabloid aspect of the London press; competing with the Murdock machine takes something a bit outrageous and Eagleton is an ideal marketing item in that sense.

His surefire willingness to take on any subject is a sign of what in Paris is laconically referred to as, *vastes connaissances*; in New York, the same

---

3 Eagleton's insistence on the use of Royal mail and not e-mail (which I am pleased to have discovered has changed just as this book was going to press) was certified by the contact-instruction attached to his University of Lancaster Faculty Page: "Eagleton, Terry: Distinguished Professor of English Literature: no _email@please see postal address on staff page." http://www.lancs.ac.uk/fass/english/profiles.

limitless opinionatedness is labeled a know-it-all. Whatever the edge of his written style, to witness him in action renders a quite different effect. Since he appears almost as often on YouTube as in the London press, for those who have the time, it is easy to see how he comes across on stage: like a bewhiskered uncle in a rocking chain. One very distinguished site of such appearances is hosted by the University of Edinburgh, where he has been invited to present lectures oriented by his writings. Although faulted for using such occasions for a relentless soft-sell of his books, what else is the choice in a world where either one is a fully commoditized author or one starves for lack of recognition? Still, it is difficult to see how Eagleton as market commodity is the proper carrying principle for a social-revolutionary call against the excesses of capital.

Yet again on YouTube, in one of his more surprising ethical positions on behalf of the downtrodden, we see his popularity; leaving the billions of starving and exploited folks around the world to fend for themselves, he has taken to defending the good name of none other than God! Invited by that Edinburgh bastion of Scottish rationality, the University of Edinburgh's Gifford Lecture Series to expound on "The God Debate," he went out of his way to argue about the rationalist position, that the 'spiritual claim' common to contemporary religion is unfounded on a 'material basis.' He was confident about this since, as he sees it, the rationalist claim is unfounded on a 'spiritual basis' as well: which is just fine since he also contends that the rationalist claim has nothing to do with faith anyway. While the result of debate on that issue is the usual standoff, thus leaving the inscrutability of God intact for another day, the fact of having talked his way calmly and cleverly around the God-issue for forty-five minutes did not go unnoticed. At the time of this writing, his video of that presentation about the justice of God, preserved for eternity in cloud-space, had been viewed more than 32,300 times and still counting![4]

That is not a record by any stretch for the University of Edinburgh site; a few years back, a fellow that Eagleton proudly admires, Noam Chomsky, was invited to speak in recognition of the work of the then recently deceased Edward Saïd. Chomsky of course is more thoughtful than most London literary critics; still it is remarkable to note that his lecture-video has been viewed nearly 50,000 times. While there is an evident difference

---

[4] *The God Debate: Eagleton on YouTube.* http://www.youtube.com/watch?v=QCqHnwIR1PY.

in the power of the position and discourse for a Chomsky over Eagleton, Eagleton makes up ground with sheer volume.[5]

In the Beginning, Lacking Uniform

In the beginning for Eagleton there was neither the word much less the opportunity to be heard had there been one; born in Salford, England (1943) of an Irish working-class family, it was surely more likely that he would have married the pub-owner's daughter, had six children and died young from cirrhosis of the liver, than to study at Cambridge and become a professor at Oxford. However, even in England, social-genetic accidents of Eagleton's type are possible. By hard work and feigned indifference to the class system, he managed to mount the obstacles between where he started, in the English out-lands and where he arrived, at Oxford, achieving from there a rare celebrity status, as among the best known literary critics in London.

Perhaps his under-privileged social class beginning explains his edge; in keeping with what we saw with Voltaire, Schiller, Foucault and Baudrillard before him, a key to being critically sensitive is to somehow arrive at the center of accomplishment after having begun in the wrong part of town. Contributing to the lucidity of critical insights can also lead to powerful pessimism and a deep distrust of accomplishment, even one's own. While that is not a terminally negative state for an active critic, it can easily turn attention away from institutional issues and structural forces, replaced as critical targets by isolated individuals or practices that are products of those structures and forces. When ordinary folks drown in a rampaging river, the point is not to blame the water but rather to call into question the work of the human damn designers.

Now seventy-years old, Eagleton is formally retired; but not entirely happily so, since with another young child by a relatively new wife, he could use a steady paycheck. We know some of these things about him from interviews where, under heavy duress, he now and again lets slip a bit of personal information. But he clearly prefers to keep his own counsel.

[5] The University of Edinburgh provides a remarkable forum for high quality conferences on the full range of issues, from politics to God. As a sign of respect for Chomsky, not for what he said about Saïd but as general testimonial, in his "Death of the Intellectual" article in *Red Pepper Magazine* (London, 2008), Eagleton refers to Chomsky as "one of the 20th century's greatest public intellectuals."

Given the contradictions of class, caste, religion, and nationality that have and continue to mark his life, and the enormous spectrum of topics that he has addressed in his writings, Eagleton is a critic who in turn draws criticism from all fronts. Some hoped that this might clear when, at age sixty, he published his memoirs; he refused to speak of autobiography, since, according to him, that is too prone to self-serving publicity. The result, a book titled *The Gatekeeper* (Eagleton 2002), disappointed many admirers and critics alike. The content revealed little about him other than that the way he engages in auto-biographical self-promotion is by practicing the selective-memory of the memoir, as if it were the full disclosure of biography.[6]

Criticism vs. History?

Eagleton's mystery, then, concerns what? What is his motive or intention? As a young man, having found himself as a student at Cambridge on the way to a doctorate (1968), he came under the influence of a prominent socialist critic, Raymond Williams.[7] Williams approached literature as more than simply the subjective expression of an artistic moment; he believed that authorship is always an expression, however veiled, of the historical conditions and situation of the author. Williams' position suggests a Marxist aesthetic: that 'art,' creativity, is issue of work done collectively, in community, about society, with the distinction of the creator linked to the originality of the forms of expression of those underlying dynamics; not as if individual originality is the sole source of that dynamic origin.

Following Williams, Eagleton turned against the then largely accepted New Criticism movement that was all the rage—and not to be confused

[6] Unrevealing Memoir: for details on what some consider the disappointing quality of Eagleton's unrevealing memoirs, see Wroe (2002). As reported in the same article, if only ironically and with evident intention to discredit, the review of this book in the *London Daily Mail* opened with the announcement (according to Eagleton) that he was "in danger of becoming a national institution." Eagleton's retort was, "But when the *Mail* says nice things about you, it makes you think."

[7] Raymond Williams was on faculty at Cambridge when Eagleton met him; concerned with the balance between practices and ideas in explaining social movements, Williams was strongly influenced by Gramsci. This drew him to revolutionary drama, where his studies of Ibsen, George Orwell and others were compelling. For a sample of this line of work, see his, "English Brecht," a review of a volume of, *Collected Plays by Bertolt Brecht* (1981).

with New History, centered in France, amounting in a way to its opposite and about which Eagleton seems to have been uninformed.[8]

In the vulgar sense, New Criticism was a somewhat 'literature for literature's sake' position: one treats a work from within its self-asserted frame, without reference to the exterior 'real world' at the time of the writing, much less to the situation or biography of the author or anything else. If generalized to all aesthetic activity, one argues that rather than expression of socio-historic cultural forces, the meaning of texts, art works and the creative act in general, is a pure ludic expression (conscious or unconsciously) of the momentary, unbounded individuality of author as creator.

As discussed in Chapter One, in connection with the work of Teresa Ebert, to take literature, art in general, as a sign concerning the under or super-structures of culture, establishes it as a fine venue for cultural criticism. Exploring that possibility was a mark of his mentor, Williams, as it became also rather quickly for Eagleton. However, the danger in this is ideological: since it is not possible to study everything, when applying the standard of the 'larger cultural significance' to a critical study of some creative work, the needed selectivity about what of peripheral content to include or downplay is often dictated by prejudice. Thus, even when couched in the language of humanity, potentially coming across as issue of dogmatism rather than logic, this mode of activity exposes the critic to counterattack on difficult to deflect formal grounds.

From there we spot an issue that critics of Eagleton might judiciously discuss. He particularly enjoys panning his 19th century predecessor, Matthew Arnold, who filled the shoes as warden of literary criticism in London under Queen Victoria. Eagleton guns at Arnold frequently, as an English-royalist-imperialist-cultural apologist, as if he had been personally responsible for generating with his writings the reactionary, conservative political line that characterized colonialist England in the 1860s.

In 1967, with Stuart Hall and Edward Thompson, Williams published the *New Left May Day Manifesto*, which continues to serve as a nostalgia alert for the London progressive movement.

[8] New History. Sometimes also referred to as Total History, this was a movement initiated by French Historians in the 1960s, away from exclusive focus on Great Personage or facts 'n dates based narratives, as a basis for historical understanding. Foucault was occasionally attributed paternity for this movement, which he denied. This movement was associated with a certain thread of French Annals epistemology. For a survey on the project, see Jacques Le Goff, Roger Chartier and Jacques Revel (1978).

While it is true that Arnold supported the English imperial politics of his age, he was hardly responsible for their content.

As for Arnold, one might well argue, that in doing what he did in the political sense, he was at least honest; not only admitting his intention in his writings, but claiming that it was the duty of "*littéraires*" to use their skill of authorship in a fashion that would help solidify national unity and firmness of mission among the people. This is the manifest point when saluting a flag or singing a national anthem; Arnold went further, arguing that within any country, the same nationalistic fidelity should pertain for literature and criticism in general.[9]

Must art always be patriotic? If this is so, then there would never be justification for oppositional literature by the nationals of any country. Since his teacher, Raymond Williams, was adamantly opposed to this view, following that lead, Eagleton attempted to express it in his critical work. The question is: how well did he do?

During the 20th century, a bit in advance of Eagleton, the German playwright Bertolt Brecht (1898–1956) applied a critical strategy quite the opposite of Arnold, favoring a progressive position rather than a conservative political objective. When called for, Brecht was convinced of the rightness of staging revolutionary theater; that the mission of authorship is not just to present the truth about subjugation in full view of the socially oppressed, but to do so in such a fashion that might stimulate movement for change.[10]

Independent of his considerable literary expertise, as a political actor, Matthew Arnold represented the politically respectable face of the cultural critical spectrum: according to him, the role of informed authorship is to overtly support and enhance the legitimacy of society and state.

Following Williams and in keeping with Brecht, as a self-announced supporter of liberty and equality, Eagleton opposed Arnold's position and goes on about it often. Yet on methodological grounds, even if aimed at audiences on opposite sides of the political aisle, the conservative Arnold and the socialist Eagleton worked with a very similar style, drawing material from the texts that they put under scrutiny to back what appears to

---

[9] For a sample of Matthew Arnold's work, see his *Essays in Criticism: Second Series* (1911/1888).

[10] Brecht texts that continue to inspire readers around the world include, *Galileo* (1966/1938: revised by Brecht for a first staging in the U.S. in 1947), along with *Mother Courage* (1939).

have been a forgone, and largely historically conditioned, political position.[11]

Turning the Eagleton critique back on Eagleton himself, we see numerous zones of ambiguity: a bit out of focus on social class tension; excessively general about what to alter if revolutionary praxis is the point; snared in a ponderous struggle between Christian pacific submission to the vicissitudes of necessity and the Marxist call for mobilization and change no matter what. Above all, working from a descriptive base largely ungrounded in theory, and resisting the use of some integrating logical model, most of his writings and interviews come across as so many bowls of potato-soup.

In his memoirs, he might have taken the opportunity to explain himself a bit, providing his readers with insight into the hidden groundings of his endlessly agitated critique. Alas, rather than furnishing material with which to better appreciate his intentions, with his memoirs he held to an imperious line of auto-referentiality, disguising his personal details with allusion (as *Gatekeeper*), as if he were not a subject of history at all, even if those whose writings he discusses supposedly are (Eagleton 2002).

This issue turns on a question of method of course, and by that on critique within history. While there is a manifest difference in manner of work between Arnold and Brecht, in keeping with the general view of Williams, this is easily explained. When Arnold was at his prime in the second half of the 19th century, the historical-materialist method developed by Marx was still more or less reserved for the study of the economy of capital. Its larger utility was not yet diffused and Arnold can not be faulted for failing to better appreciate the determinant potential of this method for his critical practice. By mid 20th century, this had shifted and Brecht, for example, was not just conscious of what he might do, but determined to put that method into practice, in formulating a theatrical aesthetic with social change as manifest prospective. By virtue of his student influences from Williams, at least as practice if not in theory, Eagleton also came to appreciate the historical-materialist call. It is still unclear, however, if he fully realizes the power of that method, and its potential for the mission he set for himself.

11 This argument about the appropriate political role for authors is related to the distinction that Kant ("What is Enlightenment?" 2007/1784) drew in that famous discussion of the public versus private role of the intellectual under the Enlightenment; a text that, Foucault used as the basis for one of his own better remembered essays ("What is Critique?" 2007/1978).

Self-Denial or Self-Deception?

Given his working-class roots it is reasonable that Eagleton would be agitated about academic institutions and disciplines. Having been an uneasy student at Cambridge, much later on, when leaving his professorial post after nine years at Oxford in 2001, he confided that he probably should have left much earlier, admitting that, "one of the least creditable reasons I stayed within Oxbridge was to prove to the bastards that I could" (Adams 2007).

Eagleton's institutional denial makes it difficult to find a solid bench before which to try him. He speaks of history, but under questioning and much as with Foucault, insists that he is neither a historian, philosopher nor social scientist. Yet his texts are salted with references that suggest a grounded judgment based on solid, deeper logic. If there is any, we should find it in that most famous of his books, the one that first set his global reputation, selling since 1983 at least a million copies: *Literary Theory: an Introduction* (Eagleton 2008a/1983).

Theory?

Even if dating from a long-generation ago, given that he just put out a new anniversary edition with a couple of added elements, what his *Theory* book says about him is evidently still pertinent. Accordingly, Eagleton pursued two objectives: to demonstrate the emptiness of all prior as well as then dominant literary-intellectual movements, and to argue that this failing of literature was less the problem than was its recurrent use as a device by which to colonize the minds of the young and innocent in keeping with the oppressive intention incarnated in the dominant ideology of the ruling class. While he offers few propositions for how to fix the affair, apparently once beyond London, the larger western world is safe: he considered that worrisome form of ideological domination via misdirected literary programming to be uniquely English in both origin and deployment.

Whatever the danger of language, the importance of theory was, for him, evident: without it, "we would not know what a literary-work was in the first place" (Eagleton 2008a/1983:xi). But a theory is not a movement: intellectual movements are mostly expressions of a "literary cannon," which is a nationalist construction hidden within which may be some malevolent ideology, ready to seduce and mislead the common mind.

Such movements often signal marking-contests among academics, such as with New Criticism, as the veiled attempt by historians to "erase the distinction between literary and non-literary works" (Eagleton 2008/1983:x) or, Reception Theory, the effort to extract the meaning of writings from the hands of authorship, with the message justified by the way a text engages or enlivens the "power of the reader" (Eagleton 2008a/1983:ix).

Working in the shadow of Raymond Williams, Eagleton was convinced that whatever the force of literature, it was definitely not "a kind of self-referential language," and something beyond the isolated text is needed to catalyze emergence of meaning (Eagleton 2008a/1983: 7). While with literary raw material, potentially anything goes, Eagleton was clear that the New York City telephone book is disqualified; still we have the question as to the difference between a good book and a simple mass of words.[12]

English on Trial

Before taking on the various unattractive literary-intellectual movements that he found littering the landscape of the humanities, Eagleton fixed his sites on "English," not just about the language as an expression of class, but the language as a way to shape people to better cohere with the ways of a class dominating society. As Eagleton judged it, the result over the past couple of centuries in England was the emergence of "a crassly philistine utilitarianism... fetishizing fact," condemning "art as unprofitable," and "converting human life into wage-slavery" (Eagleton 2008a/1983: 17).

The fault in all this was evaluated to be nothing less than literature, because, "literature, in the meaning of the word we have inherited, is an ideology" (Eagleton 2008a/1983: 19). This 'inheritance' refers to the 19th century, when he believed the true danger of English books assumed full force. The path was tight: literature served as "social cement," with English studies "constructed as a field of study to carry this ideological burden," drawing on the work of many authors of whom, "the key figure was Matthew Arnold" (Eagleton 2008a/1983: 21). Sold as protection against "philistine devaluing" of grammar and orthography, the result was a

[12] As demonstrated by the unending efforts just to make sense of the original text on the issue, namely Aristotle's *Poetics* (1997/~335BC), establishing the criteria by which to judge literature quality or even identify it is a puzzle beyond measure. See, for example, the anthology edited by Elder Olson, *Aristotle's "Poetics" and English Literature: A Collection of Critical Essays* (1965), with essays on Aristotle that date from the mid 18th century.

generation of "essential Englishness," based on having read and passively absorbed the ideological content of just the right works of literature (Eagleton 2008a/1983: 28–32). According to Eagleton, what Kitchener did with rifles in India, Matthew Arnold and other Oxford Professors accomplished domestically with their books and teachings: snuffing out rebellion against the interests of The Crown by colonizing the consciousness of unwary students with crass royalist-bourgeois ideology.[13]

Even if the perspective is negative, there is a subtle British ethnocentric celebration hidden beneath this manifestly negative talk about the need to "fortify English" against foreign invasion, particularly "French." Since Eagleton brings this up, the issue of national linguistic mentalities in Europe warrants a further word.[14] As modes of semantic construction for working the world into words, we perceive an important distinction between the English manner, in comparison to the French or German. At the level of metaphoric construction, it is my postulate that: Englishness is class-organization as adjectivization, as a lovely force of well-ordered, endlessly modified wordiness, parading in long lines across the page of time; Frenchness, on the other hand, is about sensual-extension via

---

13 Horatio Herbert Kitchener (24 June 1850 – 5 June 1916), 1st Earl Kitchener, was an Irish-born British Field Marshal who won fame for his imperial campaigns and later played a central role in the early part of the First World War, although he died halfway through it, when the ship taking him to negotiate with Russia was mysteriously sunk. He won fame in 1898 for securing control of the Sudan, after which he was given the title Lord Kitchener of Khartoum; back in London as Secretary of State for War, he miffed the general staff by ordering two-million rifles for WWI, from America, which arrived late, and then without bullets, which he may have overlooked ordering (pressure can do that to anyone); thus the fame of the Kitchener Rifle… assuming you bring your own powder.

14 Not everyone agrees on the reality of 'national mentalities'; while it seems to be a descriptively useful notion for trans-cultural studies of India compared to France, or Germany with China, its emblematic nature renders it empirically evasive. One of the more celebrated British intellectuals who stressed the importance of the notion was Alfred North Whitehead. In a still-read text, *The Aims of Education* (1923/1929), he expressed it the following ways: "Every language embodies a definite type of mentality, and two languages necessarily display to the pupil some contrast between their two types (p. 69); "Language is the incarnation of the mentality of the race which fashions it. Every phrase and word embodies some habitual idea of men and women as they ploughed their fields, tended their homes, and built their cities. For this reason there are no true synonyms as between words and phrases in different languages" (p. 71–2); "The Roman Empire and the mentality which created it absorbed the genius of Rome. … [and] The function of Latin literature is its expression of Rome" (p. 73–4).

Another example of its use which includes an outline of how it is understood, see Alon Confino (1997). Mentalities was central to one phase of a French social history movement, with much work on the topic published in the, *Annales d'Histoire Economique et Sociale* ("Annals of economic and social history"); for a representative example of how one participant in that movement explored the concept in research see Jacques Le Goff (2010).

adverbization, as a perniciously subjunctive radiant splendor, manifest in baroque twists of poetic animation on the ordinary; finally, linguistically speaking, German-ness expresses itself via technical-elongation as imposed-conjuncturization, propelled with explosive guttural power as endlessly stretched substantive roots of vocabulary, fired in volleys like mortar shells, most of which miss the mark.

Literary Verdun: Eagleton's Critical Cannon

Having dispatched in the first thirty pages of his *Theory* book the true peril of English for students, Eagleton next leveled his critical blunder-buster on literary targets that generally are treated with esteem. John Milton (1608–1674), was a "literary disaster," and T.S. Eliot (1888–1965), a poetic opportunist (Eagleton 2008a/1983: 34–8). Literary Realism was mostly emotion rather than sociology; New Criticism tore literature from the grip of not only author but reader; shorn of both "intention" and "interpretation," it "converted the poem into fetish" (Eagleton 2008a/1983: 42).

Continuing his run, the next gallery to be shot up held the icons of 20th century philosophy; words like phenomenology, hermeneutics, structuralism, and semiotics were shredded in turn, in complete indifference to everyone from Sigmund Freud (1856–1939) to Jacques Lacan (1901–1981); from Hans-Georg Gadamer (1900–2002) to Maurice Merleau-Ponty (1908–1961). This adds another one-hundred-and-fifty pages to his text. Along the way, for comic relief, he keeps dragging the wretched corpus of Matthew Arnold back on stage, since, as signaled at the outset, he is really to blame.

For a professor of literature, Eagleton gives short-shrift to pedagogy, issuing personal verdicts on these topics rather than providing readers with the basis for forming their own judgment. Take the question of structuralism; he appears to practice a certain version of that, as the basis of discrediting other versions. As regards a text, there are two major vectors of structural intrusion; one centered at the interior of the work, and the other coming from its exterior. In keeping with the cultural-critical call of his former mentor, Williams, Eagleton is an exterior or macro-structuralist sympathizer, who puts under his sights, then discredits, micro-structural critical practices. So what is the difference?

Structure invades texts from two sites, of which the first is the limit on linguistic possibility imposed by any given language for its expression as authorship. Each language is linked dialectically to the culture of its construction, which places real limits on what can be expressed and how.

This is apparent when one attempts to translate original texts, explaining the justice of the French dictum that the translator is a traitor to the original author. The political ramifications of this are limitless: a document such as the *Universal Rights of Man*, sourced in French, makes uncertain sense in India or China, or even in Norway or Wales; to use such documents as standards for international justice is an exercise in ecto-structural hegemonic domination, based on infra-structural linguistic concentration.

The other way structure imposes on a text, which in fact is always culture-structure, is by the socialization effects undergone by the author and editors of the work before the writing begins. Everyone arrives at maturity with some more or less well-formed, dissonance-reducing, apparently rational, mentality, which is put to work in adulthood.[15] While this can and is often modified at the margins by life-course experience, its force is difficult to underestimate; a potent source of which is the particular place of one's family of origin during childhood, in the pressure-cooker composed of social class, religion, and race/ethnicity.

In terms of personal biography, Eagleton was forcefully marked by conflicting structural forces; arriving early in life among elite-English-gentlemen, he was badly equipped to live on those new terms. It sometimes seems that his existence and writings are manifestation of a dialectic struggle for personal paradisiacal synthesis, driven by the confrontation within him of those opposing structural forces. In sociological terms, his existence is the lived expression of the crisis of status inconsistency.[16]

---

[15] More on mentalities. Mental formatting through socialization is assumed to be its source. The notion dates from Plato, meant as a universal disposition including both form and content, common to humanity, which for him meant Greek citizens in good standing, and thus referred only to the elite. Although Eagleton does not use the term mentality, he seems to hold a position consistent with its application, in so far as he claims that a 'national literature,' in fact, a 'national aesthetic' is active in every society. As an example of how classicists discuss this question, see Rupert C. Lodge: *Plato's Theory of Art* (2001/1953). Lodge was a Canadian, in Manitoba, where in the 1930s Marshall McLuhan was one of his students. For a contemporary example of research intended to identify what amounts to a 'team mentality' for sports groups, see Gary A. Fine : "Small Groups and Culture Creation: The Idioculture of Little League Baseball Teams" (1979).

[16] Status Inconsistency. This condition of personal disequilibrium is generated by social mobility such as might occur should a 'plumber's son goes to Yale.' It is typically a source of personal strain with institutional consequences, due to the lack of fit between the social status at birth and that attributed based on adult-life experiences; variants are associated with social class, caste, gender, race and religious orderings, varying from one country to another according to how particular societies are structured. Those who confront it, may experience it emotionally as alienation and stress, or socially by being treated in ways associated with one position in the status system that it out of fit with another, in which they also identify.

Following a Noam Chomsky or Roland Barthes, one is fully justified investigating writings' internal structure to determine 'how a text means.' This is surely an important effect to be explored. But there is also more, namely, the way in which a text expresses its times, the historical condition and conditioning of its author and editors; this is a further form of situated-structural analysis, equally justified and sound.

Unfortunately, critical studies that are empirically solid but not written into compelling narratives that inspire readers rarely hit the mark. Of course is it ethically ignoble to ignore the facts so as to generate more inspiring critical writings, which brings us back to that burdensome issue of how to tell the truth and still be read. As touched on elsewhere in this book, use of the historical-materialist method increases the ease with which factual institutional history can be effectively woven into theater, essays and books. Still navigating between the objective view of the researcher and the subjective necessity of compelling authorship is a sophisticated challenge of balance; a problem about which Eagleton is very sensitive.

A somewhat different issue concerns the multiple levels of social structure, each understandable only in relation to the others, that must be taken into account if one hopes to provide a convincing explanation for social issues and their possible amelioration. Being more technical than literary, exploration of this sort of problem is not Eagleton's strong suit.[17]

What of Unconsciousness?

A pitfall of any critical study, about which Eagleton is fully aware, is the presumption of art works as rational-consciousness expression; as if the product in view, a text, painting, music, was strategically planned and executed by the artist, conflating the fact that, often as not, even when the

---

The notion was developed in a study by Gerhard Lenski: "Status crystallisation: a non-vertical dimension of social status" (1954). See also A.S. Macke & Sheldon Stryker, "Status Inconsistency and Role Conflict" (1978).

For an opposing study by authors who attempted to debunk the unreality of this notion except in the mind of sociologists, see T.J. Blocker and P.L. Riedesel: "The Nonconsequences of Objective and Subjective Status Inconsistency: Requiem for a Moribund Concept" (1978).

[17] In France, this challenge has been taken on by Philippe Corcuff (2011/1995), in work addressing what he labels, "*Les Nouvelles Sociologies.*" His most recent publication concerning critical practice is: *Où est passée la critique sociale*? (*What has happened with Social Criticism?*) (2012).

result is as immediate as an Andy Warhol soup-can, quality writing, as with quality art of any sort, is usually unknown by the artist until it takes form. Most authors are surprised to see what runs out the end of their pen, often finding the effect on rereading to be as if issue of someone else. Criticism, however, must be targeted, and in that sense strategic; yet the result is a form of literature nonetheless. This nebulous possibility, that critical literature is of another nature, itself somehow beyond further criticism, brings us to the question of consciousness and from there to Freud.

Of course there is a psychoanalytic perspective on literature and by closing the substantive chapters of his *Theory* book with a discussion of that, Eagleton seems to unintentionally reveal his point. What he says is as uncomplicated as it is generalizable to criticism as a whole:

> Psychoanalytic literary criticism can be broadly divided into four kinds, depending on what it takes as its object of attention. It can attend to the author of the work, to the work's contents; to its formal construction; or to the reader. (Eagleton 2008a/1983: 165)

He gets to that laboriously, as if his exposure to psychoanalysis was limited as a student in Cambridge. In his later writings, having overcome somewhat a certain number of material deficits, it appears his view of this subject has evolved (Wroe 2002).[18] In his 1983 writing, Eagleton began with Freud, but tarried there only briefly, then fast forwarded to Jacques Lacan, writing on Freud, and finished with a discussion of Althusser, on Lacan, on Freud. At least concerning workings of mind, apparently even before the high-speed Eurostar train, London and Paris were too close to prevent the much feared invasion of the English mentality by the French: in this case, with Lacan and Althusser imposing Freud on at least one innocent Cambridge student, namely Eagleton.[19]

[18] According to Wroe (2002): "As a young academic, Eagleton says he never suffered any lack of intellectual confidence, but claimed his social background had severely disabled him. 'So my intellectual ability shot me into situations where I wasn't equipped to cope. It was very uncomfortable indeed.'"

[19] Psychoanalysis of Critics. In Chapter Five of his Lit-Crit study, taking off from the unsupportable tension he identifies between the 'pleasure' vs. 'reality' principle of Freud, Eagleton goes on to speculate on why work generates class effects under capitalism. Although he doesn't, I might point out that that distinction, as principle, is the expression in practice of the social class problem. Elite classes, overdetermined in pursuit of the pleasure principle, use all possible means to assure their desire by imposing on the popular classes, conditions principled by reality as necessity. From a perspective of social anthropology rather than psychiatry, Freud emphasized the neurosis-generating potential (for the bourgeois) of the necessity to temper their pursuit of pleasure with reality or necessity; Lacan adapted Freud to the postwar conditions of bounty from ruins, by transforming the

What of the English classics, concerning which Eagleton's Cambridge education is legendary? It seems not to have occurred to Eagleton that with the thumbnail sketch of the four determinant vectors of psychoanalytic oriented criticism, focusing on author, content, construction, reader, that he had rediscovered Aristotle's four causes—efficient, material, formal and final. It is surprising that he did not point this out, perhaps counting on his readers'-reception to fill it in for him. Otherwise, it seems that Freud is being unconsciously complimented by that lapse, indicating how the contents of consciousness, subtly formatted in advance, can creep out anytime, to structure a text, independent of the nominal awareness of the author or critic.

Freud's thesis was hardly a black-box, psychic-container view of human existence. His was the exploration of frustration as otherness-denied; archetypical, personal, interpersonal and historical. Psychoanalysis as cure was one thing; but as theory of being, as consciousness wrapped in unconsciousness, right from the start, Freud's was a critical perspective. The same can surely be said for phenomenology, leaving aside, of course, the first steps of that, the rather purely psychological conception as explored by early Husserl and fortunately later outdistanced by his own historical-critical take on the *Crisis of European Man* (1965).[20]

---

argument into a matter of desire as '*jouissance*.' Althusser took off from Lacan to study the collective effects of self-compounding desire as bourgeois ideology, which is unfortunately absorbed even by those from the lesser classes for whom most worldly satisfactions are but illusory. From Freud see *Interpretation of Dreams* (2010c/1899), highlighting the unconscious; then *Beyond the Pleasure Principle* (1920), shifting somewhat from being via sexuality, to death-avoidance as psychic motor force.

Lacan provided the most compelling elaboration of his project in seminars, now available in well-edited volumes, including his, *The Four Fundamental Concepts of Psycho-Analysis* (1994) where he deconstructs Freud's program according to its fundamentals of: the unconscious, repetition, transference and the drive. Also, *The Seminar of Jacques Lacan, Book VII: The Ethics of Psychoanalysis* (1997), where Lacan develops the notion of '*jouissance*' as the painful principle of the constant pursuit of pleasure.

Louis Althusser's major work on this theme was, "Ideology and Ideological State Apparatus," in his *Lenin and Philosophy*, 1971.

[20] A readable view of early Husserl is found in his *Phenomenology of Time Consciousness* (1964/1905); the crucial late work that I emphasize here is, "Philosophy and the Crisis of the European Man," in *Phenomenology and the Crisis of Philosophy* (1965). An important contribution that follows from late-Husserl was make by Alfred Schutz (see his, *Phenomenology of the Social World*, 1932). A bit later, Maurice Merleau-Ponty continued to explore this thread opened by late-Husserl, focusing on prereflective-consciousness as essential for penetrating cultural criticism; see, Merleau-Ponty's, "Le Doute de Cézanne" and "Metaphysics and the Novel" in *Sense and Non-sense*, (1996/1945). The second of these essays is a critique of the first novel by Simone de Beauvoir, *L'Invitée* [*She Came to Stay* (1967/1943)].

After-Words

The bold, high-flying critic Eagleton, attracts attention that is not always kind. In a *Guardian-Observer* article (2007) he was described as a member of an "endangered species in Britain, a public intellectual... who, having been fashionably Marxist for much of his career, is now unfashionably so"; yet counted among those, "long used to believing themselves the smartest men in the room."[21] While that last is a bit of gratuitous dig, it is surely the case that he is known for insisting that his is the final word, which, as it turns out, even applies to himself.

My copy of his *Literary Theory: An Introduction,* is a bit of a prize, being one of the highly sought examples of the Twenty-Fifth Anniversary Edition of the book. In this re-edition, Eagleton attached both a brief "New Preface" and a longer reopening of "After-Words," furnishing a basis by which we might weigh the sincerity with which he has held to his agenda over the years.

According to the original "Conclusion" for the book, to the question, "what is the point of theory," the answer was, "that the literary theory we have examined is political," that, as regards "the political system," literary theory has helped "to sustain and support its assumptions." Achieved by a "flight from real history," this "extremism of literary theory... betrays its elitism... assuming that at the center of the world is the contemplative individual self" (Eagleton 2008a/1983: 170–71). While at the center of it all there is surely more than the "contemplative individual self," the existence of that isolated, innocent, easily victimized self, hemmed-in by a commercialized, deforming capitalist society is the crux of the problem that concerns Eagleton.

As sign of his uneasiness about being too bold in his critical condemnation of capital, whenever he deals with the issue, he softens his view with irony. Thus, while literary critical exercises are necessarily political, we are relieved to read that he does "not mean by this that Matthew Arnold supported nuclear weapons." As for literature, as target of either criticism or theory, the judgment is beyond appeal: Eagleton "opened this book by arguing that literature did not exist," so, "it follows" that the object of this

[21] Eagleton maintains his stature partly by the regularity with which he produces new books. For an essay in which the sacrifice in quality is associated with that publishing strategy, excessive pressure for always a new publication, see the interview in *The Observer* (2007) where Eagleton discussed what journalist Tim Adams referred to as his Christmas Book for that year: *Jesus Christ: The Gospels,* published in the "Revolutions Series" (2007).

writing, as a "kind of metacriticism, a critical reflection on criticism… that is a non-subject" (2008a/1983: 171–72). Perhaps that doomsday proposition explains why, when I bought hi book on a recent trip to the U.S., Borders Bookstore was going bankrupt: literature having become a 'non-subject.'

His gripe against literature proceeds from the ironically morose, to the critical dark-side, to the literary graveside: "The final logical move in a process which began by recognizing that literature is an illusion is to recognize that literary theory is an illusion also," thus he announces, "this book is less an introduction than an obituary, and we have ended by burying the object we sought to unearth" (2008a/1983: 178). This problem is now clearly beyond even the well-written chicanery of Matthew Arnold since at the end, Eagleton determines that the real villain is modernity itself, couched in the verbiage of, "liberal humanism," deployed in a smog of "suburban moral ideology" (2008a/1983: 181).

The conclusions for his *Theory* book clatter like dust-bin covers at dawn: "I argued earlier, says Eagleton, that any attempt to define the study of literature in terms of either its method or its object is bound to fail." On that basis, he concludes that only major institutional changes will do, which "…would mean, for example, that departments of literature as we presently know them in higher education would cease to exist" (2008a/1983: 183–85).

Consistent with himself to the end, it is then reasonable that he should judge that, "the idea that there are non-political forms of criticism is simply a myth" because literary criticism is just a "question of different readings of history itself" (2008a/1983: 182).

Is that not only circular but contradictory? Eagleton's 19th century nemesis, Matthew Arnold, was both a cultural activist and critic: in the role of the former he stressed the value-integrating function of literature for the general order. Surely that is a political statement, but he was quite out front about it. On the other hand, concerning Arnold's criticisms, of which the one he did of Tolstoy comes to mind, while surely aimed at unveiling what he took to be the eternal messages of the famous novel, *Anna Karenina*, (justifiably critique-able for its classic Greek air), Arnold's study comes across as both pedagogically forthright and affirmative as well.[22]

[22] *Anna Karénine* (2012a/1877). Along with *War and Peace* (2012b/1869), this is Tolstoy's most studied work, of which one of the earliest critiques in the English language, "Count Tolstoy" (1887), was by Matthew Arnold, later included by Arnold in his widely circulated anthology *Essays in Criticism: Second Series* (1887–1911). With this text, Arnold provided not

Eagleton as critic seems to unknowingly shift the contents of the slide under his analytical microscope; speaking one minute of literature in the sense of Shakespeare or Joyce, and the next minute of criticism as a form of culture challenge, independent of the quality of literature in question. Is he concerned with theory and method of literature, with critical practice, or of both? Are they the same? If so within what limits?

Take Joyce for instance: if there was ever an enthusiasm for the works of a writer, it concerns this man. Yet, is not novelist Joyce overrated? As a short story writer, exemplified by his *Dubliners* (1969/1914), Joyce was competent; but the autobiographical exercise of writing his own self consciousness into life, then daring to imagine the challenge of getting through the day for his alter-ego as equivalent to the mythic challenge faced by the Homeric *Ulysses*, resulted in production of endless pages of questionable self-affirmation. Still, Joyce is uncritically admired by Eagleton: why so?[23]

Afterworlds

Eagleton added an "Afterword" meta-conclusion to his *Theory* book twenty-five years after its original composition. The world had changed a great deal: modernity is in terminal eclipse (which worries him); post-modernity is upon us (which provokes him); and Eagleton is past retirement age with a child under ten-years old, which probably helps motivate a continuing high rate of new publications.

As said a generation ago by an American sociology professor friend who shall remain anonymous, who supplemented his pay by moonlighting in the creation of algorithms to aid investment bankers beat the market: the stock in trade among academics is the citation. While universally too busy to read, university deans are never too tired to count—the number of

---

just a certain remarkable insight about challenge or authorship for Tolstoy, but in its form, the essay by Arnold demonstrated the classic method of criticism that was common until the end of the 19th century, eventually supplanted by use of the historical-materialist method as discussed in this book. For Eagleton, Arnold's work and style incarnated what he considered the ossified approach to literary criticism that characterized Oxbridge when he was a student, which, it must be recalled, was a century after Arnold did his writing. While that may justify Eagleton's not practicing the same form of critique, it is not justification for discrediting attention to the historically important work of Tolstoy.

[23] Before finding an outlet for his novel, *Ulysses* (1955/1922), Joyce published an earlier volume of short stories (*Dubliners* 1969/1914). Although his reputation is mostly based on that novel, I find his competence better established as a short-story writer.

times one's works are cited by others as certifying academic value. The win-win rule among professors is simple: if I cite you, you will cite me. The result has turned into a colossal exercise in bibliography elongating, a skill at which Eagleton excels.

In spite of his contention that literature is vacuous, method and theory are illusory, and criticism is empty, he attached to the fresh "Afterwords" of his reissued *Theory* book, footnotes containing more than two-hundred-and-fifty citations of books and articles, enthusiastically referring to what he identifies in that very book as the moribund stuff known as literature and criticism. Thus we must ask: what is Eagleton's beef?

One encouraging sign of self-enlightenment is his recognition that intellectual knowledge is historical, what I refer to as its largely archival function. Eagleton elevates this self-evident observation with reference to Hegel, who, in a famous Minerva metaphor, concludes, "Understanding is always in some sense retrospective"[24] (2008a/1983: 191). In common sense terms this is another way of saying that nothing is more acute than hindsight. As pertains for these "Afterwords," this message is a subliminal sign that twenty-five years later, Eagleton understands a bit better what he actually did with his *Theory* book.

In the original volume, he deprecated literature, theory, method, criticism, and most every major name in the business, except Joyce's. Since then, with resurgence of his interest in religion, his conscience has recovered; this leads him to the subject of values, which raises the question of where to look for their establishment. He now says values count: that "the humanities ... depend on some tacit consensus... between teachers and taught." Clearly softening his condemnation of the study of the humanities as thinly veiled elitist conspiracy, he continues to doubt, nonetheless, the constancy of "liberal humanists" (2008a/1983: 191–92).

As for movements, rather than condemning them all as empty, as was formerly his habit, he simply announces that those which so vexed him in 1983, Freudian, Marxist, Structuralist, and Reconstruction theories, each

---

24 Hegel's History. With his study of the past of culture in his, *The Philosophy of History* (1956), Hegel developed the idea of history as more than just of museum interest, but as a force of humanized movement, as the expression of humanity as such. This supplied the basis for the transformation of the exercise of just 'writing about the past' as had been done for centuries by curious and well-educated individuals with time on their hands, into history as discipline of serious study based on specialized training. The causes and consequences of that shift into discipline are central to the work of Hayden White, which is the subject of Chapter Seven. For a brief commentary on Hegel's project see Henri Lefebvre and Norbert Guterman: *Hegel: Morceaux Choisis* (1988/1939).

has since been relegated to the purgatory of dead history, beyond contemporary relevance. Were that so, then the future would be bleak: but is it?

Fortunately, Eagleton had at least one good teacher. Of course that was long ago when as a student under the influence of Raymond Williams, he was first bitten by the bug of criticism. Since the terminology with which to discuss this has drifted a bit during the last fifty years, Eagleton goes out of his way to certify his credentials by the highly unneeded announcement he makes concerning his old mentor's fame: referring to Williams as "Britain's premier socialist critic" who "coined" the term, "cultural materialism" as critical standpoint (2008a/1983: 199).

In a way which suggests this as unfortunate, he notes that the major recent carriers of the cultural-theoretical message, Barthes, Foucault, Althusser and Lacan, were "picked off by the Almighty," i.e., died (2008a/1983: 193). Is this to imply that, other than him, there is no living legacy to carry on the critical movement that he most favors?

Post-Modernists be Damned!

It is not clear whether Eagleton considers himself a historical materialist, in either theory or practice; we must assume not since he denies both. Still, he recognizes there is something there, as indicated by his injecting a reference to Mikhail Bakhtin, whose book of four essays, entitled, *The Dialogic Imagination* (1981/1930), is widely admired not just in the West but around the world. Bakhtin (1895–1975) was Russian, influenced on one side by Marx of the 19th century, and on the other side by the 20th century movement of Russian formalism.[25]

In a rather disparaging tone, Eagleton charges that, around Bakhtin, "a heavy critical industry sprang up," somehow uniting "discursive concerns of the post-structuralists with a more historical, materialist or sociological perspective" (2008a/1983: 200). In a review he published a year earlier, Eagleton had said of Bakhtin, "If he was not exactly a historical materialist, his thinking was both historical and materialist" (2007b). It is evident that

[25] Formalism. This is not the place to elaborate about Russian Formalism, but for Bakhtin (as with Lukács), the importance of that movement concerned bringing to the surface the tension, which I consider dialectic, between {content and form}; and then as concerns composition: how to express a project's creative originality, given the heavy imposition of structural forms on literature and other aesthetic works. Without form there is no way to assure that content will be understood by others; with too much emphasis on form, the content is reduced to stylized boiler-plate.

Eagleton comes to this judgment about Bakhtin and his work by implicit application of the historical-materialist method; yet, he seems uncertain just what that is.

Nothing is clearer from the use of that method in cultural criticism than that the enlightened historic-condition that sensitized the West to what is labeled modernity, is itself in a state of rapid dissolution; that a new historic-condition is on the horizon because the macro-system of cultural self-awareness known as modernity is evaporating. Like it or not, postmodernity is upon the West, and Eagleton likes it not at all; he used the last third of his fresh "Afterwords" to tell us why.

While he is appalled by the possibility, Eagleton writes that "postmodernism... is doubtless the most widely-touted term in cultural theory today," which, due to what he condemns as a horrid case of overreach, "threatens thereby to collapse into meaninglessness" (2008a/1983: 200). The evident difficulty is that just a few pages before he wrote this, he was favoring "cultural studies" as the way out of the black hole of superficial Lit-Crit; but this post-modern adventure is, for him, a worst-case scenario, an exploding star, filling the rhetorical heavens with twaddle.

My how his position-shredding word-blaster cuts in, to warn the world of this postmodern evil, intended, I suppose, to protect the naive youngsters in literature at Cambridge, Yale and Notre Dame. According to Eagleton, this postmodern talk "distracts us" with attention to a world that, "is simply chimera," a "self-divided entity," only an "extended footnote" to Nietzsche. Supplying what as alternative: nothing but, the "arbitrary... pastiche-like... contrived depthlessness; suspecting... skeptical... rejecting... negative authenticity... of ironic awareness" (2008a/1983: 200). Particularly as concerns 'ironic awareness,' I could build a strong case that the above indictment applies in spades to the majority of Eagleton's review essays published over the past twenty-five years in the *London Review of Books* and the *Guardian*.

Still he continues, certifying the substantive evil of postmodernism with more despicable modifiers than a vicar about binge-drinking from the pulpit on Sunday. For Eagleton, the plain truth is horrid: postmodern discourse is delivered by "paradoic recyclings of other works... cobbled together with the contemporary." The result is "intimidating... demotic... suspecting... radical avant-garde... transformed into a kind of aesthetic spectacle." But then what can be expected, since this evident hoax is perpetrated by, "a jaded bunch of erstwhile revolutionary western intellectuals" (2008a/1983: 202). Do we detect a slight gleeful smile on the part of our slippers-and-pipe critic?

While it is difficult to extract informed content on this issue from those rapidly drifting clouds of adjectives, Eagleton acknowledges, accurately enough, "postmodernity means the end of modernity" (2008a/1983: 200). Where he errs is in his seeming obliviousness to the nature of historical conditions and accompanying mentalities woven with practices, which, for instance, distinguished antiquity from modernity.

Admitting to being neither philosopher nor historian, sociologist or anthropologist, has he carefully considered that when Marx spoke of the question of 'who teaches the teachers,' (Marx 1992a/1845) he was not concerned with fourth-form studies, but with the expressive force of historical conditions which infuse the material of which worlds and world-views are historically constructed? So why not the possibility of a radical rupture or revolution that modifies the status quo; but next time, not from antiquity to modernity, but from modernity to something else?

While Marx never used the term postmodern, in spite of Eagleton, this rupture has opened, shifting the historical condition for the West toward the postmodern; yes, an after-modernity. And that is reference to more than literature or rhetoric, or the stuff of theory. It does not suppose an end, much less the-end of history. History as self-reflexive, world-questioning deployment of humanized-being as doing, linked to theory as action, guided by informed judgment, issue of critical practice, will be with us always: but soon, differently.

A difficulty with reading Eagleton is that his radical political halo seems overly bleached; it is said that he developed it as a student, by leading a folk singing group, while hanging out in pubs in Cambridge (Wroe 2002). This may explain a certain lack of clarity in his political register. Nonetheless, to the extent that a word constantly creeps out of his paragraphs signaling political intention, it is 'Marx.' Still, not everybody believes that Marx advanced either a philosophy or a political theory; he was a historical-materialist researcher who delved into the underbelly of capitalist society. Other than the method which he developed, which we argue is now ubiquitous in the social sciences, in spite of once 'having been right,' is the content of Marx still current? On one hand, Eagleton seems to think so, on the other not; but if not, what if anything has succeeded Marx as the guiding star toward the social revolutionary promised land?[26]

---

[26] Marxist Philosophy. In spite of use of the term in the title of the book he wrote, which has become a very popular study of Marx, the French specialist, Étienne Balibar is emphatic: properly speaking, Marx never developed a philosophy. See his *The Philosophy*

Although Eagleton finds little encouraging about English scholarship, he now and then shows some hazy appreciation for French thought: but only of now-dead thinkers. For instance, amidst the new "Afterwords" to his Lit-Theory book, he announces that, in the 1980s, "Michel Foucault rapidly overtook Karl Marx as the doyen of political theory" (2008a/1983: 196). My study of Foucault suggests otherwise; that, by the 1980s, a woefully misread Marx had already fallen from grace, tarred by the brush of the Stalinesque Gulags and that the last thing Foucault pursued was 'political theory.' While his discussion of the knowledge/power nexus is legendary, he backpedaled incessantly to discredit those who attempted to attach an active political call to his words.

Is criticism more than just words? If not, then its quality is mostly a matter of the eminence of one's expression, which it seems in the end is the judgment of Eagleton. While coy as always so as to avoid being pinned down, in the original "Conclusion" to his *Theory* book, he advanced a proposition worthy of reflection: that the step most called for to reinvigorate criticism would be a return to the principles of rhetoric (from Aristotle, we suppose). Now we know that for the Greeks this was soon turned sideways, then peddled as sophist, the idea being that effective Greek critical thinkers achieved most when they took work as rhetoric coaches, more or less as did some years ago, the former Marxist-admiring British sociologist, Anthony Giddens, who took on the role of communications coach for Tony Blair, Prime Minister of the U.K. (1997–2007). Giddens proved so effective as to ultimately save the crown not only by helping set the stage for war in Iraq against Saddam Hussein but by helping assure perpetual domestic peace in London, by advising that the town be blanketed with thousands of surveillance cameras.[27]

---

of Marx (2007/1993). However, adds Balibar, Marx is even more important for philosophy today than was the case a century ago: which is only to acknowledge that the importance of an individual's research for philosophy is not contingent on the formal development of a philosophy by that individual.

[27] Sociological Rhetoric. Anthony Giddens has had a long career; his introductory sociology book (2009a) is in its sixth edition. His early interest in macro-sociology led him to theorize on the dynamic processes by which societal systems and structures arise; the result was the book that made his name: *The Constitution of Society: Outline of the Theory of Structuration* (1984). With recognition and stature, his humanist values evolved, leading to the development of a novel position on critical change, captured in the title of one of his books, *Beyond Left and Right—the Future of Radical Politics* (1994). Thereafter, he was named Director of the London School of Economics. Now retired, he has turned to European and global political question, evidenced by: *Runaway World* (2000); *Europe in the Global Age* (2007); and *The Politics of Climate Change* (2009b).

While there is a depth side to rhetoric as pursuit, the danger of the sophist approach can not be underestimated. It often turns into the skill of aiding those in power to find the right words to sway the public in opposition to the truth. Machiavelli proposed himself as a sophist, rhetoric coach, in Italy, for *The Prince*.[28] It seems that Eagleton hopes that critics of good-judgment will somehow get the ear of those who make politics happen, and by that, turn a potentially hollow academic exercise into revolutionary praxis. The risk of going sophist as bad faith, opens the door to a litany of shabby propensities. A quick flash of the thesaurus reminds us that sophist practice tends toward doctrinaire, obscurantist, obfuscating, scholarship, driven by nitpicking, hair-splitting, dilettante theoreticians. I trust that nothing could be further from the mind of Eagleton.

The Ideology of Criticism

Another of Eagleton's important publications, *The Function of Criticism,* came out in 1984 (2005a), only one year after his *Literary Theory* book. Six years later, in 1990, another major work appeared: *The Ideology of the Aesthetic*. While in between there were others, I am going to consider the 1984 and 1990 pair as couplet. The justice of this is validated by Eagleton's own words, taken first, from his *Criticism* book: "the act of literary criticism inhabits no autonomous aesthetic sphere but belongs organically with general ideology" (2005a/1984: 33); then from his *Ideology Aesthetic* book, "The construction of the modern notion of the aesthetic artifact is thus inseparable from the construction of the dominant ideological forms of modern class society" (1990: 3). The common issue, then, is ideology.

In the classical sense, 'literature' is the defining concept of every "aesthetic artifact" including not just texts, but music, painting, sculpture, theater, dance, architecture, etc.; all are forms of creative production intended by the 'poet' to put out a message with meaning, using a particular media. Tying together the claims by Eagleton, cited just above, suggests, less antinomies than uncertainties concerning the notion of ideology.

---

[28] Sophist Politics. Machiavelli developed his position during the 16th century, based on a combination of reading the then available histories from Rome (Principally Plutarch), linked with personal experience in public administration; it is doubtful if he became an advisor for the powerful as a conscious ambition to apply the sophist skill for career building, but that is effectively what he did in practice. For his views see *The Prince* (2005/1513–32).

By any definition, cultural criticism as product is a form of literature. Guided by a certain method, it is aimed at exposing meanings as expression of political, if not manifestly ideological content; then putting that out into a community as fuel for continuity or change in social practices, depending on the circumstances. Yet if, as Eagleton says, criticism is itself but ideology, the result is an ideological synthesis of ideology as display. While perhaps not impossible as undertaking, what does that mean?

Although there exists no known, publicly accessible, comprehensive list of his work, Eagleton was recently lauded by the Rector of Edinburgh University, for having already published fifty books: a volume a year since 1961.[29] Along with a steady blizzard of essays, seminars, conferences and interviews, this suggests a furious determination, not to mention a considerable overlap of content between works. From close reading of the result, it often seems that what comes out from his pen later, frequently years later, is antecedent to something already in print.

With little time for discharging then recharging his consciousness between projects, he often addresses questions raised in his former publications, but without citing himself, yielding a curious circularity to his pronouncements. Along the way, there is often a shift in usage of terms, raising questions of authorship accountability.

Let us recall that, in 1983, in his *Lit-Theory* book, he buried his manifest object of study: literature is non-existent, theory and method illusory. If so, then why continually go on about literary criticism? He side-steps this issue by précising that his focus in 1984 (*The Function of Criticism* 2005a) was less on literature or criticism as such, than on the *function* of criticism. The implication is ambiguous: as if aimed at the meaningless, non-existent object called literature, that critical activity fills a vital function nonetheless. While communication agents for mystic economic activity often bloat press releases with well-articulated vacuities, is that what Eagleton has in mind about popular literary critics, of which he is one?

The upshot is bleak: "The argument, he asserts, of this book (*The Function of Criticism*) is that criticism today lacks all substantive social function. It is either part of the public relations branch of the literary industry, or a matter wholly internal to the academies" (2005a/1984: 8). Establishing how criticism had gotten into this decrepit state after having started out as a more honorable undertaking, required Eagleton's digging once again deep into the past; justifying, to a degree, the blurb that graces

29 The British Council provides a partial list of Eagleton's major books; see http://literature.britishcouncil.org/terry-eagleton.

the back cover of this 1984 book: "A history and critique of the last 200 years of cultural criticism from Addison and Steele to Barthes and Derrida, by Britain's most stylish critic." Apparently when done by a sufficiently "stylish critic," the power of criticism is sustained, independent of the emptiness of its object.

Eagleton used his *Function of Criticism* book to present a certain view of the development to the present of that practice. Backing up two-hundred years, takes us to 1784. Voltaire (1694–1778) was then an eighty-year old man, just finishing his last theater piece, *Irene*, which he took to Paris to direct, only to die (1788) in the process. Schiller (1759–1805) was already well accomplished and about to undertake the working relationship with Goethe, which solidified the reputation of both of them in the durable form that still holds today. Yet neither Voltaire nor Schiller are even mentioned in Eagleton's *Function of Criticism* study.[30]

Eagleton orients his *Function of Criticism* with the announcement that, "Modern European criticism was born of a struggle against the absolutist state" (2005a/1984: 13). Here he must have been speaking of cultural criticism rather than literary criticism, although he generally treats the two as if based on a single referent. Yet if so, why did he only discuss English figures, beginning with Addison and Steele? It appears this was partly an issue of timing and partly that the object of criticism for Voltaire and Schiller was different from what Eagleton had in mind; their issue was the hereditary aristocratic domination of kingdoms and principalities; linked with Christian religious fanaticism, leading to popular oppression of general liberty, and the pursuit of needless brutal war, paid for by the sweat and blood of common people.[31]

---

[30] As will be discussed later, Eagleton included a chapter on Schiller in his *The Ideology of the Aesthetic* (1990) book; but he continues to ignore Voltaire.

[31] It is difficult to escape being snared by one's times. Although I did not go into this in Chapter Two, Voltaire, who is still popular in England, dealt with certain social tensions that were rampant in mid-18th century Europe in what is judged today (2013) as a highly unsatisfactory manner. While an undeniably progressive political critic for his day, in his zeal to expose oppressive abuse, he was often too outspoken for late 20th century western comfort. Although different then, these days it is dangerous to criticize political actions linked with racial, ethnic or religious status. Specifically, Voltaire was vocal about what he judged to be the questionable ethical posture associated with the economic ambition of businessmen of Jewish origin, which was then a commonly discussed source of social tension; this in spite of insistence on religious tolerance, for all, including those of Jewish belief. Although his critical position, expressed in more carefully edited writings, is little different from that of Shakespeare with his theater, epitomized in his central character, Shylock, for the famous play, the *Merchant of Venice*, the retrospective treatment of the two authors is different.

Eagleton was perhaps less precise about the 17th century conditions that concerned him than he might have been. While the 'absolutist state' is a label for a certain form of heavy handed, over-centralized political evil, the corrosive nature of a hereditary royalist system linked with manipulative institutional religiosity was then probably more pernicious and invasive. True: Addison and Steele were in their London coffee houses, complaining because the emerging English bourgeoisie (now called middle class there) were paying taxes yet receiving few privileges. Yet was not such talk in London about the appalling effects of the 'absolutist state' largely a bargaining point aimed less at reducing absolutism than at redistributing privilege, in favor of the emerging London bourgeoisie?

From Tatler to Facebook

Admittedly predating Voltaire and Schiller, the importance of Joseph Addison (1672–1719) and Richard Steele (1672–1729) is that they founded the original popular London journals of literary opinion; first, *The Tatler*, then, *The Spectator*. Of tabloid format, each was short-lived, the first appearing in 1709–1711, the second, 1711–1712.

As Eagleton discusses, aimed at coffee-house patrons, those early printed newsletters set the pattern for the London press ever since: a mixture of gossip and personality issues, focusing on those who would be rich and famous, sprinkled with subtle fear mongering about government, prices, real-estate values, foreign worries and, above all, taxes. The readership was male, literate, economically comfortable, and without aristocratic blood: aristocrats abhor road houses, meaning that the residue lunching at the local bars each day consisted mostly of the rapidly rising, ferociously ambitious, perennially frustrated London bourgeoisie.

Those early 18th century newsletters arrived in sufficiently interesting series that the contents have been preserved in British libraries. Tucked away in those many pages of coffee-house chatter, one finds references to the 'absolutist state' on which basis Eagleton established the starting point for his 1984 historical study of criticism. Anchoring its contents in events that date from three-hundred years ago renders a bit misleading the "200 years" announcement on the book cover; should he correct that, he might also remove the cover reference to Roland Barthes, who never appears in the volume.

Announcements on his book covers are of less concern than what he says in his pages. Yet when focusing critically on a world figure like

Eagleton, known for his use of galloping synthesis as analytic tool, it does seem that one question about the punch of critical works concerns the solidity of the details on which they are based. However that is, thanks to the *Tatler*, the *Spectator* and various successor publications, the London coffee-house crowd began to read a common report, on a daily basis, of the content of the consciousness of those very bourgeois café clients. This generated increased self-awareness among members of that category, about their status and condition, leading from there to the formation of a loosely integrated, class-based public opinion. The subliminal message supported a mixture of middle-class adulation and self-asserted reclamations, which, according to Eagleton, soon transmuted into bourgeois, elitist, class ideology.

The importance of this narrative is its demonstration of how the recurrent circulation of messages, the content of which focuses on the self-absorption and topical interests of a fixed category of readers, can exert a formatting influence, generating a class or categorical awareness of common cause among dispersed members of a population, without need of formal organization. This explains one mode of the emergence of a social force as an effective and effecting institutional presence in a community, knitting together the will for action among otherwise anonymous and disconnected individuals. Although Eagleton did not stress this in the way I choose to here, the way he developed this in his, *Function of Criticism*, warrants elaboration.

The contemporary power of the web as tool for accelerating the formation and management of public opinion is inestimable. Use of Facebook as a strategy to stir up concern about social or political causes, with powerful consequences, sometimes proto-revolutionary other times reactionary, is an elaboration of the process which Eagleton spotted as having emerged two-hundred-and-fifty years ago with the London coffee-house patrons. By it, otherwise anonymous individuals can be mobilized in a network of potential action, with the result announced as 'public' opinion. While any interest might potentially benefit from this form of depersonalized multiplication of social power, as with every form of action, those with greater resources are most skillful at putting it into play.

When economic crises strike, it is usually the voice of the wealthy that is heard first. Accordingly, the hidden-hands of the market are said to function not only without arms, but brainlessly as well. Consequently, there is no particular economic actor who deserves to be blamed. Treated as if acts of the gods, one hears: 'show me the conspiracy or the guilty agent behind these difficulties.' Eagleton's observation about the emergence of a bourgeoisie coffee-house culture in London in 1750 sheds light on how this occurs.

Now at the opening of the 21st century, we see an equivalent process carried out by vastly more sophisticated means. Thanks to circulation of information via the Internet, the agents of capital are linked in a highly influential, informal system, feeding a common mentality among themselves about financial and political issues, providing useful arguments about opportunity and menace, oriented less by concern for general well-being, than for assuring continued accumulation of profits on speculation.

The annual meeting of the World Economic Forum at Davos, Switzerland is the tip of an iceberg, obscuring visibility of what amounts to a world-wide cartel of major wealth holders and controllers. Beyond the conference itself, this 'war of position' (*à la* Gramsci) on the part of the elite, aimed at convincing the world public of the rightness of unbridled profits on speculation, remains largely informal. The invisible reality of those clandestine ambitions is routinely masked by the work of media consulting firms and communication coaches, who assure that only the expression of 'compassionate capitalism,' a serious contradiction in terms, is seen when economic leaders appear in public.

Like what occurred among the London bourgeoisie in the 1750s, issuing from a 'social form without a body' (an image developed by both Boltanski and Ebert; see Chapter One), forces of this nature nonetheless give rise to powerful collective forces. They act in favor of limited interests that are very difficult to combat, due to their incarnation in a 'bodiless' institutional fashion. Usually driven by some very limited reclamation, targeted communications stressing strangely impersonal information about distant events, can set in motion social movements expressing what Eagleton identifies as ideological force. For him, that means that unreflected enthusiasm for some motivating issue is transmuted into the zone of the irrational on the part of its adherents; such that other than in very general terms, the majorities who rally to endorse these movements, often do not understand what drives the movement they back. This is achieved via an insidious form of psycho-emotive social formatting, based on highly selective content, sometimes supporting a shocking distortion of higher human values, other times favoring human liberation from oppression.

The key to understanding the power of today's web-based mobilizations seems to be alienation as false expression of freedom under real conditions of isolation and restriction. Although the research is yet to be done, I might offer a hypothesis for explaining this phenomenon, once limited in scope and now assuming global proportions. These anonymous movements draw together individuals who are not members of a true interactive community, but only a virtual, global one, yet who are tangled locally in a similar pattern of existence, leaving desires unmet and necessity unabated. The situations they face individually suggests other and better possibilities, but avenues for action appear blocked.

The logical choice these days, when searching for information, is to turn to the web. The result is often exhaustive cycles of 'surfing,' which eventually yields links with anonymous others in similarly unsatisfying local circumstances. Once this process reaches a critical level, self-styled 'moderators' and 'web-masters' establish themselves, motivated and often paid for by particular interests, the true nature of which is usually obscure. The result is a movement energized as much by common impulse as by centralized resources driven by largely unexamined ideology, with results occasionally powerful enough to reverse democratic processes or bring down a government; but usually of not much effect.

In 1710, with Addison et al., such cycles of search, location, diffusion, and linkage took much longer; information needed to be printed or speakers put on circuits, and those who might get involved needed to come together physically, with coffee-houses then serving this function in London. Until the labor-union movement developed, the common people were left out of this process; eventually they learned to mobilize thanks to it, which first resulted in a certain human progress and then union busting as liberal political response. Previously a slow, hit and miss process, today, with digital communication and satellite systems, mobilization both for-and-against almost anything is nearly instantaneous.

Alienation and existential pain are powerful motivators for concerted action but with unstable collective results. Individuals thus agitated and anonymously linked are open to the form of ideological manipulation that worries Eagleton. Because negative images are easier to simplify and transmit, the result can turn rapidly to unfounded categorical blaming if not active calls for witch-hunting. No matter what the effect, it is seldom the case that such movements generate concrete plans for affirmative social change; unfortunately, a fire-bug with a match can burn to the ground in a day an edifice that required an inspired architect and competent team years to construct. Rather than generating the basis for a concerted program of carefully studied progressive political change, this process moves more rapidly than institutions can handle; the long term consequences are uncertain.[32]

Capital Sucks the Life from Criticism

In the early years of the 18th century, for reaching a public, an Addison or Steele depended on hard-copy circulation of their tabloids, backed by printing and distributional capacity; the financial burden was considerable, explaining how moneyed-interests gradually crept in to commandeer what may have begun on neutral grounds, transforming public-opinion into a market commodity.

Whereas initially based not on "power but reason," with a "radical dissociation of politics and knowledge," coffee-house oriented journalism relied more on trust than authority, assuming, somewhat naively, that "everyone has a basic judgment capacity" (Eagleton 2005a/1984: 15–20). In those early years, while feeding the growing bourgeois appetite, according to Eagleton, this movement was "not yet struck leaden by industrial philistinism," with economic opportunists manipulating a just cause for profit (2005a/1984: 23). Still the result was a general inertia, such that, "the literary was the vanishing point of the political, its dissolution and reconstruction into polite letters" (2005a/1984: 25).

The next steps in the story are not difficult to anticipate: big money took over. As Eagleton points out, the problem was the, "intensifying penetration of capital into literary production." Whether by ownership or direct patronage, "authorship" was progressively hemmed in by "a literary mode of production ruled by the commodity" (2005a/1984: 32). The duty of authorship ceased to be representation with integrity of the general interest; writers were obligated to target some potentially remunerative public, transforming the critical process into a commercial market, obliged as result to assure reasonable financial returns. This shifted the way writers approached societal questions: by the opening of the 19th century, criticism had become, "explicitly, unabashedly political" (2005a/1984: 38).

---

32 Alienation. The notion of alienation covers two grounds: one as a personal emotional state, a form of depressive response to current conditions; the other a realization, more intellectually than only emotionally, that one is participating in doing a job or building a society or world that somehow escapes from returning its promise, becoming rather a millstone if not active menace for the general well-being. The first is the concern of therapists; the second was the interest of Marx and from there, since then, remains of major concern for critical practice.

During the 19th century, the commoditization of literature and criticism accelerated, with authors assuming their role as "enlightened discoursing subjects of the ruling class," committed to "forming public opinion" for the glory of the King and the value of the Pound. At the pinnacle of Empire, "Victorian criticism" found itself straddling two dead-end paths, "those of Hack and Sage" (Eagleton 2005a/1984: 60). As usual for Eagleton, the villain was again Matthew Arnold, who, "was dealing with social classes whose interests are historically irreconcilable" (2005a/1984: 62). The tragic end was in sight: "Criticism achieved security by committing political suicide" (2005a/1984: 65).

Ideology and Critical Aesthetics

Although the issue of dogmatic manipulation was not forcefully developed in his *Function of Criticism* book (2005a/1984), in 1990 Eagleton returned to it in his study of, *The Ideology of the Aesthetic.* This time he tied the notion of ideology to that of aesthetics, but from a critical angle, to be explored by another long historical study of literature and criticism.

Not only did ideology become a central issue for Eagleton during the 1980s, but it continues to be for him to this day; sometimes changing his angle of attack, it is uncertain if he is yet to convince himself precisely what the notion means. The same tends to pertain with the notion of aesthetics; Eagleton also uses that term without clear definition.

At the outset of his *Ideology of Aesthetics* book, we are reminded of Eagleton's earlier announcement, in 1983, of the serious nonexistence of quality literature, theory and method. Then, in 1984, noting that criticism had committed "political suicide," he seemed to suggest a cease and desist order from continuing to write as he does. Yet he strides onward for decades in pursuit of his chosen vocation. Though not exactly in the sense of Albert Camus (1913–1960) or Eugène Ionesco (1909–1994), is not his persistence in this work an exercise in the theater of the absurd?[33]

It is not that theater is inherently absurd and much less so the aesthetic of criticism. Rather, for both theater and life, when placed under a

[33] Albert Camus won the Nobel Prize for literature (1957). His works include: *L'Etranger* (2006/1942); *La Pest* (2012a/1947); *Les Justes* (2012b/1949); *The Myth of Sisyphus* (2000/1942). Eugène Ionesco is less well known in the U.S.; his works are often black-humor studies of the folly of existence, which must be lived nonetheless, including: *La Cantatrice chauve* (2011a/1950); *Les Chaises* (2011b/1952) and *Victimes du devoir* (2000/1953).

historical-materialist lens, one can perceive the rolling tension between aesthetic consciousness as humanized existence and the lived experience thereof. Depending on circumstances, this reveals the contrast between ideality as harmony, decency and compatibility in a community, versus the folly-laden tensions, conflicts, blockages and reversals that can render self-assessments disappointing and relations with others brutal. Whether exposed directly in theater, art or literature, the responsibility of critique is not to waylay authors but tell the truth about them through their work; and on the world as seen through it.

Aesthetic perplexity arises to the degree that potentially noble human action achieves drastically ignoble institutional effects. Based not on mysticism but reality, aesthetics concerns judgment; not with how what is accords with the great-beyond, but with how communities act, in accord with the standards of those who constitute communities. The community as system, as it is at any given time, constitutes standards that exert pressure to assure that when elements are added or modified, the results will not cause the community to collapse. In the critical sense, as the seeking after balance and harmony among the socially divergent, political aesthetics is the crash-test of the real.

Ideology is something else. While self-imposing and potentially dominating, and thus dangerous when unconsciously implanted in the common consciousness, there is a less onerous sense of the term that I endorse. Rather than the essence of aesthetics, ideology is a potential constituent of social systems, which when active must meet the aesthetic test. Like love or compassion, ideology is an action word, and only has meaning in reference to collective social experience. It is a predisposition toward a certain state of the future, establishing assumedly reasonable ends, which by the force of back-chaining logic, justify the necessary means of attainment as drive force for current social action. Is that goal and are those means in fit with the general well-being or not? That is the aesthetic question in the political sense, which is how it is intended in this book.

The power and danger of thoughtless ideology is evident: a group overdetermined by ideological impulse moves like a buffalo herd in stampede, trampling every obstacle in its path; if the goal is badly targeted, the herd may race off a cliff with disastrous results. Action motivated by ideology is inspired in the long term, but often thoughtless in the immediate, explaining both its energy and its peril. Affecting individual states of consciousness, motorizing individual will and action, it is a collective construction, without specific address or precise origin.

Aesthetics and Marx

In his *Ideology-Aesthetic* book, Eagleton at first sounds definitive: "this is not a history of aesthetics," but "a Marxist study... of ideological forms." His postulate is, "the construction of the modern notion of the aesthetic artifact is thus inseparable from the construction of the dominant ideological forms of modern class society."[34] At the same time he hesitates, tempering the aesthetic a bit, as if via a sort of alter-ideology or perhaps anti-ideology, judging that, "the aesthetic... provides an unusually powerful challenge and alternative to these dominant ideological forms and is in this sense an eminently contradictory phenomenon" (1990: 1–4).

As Eagleton acknowledges, the parentage of the notion, *Aesthetics*, is attributed by consensus to one Alexander Baumgarten in a book by that title published in Germany in 1750. It was picked up by Schiller who undertook a critique of the subject in his famous, *Aesthetic Letters*. In homage to that, even if neglected in his early study of criticism, Schiller is the central subject of the third chapter in Eagleton's 1990 book.

Apparently aspiring to be even more encyclopedic than usual, Eagleton laid this book out to assure that few classical critical grounds would remain unplowed. His chapter titles alone bear a long list of legendary names: Shaftesbury, Hume, Burke; Kant, Schiller; Fitch, Schelling, Hegel; Schopenhauer, Kierkegaard; Marx, Nietzsche, Freud; Heidegger, Benjamin, Adorno. The last chapter aims at exposing the fallacy in the work of that stampeding mass of intellectual bison whose works Eagleton abhors: nondescript members of the shameless multitude, today in dangerous pursuit of The Postmodern.

Given that long list of subjects, Eagleton's treatment of each could hardly be comprehensive. Further, by weaving in his own views, rarely formally detailed, with his personal reading of so many major figures, it is difficult to settle on a critical position about this undertaking. Since his book contains a major examination of Schiller's project of which I provided earlier in this book, perhaps a few words about Eagleton's treatment of that late 18th century critical poet will be instructive.

Eagleton positions Schiller on the shirttail of Kant, with the obvious bridge built from Kant's *Critique of Judgment* (1790) to Schiller's *Aesthetic*

[34] I view art as the affirmative expression of aesthetic judgment, capturing the tension of the real with its realization in some accepted media (music, text, dance, poetry), placed in a recognizable frame (whether symbolic or material) by an artist.

Letters (1795). That is a sound step, because by his own admission, while influenced by the *Judgment* text, Schiller never read Kant's first two critiques. However, it is the weight of those first two Kantian critiques, unread by Schiller, which was most heavily felt around Oxbridge when Eagleton did his studies and began his career: disposing him, as I see it, to favor an early Kant reading of the late Kant disciple, Schiller.

In his first Critique (*of Pure Reason*, 1781), the one treated most seriously by formal philosophy, Kant recognized his project as expression of 'transcendental idealism'. Soon thereafter, in his own critique of his first critique (The *Prolegomena,* 1783), Kant not only modified his view about idealism but went so far as to change the name with which he designated his program, to "transcendental critique".[35] While Eagleton is fully justified to use his reading of the Kantian aesthetic as the regulative principle by which to compare and contrast the work of Schiller and the major historical players who concern him in this book, does he not do this more as a transcendental idealist than as a critic?

Opening on Schiller by way of Kant (1990: 102), Eagleton confronts 'harmony' as factum, considered as implicit register of {object for subject}, suggesting that to know something of the world is certified by an appreciation of how it 'fits' with what one takes one's own self to be (as human existential phenomenon), including one's own stock of knowledge and appreciative experiences.

As Kant viewed it, this process of rational reasoning is sovereign over the content of what is thus understood. This left him caught in the difficulty of thinking his way from the mind to the world. That being impossible due to insurmountable antinomies, he was forced, as evidenced in his third critique, to leave somewhat aside rational understanding as sole

35 Not wanting to overburden the reader about this, critical practice as it developed since Voltaire has required that one way or the other, serious critics must confront Kant. Since the last word has yet to be said about him, there is no absolute position to be taken about cultural criticism either. In regard to the text to which this footnote is appended, given the way he emphasized terminology to capture his concepts, it is unlikely that Kant's shifting the referent for his 'idealism' to "transcendental critique" was a casual affair, and he clearly did so in the text published in 1783, *Prolegomena to any Future Metaphysics*. Given the title of that book, it seems reasonable to assert that the position he assumed in it was supposed to apply to every future form of critical metaphysics, including his own future writings. However, even if based on being convinced of the possibility of sensate confirmation of concepts, Kant's anchor was always in the mind; in that way he remained an idealist to the end, even if determined to show that there is an opening from mind into the world which can be trusted.

critical category and augment it by a further category, that of intentional experience, which is how he arrived at aesthetics.[36]

The debate continues to concern the relative primacy at the interface between {sensual-material experience and intellectual-conceptual thought}. Given that the body places pressure on existence fully as determinant, as does the mind, is not the sensuality of self-standing equivalent to the reasonable dispositions of self-concept? Is the latter (mind work) more than an archive function following from the former (sensual experience), intended to avoid being inundated by the infinite flow of worldly facts? Or are the two really so entangled as to be analytically inseparable? These were the issues about which Schiller took Kant to task and where Eagleton's admittedly non-philosophical study of that confrontation became quickly bogged down.

One difficulty with the category of intentional experience is intention itself: what is it? If intention is action aimed by thought at some worldly objective, then one is back to the difficulty of getting out of the mind into life. If intention is real, then it must be somehow implicit to action as generic fact; if so, then what is the universal, categorical virtue of action? The answer, of course, is 'harmony' or 'beauty' or 'fit'. But that fit must be with the world as well as with the preexisting categories of the mind. If not, either there is alienation (of self from its intentional acts) or there is unbearable psychic dissonance (due to the resistance of the world to comply with one's intention). Aesthetics describes this dialectic, of {intention as action}, of balancing mental categorical content with situated worldly pressure.

Although Eagleton does not theorize the aesthetic issue as I have just done above, he musters the vocabulary more customarily used to discuss it (1990: 103). The key term is 'taste,' which in its intuitive, spontaneous, personal form, labels the pressure for concordance between the next bits of the event of one's (present) existence with the residue of what was digested before, in keeping with aspirations for what may follow. This was a key point for Schiller, who supposed in a certain way that taste was a way to bridge the void between Kantian rationality and Kantian phenomenology.

---

[36] During the 20th century, concern for pragmatic experience was extended considerably, passing by the work of John Dewey (*How We Think*, 1997/1910); then William James (*Essays in Pragmatism*: 1948/~1880–1910) through to Bertrand Russell (*Let the People Think*, 2003/1941).

While it is true that Schiller did this, it does not appear that he came at it from the Kantian (mental or idealist) side of the matter; rather, he initiated his study from the real of immediate experience, and then only subsequently went into 'the mind.' This is the vector which led Schiller to discuss 'play' (the closing theme in Chapter Three): one plays, dialectically, existentially, between the formal and the factual tendencies of local experience; not as bad faith but with integrity, not as denial against alienation, but as realist engagement to avoid that snare.[37]

It is important to recall that not until midway through his career did Schiller study Kant's *Third Critique*, concerning aesthetic judgment. He decided to pass over the first two critiques because of his self-acknowledged limitations in formal philosophical training. While it seems fair to see Schiller as extending the field opened by Kant, from the zone of idealist speculation into that of practical experience, he did this with considerable independence and for that reason, originality as well.

It is thus not clear if Eagleton was fully justified in the way he speaks of Schiller as deconstructing the Kantian project, of clarifying the distinction between form and content; arriving from there to see that only a variety of meta-engagement, that is, an aesthetic-engagement, can allow one to move beyond; because following this path allows one not exactly to attain a state of synthesis as harmony in the face of tension or contradiction, but at least achieve a plateau of finer appreciation, through what amounts to good-judgment as existential expression.

As Eagleton notes without elaboration, Schiller came out of the underclass, the non-aristocratic class, yet was educated then migrated into the aristocratic milieu; for that reason Schiller was in the sensual world long before he was equipped with the intellectual formalisms to take on philosophical debate. Before he arrived at the philosophy stacks in the library to read Kant, terms like duty, obligation, nature, sensuous being, domination and, above all, freedom, were active vocabulary words for down-to-earth Schiller. But for Professor Kant, such key notions were registered in keeping with formal categories of the mind, pretty much exempt from practical considerations.

When Kant argued that a good life, a moral life, is harmonious or beautiful, this was mostly in keeping with Aristotle and classical images of heroic resolution. As considered by Schiller, it was that the aesthetic

---

37 As discussed in Chapter Three, Schiller terminated his political-aesthetic critique in the register of the sublime, suggesting that only complete horror is strong enough to mobilize revolutionary change.

impulse is the precondition for moral behavior and not its product. Ugly people are cruel, exploitive, greedy; ugly people start wars, torture others, find amusement in the destruction of cities; beautiful people do not do such things.

All along, of course, Schiller was aware of the motor force constituted by the irresolvable tension between {freedom and necessity}; were there no such tension, then the possibility of moral action would dissolve as would that of the aesthetic. Because, for him, the moral, the good, the just, the beautiful, are only certified by a certain overcoming, of a certain getting beyond the indolent, the hideous, the gruesome, the revolting. It does not seem that Eagleton was as clear about this as he might have been.

As for Marx, at least in the sense of common usage, in the text *German Ideology* that he wrote as a very young man but which was only put in circulation in the 1930s, he is generally credited with giving the notion of ideology its active political voice. This does not suggest that ideology (see my Introduction) was not used before that time, nor that Marx was the only source of inspiration on the subject; however, it does suggest that Eagleton was educated at a time when the strong ideological vector in the Marx project was not totally evident at Oxbridge.[38]

Eagleton rightly points out that ideology is not just a state of general consciousness but action that is predisposed or prejudiced in advance, oriented by what is often nearly mindless acceptance of belief or principle, the validity of which, often as not, is untested because it is untestable. Ideology for Marx was a physical expression rather than only a mental disposition, which justifies Eagleton's contention that for him, ideology attempts to go beyond a mere "incipient materialism," returning "to the body" as social action (1990: 196). This is then tied into political action: the aesthetics of collective action reveal irresolvable social class tensions, for which mobilization and revolution is the sensible response.

Were that all of it, then Eagleton would be further accurate in claiming, "Art, for Marx, is a supreme instance of this irony" (1990: 220). The irony concerns a 'cruel joke of history:' that if once successful, the class struggle, carried forward by the proletariat, would dissolve class categories and by that, eliminate the proletariat as well. This is a parallel with religious eschatology, where, speaking not of Marx but of gods, it is said that 'by his death, there is given life.' In down-to-earth terms, the same would pertain

[38] Ideology was a central issue for Marx right from the start, even if those Westerners who first studied and diffused Marx's work, other than Engels, did not know this until a couple of generations after Marx died when his early writings were published in the West.

were a total socialist revolution envisioned by Marx to be achieved; the proletariat would sacrifice itself by dissolving as a social category as an unintended but necessary step in rescuing humankind from the devilish grip of capital.

Was Marx Right?

A difficulty with this study of Eagleton's work is to decide just what his project is. We might say he is a critic of ideology, since that theme is evident in many of his books; yet, rather than laying it on about ideology as this or that thought-mongering face of capitalist repression, often as not he drifts into theology as Bible Studies; surely not condemnable, but a bit difficult to align with his announced enthusiasm for a humanist liberation movement.[39] Then there is literary critique; yet, as he's done in dozens of published reviews, when he takes on literature it is usually to find that other authors mostly generate a bourgeois decorative, criticism of pleasure, which he finds offensive in our tormented political and economic times.

As if realizing the absurdity of proposing something equivalent to the abolition of Captain Marvel comics because they celebrate capitalist power, to avoid further clatter and bang, he swings away from ideology and literature, back to Marxist revolutionary rhetoric; as if something he might write would straighten out the disengaged, impractical consciousness for his students or general reading public. Rather than a high-pressure tempest of determined critical churnings, the result is more like the restless swirl of a churning desert wind.

So, in bringing this case study to a close, attention will be given to the last book he published, prior to the beginning of this writing: *Why Marx Was Right* (2011). The title of the work is ominous, yet other than in hopes of increasing his personal capital, it is not clear just why he published this study. Political implications aside, there are very few readers who have

---

39 Good God. Eagleton has written and spoken extensively on the God-question, having conducted as careful a reading of the Bible (he's particularly taken by Paul), as he has done for Schiller or Foucault. Based on that, he has vigorously counterattacked atheists and materialist-rationalist evolutionists. Extending the list of Eagleton's already mentioned writings on God, I might mention: "The Roots of the Christian Crisis" and "Christians against Capitalism" (with Cunningham 1966); *The New Left Church* (1966); *Holy Terror* (2005b); "Religion for Radicals: An Interview with Terry Eagleton" (2009); and *On Evil* (2010).

studied *Capital* who think Marx was wrong about its inherent economic problems; the real issue is what to do about those problems.

The fact that there are important contemporary questions related to the Marx Project is surely justification enough for a new book on Marx. Unfortunately, as if he were writing half-century ago, Eagleton does not address these contemporary issues. In a review of the book by London journalist Tristram Hunt, the justice of Eagleton's taking on this project is unquestioned; he's identified as a highly esteemed and well-read, "literary critic, liberal-baiter, and Marxist man of letters." So much for the credentials. The content on the other hand is another issue since, all in all, "for any admirer of Eagleton or Marx, the book is a disappointment" (Hunt 2011).

The counter argument against the idea announced by Eagleton, namely 'why Marx was wrong,' is well known. Even if it is true that the capital machine generates fallible institutions, which regularly crash, what economic form would do differently or better? In the end, is not the capital mechanism like a giant kayak, ultimately able in any sea to right itself and carry its load onward? From there, the strategy of Marx critics is not to try to 'prove' Marx right or wrong, but only to argue that the solution for economic problems is to keep organized intervention out: to eliminate tampering by alternative, supposedly far less fail-safe institutional actors, namely governmental ones, since that will only damage the self-rectifying inner potential of the capitalist free-market system.

The clairvoyance of Marx concerning the systemic instability of capital is not a question of literature but of critical judgment. What needs to be explored, a century and one-half later, is how the current systems and structures of capital, some of which were set in place after Marx's time, provide few brakes on out-of-control economic movement and virtually no reduction at all in the world-class degree of worker exploitation; how contemporary market dynamics accelerate the global diffusion of local instabilities, such that the basic thesis of 'internal contradictions' as the inevitable worst threat possible for capital will lead to chaos; how that increases the urgency of a revolution of the common consciousness about the fundamental requisites for stable organization of society; for maximizing opportunity, security and autonomy for all western citizens, through some form of socialism.[40]

---

[40] Whereas conservatives view the socialist alternative to capitalism as a heinous option, a famous 20th century French progressive, Cornelius Castoriadis, reached quite the opposite conclusion. He argued that the real choice was either, 'socialism or barbary.'

As for Eagleton on Marx, journalist Hunt's observation is well taken. In this probably too-hastily compiled volume of lecture notes, the content is largely missing about the crucial critical issues of study related to the practical benefits of application of the Marx project for socio-political reform. Still, Eagleton's study opens on many important issues, some of which I will draw out in the following pages to provide a more complete reading not only of the underside of the Marx argument, but of the difficulty of engaging in critical practice in our contemporary liberal age, in a context of depersonalized markets of virtualized labor as inauthentic consumption, now under the specter of the hyper-speculative virtualized market of capital itself.

Born-Again Marx

This last book on Marx is certainly ambitious: Eagleton the born-again agnostic, sets out to refute what he judges to be the ten major criticisms of Marx. He covers one in each chapter, but without any evident logic as to why this is comprehensive coverage of the misunderstandings about Marx, or that the order of his chapters comply with any cumulative intention.

Each chapter follows a common template: it opens with a brief statement of a fallacious argument made against Marx, which Eagleton then sets out to refute. In my words, and not Eagleton's, as a first set of examples: there is the class issue (Chapter Seven), where he discusses why it is false to allege that Marx had a hang-up about social-class tensions; there is the utopia-issue (Chapter Four), where the demons of unjustified accusation are exposed about Marx as a bleeding heart, head-in-the sand, anti-realist Utopian; and the impractical-theory-issue (Chapter Two), where the historical record is finally set straight against those who contend, falsely, that whatever might be said about the genius of the study, the architecture proposed by Marx for restructuring the West would collapse if actualized.

The first thing to note about the bomb-squad protection offered by Eagleton's countering those ten potentially heinous critical attacks on Marx, is that there is no small risk that what will actually occur, is a

---

That image served to draw around him, in a short lived movement, a number of Paris intellectuals, including: Guy Debord, Vincent Descombes, Claude Lefort, Jean-François Lyotard and Edgar Morin.

deepening of the negative programming of even his more sympathetic readers, about the logical, practical, political shortcomings of Marx. As for anti-Marx critics: before reading this book, each had his or her one favorite issue against Marx: after reading it, all of them have ten!

As the reviewer from the London newspaper pointed out, by deciding to take the anti-Marx critics head on, to challenge "a century of misreading Marx... means he is fighting on enemy territory of dreary objections" (Hunt 2011). Courageous on the part of Eagleton as this may seem, such a strategy imprisons one in the discourse of the adversary; after sufficient time of internment, nearly everyone comes, if not to love, then at least to identify with one's captors who in this case are against Marx. Given the way he equivocates ironically about what Marx really did versus did not intend, faced with the result, readers are likely to continue to feel uncertain about Marx, which is presumably not Eagleton's hope.

To deepen an understanding of defending Marx in this way, I will focus on the contents of two particular chapters from *Why Marx Was Right*, both to better appreciate Eagleton's critical style, and to use his words as a springboard for a more general exploration of where the truth lies. Since the order he covered them followed no particular logic, it is not necessary that we follow his order. I will start with the issue at the center of his Chapter Nine (on the state), and finish with the problems raised by him in Chapter Six (about materialism).

The Power of the Social State

In Chapter Nine, Eagleton challenges the common criticism that "Marxism believes in an all-powerful state..." (2011: 196). Not so, according to Eagleton. Rather, Marx was against the abuse of power, viewing the European state-form of those times (~1850s), not wrong as principle but in practice: exerting political force, in support of the elites, land and wealth-possessors, bourgeois capitalists and other *rentiers*. He was against the state as agent of violence in support of such interests, contrary to the best interests of the people.

Marx differentiated "between class-specific and class-neutral functions of the state." He was a political realist, neither authoritarian-state maniac, nor out-of-bounds compassionate idealist; never supposing that harmony was endemic much less the automatic expression of a well-oiled state. Rather than given for eternity, the state is a project to be accomplished, a non-dramatic continuous consequence of the human civilizing drama, under vigilance of critical practice as motor force.

As Eagleton points out a bit further along, the key worry about the state on the part of Marx concerned not just its potential as source of collective alienation, i.e., that 'we the people' may build, support, then lose control of the steering of the state, and suffer domination by state power. His worry was about the dangerous fracture between state and society, with the state dominating civil society, imposing excessive burden via manipulated necessity on the majority of lesser classes, to favor the interests of ruling classes; and about the capital machine beneath it all, determining both the structure of the coercive state apparatus and of the society with liberty limiting roles and institutions.

According to Eagleton, "socialism is the completion of democracy, not the negation of it" (2011: 202). But this is Eagleton speaking, not Marx. The real problem is how to achieve it in action? In writing about, "The Civil War in France," Marx pointed to the impossibility of a revolutionary force taking over the 'old institutions,' then simply transforming them for 'the good.' For Marx, only fundamental institutional change will do, and accomplishing that is very difficult. That is why he believed in revolution, as a complete make over of social order and governance, rather than only reformation, as new paint on old ways.

The Paris Commune of 1871 was a micro-example for Marx of the possibilities for institutional change following revolutionary uprising and restoration of order: reorienting education (no longer under the Church); and justice (direct election of judges and top state agents); and referendum and recall (universal suffrage on all issues to assure that the people do not lose hold on the steering mechanism of the governance); and workers' rights (including the right to take over and direct an enterprise).[41]

More contested was that under the Commune also, private wealth ownership was to be abolished (Eagleton 2011: 204). Can we cheer Marxist inspiration on that one? Is it true that few will continue to work without the right to own more than they need to live comfortably? Are we sure that it is impossible to have a productive society without the unlimited

---

[41] The Paris Commune won in principle, what it lost in fact. The uprising installed a revolutionary government for the city that lasted only a few months (April-May, 1871), until the French bourgeois establishment incited the head of the newly chosen reactionary government under one Adolphe Thiers (1797–1877) to muster the troops in Versailles, besiege Paris and repress the uprising with fire power. Since the current order is always assumed to be legitimate, and radical change is difficult to envision much less achieve, this is the typical result of most revolutionary movements, no matter what the motive for change or what form of regime is being opposed.

right to ownership of capital and then to concentrate indefinitely its pyramidal accumulation?

Then there was "dictatorship of the proletariat." Was this Marx ironizing on participative democracy, contrasted with the form of bourgeois-aristocratic dictatorship that he hoped would be replaced? Or was it a genuine warning concerning the possibility that revolution would lead to replacement of one form of dehumanizing impersonal force, centered in a few oligarchic families, by another equally dangerous form, composed of a floating membership of inexperienced and naive republicans?

There is actually very little Marx in this chapter. As with the book in general, it is more like the transcript of a hastily prepared master class than a carefully revealed exposition. At the end, Eagleton moves from the issue of state to that of power. It seems valid to assert that there can be social power as generic potential of a collective nature for willful expression in any particular situation, as active agency aimed at getting social-work done. And there is also state power as overarching frame of presumably legitimate meaning and direction given to a government by the members of a society composed of individuals in diverse conditions, in pursuit of varying interests. Beyond Eagleton's observations, state power can easily snuff out or seriously inhibit rather than act as agency for the expression of social power. Because social power exists as *á priori* to all conditions and situations, it is the defining force of legitimate action for all significant collective events. Still, state power can either immobilize in the short run the social power on which it depends in the long run, or improve the dynamics for its amplification.

State power plays the crucial role of arbitrator between conflicting domestic interests. From this position as ultimate referee, it necessarily sets some limits on liberty in order to assure other sectors of opportunity. In keeping with the sub-structural capitalist machine, the potential for that to be turned into merchandise is evident. The balancing act is delicate: either the state manages the civil society to maximize efficiency for capital or it manages the capital mechanism for the well-being of civil society. Liberal democratic regimes favor the former, socialist democratic regimes the latter. Marx obviously favored the latter, which for now, is yet to be freely tested, much less achieved.

Socialisms (many forms of which are possible of a less total nature than first supposed) are aimed at assuring that the reason for being of state power is the protection of the expression of social power, by mediating as needed, with the resources needed, issues of priority that generate social conflict. Social conflict is a point of uncertainty in the flow of social processes; conflict resolution is the generation of decisions that unblock such system conflict. Socialism is the state in role of agent and referee, for society as composed of teams and leagues, which is to say of modifiable social categories, micro-communities and institutional forms. In all this, social categories reflect differences among social actors, in preferences for life style and productive pursuit, as subjects of distribution and consumption, associated with differential access to privileges and burdens of production.

The Realism of Historical Materialism

In Chapter Six of *Why Marx Was Right*, Eagleton was determined to expunge the common complaint that "Marx was a materialist," for being fallacious as fact, because unfounded as concept. Unfortunately Eagleton's address of the materialism issue is not very precise, which is a source of weakness in his result.

The chapter is a mixture of selected remarks by Marx on diverse subjects and a statement of Eagleton's personal view on the topic of materialism, buttressed by diverse and varied citations of classic thought. The closing is intended to assure the skeptical reader that anyone, including a Marxist, can be a materialist and at the same time a spiritualist as well. Other than Eagleton himself, exactly whom that package of remarks is intended to assure is not clear.

Avoiding opening the chapter on the manifest problem of materialism, he has difficulty finding the strike zone. For Marx, the notion of materialism cannot be divorced from historicity. What counted was less physical, mineral, or biochemical materiality, than social-materiality, as 'relations of production.' When Marx spoke of materialism, he was not decrying the excess of stone used in the construction of Buckingham palace, but of the social-institution of the monarchy hidden behind its facades: resting on the backs of the English working classes who served as fuel for the capital machine that explains both.

The family form of a people, their marriage, parental, religious form; their political or economic form, all that is historical-material: each social form being materialization in the present of a certain social history. Were that history to have been different, as with China, for instance, then its materialization via those various institutions would be different as well. It is not the function of leadership, or family, or education or parenthood which varies from one cultural system to the next, but the present materialization of the institutional forms by which such functions are resolved; with the process historically routed in the culture.

After having authored hundreds of books, reviews, and essays, Eagleton knows that talk of materialism as institutionalized history tends to be off-putting for most readers. He thus opens this chapter by reminding us that what Marx meant to say was that rather than passive material like a block of granite, as alive and dynamic, men and women are potentially political as well. At least in the West since the Revolutionary Age, as a part of normal life, people tend to be engaged reciprocally with the structures of power and opportunity that surround and protect them (Eagleton 2011: 129).

While this may be only hopeful optimism, if we take Marx via Eagleton seriously, then men and women are agents of, rather than only subjects of history: "They are creatures who transform themselves in the act of transforming their material surroundings" (2011: 130). By that, Eagleton arrives, at a core postulate of the historical-materialist method.

But then the hook, which is a puzzle that has bothered neo-Marxists for a century-and-a-half: if indeed, "ideas are deeply embedded in our actual behavior" (2011: 130), then how can any change occur? If "human consciousness is corporal" (2011: 131), if what we think is materialized, before it is intellectualized, then whether distorted or positive, how is it possible to explain collective behavior, much less alter it save by brain-washing or just plain education?

While avoiding the theorization needed to make sense of this subtle dilemma, Eagleton continues by touching on the essential: the material world, as "the object of our knowledge... is... the product of our own historical activity," so, "...we have to rethink the subject as a form of practice... and... the objective world as the result of human practice" (2011: 132).

By that we arrive at the problem of dialectics, which for some is a dead end and for others the path to liberation. The term, 'subject,' as used here by Eagleton means you and me in the collective sense, as active ingredients in making history happen. We humans are the subject of history: were we not to be, then there would be no history to report. As with Antarctica, where apparently no humans are known to have been inhabitants, there might be zoology or land-form archeology, but no history to write; if we go to the forest in Mexico, where the Aztecs once lived, even if no longer among us, that people is a subject of history.

There is a second meaning to the notion of 'subject' as Eagleton expresses it, which is why the notion is dialectic. While it is true that each people composes its own history, in the present each is also subjugated to the ways of living generated by its past; a people then, is in double sense subject, as {active-subject making history and receptive-subject determined by history}; constituting the reason for being of a certain history (as action) and not another, for a people whose existence is organized according to principles substantially drawn from their previous collective experience.

We humans create a social world with the intention of enhancing opportunity, but along the way must necessarily impose constraint on ourselves. Through time that restriction can become seriously burdensome and the intended benefit of the opportunity thus enabled may prove empty; the world of our own creation can thus become a sort of out-of-control monster. Yet the present as is, always appears justified by history; what choice is there? None, really. But there is a response, labeled 'alienation.'

Alienation: about this Eagleton is clear. It's "the condition in which we forget that history is our own production, and come to be mastered by it as by an alien force" (2011: 135). Often by good faith, we construct a world, which is later hijacked internally or by conquest, then turned against us, as a force of domination by those who become our masters. Yet once in place, due to that unexplainable force of history, since "ideas have a foundation in practice," the reproduction of historical forms tends to perpetuate a certain politically-correct materialism as well (2011: 136).

Tragic Irony

As he does often by style, Eagleton employs a figure that he appears to find comforting, that of irony: but as tragic irony in this case. He asserts that, for Marx, freedom is human, expressed as the opportunity to construct one's own history or narrative, as Eagleton puts it, which obviously animals can not do. This is tragic because most people are free in that way, but do not know that, or at least never realize it as a way of being (2011: 137). This may be deceptive; for the Greeks, tragedy was the impossible struggle to be mystically free of history as context of experience, all the time overlooking structural limitations on freedom as practical action.

According to Eagleton, "Marxist theory itself is not just a commentary on the world, but an instrument for changing it" (2011: 142). From there he introduces consideration of "emancipatory theories," which is a logical move. However, it only pertains if the mode of critical research is more than idealist rhetoric, which his largely is, without going fully historical-materialist, which he sort of approaches, but not really, because of a bit of a blind spot about method.

Rather than using the historical-materialist method as trampoline for getting a jump on the deeper issues, he takes the easier, softer way. Reactivating his irony mode, but this time as comic rather than tragic, covering his lack of foundations by belittling with a thither the significance of Marx with the line, he announces: "It is for this reason that one must take Marx's celebrated eleventh thesis on Feuerbach with a pinch of salt" (2011: 143).

From there Eagleton shows he fails the conceptual test by conflating consciousness as tactical rationality and consciousness as historical search light, claiming that:

> The philosophers, he [Marx] writes there, have only interpreted the world; the point is to change it. But how could you change the world without interpreting it? And isn't the power to interpret it in a particular light the beginnings of political change? (2011: 143–144)

Throughout this book we see Eagleton stride the stage as senior statesman of human liberation, with lines, phrases, images, all presumably tailored to convince the audience of his laudable humanist intention; but without much supporting data. The reason he offers few facts is that having conducted no research, he appears oblivious not just to the negationist potential but the productive power that can be released by judicious application of the historical-materialist method to the study of real historical circumstances.

The way he justifies his claim and his rejection of the basic position of Marx, that "it is social being that determines consciousness," (2011: 144), is by misconstruing the Marx of consciousness as if he were a Hume incarnated: which is unreceivable, as they would say in a New York courtroom. While it is true that 'before we kiss,' we have consciousness, the nature of our take on the kiss as an act of aggression turned friendly, is a determinant example of our historicized common consciousness generating our particular consciousness of a special content, known as the kiss.

As with the embrace, so it is with life, which is why corny irony comes across as a bad joke. Nonetheless he asserted, for attention-getting purposes one can only suppose, "In this sense, there is something carnivalesque about the thought of Marx, as there is about the ideas of Nietzsche and Freud" (2011: 146).[42]

He eventually confronts the dilemma, "superstructure—base" (2011: 148–50), this time defending Marx against all comers. However, he does not describe why his defense is legitimate, perhaps because he is methodologically nearsighted. He speaks of Marx about the oscillating tension between the economic underpinnings of social forms as if composing a letter to Leonard Bloom (James Joyce's hero in *Ulysses*), for whom being was all surface content. However, rather than referencing Joyce, whom he highly admires, Eagleton aims his literary spotlight on a different literary personage, Jude the Obscure (1895–2006), created by another of his favorite legendary authors, Thomas Hardy (Eagleton 2011: 154). Other than the evident parallels between the fictive biography of Jude by Hardy and the real biography of Eagleton, it is not clear just how this reference helps stabilize the argument as to *Why Marx Was Right*.[43]

Why do superstructures exist (2011: 155)? At least in their present form, they constitute overarching normative apparatuses for smoothing over social conflict associated with the essential problems facing a people. That is why, if class tensions intrinsic to capitalism were dissolved, should capitalism cease to dominate the West, the discordant tension, {base—superstructure}, would be substantially deactivated.

From there Eagleton hits on a point which might have profitably served as theme for the chapter, if not his entire book: "The base-superstructure model is a vertical one. Yet one can also think of it horizontally. If we do, the base can be seen as the outer limit of political possibility" (2011: 156). As I translate it, the 'base' of society in this lateral sense, is the level at which you and I live, as members of primary communities of action, work

---

42 The French political philosopher, Vincent Descombes produced a fascinating history of French philosophy that Eagleton seems to have overlooked: *Le même et l'autre. Quarante-cinq ans de philosophie française (1933–1978)* (1979; in English, *Modern French Philosophy*, 1980). Descombes traces the shift in orientation during the 20th century, among French intellections, from a path associated with the work of what he referred to as the 'three H's': Hegel, Husserl and Heidegger; to a new intellectual path, associated with what he labels, the 'three masters of suspicion': Marx, Nietzsche and Freud. The result provides an insightful explanation for why, at least in France, the writings of Marx, like those of Nietzsche and Freud, can not be treated as simply a set of dated documents.

43 *Jude the Obscure*. Thomas Hardy, 1895. Before coming out as a book, this story was serialized in *Harper's New Monthly Magazine* from December 1894 until November 1895. Even if the biography of Hardy himself and, more emphatically, his story of Jude is torrid, scandalous and censorial, this has nothing directly to do with the Biblical traitor, the apostle named Jude. To appreciate the lyric liaison comparison between Hardy's fictive character, Jude, and Eagleton's personal biography, I suggest reading Hardy's book.

and attainment. From there, a social revolution can do no more than establish systems and structures that accord with the fair play at that level of lived experiences. This would result in a new historical condition, where the superstructures of society are formed and reformed to fit everyday life with a certain integrity, rather than as is now the case, of the superstructures imposing categorical treatment of people as if only appendages of economic markets or international warfare. In practical terms, and reversing the image of this received from Marx, the result would be liberation of the 'base' of society from the domination by the superstructure.

He closes the chapter with three pages of religious apologetics: affirming how everyone might be a metaphysical believer and embrace meta-materialist Marx anyway (2011: 157). He decides that Marx was an ethical fellow, a moral fellow, an all-around nice guy; with that, Eagleton closes his discussion of the materialism of Marx. The result seems an unusual terminating twist, but he had to get off stage somehow: softening the critical capitalist concerns of Marx, basking his commentary in the soft light of spiritual other-worldliness, which seems a strange defense against all comers who fail to see *Why Marx was Right*.

Socialism?

Since taking Marx seriously naturally led Eagleton to favor socialism, it is unconscionable that I would finish without examining how he defends that argument. I will focus briefly on what he said in an article he contributed to a left-leaning political magazine, called *Red Pepper*: "A Shelter in the Tempest of History" (Eagleton 2002): just what does that mean?[44]

In this interview, Eagleton gets to the polemic about socialism without ever specifying what he takes that to be; this lack of pedagogical deployment tends to transform his position into a Don Quixoté combat. Not exactly as if sparring with windmills but surely confronting with a weapon of unspecified potential an opposition that is expected to collapse under the weight of its armor before the battle even begins.

A number of paragraphs from his opening, after having taken time to name-drop the "IMF" (International Monetary Fund, close collaborator of

---

[44] As stated on its website, "*Red Pepper* is a magazine of political rebellion and dissent, influenced by socialism, feminism and green politics." Find this short essay by Eagleton online at: http://www.redpepper.org.uk/A-shelter-in-the-tempest-of/.

World Bank) as warning in advance about where he is going with this essay, he says, "It's highly probably that there will be a major crisis of capitalism in the coming decades." He wrote that about five years before the fall of 2007, when the sub-prime crisis caused by irresponsible bank lending first ignited the fuse that led to the collapse of Lehman Brothers, which at the time was distributing bonuses on $600 Billion in assets. While this suggests visionary talent, in his warm-up for this article Eagleton equivocated about futuring; contrasting the prognostications of the soothsayer, whom he deprecates, with the work of the prophet, in whom he sees himself and thus admires.

While it is dramatic to cite recent examples of market failure as signifying that the end is near, what proof is there that, "The System undermines its own hegemony without much need of help from the Left"? In fact, capital is indifferent to the details of the corporate agents that execute its dreary mission, even those with hundreds of billions of digital dollars in their virtual investment accounts. It is as if Eagleton forgets that capital has its own agents of superstructure, battling it out for breathing space in the commons of western Communities, and that there is no passive way to bring that into question without fermenting revolt, not because of hyperbole about 'debt problems' that will be left for 'our grand children,' but about the abominable differences between the conditions of life of those that exit in their fine cars from the garages of the corporate towers in the evening, and those who arrive on the night shift by bus, to restock the water coolers and shine the floors.

Glancing again at the title, ("A Shelter in the Tempest of History"), we see that Eagleton's narrative for this story is simple: leftist humanists need not unite, much less engage the revolution, but only be on the alert and keep their powder dry. The storm is surely on the horizon, bringing a violent "tempest" of civil woes due to economic breakdown. When that occurs, socialism will appear, offering a glimmering shelter of protection in the chaos. We can be confident of that because, as he says, speaking of Socialism, "all it wants are" enough to eat, a job, freedom, dignity, for all on the planet.

Even if, "the point is to be gloomy for the right reasons," my right reasons are not necessarily my banker's. Nonetheless, he says, given the current state of disorganization among left-leaning political parties and groups, it is likely that when the big one (the final untreatable global financial implosion) finally comes, we will find "the Left is disheveled, disorganized and incapable of steering ragged, spontaneous revolt into productive channels." This is certainly gloomy to consider. Would it not seem better that the socialist movement actively recruit participation, even using a bit of its already too-dry powder to stimulate timely episodes of de-leveraged dishevelment. Why not a day, say, February 14, Valentine's Day in the U.S., to agree that no one pays their Visa card bills for a month. Rather, send our bankers a paper heart: they could use one.

This would require collaborators, from "liberals, pragmatists and modernizers," three categories of social actors that Eagleton condemns with greater virulence than he does Hedge Fund Operators, for displaying a "naive form of idealism." Is not Eagleton forgetting that a human liberation movement will never succeed based only on the energy of a militant core? Without mobilizing the 'army of reserves,' most of whom will necessarily come from the ranks of "liberals, pragmatists and modernizers," nothing will be achieved but pointless destruction and post-movement retaliation.

While I agree that "it is not that the system is monumentally stable, just formidably powerful," it is also not intuitively evident that critical short-hitting will pay off here anymore than in baseball. While indeed, "it doesn't take Socialism to bring Capitalism crashing down; it only takes Capitalism itself," having the timber fall this way rather than that depends mostly on how the wedge is set.

In the end, Eagleton's millenarian utopian confidence as to a better future via socialism seems unduly tempered by fear of the lightning and thunder that will mark the day of reckoning needed to set things off in that direction. While it is surely true that there is more to launching a ship than the splintering of a champagne bottle, the socialist movement must start someplace and if a bit of marble is cracked by that announcement, there will be no shortage of brooms in the aftermath.

The Public Intellectual

Although there is not time to pursue this too far, in another more recent article in *Red Pepper*, "Death of the Intellectual" (2008b), Eagleton laments the vaporization of, if not exactly the role of critical intellectual, at least of some place to concentrate them sufficiently to assure a critical mass. A generation ago, universities were such places, havens of independent thinking, ringed by professional schools of institutionally complacent technicians. Since then the core of universities has been progressively emptied, reoccupied by shallow-thinking representatives of the liberal professions and technical specialties, who have allowed the needed insulation between town and gown to be breached.[45]

The invasion by capital of centers of research, the transformation of instruction into services rendered, the reversal of the role of supply and demand such that the student does the demanding and the professor the supplying, with good grades assured in advance or else; there is now no systemic center for "bringing ideas to bear on society as a whole," shifting "the role of the critical intellectual to outside the college walls, to (freelance) writers and artists" (Eagleton 2008b).

In this tribune of desperation, the recently forced-to-retire Eagleton laments how, "the free play of the mind has been managerialized." On the campus, like elsewhere, "utility is now the touchstone of reality."

With that, we leave this strong-spirited, but now freelance intellectual, who, in spite of being an institutional orphan, is still able to find a nearly poetic manner to capture the challenge of critical practice:

> Whereas critique assesses actuality in the light of possibility, measuring the indicative by the yardstick of the subjunctive, the ambition of advanced capitalism is not simply to combat radical ideas, or even to discredit them. It is to abolish the very notion that there could be a serious alternative to the present. (Eagleton 2008b)

---

45 Intellectual Banishment. In this brief article oriented by the work of Noam Chomsky, Eagleton is violently critical of the anti-intellectualism that has gradually infested Anglo-American Universities. Part of the problem as he sees it is that once critical in outlook, in recent years not only have many academics of stature "defected to the political right," but in terms of budget and curricular content, the critical intellectual mission of the social sciences and humanities in universities has been supplanted by the career training mission of the technical departments and professional programs of universities. In the course of the article, Eagleton points to a couple of those whom he identifies as big-name defectors, including the influential former progressive English author and critic, Christopher Hitchens, and the internationally known and highly reputed German sociologist, Jürgen Habermas. As will become clear in my own closing for this book in Chapter Eight, even if on somewhat different technical grounds, at least in regard to Habermas, I am in high agreement with that assessment. Still, these harsh words against universities and other intellectuals on the part of Eagleton can not be separated from the personal difficulties he has had with university administrators throughout his career. This must be understood to appreciate the cryptic note appended to the end of Eagleton's essay, where the Red Pepper editors provide the following laconic information: "Terry Eagleton was forced to retire from his post as John Edward Taylor Professor of English Literature at Manchester University in July 2008." http://www.redpepper.org.uk/death-of-the-intellectual/.

CHAPTER SEVEN

HAYDEN WHITE: HISTORIC TRUTH AS STORY TELLING

Against Historical Formatting

Born in the hills of middle-Tennessee in 1928, as a student, Hayden White went North, to Michigan, studying first in Detroit at Wayne State University, then on to Ann Arbor for his MA and PhD in history (1958). Now in his 80s, he has yet to say his last words. His specialty is difficult to peg; a volatile critical mixture aimed at cultural history as expressed via texts and literature, with a world-spanning readership centered in the nether-land known as the humanities. From a distance, what he does is social-philosophy, concerned with truth and how to put it into life; too practical for philosophers, too thoughtful for most social scientists, too a-typical for ordinary historians. For lack of clear identity his books are generally placed in the philosophy zone of major book stores.

White's place here is similar to Eagleton's and by that different from the place occupied by the first four major figures of this study. Rather than only examining the work of the subjects of these last two chapters in order to better understand their methods of practice, I am concerned also with the political consequences of such practice, as illuminated by theirs.

By legend, the West is democratic and free. Yet as with every cultural system, it generates and is sustained by particular ways for organizing everyday life. Whatever the benefits, even the best intended institutions weigh heavily on individuals, throwing relations between different categories of citizens out of balance, often threatening freedom by imposing burdensome obligation as enforced security.

Western institutions are chronically out of fit with the demands of their citizens and natural condition: constant adjustment is necessary. Properly informed criticism concerning the need for liberation as direction is thus crucial for a free society, focusing on the agents of society that are working in a progressive fashion versus those who impede the general well-being. Whatever the sector, key actors and agencies dislike being graded. Like the tax-assessor, critical practitioners are both necessary to refine social order and considered dangerous; yet for different reasons.

Militant Accretion

Before he was forty years old, White had become a challenge not only to his chosen discipline but to the political status quo as well. Although he was respected wherever he worked, for reasons immediately associated with his critical attitude he ended up being a bit of a disciplinary nomad.

After finishing his studies in Michigan (1958), he spent ten years teaching in the history department at the University of Rochester, New York, then, after 1968, five years more at UCLA. Next (1973) he accepted the position of Director of the Center for Humanities at Wesleyan University, Connecticut, and fifteen years later, in 1978, he moved to UC Santa Cruz, California, as Professor of the History of Consciousness from which post he eventually retired, migrating a final time to an emeritus post at Stanford as Professor of Comparative literature. The only brief stop in this story was at UCLA and the circumstances leading to his abrupt move from there, in 1973, merits a comment.

Hayden White gained his tenure and a stable place in academe in the mid-1960s, when cultural criticism in the U.S. had taken to the streets. Being mostly conservative, the established powers retaliated, attempting to snuff-out the protest movements. When White arrived in Los Angeles in 1968, the reactionary gaze of anti-protest response was well in place; civil authorities began to use security agents, in fact domestic spies who infiltrated groups of all sorts from bicycle clubs to university organizations, intending to smoke out non-conformists.

White refused to be intimidated, particularly when it became apparent that police agents were mixed among his students, as if nothing is more dangerous for the nation than a gaggle of grumbling history majors eating peanut-butter sandwiches in a park. In 1972, he struck back, constituting himself sole plaintiff in a case against the Chief of Police of the Los Angeles Police Department. Three years later, in 1975, by which time he was already in Connecticut, under appeal, the judgment came from the California Supreme Court, vindicating White's position, in defense of freedom of speech and association at universities. A certain practical notoriety as defender of the right to speak out has preceded him ever since, for protecting students from illegal intrusion by the social control apparatus of the state.[1]

---

1 "HAYDEN V. WHITE, Plaintiff and Appellant, v. EDWARD M. DAVIS, as Chief of Police, etc., Defendant and Respondent." *Supreme Court of California: L.A. No. 30348.* 24 March 1975. The unanimous judgment included the following:

Beyond simply a review of his most representative writings, I will attempt to display his method by applying it, with particular concern for the relationship between the method used in critical practice and the political punch of the results.

The core of White's argument is found in the contents of two collections of his essays and one large, historically burdensome book. In the first of these anthologies, *Tropics of Discourse: Essays in Cultural Criticism* (1978), there is a reprint of a crucial journal article: "The Burden of History." Published in 1966, this paper constituted the foundational move in his project, where he boldly and unambiguously challenged the way work is done by academic historians. In combination with the other essays contained in that anthology, this work established White's intellectual signature: using the tools of history to examine the product of historical study, buttressing in the end a manifestly outrageous counter-intuitive position about its conduct.

Next there was his major theoretical work, *Metahistory* (1973), where White provided a detailed description of his model for the study of history, coupled with an empirical demonstration of the use of that model, consisting of case studies of the work of eight major 19th century European historians.

Finally, there is a second anthology of his more recent essays, *The Content of the Form: Narrative Discourse and Historical Representation* (1987). Here, White develops his position about the narrative form as historical-literary archetype.

I will explore the methodological underpinnings and practical findings revealed in those pages of White's scrupulous erudition. Along the way, I will use what this establishes about White's program as the basis for speculating on the blockage that continues to reduce the practical political clout of even the most carefully conduced cultural criticism.

Historical Half-Measures

With his 1966 paper, "The Burden of History" (1978: 27ff), White challenged the disciplined tradition of history. This paper came out just after he

"We conclude that the allegations of the complaint state a prima facie violation of freedom of speech and of assembly as well as of the state constitutional right of privacy. As we shall explain, a host of decisions of both the United States Supreme Court and of this court firmly establish the constitutionally enshrined status of freedom of [13 Cal.3d 761] speech and freedom of association in our nation's universities and colleges." http://scocal.stanford.edu/opinion/white-v-davis-27879.

had been granted tenure, minimizing the danger for his career. In that nearly legendary essay, he accused his fellow historians of unintentionally plying their professional trade in an intellectually duplicitous fashion, straddling the fence between fact-based analysis of past events, as if an exercise of the empirical sciences, and using artistic license to fill in the gaps, smoothing out the narrative by applying the acumen of the gifted creative writer, to bring the past back into life in their texts.

White decried this form of intellectual equivocation, not as morally wrong or strategically unjustified, but as a practice linked to institutional denial on the part of professional historians; they pretended one thing and wrote otherwise. He advocated greater professional integrity, and greater transparency concerning the fundamental fact of history: even concerning yesterday, no one is sure just what occurred, much less why or what to say about it.

No matter what the pragmatic intent, since the facts about past events are partial and the historian is obliged to make a coherent story (narrative) of them anyway, it is evident that the author must fill in the gaps and thus portray those events in a fashion that is, at least to some degree, fictional. White was particularly bothered about the practical consequences of this form of erudite complicity: the difficulty with it is that, time and again, the work of historians is used as a guide for political action. Even when motivated by the desire to contribute to future improvement, being always based on the past, critical histories are stories involving a substantial degree of uncertainty, the ambiguity of which is so severe as to call into question the timeless practice of using history as a guide. About this he is clear, because historians, "should no longer naively expect that statements about a given epoch or complex of events in the past 'correspond' to some preexistent body of 'raw facts'" (1978: 47).

Apostates being rarely much loved, as a by then (1966) recognized history professor, young man White was obligated to answer his own accusation: was he symbolically similar to the fictional character, Elmer Gantry, preaching in public against the very professional malpractice that he pursued in private; or an enlightened Luther, pinning his critical thesis on the bulletin-boards in university corridors, using the findings from his own research on the history of History to condemn as unjustified the rightness of the archival research of his disciplinary compatriots?

Seven years later he published the book, *Metahistory: The Historical Imagination in Nineteenth-Century Europe* (1973). There he summarized his study of history upon which he had based the position announced in 1966. Forty years later, this book continues to broaden the knowing smiles of humanities students the world over, equaled in intensity only by the dour despondence of many ordinary history professors, faced with the need to impress on their students the superlative quality of 'objective' historical understanding.

White did not dispute what most readers take to be the task of history as the critical study of the past or the importance of disseminating such understanding for every generation. What he questioned was not the process of historical research but the indeterminate quality of what he irreverently referred to as 'raw facts' concerning historical events. His thesis was simple, repeated in nuanced forms, popping up in most of his important texts ever since, reminding his listeners and readers that rather than heresy, his critical position is fully reasonable: "In my view"... and he was quick to affirm that this was only his personal judgment:

> ...'history'... as a plenum of documents that attest to the occurrence of events, can be put together in a number of different and equally plausible narrative accounts of 'what happened in the past,' accounts from which the reader, or the historian himself, may draw different conclusions about 'what must be done' in the present. (1973: 283)

Historical study is necessarily interpretive. For any culture system, while there surely are anterior circumstances that bear on the present with significance for the future, there is no single determinant truthful recounting as to the particular form of those past conditions, much less of their causes, effects or future pertinence.

Far from skeptical or cynical, White spoke with authority about the poetic, creative aspect of historical narratives, leveling an announcement that continues to raise the eyebrows of rationalists. As he put it in another paper, "The Fictions of Factual Representations" (1976): between, "the discourse of the historian and that of the imaginative writer," although they deal with different sorts of events, "the techniques or strategies that they use in the composition of their discourses can be shown to be substantially the same" (1978: 121). This is another way of asserting that, as texts, there is no *a priori* difference between history and literature.

Although he attempted to buttress this argument in more sophisticated ways, he was not beyond direct appeal to common good judgment:

> Readers of histories and novels can hardly fail to be struck by their similarities. There are many histories that could pass for novels, and many novels that could pass for histories. ... Viewed simply as verbal artifacts histories and novels are indistinguishable from one another. (in 1978: 121–22)

Is not philosophy in its way literature also, and if so, what of its facticity? Why not the same concerning all academic books and scholarly journal articles, suggesting that the treaties of Darwin, Newton, Einstein, Freud, Marx, Nietzsche: each is some mixture of well-crafted history and imaginative construction, with the power of the result depending on how one prefers to judge it.

History as Irony

Irony can be defined as the convincing portrayal of stories that are less than completely truthful, about which doubts are actively harbored by—the storyteller. Yet speaking of disciplined research, the more informed the historian, the more likely and well reasoned ought to be her or his doubts about the adequacy and truth of those past facts and texts. Thus the door into the field of irony: even from respected historians, the facts of past matters are to some degree stories told, presented to the public as otherwise.[2]

Beyond the details of how White developed his argument, the important point for us is its practical implication. According to him, on a stage set during the 19th century by excessive attention for rational empirical certitude about the human condition, thanks to advanced techniques of communication, the 20th century became a period of invasive, profound irony. With information now employed more for distraction and persuasion than for enlightenment, the result is an almost insurmountable discrepancy between what is said versus done, between the intended and understood, constituting a serious challenge for social action, radical political modifications and, above all, for liberation movements.

Not just for political leaders but professors as well: are there bounds on historical truth other than those established by the current moment? Critical method necessarily relies on some form of literature for its expression it's target being current social practices (purportedly misinformed or poorly appreciated) animated by the residual energy from past events, consisting of politically significant action in the largest sense. Criticism thus generates a history in the present, usually aimed at the short term future; yet it is

---

2 Facts. In keeping with White's preference for what the rhetoricians call middle-voice, the word 'fact' appears frequently but ironically throughout this chapter. White opposed the claim that the fictive nature of the past as narrated was surmounted by attaching a statement about 'rules of evidence' to one's writing.

history nonetheless. To believe White, necessarily depending on interpretation, the factual basis of the best historian's work is always debatable and because of that, so too are the normative implications of the findings. Critical histories are often politically offensive in a boldly out-front manner: yet even when intended otherwise, based on some twisted optic or selective perception, they it may be largely unfounded in fact.

Irony involves reversals of expectations: for example, treating political events as due to the gods rather than humans or the transmission of evidence intended to convey double meaning associated with specific words and actions. When the results of critical studies are picked up and diffused in the ironic mode, the result is conventionally equated to a magic show, where the public is fooled thanks to the clever employment of smoke and mirrors. To hijack the critical enterprise and transform it into a gag, to express its results with a 'knowing wink,' to ironize rather than theorize, buries the vital call for needed surveillance of socio-political practices. In my judgment, by drawing scholarly attention to the bad-faith potential of irony for history, White identified one of the factors that may explain why, during the 20th century, the products of quality critical practice were often sentenced to the graveyard of political irrelevance.

Metahistory as Postulate

Since the book *Metahistory* is White's signature text, I will concentrate on it. In the "Preface," he boldly announced his ambition: the "analysis of the deep structure of historical imagination," using a set of "interpretative principles" to be described "explicitly" in his introductory chapter. His goal: nothing less than "a formal theory of historical work." Accordingly, historians produce "histories," consisting of "a certain amount of 'data'... and a narrative structure for their presentation," following a schema chosen in advance for presenting those data, "as an icon... of events presumed to have occurred in times past." The nature of the result "is generally poetic and specifically linguistic in nature," exemplifying what a "distinctively 'historical' explanation should be." This supposes one is faithful to some generally accepted historical "paradigm" which "functions as the 'metahistorical' element in all historical works"(White 1973:ix).

White's objective was overtly methodological. He was perplexed with "the problem of historical knowledge" that at the time seemed to be turning historians away from their subject and against each other. The result was announced in this book as "a history of historical consciousness in

19th century Europe," aimed at determining "what does it mean to think historically and what are the unique characteristics of a specifically historical method of inquiry?" (1973: 1). He decided that the key is a certain "historical imagination," the "deep structure" of which he set out to explore (1973: 2). This led him to identify a topology of tropes as guides for 'historical imagination,' and to his choice of the six major historians whom he focused on in the case studies that fill the central chapters of this book.[3]

Since the key issue here is his method, most of what follows concentrates on the derivation and effectiveness of the "theory of tropes," that he says underlie the various "historiographical styles" that he asserts dominated 19th century historical thought. He laid that out in a dense, formal fashion in his Introduction (see particularly 1973: 29ff), thus setting the stage to explore with his in-depth case studies the veracity of his model; to demonstrate in practical terms the approach he believes dominated critical interpretive writing since history became a serious discipline two hundred years ago.

It is not every day that an attempt is made to re-theorize an entire discipline of knowledge; unsurprisingly, White's ambitious project generated waves of agitated response. He did not approach the task casually, but anchored his position in an encyclopedic study of eight major intellectual figures from 19th century Europe. Beyond describing their singular contributions, about each of whom he seems to have been well informed, he applied the framework from his model to classify their work as if they were representative members of certain sociological categories. This is not unlike what occurs in studies of the history of religion, when an author claims that rather than divinely inspired, great religious figures are only spokespersons for their times. White's book left the historical purists gasping.

I generally draw sparingly from the commentaries associated with the work of those featured in my case studies in this book, preferring to let them speak for themselves. Because of White's unprecedented angle of attack on the rational-empirical, epistemological base of the historical sciences, it may be useful to include material from one representative example of the critical response that his work generated.

Ewa Domanska, a professor at Stanford, is one of White's profligate biographers. In a 1998 paper, she refers to White's *Metahistory* as a "cult

---

[3] The similarity between the "sociological imagination" as discussed by C.W. Mills (1959) and the "historical imagination" as discussed here (1973) by White should not be overlooked.

book," a rare attribution in contemporary critical studies. Yet she also judges the text "tiresome and repetitive," which makes its popularity difficult to explain. Of course as marketers know, many reasons motivate purchase of a book other than to read it.

Writing twenty-five years after White's seminal *Metahistory* appeared, Domanska (1998) shed additional light on White's intellectual road-map. After addressing an extensive list of the major historical figures that he recurrently drew on during the early years of his research, she looked for some common "intellectual sensitivity," "point of view," or "vision of the world," which she assumed the individuals whose inspiration White relied upon must share at least implicitly, else why would White so often turn to them? As for, "what links all of these individuals together (and with White himself)," her summary observation is telling: speaking effectively of his intellectual reference group, "they were very influential 'rebels,' 'heretics,' challenging the legitimate (in their times) way of thinking (of their times) about the world and modes of its representation."[4]

While she admired White's discipline, she claimed that, "especially in *Metahistory*," he was so occupied with the "exposition of the writers, literary critics, philosophers, and historians that constitute his own object of analysis," as to "interfere with his own philosophy" (1998: 174). Domanska thus reflected White's critical strategy back on him, a common approach among practitioners of the critical art.

Still, to contend that White had a 'philosophy' which somehow got lost in his attention for archives and writings of others is probably less valid an observation than to say that, as with many who practice social-philosophy, his theory emerged from his work rather than purposefully informing it in advance; with that 'informing,' such as it was, due rather to his aesthetic engagement resulting from an almost too serious personal confrontation with the ponderous question: 'what does the word, history, say'?

While the debate is open, it is probably worthwhile to consider carefully the line that White selected as dedication for his *Metahistory* study. Taken from a text (*The Psychoanalysis of Fire*) by the French philosopher of science and literary critic, Gaston Bachelard (1938/1964: 22), it says:

[4] The list of 'influential rebels' that fascinated White, much longer than only the eight whom he attended to in his *Metahistory*, includes: Auerbach, St. Augustine, Balzac, Bergson, Burckhardt, Camus, Collingwood, Croce, Dawson, Dilthey, Freud, Frey, Gombrich, Hegel, Herder, Ibsen, Jaspers, Joyce, Kafka, Kant, Mann, Marx, Michelet, Nietzsche, Popper, Ranke, Sartre, Spengler, Tocqueville, Toynbee, Vico and Weber.

"One can study only what one has first dreamed about" (in White 1973: Front piece).[5]

While thus perhaps too rational in her quest to establish White's manifestly poetic motive, with her 1998 study Domanska nonetheless put her finger on what appears to have been the central issue, preoccupying White's thinking: "how to structure the world and produce meaning for a chaotic reality" (Domanska1998: 175).

The way she saw it, in the wake of the political churning of 19th century Europe, in the interest of domestic harmony, the West took a major ironic turn. The point was to justify the continuing subservience of the working classes to a system that had little payoff for them. Yet how to disguise the suffering of the masses behind the illusion of enlightenment progress? The truth was that most of the benefit from the production of society was delivered to those in the elite classes, among whom delayed gratification, occupational discipline and difficult living conditions were rarely seen.

Political irony proved to be a less violent strategy for muting popular agitation against the inequality of the system, which had been the major domestic political worry since the French Revolution. In order to reinforce the illusion of general progress, in spite of the selective benefit of its fruits, required finding a way to put a smile on the face of the empirical evidence. Irony, of the political rather than only the vaudeville variety, was found to help soften the sense of indignation against occupational exploitation and rude life for the poor, by masking with a snicker the tragedy of the masses and the opulence of the elites. Accordingly, intellectual double-talk was used as camouflage, rendering less apparent the failure of "reality to fulfill (its) expectations," while continuing nonetheless to calling for greater sacrifice by 'others.' This left both common citizens and the elites in a state of "ironic apprehension," generated by the unspoken and thus consciously denied truth about "social breakdown" and "cultural decline." Not only is the effect not really funny, but its false

---

5 Fiery Dreams. The source of this line for White's Front-Piece, Gaston Bachelard (1884–1962), was very influential in France, but not well-known elsewhere. His criticism was oriented by metaphorical reference to the four elements—earth, water, fire, and air, which, since Classical Greece, have been treated as the material source from which all else is created. Developed in his most recognized essay, *The Psychoanalysis of Fire,* (1964/1938), Bachelard subsequently applied those symbols—metaphorically, in his historical-critical study of creativity through world literature, touching the work of major figures including Charles Baudelaire, Edgar Allan Poe, Lautréamont and Friedrich Nietzsche. Although White does not cite Bachelard in the body of this text, it appears that Bachelard may have been a source of inspiration for the metaphorical figure-based architecture that White used as critical method throughout his career.

nature rather quickly contributes to the alienation, not just of the poor, but for the elites as well (Domanska1998: 173).

At the time of that writing, the burden of history must have weighed heavily on Domanska, since she identified as her "main purpose" for the 1998 paper: "to answer the question, how can we go beyond irony?" (1998: 173). As we will see, according to White, such a move would be Utopian, a possibility that as far as he was concerned, was banished from the intellectual horizon of late modernity. If so, then to move beyond irony would require going beyond modernity, which, rather than Utopianism, would imply the ultimate in postmodern realism.

Four Figures of Interpretation

White is no late blooming European romantic or postmodern relativist in the vulgar sense. Still, in spite of his training in empirical exactitude, he sometimes comes across like an unconvinced archivist in the Paris Picasso museum. To justify arguing that the key to history depends on its execution as a literary undertaking, he was obligated by his own standards to detail just how historical texts are structured. This was the point of his *Metahistory* study, in which he not only laid out his complex topology of alternatives for action when writers take to historicizing past events into text, but with considerable care he applied his topology to the working ways of eight major figures of 19th century historiography: Hegel, Michelet, Ranke, Tocqueville, Burckhardt, Marx, Nietzsche and Croce.[6] Since the typology he proposed is key for understanding his theory of historiography, I must pause to put it in relief.

White argues that, at least for the eight cases he studied, one or some combination of four master figures of style was used to build most every

---

6 Nineteenth-Century Actors. In this order, the historical targets that White put in his sights were: G.W.F. Hegel: 1770–1831; Jules Michelet: 1798–1874; Léopold von Ranke: 1795–1886; Alexis de Tocqueville: 1805–1859; Jacob Burckhardt: 1818–1897. Karl Marx: 1818–1883; Friedrich Nietzsche: 1844–1900; and, Benedetto Croce: 1866–1952.

Overcoming the manifest divergence in the mass of work generated by those eight master historians, in his book White demonstrated unusual facility with the art of historical narrative construction; not only covering each case in a single readable chapter, but weaving this diversity together as if, beneath appearances, the chaotic 19th-century in Europe followed a rational plot line of movement-check-countermove, such that the West was very much on its feet, ready for one more round, at the opening of the 20th-century. In spite of the facility of historian White's reassurances, by exposing retrospectively the comic aspect of the hell on earth that was the 19th century for the West, I wonder if the same level of human vitality with which he claimed the 20th century opened will still pertain by the end of the 21st century.

text, guiding decisions about inclusion, emphasis and order of details, as well as about the logical ties between elements which define and integrate (or not), the relations between elements. This allows the resulting narrative both to convincingly capture with necessary authority the historical image that the author has in mind and to pass it along understandably and forcefully, to his or her audience.

The term used to label these four figures is 'trope.' Toward the end of the well developed paper where he delves into the derivation of this strategy, he adds a definition for the term, inspiration for which he attributes to Kenneth Burke. Accordingly,

> ...we may say that the four 'master tropes' deal in relationships that are experienced as inhering within or among phenomena, but which are in reality relationships existing between consciousness and a world of experience calling for a provision of its meaning. (White 1978: 72)[7]

The four figures deployed by White are *metaphor*, *metonymy*, *synecdoche*, and *irony*. These describe somewhat different strategies by which modifiers are linked to referents, generating images of events or individuals described in a text in such a way as to assure some intended meaning at the time of its reception; images which might otherwise come across confusedly or text which might later be read by others as dreadfully dull.[8]

---

7 Tropes. "Interpretation in History" (orig. 1972). While in his *Metahistory* study, White described and applied this tropic strategy, whether by desire or obligation, in this paper published about the same time, he provided a more elaborate review of its derivation. Avoiding extensive logical development, as is also characteristic of his style, he attempted to justify use of that mode or 'empirical' study, oriented by what some critics consider the imaginary, subjective, ethereal or metaphysical qualities of the trope. Given the definition cited above, it might be concluded that every expression of knowledge of any world-given stimulation is a 'trope,' rendering virtually every substantive noun a 'trope.' As methodological strategy it is thus a dangerous device, but so poetically attractive.

8 Defense of a Method. In addition to Kenneth Burke, and the less direct influence of Bachelard, White acknowledges two sources of inspiration for his use of those figures as the basis of his comparative historical study. Foremost is Giambattista Vico who discussed them in his, *New Science* (1725). White mentions this in a footnote in his *Metahistory* (1973: 31ff), and again in the same year in his, "The Irrational and the Problem of Historical Knowledge in the Enlightenment" (1972, in *Tropics of Discourse*, 1978, Note 42, p.80), where he labored just a bit in justification of his reliance on such a symbolically wispy logic for classifying a century of historical production; where he also references the influence of another 'Burke,' this time Edmund Burke whose most recognized writing is, *Reflections on the Revolution in France* (2004/1790). The following year, by then probably much on the defensive about his critique of history, in another essay, "The Historical Text as Literary Artifact," (1974, in *Tropics of Discourse*, 1978; 94–5), in direct reference to Vico, he acknowledged having been "taken by ...Vico's notion that the logic of all 'poetic wisdom' was contained... in [the] four principal modes of figurative representation," listed above.

With *Metaphor*, one associates some quality with a referent so as to lessen, embellish, or otherwise alter, often by innuendo, the received image of the referent by one's audience. Both modifier and referent are commonly recognized on their own, but not immediately, perhaps never really associable in the way they are presented in the text; a human quality may be attributed to a non-human event, ('an angry storm') or vice-versa ('a thunderous disposition'), intended to attribute or alter perception or understanding of some dynamic attribute of the person, place or thing of reference.

In *Metonymy*, a part of a system is taken for the all of it, usually mixing up or reversing cause and effect, as if some mechanical connection between the comparative elements explains the one by the other. For example, a 'man that is all heart' or a 'society that is all economy.' Thus understood, it is no surprise that this is the mode that White attributes to the historian Marx, in his study of *Capital*; except, there is more to Marx than that. Nonetheless, it exemplifies the logic.

In *Synecdoche*, an aspect of some target phenomenon is taken as if the essence thereof ('the breath of life'), or the contemporary presence of elements is taken to mean their inherent harmony, functional fit, aesthetic resonance, or otherwise (a 'dream team').

Irony is the use of double-meaning language to manipulate the truth of announced elements: perhaps false allegories, unjustified illusion to hyper-real extremes, bombastic hyperbole, the raising of false questions, or disguised assertions as innuendo, depicting by description as if palpably true, some quality of the referent, in spite of the fact that the claim is unlikely, if not patently false. As only the desperately hopeful might appreciate, the boldest of irony is when the lie is the truth.[9]

While unavoidably necessary to bring life into communication, often revealing unexpected insight, the use of tropes also tends to attach, consciously or not, a certain amount of subversive or deific baggage to the

---

Three years after *Metahistory*, White returned again to Vico in another essay, "The Tropics of History: The Deep Structure of the New Science" (1976, in *Tropics of Discourse*, 1978; 197ff), where he as much as admitted that the strategy used in his 1973 monograph was a reworked update of Vico's original project.

[9] Meaning Construction. Dating from Classic Greece, specialists in rhetoric and literature have studied these various constructive strategies of language, pointing to the importance of how what is said about any subject is determinant for what is understood about it. Owing to the difficulty of finding accurate vocabulary to discuss how the association of words drives the meaning of communication, these issues are deceptively complex. For a brief, technically precise discussion of the issue, see Catherine Fromilhague, *Les Figures De Style* [*Figures of Style*] (1995).

result, one way or the other informing a message with moral, political or aesthetic bias. For instance, while there is nothing inherently violating to describe Bill Gates as 'a giant of a man,' pursing a 'life of service,' in an otherwise 'heartless society,' as a 'compassionate capitalist,' the effect is clearly loaded in the direction of the absurd.[10]

Use of tropes implies selective judgment. When applied to familiar incidents, the effect is achieved essentially with adjectival modifications, which are relatively easy to spot and unmask by the vigilant observer. Applied by historians to entire historic epochs, world class events, or major historical figures, the result is a complex narrative that dissimulates the facts of the matter within its style of presentation. While this is done routinely for cinema or fictional novels, White's point was to alert his professional colleagues about how the use of these tropic strategies colors their work in ways that are often unrecognized not just by the reader but, more importantly, by the writer.

No matter which of the four tropic styles are deployed, the result is usually some degree of misrepresentation, if not fiction dressed up as fact. Still, the choice of authorship is to decide on one, or perhaps some mixture, of them, for structuring a purportedly evidence-based writing exercise, knitting together the details as if revealing a convincingly reasoned historical plot.[11]

---

[10] Transferring a 2012 image from quantum physics to criticism: since one is known only by the relationships it establishes, the trope might be considered as the Higgs Boson of idiom; as said about the cyclotron of the other one, 'because it has so much mass it takes a lot of energy to create one.' White does it with words.

[11] Authorship freedom. Since the message at its core is the central concern of serious authorship, it should not make much difference how a work is framed: but it does. This applies not just to fiction but to 'fact-' oriented writings. The framing process is cultural, serving as the basis of differences between works that are produced in different national languages at the same time on the same theme, generating differences in 'meaning' of how issues are understood between countries and explaining why translations are always approximate. In Europe, more or less prior to the French Revolution, during 'the Classic Period' as it is said, there was one dominant style of writing that all authors were obliged to use if the result was to be taken seriously. By the 20th century that had changed; not that one might suddenly compose any way at all, but that there developed a limited number of styles of '*écriture*' as Roland Barthes referred to it. Specifically, in reference to France, on sitting down to write, the author was free to choose her *écriture*, but once having done so, was obligated to stick to it throughout a work, less the audience become confused and the result be degraded. Effectively, White is making the same argument about the modes of historiography used during the 19th century: but in his case, he refers to the use of one or another dominant '*tropes*' as framing principle for the construction of narratives. As I discussed in Chapter Four, Foucault emphasized the same sort of effect, using the notion of '*épisteme*' to identify the characteristic style of writing of an historical epoch. Since I am covering this issue as practice for White in this chapter, and have discussed it in

While this use of literary devices is apparently necessary to glue the elements together into some comprehensible whole, if the result in the end is a sort of put-on, the question is, why do it? A comic might do this as a spoof to entertain an audience; an ad-person to mislead a market; a pundit to rally political support; a preacher to fill a contract with the gods; but, assuming they already have tenure, why would serious historians or cultural critics bother with the tropic art?

Irony: More Than Staged Technique

If White is accurate, that today the West is blanketed by a culture of irony, a first question to pose concerns its durability. If our standard is ancient Greece, the earliest known instance of this phenomenon, then our present indeterminate condition may endure for centuries. The next question is, what might we anticipate in the long run? The answer is a bit cruel: if we follow the Greek path and there is no rupture in our historic condition, rather than toward a new golden age, we are on the road toward cultural collapse.

Since the usefulness of a trope depends on its imprecision, it is difficult to pin down precisely the definition of, irony. By convention it is said to be feigned ignorance in situations of sharp discordance, not just in the words used to express conditions by official spokespeople, but between what is known to be the truth of those conditions and how they are broadcast. One can assert that the U.S. Constitution is 'clear as mud' and by that play of words, tell an important truth; but to paint a picture of social justice under political regimes dominated by speculative capitalism as if it is the best the West can do, is conscious distortion of the truth. When generated by the popular press, political leaders, or hired agents of capital, that fact is ironic: a dissimulation of actuality. So: why would a society want to hide the truth from itself?

In Greece of about 450 BCE, the newly emergent culture of irony was manifest as a theatrical device, demonstrated dramatically by Sophocles (~497–405 BCE) in his *Oedipus Rex*. That was tragic theater, intended to impress Greek citizens with the importance of remaining loyal and in service to the Republic; not because it was a perfect society, but because the

reference to Foucault in Chapter Four, I might point to a set of texts where Barthes confronts this problem. See his *Le Degré zéro de l'écriture: suivi de Nouveaux Essais Critiques* (1972 and 2004/1981).

power of human agency was invariably exceeded by the unknowable countenance of the future. To act in good judgment is to trust the gods, clean house and face the music.

Beyond its existential message, that state of irony expressed a political warning: the sustainability of the Greek society was threatened by the refusal of the city to be realistic about its internal responsibilities. Rather than living within their means, the grandeur of that people during its golden age was sustained principally by pillage and colonial exploitation, issue of military aggression. The tragic announcement was a wakeup call, ignored by the Greeks, with disastrous consequences some centuries later.[12]

The ironic message of tragic theater became too heavy for the Athenians to accept. They apparently could not imagine the possibility of major societal change. The solution was institutional denial: not replacement of societal irresponsibility by something different, but by an aesthetic of ethical compromise, by the substitution of tragedy with comedy.

The greatest of the Attic comic poets was Euripides (480–406 BCE). His work turned drama into melodrama, with the sublime refracted as emotional pathos. By that, irony doubled its force; everyone knew that no one was telling the truth, but instead of being horrified, this was passed off with a simper. The key in comedy is to disguise the tragic limits of humans and their society as if only a case of periodic collective misfortune or personal distress, treated as if accidental and rare, or else the product of the misguided actions of 'others,' in comparison to which most ordinary viewers consider themselves sympathetically superior.[13]

What were the Greeks denying during their post-golden age of irony? Nothing less than the eminent collapse of their society, due to the

---

12 Decadence. A major inspiration for the metaphorical use during the 20th century of the Decline of Ancient Greece (the actual details of which are obscure), is Nietzsche. Indeed, his famous 'pessimism' was mostly a derivative of his aesthetic awareness of the proximity of a Fall for the Modern West, equivalent in brutality with what occurred 2500 years ago. He dealt with this theme a bit everywhere in his writing; two points in particular are his *Beyond Good and Evil* (1989/1886) and *The Birth of Tragedy* (2000/1872), the latter originally titled, *Socrates and The Greek Tragedy*, before it was lengthened a bit as final form. See the Oxford Edition, 2000, Note p. 155.

13 Tragicomic. As we will see later, White's study of 19th century historians starts with G.W.F. Hegel. As White saw it, Hegel followed the Classic Greek sequence for his own work: considering the world movement of the ideal of humanity, as represented by its history, as the dialectic between tragedy (humankind can not achieve in reality its own noble potential), and comedy (humankind must nevertheless move onward, accepting the frustrating limits of its worldly social achievement). In this regard, White's personal philosophy of history appears to be neo-Hegelian, even if he carefully avoids such labeling.

misshaping effects of the oligarch families that continually drained vital resources, human, financial and intellectual, from the mainline of the city. Decadence is a golden age based on hijacked booty.

Thus it was: the Greek democratic republic got its start about 500 BCE and its hegemonic prominence peaked about 325 BCE. Then, in 146 BCE, following a steady decline and one war too many, the country was forced to submit to foreign authority. To preserve a minimum of independence, the Athenians were obligated to replace their democratic regime with a manifest oligarchy. As discovered long ago by the oligarchs, when given a political voice, the popular economic classes are prone to militate for equality and liberation from the bonds of necessity. Under the sway of Roman hegemony, popular democracy was abolished and only the well-to-do were henceforth allowed to participate in government. Unfortunately, when they take all political control, in the hands of the elites the chariot of the gods is certain to crash; and it did.[14]

The Poetics of History

Sub-titling the "Introduction" for his 1973 monograph, "The Poetics of History," White challenged his historian colleagues by proposing that their studies are as much the expression of an informed poetics as the objective analysis of an empirical past.[15] The way history is recounted in a

---

[14] Greece goes Roman. As for the terminal phases of its irreversible decline, after a couple of generations of oligarchic governance, in 86 BCE, Athens was sacked for the first time, and its schools were closed. Pillage is always similar: burn the books, take the money and run. Athens gradually recovered, only to be sacked a second time in 267 AD, leading, eventually, to the abolition, in 529 AD, under Roman Emperor Justinian, of the Academy, established by Aristotle five hundred years earlier. By then the Greek spirit was rapidly evaporating from European consciousness, replaced by the low-brow view of feudal principalities, with lifestyle privilege for the few generated by exploitation of the domestic masses, marking the effective end of the institutional prominence in Europe of the Greek Republic as ideal; although not ending its romantic recall in the hands of later historians of philosophy, most famously, in Late Modernity, by Hegel.

[15] The term, 'poetics,' appeared very often in White's early writings; but as with any important text, its meaning must be drawn out from his usage. To say that a text is deployed with a certain poetics is less to compliment its inherent charm as to warn readers of its lack of political innocence; this is irony. Like most of his important vocabulary, White's attaching here the notion of poetics to the writing of history is not intended to suggest that the Durant's, *Story of Civilization* (12 volumes, 1935–1975), is little different from the work of Robert Frost. Poetics is used here in its ironic expression, referring to a form of literary attentiveness, which beyond care in composition, draws images slanted to convey a combination of facts and emotion. Due to the resonance it assures on the part of the ordinary reader, the dependence of serious critical texts on the use of a certain poetics, means that

text, after the fact and by whom, is substantially colored by the interpretive mode of the story teller. White provided a further detail: "This book is a history of historical consciousness in nineteenth-century Europe..." (1973: 1).

He did not assert that historical studies are wildly subjective, that no effort is made to be factual, that the point is systematic manipulation for political or other ideological ends. While not denying the possibility of out and out historical dishonesty, White's argument was more fundamental: what we label the active expression of the historic condition imposes itself not just on ordinary people, but on intellectuals of every stripe as well.

Diffused by the subtle workings of the cultural life of a population, the historical condition that dominates a people in an epoch is constituted by an ideological aura, diffusing a dominant world view, a narrow range of ways of describing experience, a limited set of expressive images that define the historical style or common consciousness of the moment. Historians, critics, scientists, like everyone else, must rely on that language, those modes of description, and images for writing-up their studies; else few will understand what is said.

In order to be published, whether consciously or not, all types of writing, from journalism to Nobel Science must fit with the cultural expressive-fashion of the times. However, by complying with a particular linguistic code, chosen at least implicitly in advance of the work, much of what appears in the most serious forms of scholarly writing, not to mention political or economic journalism, is thus heavily filtered, informing the public and specialists alike only about the selected material that fits with the code.

When they arrive before the public, the resulting reports of research, like texts of any sort, are necessarily in form, and by that also in content, shaped by the cultural style of the time of their authorship. While the process is potentially distorting for current studies, White was concerned about the quality of the result when, say, a 21st century cultural critic writes about a 19th century historical event.

Even when based on documented evidence, the way one writes or communicates the result of a study heavily determines the view of the truth exposed in one's text. While this is generally accepted as a thesis,

---

they can sway the reader, this way or that, not only as conscious manipulation based on intellectual argument, but as imminent result of unconscious compositional choice. This disposition associated with certain forms of composition was also explored at about the same time by Roland Barthes (2005/1977).

the question concerns the amount of variance that it explains compared to other factors which influence the content and meaning of literature. While this does not eliminate the possibility that the work of a critique will have cultural-revolutionary impact, even when that occurs, it is difficult to evaluate its justification.

For instance, it seems clear that after Descartes (1650), there was a shift in the way science was thought-out, conducted and reported; the same occurred with issues of government after the French Revolution (1789); with questions of political-economy after Marx (1875), with human psychology after Freud (1920) and with considerations of the ethical disposition of humanity after the Bomb that ended WWII (1945). Accepting this form of evidential fine-tuning of the educated historical consciousness is one thing, but deciding what it means for people in subsequent ages is another. This is the problem of history and with contemporary compositions about past events, which motivated White to write his 1973 book.

In the 1960s, when White launched his career, there were serious questions about the epistemological status of historical research. This hesitation extended to all realms of scholarly activity, since the possibility had been raised that intellectuals may be no more qualified than anyone else to offer guidance for the practical affairs of the human community.

Western civilization owes its origins to classic Greek thought; at the center of Plato's *Republic* was the philosopher as supreme guide and judge. Over the centuries since then, a special status of practical relevance has been granted to intellectuals. Then WWII in Europe cracked the faith in that form of guidance, since what the Continental Philosophers took to be the pinnacle of advanced humanist culture, namely Germany, proved itself capable of the highest crimes against humanity. In this 'crack,' the historical-critical fields, the human and social sciences, and philosophy, played a part; by articulating this touchy issue as he did, White put his finger on what was and continues to be a major meta-problem facing critical practitioners in the West: can intellectuals be believed?

There are two ways to consider the sometimes failure of the intellectual guidance of western civilization. First is to recognize that over the past two centuries, yielding to the forces of capital, intellectual productions, books written by historians, like everything else, have gradually been transformed into market commodities. Accordingly, the dominant ideology of Western nations, which is to say the ideas that fit with the desires and ambitions of the elites that dominate western civilization, are the ideas that must be supported or at least not denied by intellectual production. If so, then ordinary intellectual work follows from, rather than leads, the socio-political status quo, at least implicitly supporting the rightness and legitimacy of current structures and systems rather than challenging or proposing major modifications of them.

Even if the current direction of society is dangerous for humanity, White's thesis implies that there will be no corrective action provided by ordinary intellectual work: because normal science is normative before it is scientific. This reading of the problem of conventional scholarly activity on the part of critical-historians was at the center of the writings of Karl Marx. He attempted to work differently, resulting in his revolutionary discourse, which is why his historical studies received the negative response as they did, why he was censored in Berlin, was stripped of his German nationality, chased from Belgium, and threatened with arrest in Paris until he finally fled to spend the rest of his life in the library in London.

For his own purposes, Hayden White provides an alternative to the Marxist reading of the crisis of historical studies. He argued that, like everyone else, intellectuals are caught in the cultural-historical web of their era and, for that reason, cannot describe the world differently. Rather than being seduced by state ideology or purchased by the economy to serve as apologists for the status quo, historical-critical intellectuals are necessarily led to see the world and its past, as guide for its future in a way which is more or less politically correct. Rather than judging the world differently because of having seen its history better, even Karl Marx, according to White, was just another contextually determined historian, no more clairvoyant that the rest.[16]

---

16 Marx as Historical Object. White acknowledged the importance of Karl Marx as among the "masters" of 19th century history, devoting Chapter Eight in *Metahistory* to him ("Marx: The Philosophical Defense of History in the Metonymical Mode"). Elsewhere, in traversing his many lesser texts, White seems to have devoted more paragraphs to Marx than any other historical figure. White seemed perpetually stumped about just how to 'interpret' Marx. Marx is a project more than a man, which is easily ignored but nearly impossible to interpret.

For White, who based his fame on the assertion that history is always interpretation, this left nothing specific to say. Not easily stopped, he incessantly returned to Marx, as if trying to find a more precocious linguistic mode of expression by which to overcome the cruel fact: the problem with capital-driven society is that the same social categories benefit from the work of the same other social categories; this effect is largely hereditary, with this benefit not as reward for honor or service or capacity, but as issue of aggressive, obstinate exploitation.

White did not try to defend a different reading of the facts of capitalism, facts which he assiduously avoided discussing anyway. Rather, he argued that Marx was a man of his times; that Marx saw a certain temporary problem with the lack of fit between economic form and political regime, and put this into language in keeping with a post-romantic, somewhat Utopian world view that floated about Europe in the middle of the

As curious consequence of what he probably supposed was only his determined ideological even-handedness, White managed to alienate nearly everyone. Historians of the right, those believing in history as positive-empirical, truth-oriented practice, were incensed to be accused of generating little more than subjective historic fables. Historians of the left, more aligned with Marx's materialist conception of history, were aghast to think that White took the movement of cultural history as a giant impersonal force, with no accountability either at the level of state leadership or in intellectual vision; as if members of all classes and categories, from those on the state-house to the university-hall, from those on the back of the elephant to the fellows in the dust beneath, were but passive players in this historical chess game.

As the saying goes, 'every golf shot pleases someone.' The sectors that benefit most from the brouhaha associated with White's form of discourse are the technical fields (business, medicine, engineering, and the applied sciences that drive them); whose leaders take White's objection as a final discrediting not only of political leadership but of the practical importance of the humanities as intellectual undertaking; proving that the direction of society ought properly be left in the hands of material-scientists, engineers, and MBAs. What is good for industrial chemistry is good for humanity is it not? Or is that irony?

Imaginary Mastery

White drew attention to his work by the use of uncommon vocabulary, at once baroque and grandiose. His was to be an "analysis of the deep structure of the historical imagination of 19th century Europe," with minute attention paid to "the works of the recognized masters of 19th century European historiography." Still, he would focus on those masters, not as human beings or engaged political actors, but on their writing as what they "manifestly are... a narrative prose discourse that purports to be a model, or icon of past structures and processes in the interests of

19th century. As I mentioned in the previous chapter on Eagleton, at the time Marx wrote (~1860s), Matthew Arnold was very active about London, using quite other language to draw readers to quite another position, which was politically legitimist and not at all social-revolutionary. Drinking from the same well of history, at the same time, there is no comparison between Arnold's critical project and Marx's projective statement; this in itself seems to constitute an irresolvable dialectic test of White's situated-historicist postulate.

explaining what they were by representing them" (White 1973: 2 emphasis in original).[17]

Those he considered of masterly stature consisted of four "historians" (Michelet, Ranke, Tocqueville and Burckhardt), and four "philosophers of history" (Hegel, Marx, Nietzsche, and Croce). While the result would necessarily be comparative, White insisted that this would be of a "formalist" rather than evaluative nature: "I will not try to decide whether a given historian's work is better, or more correct," but only, "seek to identify the structural components of their (respective historical) accounts" (1973: 4). From a distance, it seems that White imagined himself able to rise beyond his own historical condition, so as to produce an 'objective' reading of these past-masters, all of whom he claimed had been largely locked within theirs.[18]

---

[17] Imaginative Reality. While often decried as empty dream work, John Dewey, famously, has argued that rather than necessarily 'unreal,' imagination allows images of "realities that cannot be exhibited under existing conditions of sense-perception." (See Dewey: *How We Think*, 1997/1910: Chapter 16). This appears on the surface to contradict the statement by Kant that imagination is a 'blind faculty'; but there is more to it because, to cite the infamous line from *Critique of Pure Reason*: "concepts without intuitions are empty, intuitions without concepts are blind" (1781/1787).

The more general claim, that aesthetic-expressive creativity precedes intellectual-conceptual knowledge of what one creates, dates from Plato. See Rupert C. Lodge, *Plato's Theory of Art* (2000/1953). In Lodge's Chapter 10, "The Judge in Matters of Art," the question occurs, not only what there is to judge about art, (whether there is some sort of truth in art, which, according to Hans-Georg Gadamer in his *Truth and Method* (1960), there is), but whether perhaps only the artist knows what it is for her works.

Summarizing the Platonic standard, which I generally support, Lodge cites a commentary that he evidently admired (Samuel Alexander, *Beauty and the other Forms of Value*, 1933), that, "the poet does not know till he has said it, either what he wants to say or how he shall say it. Excitement caused by the subject bubbles over into words or the movements of the brush or chisel. When the artist has achieved his product, he knows from seeing it or hearing it what the purpose of his artistic effort was." Further, says Lodge, "… it often takes someone else, a later artist or critic, to tell us what the (unconscious) purpose was. It seems to be irrelevant to artistic creation, that the artist should at anytime (before, during or after) know clearly and correctly the purpose of her work" (in Lodge 2000/1953: 206, Note 39).

[18] Formalism as Method. Sensitive about the formalist accusation, White responded as follows: "It is often alleged that 'formalists' such as myself, who hold that any historical object can sustain a number of equally plausible descriptions or narratives of its processes, effectively deny the reality of the referent, promote a debilitating relativism that permits any manipulation of evidence as long as the account produced is structurally coherent, and thereby allow the kind of perspectivism that permits even a Nazi version of Nazism's history to claim a certain minimal credibility."

He refused this charge, and filled many pages attempting to explain why, all the time rejecting a materialist conception of history (which would transform history dangerously close to sociology, a move to be avoided at all costs); but by refusing the only alternative to free-floating symbolic anti-factuality, he thus opened himself up to the formalist charge of

White's study, then, is a methodic analysis of the styles of composition used by 19th century historians: essentially, this implies that history is but its composition. In the interests of subjective impartiality, he applied that complex typology, the elements of which he laboriously argued, with each component identified and placed within a logical tree that he captured in a single schema (White 1973: 29). While the details are available for anyone who wishes to pursue them, White's enthusiasm for the procedure led him to elevate it to a most noble status: applying, as he put, from, "modern language theory... (the) four basic tropes for the analysis of poetic or figurative language" (1973: 31).[19]

He was concerned with the impact on what is said of the form of verbal or written expression of that content, constrained always by the objective of clarity and persuasiveness. To announce, 'it is raining' implies little action; to say 'it is raining cats and dogs,' is a call for at least an umbrella. For the teacher to state, 'here is the problem,' is hardly worrisome news; to put it otherwise, as, 'here is a most intricate problem,' is a call for intensified discipline and concentration. Whatever their purely intellectual interest, in the last hundred years, considerable analysis has been undertaken of

---

unjustified imposition of structure on innocent scholarly works. For the above citation, followed by his efforts to rebut the accusation, see his "Politics of Historical Interpretation: Discipline and De-Sublimation" (1982), in *Content of Form*, 1990, p.76.

White's calling into this debate the image of the Holocaust signals a problem which bears notice in any contemporary critical text; however horrid the incident, that heinous tragedy was a non-recurring event, unlike, for instance, the repeated usurpation for autocratic reasons of the power democratically allocated to political leaders by their people, or the international crime of aiming wars of aggression by superpowers against defenseless lesser powers, or of the cycles of profit bulging speculative hubris for the benefit of the elite social classes, followed by selective deflation to assure that members of the lesser social classes pay for the crisis. Rather than calling on the Nazi incident as a straw-man for debate, might it not be more valuable to focus on recurrent forms of societal dysfunction as a means to test the practical humanist value of what might otherwise be mistaken as neutral or defective historic interpretations?

[19] Deep Structure. White's formative idea is of the existence of 'deep structure' in any text, and it is this which he studies in his own case studies. His tool for investigation is the typology of tropes, which he asserted offered a means for categorization of the work of real historians. From there, he applied the model of deep structure with considerable bravado, sifting and comparing the individual strategies of each of his eight 'masters' of 19th century thought. Simply to propose such a move is enough to stretch the critical nerve to the breaking point. It appears that this proposition proved to be too much for one of the reviewers of the manuscript for his book; why else would he have attached a two-page footnote of very small print to the brief paragraph where he explains the logic of his book and his model (See 1973: 27ff), charged with energetic referencing, considerable justifying, broaching on the defensive. White's determination to overcome all obstacles and publish this book, demonstrates an admirable virtue for any critical practitioner.

the use of these figures for strategic communication, which is to say, for politics.

Style as Consciousness Figured-out

White wraps up the Introductory Chapter to his *Metahistory* with a section entitled, "The Phases of Nineteenth-Century Historical Consciousness." There he sealed the argument which drives the rest of the book: not only do those four fundamental tropes exhaustively cover how 19th century historical-critical studies were conducted (i.e., how history was transformed into literary texts to be read), but that in the course of the 19th century, there was a gradual shift in the historical-consciousness, moving through the four as successive phases of style: metaphor to metonymy, to synecdoche to irony. He theorized that the movement through these phases was attested to by the successive modification in the historiographical method, put in evidence chronologically, by the work of the eight history masters he studied.

In his 1973 text, White did not dwell on the derivation of those four figures of style, which date from Ancient Greece; nor did he explore the possibility that their meaning and application had changed over the centuries, or that they held local, national-cultural signification, varying, for instance, between the German Marx and the French Michelet. Rather, he focused on the phases of their chronological use in one single century as if the expression of a single European consciousness.

A difficulty with that postulate is that, as he acknowledged in passing, "Thinkers such as Voltaire (among others from the 18th century)... came to view history in essentially Ironic terms" (White 1973: 39). That observation seems ambiguous since, according to him also, irony is the endpoint rather than an aspect of origin for the 19th century historic-literary cycle. Nonetheless, this detail is explainable in part to the extent that the irony deployed by the 18th century figures was muted a bit, and then countered by other movements including that of the *Sturm und Drang* ('storm and stress' or 'turbulence and urgency') in which Goethe and Schiller were major participants, and later by the German romantic movement, which eventually shunned Goethe.

White interpreted the above set of events as a sort of convergence of movements and as a sign of "a genuine crisis of historical thinking" as the 18th century closed, setting in motion the cycle of changes in modes of interpretation that he asserts characterized the 19th century (1973: 38).

Even if it is true that the century he focused on saw the shifts in style as he claimed, it seems that, by his own admission, there was an equivalent shifting about as prelude to that century as well. If not, then what is so distinctive about the 19th century, and if so, then what is the special justification for his purported typology of phases?

Most commentators consider that the crisis which opened the 19th century in Europe and continues to agitate the West two centuries later, is associated less with historian's tropes than with the French Revolution (and its U.S. cousin) and general political-economic upheaval, related to the emergence and conquest by bourgeois-capitalist elite of political terrain formerly occupied by royalist-aristocrats. White focused instead on the crisis in historical consciousness that also occurred in keeping with the breakdown of the Ancient Regime of governance and its hesitant and uncertain replacement by systems and structures of capital market-determined democracy. While the interplay between the common state-of-mind and patterns of societal-organization are descriptively evident, it is not certain that White got their order of priority correct in conditioning social change.

White was convinced that the importance of those shifting historical conditions was principally materialized as modifications in common consciousness, or at least educated historical-consciousness, which followed from the crisis opening the 19th century. Having satisfied at least himself as to how that came about, he was on his way, leading off with Hegel, "the philosopher who gave this problem its most profound formulation," then following along chronologically, covering in considerable detail the serious work of the remaining magnificent seven of his historical masters (White 1973, Chapter Three).

White was obliged to carefully choose what he cited and how he used what he took from the works of the historians he studied, to demonstrate both his hypothesized use of particular tropic-forms in their work, as well as demonstrate the century-traversing shift in tropic emphasis as predicted by his 'theory.' Others can judge whether or not the effort was unduly forced.

At the end of the book, he admits that one may question the justice of his categorical, formalist approach: "I do not know whether the four interpretive strategies I have identified exhaust all the possibilities contained in language for the representation of historical phenomena" (White 1973: 429). Still, he proceeded with confidence, building a complex historical narrative, covering the 19th century, with the works of his Masters serving as markers, revealing unexpected seams in that complex and crisis-stained tapestry. Further evaluation of his mega-narrative aside, once having read what he wrote imposes a considerable burden of intellectual self-responsibility on anyone who subsequently sets out to compose a critical-historical text as if an entirely factual report.

The Irony of Irony

A particular question motivated my inclusion of White in this book: what can we learn from him about how the content and presentation of critical work might be deployed with greater political impact? To believe him, there is an interpretive, filtering effect resulting from the way that critical studies are transformed into literature, which enhances or limits their force. What he claims is, "any theory which is framed in a given mode is foredoomed to failure in any public which is committed to a different mode of prefiguration" (1973: 430). That contention is compatible with the position of Bertolt Brecht (1898–1956) about revolutionary theater: he was convinced that to produce theater that appealed to the bourgeois would mean little to members of the common classes (Brecht 1991/1934; 1997).

Suppose one's literary mission is to alert the under-classes to recognize the exploitative, elitist abuse they suffer and then to see collective mobilization as a way of redressing this problem. If so, then particular stagecraft must be used to reach the popular audiences in a way that they can appreciate. Theodor Adorno, who otherwise appreciated the political commitment of Brecht, famously differed about the potential of 'revolutionary theater,' contending that to stage theater or compose texts with an ideological undercurrent, even if it is of a most noble humanist nature, is a manipulation nonetheless. Thus the interesting possibility and attendant ethical problem: of using a consciously managed ideological appeal for liberation as counter force to an existing unconsciously powerful ideology of domination, when composing a text.[20]

[20] Ethical ferment. Theodor W. Adorno (1903–1969) was a committed and gifted culture critic. In spite of the brilliant work done with Max Horkheimer on the *Dialectic of Enlightenment* (1944), Adorno could not escape (*à la* White) from being formed by his times. As for master-narratives, in Nietzschean terms, Adorno was probably 'too modern,' placing excessive emphasis on the rational faculties and not sufficiently sensitive to the perceptive-expressive faculties. The result was a certain tunnel vision on the politics of criticism, generating a swirl in his inconclusive study of, *Aesthetic Theory* (1995b/1970), which I will return to briefly in Chapter Eight. For Adorno on Brecht (among other issues) see his essay, "Commitment" in *Aesthetics and Politics* (Adorno et al. 2002/1977).

To reach others with an existentially pertinent message, rather than channeled primarily via the intellect, where it is easily deflected, difficult to do with precision

In spite of his expressed disavowal of revolutionary motives, White implicitly sides with Brecht, concerning how the interpretive strategy that informs one's work has major influences on its receptivity. Take the work of Karl Marx, for instance, one of the eight Masters of historical thought that White elucidated in his *Metahistory*.

To believe White, like any other composer of texts, in order to assure the clarity of his work, consciously or not, Marx necessarily selected one (or a combination) of the four modes of interpretation that White identified as active during the 19th century in Europe, and stuck to that style for his project. While that assured a minimum of understandable consistency for his writings, at the same time it necessarily limited the practical reach of Marx's work. Unfortunately, only that portion of his potential readership that was tuned into the tropic form that Marx favored, would get the full meaning out of his texts.

On that basis, White judged that Marx had unintentionally marginalized the influence of his writings. As White put this:

> A historian such as Marx, employing a Mechanistic (metonymic) explanatory theory, has no authority in a public which is precritically committed to the prefiguration of the historical field in the mode of Irony, Synecdoche, or Metaphor. (1973: 430)

While we might argue about the four tropic modes in which White contended historical discourse has been trapped for the past two-hundred years, and while we may differ also about how he categorized the work of Marx, the logic of White's argument seems legitimate. Like it or not, unframed art hangs poorly and imprecisely framed critical works are confusing. Yet once selected, the chosen frame sets definite limits on critical content, risking to transform the most consciously intended critical text into Bourgeois Decorative Art.

At least to believe White, we already know that, since early in the 20th century, the West has been mired in a culture of irony. This, according to

---

and thus highly variable in effect, is it not better to approach humans from their aesthetic side which is linked, after all, to the universal base of humanized existence? (This is admittedly a retooling of Plato, but as if he were also an existentialist, which he was, rather than as if he were only an idealist). It seems that the latter was Brecht's point, and why he militated for the staging of revolutionary theater in the way he did. At the same time, as demonstrated by his brief exploration of the challenge of "Writing the Truth," Brecht [1991 (1934)] was not politically naive; he recognized the importance of speaking in epistemologically clear fashion. However, theater, art in general, is less about rhetoric than immediate human enactment; when effective it is performative literature in the true sense, which is received more as a function of its humanized resonance than according to its rational-intellectual relief.

White, invalidates Marx, the master neg-ironist, more effectively that any neo-conservative publicity campaign might ever achieve. Marx conducted research to establish the truth and to 'tell it as it is.' But under the specter of Irony, the common consciousness is so accustomed to communicative duplicity that the truth will be rejected as if it is but a manipulation.

This suggests that the only way to get his message of human liberation effectively across would be to re-spin Marx, by the use of images intended to express or reinforce meanings that are opposed to the truth. For instance, to dramatically understate the factual connection between the class-thing, elite privilege, exploitation of the popular classes and domination diffused in society by the workings of the capital-concentrating machine. Achieving this would be like having Stanley Kubrick, director of the movie *Full Metal Jacket* (1987), produce a contemporary version of *Brave New World* (1931): as if only by re-wording the truth as the lie might sincere critical practice compete on even terms with the dominant mode of communicative discourse, which is the incessant packaging of the lie as the truth. Now that is irony.

Even White, determined as he was to be a value-neutral historian, apparently found the practical implications of his research aesthetically unappealing; not so much so as to lead him to supply a source of hope about a way beyond Irony, but at least to allow him space for an occasional line about the effort to surmount this cultural impasse.

He announced, then, that "much of the best historical reflection of the 20th century has been concerned... to overcome the condition of Irony." This, he contends, explains the "revival of interest in the work of the great historical theorists of the pre-Ironic period: Hegel, Marx and Nietzsche." Further, he sees signs of "interest in speculative philosophy of history... to generate systems of historiology which challenge the Ironic perspective." Apparently, he is not entirely confident in this effort toward truth-telling, since he adds the note that, under any circumstances, "contemporary academic historiography remains locked within the Ironic perspective" (White 1973: 433). University students: be forewarned!

What is the truth or how might it be judged? Is this only a matter of style, or is there some basis to evaluate the rightness of alternative representations of the historical tableau? In spite of his formalist inclinations, White shows that he is an idealist after all, because in the end, while he admits that each researcher or intellectual critic is free to choose his or her mode of interpretive discourse as study guide, there is no rational-conceptual, epistemological basis for deciding that one is superior, more desirable or believable than the other. Rather, "When it is a matter of choosing among these alternative visions of history, the only grounds for preferring one over another are *moral or aesthetic* ones" (1973: 433). That being the case, and I fully agree that it is, then the world continues to wait for a sequel to this diligent effort by White, that might explain the underpinnings and expression of moral-aesthetic judgment, and the dynamics of its progressive, but hopefully not irreversible, deactivation over the centuries in the West.

Behind the Veil: Culture Failure?

Earlier I speculated about the ironic eclipse the Classic Greek culture; even if the West is now on a similar trajectory, is there not plenty of time to redirect this negative socio-cultural decline? Or is the question only a sign of excessive trust in metaphor?

Two-thousand years ago, cultures were 'lazy-systems,' possessing equivalent domains as characterize cultural systems today, but with relations among those domains loose rather than rigid. Information moved slowly and erratically, energy drive was minimum, action/reaction times were slow and unpredictable, rendering centralization, formalization, and routinization virtually impossible. Back then, independent of content, tropic or otherwise, disfigurations or emergences in one zone of cultural importance were only loosely connected to other zones; diffusion of effects was sluggish, often with few long term consequences on the system as a whole. That is probably why the 'fall' of the Greek Republic as institutional embodiment of the Greek cultural system, took a number of centuries. As demonstrated more recently by the French Empire under Napoleon, the British Empire under Queen Victoria, or the German Third Reich under Hitler, it is now possible for massive cultural developments to emerge, take form, diffuse effects, and decline or be defeated and absorbed in a generation or two.

Since dissimulation of truth is its trademark, only a culture system in a tragic state of decadence goes ironic. While with the Greeks this occurred with innocence, today, due to what we might learn from history, it is evident in advance. Still, our late-modern agents of the elites continue to sing the false notes of progress and stability, and official pronouncements prop up this claim. The myth of humanity, 'to find a way around any difficulty,' is repeated as a form of ideological drug, intended to calm the common consciousness. The late modern west seems to be on the path of cultural dementia as occurred with the Greeks long ago, probably with the same inevitable consequences: collapse, conquest, absorption by some other cultural force with superior integrity. That is, assuming the natural environment does not reach such a state of depletion that the human race itself goes extinct.

As pretense about the truth, Irony as culture of domination might only occur when the facts that matter are not in fit with the accepted view of the truth. The circuit is vicious, if not circular: cultural truth is ideological matter, and the ideas that matter are those of the elite. For all parties, institutional denial wears thin; people and institutions snap under the load. Is there a way out: probably, but only if the West reconstitutes itself in keeping with, rather than in resistance to, the postmodern condition which now presents itself.[21]

What Historians Do

If, in spite of good intentions, they do not entirely tell the truth with their writings, (because they cannot), and yet they hope to be taken seriously, then what is it that historians or cultural critics accomplish? As specialists in the management of proximate truth, they generate well informed literature. Covering virtually every major published announcement that goes beyond the minutia of a daily chronicle, the same is the case for most philosophers and social scientists. If we take Hayden White seriously, then not just leaders who seek counsel from serious intellectuals, but we humans in general, base our action on unsure accounts of events and their causes, presented to us and taken into mind as if hard fact. Yet, White avoids cynicism, never calling for an end to scholarship, much less social actions based on uncritical judgments; concentrating rather on what constitutes intellectual work, when the point is to turn its object into literature.

---

[21] Ironic Cracks. In his essay "Politics of Historical Interpretation" (1987: 83), White notes that the ethics of history and politics of history carry the same meaning. He also makes the claim that we can not learn anything by studying history; but we can learn a great deal from 'how' those before us have studied history, an observation he acknowledges as of Hegelian inspiration.

In another paper, based on a careful reading of Vico, he not only shows how he was inspired to use his four-fold tropic model by Vico's use of it also, but that Vico applied this to a study of the movement of history as cultural emergence, decline and succession. For us here, the important thing to note is Vico's conclusion: that once the decline sets in, the stage of Irony becomes dominant and there are only three possibilities as outcome: internal cultural collapse, foreign conquest by a superior culture, or—intervention of the gods! Perhaps the West can be saved from disaster by spirituality (Vico 1976; White 1978: 197ff)!

He draws attention to the unintended result of mindless pursuit of historically guided political order. Historians, critics, researchers, and ordinary individuals work by framing their projects in advance. As with the chef and her menu, the plan as prepared allows selection of ingredients, then arranging the dishes, to serve it up in a way that achieves her objective. The point is to have a method of procedure, not necessarily as ironclad as that may sound, but with clarity of guidelines.

Without clear method, research easily turns into a random fishing expedition, the eclectic gathering of facts, the helter-skelter assemblage of the results, occasionally yielding a serendipitous finding, but usually not.[22] For historians as well as for social scientists and philosophers, the point is to compose a text, focusing on particular 'evidence,' in keeping with certain logic, extracted to illuminate particular notions, relationships, events, in support of an argument. In the physical sciences this is achieved by use of some proscribed method of research; why not the same for the study of society?

Whatever the quality of data, the result, in the end, is a literary performance of sorts, a present interpretation of a certain past, framed this way rather than otherwise by one's method; as with a symphony, change the maestro, and the music as played will be modified. With each version true to the ear of its interpreter, is any one orchestration certifiably superior to others? The same question arises for most academic work and forms of criticism as well, more so to the degree that the studies are conducted with methodological rigor: more irony.

So far, so good: Hayden White has blown the factual cover off the surface of texts, revealing not exactly the subjectivity of critical studies, but the shimmering nature of the revealed secrets. What to make of it, then? White is definite on this: the standard of evaluation must be ethical or aesthetic rather than epistemological. The full reach of judgment must be engaged if the significance of historical studies is to be realized, which

---

22 As Jean Strobinski (1970) underlines in the essay that introduces his volume, *The Critical Relationship*, while particular methods of research have the advantage of better bringing to light certain 'facts' of reality than do other methods, use of any one of them also blinds the researcher to other equivalently valid facts. While I couldn't agree more with this assessment, the choices are limited: the form of rigor I favor is a question of discipline and method, with the alternative usually leading to imprecision if not confusion. The advantages of the historical-materialist method is its double dialecticity, which in a way transforms it into a multi-method strategy, which in the end proves most useful for studying the human condition.

is an aesthetic problem in the political sense, as much as a rational-intellectual one.[23]

While the process is more mechanistically replicable by a chemist or astrophysicist than by a historian or other cultural critic, the difficulty with intending in advance to be precise about one's work heavily colors its accomplishment. The resulting tangle between one's approach to the problem and its analysis, between its stylized frame and the content of one's research is too great to be resolved. Whether concerning the use of quantum-theory to explain the dynamics of the physical world, or the use of macro-economic theory to explain marked failure under capitalism, the approach to one's study heavily determines the answer it generates.[24]

Trapped by the Trope of Progress

If we are blocked from really knowing reality anyway, why are historians obligated to conduct critical studies with maximum rigor, then veil the results ironically? The problem, at root, must be blamed on 'historical

---

23 Poetic figuration. White plowed through the thorny thicket of historical considerations associated with the conception of judgment under the Western Enlightenment, revealing for us the extent to which the 'irrational' is so entwined with the 'rational,' that rational judgment is ironically limited by its inherent irrationality. See "The Irrational and the Problem of Historical Knowledge in the Enlightenment," (White 1972; 1978: 142ff).

24 Interactivity. While it is clear to most observers that the human historical past is as impossible to know as the future, the physical sciences are considered exact, and technical knowing precise. Under scrutiny, the exactness of the physical sciences is just as furtive as the Social Sciences (consider Einstein and his Quantum Theory, or Stephen Hawking and his Big Bang Theory).

The problem is interactivity; when a study is conducted, the instrument used interacts so immediately with the event under scrutiny that no one can be sure what the results reveal about the world, versus what they demonstrate to be the real effect of the use of the tool. In what is considered a cult book, concerning the relationship of science and consciousness, the theoretical physicist, David Bohm, tried to tease out the ambiguities associated with what we human beings are as knowing consciousnesses, and what the world is in so far as we know it. His conclusion is no different about physics than is Hayden White's about the historical sciences: as Bohm put it, (back to Einstein) "The result of the (research operation) of the whole experimental set-up does not tell us about the (quantum) system that we wish to observe but, rather, only about itself as a whole (system of inquiry)" (Bohm 2008/1980: 74).

Conventional historians tend to reject Hayden's White's writings as somewhat folklorist, as conventional physicists deplore the work of Bohm. This signals what is perhaps the most difficult block for cultural criticism: the insistence in the Modern West that knowledge be objective and independent of common consciousness, rejecting the alternative, that the common consciousness is issue of cultural processes, such that what is known in every field of inquiry is as much a cultural production as it is a certifiable indicator of the structure of some non-human reality.

consciousnesses.' One of the heavy legacies of the Western Enlightenment is that, having liberated ourselves from the sacred obligation to work to save our soul, we westerners are now committed to the secular obligation of working as progress, to save our modernist reputation. Presumably there is worldly payoff from this, leading to increased knowledge of the secrets of nature and anticipation, if not control, of future events. To demonstrate progress we must compare the present with the past, and therein lays the essential burden of history.[25]

The only way to know we are succeeding in our modern mission is historical, by placing the contemporary in the spotlight of the past, either to learn how to change for the better or to demonstrate that what is now done is advancing properly. This suggests that progress is assured by running forward with ours eyes fixed over the shoulder, focused on what has just passed by; since a crash seems inevitable, the folly of that strategy is striking.[26]

Obsessed with making sense of history in order to certify progress, modern westerners generate a continuous stream of narrative understandings which allegedly demonstrate forward movement guided by, or at least conceptually consistent with, the past, yet surpassing that. History is demanded for self realization of the modern enlightened consciousness, explaining why today we pay attention to history, while doubting the historical story as told; reading it ironically, then placing our faith in it even if we are rather sure of its misleading quality.

While irony is a fine figure to use for a critic seeking public attention, with its contemporary large-scale application to shroud the truth with insincere ridicule, it has lost the capacity to stimulate political mobilization. The failure of irony to achieve its political mission is largely due to the modern western version of bad historical consciousness: who can take critique seriously, when its content is routinely distributed in the form of bad jokes? The only space left for sincere critical formulation lies in the nowhere land between brutality and lassitude.

25 Historical Salvation. Salvation transformed into secular progress, via pursuit of full expression of historical consciousness, as replacement for spiritual calling as higher holy mission, is an image that surfaces in many of White's essays.

26 Hot pursuit of The Past. Today the notion of Modern Progress as both promise and fact is taken as gospel, even if, when the idea first arrived in the West, it was hotly contested, often ridiculed, and sometimes proven false. For a readable set of writings on this fascinating debate that erupted at the end of the 17th century in Paris at the *Académie Française* see Fumaroli, 2001.

Now largely sedated by irony, tragedy is no longer embraced as serious exposition of social malaise. The effect is so deadening in aesthetic affect that comedy can no longer amuse. How else to explain the depressing effects of being constantly bathed with the illusion of progress, supported by real-life grimace-driven, comic book characters addressing the public as if experts in economics or politics; or public action in the face of crisis displaying the hapless heroics of shocker cinema scenarios. Given the crumbling facade of critique under the overbearing weight of irony would almost lead one to believe the time is right for a rebirth of film noir![27]

It is old-fashioned in the 21st century to mention what the French label the existential crisis, much less the Marxist crisis that often materializes it. For Marx, that occurs when the work done by a community to transform the world for general well-being has results that turn back against the workers. For Sartre and other French existentialists, the crisis came from the impossibility of transcendental fulfillment from any life-course engagement due to the inevitable complicity this will sooner or later require with forces and interests that are displeasing and unadvisable, if not downright dangerous for self and others.

In order to be identity sustaining, collective action as work done with discipline and energy must have world-altering effects of a meaningful symbolic nature. When the material evidence of that work is constantly discredited, as is now the case in our image-shifting world of planned obsolescence, no matter what the effort, the mirror of existence is marred and the affirmative common view of the structures of society evaporate. Thus violating the standards of authenticity, the more individuals work together, the more alienated they become. Rather than social reform, which is risky to propose and difficult to execute, the popular choice is to blame government, and then chase distraction, such as television or micro-screen scratchings: chewing gum for the mind. When the Greeks faced the same predicament, they went Stoic. Might not radical social change be better?[28]

27 For an extensive study of how frustrated heroics can reveal the truth of cultural contradiction, see the exhaustive study of 20th century American Film Noir by Dennis Broe (2009).

28 Being Ironically. The existential crisis generated by this cultural impasse has been discussed from Kierkegaard to Sartre; in fact, Soren Kierkegaard's first study, for his thesis, was: *The Concept of Irony with Continual Reference to Socrates* (1841). Not formally addressing it theoretically, Sartre captured this tension in the line, "condemned to be free." Although he had other difficulties, Kierkegaard knew irony for what it was, without being personally trapped in it; Sartre, on the other hand, appears to have practiced a life of irony, but unknowingly.

Even serious historical stories must be told so that we humans can grasp them as actual; beyond historical-consciousness, this gets into the realm of consciousness as such. The dispositions of contemporary consciousness must pertain to historical narratives or else they will be denied as inauthentic. This is the problem with mythology, being narrative histories that violate the rules of western modern consciousness as locale for 'rational' understanding and general sense making. The essential compromise is use of figurative adjectives, with which brute facts from the past are conceptualized, allowing the generation and reception of aesthetic resonance by which to actively link spectator to theater, or reader to text. Misuse of the process hardly justifies its abandonment; as White notes in reference to Voltaire, it is vital to see "that figurative language is just as often a way of expressing a truth incompletely grasped as it is of concealing an error or falsehood incompletely recognized" (White 1972 in 1985/1978: 142).[29]

Inescapably Ironic

What are the basic rules for structuring story telling as narrative in the consciousness of westerners? White claims that the four modes of ideal style he identified are just that, which is why one or the other must be applied as the frame of inclusion for all historical texts if they are to be taken seriously by readers.[30]

---

[29] Candid(e). Having opened this book with a chapter on him, it is evident that there is more to be said about that Grinning Critical Gladiator named Voltaire than White includes in this book. It is valid enough to note, as White does, that Voltaire, along with others of his century, was caught in the tormenting shift from a religious-ideological view to a rational-enlightened view of truth. They thus distrusted subjective figuration as if it were conscious manipulation, leading some to overplay the power of rational objectivity, not seeing that this was in its way another ideological extreme. However, when it gets to Voltaire, surely with his *Philosophical Dictionary*, or with *Candide* for that matter, he was boldly challenging the unjustified posturing both of the scientific minds of his day, as well political and ecclesiastic leaders although less for reasons of Intellectual style than because of the horrid political effects that this had for society and its people. Voltaire's was hard hitting, first stage, political criticism with a jack-hammer; which it seems the gentle spirited, and curiously politically hesitant White, finds a bit harsh.

[30] Framed. As developed by White, this argument is similar to one advanced by Georg Lukács: that an aesthetic work must be 'framed' or structured, or informed in such a way that the particular 'content' (often very original), will arrive in the world (gallery, bookstore, symphony hall, etc.) in such a fashion that it can be appreciated by members of the culture group for whom it is intended.

Here, White speaks of four figures of style, which might 'structure' literature. This implies an architectural distinction: use of an 'in-forming' structure rather than external

He contends the setup for this emerged during the 19th century, opening with G.W.F. Hegel, according to whose reading, across the long reach of history, comedy trumps tragedy and the rationalist-progressive joke is on us individually; because all truth, as that which does not contradict itself, lies with the ineffable Idea of History as Humanity incarnated in Society. In spite of our transient frailty, the idea of civilization lives on nonetheless, expressing itself as the unstoppable pursuit of Its perfection, validating by that pursuit the final achievement of human nature. Accordingly, we are pawns in the jousting match of civilization through society; all the time plagued by the gift of historical-consciousness, a source of questions without answers, of premises without resolution.

Hegel's detailing of the past rising, and collapse of actual societies, surely comes across as tragic in common sense terms (Hegel 2004/1837). Yet tragic for a classic historian is not a reference to everyday suffering but to the lack of human attainment of an ideal of reason, for reasons beyond human comprehension. Tragic events concern larger-than-life forces, setting the stage for contemporary experience and loading the dice in advance. Comedy occurs as ordinary humans, at the level of existence, struggle to overcome or deny the unassailable results of those tragic truths. The inevitability of death is the baseline for tragedy and the struggle to escape it the parody in comedy. By common sense, a comic condition suggests amusement when, for Hegel, tragedy suggested relief gained by surrendering to the uncontrollable power of history.

In laying the basis for his metahistorical study, White depended on a particular view of the tragic-comic tension as starting point, which he identified as inherent in the work of Hegel. But, the way he expresses this is deceptive, partly because of common sense confusion over the use of those terms, linked with White's personal style of address. For purposes of clarity, I suppose, White is prone to open a section of text with a strong declarative sentence, which attracts the eye and forces concentration by the reader. Thereafter, he tends to soften the commentary on the bold point and by that appear reasonable rather than dogmatic. As a matter of style, this is an ironic strategy for composition, using the declarative form

framing device for a text. Roland Barthes discusses something analogous in reference to 'classic style,' which, until the end of the 19th century, was mandatory, at least in France, if an author hoped to be taken seriously. As I discussed elsewhere, to believe Barthes, this rigidity diminished during the 20th century, allowing now a certain plurality of styles to emerge and by that an increased freedom of authorship. To examine White under the lens of Barthes, suggests that even if White's notion of master trope domination was valid for the 19th century, that was but a passing phase that has since been supplanted: but by what?

as a mask for the hypothetically or only marginally true. Thus suffering a bit from the ill he diagnoses, care must be taken to assure that meaning is accurately drawn from White's lines.

In his chapter in *Metahistory* on Marx, White announces boldly that, "Hegel's Comic conception of history was based ultimately on his belief in the right of life over death," where "life" guarantees "the possibility of an ever more adequate form of social life throughout the historical future" (1973: 281). This is equivalent to saying that it is figuratively comic to suppose that there will be a day when automatically driven automobiles will eliminate accidental deaths in auto accidents; in the meantime we continue to fool ourselves and not be concerned with the tragic fact that we are killing one another while driving today with reckless abandon. While the comic in that form is a classical figure, to take the second portion of the argument as reactionary justification for current denial of social responsibility is no laughing matter; which is what Hegel did in a way, rendering his reading of history both unamusing and inexact.[31]

Hegel rightly saw human history as tragic: the repeated failure of ordinary individuals, in everyday society, to get the better of nature, of their neighbors or even of themselves; thus, civilizations come and go, 'rise and fall.' But, then there is classic 'comic relief,' the good news issue of the horrid. According to White: "In the cycle of moral attitudes, Comedy is logically posterior to Tragedy, for it represents an affirmation of the needs of life and its rights against the Tragic insight that all things existing in time are doomed to destruction" (1973: 117). It is unclear if such a reading transforms the Normandy Beach cemetery memorial into tragedy or comedy.

Is this not salvation by metaphysics over physics, because in the Hegelian project, the 'existing in time' refers to this or that society or state, with its comic ongoingness and unstoppable vitality driven by the virtue of humanity. The result is the practical struggle to build and assure a

---

[31] Chiding without a Wink. Kierkegaard focused the second part of his (1841) study of irony since Socrates on Hegel. Some years later, he noted in a journal entry that he initially failed to recognize that Hegel missed the truth, by taking Socrates' Irony as serious; that effectively, 'Hegel missed the joke' (concerning Socrates' pretending not to know, to be but a bumbling Columbo-like philosopher, surely guilty of no crime greater than verbal clumsiness, never intending sedition, etc). In that same entry, Kierkegaard went on to observe that for a rational-idealist this was not a great failing on the part of Hegel, since, in his judgment, Plato himself was too much of a rationalist to appreciate what today we would consider the aesthetic of irony as played out in life by, and ultimately paid for with the life of, Socrates. Kierkegaard's personal Journals count ~ 7,000 pages (Kierkegaard 1996). References in this note are to Volume X, Book 3, 1851; for details see Anthony. D. Storm's "Commentaries on Kierkegaard": http://www.sorenkierkegaard.org/.

sustainable society, which in the end always proves to be a mission impossible. Humanity as idea, on the other hand, marches on, in spite of what occurs along the way with the misfortune of any actual society. A certain form of Hegelian optimism dominated western civilization until it was seriously challenged by the Nazi period in Germany.[32]

Hegel supposed there to be heroic people and life-forms of the human race equivalent to the classic images of Hero. The "tragic flaw" is represented by the way the society realizes itself as social form, always less than the higher aspirations it has of its being as civilization. Decadence comes next, and deceptive talk of the ideal replaces its practice. However, reflective consciousness continues, as common consciousness, such that the Ideal of Greek Civilization lives on, even today, two thousand years after it stopped existing as organizing power.

The next stage in the historical story for the 19th century was *realism*: the truth of the human condition cried out for better things than Hegel had foreseen: Michelet in France, Ranke in Germany, Tocqueville in France about America, Burckhardt in Switzerland about European civilization. Each set out to show how the lived promise of individual-being exposed loopholes in the evident, as windows of escape from the Hegelian Leviathan; that generally better days are realizable, if only individuals would work together for that.

By mid-19th century, as crises continued to plague Europe, confidence in the individual potential to cope with real conditions went sour and the force of history took charge once again. A third strain of historical authorship emerged as Marx, Nietzsche and Croce assessed the pall of historical forces as both brutal and glum, focusing on history as the story of practical philosophy, as human struggle not just to cope, but for movement beyond

---

[32] Historical Limits. In his essay on the "Politics of Historical Interpretation" (White 1987: 58ff), and with inconclusive results, White raised the issue of Nazi Germany as evidence of the inadequacy of the Hegelian rendering of history. He also explored the issue in his writings on Paul Ricoeur. Ricoeur was committed mystically to the super-historical power of collective memory as lived history; in that sense, for him personally, no lesson of history is equivalent to that of the Holocaust. For geopolitical reasons, unlike even a phenomenon as unthinkable as the Inquisition, it is still not acceptable to integrate the Holocaust phenomenon into any 'normal' history; for that reason, the clarity of White's typical capacity to absorb every major past event in his historical narrative remained curiously ambiguous in regard to this subject. Apparently recognizing that silence makes poor history, White returned inconclusively to the subject in: "Historical Emplotment and the Problem of Truth" (1992: 37–53).

Two of his papers on Ricoeur: "The Metaphysics of Narrativity: Time and Symbol in Ricoeur's Philosophy of History;" in *Content and Form*, 1987, and "Guilty of History? The longue durée of Paul Ricoeur," 2007.

the actual; toward liberation of history as social philosophy, of human community engaged with willful resistance, or toward at least Stoic acceptance, with social revolution as the hope for humankind against nihilist finality as ultimate comedy.

As that dark 19th century of sweeping history continued, the facts looked not progressively better but repressively morose; was resistance, acceptance, rebellion likely to payoff? Could the behemoth of society, the instrument of history, techno-instrumentalized to the hilt, be defended against, much less beaten into plowshares through collective engagement as expression of good conscience? While no one was sure, the story was told 'as if it were sure,' which, as White saw it, reached its terminus as comically-ironic.

The 20th century opened with the thunder of cannon and the threat of market collapse. On that basis, how might sincere anticipation be entertained in Europe or America? There was none, which for the western enlightened people, always confidently progressing against all evidence, was and continues to be, tragically-ironic.

According to White's study, since its opening, 20th century literary scholarship, theoretical and practical, social and political, has been under the spell of irony as its dominant trope. With origins in the perspective of the German, Nietzsche, and the Italian, Croce, the West continues to wait for rescue from this higher formatting of intellectual consciousness that continues to impose itself more than a century later.

The Tragic Fault of Disciplined History

As an objective historian at least by intention, White portrays the current 20th century ironic impasse as if the inevitable outcome of a battle for survival among historical-interpretative possibilities. This recalls neo-liberal economics, as if today's dynamic were due to the hidden hands of the historical marketplace. As if from Hegel to Nietzsche and beyond, passing by Marx among others, the various figures of style were systematically profaned, until nothing is left but the grimace; with the burning potential of acrid criticism forever soothed with stories of historical irony: that henceforth, rather than those that count, the only historical facts put in evidence are those that feel-good.

Beyond human agency, is there no one to blame? Hayden White is also a realist from the Tennessee Hills, where they reckoned distance on country roads when he was a boy, by the "far see." He knows that all those pages of text that he studied were produced by very real human hands, connected to historically situated heads; whatever the greater degree of insight at the end of the 20th century among historians, the discipline itself has been around a long time. As far as he can see, that is a major part of the problem.

The study of social organizations (schools, businesses, families, associations, etc.), reveals the existence of principles of establishment, consisting of a loose cultural template, held in the consciousness of the founders if not formally detailed in a constitutional document. These principles provide the symbolic skeleton to which the techno-organizational structures of the unit are attached. They establish the moral boundaries and the normative central tendencies of organization, defining values and beliefs as to its mission and images of collective action imputed to be rational for members. Like any other institutionalized undertaking, this has occurred with history as a discipline.

Whether for money or love, salvation or education, political guidance or existential reform, some such set of principles informs each social organization, knitting together participants in webs of communication and action, in pursuit of its goal. While useful for assuring orderly procedure for their members or users, such systems of organization are nonetheless rather rigid, non living, historic objects; they come into being due to certain demands from a population (of potential users or members), given certain opportunities and constraints from an operating environment. As the population demand and/or environment qualities shift, the initial fit of the organization and its conditions, which was presumably maximized at the time of establishment, may be degraded, leading to potentially crippling operational weakness.

With that as background it is easier to appreciate Hayden White's analysis of the political history of history, exposing how, in order to assure the quality of the work of its disciplinarians, the strength of its discipline necessarily imposes serious restrictions on the definition of what counts as a historical event for study and how to report on it. Due to the political climate at the time of its founding, the principles of establishment of history as discipline now contribute to the perpetuation of the 20th century Ironic log-jam, by imposing epistemological barriers against recognizing the possibilities for fundamental societal reform.[33]

---

[33] Unnatural Selection. Formal organizations exhibit systems-ecological properties, for which survival depends on accommodation to demands balanced between the

History Rules: Utopia is Disqualified

After putting students of history on guard about it in his 1966 "Burden of History" paper, with his theoretical monograph of 1973, White detailed the 19th century development of what proves to be our corrosively enduring, ironic historic condition. Nine years later, in a 1982 paper, he returned to the issue, discussing how the formal establishment of history as academic discipline (early in the 19th century) played a crucial part in this process. The good news is that his study demonstrated the practical worldly power of history; the bad news is that this power is substantially negative.

A brief overview of his 1982 work, "The Politics of Historical Interpretation," will serve us two ways. It provides a final study of how White plied his critical intellectual craft, and it serves to demonstrate, in intellectual institutional terms, why a human liberation movement within western society is not likely to arrive anytime soon.

Framed by principles of establishment dating from more than a century ago, the discipline of history blocks movement toward all possible futures but one: the reactionary one of bourgeois positivist progressivism. According to White (and in keeping with Horkheimer as I discussed in my Introduction), the fact of the fit between the *modus-operandi* of history and a reactionary bourgeois world-view is logical, since that ideology defined the 19th century cultural niche in which formal history planted its roots.[34] Defining realism as negation of the imaginary, serious historical study of Utopian possibilities became illegitimate, forcing the West by grim necessity to march to the tune of the dehumanizing techno-mechanical drummer, as if it is progress for humanity rather than principally privilege-assuring for bourgeois entrepreneurs.

---

population they serve and the operating environment in which they find themselves. This applies for every form of social system, including universities within nations or and academic departments within universities. In reference to the model presented in my Technical Appendix, White is tacitly acknowledging that the force dominating history as discipline comes from the symbolic aura of western modernity, which is what Horkheimer attempted to describe in his study of the bourgeois philosophy of history. While individual initiatives by renegade historians (like White) is always possible, if it hopes to thrive in organized form, the discipline of history, or for that matter sociology or any other, will not modify its trajectory until the philosophy of history that underwrites it, does.

34 Why History. For a concrete example of the insistence within the organized Historical Community about the rightness of its calling, on the web-site of the American Historical Association, see Peter Stearns, "Why Study History." *The American Historical Association*, 2008/1998. http://www.historians.org/pubs/free/WhyStudyHistory.htm.

White postulates that interpretation is a political act, and by that, history also. His reasoning rests on the classical position since Socrates: to know the world is to engage in it. Yet to engage is to alter the world. Hence, the world is composed for a community via personal engagement of its people, motivated by the need to know it in order to survive, along the way keeping track of the process by interpreting it. To draw meaning from that world of collective engagement, as do historians or others less formally, is thus a political act.

Criticism begins with historical study; even if only yesterday's, some past is assessed, its strength and limitations identified. While objective historians are often content to assess the past while resting neutral about its action implication, critical practice implies a further step of proposing how to put into action affirmative recommendations based on that analysis.

The separation between passive historical-assessment and activist-criticism is practically impossible to sustain in practice, which explains the ambivalence of White's own purportedly 'objective historical' commentary. To avoid taking a political stand, he is forced to contend that there is nothing to learn from history, except concerning how those before us have studied it. This is a rather curious contention, since, in what follows, I will show how he argued that history holds a power over the future of historical studies, unmediated by human social actors, implying a form of historicism in the construction of history as a discipline that he rejects in reference to society at large.[35]

Interpretation is political, having to do "with the kind of authority the interpreter claims" in reference to the general community and others from her field of study; it "presupposes politics as one of the conditions of its possibility as a social activity," leading directly to the observation that, "pure interpretation, the disinterested inquiry into anything, whatsoever, is unthinkable" (White 1982: 58–59).

White acknowledges that the usual distinction between the natural (fact driven) versus logical-meaningful (value driven) sciences concerns the difference in interactivity of the object of study with the method of study. Beyond the fact that this is a valid formal claim, the real difference between disciplines in terms of their object of study is less the result of natural qualities than political choice. To establish this, he focuses on the

---

35 Learning. White based this position on Hegel: that the critical importance of history is not from its study directly, but rather "from the study of the study of history" (White 1987: 82), which is precisely the logic driving this book.

process by which history was taken from the writing tables of aristocratic 'women of letters,' then institutionalized as recognized academic field, revealing, "what was involved in the transformation of historical studies into a discipline that applied rules for construing and studying their objects of interest" (1982: 60).

With the past as the total field of historical possibility, to apply discipline is to place limits on what is to be considered pertinent. Or, and somewhat counterintuitive at first glance, "discipline consists less of prescriptions of what must be done than of exclusions or proscriptions of certain ways of imagining historical reality" (White 1982: 68).

Disciplining history is similar to disciplining a child: providing a set of 'dos and don'ts,' with major emphasis on the 'don'ts.' For children, it is the structure of the family that holds authority, from which the rules for their discipline are derived. In a society, it is the culture as a whole that holds authority, establishing the rules of discipline with which social organization of sound standing is expected to comply (roughly), including (even more roughly) fields of academic study.

Social organizations are not living or fully dynamic; being more rigid than not, the discipline imposed on a social system at the time of its origin is infused into its structure as principles of establishment, which then rest pretty much invariant until the organization dissolves (to be completely reconstituted) or until the sustaining society which houses it, does. This is why it is very difficult to restructure any social organization.

White underlines the importance of the timing and circumstances of the birth of history (recalling Foucault's, *Birth of the Clinic,* 1963); the forces behind-, and the consequences of-, the disciplining of history, are evident:

> The social function of a properly disciplined study of history and the political interests it served at its inception in the early nineteenth century, the period of the consolidation of the (bourgeois) nation-state, are well-known and hardly need documentation... (including its) ideological benefits to the new social classes and political constituencies that professional, academic historiography served and continues to serve down to our own time. (White 1982: 60)

Why the interest, one must ask, on the part of the bourgeois establishment, in disciplining history this way versus that? History is supposedly responsible for establishing the facts from the past, which in turn are used to rationalize current action. Throughout the 19th century, various competing grand historical narratives were proposed, on the validity of which depended the legitimacy of competing political philosophies.

Were historians to determine from past 'evidence' that an interpretation of history inconsistent with the bourgeois political-economic philosophy was valid, this would undermine bourgeois domination. If the discipline is going to "determine the facts of history, by which to assess the objectivity, veridicality and realism of the philosophies of history that authorize the different political programs," it is clear that the political stake in the working of history is immense (White 1982: 61).

The liberation-negationist disposition of history, by history, is not really the fault of historians, but of the politics that assures their livelihood. As White underlines, "the politics of this disciplinization... as a set of negations, consists of what it marks out for repression for those who wish to claim the authority of discipline itself for their learning." And, "what ... history... marks out for repression in general is utopian thinking—the kind of thinking without which revolutionary politics... become unthinkable" (1982: 62).[36]

The conclusion is evident: by imposing informative influences at the time of its establishment, bourgeois political domination assured that the guiding principles of the discipline of history fit its political agenda; specifically, "by disciplining historical consciousness so as to make realism effectively identical with antiutopianism," thereby, "ruling out as unrealistic any political program of thought in the least tinged with utopianism" (White 1982: 63).

In the end, the result is soothing bourgeois decorative literature; soothing, that is, if one shares the bourgeois entrepreneurial attitude, since, by the politics of its establishment, the range of content for the narrative interpretation of history is limited to the politically correct, and that because:

> The means by which (historical) understanding is provided is *interpretation*. *Narration* is both the way in which a historical interpretation is achieved and the mode of discourse in which a successful understanding of historical matters is represented. (White 1982: 60)

---

36 Unthinkably Revolting. The object of this well disciplined ploy is not exactly for History to overtly laud the virtues of its Bourgeois Philosophy, but to constitute the blockage needed to assure that the momentary flash of utopian potential associated with the French Revolution and its enduring possibility exposed by Marx with his critique of Capital, could never occupy the center of the political agenda for the West. As exemplified by Eric Hobsbawm, there were numerous individual historians who rebelled against this disciplined censorship. But the structuring process of the Discipline of History (and of all the Normal Social Sciences for that matter) allowed such critique to be deflected as 'merely ideological' rather than 'seriously empirical.'

In other writing from that same period, (not to be confused with his elaboration of what he considers the four master 'tropes' of the 19th century), White discussed four "master narratives from among which western man may choose," for "construing the meaning of history":

a) "Bourgeois Progressivism," according to which the West is making progress, with more good for more people, thanks to better living through chemistry, with a bit of unfortunate wear and tear along the way, such as vicious warfare, exploitation, miserable lives for underclasses, which is a price not too high to pay for the ever more splendidly progressive results, for the elite;
b) "Marxist Utopianism," according to which it is possible to leave behind not just royalist domination of people by brute force but their transformation by capital into commodities and debt slaves, to arrive at a society without class tension as its defining structural quality, shorn of (structurally inherited) economic inequality that transforms everyone into merchandise, thus opening the way to realization, however imperfectly, of the noble civic qualities of solidarity, opportunity and security, in that order;
c) "Greek Fatalism," according to which, since decadence eventually overtakes every cultural system, after peaking at its golden age, all people will be like hooked fish, struggling to escape the trap of life under decadence, enduring more and more painful struggle, until exhaustion brings their culture to its end; and
d) "Christian Redemptionism," according to which life is hell on earth, and then we die; but "*ça va quand même*'," that's ok, no problem, because next comes Paradise, for those who merit ideal existence for ever and ever (White 1987: 151; my paraphrasing).

Of the four scenarios, only the second Marxist narrative is a threat to bourgeois hegemony, which is why it was disqualified from inclusion under the rubric of historical realism. However, this authority is exercised not by slapping the knuckles of historians who dream of human liberation with a copy of *The Communist Manifesto* on their night stand, but by imposing restrictive standards of narrative style which must be complied with as they write the past into life.

For those who have not considered it, by the classic standards of expression, there are three ranges of language style: low, middle and high. The use of high style language in speaking and in most texts is taboo, being too formal, educated, refined, as if carefully worded, thoughtful, mannerliness equals decadence, which is ironic. Low style usage is uncouth, street-talk, slang ridden and inexact, so it too is taboo. As White sees it, history must be told in middle style. Alas:

> The subordination of historical narrative to the deliberative mode of the middle style entails stylist exclusions... [which] consigns to historical thinking the kinds of events that lend themselves to the understanding of whatever currently passes for educated common sense. (White 1982: 66)

When speaking historically in middle style, while Santa Claus as allegory is a fully discussable category, as a violation of 'common sense' it is not seriously imaginable that there be Christmas Time in Hell.

The Subliminal Becomes Unimaginable

Following the dictates of bourgeois history, the discipline found itself unable to study anything considered imaginary; this was a major shift from the Greek past, where, without the intervention of the gods, life on earth was impossible. Fortunately, a deal was struck between modern history and Christian theology, leaving the realm of the materially unverifiable in the hands of preachers and confessors, exorcists and inquisitors. The evident discontinuity this generated between Sunday truth and what counts during the rest of the week, spilled over conveniently to cover politics and business economics, assuring ever more that money does not smell and no one shall dress prettier than a queen.

The banishment of Utopian possibility from historical reality still left the patina of overcharged emotion to deal with; what was one to do, historically speaking, with out of bounds enthusiasm? Clearly too risky, a further step was necessary to assure a proper intellectual hygiene for history: not just the Utopian but all measure of the sublime was banished as well. As White put this in reference to the "stylist exclusions" discussed above:

> Excluded are the kinds of events traditionally conceived to be the stuff of religious belief and ritual... [as well as] 'grotesque' events that are the stuff of farce, satire, and calumny. (White 1982: 66)

As a result, among serious historians, there was to be no more consideration of 'peak' experience, either the fantastic or magically wondrous. The discipline fell under the 19th century spell of the then newly diffusing aesthetic movement, which brought to the forefront the formerly silent debate about the beautiful versus sublime. The judgment fell rapidly, such that the rules of the new discipline of history,

> ...entailed regulation, not only of what could count as a proper object of historical study but also of what could count as a proper representation of that object in a discourse, discipline consisted in subordinating written history to the categories of the 'beautiful' and suppressing those of the 'sublime.' (White 1982: 66–67)

It thus came to be, for political reasons certainly, that "disciplined historical style" entailed nothing less than "an aesthetic regulation." History was determined to be rational: the "rule of evidence" would pertain, no matter what truth that forced one to ignore.

Being appropriately well-read, at this point White turned to Schiller, to concretize the issue of what is missed when one only speaks of the beautiful while denying the sublime. Since I have dealt with Schiller elsewhere in this book, it is not necessary here to follow White on this vector. Suffice it to say, the *Aesthetic Education of Humankind* (Schiller's theme for cultural reform) would involve not just helping individuals intensify their regard for the given, but he proposed this based on the postulate that openly appreciating one's circumstance is the first step to changing it. Stripped of sublime potential, beauty is frigid and fixed; not femininity enlivened from within as is the stature of Venus, but womanliness transformed into cellulose in a world of Marlboro Men.

Beauty is harmoniously there, to be contemplated as distraction from the real; the sublime is an inner tension for action aroused by being before the potential totality of the unrealizable, because artificial, 'merely beautiful'. Beauty is appropriate, the correct measure in all things, where no violation of perspective is allowed; the sublime is disturbingly passionate, violently compelling, the true sign that, more than the ability to draw better than a baboon, what renders humankind human is the emotional charge generated in response to the footprints of others in the sands of time.

As one might suppose, since his subliminal tendencies were shocking, Nietzsche was banished by most conventional historians to the philosophy department. Even Marx was sidelined by many progressive historians because of ambiguities in his aesthetic. White indicts him, or at least his followers, on these grounds:

> The gradual displacement of the sublime by the beautiful in a generally accredited aesthetic theory, as uncritically accepted by Marxists... had the effect of restricting speculation on any ideal social order to some variant in which freedom was apprehended less as an exercise of individual will than as a release of beautiful 'feelings.' (White 1982: 69)

It is surely true that some of his followers misread Marx on the aesthetic question, and that Marx positioned himself on the issue of humanity and consciousness differently when considering the preconditions for revolution as opposed to the requirements for engagement in it. It is also true that with his historical materialist method, Marx revealed the aesthetic tension between the stability of given social arrangements and the sublime horror generated by the realization of how those are propagated through time. Although the Marx aesthetic is extremely complex and thus open to a variety of readings, it seems substantially uninformed to suppose that he based his study of the crisis of Capital and his program for revolution out of that, on a view of "freedom... as a release of beautiful feelings."

Apparently White recognized the shaky grounds beneath that claim, because he spent much of the rest of this otherwise erudite essay (1982) trying to shore it up. As if his conscience was bothering him, he even went so far as to prelude one of his negative pitches against Marx with the classic ironic quip, "I am not suggesting that Marxists have got history wrong" (White 1982: 73): quite. In spite of being as far as a humanist historian could get from the left of the political spectrum without decidedly shifting to the political right, White nevertheless showed sincere appreciation for the power of the historical materialist project. In the chapter of his *Metahistory* that he devoted to that world view, he had the following to say about Marx:

> He was a prophet of social innovation, and he conceived historical consciousness as an instrument of human liberation in a way that no other 19th-century thinker of similar status ever tried to do. [Consequently], he envisaged his theory of history as a means of liberating men... so that they might finally realize their humanity fully. (White 1973: 285)

Historical Limits on Being

Demanding realism, rejecting imagination; stressing the empirical, denying the intuitive; the discipline of history became anti-utopian in its political posture and anti-subliminal in its aesthetics. Although Schiller appreciated the sublime as motive for radical rupture and valued it for that, unlike White, his was a more decidedly philosophical, and by that a somewhat distanced, take on the problem.

By the end of the 19th century, other than a bit of distraction by romanticism, Nietzschean nihilism was the only reasonable response to the crushing truth, by then appreciated, about the sublime state of the West: that using modern means, knowledge, know-how and techno-tactics, westerners were stuck in their existential mud. A superhero might carry him or herself beyond the crisis, against all odds, by a sort of existential retreat; but in collective terms, there appeared no way out, which is to say, no way of reinvesting meaning in western existence. This was quite a conclusion, since it was a couple of generations before the Holocaust, which proved to be an even more horrid provocateur of the sublime than were the senseless wars and economic posturing of 19th century Europe that so exercised the romantics.

Sticking to his historical agenda as basically a specialist in 19th century Europe, White had to back up to Schiller, at the end of the 18th century, to find exemplified the demand of the sublime as existential propellant. In the 20th century, there were few who dared to approach this as even marginally embraceable. One who did was Walter Benjamin and he got to it very much at the end of his life, at a time when the absolute meaninglessness of The West as cultural configuration imposed itself repulsively on him. His last text, written in 1940, a "Thesis on the Philosophy of History," (in Benjamin 1968) is a chilling example of why ordinary intellectual positivists and political legitimatists dare not deal with the danger of the sublime. That which evokes a sublime response constitutes the total check of one's cultural system, indicating an irreparable state; as sign not of courage but desperation, the only response is ghastly, with the choice to lunge toward revolution as the sole beautiful possibility.

Benjamin developed his philosophy of history in eighteen theses; accordingly, his message of history as movement was as a 'one way street'. The issue is not death, but life, which we can not do alone, yet have totally failed to achieve together (Benjamin 1968). The sublime response signals the panic of the ordinary.

Beauty or its lack will rarely motivate reform and never revolution; only uncompromising disgust with the past, the unconscionable possibility of continuing to allow it to influence, much less determine, the future, must be attained before revolutionary praxis, as consciousness in action, against current social order, can happen. To achieve such a state in the moment is the Sublime. The following slices of text from Benjamin express the attitude of capitulation to existence that defines such as state; the sublime can only arrive in accepting the past, while never staring back: it is historicity as life.

Excerpted from his *Theses on the Philosophy of History*, the following image of the Sublime was captured just as Benjamin accepted the need to run for his life from the Nazis, from Paris toward Spain. So close and yet so far, with his passage to freedom blocked, in a village on the border, allegedly he ingested enough morphine to die. He felt history was upon him in a very personal way, and he set the scene this way:

> The past… flashes up at the instant [I]…. at a moment of danger [II]… in a state of emergency [III]… to make the continuum of history explode [XV]… at the moment of their action [XV]… that defines the present in which he himself is writing history [XVI]. (Benjamin 1968)

From whence there is nothing left but encounter with the Angle of Historical Being; Benjamin expressed it this way in his famous Ninth Thesis:

> A Klee painting named 'Angelus Novus' shows an angel looking as though he is about to move away from something he is fixedly contemplating. His eyes are staring, his mouth is open, his wings are spread. This is how one pictures the angel of history. His face is turned toward the past. Where we perceive a chain of events, he sees one single catastrophe which keeps piling wreckage upon wreckage and hurls it in front of his feet. The angel would like to stay, awaken the dead, and make whole what has been smashed. But a storm is blowing from Paradise; it has got caught in his wings with such violence that the angel can no longer close them. This storm irresistibly propels him into the future to which his back is turned, while the pile of debris before him grows skyward. This storm is what we call progress. (1968: 257–258)

Narrative Flaw?

To close this chapter on Hayden White, I will return to the issue of narrativity. Although he is a critique of its use as a bit of a *trompe l'oeil* for the real, he nonetheless depends on it, but as meta-narrative, to invalidate other people's use of it in their studies of the Past. While on the one hand implying an admirable theoretical posture of open-mindedness, the practical effect is radical skepticism; in support of his position, he systematically denigrates most former historical studies as so localized or historically situated that, even if valid in some limited sense, in terms of substance, the results have little to teach us today. His insistence on narrative as a limiting trope for dealing with historical truth, suggests that he and his discipline are caught in the very meta-historical trap, the elaboration of which established White's reputation.

Narrativity is imposition of plot on past events to knit together the details of history; thus, "the production of meaning in this case can be regarded as a performance, because any given set of real events can be emplotted … as any number of different kinds of stories"

(White 1987: 44).[37] This suggests high level doubt about the truth of historical study, justifying his claim that no given historical interpretation can be certified as more valid than any other.

Is White a radical relativist, denying truth to statements beyond their moment of immediate expression? As if to avoid that charge, in the paragraph following the above citation, he adds a further line that softens his position; that, even if,

> ...narrative history can legitimately be regarded as something other than a scientific account of the events of which it speaks... it is not sufficient reason to deny to narrative history substantial truth value. (White 1987: 44)

As a debate technique, the use of this sort of back-chaining clarification is a classic maneuver to convince one's opponents of the rightness of an initial announcement, but only after the fact. Descartes did it famously in his *Metaphysical Mediations*, where he fell back on the alleged ever-presence of the Divine Hand to reassure the Jesuit critics at the Sorbonne; that his argument about the humanist capacity of reasoned good judgment, as developed in his *Discourse on Method*, was not a heretical claim. Rather, it was only his discussion of a faculty (the thinking-soul) that is hard-wired into human being as the benevolent gift of the gods, who we can be sure would never fool us. As for White, not suggesting recourse to aid from the gods, he leaves the interpretive issue hanging. Yet, in reference to a Hegel or Marx, a Nietzsche or even White for that matter, how can any of us know just what aspects of history carry "substantial truth value," and which are only inspiration for various stories to be told?

Exploring this irresolvable perplexity is one of White's recurring themes. While theoretically engaging and harmless as seminar topic, roughly equivalent to the debate about the number of angels that might perch on the head of a pin, left as it is, does not his position silently justify a form of crass cynicism as displayed in the mainstream, non-critical journalism which now floods the common consciousness of unwary westerners?

For undisclosed purposes, White uses this meta-narrative scheme in paradigm fashion to discredit the use of narrative style by other historians, who are supposedly aiming not at the production of literature, but at a certain truth, drawn from history. Rather than historic truth, what they generate, he says, is 'only narrative literature.' Is there more to the project of Marx (or Hegel, or Nietzsche) than that? One possibility is confusion

[37] Plotting Performance. See White's "The Question of Narrative in Contemporary Historical Theory" (1984; in *The Content of the Form*, 1987).

between their mission and their writings: to the extent that a project is more than a sum of its texts, it is probably true that a critical product deserves more than just literary criticism.

Is History Really There?

Denying transcendental historical force to the judgments of other critical historians, due to the deceptive face of narrativity, White nonetheless applies the narrative form for everything he writes, using it to back the work of others straight into the grave, refusing to acknowledge their potential value as a basis for future social movement. Is this enlightened erudition or the use of narrative history to condemn its own process?

White confronted this issue head-on in the paper, "The Value of Narrativity in the Representation of Reality" (1980). There he carefully elaborated a judgment about the overvalued use of narrative interpretation for generating histories. As a historian himself, he under-theorizes reality philosophically and under-describes existence sociologically, making it difficult to decide just what to make of his observations.

The narrative mode of interpretation is commonly applied in the construction of all critical historical work: can it be trusted? White focuses on composition issues rather than content, justified by the postulate that there is no evidence other than written texts as to the existence of historical study. If so, then literary issues are paramount in evaluating the quality of historical judgments. White denies that there is anything about the past which is there, "speaking for itself"; what we understand of the past is entirely a function of the story told about it by critics and historians. This reveals the speculative quality of his formative postulate, which comes across as perhaps too simple to handle the subject he addresses. As William James was wont to repeat, in spite of the struggle to render it otherwise, existence is a mighty complex affair.

As exemplified by this 1980 essay on narrativity, when White writes, he starts with evidence consisting of historical documents, with the purported intention of drawing out a conclusion based on logical study of those facts. This defines the inductive approach to research, from data to generalization. Starting with a theory, extruding a hypothesis, setting up a plan to test it empirically, then comparing results to prediction, is deduction.

In most of his essays (and markedly different from his strategy in his *Metahistory* book), White complies with the rules of induction, arriving at his generalization at the end, avoiding prejudgment, by not stipulating in advance the conceptualization that he believes will be applicable to the study. Technically speaking, this suggests open-minded, methodological-objectivity.

Still, we must ask: does he not really construct a methodological facade, hiding his *a priori* theorizing under an inductive narrative cover? Generally at the end of his essays, there is the denouement, exposing the thesis that rationalizes the study, and *voilà*: like the Sherlock of literary history, we imagine his rather remarkable pleasure, since from the beginning, he was right one more time.

For an Agatha Christie, a history structured in that fashion is said to possess plot; since Aristotle, as concerns literature, the basic rule is: no plot, no story. White seems faithful to the principle of plot, with the result that his essays are a pleasure to read. There is always closure of a most satisfying form: before it is over, we clearly understand the solution for the intellectual conundrum at the center of the paper, as revealed to us by White with absolute intellectual transparency: we finally know 'why,' thus eliminating the pernicious confusion that would otherwise turn us off.

The comfort comes from White's application of narrative emplotment, which on the one hand he discusses with unmatched erudite sophistication, and on the other hand, applies to show why the use of narrativity for the generation of histories is a sort of con-job against science itself. If so, does this not include him? In his pivotal essay on narrativity he employs that double-edged strategy with aplomb, indicating why we should never believe histories—other than his.

Behind writing in general, and historical studies in particular, is the working of "historical consciousness." Although White does not expand on this, it is assumedly a universal human attribute, perhaps his way of identifying the core feature of consciousness itself. If a historian, imbued with such consciousness, wishes to generate a study of history that appeals to readers, then he or she must comply with the demands placed on reality by humans thus disposed. Historical consciousness demands nothing more or less than that history has 'meaning.'[38]

[38] Consciousness. White favors the view of the French psychoanalyst, Jacques Lacan, over that of Freud. In general, that places him in the mainstream of the last half of the 20th century, when discrediting Freud was the trend. As an alternative, not all preferred Lacan. Many, such as the Anglo-Saxons in general, never took Freud seriously in the first place, other than as a danger for positivist rationality. Against the baseline of the *Bourgeois Philosophy of History* as laid out in my Introduction, it can be argued that, whereas Freud posed a critique of the bourgeois model of human being, with negative results for the

We humans are vulnerable to manipulation by meaning. Without plunging into the structure of the psyche, it is clear that uncertainty begets agitation, the antidote for which is 'meaning'; understanding 'why' is comforting even if that about which we thus understand is materially horrid. Formal authority is identified by the legitimate right to generate and reinforce meaning-wrappers around reality, some degree of which historians, cultural critics in general, strive for. This is why there is an important core to the call for vigilance that White suggests when faced with any purportedly authoritative text.

Manipulation of meaning can be overridden by personal reflection, anchored within an informed community, a defense now losing its potency due to the increasing rapidity of western life that eliminates the time for reflection, coupled with the isolation generated by the false note of liberty as radical individuality. Our all too humanized historical consciousness refuses ambiguity, while demanding meaning with such violence that, to paraphrase Alfred North Whitehead: when there is no logical resolution for a major point of confusion, we will invent one ourselves, or more likely, embrace one of someone else's invention, whether it supposes any logical justification or not.

"Plot" gives to "reality the odor of the ideal," which humans require if they are expected to take a text seriously; insisting that existence be described as a "moral drama," there is unspoken "demand for closure in the historical story," carrying compelling "moral meaning" (White 1980: 21). The result, according to White, is persuasive because, "the plot of a narrative imposes a meaning on the events that make up its story... revealing at the end a structure that was (purportedly) immanent in the events all along" (1980: 20).

In this 1980 essay on narrativity, White complies with this readerly-credibility requirement with aplomb: right at the end of it he comes out of

philosophy that drives it, Lacan's critique yields a much more flattering judgment of the bourgeois psyche. The lacuna for Freudian Man is the tension between human being as humanity expressed, forced to exist in the side-slipping region of manipulated meaning generated by bourgeois society. The result, sociologically, is existential crisis, for which there is no fix other than intra-psychic maneuvers or extra-psychic social revolution. For a Lacanian, on the other hand, the pit for consciousness is not really 'unconscious' tension, but rather '*Jouissance*': oversaturated desire driving individuals loony because of blocks on the rational payoff of worldly satisfaction for that desire. Lacan never posed a negative critique of bourgeois society, as did Freud, which is probably why Lacan emerged as a popular offering in the 20th century while Freud, for reasons similar to those used against Marx, continues to be one of the most influential intellectuals ever to suffer from a tarnished reputation.

the closet to tell us that he knew all along how it would work out, because it could not have been otherwise. In this twenty-five page paper, he gets to that point on page twenty-four. Showing a certain operatic flair, he backs into it coyly: "It may be thought that I have stacked the cards in favor of my thesis—that narrativizing discourse serves the purpose of moralizing judgments..." (p. 24) in the writing of history. The structure of this phrase implies that we 'all knew' what his thesis was, that it was 'immanent' in the preceding twenty-four pages of the essay; in fact, it was not evident at all, and as for its formal precision, it was not until the above line was dropped that he stated it himself.

Plot embodies a moral principle, for which a secular morality is fully acceptable; revealed in the denouement, at "the end of the discourse," which then can "cast its light back over the events originally recorded (in the text) in order to redistribute the force of a (supposed) meaning that was immanent in all of the events from the beginning" (White 1980: 20).

I add reference to the 'supposed' nature of this backward chaining effect of narrative meaning, without which the popular consciousness will refuse to read on, the truth of which is less important than the sense of closure it provides. This generates among historians, says White, "the embarrassment of plot to historical narrative." For a crime writer such as Dorothy Sayers, the use of emplotment is a sign of fiction-generating genius. When historians do it to manufacture an appealing story out of the U.S. Civil War or the Fall of Rome, is it all just imagination? What else can White say, but: "This is why the plot of a historical narrative is always an embarrassment and has to be presented as (if) 'found' in the events rather than put there by narrative techniques" (1980: 21).

If plot is absent, the text is discredited if indeed ever read; when present, it answers to the demand "for moral meaning... that sequences of real events be assessed as to their significance as elements of a moral drama." The result is "narrativity... (as) representations of reality... embodied in historical discourse." Is that not just to say that every critical study is largely fiction with footnotes (White 1980: 21)?

Who is responsible? Evidently, "it is historians themselves who have transformed narrativity from a manner of speaking into a paradigm of the form that reality itself displays to a 'realistic' consciousness" (White 1980: 24). Is there an alternative? Not really, or at least, as White admits:

> I confess that I cannot think of any other way of 'concluding' an account of real events, for we cannot say, surely that any sequence of real events actually comes to an end, that reality itself disappears, that events of the order of the real have ceased to exist. (1980: 23)

Which leaves us where? History does not end or cease to exist; so it is there for us, yet inaccessibly so according to White. Is there no way to know anything about that process called the past? Are we obliged to accept story telling as our only access to history? Are we confronted with a truth, otherwise denied, that not just the future is an unknowable force for our existence, but the past as well?

Suspended in the present: is that the truth of White's reading of historical studies? Neither theology, nor anarchy, nor fatality, nor utopia, but only the slow pirouette of present-existence, twisting slowly, slowly in the liminal state between two times (past and future), neither of which is specifiable?

In the moment as movement of now-thens, neither tragic nor comic, nor even history as ironic put-on, Hayden White's study of history frames a canvas for another possible future. Earlier we viewed the modern condition through Benjamin's angel's gaze, with the sublime force of cluttered being and the need not just to sanitize the vacant canvas of existence, but to fill it with material that is other than modern. As they say in banking, so it is true in life: only new deposits count.

Defenselessly True

In the midst of editing these pages on social criticism in a Paris café, using as background the even flow of music from a Paris radio station (FIP), what should pop out of my ear-buds to force its way into consciousness but the opening call for the "War of the Worlds" radio program. Direct from the audio archives, it was Orson Welles: raising the verbal curtain for the Mercury Radio Theater on the Air, opening the show (30 October 1938) that terrified a large number of his estimated thirty-million weekly listeners, completely duped, then panic-stricken, in a state of terror. Given today's war of worlds of meaning, how might we introduce the Welles aesthetic for the use of those who dare to take on the cultural malaise in our tumultuous 21st century?

It is clear from that work by Welles that, when properly generated as plausible narrative, even if linked with fantasy or illusion, well plotted meaning can mobilize enormous human energy. Such is the power of art. Yet why is it so difficult to generate the same energy from thoughtful exposure to the real conditions of existence? What is it about the method of critical inquiry that defuses the power of its truth, seemingly to leave space only for the make-believe to rise from its ashes?

In the preceding chapter, my study of the work and workings of Terry Eagleton provided evidence in support of a central claim by Hayden White: 20th century expression became entrenched in irony to an extent that is not even funny. Unlike White, Eagleton hammers and sickles away relentlessly at the structures of unjustified social class differences hidden in the dune grass on the shores of the ocean of life; we know that he knows that the current crisis of the West is democratically generated and reproduced social injustice, driven by the crass concentrating ambition of capital. He publishes his words in a nearly continuous stream, with plenty of evidence that they are read if not listened to; yet the fact that he must couch his delivery in irony drains the pique from his discourse and the result is comforting to the upper, so called entrepreneurial classes rather than consciousness raising for the lesser classes.

As for White, while instructing us as to the ironic hijacking of the West during the 20th century, he largely avoids falling into it himself. Rather than using that (ironic) tactic to incidentalize the shortfall of modern liberty under democracy, he draws our attention to it by exposing its historical roots and development as over-determined by bourgeois intention. But to achieve this effect he is obliged to treat history as if it has consequences; which can only be done by writing up his cultural criticism in narrative form. This in turn requires the false factum of artificial closure, of everything ending well, of the insipid details working out in an 'all and all' fashion. That can only be achieved, as he also underlines in his writings, by a considerable degree of fictionalizing of the facts.

If it is true, as White believes, that history is always political and that the poetics of an epic are associated with the common consciousness of the times, and I am accurate in my hypothesis, then the drive force behind the manipulation of historical reporting that so unnerves him is probably the bourgeois philosophy of history as detailed by Horkheimer. Even if Eagleton himself, in his irony, is clearly aware that the current cultural crisis is no laughing matter, and if White is convinced of the necessity of sincerity when describing how the force of the past shapes current experience, still, it seems that, in terms of packaging and delivery, oscillating between irony and narrative, critical practice today is caught in the jaws of a deforming vice, locked in a struggle between the joke and the lie.

Accepting that tense condition as a challenge rather than a dead-end, I will close these case studies with a few last words from White, demonstrating the dialectics of possibility that is intrinsic to the burden of history:

> My own view is that all theoretical discussions of historiography become enmeshed in the ambiguity contained in the notion of history itself. This ambiguity derives, not from the fact that the term history refers both to an object of study and to an account of this object, but from the fact that the object of study itself can be conceived only on the basis of an equivocation. (from 1984, in 1987: 54)

It would seem that the very equivocating interface of the past that White speaks of, provides the opening by which a critical dialectic might get the better of history; and soon, we would hope.

CHAPTER EIGHT

LIBERATION: PROJECT, METHOD, OBJECT

Beyond Domination by Necessity

What does this study of critical practice tell us about the nature and expression of that role, and about the potential for liberation of westerners from the grip of a rigid societal organization, mobilized by a hegemonic political-economy and sold to its publics as inevitable in form, and timelessly cyclic in passage. Are current conditions of domination as necessity beyond either fundamental modification or replacement, frustrating the very call for freedom, equality and justice which gave rise to the modern democratic nation state in the first place?

I have presented six case studies of major figures, who have put themselves out at considerable risk, some for their physical freedom, all for their professional reputation, calling into question with particular acuity the false note of the modern west. I have demonstrated that critical practice is issue of a perceptive individual, fully and consciously engaged in a particular historical situation and that the resulting working-through of that contemporary history by writing it into life, using some form of humanly resonant narrative, is not just part of the process needed to display the content of the critical consciousness, but that this narrative-generating process is the crucial expression of critical practice in action.

Critical practice of the form exposed by these case studies is the generic expression of civic responsibility pushed to the height of aspiration in an open society. Its pursuit is material evidence of judgment as movement in a democratic community, reinforcing the validity of the Socratic dictum that as a work of art, even if not science, every public act is political. It brings into focus the fine structure among social classes and categories, by which the pain and benefit of life in common is attributed, and about the need and opportunity to better manage those distributive and allocation processes. For any society, this is essential in establishing the moral boundaries of preference and obligation that frame the existence of the members, linked to the life and death process of having, using and bequeathing to posterity the means at the disposal of a people.[1]

How well does this work out, for whom and at what costs? To what extent do these studies exemplify the qualities of a generic process even if of rare pursuit, cumulatively presenting a legitimate profile of critical practice, with its place in the sociology of everyday life in democratic society? While empirical certification is impossible, given their exceptional tenacity, discipline and perspicacity, I consider the figures I studied here to have set themselves apart in this crucial critical role.

Critical Profiling

Turning first to the question, 'liberation from what,' I draw attention again to Horkheimer's thesis concerning the *Origins of Bourgeois Philosophy of History* (1930). I treat as valid his premise that this view of societal reality underwrites both the dominant institutions and ideology of the West, as materialized historically in practical productive relations and action. I propose also that the six figures that I have studied were on the mark about the somber failings evidenced by the various institutional arrangements on which they focused, as perpetrated in pursuit of that world view.

To take these six critics seriously is not entertaining. The West as a system is prone to the tyrannical perpetuation of oligarchic power (Voltaire), and to political despotism generating horrid domestic inequality and dangerous foreign wars (Schiller). Prone to a lattice of manipulated knowledge and expertise that drains resources from the general well-being through the deformation of rationality as instrument for the concentration and preservation of power (Foucault), and to the mutation of technological capacity for the development of tools that free humans from drudgery, transformed into a system of self-serving objects that trap

---

[1] As the Greeks since Socrates and his student, Plato, were concerned, any public act intended to influence one's community, is political, aimed at reinforcing or weakening, understanding or modifying, civic convention. Furthermore, Socrates assumed that those who take seriously the call to 'know thyself' would be acting 'philosophically' in public with the interests of Higher Humanity as guide. Perhaps as a result of seeing his mentor, Socrates, executed for his critical practices, for Plato, politics was a necessity, a way of strategically organizing to avoid the disaster of confusion and menace that humans face. Political action was a tactical skill and not a form of higher knowledge or wisdom in action. This tension, between politics as 'science' versus 'art,' is explored at various places in the Platonic dialogues (and recurrently since then): see for example, Zukert (2005).

citizens in cycles of useless and meaningless consumption (Baudrillard). Prone to the taking in charge of the linguistic aptitude of culture as such, of English and its literature in particular, turning the very humanizing capacity of verbal expression and forthright communication into a tool for the perpetuation and extension of systems of domination of lesser classes by those ensconced in self-defined advantage (Eagleton) And prone to the hijacking of the study of what culture is as a time-binding system, by manipulation via neo-mythic story-telling the facts of the historical past, carried out by reputed scholars, to render a continuing basis of deceptive justification for whatever occurs, including current schemes of injustice, inequality, blocked opportunity and frustrated creativity, as needed for the perpetuation of the hegemonic west (White).

Engagement

As shown by these case studies, determined cultural critics first enter the contested arena for personal, often dramatically idiosyncratic reasons. Once faced with the challenge, like toreadors in Madrid, all tend to work in a similar fashion. They set their sights on a particular historical object, to study both why and how it came into being and/or its basis of continuation, and what this says about the historical context that explains and perpetuates that emergence. They asses its effect (positive or otherwise) for the general well-being and what might be done to modify the constitution of that object, exploring its reach and power, perhaps its elimination or renaissance in greater force, so as to fit better with some view of the human, social potential. This demands a nested set of interlaced judgments.

As noted in the preceding chapters, societies are organized to fit with the avowed interests of the dominating elites. Meeting those interests does not necessarily mean denying all other interests. It is the role of government to put in check the boundless pursuit of every category of self-interest, so as to protect the common-interest in favor of the general good. The *raison d'être* of government is not only to assure good orderly direction for a population, but to assure also that the hubris of limitless pursuit of self-interest among members of elite classes does not destroy the self-reckoning potential of a society.

To arrive at some critical conclusion is one thing; to lay it out convincingly requires packaging the process in a fashion that is reasonable, explainable and understandable, linked to real conditions by active observation. This involves considerable study of the components, qualities and goals of the cultural system, of the critical object, and of the meaning of the object for or within it. There is no way to untangle the evaluative or normative aspects of the operation from the positive or empirical steps needed to anchor it in social action. The test of the undertaking is ultimately established by the ability of the critic to reach an intended audience, in a plausible fashion that resonates with their frame of meaning and action, even if negatively. This imposes enormous burden on the critic and helps to explain why the task is generally the undertaking of a lifetime and even then, for very few.

Objects of cultural criticism are historic in that they are 'humanized,' which is to say otherwise than they might have been due to the intervention of humans. This historic quality certifies the potential for their future change based on different human interventions. Some points of critique are natural objects, but transformed by labor: a North American Indian arrowhead is a 'humanized' piece of flint-rock. Other historical objects, including most that attract the attention of major critics, are exclusively 'social' objects, having come into being and owing their existence entirely to the collective human labor of their creation and maintenance. Called social-institutions, these include government and economic structures, forms of industry, organization of cities, modes of transportation, strategies for production and use of food, as well as the way that knowledge or expertise is cultivated, refined and transformed into practice.

When aimed at more than just decrying current practices, affirmative criticism demands a lucid appreciation of history. Whether initially natural objects or pure social forms from the start, owing to the human work done either as modification or creation, in the event that the object of study is negatively evaluated, it is reasonable to assume its possible modification and by that a shift in its cultural meaning. In other words, the historicity of the institutional objects around us is the crucial quality of study for critics and all humans, as the foundation for sound judgment. When well chosen, the work serves not just as a window for better appreciating the dynamics of a society and its cultural system, but can identify points of leverage for reform, restructuring or even dramatic revolutionary action.

Genre Criticism

Rather than aimed at fundamental modification or renewal of the cultural apparatus and the societal forms that it seeds, most professional critical activity is of much reduced ambition, carried out by what I identify as genre or first-level cultural critics. They focus on evident, popular and usually less highly contested aspects of society, sometimes elements of high-culture, other times of popular-culture. They generate the ubiquitous examples of critical work found in newspapers, television and radio broadcasts, magazines, in print and on the web, covering diverse subjects including literature, film, self-help programs, theater, educational programs, art, architecture, and the many forms of music that animate society.

While the manifest point of genre-criticism is to aid clients or consumers to make better choices and improve the special art or cultural form under review, such work is not necessarily concerned with the significance for society or culture as a whole. This is not to suggest that these forms of cultural material are without meaning beyond their value as entertainment, distraction or personal improvement. Any genre of fiction, from science fiction to online empire games, for example, may well impart a gripping message for the reader or user, infusing their consciousness with a particular ideological orientation that may or may not accord with the humanist goal of western civilization. Most often genre-critics are attentive to sustaining or expanding the market for their favored genre, even when the works that are put under their critical eye are of low quality or potentially distorting in impact.[2]

The Radical Benchmark

The benchmark example of cultural criticism is the research of Karl Marx. He targeted a vital historical object (the capital economy), then pushed its study to the limit by addressing the political issues thus exposed. What marked his originality was that he studied the economic mainspring of western societal organization by exploring its positive and negative consequences for both the technical stability and social responsibility of western nations.

Independent of the fact that his terminal judgment about capitalism was extremely threatening for the status quo, even most of his critics admit that the Marx study was a landmark. Due to what he considered the contradictions inherent in the constant accumulation, and, above all, hardnosed concentration of capital associated with this mode of

[2] Critical Acumen. As I discussed in my Introduction, to a certain extent, the work of the French sociologist, Boltanski, and, above all, that of the American humanist, Ebert, demonstrates the powerful potential of the use of literature as window for access to deeper cultural critical issues.

political-economy, and due to the necessity of generating an ever increasingly surplus value based on a societal infrastructure fractured by class and categorical differences, from this he concluded that only a total reform of the status quo would do. For Marx, societal renewal could not be achieved unless that form of political-economy was surpassed, with some form of socialism replacing the monolith of capitalism. He went further, of course, in asserting that this rupture and replacement would inevitably occur, a possibility on which the West continues to wait.[3]

No single one of my case studies demonstrates an equivalently vast, proto-revolutionary calling for radical societal change based on critical study of a major institution; rather, each of the figures I've studied here seem to leave open the possibility that the western system might be repaired, and by that preserve its modern enlightened form. This suggests that, to some extent, they each remained faithful to the bourgeois philosophy of history as profiled by Horkheimer: as if there is no other way for society to be constituted. This may signal the inherent rightness of that world view as guide for social practices: as if the current way of responding to the humanist call of the western enlightenment is fundamentally beyond reproach. It is always possible that, even if his method was of enduring quality, the substantive content of Marx's final observations is no longer in step with contemporary conditions due to changes over recent generations in the mode of expression of capitalism in society. Or, though not flawed in method, the Marx critique was perhaps misshapen by the normative assessment he applied to the results of his work. Clearly these are issues about which reasoning individuals differ.[4]

---

[3] Bourgeois Glorification. I mention again the writings by the American, Deirdre McCloskey (2006, 2010), who discuses bourgeois dignity and bourgeois virtue as a platform to argue not just that Marx was dead-wrong, but that everything that is admirable about the world today is expression of and validation of the rightness of the bourgeois attitude.

[4] A Pragmatic Sociology of Critique. From my discussion in Chapter One of the work of Boltanski, it may be recalled that he is specific in distinguishing the empirical phase of social research from the political-evaluative phase in critical studies. The Marx critique exemplifies this distinction, which is why many critiques who are loyal supporters of radical capitalism accept and use the empirical aspect of the Marx research for their own purposes, denying on the other hand the evaluative judgment that he reached about the 'pragmatic' consequences of the result, and above all rejecting the proposition that western conditions would be better for general well-being if some form of socialism were adopted by western countries.

None can say what might occur if the U.S. or Germany were to follow China and India, and reconstitute themselves around some set of socialist principles. However, at the time of this writing (2013), following a very tumultuous free democratic election, a shift toward a mild form of state socialism became possible in France, providing an important five-year long case study of the process.

Cases of Critical Objectification

For the cases I considered, compared to Marx, the objects and objectives of critique were of a much less fundamental nature. The first two, Voltaire and Schiller, were necessarily so, having preceded by many generations his work and development of his method. Still, the results were politically confronting in a way that few critics would dare to match today.

Voltaire took on as historic object the tyranny of self-perpetuating oligarchy, the arrangements on the part of the elites of his day, that generation after generation dominated society to its detriment. He saw that his society was overwhelmed by autocratic nobility, reactionary religious hierarchy and arrogant intellectuals who imposed their whim and desire as if *raison d'état*, perverting the principles of human decency as if it were achievement toward creativity, discovery and freedom.

Schiller set his critical sights on despotism: cruel, greedy, vicious, pride driven, war-mongering tyrannical rulers who subjugated people in cycles of senseless, bloody warfare. Entire populations were enslaved in chains of necessity, exploiting their labor, shortening their lives, in a general pall of hopeless confusion.

In spite of being largely descriptive, in a way superficial, somewhat over stylized in current terms and almost of a cliché form, the work of these first two of the central figures in these case studies was, nonetheless, compelling. Yet, in spite of the ensuing dramatic revolutionary phase of upheaval in Europe at the end of the 18th century, the core tendencies criticized by Voltaire and Schiller, toward abuse of power, are as common now as then, even if the way this is manifest in the West today is (usually) less bloody for the domestic population of the war-makers. Were they to

---

The challenge facing a socialist movement (like any other) is its own stability. Paradoxically this is made difficult by the fact that since Marx, socialism is driven by a social philosophy based on ethical, esthetic and civic standards associated with practical values such as liberty, equality, fraternity, etc. Once in action, expectations tend to rise in every direction favoring the good life, resulting in enormous differences in judgment about how that might be achieved. This can generate internal discord of a form that is absent under its alternative of radical capitalism, which is bereft of higher principle.

In a flash of insight, the process by which this occurs was summarized by Michael Burawoy, now professor at UC-Berkeley, recent (2004) President of the American Sociological Society and current (2011–2014) President of the International Sociological Association. At the time of his election to the U.S. post, he composed a limpidly frank intellectual autobiography entitled, "Antinomian Marxist" (2005b). There he described what he learned at various points of his career, from field work in factories around the world. One observation he offers from his experience working in a steel mill in Hungary in the 1980s is that: "State socialism had the paradoxical effect of manufacturing dissent to the socialist regime for failing to live up to its socialist claims" (p. 65).

be among us, Voltaire and Schiller would probably be jailed for life for advocating sedition, indicating that political progress in the West has not yielded greater justice and equity but rather greater technical capacity for suppression of opposition. This explains, no doubt, the difficulty in today's western societies for well-reasoned critics to find an outlet for their views, unless of course, they are aiming their critical arrows at non-western countries and leaders.

Foucault put in his sights the truly byzantine organization of the fields of knowledge and expertise that establish the dominion of rational wisdom in the West. He detailed how this has produced a balkanized division of intellectual territory, vitiating not just the freedom and creativity of intellectuals of every specialty, but by its usurpation of power, perverting also the general liberty of all western citizens.

Baudrillard challenged the proliferation without logic or anchoring of the means of production of objects of consumption and of the consumers of such objects, with so much techno-instrumental efficacy. According to his analysis, modern westerners are now trapped within, saddled beneath and chained to an unfathomable myriad of objectified gadgets, truncating the free, meaningful expression of their full human potential.

Eagleton's object of concern is English as expression and literature. He is relentless in exposing the degree to which its content as formulated achieves what he considers to be ideologically distorting, if not actively perilous effects. He continues from there to describes how this contributes to the twisting of public opinion by disguising the truth of the social dynamics with which literature is necessarily concerned, masking the reality of inequality and exploitation by the elite classes, for self-serving reasons, vis-à-vis vulnerable members of lesser social classes.

Hayden White took on the discipline of history and unraveled its mystery with his penetrating study of 19th century developments in Europe, shaped by the politically determined emergence of that discipline. He revealed how the way history is written, concerning institutional events in the West, is put forward as fact, but is actually heavily contorted by fictions, in ways so convoluted as to be often unrecognized even by the historians who create it as literature. This generates uncertain if not misleading narrative story-telling about western life and work done in the past, which, as a guide for future action, is often groundless, illusory and desperate.

While structural change may be difficult, is there reason to be politically submissive in face of this stream of observations about the dysfunction of society? Yet the four figures I studied from the 20th century were amazingly passive about fundamental issues, as if the intellectual basis of their critiques was sound yet the political relevance of the result was questionable. Since apologists of the status-quo are unhesitatingly vocal about their conservative, often reactionary positions, this meekness on the part of sensible cultural critics is difficult to understand.

Justification or Demagogy?

Criticism questions the justification or power of its target object (an economic strategy, a political form, a populist mobilization), investigating and exposing its believability or truth-content and what that says about the object, given its momentum in the world. Based on a synthetic judgment in the form of a hypothesis, the meaning of the object of study is identified by the critic as both a discovery and an analytic fact. This is established in reference to practices in which that object plays a part, and how that contributes, for better or worse, to the work of society.

Expressed as the second-degree of the real, well formulated critique is often worded in the extreme. Necessarily defaming the usual appeal of the *juste milieu*, its severe words and images often render suspect the critic's work. Is the result well-founded wisdom, one-dimensional dogmatism or hyperbolic attention seeking? Is it indicative of a path to be followed or a fantasy to be avoided? As with every expression of strength, the danger of excess or misapplication is palpable, but without such potency, critical imagination, discovery and innovation are impossible.

Historical objects sprout in the cultural field composed of the residue of the history of a society as system of practices, of collective achievements and errors, of confrontations, oppositions and reversals. Yet being historical is to say that every such object is limited: there was an era before which the sonnet as poetic form did not exist, the same goes for the novel or rap music. This applies as well to each religion, way of organizing the family, or system of government. For a new type of airplane, the technical factors explain whether or not it flies. But for pure social-cultural objects, like a new music or literary form or new way of governance or mode of production for a country, there is no necessary material criterion that determines the success of failure of innovation.

Many aspects of society demonstrate a similar transient quality, suggesting that none in particular deserves more than superficial concern. Beyond that, it is often argued that if a given practice is really negative, it will dissolve all its own. If so, then why should anyone be concerned with what critics study or conclude? Even if not overtly dangerous, like theater pieces that fail to attract support and fold after the first night, most cultural innovations are of flitting appearance. Other than for the select individuals who are directly frustrated or inconvenienced, or perhaps those who give birth to some new idea in the first place, on what basis is any property of society sufficiently important to merit serious critical analysis?

While the vast majority of social practices are of minimal cultural significance, when it comes to the systems of production and allocation that sustain a population and determine individual well-being, we arrive at the life and death reality of the political-economy. This sector is not optional or superficial. It establishes the range of possibilities for emergence of new institutions and for maintenance or reform of existing ones. This is how the political-economy of a country influences not just the life chances for the members of a society, but the potential for the opportunity and freedom, and the distribution of burden and privilege among them. What occurs with the political-economy is worthy of more than just passing interest, since in one form or another it must exist if the society does.

No social form will be sustained if it violates beyond reasonable limits the principles of the field of action in which it is operative. As not just any biological species can thrive just anywhere in the physical-organic environment, not just any social form can thrive in just any socio-cultural environment. Cultural critics attempt to understand the conditions of existence of historical objects, such that their change, difficult and dangerous as that may be, might shift the probability of perpetuation or emergence of particular socio-cultural effects.

The targets for cultural critics tend to be faceless, institutional forces without material bodies, and the criteria for redress are based on similarly non-material entities. This explains, for instance, why attacks against an out of control banking system can be argued away as if for lack of material foundation. Because we humans are symbolically-minded creatures, the very immateriality of institutions without bodies explains in large part their authority.

Is Jail Necessary?

If you avoid direct political confrontation and do not excessively irritate the pride issues of the elites that dominate your society, it is possible to be a cultural critic and never see the inside of a jail cell; this was the case with both Baudrillard and Eagleton. However, to keep the police record clean is not to say that one's professional colleagues will respect your stance. Baudrillard was poorly accepted within the usual university circles in Paris. After securing a teaching post at Oxford, Eagleton was driven nearly to despair by the ceaseless nay-saying of his more properly profiled colleagues. As he put it, when finally yielding to the pressure and resigning, he stayed on as long as he had mostly to prove that he could.

In the interests of notoriety and perhaps even practical effectiveness, it is probably preferable to have the outrage of critique validated by a subsequent, but hopefully brief, jailing of the critic. Voltaire spent six months in prison in Paris for a couple of accusatory poems that cast inflammatory aspersions on the moral un-rightness and religious duplicity of members of the French Royal family. He persisted, nonetheless, eventually certifying his position as first Enlightenment public intellectual. On the one hand, he so irritated Frederick the Great in Germany, that he was evicted from that royal court after a three year tenure, yet also is so well remembered for having been there, that in the Château in Potsdam where he spent those years with Frederick, his room has been preserved as a tourist attraction.

Schiller also was able to recover form his initial run-in with the law, for the outrage expressed in a play he began writing while still a student, that earned him two weeks in jail and a court order never to write again (which he ignored, or course), because of the vehemence with which he attacked the despotic political system in the German principalities. Three centuries later, his first play, *The Robbers*, is still produced, and the theater in Berlin where his works are staged regularly, and continue to inspire students, is named after him. Demonstrating again that genius and discipline can overcome shocking political repression, he went on to attract the attention of, then was sponsored by, then worked with and eventually became the beacon of inspiration for the fellow widely considered to be the major literary figure of post-enlightenment European high culture, Goethe.

Objectively, Foucault's one night in jail hardly measures up; yet, in France, the symbol weighs more than the gem. The fact that he was whisked off by the police for a night in jail, along with a couple of busloads of long haired student demonstrators who had just been evicted from a Dean's Office at a Paris University building; well, the result was simply too-'60s not to serve Foucault for the rest of his unfortunately shortened life, as evidence of an uncompromising anti-authority attitude.

Hayden White's anti-establishment status was certified by the risky public challenge he posed to the established order of the state. While a

California history professor, he single-handedly took to court the LA police chief and won his judgment, against the planting of thought-police in his history seminars at UCLA in hopes of snaring humanities students whose critical thinking had apparently become a public danger. This signaled a deep appreciation on his part for the true political danger of late-modernity, that of insidious intrusion into the private life and experience of citizens. Yet he never spent a single night in jail as a result.

As for Terry Eagleton: no jail sentences, no courtroom drama in defense of the right of free-thinking on the part of students. The most we can point to as certification of his critical determination is that he generates more rabid reader response from his agitated London audiences than Larry King could do with his prime-time pyrotechnics on the CNN cable news channel in the U.S. He has found a less politically dangerous way of spawning public outrage while staying out of jail: by slandering the reputation of defenseless image holders. His preferred target consists of other hapless intellectuals, unusual university types like himself, but posted at right-places like Yale or Oxford. He's particularly good at roasting poets, medieval historians or back-sliding theologians, who, of course, are able to be hurt over and over again, and willingly so, since it is the only way that the public will ever hear of them. While the result clearly sells London newspapers and airport newsstand books, in terms of political change, just what service is provided from this form of intellectual sadomasochism?

Disciplinary Irreverence

Some form of turncoatism seems inevitable as intention for higher-grade critical practice. The question concerns what aspects of one's own origins and profession one turns against and with what determination and follow-through, which brings us to the scandalous question of criticism as sedition.

The leaders of all corporate entities share a common worry and are thus ready to share resources to combat an ultimate enemy: rebellion. Formal organizations exist for assuring orderly direction of proscribed activity, channeling behavior and mental activity in fit with an ideology linked to an earthly mission. Whether the end is foreign conquest, paradise, or sale of a trainload of luxury cars, no responsible leader of any formal organization or body of practice can tolerate a basic challenge to its right to exist. Moreover, sedition is contagious: at any given time, many different organizations and systems of action are out of fit with their demands, and need serious overhauling. If revolt, rebellion, and revolution lead to the upending of any one of them, the fact that members of other societies witness this event, often leads, on a comparative deprivation and opportunity basis, to the view that 'we also' ought to rebel.

Beyond the limited desires of their founders, the larger justification of every social organization is open to question. While perhaps at their inception most are more beneficial than not, as time wears on, many engage in less justifiable border warfare, symbolic or open, with competitors, or impose unnecessary or unequal constraint on members. Most could probably benefit from major overhaul if not rupture, destruction and reconstitution. To forestall this, their leaders often engage in dissimulation, or identify other organizations or systems of practices in their operating environment as if the source of their internal difficulties. When agents are not deployed to spy on one another, or provoke rebellion elsewhere, propaganda is circulated as if reliable information, in hopes of buttressing the image of their own enterprise.

The position of radical cultural critics is paradoxical. If they remain at the margins of the acceptable, condemning by faint praise the internal workings of the systems of which they are members, the result is decorative rather than threatening, and the complaint will usually be hijacked and buried by publicity agents. In a way this was the case with Foucault. The only areas where his critical bite was strong concerned universally popular zones of complaint, such as the treatment of inmates in prisons or psychiatric institutions. At present, with five percent of the world's population, the U.S. has twenty-percent of the prison inmates, many of them shackled by private businesses, with a gross bite, paid for by taxes, of about three-billion dollars annually. Evidently, unlike every 'real dictatorship,' no 'real democracy' is ever placed in jeopardy because of how those who are rounded up by the police are treated, rendering such objects of criticism as entertaining diversion for Sunday supplement press, rather than a profound call for change.

But, Foucault also turned against academic disciplines and professions in general, arguing that most are set up to claim authority concerning a body of resources (as is so prominently evident in major universities), allowing the members to monopolize a certain expertise regarding this or that social issue or scientific problem. This is continually redefined to their advantage, generating a market for their professional wears, assuring as lucrative a return from their work as possible and the expansive power of its application. It is true enough that, as he suggested, most police and legal corrections activity is aimed at control of political crime, and most treatment of mental health problems is oriented by the worry that, without treating affected people as 'crazy,' those who do not work might spread the infectious example of how to avoid the underpaid exploitation of most ordinary labor, carried out for the privilege and profit of the elite classes in society.

However, Foucault was just as determined to expose the abuses on the part of the high-priests of health-care in western society, of overpaid doctors, justified politically by the medical-product multinationals that they are in service to, or against professional bodies representing the Nobel-Prize sciences, that spread shrouds of mythology in the West to justify astronomical research budgets and consulting fees for their members.

Trained as a sociologist, Baudrillard later admitted that he only took that degree for lack of other options, and then, as was the French system of the early 1960s, his training was as much philosophical as sociological. Nonetheless, he never openly attacked either the discipline of his origin or academics in general, even if he personally preferred to keep his professional distance from them. He resisted being captured by ideology, including the revolutionary line of the radical Marxists that was still common when he went to school, and never really attacked capitalism as universal sub-structural machine and as explanation for the evils of the consumer society that he exposed in his writing. Still, his attitude was manifestly anti-capitalist, the question of authenticity of work and value creation concerned him deeply, and the misuse of contemporary methods of social research as a basis for designing invasive and misleading advertising, was painful for him to accept.

Voltaire and Schiller were more direct in their political attacks; both were determined to expose abuses of power, the misappropriation of privilege by those of advantaged birth, and the disguising beneath robes of spiritual calling the pernicious and salacious behavior of prelates and church leaders. In other words, both Voltaire and Schiller took on directly the formal power structure of the society in which they lived, and both paid the price for this opposition by facing legal pursuit and jail. Each was able, nonetheless, to recuperate a respected reputation, but this was gained by often turning sideways, at least a bit, their penetrating political regard, so as to create more entertaining, distracting, less openly rebellion-inciting literature.

As for profaning the intellectual cemetery in which one's own ashes of erudition will eventually be spread, the work of both Eagleton and White is remarkable. Eagleton was trained in English literature at Cambridge, then went to Oxford as an English professor, from which post he not only condemned the emergence of the discipline of 'English' as an unjustified political travesty, but went so far as to argue that for the best interests of serious scholarship, British universities would be very well served by disbanding those faculties and closing their departments of English altogether.

While Hayden White was equally tough on the discipline of history, he based his critique of the field on a careful historical study of its emergence. In a language remarkably similar to that later used by Eagleton to discuss what had occurred with English, White judged that history as a discipline emerged as expression of the need of bourgeois society for a reading of the past that would provide ideological justification for its present practices and future direction. Those origins resulted in heavy constraint on what is now taken to be historical evidence as well as the forms of interpretive narrative writing that is accepted as valid for presenting the findings from historical research.

The cumulative weight of these insider, critical-reports is horrid: politics tends toward corruption, economic production is self-serving, systems of learning, knowledge and expertise are distorting, disciplines for the expression of language, the tacking of the past, are misleading. As previously noted (see the Introduction) 'institutions without bodies' seem to be systematically twisting the base of everyday life: it is as if there is no one to blame for the crises within the West. Are we to conclude that the many zones of questionable activity, in the financial world, for instance, is only a situational accident, due to an unfortunate conjuncture of unrelated circumstance? Or is there some underlying motor force behind this travesty of freedom, justice and equality?

No matter the method or quality of its production, when the content of critical judgment appears to be on target, the resistance is immediate. On the other hand, critical positions that justify the reach of bourgeois domination are always welcome. That is only a sign of the validity of the Althusserian observation that the ideas that dominate a society are those of its dominant classes. Since they rarely ferment mobilization for change, apologist critiques in favor of the dominant discourse may not always sell, but at least they will rarely be muzzled.

By legal tradition, identified by means, opportunity and motive, the search for explanation of wrong-doing focuses on spotting likely suspects. On this basis I believe that there is a likely suspect lurking beneath these fissures in the social contract: the one identified by Horkheimer in his 1930 essay, and clearly of a 'bodiless institutional' nature. Before elaborating further on that, attention must be turned to the question of method at the center of this small study.

The Issue of Method

During the 20th century, the historical-materialist method became the approach of choice for critical studies, reaching well beyond the social sciences and humanities to include other fields from psychiatry to philosophy.[5] Still, as the 21st century opens, it is audacious to claim that the dominant mode of investigation of the human condition is now driven by the methodological motor developed by Karl Marx in his study of *Capital*. Given our extremely reactionary age, that conclusion has a dogmatically unacceptable ring to it in the West.[6]

Further, the validity of the interpretation of results generated by use of this method requires adhering to the postulate that society and culture are real, dynamic systems, which, while not determinant in mechanical terms, exert preconditioning forces related to their being far more than only a sum of autonomous parts. For reasons related to the political extremism from both the Left and the Right that marked the world during the 20th century, we are today in an atmosphere of profound renouncement of 'totality' as concept, favoring instead a crude version of individuality and anti-structural-functionality in which every-person is treated as if his or her own demiurge.[7] When cast from an anti-totality stance, the results generated from studies oriented by a historical-materialist design are easily dispatched as if mere artifacts of method, condemning the products of critical research as if little more than extremist incidentalism.[8]

---

5 Extensible Method. Parallel to the study by Eagleton of the 'origin' of English, or that by White concerning History, the French philosopher Pierre Hadot used the H-M method to determine the nature of his discipline, beginning with the question of, what 'philosophy before Philosophy'? See his, *Qu'est-ce que la philosophie antique* (1995). Freud also used that method in his study of religion as cultural ritual, see his *L'Avenir d'une illusion* (2010a/1927).

As with Eagleton and White, both Freud and Hadot judged that one of the limiting aspects of the modern movement is the misdirected insistence on centering intellectual work in the rational, which is to say {intellectual—conceptual} faculties.

6 Bourgeois Capture of Marx. In an interview given just before his death, Eric Hobsbawm (2012) discussed the recent revival in reading of Marx, not on the part of progressives, but rather by the minions from right-wing think-tanks, seeking insight on how to short-circuit political opposition to capital structures.

7 Totality. This theme has been taken up at least indirectly by all of the critics who play a part in this book. Without going into detail, Adorno accepted it as the aesthetic truth, necessary to allow the workings of dialectic; Foucault treated totality as a menace against liberty; Baudrillard considered that Westerners live beneath a sort of totalizing fetish cloud; Gramsci took totality as the evident fact of society; Marx accepted it as a given, without which his critical project would have been pointless. To render the concept real, I use the system model presented in the Technical Appendix.

8 Does Society Exist? For those who are not sociologists, it is undoubtedly difficult to accept the confusion related to the debate as to 'whether or not society exists.' Given that

This is not to suggest that all studies of the human condition pursue the search for historical material groundings for social action as completely as did Marx, much less evaluate their findings on the criteria that he endorsed. Even when borrowing heavily on his method, most critics sidestep the Marx issue for fear of jeopardizing their legitimacy. However, studies which do not go to equivalent lengths usually rest on description rather than analysis and thus are not particularly important other than as sources of information for further research. The in-depth case material developed in this book can be used to demonstrate this range of application of the method, and I will begin with the last pair of cases first.

Limits on the Reach of History

Although on different bases, both White and Eagleton questioned the validity of historical texts as the basis for future guidance. Independent of the resolution of that issue, two questions remain that are pertinent for the structure of this book: does their work show evidence of application of the historical-materialist method and did its application contribute or hinder the political effectiveness of the critical practice?

Since White and Eagleton are both still active, high-profile cultural critics, their real-world importance is then of two natures. Through mass communication and professional networks, they each have access to an important audience. If they generate a position, its diffusion is more or less instantaneous and once in the air is taken seriously. The same was

---

Auguste Comte is conventionally viewed as the 'father of sociology,' having been the source of the notion, 'scientific sociology,' if there is no such entity as 'society,' the meaning of the discipline is empty.

In recent years, Burawoy has attempted to stabilize the issue, by placing it at the center of a seminar on Global Sociology that he organized at the University of California, Berkeley, during the first session of which, after some back and forth with participating students, he came down hard concerning the undeniable truth: the essential unit of analysis for sociology is society. See: http://www.academicroom.com/video/global-sociology-sociology-185-introduction-michael-burawoy-lecture-1–12-berkeley-spring-2011.

Still, Burawoy is unclear as to just how to 'study society.' For instance, he has disputed the position by another well-known sociologist, Immanuel Wallerstein, who argues that the only sensible way to study society as a whole and particularly the 'world system' is by developing a new unified social science discipline. By contrast, while Burawoy stresses a unified object of sociological study, he denies the justice of a unification of the many disciplines other than sociology that are needed for its comprehensive study.

Wallerstein's project is presented in his four volume, *The Modern World System*, (1974, 1980, 1989, 2011). Denying existence of a world-system 'theory', he insists that there is a world-system as social-fact: as a social system integrated or unified by a single internal mode of capital-driven division of labor. Still, he considers the world-system to be based on integration of a plurality of distinct cultural-systems.

true in their day for the other four subjects of this book (Voltaire, Schiller, Foucault and Baudrillard), which is not pertinent today in the same sense, since now all four of the others are dead.

If we take Hayden White's 'master narrative' categorizations as a heuristic guide for reflecting on the intention of critique, there are four traditions for consideration of the flow of history in the West: the Theological, the Bourgeois, the Utopian, and the Fatalist. We can examine the utility of that assertion by considering the case studies in that light.

Voltaire and Schiller were Utopian; their criticism was aimed at the theological elites and bourgeois-royalists, with the warning that the world was poised to achieve its own fatality unless major social-political change occurred. Their critical announcements carried a sense of urgency, a call for mobilization and action without delay. There was a phenomenological pressure in their exposition, aimed not at decorating or comforting but at rescuing humanity from pain and danger, due to the arrogant, exploitive, thoughtless practices of the elite classes. But this principally concerned changes in the direction of enlightened leadership, which is rarely possible when the sustaining logic of the West is Machiavellian and elitist at base. However, neither Voltaire nor Schiller were sensitive to that deeper cultural-structural blockage.

By the 20th century, the theological category found itself at least formally distanced from political criticism; this was a major accomplishment, since its political manipulation and misuse is still very alarming. However, this distancing was less a sign of a new independent stature of theological positions than of the expansion over the past couple of hundred years of bourgeois ideology to include theological issues. Deciding that the modern west is based on the concept (among others) of 'separation of church and state' is only to say that theology is now either totally internalized into the bourgeois philosophy of life (i.e., as generic Christianity), treated as 'only exotic' (i.e., as with Buddhism), or condemned for being radically foreign and dangerous (i.e., as with Islam). Again, the dominant ideas that fit in western society, theological or secular, are those that fit the needs of the western elite.

Baudrillard started off down the path of Utopian thinking, not really at the scale of a world movement, but more at the level of locality as community, and what might allow ideal relations of each with all. His critique of the negationist expression of the market against humanity through economic determination, led him to unveil with remarkable acuity the proliferation of systems of production of objects, and by that of domination of social categories less by manipulation of labor than by consumption. He exposed how the economy fabricates consumers by the generation of objects as socio-symbolic intoxicants, hooking people, addict-like, to pernicious cycles of demand for more, which eventually overwhelms and buries them under mountains of senseless junk.

Baudrillard's critique was aimed at the bourgeois supremacy, yet he seems to have been intentionally politically cautious, minimizing his commentary about policy and theology. He rarely called for action or provided suggestions about how to overcome or outwit the pernicious steamroller of consumer object-isation that concerned him. He never actually called for breaking the chains of consumer domination; he was no Voltaire or Schiller.

While remaining mute on theology, Foucault also started out down a utopian path. But his own biographical contradictions, associated with his family, his sexual identity, his difficulties with authority, set him on a quest for some form of legitimate public right to be. That insistence on personal non-conformity as public life-style appears to have distorted the political region of his critique. Nonetheless, a critic he was, and of the bourgeois structures in particular. Unfortunately, he downplayed the political aspect of that, focusing rather on how bourgeois society dominates, not by its production of consumption as behavioral seduction, as did Baudrillard, but by the production of intellectualizations as mental domination. In a way, this restricted his culture critique to the academic, intellectual world, allowing it to be ignored on the political front.

Foucault underestimated the force of social institutions and the practical political capacity to manage the immediate workings of a society. As if an institutional phobic, he supposed that the better society would be one without any; this is a false hope of political libertarians, which Foucault was to a degree. Society without institutional structure is as impossible as is a human body without a skeleton. The skeletal structure of society is malleable in constitution, but essential elements are necessary. Institutional restructuring is one thing, but elimination of institutions is out of the question. Foucault had little tolerance for the institutions that are the vectors of societal authority, by which the personal opportunity as the liberty which he so craved, is enabled.

Unlike Voltaire and Schiller, who remained critical on the surface of public tensions, Baudrillard and Foucault achieved deeper penetration by applying the historical-materialist method. Each of the latter pair saw that there are issues out of sight, at the foundation of social experience, which are determinate for the expression of more evident social practices. Foucault saw the under-forces to be intellectual, linked to the generation and manipulation of fields of knowledge, expertise, professional specialization, etc, attacking more or less directly the zone of ideology rather than the sector of public action.

Bourgeois political action has as one of its goals to insulate itself from contrary ideological intrusion, to assure that ideas which do not fit with its immediate interests will be deflected, rendered illegitimate, banned from circulation or reworked into a harmless form.[9] Thus whatever the eminence of Foucault, and whatever his critical edge, he raised very little political dust. Even early in his career, rather than holding to a role of public leadership, he backed away from not just the Paris student movement, but the north-African post-colonial Arab liberation movement. He was angry, a bit of a political anarchist, but incapable, or at least unwilling, to discuss some alternative construction of a well-integrated just society; this identifies his as a 20th century example of the Greek fatalist narrative.

White is the only formal historian featured in this study, and among the preeminent theoreticians of historical studies of the 20th century. So, did he base his work on application, at least implicitly, of the historical-materialist method? The answer seems to be yes.

Again, compared to Voltaire and Schiller, the point is obvious. Imagine the problem of segregation in public transportation where blacks are forced to sit in the back of the bus. Martin Luther King worked like Schiller and Voltaire, only more immediately politically, rather than intellectually. Nonetheless, King was a cultural critic of the classic form, applying a Voltairesque mode of cultural critique. If one attacks the way seats are assigned, or toilet access in train stations controlled, this is surface criticism, aimed at modifying the distribution of space on the chessboard of the everyday; 'men will be obliged to do more childcare as expression of female liberation,' etc. An important limitation of this sort of first-stage or surface-focused cultural criticism is that it does not involve penetration to the underlying forces, and the historical sources. which produce and reproduce the distortions in social arrangements against which the critique is mobilized.

By contrast, Baudrillard explored the economic forces beneath the evident features of the markets, which generate demand for objects of

---

9 Deflecting Critique. One tactic for the transforming threats to the cultural order into complacent indifference is to universalize the substance of critique, or better yet, the critic as individual, in such a way as to depersonalize the message and thus defuse its human power. This is achieved through a process of 'fetishism,' or if one prefers, 'iconization.' An example is the t-shirt image of Albert Einstein, as mostly a head of hair with a tongue sticking out; as if to treat his thought as really a joke.

consumption, put into the world in such a way as to take over the general population by a distortion of consumer liberty. Foucault worked similarly, focusing rather on the ideational, intellectual, knowledge centers, beneath the surface of society, which define and compartmentalize the discourse of rationality in ways that dehumanize it, fracturing experience into specialized sectors of concern and expertise; where communities of professional and intellectual specialists dominate the respective sectors, stripping the integral capacity of self-defining action from the range of possibilities of ordinary human beings.

Although Foucault did not elaborate on it, by splintering the field of *savoir faire*, the potential for *vastes connaissances* is dis-integrated into isolated regions. This suggests a destabilization of the integrative potential of appreciative consciousness that all people possess. To the extent that this dis-integration or radical sectorization of knowledge is carried though to its logical end, the effect is to deactivate good-judgment as guiding principle for social action.

White worked similarly, but considered the workings of history as a problem of its composition. He accepted that there was a past and that it had consequences for the present, toward the future, but he was convinced that there was no definitive way we might know that. The best we might do is appreciate this chain of forces aesthetically, which is to say in moral or ethical terms. Unfortunately he never elaborated his views about political aesthetics, although he may get to it before his days are up.

For White, the substructure of the present is history, which is, formally, an insight accessible only if one approaches existence with a material conception of history (in the Marxist sense, that 'material' includes 'symbolic' material as well). The confusion for White is linked to the way he became convinced that there is no real access to the truth of the past, as if we were in the pre-DNA epoch, with 'no real access' to the genetic history of living things. White was not denying the findings from his own application of the historical-materialist method for the study of history itself, but only concluding that the phenomenalization of history as contemporary reality is, at least for now, still a mystery. There is no 'objective' way to study history in a fashion that yields interpretive certitude. In a way, he applied his narrative-constructionist theory of history as a critique of the historical-materialist method, rather than using that method to study the reach and limitations of his theory.[10]

---

[10] Historicism. It is common to criticize historicism as the unjustified overplaying of the assumed determinant force of history for explaining current or future social action.

What of Eagleton? His project also generated results by application of the historical-materialist method. He sees the sinister forces of class domination, as human necessity generated necessarily by the motor force of capital, lurking beneath everything, and he backed up historically to the time that he took as vital in this regard, at the beginning of the 18th century. Yet, this everything-and-always aspect of his study is also a weakness for his project, since it provides no view as to mobilization, no starting point from which, or objective toward which, political action might be directed.

Both White and Eagleton have had limited political influence. What might occur if their modes of critical practice were generalized, multiplied a thousand-fold? Not much: either there would be a proliferation of Hyde-Park barkers, railing against the exploitive evils of capital, or there would be many more op-ed contributors, applying the incompleteness theory or 'fails to criticism' to most public initiatives. Expressed principally through irony, or black humor if you wish, I fear that little would be accomplished.

The Historicity of the H-M Method

The historical-materialist method is now so widely used as to seduce critics who are not only dogmatic anti-Marxists, but who are out to demonstrate that the political position associated with his work is unfounded, wrong, even dangerous. While this use of his method to build a case against Marx is not quite equivalent to employing a vaccine to accelerate the infection it was intended to prevent, the analogy is apt (for what I consider as the signature example of this, see McCloskey, 2010).

Associated with this strategy, over the past century there has been a curious shift, often on the part of critics who take Marx seriously, away from the study of the structural confrontations, tensions and contradictions occasioned by the organization of labor, the possession and manipulation of capital and its derivative effects, to focus more on ideological issues and their consequences. While this latter position, sometimes

---

Excessive enthusiasm of that sort in social research is said to be associated with the "genetic fallacy," as expressed in the U.S. by Burawoy (Burawoy 2005) and in France by Philippe Corcuff (Corcuff 2012). As elaborated below, (see section "History's Double Dialectic"), I deal with this issue by treating the expression of history as a doubly-dialectic rather than linear-determinist force, which is how it is treated when applying the H-M method in research.

referred to as neo-Marxism, or 'Marxism without class' is explainable, it is not particularly fruitful as a guide for fundamental structural change.

A virtue of the historical-materialist strategy is the ability to shift attention from ideological hyper-structure to the productive substructure of society, to better expose the interest seeking drive-forces beneath collective social action, of which for Marx, ideology was in a way only an important artifact. This is what he intended by recommending that Hegel 'be turned on his head.' As background for Marx, Hegel believed that the force of history as metaphysical idea and ideal, carried in the spirit of humanity, is actualized as well as might be during any given epoch, in existing social practices. As sequel to Marx, Gramsci proposed what amounts to a third alternative, that both structural issues of production and the content of common consciousness are important for explaining the durability of the current conditions of society. Hence both the technical and symbolic expressions of the dominant order must be confronted and altered if a social movement toward liberation is to have durable effects.

My position inclines in favor of Gramsci, but is levered in the direction of early-Lukács and the technical forces linked to the pursuit by capital of its own concentration, and the way this imposes injustices on many social categories both within and beyond the western countries. However, the legitimizing force of common consciousness is powerful, and its acquisition, perpetuation and constant reinforcement explains the immediate capacity for resistance to change at the level, for instance, of the ordinary electoral processes of western democracy. I consider this to have its origins in the bourgeois strategy of domination through interest-politics and regime determination. While this has both ideological and material consequences, any critical study that remains exclusively a critique, either of communication or of ideology, but which does not continue through to explore the collective-action consequences of that, while often intellectually or esthetically illuminating, is unlikely to lead to change.

Ideological Flux

Even if ideas are ethereal, fascination with the symbolic realm of society has gradually gripped the attention of critics, leading, I believe, to a drift in critical practice during the last half of 20th century, from the more manifestly material social class issues in the direction of ideological ones. This suggests that critics have been using the method of Marx to approach the study of society more in keeping with the vision of Hegel (or Kant), which is quite the opposite of the intention that motivated Marx to develop that method in the first place, or motivated Horkheimer to approach it as he did.

This is not to suggest that ideology was of a trivial issue for Marx; after all, in his foundational study (with Engels) of *German Ideology*, he established the functional definition for the term as it is generally used today. Thus to contend that ideology is a sort of epiphenomena of society in action is not to diminish its importance. As he pointed out in his study of the market process by which undifferentiated merchandise as symbol of the real achieves its status of pure symbol, for us as symbol-dependent humans, fetish can exert as much if not more force on social action than the palpably real itself.

Money as fetish of value can exert more coercive symbolic effect on human social action than does most of the products to which such value is attached, surely more than the real human labor that creates the value as product, for which money as fetish, stands. Although Marx did not go this far, extending that logic, I would say that a national ideology (such as that incanted by the notion of an American Way of Life) is the society of a nation as fetish.

Even when recognizing the dialectic dynamics of general system properties, consistent with the position of Marx, ideology is a secondary feature that is derived from the fact-in-action of society. This is why the national ideology of societies may differ, even if a certain number of infrastructural similarities may pertain across them. This explains the powerful para-linguistic cultural filters that affect the interaction of foreigners when beyond their accustomed home-range, as well as the geopolitical tensions among manifestly cooperative, non-belligerent nations, or the difficulty of attempting to do business in foreign places.

Whatever the structural components and dynamics, societies can and do change, occasionally undergoing revolutions, bloody or not. Since little if anything about human experience is historically fixed, ideology and the modes of communication that diffuse it can shift as well, as can the patterns of organization by which the labor of the production of value is assigned and rewarded. Critical practice is intended to specify those means and ways of social organization, and propose points of entry for modification. While the process must not ignore the ideational content of regimes of collective action, focusing exclusively on that is more useful for generating agitation, than for mobilizing change.

Critical Vision: More than Meets the Eye

As elaborated in the Technical Appendix, my work is thus positioned in the fluid zone of triangulated tension associated with, respectively, the work of Hegel, Marx and Gramsci. Far from proposing a grand synthetic narrative, I choose to exemplify certain aspects of that tension and the effects of its confrontation by reference to my case studies.

Since he predated its time, Voltaire's work neither depended on nor even anticipated the historical-materialist method. He approached society as a historically given arrangement, without examining its human origins. He nonetheless appreciated how political leadership often turns against the interests of the common people (and in times of war, against everyone), with equivalent peril concerning major figures in the hereditary nobility and ecclesiastical hierarchy. However, he seemed to consider those players and forces to be located on the same level of battle ground, more or less like a chess board. Despotism, for example, was considered by him to be a personal weakness of a prince, and not a tendency largely predisposed (or constrained) by structural forces, and thus built into the throne, so to speak, and largely beyond the management of anyone.

Culturally speaking, Voltaire's was a flatland view of society and its problems, as a labyrinth of rings of power and influence, privilege and opportunity.[11] While centrality counted in that setup and autocracy in vital positions was to be exposed and rallied against, his writings show little appreciation of the existence of hierarchy or vertical layering in the social order of his day. Even if he often called for changing the heads of leadership, by the end of his life he came to see that subsequent occupants of roles of importance were likely to be as thoughtless, ruthless or opportunistic as were their predecessors.

Voltaire also worked at a time before the force of secular ideology was fully appreciated. Although that force had gathered steam beforehand and contributed to it, appreciation of its active power did not occur until the violent phase of the French Revolution was past, and efforts were undertaken (largely unsuccessful) to negotiate the transition to a

[11] One Dimensionality. I make oblique reference here to a book by Edwin A. Abbott, *Flatland: A Romance of Many Dimensions* (1982/1884), re-edited and translated on a worldwide basis ever since its composition. It is an allegorical and satirical fable about a two-dimensional world, exploring in dramatic fashion how what we humans perceive is determined by the contextual characteristics of the events in which we are engaged. For one study of that work by a critical mathematician see Thomas F. Banchoff, "From Flatland to Hypergraphics: Interacting with Higher Dimensions" (1990).

republican form of government where the rights of humankind might be respected.[12]

Although separate moments in the process, the same events that forced recognition of the power of ideology also brought into view the potent, explosive mix of social classes (or 'social estates' as they were then labeled), for European society. Even if these forces helped set the agenda of tension that led to the toppling of the French Monarchy in 1789, none of this was in the air during Voltaire's productive period, sparing him responsibility for not confronting the issues subsequently central to Hegel, then Marx, then Gramsci. In sum, since structural change was not on his horizon of possibilities, though often scathingly irreverent against the pretentious posturing of the powerful, Voltaire's critical message comes across a bit soft on overthrow rhetoric and long on ironic pacifist resistance.

Schiller arrived on the scene in Europe when the dust was far from settled after the historical explosion of the French Revolution that left in plain view the disturbing fact of both social class and ideology. While that upheaval set the stage for Hegel to pose the questions that drove the Marx project, these forces were not sufficiently manifest to have a clear effect on Schiller. Still, there was an undeniable air of both social-class and ideological tension (almost in the Gramscian sense) in both his aesthetic writings and his theater, suggesting that as much as contributing foundational energy, Schiller's writing contributed to the elaboration and the eventual force of conviction that major political change was essential.

The trigger for this change in awareness was the patent facticity of the layering and historical stretch of the social ordering that dominated Europe toward the end of the 18th century, highlighted not just within France after the Revolution, but elsewhere in Europe by the military conflict that this engendered. Serving as a sort of societal x-ray, that revolutionary event blew the cover from the complicity of political power with economic ambitions, revealing the extent to which a society is not only multi-cellular in horizontal terms, but vertically multi-leveled as well, with the interplay of those layerings as present-forces, not quite determined by, but heavily preconditioned by the past of a society, generating the sustaining energy that informs its present and strongly frames its future movement.[13]

12 Secular Ideology. For a study of its origins see Kelly, 1981.

13 The Language of Radical Change. A major revolutionary problem is to find the language to express the change it attends or achieves, and by that to re-view the history up to the change. For a refresher on the battle of words at the center of the post-revolution

While Schiller seemed to have been intuitively aware of this, he was not equipped to inquire further as to the dynamics of those relations, between the past and present as pointer to the future, with the interplay of the vertical societal layerings heavily influencing the timing and content of that horizontal historical movement. For lack of study or precision, while surely advancing on this front farther than had Voltaire, the best that Schiller might do was to anticipate the historical-materialist moment, as eventually formalized methodologically some generations later by Marx, during his study of *Capital*.

In intellectual territory yet unexplored in the West, relying only on vivid recognition and a keen political sixth-sense, Schiller worked without conceptual assistance about social structure. However, due to his highly sensitive personal constitution, his attempts to untangle the causative links between the decrepitude of then-current political practices and the potential of alternatives, led him to make what some might (anachronistically) consider the neo-Marxist category error mentioned earlier. Rather than localizing the causal dynamics of social malaise in the understructures of wealth/power concentration that fuel collective action, including privilege and exploitation, Schiller looked to the sky, toward the heavens, and sought the remedy (if not attributing the cause) for societal mayhem in the ideological hyper-structure of society. Apropos of my earlier discussion on the topic, he mis-attributed as most promising target for reform, the ideological awareness of westerners, as if a change in common consciousness (as sufficient-cause) would necessarily lead to reduction in support for, and then discontinuity of, dangerous and inhuman action on the part of political leaders.

While it is surely important (*à la* Gramsci) that common consciousness be altered so as not to impede collective action for the better, when faced with the drudgery of necessity, (which is a condition easily assured by corrupt authority), no matter what their state of mind, it is difficult for the repressed to mobilize resources to combat that same authority. Unlike Marx, but in keeping with many who today still fail to push their critique to those foundations, Schiller did not see that the structures of domination of wealth and its accumulation that compel the productive forces of labor and land in society are responsible for radical inequality in liberty,

---

drama in France, I refer the reader to a volume of writings by one of the individuals who played a central role in the deployment of post revolutionary, republican ideas, and for that effort at progressive leadership, was eventually rewarded by losing his head to the Guillotine. See *Robespierre: Écrits* (1989/1789–1794).

privilege and pain, and that change at the structural level is needed to relieve the surface tensions of misery and alienation that are symptoms of those deeper issues.

20th Century Openings

When we get to the 20th century with Foucault and Baudrillard, in the wake of the incisive work of Marx (and facilitated surely by the work of Nietzsche and Freud among others), the methodological scene had shifted dramatically. It was now evident that the horizontal, forward movement of the material mass of history, which is to say, society, mechanized by capitalism and oxygenated by ideology, was animated by the dialectic tensions generated by the vertical layers of inequality and competition among the various categories of citizens and agencies. Considering this movement as linear, but surely not in a straight line, its front was advancing due to the self-perpetuating eruption and calming of relations of production (conflicts and negotiations) among those social forces, linked to categorical interests.

Under those circumstances, the universal standard of efficiency applied: the continuous concentration of capital, of wealth and its means of production was the top priority. The relative equilibrium of that movement was explained from 'above' by the state(s) of common consciousness or shared ideology of the sort pointed out by Schiller, and from 'below' by the structural, productive motor-forces that feed the different categories and classes of members; together these provided the resources (technical, organizational and symbolic) that fuel the societal enterprise, by selectively distributing opportunities and burdens among different categories of members.

While political or economic leadership makes a difference, in the short term the momentum of society is so heavily fueled by a combination of {ideological and productive} apparatus as to be largely unresponsive to immediate human intervention. However, unlike the natural environment, where turbulence or calm are beyond local control, tensions and explosions in the human social environment are generated by the ongoing struggle among different categories of members, which, like so many vacuum cleaners, attempt to suck resources from available sources, and like so many conduits, funnel the take in ways favorable for the various competing interests. Evidently: under capital, power counts, and economic power most of all.

Even if their zone of concern was markedly different, both Foucault and Baudrillard appreciated the dynamics of this drama in a similar fashion.

Foucault's application of the historical-materialist method involved a back-chaining movement, along various fronts of domination and repression. He receded with his studies in historical time until the point where, at least to his personal satisfaction, he localized the initial confrontation by which some category of social actor or agency wrestled control over some area of common experience, transforming that domain into a worry and menace; the resolution for which was achieved by the development of a new discipline or profession, under control of those responsible for its emergence.

Foucault focused on the manipulation of ideas as vectors of power, due to the contrived workings of rationality, lending a make-believe quality to many sectors of knowledge which are hatched and diffused in such a way as to take hostage a substantial slice of a domestic population, if not of the world. However, with his emphasis on 'knowledges' and their diffusion and use for domination, he more or less fell into the same category-error as had Schiller, focusing on the circulation of ideas and images about social problems and solutions, at the hands of various warring disciplines and professions, as if the remedy for the resulting limitations of freedom, justice and equality would be substantially redressed if only the 'order' of ideas and the words used to express them were different.

Since Foucault (unlike Schiller) clearly new better, because of having been exposed to the writings of Marx as a student, it is uncertain why he chose to work as he did. While as a forceful critic of practices, indicting all the disciplines and domains that he studied, in foundational terms, his historical-materialist studies were far less original than is conventionally considered. However, his work does underline how an undertaking such as the ongoing 'war on terrorism' can be used by particular enterprises to hold hostage the U.S. public and drain an enormous amount of resources from the common purse.

Foucault used the historical-materialist method somewhat in stages: sometimes digging vertically beneath the systems of rhetoric that shroud the intellectual structures of domination (i.e., his genealogy activity), which in the end, limit general freedom in areas of life which concerned him; other times, as if with the trowel of an archaeologist, he worked his way back to a point of historical origin, in western institutional terms, to localize the events that conditioned the emergence of that pattern in the first place. His well-known interest of this sort concerned the structure of domination, or the 'power/knowledge' nexus, that allowed mental-health professionals to emerge then dominate directly the mentally ill, then due to the propagation of a general worry factor, indirectly dominate also a certain dimension of general experience for the entire society.[14]

While it appears that his attention to this issue was motivated in part by his personal experience, (after being treated as a bit off the mental-health beam for twice attempting suicide as a student), he was accurate in concluding that, once upon a time, the form of deviance that he expressed (refusing to go along with the rules of institutional life in normal society) was not treated as illness, that even suicide was once considered just another of life's choices. Whatever the rightness of the facts, he investigated this process, not of suicide or mental organization, but of the labeling and treatment process that has by now elevated that to a first-order moral and legal affair, tracing the lines back to the time when the distinction between the hierarchical layering of dominant versus dominated dissolved with regard to mental-health professionals versus those with mental illness. He then studied the dynamics of the era which marked the transition leading to the emergence of that layering of classes, categories and forces.

To his own satisfaction, Foucault demonstrated the convergence of factors that was generative of new forms of social ordering, controlled by previously inexistent disciplines and professions, which emerged and took charge of entire zones of knowledge, expertise and practice. This occurred in cycles of self-affirming justification, allowing not only intervention in community life, but the reconfiguration of the standards of such communities. Forms of personal activity (such as sex behavior) and disability (such as diminished mental capacity) were redefined and elevated in dramatic importance. Suddenly, new social labels appeared, such as the sexual deviant or the mentally ill, based on the condemnation of forms of behavior that have been ubiquitous features of the human condition since the dawn of time. Yet all was packaged and well recompensed as if the resulting regimes of social control, intervention and treatment were in the best interests of society.

While specialists continue to argue about the validity and originality of the results, Foucault's somewhat fragmented application of the

[14] Foucauldian Method. As discussed in Chapter Four, my description of the use of the H-M method is somewhat equivalent to simultaneously and consciously applying the chained application of the Archaeology and Genealogy strategies deployed separately (in different studies) by Foucault. It is curious that he never formally recognized the dialectic interplay between the two strategies and the benefit of their simultaneous application, explaining a certain confusion on the part of his readers about his method, and perhaps on his part, about that, as well.

historical-materialist method provided him with a convincing basis with which to assail the way society is organized and managed, for the benefit of special interests and at the cost of general freedoms. While thereby demonstrating the descriptive power of arguments based on strategic application of this method, he did so without using the term.

Baudrillard's Bold Move

Being formally trained as a sociologist, in French style of course, Baudrillard, had little difficulty appreciating the complex dynamics of social order and the way powerful interests can use the resources under their control to twist the options for ordinary people. He saw that these forces deadened the quality of personal judgment by appealing to a misunderstanding of technical progress, leading large slices of the population to 'freely act irrationality' as concerns their personal well being. What bothered him most was the way that techno-instrumental production and marketing of commercial gadgets had crippled western civilization, due to the tragic tendency of hundreds of millions of sadly duped individuals to spend money they do not have, to buy things they do not need, to impress people they do not like.

As critic, Baudrillard distinguished himself less due to the ability to see this problem, than to apply the historical-materialist method in a masterly fashion to lay open, with surgical skill, the inner workings and hidden mechanisms that explain how society as a system, works; how particular interests grab control, often as not, quite accidentally, of this or that sector of technical novelty, then over time, find willing middle-persons, eager to mobilize markets for the explosive expansion of the production and distribution of the result. This is followed by replacement, often due to built-in planned obsolescence, modifying the gadget or process at the margins, giving the result a fresh coat of color, and allowing the marketing forces to generate another tidal wave of illogical, ultimately disappointing consumption. Inevitable cycles of buyer's-regrets are soothed by promises that whatever the failure of this or that item, the process itself is not just a sign of progress but evidence that those who consume more are participating in the making of history as progress, helping proclaim the enlightenment promise touted as western history. As a lucid demonstration of the how the forces of history take on material form, then inform human action as the ultimate material of society, little surpasses the relentless research of Baudrillard.

Trapped by One's Critical Object?

In spite of the perspicacity of each of them, there is nonetheless a curious shortcoming in the critical work of both Foucault and Baudrillard. Unlike Marx, who developed the research method that both of them depended upon, and Horkheimer, upon whom I drew in Chapter One, each underplayed the idea of society as totalization. They cannot be blamed entirely on this point, since that was also the position of Immanuel Kant, whose influence has underwritten (one way or the other) most European critical research ever since. The originality of the Marx method was the intention not just to reverse the ideality of Hegel, but to reform the anthropology of Kant. The fact that Foucault worked on the Kantian question in the theoretical volume of his double doctoral-thesis probably explains his drift away from the idea of totality; the equivalent move by Baudrillard is less easily traceable.

Side-stepping the totalization postulate, both Foucault and Baudrillard remained what I identify as sectorial-systemists rather than general-systemists. On the side of clairvoyance, Foucault could see that disciplines like physics or psychology had been transformed into icons of western rationality, and Baudrillard rightly identified, how progressively high-tech consumer objects had become, as a block, a crippling fetish of western instrumental progress. Beyond drawing attention to those dysfunctional achievements of the techno-rational promise of modernity, neither of them pursued their analysis to the level of the total society. Thus their readers are not carried far enough to see that these devastating developments are not simply accidents of history due to confusion or malfeasance on the part of misdirected intellectuals or technically intoxicated design engineers; rather, they are an inevitable materialization of the underlying productive force that motorizes what has come to be defined as modern progress, because under domination of the logic of capital, it might not be otherwise.[15]

---

[15] Intellectuals? Use of this term is debated among cultural critics, many of whom deny existence of the status, while all time depending on it as justification for taking seriously their critiques. Compared to the U.S. or England (what I consider the Anglo-American world—another term often considered illegitimate), at least in France it is still possible to use the label. Pierre Bourdieu (1979) decided that the term should be reduced from its capital letter status, since whatever it is constitutes an Intellectual is a historic construction like all other human facilities. Unsurprisingly, Foucault went further, deciding that the age of the Grand Ideology is passed, and today there are at best 'specific' intellectuals, with a view limited by a particular range of technical expertise; but that it is no longer possible for individuals like Voltaire (who Foucault specifically recognized as having been the first to play that role in the West), and that there is no longer a place for it today. For Foucault on

I am not accusing either Foucault or Baudrillard of causal faults or shoddy workmanship. Both were a product of their times in Europe, when seeking solace in a detached Kantianized Hegelianism was somehow seen as a tragically comforting and politically neutral alternative to vulgar Marxism or deceptive liberal capitalism, each of which European intellectuals were then fleeing from like the plague.[16]

For good if not exactly sufficient reasons, following WWII, in the shadow of German Nazism and Stalinist Communism, due to the general political anxiety about over-centralized state power, intellectual deliberation on the full potential of social system dynamics was cut unfortunately short. This neglect of totalizing expression of society as culture on the move, allowed treatment of societal dynamics as if heteroclite, disconnected circumstances, bereft of logic or inner connections. This in turn allowed for the instrumentalization of rationality, as different domains of knowledge (*chez* Foucault) and different domains of consumer-oriented technical productivity (*chez* Baudrillard), without any call for collective responsibility to reign-in the corroding and corrupting effects of displaced *technique* and *savoir-faire*.

This line of exposition can be illustrated practically by returning to the fact of ideology and the notion of fetish. As an item of social intercourse, money is the fetish of the value of merchandise, stripped of the use value of such products and the labor value of their production. A fetish is the icon or nutshell of the real, the concentrator, carrier and diffuser for some aspect of the dominant ideology in the society in which it is present.

As if with a Christmas tree expressing the joyous if illusionary promise of society, each fetish is a decoration for one of its branches. If a fetish is not consistent with expression of some affirmative aspect of the dominant ideology, it will be treated as weird, dangerous or both; consider

---

this topic, including what amounts to a mild tribute to Voltaire, see his, "Truth and Power," in *Power/Knowledge* (1980/1977).

16 Persistent Marxists. While even in Europe it became progressively out of style to speak favorably of any form of Marxism during the last decades of the 20th century, two French specialists who remained unvarying in their position were Louis Althusser and Alain Badiou; with no small irony connected to Badiou since now, in the early years of the 21st century, he is the most translated French author into English. A possible 21st century Intellectual (of a profile that Foucault denied to be any longer possible) is the Slovenian cultural critic Slavoj Žižek. After spending his early years as a translator, having developed an exceptional skill for careful reading, even when he is on a radical slant, he is able to weave his ideas into texts in a way that come across 'comfortably.' He considers himself a communist, in the humanist sense of the word, and thus what I might label, a Humanist Marxist as well. Among his many works, I point to: *The Sublime Object of Ideology* (1989), *The Indivisible Remainder* (1996), and *Less Than Nothing* (2010).

voodoo dolls near the Vatican or an installation of the Stations of the Cross in Mecca. Still, one does not change a society by redecorating the Christmas tree or banning the sale of stick-pins in boutiques that sell miniature replicas of well-known personages. Beneath it all, surface evident structural problems demand sub-structural interventions.

Materialized History with Eagleton and White

How well did the subjects of this study avoid being sidetracked by the ironization of critique, resting instead within the zone of the real, where social change is possible? Coming from a student of literature and language, Eagleton's work provides a lucid view of the use and misuse of the historical-materialist method. As an avowed socialist, he accepts the Marx critique of the capitalist political-economy. However, not trained as a social scientist, he does not raise questions about his extension of Marx by his own work.

Eagleton appears to consider use of the historical-materialist method as if inevitable, which is to say uncritically, rendering a certain lack of precision in application. Further, having jumped into cultural criticism from the literature rather than social science side of academe, the pressure one detects when reading his writings suggests that he came to Marx as justification or rationalization for the view of the elitist world that he reproached due to his personal frustration about that based on his own rearing, rather than attacking socioeconomic injustice because of the theoretical-practical issues raised by Marx or anyone else.

Above all, Eagleton is agitated by the fact of social class differentials, which is the singular evidence of his enduring subscription to the Marx project. For him, this problem arose as a practical immediacy: he was not born into the middle nor the elite classes. Then, rather than staying in the place normally proscribed for a fellow of humble origins, he migrated across class lines to arrive in circumstances dominated by individuals who pursue the ultimate elite-class intellectual life of English society.

Considering that England is today the most rigidly class-based society in the West, and given its reach into the world, the fact of having successfully made the dramatic upward-mobility move as he did is amazing in itself. In existential terms, there is no way that such a migration might be satisfying without being at the same time disturbing, even if his having accomplished it was enormously valuable in terms of the eventual reach of his work. In sum, Eagleton is a fascinating case of the incarnation of the pain and benefit of upward social mobility, a highly gifted, text-composing, personified example of the contradiction of class that plays the axial role in the Marxist critique of capitalism.

In status terms, having gone early in life from nowhere, socially speaking, to somewhere, namely from *villageois invisible* to Cambridge, was one step. However, that was incomparably tiny considering the next one that he made to arrive at the ultimate perch of scholarly status in England, namely from Cambridge as student to a professorship at Oxford. Perhaps I overplay this social moment, which in the academic world is more common than most people consider, but it usually occurs for bright students in technical fields, who work with equations or equipment and thus rarely come to the attention of the general public. However, given the nature of his field of study, the innocence with which Eagleton undoubtedly started his transition was quickly overwhelmed and replaced by well informed intellectual awareness. The tension between his past as life-style of burden and his present as opportunity for a very stylish life, undoubtedly contributed to the profound disapproval of the fundamental injustice of the social class apparatus, which he expresses in his writings.

After arriving at Oxford, he was surrounded by the British version of high bourgeoisie, referred to in London as the middle-class: strategically positioned as far above the commoners as possible, without encroaching on the royals. Even then, Eagleton would have had little refined knowledge of the life of the elite. It is hardly surprising that he oscillated between an uneasy attempt to find salvation with the gods, and an irreverent critical wailing about the self-serving injustice of the English and their language as mirrored and reinforced by the professorial antics of high scholarship.

Eagleton's Methodological Frame

When doing serious work, cultural critics are not fiction writers: they can only take to task what they know in reality. The target for Eagleton was the study of literature at Oxbridge, the texts that were used, the professors that used them, the key writings and writers from the past that marked the tradition of English as a discipline itself. Since England is above all the phenomenal realization of its own tongue, to take on its language as transmission of culture, as deployment of a structure of domination through English, imposed on the English and the world, entirely in service of high society, was to rather directly take on England as a way of life.

The methodological frame of Eagleton's work consisted of the English language, not as naturally evolving form of expression, but as artificial contrivance, generated for political reasons during the 19th century, as a way of colonizing the minds of the unwary, rendering them docile to the needs of middle-class attainment and royalist legitimacy. He judged the result to have been a success, yielding unending rewards for the elite and an indescribable sense of subservience for the rest, such that there is rarely a whimper from the oppressed lesser classes concerning change in the structures of distribution of advantage in their country, much less major revolution at base.

While this is clearly part of the institutional deployment that in England reinforces the structure of social class that he abhors, it is doubtful that banning the Encyclopedia Britannica from libraries or closing the English Department at Oxford would accomplish much other than to further refine the inside talk of the public school boys (and now some girls), rendering even more difficult the ascendance from lesser ones into the elite classes as expression of the very form of social mobility from which Eagleton himself benefited.

Were serious social change to be envisioned for England a more direct target might be land reform; this would finally end the continuing right to royal grants on property that date from Henry the VIII. Or banish the royal family to somewhere in the U.S., where there is plenty of farmland suitable for the hunt. Or perhaps throw out the British Pound and join Europe's Euro, putting an end to the particularly well protected financial practices that continue to enhance the splendor of the City of London, to the detriment not just of most ordinary English folk, but much of the world.

For his own reasons, Eagleton remains silent on such issues, which for a Marxist romantic seems a bit of an internal contradiction.

White and History's Historicity

As a final plowing in the grounds of these case studies, in search of nuggets of proof of the justice of the use of the historical-materialist method, the work of Hayden White is particularly illuminating. Not only does he apply the method with resolve, but the material object of that application is history itself.

To review it in a nutshell, the argument on which his frame principally rests is that using history as a guide for current strategies about future possibility is risky, neither because of ignorance about the past, which is part of the issue of course, nor because present conditions are too different for past material to remain greatly pertinent. Rather, White's indictment of history as guide is less about its content than its guides, namely professional historians.

As he sees it, in order to render what they take to be the truth of the past understandable and believable for contemporary audiences, historians are obliged to construct narrative interpretations axed on certain over used tropes, requiring such refined compositional gymnastics that the perceived integrity of the result is achieved principally by sacrificing its truth content. Hayden White's historical object of critique is thus of a radically different nature from that which incensed the acumen of the other five of my critical figures. Rather than taking to task political leadership or purveyors of ideological intoxicants as did Voltaire and Schiller; rather than taking on the production of objects and the objectification of existence generated by the consumption thereof, or the production of knowledges and the expression of power over common behavior that this allows, as did Baudrillard and Foucault; rather than taking on literature and language as an insidious arrangement for choking the world in knots of pseudo-correct thought-less expression, as did Eagleton, White challenged the very texts by which history is concretized in writing.

If he is exact, there is no more justification for faith in the empirical foundation of the many thousands of volumes of historical writings found in the Bibliothèque Nationale in Paris, than in the thousands of paintings in the Musée de Louvre, no more truth value, and considerably less beauty, which may explain why it costs to get into that museum but not into the library.

In order to build this case, White focused on the rather remarkable set of historians and texts from the 19th century. That period was exceptionally fecund for a number of reasons, including the development of history as a bourgeois discipline, an issue to which White devotes considerable importance. From Hegel to Nietzsche, passing by Tocqueville and Marx among others, his reading of the narrative result of history thus told reveals a considerable amount of interpretive pirouetting, as the various historians attempted to find a way to discuss the movement of the past in a fashion that we would today label politically-correct. For the time, this meant writing the story of history so that it fit with, or at least failed to threaten, the insistence on superiority and justice of the bourgeois way of life.

Configured by the judicious use of appropriate tropic modes, his study revealed how the mix of narrative writings of history established that the past can be slanted as one wishes, yet with such seeming authority that there is no way to filter the fantasy from the fact. While some are more reader friendly than others, effectively, history books constitute only a special form of literature. He concluded, for instance, that what Hegel said about the West, based on his reading of history, is no more or less valid than what Marx said about it, this in spite of the manifest intention of Marx to 'stand Hegel on his head.'

History's Line of Defense

Having avowed from the onset my penchant favoring the truth-value of Marx over Hegel, are we to believe White's denial of the enduring significance of both? Rather than attempting to resolve this question on evaluative grounds, by arguing that somehow the humanist benefit of the Marx critique puts to shame that of Hegel, since to do that would lead to the accusation of dogmatism, better I attempt to deal with this conundrum, not by arguing Hegel versus Marx, but rather by sticking to my methodological critical guns and putting Hayden White himself beneath the unforgiving gaze of the historical-materialist spy-glass.

I begin by agreeing that, during the 19th century, the proliferation of formal, one might say 'scientific' historical efforts, to weave the past into the future in a way that best fit politically, was associated with the transition from the previous pattern of the writings of history as a form of free literary art, replaced by development of history as formal discipline, henceforth to be put out to the world as if objectively based on the documented facts of the past. Further, there is little doubt that the result was considerable cacophony about what really had happened in the past as precursor for the present: for what causes, and with what consequences for the West, about how various events did or did not fit with the call of the western enlightenment, and, to the extent that it is believable, what this story of history announces for the future of westerners. Further, I agree whole-heartedly with White that the discipline of history was a product of bourgeois ambition, every bit as much as was the steam-engine, the Ferris wheel, Victorian London, the Tour Eiffel or the 1900 *Exposition Universelle* in Paris.

Still, we must face the question: whatever the evident similarities between the work of professional historians and the Ferris wheel, since history is arguably only about words anyway, why would the bourgeois movement have need for the professionalization of the discipline? And why the attendant slapping of censure disguised as restrictions via occult standards of solemn objectively by the historical community, to discredit the Marx reading of the western past? And along the way, to set the stage for shelving the Marx critique, why was history called on to do away with utopia as possibility, even if progress is to be announced as endless? While on the one hand, utopia and Marx were never on the same playing field, it seems undeniable that some dangerous aspect of the operation of society was being covered up by this process: what might that have been?

When I pose the question this way, it is clear that White failed to address it. Why so, if it is the issue most central to the question that he did pose?

Disciplined History: Counter Revolution from Above?

I dare to venture that the historian White suffered from a case of excessive enthusiasm for his period of study, namely the 19th century. He neglected to apply the historical-materialist method to the material of his own critical study. He overlooked that, rather than just a better way to beat plowshares into swords, the material necessity that demanded that the bourgeois celebration of itself be interrupted long enough to assure the coming into being of the discipline of history is explainable in reference to the defense of the underlying philosophy that sustains it, against the nearly deadly attack on that world view by events attendant to the French Revolution.

It is not just, as well-noted by White, that the 19th century followed the 18th chronologically. More importantly, the latter was radically marked by the culture-rupture of the French Revolution, signaling the irreversible decline of the aristocratic structures that had dominated Europe for a millennium. The fact that most 19th century historians were overtaxed to make sense of those events and their consequences is a sign of the radical nature of that rupture, coupled with a certain misreading due to a lack of images and language appropriate for describing it. Those difficulties were overcome famously by Marx, providing the methodological focus for this study.[17]

---

[17] Selective Celebrations. In spite of the military campaigns and domestic chaos, at the end of the 19th century, France (like England) was a thriving center of western capitalism, advancing primarily thanks to domestic industrial production and foreign colonial exploitation. Paris celebrated this 'progress' with two different *Expositions Universelles*, one in 1889, the other only eleven years later, in 1900. While that distinction is blurred in most memories, for the record, the first was marked by opening the Tour Eiffel for tourists. However, the second of the two was more massive, longer lasting, better attended and more costly. The difference in amplitude as well as the staging of the second so soon after the former one is largely explained by political-ideological issues: the first was specifically intended to celebrate the 100th anniversary of the French Revolution and the destruction of the Prison de Bastille by the revolutionaries. Following that, as is well known, the Guillotine was used to remove a number of heads of the state, not the least of which was that of King Louis XVI. As a sign of the fact that this event was denied its legitimate acceptance by the bourgeois successors who, in fact, colonized the European capitals during the 19th century, most of the major European principalities boycotted the 1889 Paris

The discipline of history was invented on behalf of bourgeois interests to whitewash the truth signaled by the events associated with what occurred during the generation either side of the French Revolution. Development of formal history was authorized and demanded, as if empirically positive and value neutral, to help prop-up the logic exemplified by the restoration of the monarchy after the revolutionary smoke had settled, to aid in protecting that world-view from the dramatically intensified awareness of the inconsistencies of its underlying philosophy of history, as exposed by the anti-aristocratic movement.

Today the same quality of historical erudition (as exercise of purification and justification for the bourgeois philosophy of history) continues to hold sway, white-washing (among other matters) the extreme roots of fascism that are an inevitable product of out of control pursuit of technical progress. Such tactics include reducing WWII to a story about one nasty German and a huge number of Jews; of white-washing the extreme roots of xenophobia implicit in a culture of fear, intolerance and domination, put forth as if of eternal rightness and thus imperialistically sanctioned, by reducing the attack on the New York World Trade Center to a story about a restless, irritable and discontent Arab; or white-washing the collapse of the western capital market system in the late 1920s, or more recently in 2008, as a sign of the necessity to constantly destroy capital (as long as it's not 'ours'). The latter assures sufficient scarcity to terrorize the petite-bourgeoisie into compliance, by the interpretive description of recurrent life-shortening economic upheavals as if only minor cyclic adjustments.

Events associated with the French Revolution constituted the first frontal attack against the justice of the bourgeois philosophy of history. Since that truth of revolt could not be suppressed, the second best alternative was to re-spin it as epic narrative, achieving a number of otherwise impossible missions, such as converting Napoleon into a hero for saving France and by that Europe from itself with his autocratic imposition of the restoration. Bonaparte not only achieved power thanks to a decidedly non-democratic coups d'état (then crowning himself emperor), but went on to destructive war-making and manipulative international diplomacy that renders him easier understood if one ignores the usual telling by legitimate historians and supposes that, for his day, he was an explosive mixture of a medieval Italian Borgia and a hyper-modern Libyan Gaddafi.

Exposition. However, when the subsequent one was planned entirely as a celebration of bourgeois economic progress, all of Europe, as well as most of the world, came to the party.

Imagine what might have occurred if the adversaries in the various 20th century wars had found in their briefing books the texts of a Victor Hugo or a Charles Dickens rather than some rationally told, data dense, solid historical biography of the father of European realpolitic, Bismarck? There might have been consideration of the human consequences of war, the suffering of ordinary people, the sacrifice of the many due to the devastating destruction imposed on Europe and the world in an attempt by the leaders of a few nations to balance their economic accounts as service for their elite classes.

But no, novelists cannot write history, it is now argued; only professional historians might do that correctly. Yet what we learn from Hayden White is that the result is not better foundation in fact of our understanding of the past and its implications, but a generally shabbier construction of literature. The way this comes about is itself a sad history. The demands of narrative interpretation seeded with spicy literary tropes requires so much selective attention about the past, and so much artificial build up about what is said of it, that in the end, like Penelope's weaving, there is no way to untangle the historical beauty of truth from the politically dominated garret in which it is caged.

History's Double Dialectic

With his *Metahistory*, White deployed a meta historical-materialist method, as a highly baroque effort to turn the dialectic of the procedure back on itself. As I have attempted to point out, the method is already doubly dialectic. On one hand, there is the non-evident sub-structure that drives society, as put in evidence by the visible institutions that organize collective action. By attention to the playing out of that vertical dialectic, we can explore the causal elements of, say, the organization of residential areas in cities or the structure of labor, by looking beneath at the economic mechanisms that determine the allocation of price to property and of wages to work.

However, sustained so to speak from above, by a common consciousness of the rightness of its arrangement, those vertical dynamics are further convoluted by a hyper-structural reality. This symbolic level, constitutes a sort of ideological cloud of meanings, images and understandings that infuse a common world view about, among other things, the rightness (in Hegelian terms) of the economic priorities of values, prices and wages, and the consequences for people in families, in residences, in industries, in cities.

While I describe those levels of vertical structure as if hierarchical, being in dialectic relation is to say that the constitutions of each domain, {Technical, Organizational and Symbolic}, involves both of the others. None can be understood except in relation to all. This explains one aspect of the dance of the real that constitutes actual social experience, comprising the challenge for which political processes are called, to maintain a minimum of societal order.[18]

Were that three-element synchronic composition of the contemporary the all of the story, then every society would be overdetermined, and the result would be what William James referred to as a block-universe. While there would be constant possibility to vary priorities among the three domains of the present, {T-O-S}, true novelty would be precluded. All that might differ would be a combination of that which is, with the limits of the already existent setting the outer limits on future possibility. The result would be a perpetual present, not necessarily utopian, nor necessarily hell on earth, but simply the continuation of the as-is, unabated until the balance between the population sustained by the society and its operating environment became so radically out of fit that the self-perpetuating dynamics of the present were exceeded, to send the system into decline.

History is not only the precondition for the possibility and the measure of the reality of novelty. As the chart-book for change, history is also the fact of freedom. Thus the paradox: history is in dialectic relationship to itself.

However, rather than putting it that way, we customarily refer to history as somehow associated with the past, in reference to which the present is its alternative; the present is that which is no longer history, yet knowable only in so far as there was a history leading to it. Without history as frame of reference, the notion of present would dissolve and we humans would be in an existential state like that which we attribute to a tree or flower: in a permanent condition of as-is-ness.[19]

---

18 Dynamic Totality. See the Technical Appendix where the model supporting this discussion is presented and its main lines explained.

19 Presentism. As I see it, the ill-defined notion of 'presentism' suggests that the real be limited by an ideology of timelessness, or at least timeless contents, which, for those against progressivism, assures justification for the status quo, inaction in the face of eminent need for change, and a general inability to apply comparison between events. However vague and diverse its various definitions, this notion implies a position quite opposed to the postulate on which rests use of the historical-materialist method.

In more mechanical terms, this concept is used among some historians to refer to the introduction into 'the past' of images or ideas from the present which were absent at the time under investigation. The difficulty with this position is that timeless psychological

Perhaps it should be blamed on death, but change happens in spite of us. Others around us die and we are forced to be conscious of that. By extrapolation, by interpretation of the fact of the death of others, we come to decide that death awaits each of us, even if none is ever known to have been conscious of his or her own death. From this line of argument, I see a dialectics of horizontal temporality: each of the three temporal moments, the {Past-Present-Future}, are only comprehensible by including the others as constitutional facts.

When the tripartite horizontal dynamic of temporality is brought into conjunction with the tripartite vertical presence called society, we are confronted with a triple possibility of novelty or freedom, ideological (in the Symbolic relations of meanings and value), institutional (in the patterns of Organization of social relations), and productive (in the Technical arrangements by which solutions to material necessity are generated). It must be understood, however, that this novelty or freedom pertains not for individuals as monads but for a society, understood historically as encompassing a population, in an operating environment.

From there, one might better appreciate the rather unusual work of Hayden White. More like an aesthetician than social scientist, he attempts to unravel the interpretive or meaning-laden problem of sense-making on the part of the members of a society from the facticity of the past, with its monuments, tragedies, victories, disasters and advances. He concludes that history is like the cement, which, when mixed with sand, contributes to the solidification of the social-construction of present reality. Yet the very granularity of that past historical-material defines the present as but an aggregate, prone to weakness, erosion, inner deterioration, and ultimate collapse, as well as fluid plasticity, expansion, and self-reformation. The result is not to suggest that the foundation for the present is historical quick-sand, but that the very inner constitution of the socially real owes its solidity, durability and fluidity to the interpretive historical grains of the concrete which are molecularly called on to render resilient force to the societal structures on which we humans depend. The discipline of history is like a giant concrete mixer: essential for constituting the possibilities for truth in social experience, but not to be confused with the

---

facts like the 'unconscious' which was first articulated by Freud in the 19th century, were as equally active for Alexander the Great as for Charles Darwin or Albert Einstein, and the same for the material facts such as relativity or evolution. However, when it comes to invention rather than discovery, it is clear that the atom-bomb was not available for use by Napoleon, otherwise he surely would have put it into action against the Russian Army... and the English Navy.

architectural, which is to say aesthetic challenge of putting that mass of historical-material into livable form by the collective and creative work of a people. History is the potter's clay of life.

History as Apology?

Is it reasonable to indict a philosophy of history? If history is the potter's clay of humanized existence, can it go wrong? Since there are no specifically evident hands shaping the contours of its expression, was Leibniz correct: is the world as given necessarily the best that might be? If so, then there is little justification for cultural criticism other than in the decorative sense. To consider that further, I will continue to mine my case studies.

Even if historical necessity denied them use of the H-M method, the critiques of both Voltaire and Schiller constituted a dramatic and open call for change, dispensed with a rebellious fervor, which has served well through the years as ammunition for no-nonsense political mobilization. While their work demonstrates the value of head-on critical action, over the centuries the ability of modern systems and structures to resist being sunk by that form of frontal critical torpedo certifies the survival capacities of the structures of governance actively sustained by the bourgeois philosophy of history.

As for the 20th century non-western world, the geopolitics of stability and revolution demonstrate that one way that governments can be put in jeopardy is by critical aggression from foreign sources, based on an ideological attack as cover for the clandestine invasion by agents of destabilization, which bring down regimes in a fashion that seems both justified and inevitable. This is exemplified by the questionable but successful fifty-year Cold War waged by a united front of western governments, determined to destroy the Soviet Union, or the more recent use of the same strategy to destabilize the Arab countries on the south shore of the Mediterranean.

However, the western countries themselves continue to resist such intrusive attacks, deploying ideologically self-justifying anti-terrorist counter forces with draconian results for their own domestic populations. The progressive limitation of freedom of movement and expression in western countries has begun to match in amplitude the dangerous levels of economic inequality that characterizes them. Still, for reasons mentioned above, the capacity of modern western regimes to internalize all challenges to their legitimacy, not, however, without ever growing costs, is truly remarkable, such that their durability remains largely unthreatened even as the level of legitimization among their own citizens is falling.

As concerns the West, then, apparently non-violent social change can only be mobilized by critical attention from within free democratic society itself. I thus suggest that the sole strategy with which critics might work and that is likely to measure up to the test, must draw on the one form of critical ammunition against which the West is vulnerable: that of its own history.

Beyond intellectually fascinating, the political utility of the historical-materialist method is simple. With it, one way or another, in one sector or another of social action, the critic is able to put the West on the spot in a fashion that no amount of ideological double talk can pervert. Because, whenever current practices within the West are judged against its announced intentions from the past, it is clear that western society is failing to live up to its own promise.

As if indifferent to that potential, a tragic aspect of 20th century criticism is that by putting in practice as half-measures the historical-materialist method, it turned soft on history, and by that, let the West off the hook. The result was a form of complicity with the Machiavellian main-spring of the bourgeois philosophy of history: that the lie is truth.

The analytic philosophy movement that was all the rage in Anglo-American circles played into this famously, proposing that truth is no more than the matter of its expression. Among continental social philosophers a similar move was labeled deconstruction, assuring the systematic de-systemization of everything. Together those movements justified denial of the existence of an integral-society to critique, and when attempted anyway, it undercut the rightness of critics who proposed application of a humanity-driven truth-test to the results.

Intention as Potency

As pointed out so far, all four of the 20th century case studies, of Foucault, Baudrillard, Eagleton and White, showed the footprints of the H-M method, a sign that each of them was educated and had debated not just its use as procedure, but the concrete historical work by Marx on *Capital* that had occasioned it. Yet the paradox: although for different reasons and ideologically opposing directions, both Foucault and Baudrillard turned away from the Marx critique as guide. In spite of the lucidity of their studies, this may explain their rather tepid appeal for basic societal change. White, by comparison, in spite of careful reading, appears to have never taken the critical substance of the Marx project seriously, although it is clear that without use of the historical-materialist method, even if only tacit in application, his work would have been unconscionable. Eagleton, on the other hand, rather than being educated about Marx from the perspective of a critical social science, seems to have fallen upon him a bit by accident, which may explain a certain effervescence to the way he introduces Marx in almost all of his voluminous of writings.

In other words, while the writings by Voltaire and Schiller seemed to have been a source of nightmares for the harbingers of civil and church authority of their day, and constant agitation for the social elites who benefited from its twisted economic structures, other than the graduate students who have been called on by their professors to work the material into a qualifying exam, virtually no one has ever taken to the streets over the critical address delivered by Foucault, Baudrillard, White or Eagleton. Each of them scores ten on literary elegance, but for political impact, their marks are considerably lower.

One way to let them off the hook and hang ourselves instead would be to argue that social change was never their point. Little different in motivation from the movie critics who write for *Variety*, it might be argued that all they were doing was engaging in bourgeois decorative criticism. If so, we are unjustified in posing questions as to a deeper search for truth, a more profound methodological discipline or a greater dedication to care in describing the cases that attracted their respective gaze. This suggests itself as hollow. Is it conceivable that there was nothing serious in the indictment by Foucault of the various disciplines and professions that he studied, specifically concerning the 'abuse of power' implied in the distorted and overblown seriousness by which domains of knowledge are carved out and colonized, then turned to advantage by 'specialists' to the detriment of the common good? Might we actually suppose that, in spite of what Baudrillard's study exposed concerning the commercial process associated with the production of objects and their diffusion through markets to the general peril of all, that his long suffering and relentless voice was only motivated by an interest in generating speaker-fees or book-sales? Or that whatever the astounding insights revealed by White about the hijacking of the study of history by the interests of bourgeois society, that he harbored no ambition for its reform? Or that the veritable blizzard of book reviews and monographs by Eagleton, always hounding those with class about its misuse, and those who worked on the subject, for being soft in position, that all this bristling rhetoric had no higher ambition than filling the pages of the Sunday supplements of London newspapers with entertainment? I think not.

What Critique of the Critical Industry?

Criticism is reflection of some operation that emanates from a socio-cultural system back on its source, in search of practical knowledge aimed at changing what one might, and presumably for the better. What first comes to mind is personal and mental, when critical consciousness takes under review its own structure and process. Socrates did this and came up with the view that being human is the seeking of self-knowledge. With his study of human understanding, Hume decided that consciousness is aimed at self-assertion. Kant undertook such a critique also and decided that rationality is driven by the appetite for well-ordered conceptualizations. Adam Smith followed a similar path and decided that the nexus of human being is the seeking of self-satisfaction. Descartes concluded from the point of view of the thinking-soul that the object is good judgment based on analytical-knowledge. Freud did similarly and observed that consciousness is self-deluding except in so far as its unconscious allusions are taken into account. While the result of such lines of attention are neither inconsequential nor fictive, criticism of consciousness is not directly cultural criticism.

What I am concerned with in this volume is more complex than only critique of mind or consciousness. For me, cultural critique as strategy is architectural in nature. It is aimed at understanding not the place of self in the world, but of the social world using one's own place in it as point of reference. From there, one reflects some object of social construction, down to its roots and back to its origins. To achieve this, the critic must hold in abeyance the causal forces of self-consciousness, to work on the social world from a posture of full-engagement. While some degree of subjective detachment, (bracketing, according to Husserl, or application of what Descartes labeled methodological-doubt), is essential for any serious research, with the conduct of cultural criticism that exigency is doubly demanding.

Posing the problem thusly shifts the undertaking of critique away from the ordinary problems of clarity of mission or eloquence of its literary productivity, away from polemics concerning the local troubles of society and the need for amelioration thereof, forcing us to consider a more fundamental issue: as currently configured and deployed by its practitioners, to what extent is the *core technology* of critical practice suitable for attaining its objective?

I believe the political effectiveness of critical practice during the 20th century has been under-realized due to a perhaps unintended misapplication of the technique on which the industry depends. This shortcoming results from a particular side-slippage of critical intention, reinforced by what eventually emerged as the heritage of the Frankfurt School of Critical Theory.[20]

While the resulting shift of emphasis proved useful and informative for the description of certain tensions in ordinary social experience, it directed attention away from the more looming task of societal revolution. The way that occurred was that the critique of society as rational organization in pursuit of gain measured in irrational instrumental terms was set aside, in favor of a critique of rationality itself, which exposes, unsurprisingly, that the pursuit of instrumental rationality at all costs is irrational to the extent that human well-being is at stake.

Give the centrality of the problem of method for this study, drawing on inspiration for the case studies, it is possible to propose how this difficulty for critique came about. I set out to demonstrate the power and limitations of critical studies that employ a historical-materialist method. Comparing the work of Voltaire and Schiller to that of Foucault and Baudrillard, then Eagleton and White, I described the potency of this method for exposing the deeper and anterior sources of current practices that explain societal movement. However, once the data are in, one must then reach an evaluative judgment about the justice of the historic object under review, the current result and the future direction implicated thereof, as the basis for a countervailing possibility should that be proposed. The crucial issue is the shift from data, to judgment, to affirmative alternative.

For instance, following from the work of Baudrillard, one might evaluate the technical domination of westerners to be the sign of a major existential problem which must be combated at all costs; or, conversely, the plethora of technical gadgets that so irked him can be judged as simply a minor inconvenience, to be overlooked in favor of the presumed benefits from economic development. This points to the distinction between the material facts of some matter and the interpretive signification thereof; consensus about a benign condition or even a crisis is almost always followed by conflict about its meaning and resolution.

Or, to shift register a bit, assume that I take as valid the postulate supported by Hayden White's study of history as discipline: that the construction of histories is a narrative exercise of fact based story telling. From there, however, rather than evaluating historical writing as a

[20] For an informed, brief summary of the key issues and individuals associated with The Frankfurt School, see the book by that title by Tom Bottomore in the Key Sociologists series of Tavistock Publications (1984).

conspiracy in the interests of the elites against the best interests of humanity, or denigrating their work in comparison to that of detached natural scientists, why not consider historians as engaging in a form of practice analogically similar to the work of religious apologists? If so, I might compliment the community of historians for their services, since they do their best to write up the past in such a way as to soothe the consciousness of the people in the present, minimizing guilt about what has been done in the past and anxiety about future possibilities, by depersonalizing and embellishing their narrative accounts of what occurred.

Were this last path to be followed, historians might be treated as if shamans for civic consciousness, similar in function to religious prelates as inspiration for the tortured soul. As critical judgment, reaching that conclusion would require disconnecting debate about the veracity of knowledge concerning historical facts, from the interpretive function as pursued by the specialists who draw on those past facts as a source of guidance for the disturbances of conscience and/or consciousness that plague the contemporary population. The result would be the radical separation of the problem of objectivity when attempting to establish historical facts from past material for present social production and from the problem of establishing the meaning or implications of alternative ways of gaining knowledge, evaluating and generating texts about past events. Referencing Dilthey, as I did in Chapter I, in terms of historical understanding, this would require accepting as unbridgeable the gap between fact and value.

If there is no intrinsic connection between fact and value, then any fact can be evaluated in any possible fashion. While that possibility would not silence the matter as a source of debate for philosophy, it would sentence critical practice to the purgatory of irrelevance. There would never be any sound basis for judging one way of organizing society or of sustaining productive patterns of social relations as more or less desirable than any other. In spite of this lacuna, it appears to me that during the last half of the 20th century, the critical community drifted in that direction, and in the process substantially disqualified the validity of its enterprise.

Why would a community of scholars violate the basis of their own justification; at least to believe Foucault, this would be madness. My hypothesis is horrid to consider: western cultural critics appear infected tragically by the call of humanity, which, as Schiller noted in his story of Don Carlos, is a dangerously infectious disposition. The danger comes from the way that being struck by an excess of concern for moral responsibility disqualifies successful participation in the game of real politics.

Once 20th century critics decided that declarations concerning 'one best way to organize society' was an opening to autocratic imposition of government, then serious debate of the sort that spices this book, such as that capitalism might be ruinous for society, or that some form of socialism is the only possible path of repair, receded. Most cultural critics felt that strong pronouncements in favor of any particular political change was only dogmatism. Since dogmatic positions appear to violate the enlightenment ethics of Humanity, the result was to silence cultural critics about radical societal change. This voluntary retreat of many otherwise responsible critics from the field of political battle, left it open for domination by those interests that are unbothered by humanist ideals.

Because of justifiable disputes about the criteria for interpretation of the results of critical research, linked with worry about being accused of dogmatism, critical practice was thus allowed to collapse downward and backward upon itself rather than pulsing upward and outward into the social world. In topological terms, critical studies thus tended to sink into the historical-material morass of their own research, as if playing with the historical-materialist method were a sufficient end in itself.[21]

Unfortunately this critical misstep (as I see it) contributes to furthering what Horkheimer exposed as the global problem with the Occident. Domination by the bourgeois philosophy of history has become so massive that, like a school of fish in the ocean, from totally within it, bereft of visionary work of cultural critics, Westerners are unable to imagine any other way of life. Thus the withdrawal of most critics from the political arena helps buttress the ramparts of the system that most of them do not admire.

In spite of it all, the in-depth case studies here bear witness to a certain persistence of critical activity, though be it of a minority, if energetic voice. Although this demonstrates that there are feasible alternatives to current unjust social practices, a look at those who work more directly in the wake of the Frankfurt School movement is much less encouraging.

We might consider, for instance, the work of Jürgen Habermas or his recent successor as current director of the Institute for Social Research in Frankfurt, Axel Honneth. In spite of the elegance of composition, their work provides little guidance for rescuing the modern west from self-destruction other than by minor institutional repair. And neither of

[21] Critical Hubris. The ease with which critics can become snarled internally to their own process is analogous to the problem of 'out of control' psychoanalysis, which can strap a misguided 'patient' to the analytical couch for decades.

them speaks at all of a refounding of the West on a different basis. It is as if they are comfortably under the cover of the very bourgeois philosophy of history which Horkheimer identified as a menace.

The two of them seem to epitomize the contemporary paradox of critical practice. There is a tendency to confuse the means by which a critical position is formulated, namely by application of a certain form of rationality for the study of social relations, with the forces that drive society, namely the material facts of the production of life by people in a community of action based on those social relations. Even if thought's work is the tool of critique, it is not the driving force of society at work.

The form of 'rationality' that assures a certain constancy to critical appreciation, analysis and judgment about society among critics does not imply that a similar form of subject-centered rationality drives society. Critique is individual action propelled by thought, while society is collective action driving common consciousness. There is no direct rational bridge from the mind to collective action, even when sophisticated critics are doing the thinking.

This confusion about rationality is a major contradiction in social practices that are over determined by the bourgeois philosophy of history, This explains why it is so difficult in late modernity for even well educated critics to think a way out of the problems generated by the mindless application of its principles. Yet, having failed, in my judgment, to recognize this difficulty, during the past half-century, most cultural critics have stopped examining the material facts of societal organization, so as to concentrate their intellectual analysis on critical thought itself. This drifting of critique back on itself explains the energetic generation of texts of elegant allure, that go nowhere politically, while often intensifying the alienation, if not the despair, among the critics themselves.

Excessively Reasonable

To exemplify this trap of misplaced critique of rationality, generated entirely by reliance on the techniques of rationality which, at least in the eyes of Horkheimer, are the supposed target of critical theory as practice, I will examine a bit further the passionate work of Theodor Adorno.

Without doubt, Adorno was a leader among 20th century cultural critics in lucidity, creativity and realism. He never minced his words or pulled his punches, determined to find a way to theorize a just society of harmonious humanist disposition, or die trying. Unfortunately the latter was what occurred, and a bit of an intellectual autopsy may serve us well.

Unavoidably, Adorno did not work in a historical vacuum, which is precisely the source of the problem. Throughout the second half of the 20th century there was intense pressure within the social sciences and humanities to justify work in keeping with standards of the natural sciences. This influence was not lost on cultural critics, even if they were working on issues within which it is more appropriate to place in question the standards of 'normal science' and positivist methods than to apply those standards and methods blindly. In fact, this very critique was the central point that Horkheimer attempted to express in his movement founding essay, "Traditional and Critical Theory" (Horkheimer 1937).

Normal science, oriented by "traditional" epistemological theory is idealist and Kantian: one thinks, assesses, classifies what one finds, and interprets what is, entirely from the mind as both view-point and end-point. In his study of the difference between traditional and critical theory, Horkheimer demonstrated that the value of "critical" theory is precisely the bypassing and replacement of a rational, idealist, Kantian view by a historical material view, for which some sort of mental activity is the instrument but not the objective, aimed at learning about the world as revealed by the worldly engagement of the researcher in it.

Somehow, there was a serious misappropriation of the critical call issued by Horkheimer, which plunged critics back into the idealist soup from which he intended to extract them. His interpreters failed to take into account that the founding essay of the critical theory movement was itself historical material, that there was something behind and beneath that essay, a historical residue if you will, which was active in the consciousness of Horkheimer when he composed that text, shaping his view of the critical project that he set in motion. That 'something else' was his reading of the western history associated with his place in it.

We have access to the material that occupied his prior state of mind as experience not because he confided it to his psychiatrist, but because he wrote an entire text on the subject, namely that of, *The Origins of the Bourgeois Philosophy of History*, which I discussed in Chapter One. I believe that the methodological manifesto Horkheimer wrote in 1937 makes sense only when read in reference to the 1930 text where he sketched a thundering view of the object of critique. However, for unspecified reasons, that earlier text was never widely circulated, leading to the misreading of his second (1937) more methodological treatise, with the fault probably lying more with lack of accessibility of the earlier text than as error on the part of interpreters.[22]

---

[22] My argument here about the work of Horkheimer is revisionist in nature, not unlike what developed since the 1930s, around the project of Marx, when a block of his early

The problem that critical theory was called on to redresss was not simply the misuses of 'modern rationality,' as discussed in the 1937 text, but the bourgeois philosophy of history, which in fact is the material basis for (among other factors) the manipulated version of intellectual rationality that has led to such tragic disorientation of western life over recent centuries. The devil, if you will, is not in a misuse of the 'tools of the mind,' nor even the abuse of the political space by bourgeois interests; the demon is the very philosophy of history that feeds both the collective distortions that make possible the legitimate continuation of bourgeois domination to this day, and the individual limitation of the view that freezes intellectuals at the interior of their criticism, such that a serious political call is rarely produced by their work.

Little surprise then, if the voices of critical studies have been discounted as ephemeral or inconsequential, as if the problems they identify are due to individual limitations or purposive deviance on the part of the critics, rather than generated by the structures of social organization that shape ordinary behavior, as if human need, desire and opportunity are not collective issues.

Prolific Irrationality

I venture to assert that the relative ineffectiveness of critique during the second half of the 20th century was due both to a misunderstanding of its object and of the potential of its work, based on the mistaken postulates that a critique of rationality is equivalent to a critique of society, and that the possibility of a radical rupture as opening to a truly different future is empty utopianism.

Among the four final figures included in my case studies, Baudrillard was the most determinedly resistant to this trap, avoiding even tacit

---

writings previous unavailable, were published, necessitating a major rethinking of the social-philosophical underpinnings of his very practical and revolutionary later study of *Capital.* (See, Karl Marx, *Economic and Philosophical Manuscripts of 1844*, 1992b/1844 [first published in 1932]).

The question of historical accountability through the lifetime of an intellectual is difficult to resolve. Might there be a radical rupture between a prior and later phase of work due to some major new historical experience for a cultural critic (as Althusser argued to be the case with Marx, in his *For Marx*, 1965), or is personal history necessarily a form of continuous causal energy, on the basis of which all subsequent work is accomplished? I favor treatment of history as a powerful force in shaping the environment within which later development occurs. This pertains, as I see it, for both individuals and societal systems; however, there is no iron-law of historical development, such that, even if rare, radical rupture is possible both personally and systemically.

complicity with the forces of the consumerist, objectified society of domination that drew his critical ire. Yet even he was hesitant to call for radical rupture in structures, as if the unhinging of humanity from the levers of modernist social control would lead either to anarchy or to the dogmatic imposition of an even more monstrous form of capitalist-market dominated structure, i.e., fascism.

As an impractical libertarian, Foucault rejected the promotion of a fundamental political alternative since he believed that every form of government was an encroachment on freedom, rendering none more desirable even in principle. Hayden White issued a powerful indictment of the perversion of history due to the intrusion of bourgeois political intention into the foundation of its discipline, but remained aloof as to active political issues as if that were a sign of well-reasoned intellectual work. Bothered from early in life by the class issue, Terry Eagleton seemed to conclude that the English are so dominated by their status as to be beyond durable activist mobilization no matter what the cause or who their spokesperson.

Reason against Reason?

If I am right, a pivotal error in contemporary criticism continues to be the mistaken postulate that individual agency, expressed via modernist rationality, ought to be the principal target for critical work. From a distance that seems justified: the society is said to be the product of rational engagement as collective work done, in pursuit of coherent objectives. If the result is unproductive, unjust or inequitable, then there must be something faulty about the application of the rational process by the agents who mobilize action. Since only human individuals 'act,' ought not the critic focus on state-of-mind issues as the source of problems and site for improvement?

Is it reasonable to argue against reason? Most accept the Enlightenment belief that rational processes are those that deliver a maximum of truth content, which is politically vital since it is further assumed that 'the truth will set us free.' When placed in motion, should not modern rationality thus assure a maximum benefit? Indeed it ought to, as long as one restricts interests to mechanical features of a fully material reality, which is necessary to the extent that another key postulate of modern progress is that technical measures are the only ones that count.

Humanity concerns something quite different, the symbolic linkages among self-propagating entities (individual and collective). Applying the modern rational attitude to conditions of that sort restricts one's study and dehumanizes the outcome. The result is equivalent to the difficulty with postmortem studies: they provide plenty of evidence about the cause of death, but contribute little to explain the cause of life, growth and dynamic development.

Today there is unbounded enthusiasm for a critique of rationality, as if the unacceptable results of institutional action are due to a block in the capacity to think ahead or to heed evident warnings, or clumsiness in deploying the findings from such studies for everyday use. The standard of freedom is then interpreted in reference to this argument, with limitations on it said to indicate that the rational processes are being misused, as if some form of false-truth is being treated as canonic. Considered conversely, is it not possible that modern rationality is misconceived, or the priority assigned to it vastly overvalued?

Confusion in the Frankfurt Schoolroom?

Perhaps unavoidable from the start, this exploration of critical practice via the historical-materialist method takes us ultimately to the doors of the Frankfurt School of Critical Theory itself, the agents of which have been and continue to be, at least in principle, its flag bearers.[23]

Perhaps less specifically than might have been expressed in its initial formulation, the mission identified by Horkheimer was clear: to study western society, identify its shortcomings and offer proposals for amelioration, with, as end-point, not just the description of reality, but its change for the better. Yet things did not work out that way.

The challenge when putting the emphasis on rationality is to avoid taking it personally. This is needed to keep clearly in view the differences between its means and its ends, as well as to avoid being seduced into applying those means as a tool in pursuit of their own critical ends. Horkheimer (and Marx, it must be noted) seem to have recognized that risk in a fashion that gradually dropped from sight during the following generations. Thus, while successive promotions from the Frankfurt School continued to attack the despicable effects for the human condition of the modern project in action, those aims were distorted due to an excess

[23] Frankfurt School Dropouts. In the same way that Marx famously, declared, "I am not a Marxist!," both Habermas and Honneth deny allegiance to the Frankfurt School movement. Still, they work in evident pursuit of a Critical Theory, which, if not oriented by that earlier history, comes from where, then?

enthusiasm for rationalist progress as work of the mind, applied instrumentally to every sector of institutional life, from the work place to the family.[24]

As Horkheimer saw it, the underlying motor-force of the social, including thought's work, is determined by the social relations inherent to the capital process, which, due to its unyielding determination to assure the continuous concentration of itself, achieves economic 'progress,' at the cost of dehumanizing social practices. While he certainly acknowledged that humans work on the world with their mind, he was critically aware that the meaning of mental work is informed by collective experience in real social action. Accordingly, experience and not just thought must be the object of critique.

While surely embracing the centrality of the liberation theme for critical practice, the successive directors of the Institute of Social Research in Frankfurt progressively distanced themselves from a focus on the misshaping effects of underlying economic process as stressed by Horkheimer and derived from Marx. By the end of the 20th century, this yielded a rather unfathomable form of neo-Marxism: a critique of liberation with *la lutte des classes—déclassé*! Even if Habermas and Honneth attempt to excuse themselves by refusing to identify as harbingers of any movement or orthodoxy, the spread of this view by other means, to cultural critics in general, has contributed in a major way to what I view as the progressive depoliticization of cultural criticism.[25]

A turn away from the contradictions generated by the internal production of society, leaves the liberation call shorn from the economic roots of the predicament for which it is a solution. Thereafter, the humanist crisis of alienation generated by deranged social experience appears as

---

24 Unbound Irrationality. This danger was explored famously by Herbert Marcuse, another of Horkheimer's brilliant recruits, in his: *Eros and Civilization* (1955), and, *One Dimensional Man* (1964). Apropos the question I raised earlier about continuity versus rupture in the perspective of an intellectual, Marcuse assumed (not unlike my position regarding Horkheimer) that the early work of Marx was of preeminent value in understanding his critical posture during his mature years struggling with *Capital*. Reinstalled, the 'humanist' theme at the center of the Marx project, with individual-sensitive factors such as alienation (or its absences) occupying a vital position, fit with the '60s attitude in the U.S., on the basis of which Marcuse played a major role in mobilizing the New Left movement that marked that generation.

25 I am Not of the Frankfurt School. This negation of allegiance on the part of both Habermas and Honneth is explored in a carefully-drafted journal article, tracing the three generations of the Frankfurt School, with particular ambition to identify Axel Honneth's historical roots by the principal translator into English of Habermas writings. See Anderson (Forthcoming): http://phil.uu.nl/~joel/research/publications/Anderson-SituatingHonnethinthe3rdGen.pdf.

something like the result of a bad-trip on drugs: as if in a causal vacuum in structural terms, the solution is not institutional change but only attitude-altering social therapy.

Again I must stress, quality critical work is necessarily anchored in the material conditions within which the critic is participant and spectator, yielding an interpretive reading of those circumstances, limitations and potential, the meaning of which is understood in reference to how it was historically rooted, given where the critic supposes the system of interest is or should be heading. Investigating not its causes for their own sake, but the origin of which it is a sign as information about the future, requires first attempting to locate the deeper structures that serve as its constitutional basis, and then the historic source of those underlying cultural roots. Thus a cultural critic is a contemporary spokesperson about the historic forces of change or tension, which is dialectic in nature, generating contemporary challenges about alternative possible futures.

The Limits of Critical Rationalism

If Horkheimer was right, once having achieved its original objective of recovery from ecclesiastical-royalist domination, the humanist goal that set bourgeois society in motion over five centuries ago might only be fully attained by eventually dissolving its own institutional base, so as to reconstitute western society, perhaps around similar goals, but on a radically different operational basis. This is a very radical proposition.[26]

Still, we have the operational conundrum: since a certain sort of instrumental-rationality is the core personal quality inherent to the propagation of the bourgeois philosophy of history in action, other than by being mad, how else might one be 'modern' except rationally, in that way? Yet if exclusively so, exclusively instrumentally-rational that is, it would seem to be possible only to the extent that one become a fully-modern individual, foreclosing the possibility of the repudiation by critics of the very modernity that legitimizes their self-definition. Thus the devilish circularity of critical problem: unless reconceptualized otherwise, a rational assessment of the limits of instrumental-rationality will roll along like a Möbius ribbon, not really forward, but deceptively back on itself.

---

[26] Auto Dissolution. This insistence by Horkheimer on the necessary *dépassement* of bourgeois society once its initial success was achieved, is analogous to the argument by Marx, that once the proletariat have successfully led the way to a liberation revolution, society would be reconstructed in such a manner (no longer organized on a class basis) that the proletariat as social class would necessarily cease to exist.

Horkheimer's immediate successor was Adorno. Although Adorno's early work was oriented more traditionally in the Marxist sense, his later difficulty confronting the dialectic of rationality surfaced with particular force when he tackled the aesthetic question. Aesthetics is concerned with the fact of harmony, of the good, the right and the beautiful. Political aesthetics, which was Adorno's concern at the end of his life, attends to the argument that, when well functioning, aesthetic forces promote societal balance as a natural disposition or pre-instrumental mode of direct exercise of human liberty and responsibility. (Formally, this is a continuity of the position of Socrates). However, critics such as Adorno contend that the excessive instrumentalization of society erodes the web of aesthetic transaction, destroying its ambiance, propagating alienation rather than good will.[27]

Instrumentalization of production and consumption, as necessary for assuring the material demands of the capital motor force, is clearly an argument drawn from Marx. The difficulty with the broader *aesthetic* alternative as opposed to the more restricted *instrumental* one is that the latter can be demonstrated to explain a certain integration and stability of the social order (albeit an exploitive, class-based and far from free social order); but the aesthetic view, attractive as it may seem as concept, is very elusive to study by the usual techniques of science. Adorno set out to develop an aesthetic theory that would overcome those difficulties. He attempted to establish that rather than only technical-instrumental relations, an aesthetic web of civic morality could be consistent with the higher call of humanity (and with the view of Schiller it should be noted), and ought to be the principle governing force for western society.

---

[27] Adorno's critical grounds were vast. While in the U.S. during WWII, in addition to collaboration with Horkheimer, he generated the content for his most cited work, *Minima Moralia: Reflections from Damaged Life* (1951), a brief collection of daily journal entries, elaborating extremely acrid critical aphorisms, with a remarkable and convincing dialectic allure.

It was also in America that Adorno (the dialectically disposed critical musical classicist) took on the question of jazz, which he criticized as much more formatted than spontaneous, and for which he was chastised for a lack of romantic sensibilities (*Essays on Music*, 2002). He argued, effectively that jazz is fully formatted in advance to give the impression that from time to time during its play, the musicians perform with total spontaneity; he evaluated this as technical domination masquerading as freedom, and the California music world took offense. Seventy years later, the issue is yet to be settled, as signaled by the fact that it came up recently when Toni Morrison, Pulitzer Prize Winner (1988) and first black woman to win the Nobel Prize in Literature (1993), was interviewed on CBC radio about her latest novel, *Home* (2012); unknowingly or not, Morrison's opinion agreed with Adorno about jazz.

A minor chord of that argument is the proposition that societal ethics, rather than economic efficiency (the common interest rather than self interest), ought to be the first priority as valuing criteria when judging social performance or proposing corrective measures. While the attractiveness of this approach to the problem of societal integration is undeniable, Adorno ran into difficulties of execution that he never overcame. We cannot say whether he might have succeeded had he lived longer; unfortunately, his premature death at age 65, left that study unfinished, and what was ultimately put into print as his *Aesthetic Theory*, consists of an arrangement in chapters of elements about which the linear development he intended cannot be certified. A striking feature of that work is Adorno's determined effort to logically explain the aesthetic force, but this was to be achieved 'rationally,' which as a tool (rationality that is), proved insufficient for the job.

Like the two who succeeded him at the helm of the Institute in Frankfurt (Habermas, then Honneth), Adorno was blocked by his determination not to fall into metaphysics, which might have invalidated the work of Marx, by a return to rational idealism associated with Kant and Hegel. Yet this insistence on avoiding metaphysics precluded consideration of a non-rationalist perspective on aesthetic appreciation as central component of the aesthetic theory that he hoped to articulate.

The strange feature of this impasse was that when writing on music, about which Adorno was a specialist, he was quite able to articulate the aesthetic deployment of the understructure of music without drawing on an excessively rationalist positivism. He recognized that there is more to music than can be captured by its mathematical formulae, and that this extra quality, its meaningful 'musicality,' is accessible via direct, pre-analytic appreciation. Yet, when attempting to articulate a general aesthetic theory, he fell back into a rather formal rationalist discourse, which, in spite of his being the finest dialectician of the 20th century, in my opinion, left him hooked in his anti-thesis.

From the perspective of positive rationalism, aesthetic qualities, (the good, just and beautiful) are attributes of existents, and not states of being in and of themselves. If so, then appreciation of aesthetic qualities depends on the situated presence and judgment of a human subject, precluding (it would seem) material transcendence and impersonal detachment, denying by that some of the central postulates of normal science.

Positive science, applying rational analytics from a depersonalized point of view, is thus denied direct access to aesthetic matter, and is forced to refer to it as approachable only by intuition, which is not a rational category. Rather, for a rationalist, intuition participates in the metaphysical category, as do, for instance, faith, hope and love, which returns the aesthetic issue to the realm of metaphysics, which Adorno was determined to avoid.

There is a radical difference between beauty as attribute and hope as existent. Beauty is directly associated with material experience, while hope can exist independent of it. This suggests that the aesthetic expressions of harmony, goodness and justice are considerably less 'metaphysical' than, say, faith, hope and love. Still, all of those qualities are difficult to access by way of a rational analytic. In spite of his struggle to develop this work as justification for the claim that society is held together by aesthetic forces, that contradiction in his method largely explains why Adorno's effort at constituting an aesthetic theory remained unfinished.

Why not consider a non-rationalist (which is not to say irrational) possibility for the recognition of radically humanized, which is to say, aesthetic dynamics, namely, phenomenology? For various reasons, during the 20th century, even branches of this theory that propose the direct, non-intellectualist appreciation of aesthetic states of being, were rejected as excessively psychological and no workable alternative was admitted.[28]

In the wake of Adorno's difficulties, his successor as director of the Frankfurt School, Jürgen Habermas took a different tack. Still determined to explain social cohesion in a fashion that articulated with the modern view of higher humanity, he proposed that the essential social-glue consists of webs of communicative action as expression of what westerners take as rational. He developed this position during the long middle period of his career and it is from this angle that his enduring reputation seems to be maintained. It is a view that allows him to compose and lecture with conviction, stimulating reflection and research in a fashion that is understandable and thus supported by the positive science community that dominates western intellectual circles.

In his early work, he focused on how to straighten out the capital mechanism as drive force so as to assure popular political support for it (see his

---

28 Phenomenology. Husserl's early approach to the subject was too psychological for my taste, dealing with things-in-themselves, via bracketing, being a matter of mind over its own historical matters. That this was a limiting view of social action was later attested to by Husserl himself, when, toward the end of his life, facing the difficulties in Europe under mounting fascism, he radically modified his view in his text on the *Crisis of European Man* (1936). This thread of phenomenology was picked up and amplified in France by Maurice Merleau-Ponty, who, for post-WWII political reasons, unfortunately lost confidence in the original potential of his own work.

first major internationally recognized title: *Legitimacy Crisis,* 1975). This work was the most tightly connected of his writings with a material critique of capital in the Marxist tradition.

During the extended middle phase of his career, Habermas shifted attention to the symbolic texture of society, focusing on instrumental rationality as the problem, in so far as its centrality to public discourse distorts communication, leading to unresponsive institutional leadership and ineffective political action. The principal works here are *Communication and the Evolution of Society* (1979), and the two-volume *The Theory of Communicative Action* (1981). Recently, focusing specifically on Europe, Habermas has turned more directly to the political process itself, claiming that the problem with democratic Europe is an insufficiency of institutions by which to effectively mediate popular political action via representative government agents and institutions.[29]

From a distance, taking together the views he expressed during the three phases of his impressive career, this amounts to the judgment that due to distorted standards of instrumental-rationality: a) the capital mechanism under-delivers, in general, well-being; b) the communicative web needed to assure societal stability is not only splintered, but, by being detached from history, generates what amounts to a crisis of existential meaning for westerners; and c) the formal apparatus of representative government needed to realize democracy in action are woefully underdeveloped, generating a European state system without steering capacity, thus defenselessly exposed to one crisis (either economic or military) after another.

Although trained in sociology, Habermas refuses to endorse (as did his compatriot Niklas Luhmann, for instance) a general-system view of society.[30] While effectively covering the three domains that I depict in my model (see Technical Appendix) as the institutional infrastructure of the West, he can only approach the workings thereof from the point of view of the individual political agent. Sidestepping the issue of totality, this necessarily results in his judging that the problem in the West is linked to misdirected, misconceived individual rationality, because given the modern

---

[29] Historical Material Rediscovered. In the last five years, Habermas has re-centered his writings on democracy as something other, he hopes, than mass deception, proposing strategies for political repair, particularly of the ethereal entity known as the European Community, now transformed into an unworkable European Economic Union. See two of his recent books: *Europe. The Faltering Project* (2009), and *The Crisis of the European Union* (2012).

[30] Systems Perspective. See Niklas Luhmann's, *Differentiation of Society* (1982), and *Theory of Society* (2012/1997).

reductionist viewpoint, that is what drives social, political and economic action. At the same time, this anti-system view (generally characteristic, I must repeat, of most critical theorists today), prevents Habermas from seeing that the system cannot be repaired by re-fashioning human rationality as simple correction at the interface between economics and politics.

Reading through the immense work of Habermas, the image of the Möbius ribbon returns. While communication is its own support, and while it is surely a humanism as well, it is probably impossible to attribute causal force to the way humans communicate as explanation of the survival and social structure of a population. While Habermas continues to display a provoking political determination as to the potential reform of society in an affirmative humanist direction, there is little evident connection between his elaborate writings on communicative truth, rightness and appropriateness, and justification for political mobilization. Again, not just his excessive concern for the abuse of rationality but a certain display of the very tendency he critiques leads him into a closed metaphysical loop.

For Axel Honneth, the current director of the Institute at Frankfurt, I see a continuing momentum favoring the rational in analysis, but this time focusing on an issue that is even more ethereal than communication, that of recognition. However, even if his central concept is more intra-subjective than extra-structural, my issue with Honneth concerns less the historical object of his interest (recognition) than the intense determination he displays to approach it critically via the work of the mind. The result, I must add, is that he finds himself in a precarious position not unlike that which haunted Adorno with his aesthetic. Recognition is itself a decidedly non material, metaphysical-appearing phenomenon, the appreciation of which contradicts in essential ways the logic of rationality with which he attempts to deal with it.[31]

---

[31] Saving Criticism. Axel Honneth's vast production is not easily summarized, although common points of entry into his works are: *The Struggle for Recognition: The Moral Grammar of Social Conflict* (1996), and *Pathologies of Reason: On the Legacy of Critical Theory* (2009).

Distancing himself in general from a Marxist discourse, Honneth made a recent appearance in the Paris, *Philosophie Magazine* (No. 52, 2012), for which he wrote a short overview essay as Preface for a centerfold attachment consisting of the essential pages from First Part of Volume I of *Capital* where Marx discussed "The Fetish Character of Merchandise and its Secret." There is an air to his Preface suggesting that Honneth considers himself somehow 'beyond Marx,' or at least that Marx is now largely museum material. Although he claims elsewhere that he is not a carrier of a particular intellectual heritage, he evidently failed to underline that for the Paris journalist who translated his comments

It is not so much that rationality yields falsehood and thus is a deceptive guide for action, as it is an insufficient tool for the perception or expression of existential truth. Its yield is too limited to serve as a guide for social restructuration. Unfortunately, not just Honneth and Habermas, but the majority of 20th century critics relied on a similarly rational analytic. The result is like attempting to build a wood-frame house using a rubber carpenter's rule: not only is the process prone to deformation, but there is no way to differentiate the accurate from the distorted measure. Not only will a critique of rationality not yield results that are up to the task for which cultural criticism is undertaken, but the insistence on or confidence in the rational processes as source of trusted assessment of existential conditions and possibilities, even of rationality itself, is without justification. At least within the late modern condition, it is irrational to overly rely on the rational faculties.

Since I introduce Honneth here only as a collateral source to help clarify a view of critical practice drawn from my in-depth case studies, I will not delve further into his writings. However, as the current Director of the Institute in Frankfurt, coming as he does on the heels of Habermas, who is still much cited and active, it is no small testimony to note Honneth's success at attracting a sizable audience with his work. He does this by approaching the issue of social problems a bit in keeping with the strategy of R.K. Merton fifty years ago in the U.S.: by what amounts to a middle-range strategy. Although, unlike Merton, who did similarly in order to carve out a bit of personal space from what he considered to be the excessive macro-systemic structuralism of his mentor, Talcott Parsons, with Honneth, it is as if he is attempting to achieve quite the opposite topological effect: to restore a bit of structure to the critique of subjective rationality of Habermas. In the sense that Merton's program was more appealing or at least less daunting than was that of Parsons,' the same pertains for Honneth by comparison to Habermas. But: what about the inclusiveness and internal consistency of the result?

What Future for Critical Practice?

This elaborate study of critical practice provides a rather gloomy up-date about the playing out of a world condition in keeping with the 1930 thesis

for the magazine, since the journalist introduced Honneth as, "Professor of Philosophy and Sociology... [and] principal contemporary representative of the School of Frankfurt."

by Horkheimer. It seems unarguable that the formally unannounced, yet very real domination of the bourgeois philosophy of history (BPH) as world view constitutes an immanent danger. This world view is so pervasive that it veils the capital mechanism, thereby defusing serious criticism of capitalism. This allows free hand to the capital machine, supported by political institutions and practices that sustain it, no matter what the cost in environmental damage, social inequality or individual alienation. The reason for this distorted effect is that under the specter of capital, public action is evaluated in the short term exclusively against the limited standards of instrumental-rationality.

Since I feel reassured by my case studies in the conviction that the generalized use of the historical-materialist method has resulted in a superior quality of critique, and since critical projects continue to be conducted, what might explain the inability of its products to cut through this ideological fog which serves as a convoluted cover for the anti-humanist consequences of the accepted Western model of political-economy? Either I am wrong in my judgment about the power of critique, or, at some deeper level, while the method being used is appropriate, the object of critique is poorly informed by cultural blockages that in all justice ought to be the point of critique in the first place. A brief summary of my view of that puzzle will serve to close this volume.

After pushing an examination of the foundations and heritage of the Frankfurt School back to Horkheimer as professor of social philosophy in 1930, a new interpretation of these events came into view.

The bourgeois philosophy of history was constituted in keeping with a small set of pragmatic and politically interventionist principles associated with the work of Machiavelli, Hobbes and Vico. The action principle of this world view is that a stable political order depends on support of the grand bourgeoisie: the economic elite will only support the political order if their economic means are assured by executive political power.

In pursuit of that objective, a political regime that incarnates the principles of, *The Prince*, is justified in doing anything needed to eliminate the risk of popular rebellion or refusal to work, so as to assure the level of production needed to guarantee the perpetual comfort of the wealthy. This implies general indifference about the conditions of existence of the common classes, and the willingness to perpetuate domestic exploitation or foreign warfare if the cost-benefit equation is favorable for wealth enhancement.

Over the centuries, that social compromise between the bourgeoisie or economic elite and the political regimes in the West has been materialized in various ways, favoring a particular system of technical organization for the economy, and a particular symbolic content for the common consciousness. Initially, this mode of societal organization was centered on the productive capital process and military preparedness. From there, the notion of progress that dated from earlier in the Italian Renaissance was reconfigured as capital concentration (i.e., technological advances) and eminent domain (i.e., monopoly).

Another post-renaissance figure was also re-materialized, that of rationality. But rationality in action requires some determinant criterion of evaluation, such that choices can be compared in terms of their effectiveness. In this case, rationality became defined as instrumental-rationality, hooking the measure of individual performance back on the scale of economic concentration and power. If that conjecture is accurate, rather than foundational historic-objects, as materialized in the contemporary west, both the capital mechanism and instrumental-rationality are only epiphenomena of the bourgeois philosophy of history. This suggests a significant rethinking not only of the 20th century critical theory movement, but of the Marx critique that lies behind it.

As for Marx, then: his early writings on *German Ideology* demonstrate that right from the start, he was on a track more or less consistent with the conjecture developed in this book, that ideological distortions prepared the grounds for takeover by the logic of capital. He thereafter shifted attention to a critique of *Capital*, because, as he was rightly aware, and as reinforced in practical terms by his new life of exile, in London, this is the most durable structuring mechanism of society and a key point of action should fundamental social change be pursued.

However, as Marx saw in a way that gradually was lost on the part of his followers, if one remains exclusively at the level of a critique of capital, one will overlook the intention as world view that legitimizes that mechanism, arriving at the conclusion that conditions might be better if only one were to repair or fine-tune the capital system and/or the social relations of production that it underwrites. In and of itself, a critique of capital in its material manifestations will not open the way to social revolution, as a political aesthetic fact, which explains in part (*à la* Gramsci) why the Marx critique, as carried out somewhat misguidedly by his followers, has yet to have much revolutionary yield in the West.

It does not appear that Horkheimer was entirely innocent in this affair of misdirection. For political reasons during 1930s, due to the danger of advancing a Marxist profile under the nose of the newly emerging Nazi regime in Germany, he felt obliged to go soft on his capital based materialist critique.[32] As it turned out, however, that caution did not really pay off, since he was soon evicted from his post and forced to flee Frankfurt less because of being Marxist, than for being a Jew. For a while after WWII when the Institute for Social Research returned to Germany under different political circumstances, his successors reengaged in the materialist critique with considerable sincerity (Marcuse in particular, very early Habermas, somewhat). But by the end of the 1960s, momentum shifted once more away from the Marxist image, for effectively the same reason that motivated Horkheimer to do so a generation earlier. To be frank about it, to persist in a critique of the capital mechanism, is a major danger for one's career if not one's freedom. Things have not changed in that sense since Voltaire.

In the long term, Horkheimer's successors gradually displaced their critical ire, away from contradictions forced by the capital mechanism, in the direction of the excesses of instrumental-rationality. As developed above, this is not unjustified, but only to say that such a critique cannot have immediate effect since (assuming the justice of our conjecture) instrumental rationality is an epiphenomenon of the social organization by which the BPH is materialized and not its fundamental condition. Parallel with the way a mainstream critique of capital leads only to suggestions for its improvements at the margins, critique of instrumental-rationality leads to marginal corrective measures, such as using pedagogical tactics and modifications in communication and image of the sort tacitly called for by Habermas.

This is not to condemn as unjustified a frontal critique of means of production or of the basis of rationality: each counts. But, since contemporary social practices are lodged in concrete for which the bourgeois philosophy of history lays the forms, only by somehow dissipating the BPH might it be possible to openly consider a major reworking of both the economy and the basis of rationality.

As I see it, that necessary reworking is very possible, but only to the extent that the world view of late modernity is scrapped. This would be achieved by migrating the West away from grounds anchored in systems of societal organization for which the skeletal structure is formatted in keeping with the BPH. This would mean migrating toward a new historical condition for the West, the contours of which are yet to be constituted, but which would bear the identity of a post-modernity. Among other

[32] Repressed Expression. For details on the conditions in Frankfurt at the time Horkheimer assumed directorship of the Institute, see Durand-Gasselin (2012).

practical benefits, such a program would allow acceptance that the problem is not the presence of capital or particular capital process within a well-ordered society, but domination of society by the capital process, as if it were the only mechanism for successful societal ordering.

Promising Leads

While surely no minor undertaking, a shift to a post-modern condition for the organization of western society (from a systemic perspective as I conceive that) can be achieved. A major barrier to such a move is the dogmatic claim that it is impossible to seriously consider alternative possible futures because of the implausibility of reconceptualizing the nature of truth and being. This is equivalent to claiming that the BPH contains the ultimate statement of truth and human existence, a position that critical theory was set up to counter. The needed reconceptualization is very possible, as long as the transformative process is judicious in drawing on existing elements of culture and practice for use under greatly reconfigured conditions.

Even if not determinant, what the people in any society do collectively can make a difference in the way their world is structured. Speaking in the spirit of Gregory Bateson, important steps toward achieving a humanist ecology for the West might include the following:

In politics it might be decided that rather than the truth, a lie is a lie. This would not of course eliminate the possibility of despotism based on a public lie, but only expose it more rapidly when it erupts. Under more accommodating leadership, this could lead to substantial transparency in public decision-making, opening the way to a revolutionary change from a democracy of form, to a democracy of process.

At the level of societal organization, the legitimacy of utopian world views might be reinstated, providing confidence in the capacity to conceive and realize entirely different possible futures. This is not to assume reality as utopia but only to authorize evaluation of options against utopian visions, allowing the basis of planning to shift from reactionary focus on disaster avoidance or recovery of some romantic past, to a progressive agenda of principle optimization.

The notion of being-rationally might be reconsidered, shifting priority from a critique of instrumental-rationality (a 'because of' logic), to a critique of prospective-rationality (an 'in order to' logic). This would rebalance concern for the past as constraint with attention on a present guided by the future as a field of choice, which is to say with a view of the future as freedom-expressed.

Human consciousness might be placed under serious critique. Rather than shying away from this for excuses linked to misconstrued neo-Marxist materialisms or neo-Freudian psychicisms, or for fear of guilt by association with denatured metaphysics, an opening could be acknowledged for a reinvigorated aesthetic of collective action, thus shifting from conflict management to harmony enhancement as orienting political fact.

While not accessible by the currently accepted means of positive science, the practical elements of the critical program outlined above might be appreciated and mobilized by deployment of the sort of iterative-phenomenology advocated by Maurice Merleau-Ponty. This implies resurrection of phenomenal-existentialism, for a society reconstituted on the basis of a phenomenological epistemo-ontology, in contrast to a positivist onto-epistemology of the type associated with Heidegger that is largely dominant today.

These are only suggestions for a reinvigorated critique not just of capital or of instrumental-rationality, but of the materialized fundamentals of late modernity itself. While admittedly heavy on the philosophical side of social-philosophical engagement, each of the outlined issues touches human experience in a direct way, the detailing of which would constitute fertile grounds for theorization, research and political debate. At present there is plenty of work already being done regarding the proposals listed above. A first step to change would be to pull that work out of the archives where it tends to be buried and off the back burners where it tends to simmer listlessly, putting it on the table for discussion in order to draw out its potential in an integrated fashion.

As concerns the role of critical practitioner, independent of tactics or resources, a dominant feature of the six individuals studied here in depth was their force of conviction, associated with a willingness to plunge into zones of uncertainty, no matter what the risk of futility or failure. It takes uncommon verve to spend a lifetime challenging conventional ways of understanding and action, since the destination of a path into the unknown is never assured in advance. At the opening of this volume, I pointed out the atypical key figure with which this study would be signed. In that light, to close this book on critical practice, it seems appropriate to report that the crucial unspoken quality of character for higher grade critics appears to be an enormous tolerance for ambiguity.

APPENDIX

TECHNICAL NOTE

1. This Note is provided to clarify the architecture of a general-system model that underwrites my commentary in this book concerning the organization of society, its critique and potential. It is depicted by the following schemata diagram, of my own design, which I find heuristically useful as conceptual aid, when studying or lecturing about 'social facts' such as a society, family, the western cultural system, a business enterprise, a religion, a state system, and similar institutionalized patterns of social relations that give order (i.e., opportunity and constraint) to human social experience.

System-Ecology Model:{P-E-T-O-S}

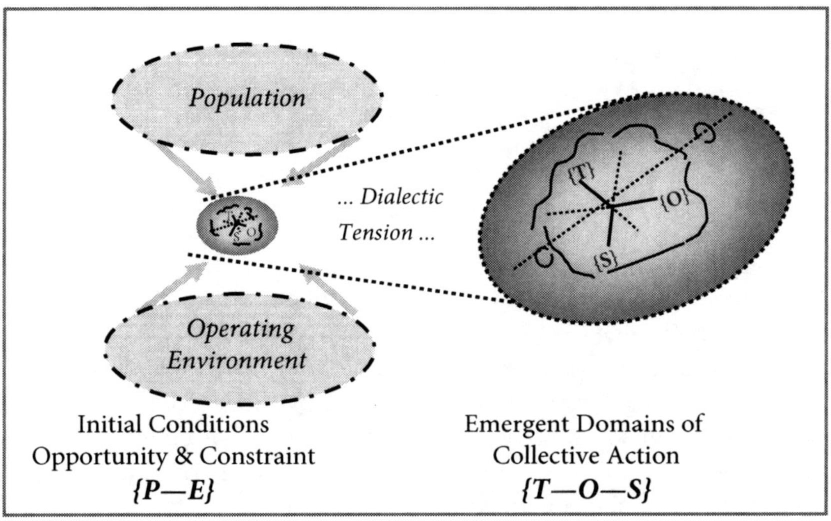

Diagram 1. Schematic representation of {PETOS} General-systems model

As an important component of the conceptual apparatus with which I study and analyze social dynamics, the model is used in this book to provide an architectonic language for specifying the strategy and methods of critical practice. Since the model is used in this book mostly as a source of vocabulary and not as a formal component of the study, it is relegated to this Appendix rather than introduced in the body of the work. It is presented here, not as a statement of dogmatic certainty about the nature of social reality but only in the interests of intellectual transparency concerning how I deal consciously with the systemic aspects of such reality.

2. In addition to providing a static representation of any social-cultural system, the model is intended to highlight the historical nature of such systems, by drawing attention to the social-ecology dynamics that precondition their coming into being and continuity. The model isolates for emphasis five domains:

Social System Defined

- Model of Five Domains: **{P-E-T-O-S}**
- Initial Conditions :
  {P} :: **Population** (Served by System)
  {E} :: **Environment** (A set of Rules)
- Emergent Domains of Action:
  {T} :: **Technical**
  {O} :: **Organizational**
  {S} :: **Symbolic**

Diagram 2. The five domains of our General-system model

Use of the model implies a set of nested postulates. Socio-cultural systems come into being due to the collective work of a population {P} (of varying size and which may or may not constitute a formally organized group) that is attempting to resolve some issue (of survival or productivity in the largest sense) in confrontation with its operating environment {E}. Such systems arise as the result of collective work done, thereby defining and setting the constraints on individual necessity, opportunity and liberty for those engaged in the system, within its range of action. Relations between the domains are dynamic, iterative and dialectic.

Such systems tend to be evolutive, exhibiting a capacity for adaptation and autonomous continuity that is, in the short run, independent of control even by key actors. However, they can be 'steered' to some extent by recasting components and linkages within and among the various domains, the potential of which justifies critical practice as discussed in this book. Even if difficult to modify, socio-cultural systems of this type can be destroyed by acts of aggression from the environment (usually by limiting resource transactions) or due to internal imbalances or conflict, which dissipates their vital force, allows for a breakdown of their frontiers, with a loss of integrity and progressive levels of internal disorder, terminating in exhaustion.

3. Since the normative demand on social experiences for the people engaged in them is experienced internally to such systems, the contents, configuration and discursive priorities of the three domains of internal action are a frequent point of attention. Within constraints set by the {P—E} relationship, it is within or between one of the three internal domains that problems are assessed or modifications attempted. Use of the model as heuristic guide allows greater precision for understanding and action. That internal content can be represented as follows:

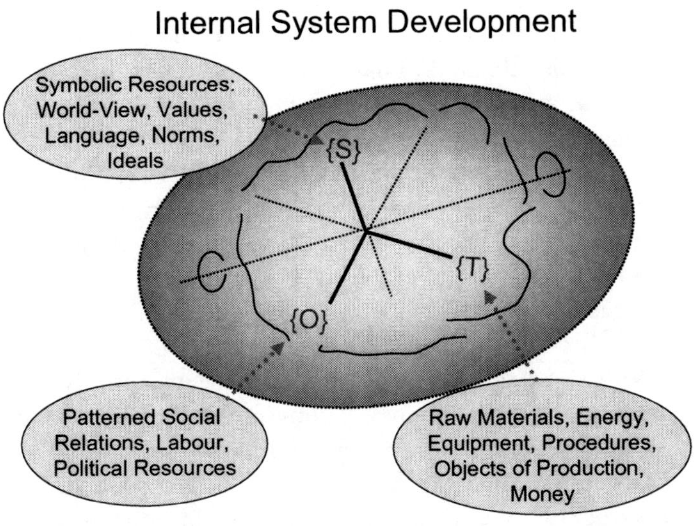

Diagram 3. The internal domains of General-systems: {T-O-S}

A logic of macro- and micro-system architecture necessarily applies for all general-system models: each domain is both a sub-structure of some larger system, and internally sub-structurable according to the same {T-O-S} configuration. A famous demonstration of that generic quality of social systems was articulated by Talcott Parsons (see Parsons and Smelser 1956; Parsons and Platt 1973). Since his reputation was demolished toward the end of his career in part due to his insistence on wording his work in keeping with the system model of his personal design, I advance mine here with full awareness of the danger of the undertaking. For what it is worth, the current proposal was intended to advantage the one used by Parsons, by placing history, temporality and an environmental dynamic into the model.

4. Derivation and Use of this Model. The {PETOS} Model depicted schematically here was developed in connection with a series of studies conducted on more than 300 complex corporate organizations, private and public, principally in connection with policy research studies that I directed from Portland State University, Oregon, and at the University of Minnesota. The model was first presented professionally in a paper, "Organizations as Systems" at the 1989 Annual Meeting of the Oregon Academy of Sciences.

The structure of the model was inspired by a somewhat similar one developed by Otis Dudley Duncan. His model was known by the anagram: (POET) (Duncan 1964; Blau and Duncan 1967; Duncan 1984). My {PETOS} model differs in two ways: first, the {Symbolic} domain is added, and the assemblage reconfigured to highlight the complex internal structure of socio-cultural systems, as a three domain field of action, Technical, Organizational, and Symbolic ({T—O—S}).

The other difference with my model is that it is dialectically dynamic by design: there is no assumed 'one way determination' or, once in existence, of hierarchy between domains; but only bi-directional influences among them, such that the nature of each can only be appreciated by taking the others into account. That having been said, in the end, the environment has the final word for system formation and survival.

In application, use of this model implies that one conceives of socio-cultural systems as real social constructions (or 'facts'), with major dynamic properties, and not simply of social systems as the inert historical residue of past social action. Since the relation between that past and the present social construction is also dialectic, this explains the future-oriented dynamics of systems of this nature, not to mention the fit between conceiving of social systems in this way and their study with a historical-materialist method.

BIBLIOGRAPHY

Abbott, Edwin A. 1982 [1884]. *Flatland: A Romance of Many Dimensions*. New York: Dover Press.

Adams, Tim. 2007. "Eagleton: The armchair revolutionary." London, *The Observer*, 16 December. http://www.guardian.co.uk/books/2007/dec/16/martinamis.

Adorno, Theodor W. 2004. *The Culture Industry: Selected Essays on Mass Culture*, edited by J.M. Bernstein. London: Routledge.

——. 2002. *Essays on Music: Theodore W. Adorno*, edited by R.D. Leppert. Berkeley: University of California Press.

——. 2001 [1966]. *Dialectique Négative*. [*Negative Dialectics*]. Paris: Payot.

——. 2000 [1963]. *Problems of Moral Philosophy*. Cambridge: Cambridge University Press.

——. 1999 [1970]. *Sur Walter Benjamin*, edited by Rolf Tiedemann. Paris: Gallimard.

——. 1995a [1955]. *Prisms*. Cambridge: MIT Press.

——. 1995b [1970]. *Théorie esthétique.* [*Aesthetic Theory*]. Paris: Klincksieck.

——. 1951. *Minima Moralia: Reflections from Damaged Life*. London: NLB.

——. E. Frenkel-Brunswik, D. Levinson and N. Sanford. 1993 [1950]. *The Authoritarian Personality*. New York: Norton.

——. and Max Horkheimer. 2001 [1944]. *The Dialectic of Enlightenment*. New York: Continuum.

——. W. Benjamin, E. Bloch, B. Brecht and G. Lukács. 2002 [1977]. *Aesthetics and Politics*. London: Verso.

D'Alembert, Jean-Baptiste and Denis Diderot. (eds.). 1751–1765. *L'Encyclopédie ou Dictionnaire Raisonné Des Sciences, Des Arts et Des Métiers*. [*Encyclopaedia or a Systematic Dictionary of the Sciences, Arts and Crafts*]. http://quod.lib.umich.edu/d/did/index.html.

Alexander, Samuel. 2003 [1933]. *Beauty and the other Forms of Value*. London: Macmillan.

Althusser, Louis. 2008 [1971]. "Ideology and Ideological State Apparatuses." Pp. 1–60 in *On Ideology*. Verso: London.

——. 2005 [1965]. *For Marx*. London: Verso.

Anderson Joel. (Forthcoming). "Situating Axel Honneth in the Frankfurt School Tradition." In *The Critical Theory of Axel Honneth,* Danielle Petherbridge (ed). Leiden: Brill.

Araújo, Ana C. 2006. "The Lisbon Earthquake of 1755 – Public Distress and Political Propaganda." *E-journal of Portuguese History* 4(1). www.brown.edu/Departments/Portuguese_Brazilian_Studies/ejph/html/Summer06.html.

Arendt, Hannah. 1963. *Eichmann in Jerusalem: A Report on the Banality of Evil*. New York: Viking.

——. 1951. *The Origins of Totalitarianism*. New York: Schocken.

Aristotle. 1997 [~335 BCE]. *Poetics*. New York: Dover Publications.

Arnold, Matthew. 1911 [1888]. *Essays in Criticism: Second Series*. London: MacMillan.

Aronowitz, Stanley. 2005. "Comments on Michael Burawoy's 'The Critical Turn to Public Sociology.'" *Critical Sociology* 31(3): 333–338.

——. 2003. "A Mills Revival?" *Logos* 2(3). http://www.logosjournal.com/aronowitz.htm.

Aubel, Francois and Michel Delon. 2008. "Dossier: Voltaire, Ici et Maintenant." Pp. 58ff, in *Magazine Littéraire*, Paris, August 8, No. 478. www.magazine-litteraire.com/mensuel/478/voltaire-maintenant-01-09-2008-28788.

Bachelard, Gaston. 1964 [1938]. *The Psychoanalysis of Fire*. Beacon Press.

Badiou, Alain. 1988. *L'Être et l'Événement*. [*Being and Event*, 2002]. Paris: Seuil.

Bakhtin, Mikhail. 1981 [1930]. *The Dialogic Imagination: Four Essays*. Edited by Michael Holquist. Austin: University of Texas Press.

Ballibar, Étienne. 2010 [1993]. *La Philosophie de Marx.* Paris: La Découverte.

Banchoff, Thomas F. 1990. "From Flatland to Hypergraphics: Interacting with Higher Dimensions." *Interdisciplinary Science Reviews.* 15(4): 364–372.

Barthes, Roland. 2012 [1957]. *Mythologies.* New York: Hill and Wang.

——. 2007 [1970]. *L'Empire des Signes.* [*Empire of Signs*]. Paris: Seuil.

——. 2005 [1977]. *Image-Music-Text.* New York: Hill and Wang.

——. 1972. *Le Degré zéro de l'écriture: suivi par les Nouveaux Essais Critiques.* [*Writing Degree Zero*]. Paris: Seuil.

——. 1967. "Death of the Author." *Aspen Review* 5–6.

Bateson, Gregory. 2008 [1972]. *Steps to an Ecology of the Mind.* Chicago: University of Chicago Press.

Baudrillard, Jean. 2010a. *The Agony of Power.* Los Angeles: Semiotext(e).

——. 2010b. *Carnival and Cannibal: Or the Play of Global Antagonisms.* London: Seagull Books.

——. 2010 [1970]. *La Société de Consommation: ses Mythes, ses Structures.* [The Consumer Society: Myths and Structures.] Paris: Denoël.

——. 2003. "Matrix, The Film?" [Interview. Aude Lancelin.] In: *Le Nouvel Observateur* No. 2015. http://web.archive.org/web/20080113012028/http://www.empyree.org/divers/Matrix-Baudrillard_english.html.

——. 2002. *The Spirit of Terrorism: And Requiem for the Twin Towers.* London: Verso.

——. 2001. "L'esprit du terrorisme." ["The Spirit of Terrorism"]. *Le Monde.* 03 November. http://www.lemonde.fr/cgi-bin/ACHATS/acheter.cgi?offre=ARCHIVES&type_item=ART_ARCH_30J&objet_id=677599&xtmc=baudrillard&xtcr=142.

——. 1999a. *Sur la photographie.* [*On Photography*]. Paris: Sens and Tonka.

——. 1999b. *L'Echange Impossible.* [*The Impossible Exchange*]. Paris: Galilée.

——. 1995. *La Crime Parfait.* [The Perfect Crime: Verso, 2008.] Paris: Galilée.

——. 1986. *Amérique.* [America: Verso, 1988.] Paris: Grasset.

——. 1981. *Simulacres et Simulation.* [*Simulacra and Simulation.*] Paris: Galilée.

——. 1968. *Le Système des objets.* [*The System of Objects*, Verso, 1996.] Paris: Gallimard.

Baumgarten, Alexander G. 1988 [1750–1758]. *Aesthetics.* [*Esthétique; précédée des, Méditations philosophiques sur quelques sujets se rapportant à l'essence du poème et de la Métaphysique.* Jean-Yves Pranchère (ed). Paris: L'Hern.]. http://www.britannica.com/EBchecked/topic/56478/Alexander-Gottlieb-Baumgarten.

Benjamin, Walter. 1986 [1934]. "Paris, Capital of the Nineteenth Century." Pp. 146–162 in *Reflections: Essays, Aphorisms, Autobiographical Writings*, edited by P. Demetz. New York: Schocken.

——.1968. *Illuminations: Essays and Reflections,* edited by Hannah Arendt. New York: Schocken.

Bergson, Henri. 2011 [1889]. *Essai sur les données immédiates de la conscience.* [*Essay on the Immediately Given to Consciousness.*] Paris: Presses Universitaires de France.

——. 2010 [1896]. *Matière et mémoire.* [*Matter and Memory.*] Paris: PUF.

——. 1981 [1907]. *L'Evolution créatrice.* [*Creative Evolution.*] Paris: PUF.

Berlin, Isaiah. 2002 [1958]. "Two Concepts of Liberty." Pp. 118–172 in *Four Essays on Liberty* by Isaiah Berlin. Oxford: Oxford University Press.

Billington, Michael. 2005."The German Shakespeare." *The Guardian* of London, 26 January.

Birnbaum, Jean. 2012. "Boltanski, détective critique." *Le Monde des Livres,* 17 Février: lemonde.fr.

Blau, Peter and Otis Dudley Duncan. 1967. *The American Occupational Structure.* New York: Wiley and Sons.

Boethius. 1957 [524]. *The Consolation of Philosophy.* New York: Ungar Pub. Co.

Bohm, David. 2008 [1980]. *Wholeness and the Implicate Order.* London: Routledge and Kegan Paul.

Boltanski, Luc. 2012a. La Suite dans les idées. [Radio Interview] Paris: *France-Inter,* 18 Février.

——. 2012b. *Énigmes et Complots: Une enquête à propos d'enquêtes.* Paris: Gallimard.

——. 2012c. La figure de Sherlock Holmes aujourd'hui. [Radio Interview.] Paris: *France-Culture*, 20 Février.

——. 2009. *De la Critique: Précis de sociologie de l'émancipation*. [*On Critique: A Sociology of Emancipation*, 2011.] Paris: Gallimard.

——. 1990. "Sociologie critique et sociologie de la critique." *Politix* 10(11): 124–134.

——. and E. Chiapello. 2005 [1999]. *The New Spirit of Capitalism*. London: Verso.

——. and L. Thévenot. 1991. *De la justification. Les économies de la grandeur*. Paris: Gallimard.

Bonfiglio, Thomas P. 1994. "The Patrilineal Discourse of Enlightenment: Reading Foucault Reading Kant." *Bulletin de la Société Américaine de Philosophie de Langue Française* 6(1–2): 104–115.

Bottomore, Tom. 1984. *The Frankfurt School of Critical Theory*. London: Tavistock.

Boulding, Kenneth. 1956. "General Systems Theory: The Skeleton of Science." In *Management Science* 2(3): 197–208.

Bourdieu, Pierre. 2012. *Sur l'État: Cours au Collège de France 1989–1992*. Paris: Seuil.

——. 1989 *La noblesse d'État: grandes écoles et esprit de corps*. Paris: Éditions de Minuit.

——. 1979. *La distinction: critique sociale du jugement*. [Distinction: a Social Critique of the Jugement of Taste.] Paris: Éditions de Minuit.

——. 1970. *La reproduction: Éléments d'une théorie du système d'enseignement*. Paris: Éditions de Minuit.

——. and Jean-Claude Passeron. 1964. *Les héritiers: les étudiants et la culture*. Paris: Éditions de Minuit.

Bove, Arianna. 2004. *A Critical Ontology of the Present*. Doctoral Dissertation. University of Sussex, England.

Brantley, Ben. 2011. "Wizard of Corporate Climbing." *The New York Times*. March 28, C1.

Brecht, Bertolt. 2010 [1939]. *Mother Courage*. London: Methuen.

——. 1997. *Brecht on Theater: The Development of an Aesthetic*. Edited by J. Willett J. New York: Hill and Wang.

——. 1991 [1934]. "Writing the Truth: Five Difficulties." Pp. 131–150 in *Galileo*, by Bertolt Brecht, edited by Eric Bentley. New York: Grove Press.

——. 1966 [1938]. *Galileo*. Edited by Eric Bentley. New York: Grove Press.

Broe, Dennis. 2009. *Film Noir, American Workers and Postwar Hollywood*. University Press: Florida.

Burawoy, Michael. 2011. *Global Sociology* [Online Seminar.] Berkeley: The University of California. http://www.academicroom.com/video/global-sociology-sociology-185-introduction-michael-burawoy-lecture-1-12-berkeley-spring-2011.

——. 2005a. "The Critical Turn to Public Sociology." *Critical Sociology* 31(3): 313–326.

——. 2005b. "Antinomian Marxist." Pp. 48–71 in *The Disobedient Generation: Social Theorists in the Sixties*, edited by Alan Sica and Stephen Turner. Chicago: University of Chicago Press.

——. 2005c. "For Public Sociology." *American Sociological Review* 70(1): 4–28.

——. 2000 [1991]. *Ethnography Unbound: Power and Resistance in the Modern Metropolis*. Berkeley: University of California Press.

Burckhardt, Jakob. 1990 [1860]. *The Civilization of the Renaissance in Italy*. New York: Penguin Books.

Burke, Edmund. 2004 [1790]. *Reflections on the Revolution in France*. New York: Penguin.

Butler, Judith. 2012 [1984]. *Subjects of Desire: Hegelian Reflections in Twentieth-Century France*. New York: Columbia University Press.

Camus, Albert. 2012a [1947]. *La Pest*. [The Plague]. Paris: Gallimard.

——. 2012b [1946]. *Les Justes*. [The Self-Righteous Assassins]. Paris: Gallimard.

——. 2006 [1947]. *L'Etranger* [The Stranger]. Paris: Gallimard.

——. 2000 [1942]. *The Myth of Sisyphus*. London: Penguin.

Capote, Truman. 1966. *In Cold Blood*. New York: Random House.

Carlyle, Thomas. 2010 [1858]. *History of Friedrich II of Prussia*. Cambridge: Cambridge University Press.

——. 2005 [1843]. *Past and Present.* Berkeley: University of California Press.

Cassé, Michel. 2001. *De Vide et de la Création.* Paris: Odile Jacob.

Cervantes, Miguel de. 2008 [1605 and 1615]. *Don Quixote.* Oxford: Oxford University Press.

Chomsky, Noam. 2006 [1971]. "Human Nature: Justice vs. Power: A Debate Between Noam Chomsky and Michel Foucault." Pp. 1–67 in *The Chomsky-Foucault Debate on Human Nature.* New York: The New Press.

Collingwood, Robin G. 1993 [1946]. *The Idea of History.* Oxford: Oxford University Press.

Comte, August. 1999 [1851–1854]. *Cours de philosophie positive: Leçons 47–51 sur la Sociologie.* Paris: Flammarion.

Corcuff, Philippe. 2012. *Où est passée la critique sociale?* [*What has happened with Social Criticism?*] Paris: La Décuvert.

——. 2011 [1995]. *Les Nouvelles Sociologies: Entre le collectif et l'individuel.* Paris: Armand Colin.

Coulter, Gerry. 2007. "BHL and JB in America: Review and Virtual Dialogue." *International Journal of Baudrillard Studies* 4(1). http://www.ubishops.ca/baudrillardstudies/vol4_1/levy.htm.

Culler, Jonathan. 2007. *The Literary in Theory.* Stanford California, Stanford University Press.

——. 1988. *Framing the Sign: Criticism and its Institutions.* Norman Oklahoma: University of Oklahoma Press.

De Beauvoir, Simone. 1967 [1943]. *L'Invitée.* [*She Came to Stay.*] Paris: Gallimard.

——. 1948 *"Littérature et métaphysique: Existentialisme et la sagesse des nations.* [*Les Temps modernes*: 1.7: 1946.] *Paris: Nagel.*

Defert, Daniel. 2004. "Les Derniers jours." [Interview by Eric Favereau.] Paris: *Libération,* 19 June. www.liberation.fr/cahier-special/0101492961-les-derniers-jours.

——. 2001. "Chronology of Foucault." In *Dits et Écrits I: 1954–1975.* Paris: Gallimard.

Defoe, Daniel. 2000 [1719]. *The Life and Strange Surprising Adventures of Robinson Crusoe.* Oxford: Oxford University Press.

de Man, Paul. 2006 [1983]. *Blindness and Insight: Essays in the Rhetoric of Contemporary Criticism.* Minneapolis: University of Minnesota Press.

Descartes, René. 2004 [1641]. *Méditations Métaphysiques.* Paris: PUF.

——. 1999 [1637]. *Discours de la méthode: pour bien conduire sa raison, et chercher la vérité dans les sciences.* Paris: Flammarion.

Dewey, John. 1997 [1910]. *How We Think.* New York: Dover Publications.

——. 1981. *The Philosophy of John Dewey.* Edited by John J. McDermott. Chicago: University of Chicago Press.

——. 1950 [1920]. *Reconstruction in Philosophy.* Boston: Beacon Press.

——. 1922. *Human Nature and Conduct: An Introduction to Social Psychology.* New York: Carlton House.

——. 1927. *The Public and its Problems.* New York: Henry Holt.

Dilthey, Wilhelm. 1991 [1883]. *Introduction to the Human Sciences.* Princeton: Princeton University Press.

Djian, Jean-Michel. 2009. *Vincennes. Une aventure de la pensée critique.* Paris: Flammarion.

Domanska, Ewa. 1998. "Hayden White: Beyond Irony." *History and Theory* 37(2): 173–181.

Duncan, Otis Dudley. 1984. *Notes on Social Measurement, Historical and Critical.* New York: Russell Sage Foundation.

Duncan, Otis Dudley. 1964. "From Social System to Ecosystem." *Sociological Inquiry* 31: 140–149.

Durand-Gasselin, Jean-Marc. 2012. *L'École de Francfort.* Paris: Gallimard.

Durant, Will and Ariel Durant. 1935–1975. *The Story of Civilization.* [Eleven Volumes.] New York: Simon and Schuster.

Durkheim, Emile. 1982 [1895]. *Rules of the Sociological Method.* New York: Free Press.

——. 1965 [1912]. *The Elementary Forms of Religious Life.* New York: Free Press.

——. 1964 [1893]. *The Division of Labor in Society.* New York: Free Press.

Dworkin, Ronald. 1986. *Law's Empire*. Cambridge: Belknap Press.
Eagleton, Terry. 2011. *Why Marx was Right*. New Haven and London: Yale University Press.
——. 2010. *On Evil*. New Haven: Yale University Press.
——. 2009. *Reason, Faith, and Revolution: Reflections on the God Debate*. New Haven: Yale University Press.
——. 2008a [1983]. *Literary Theory: an Introduction*. Minneapolis: University of Minnesota Press.
——. 2008b. "Death of the Intellectual." London: *Red Pepper magazine*. October. http://www.redpepper.org.uk/death-of-the-intellectual/.
——. 2007a. *The Gospels—Jesus Christ*. London: Verso.
——. 2007b. "I Contain Multitudes." *London Review of Books* June 19(12): 13–15.
——. 2005a [1984]. *The Function of Criticism*. London: Verso.
——. 2005b. *Holy Terror*. Oxford: Oxford University Press.
——. 2004. "A Shelter in the Tempest of History." *Red Pepper magazine*. http://www.redpepper.org.uk/A-shelter-in-the-tempest-of/.
——. 2002. *The Gatekeeper*. New York: St. Martins.
——. 1990. *The Ideology of The Aesthetic*. London: Blackwell.
——. 1969. "Priesthood and Leninism." *Slant* 5(4): 12–17.
——. 1968. "Language, Reality and the Eucharist." *Slant* 4(3): 18–23.
——. 1967. "Why We Are Still in the Church." *Slant* 3(2): 25–28.
——. 1966. *The New Left Church*. London: Sheed and Ward.
—— and Adrian Cunningham. 1966. *Slant Manifesto: Catholics and the Left*, edited by Adrian Cunningham et al. London: Sheed and Ward.
—— and Nathan Schneider. 2009. "Religion for Radicals: An Interview with Terry Eagleton." *The Monthly Review* 61(4). First published in *The Immanent Frame* on 17 September 2009.
Ebert, Teresa L. 2009. *The Task of Cultural Critique*. Urbana and Chicago: University of Illinois Press.
—— and Mas'ud Zavarzadeh. (forthcoming). *Marxism and the Task of the (Post) Humanities*. New York: Macmillan Palgrave.
Einstein, Albert. 2002. *Physique, Philosophie Politique*. Paris: Seuil.
Fine, Gary A. 1979. "Small Groups and Culture Creation: The Idioculture of Little League Baseball Teams." *American Sociological Review* 44(5): 733–745.
Foucault, Michel. 2007 [1978]. "Qu'est-ce que la critique?" [What is Critique?] In The Politics of Truth. Edited by S. Lotringer. Los Angeles: Semiotext(e).
——. 2004. *Naissance de la biopolitique*. [Cours au College de France, 1978–79.] Paris: Gallimard.
——. 2002 [1969]. *L'archéologie du savoir*. [*Archaeology of Knowledge*. Routledge, 2002.] Paris: Gallimard.
——. 2001a. *Dits et Écrits I: 1954–1975*. Paris: Gallimard.
——. 2001b. *Dits et Écrits II: 1976–1988*. Paris: Gallimard.
——. 1984a. *Histoire de la sexualité: Tome II: L'Usage des plaisirs*. Paris: Gallimard.
——. 1984b. *Histoire de la sexualité: Tome III: Le Souci de soi*. Paris: Gallimard.
——. 1980 [1972–1977]. *Power/Knowledge: Selected Interviews and Other Writings*. Edited by Colin Gordon. New York: Pantheon Books.
——. 1976. *Histoire de la sexualité: Tome I: La Volonté de savoir*. Paris: Gallimard.
——. 1975. *Surveiller et punir: Naissance de la prison*. Paris: Gallimard.
——. 1972. "Mon corps, ce papier, ce feu." [My body, this paper, this fire.] Pp. 583–603 in *Histoire de la folie: Appendix* II by Michel Foucault. Paris: Gallimard.
——. 1971. *L'Ordre du Discours*. [The Discourse on Language.] Paris: Gallimard.
——. 1966. *Les Mots et les choses: Une archéologie des sciences humaines*. [*The Order of Things: an Archaeology of the Human Sciences*.] Paris: Gallimard.
——. 1963. *Naissance de la clinique: une archéologie du regard médical*. [*Birth of the Clinic*.] Paris: PUF.

——. 1961a. *Folie et Déraison: Histoire de la Folie à l'âge classique.* [*Madness and Civilization*] Paris: Plon.

——. 1961b. *Introduction à l'Anthropologie de Kant:* [Vol-I of *Thèse Complémentaire.*] Paris: Sorbonne Université Librarie.

——. 1954. *Maladie mentale et personnalité.* Paris: PUF.

Freud, Sigmund. 2010a [1927]. *L'Avenir d'Une Illusion.* [*The Future of an Illusion.*] Paris: Hatier.

——. 2010b [1930]. *Civilization and its Discontents.* New York, Norton.

——. 2010c [1989]. *Interpretation of Dreams.* New York: Norton.

——. 1998 [1913]. *Totem and Taboo.* New York: Dover.

——. 1989 [1920]. *Beyond the Pleasure Principle.* New York: Norton.

Fromilhague, Catherine. 1995. *Les Figures De Style/Figures of Style.* Paris: Editions Nathan.

Fukuyama, Francis. 2006 [1992]. *The End of History and the Last Man.* New York: Free Press.

Gadamer, Hans-Georg. 1989 [1960]. *Truth and Method.* London: Sheed and Ward.

Garo, Isabelle. 2011. *Foucault, Deleuze, Althusser and Marx.* Paris: Éditions Demopolis.

Geertz, Clifford. 1973. "Thick Description: Toward an Interpretive Theory of Culture." Pp.3–30 in *The Interpretation of Cultures: Selected Essays* by Clifford Geertz. New York: Basic Books.

Gennep, Arnold van. 1977 [1909]. *The Rites of Passage.* London: Routledge.

Genosko Gary and Bryx A. (eds.). 2004. "The Matrix Decoded: Nouvel Observateur Interview With Jean Baudrillard." *International Journal of Baudrillard Studies.* 1(2). http://www.ubishops.ca/baudrillardstudies/vol1_2/genosko.htm.

Giddens, Anthony. 2009a. *Sociology.* Cambridge: Polity Press.

——. 2009b. *The Politics of Climate Change.* Cambridge: Polity Press.

——. 2007. *Europe In The Global Age.* Cambridge: Polity Press.

——. 2000. *Runaway World.* London: Routledge.

——. 1994. *Beyond Left and Right—the Future of Radical Politics.* Cambridge: Polity Press.

——. 1990. *The Consequences of Modernity.* Cambridge: Polity Press.

——. 1984. *The Constitution of Society. Outline of the Theory of Structuration.* Cambridge: Polity Press.

Glaser, Barney G. and Anselm Strauss. 1967. *The Discovery of Grounded Theory.* Chicago: Aldine.

Gödel, Kurt. 1967 [1931]. "On Formally Undecidable Propositions of 'Principia Mathematica' and Related Systems." In *From Frege to Gödel: A Source Book in Mathematical Logic,* edited by Jean van Heijenoort. Cambridge, MA: Harvard University Press.

Goethe, Johann W. 1987 [1808]. *Faust. Part I.* Cambridge: Cambridge University Press.

——. 1980 [1809]. *Les Affinités Electives.* Paris: Gallimard.

Goffman, Erving. 1974. *Frame Analysis: An Essay on the Organization of Experience.* Boston: Northeastern University Press.

——. 1963. *Stigma: Notes on the Management of Spoiled Identity.* Boston: Prentice-Hall.

——. 1961. *Asylums: Essays on the Social Situation of Mental Patients and Other Inmates.* New York: Doubleday.

——. 1959. *The Presentation of Self in Everyday Life.* New York: Anchor Books.

Gonzalez, Madalena. 2008. "Pourquoi y a-t-il Baudrillard Plutôt Que Rien? The Reception and Perception of Jean Baudrillard in France." [Why was there Baudrillard rather than nothing?] *French Cultural Studies* 19(3): 287–303.

Gramsci, Antonio. 1971 [1929–1935]. *Selections from the Prison Notebooks.* London: Lawrence and Wishart.

Habermas, Jürgen. 2012. *The Crisis of the European Union.* Cambridge: Polity Press.

——. 2009. *Europe. The Faltering Project.* Cambridge: Polity Press.

——. 2005 [1975]. *Legitimacy Crisis.* Boston: Beacon Press.

——. 2007 [1981]. *The Theory of Communicative Action.* Cambridge: Polity Press.

——. 1979 [1976]. *Communication and the Evolution of Society.* Boston: Beacon Press.

Hadot, Pierre. 1995. *Qu'est-ce que la philosophie Antique?* [What is the Philosophy of Antiquity?] Paris: Gallimard.

Hall, Edward T. 1990 [1959]. *The Silent Language*. New York: Anchor Books.

Hardy, Thomas. 2006 [1895]. *Jude the Obscure*. New York: Dover.

Hartnack, Justus. 1967. *Kant's Theory of Knowledge*. New York: Harcourt Brace.

Hegel, Georg W.F. 2004 [1837]. *The Philosophy of History*. New York: Dover.

Heisenberg, Werner K. 1983 [1927]. *On the Perceptual Content of Quantum Theoretical Kinematics and Mechanics*. Pp. 62–84 in *Quantum Theory and Measurement*. English Translation by John A. Wheeler and Wojciech Zurek, eds. Princeton: Princeton University Press.

Herder, Johann G. 2000 [1774]. *Histoire et Cultures avec Une Autre Philosophie de L'Histoire-extraits*. Paris: Flammarion.

Hobsbawm, Eric. 2012. "À présent, ce sont les capitalistes qui cherchent des solutions chez Marx." [Presently, it is the capitalists who search solutions in Marx.] Paris: *Magazine Philosophie*, 62, 01 Sept.

——. 2011. *How to Change the World: Tales of Marx and Marxism*. London: Little Brown.

——. 1994. *The Age of Extremes: The Short Twentieth Century, 1914–1991*. New York: Pantheon Books.

Hofmannsthal, Hugo von. (ed.). 2004 [1926]. *Friedrich Schiller: Autoportrait*. Paris: Klincksieck.

Honneth, Axel. 2012. "Marx and the Merchandise Fetish: Preface." Paris: *Magazine Philosophie*, 62: pamphlet insert.

——. 2009. *Pathologies of Reason: On the Legacy of Critical Theory*. New York: Columbia University Press.

——. 1996. *The Struggle for Recognition: The Moral Grammar of Social Conflict*. Cambridge: Polity Press.

——. 2010 [1930]. *Les débuts de la philosophie bourgeoise: suivi de Hegel et le problem de la metaphysique*. Paris: Payot.

——. 1999. *Critical and Traditional Theory*. Pp. 188–243 in *Critical Theory: Selected Essays*, edited by M. O'Connell. New York: Continuum Press.

Hunt, Tristram. 2011. "Why Marx Was Right by Terry Eagleton." London: *The Observer*, 29 May. http://www.guardian.co.uk/books/2011/may/29/why-marx-was-right-eagleton-review.

Husserl, Edmund. 2000 [1936]. *Crisis of European Sciences and Transcendental Phenomenology*. Evanston Illinois: Northwestern University Press.

——. 1965. Philosophy and the Crisis of the European Man. Pp. 149–192 in *Phenomenology and the Crisis of Philosophy* by Edmund Husserl. New York: Harper and Row.

——. 1964 [1905]. *Phenomenology of Time Consciousness*. Edited by Martin Heidegger. Bloomington, Indiana: University Press.

Ionesco, Eugène. 2011a [1950]. *La Cantatrice chauve*. Paris: Gallimard.

——. 2011b [1952]. *Les Chaises*. Paris: Gallimard.

——. 2000 [1953]. *Victimes du devoir*. Paris: Gallimard.

"ISI Web Monitor." Times of London Higher Education website. www.timeshighereducation.co.uk.

James, William. 2003 [1877]. *The Will to Believe and Other Essays in Popular Philosophy*. New York: Longmans, Green.

——. 1996a [1909]. *A Pluralistic Universe*. Lincoln: University of Nebraska Press.

——. 1996b [1911]. *Some Problems of Philosophy: A Beginning of an Introduction to Philosophy*. Lincoln: University of Nebraska Press.

——. 1948 [1879–1907]. *Essays in Pragmatism*. Edited by Alburey Castell. New York: Macmillan.

Jameson, Fredric. 2007 [1990]. *Late Marxism: Adorno or the Persistence of the Dialectic*. London: Verso.

Jay, Martin. 1996 *The Dialectical Imagination: A History of the Frankfurt School and the Institute of Social Research, 1923–1950*. Berkeley: University of California Press.

Joyce, James. 1996 [1914]. *Dubliners*. Edited by A. Walton Litz. New York: Viking Press.

——. 1922. *Ulysses*. Paris: Shakespeare and Company.

Kant, Immanuel. 2009 [1795]. *Perpetual Peace*. London: Penguin.

——. 2008 [1790]. *Critique de la Faculté de Juger*. Paris: Flammarion.

——. 2007a [1788]. *Critique of Practical Reason*. Cambridge: Cambridge University Press.

——. 2007b [1784]. "Answer to the Question: What is Aufklärung." Pp. 29–37 in *The Politics of Truth* by Michel Foucault. Edited by S. Lotringer. Los Angeles: Semiotext(e).

——. 2006 [1798]. *Anthropology from a Pragmatic Point of View*. Cambridge: Cambridge University Press.

——. 2004 [1783]. *Prolegomena to any Future Metaphysics*. Cambridge: Cambridge University Press.

——. 1996 [1797]. *Metaphysics of Morals*. Cambridge: Cambridge University Press.

——. 1981 [1785]. *Groundwork of the Metaphysic of Morals*. Indianapolis: Hackett.

——. 1968 [1781 and 1787]. *Critique of Pure Reason*. Oxford: Clarendon Press.

Kelley, Donald R. 1981. *The Beginning of Ideology: Consciousness and Society in the French Reformation*. Cambridge: Cambridge University Press.

Kellner, Douglas. 2009. Jean Baudrillard. In E.N. Zalta (ed.), *The Stanford Encyclopedia of Philosophy*. Winter Edition. http://plato.stanford.edu/archives/win2009/entries/baudrillard/.

Kennedy, Emmet. 1979. "Ideology from Destutt De Tracy to Marx." Journal of the History of Ideas 40(3): 353–368.

Kierkegaard, Soren. 2000. *The Essential Kierkegaard*. Edited by Howard V. Hong and Edna H. Hong. Princeton: Princeton University Press.

——. 1996. *Soren Kierkegaard—Papers and Journals: A Selection*. Edited by A. Hannay. New York: Penguin.

——. 1992 [1841]. *The Concept of Irony with Continual Reference to Socrates*. Princeton, N.J.: Princeton University Press.

Konstan, David. 2010. *Before Forgiveness: The Origins of a Moral Idea*. Cambridge: Cambridge University Press.

Korzybski, Alfred. 1924. "Time-Binding: The General Theory." http://esgs.free.fr/uk/art/ak5.htm.

Kuhn, Thomas. 2012 [1962]. *The Structure of Scientific Revolutions*. Chicago: University of Chicago Press.

Lacan, Jacques. 2006 [1966]. *Écrits*. Trans. Bruce Fink. New York: Norton.

——. 2005 [1964]. *The Four Fundamental Concepts of Psycho-Analysis*. New York: Norton.

——. 1997 [1959–60]. *The Ethics of Psychoanalysis: The Seminar of Jacques Lacan Book VII*. Edited by Jacques-Alain Miller. New York: Norton.

Latour, Bruno. 2012. "Hygiène de la suspision." *Philosophie Magazine*. No. 57, Mars. http://www.philomag.com/les-livres/notre-selection/hygiene-de-la-suspicion-1984.

Lefebvre, Henri. 1992 [1940]. *Matérialisme Dialectique*. [*Dialectical Materialism*. University of Minnesota Press, 2009.] Paris: PUF.

——. 1991 [1974]. *The Production of Space*. Oxford: Blackwell.

——. 1973 [1968]. *Le Droit à la ville*. [*The Right to the City*.] Paris: Ed. Anthropos.

——. 1968. *La vie quotidienne dans le monde moderne*. [*Everyday Life in the Modern World*.] Paris: Gallimard.

——. 1947, 1961, 1981. *Critique de la vie quotidienne*. [Three Volumes: *Critique of Everyday Life*.] Paris: L'Arche.

—— and N. Guterman. 1988 [1939]. *Hegel: Morceaux Chosis*. Paris: Gallimard.

—— and N. Guterman. 1969 [1934]. *Introduction aux Morceaux Choisis de Karl Marx*. Paris: Gallimard.

Le Goff, Jacques. 2011 [1526]. *Marchads et banquiers du Moyen âge*. [*Merchants and Bankers of the Middle Ages*.] Paris: PUF.

——. 1996. *Saint Louis*. Paris: Gallimard.

——. 1981. *La Naissance du Purgatoire*. [*The Birth of Purgatory*.] Paris: Gallimard.

——. 1979. "The Usurer and Purgatory." Pp. 25–52 in *The Dawn of Modern Banking*, edited by Fredi Chiappelli. New Haven, Center for Medieval and Renaissance Studies, UCLA.

Leibniz, Gottfried W. 1969 [1710]. *Essais de Théodicée : Sur La Bonté de Dieu, La Libérté de l'Homme et l'Origine du Mal*. Paris: Flammarion.
——. 1968 [1714]. *La Monadologie*. Paris: Delagrave.
Leitch, Vincent B. (ed.). 2001. *The Norton Anthology of Theory and Criticism*. New York: Norton.
Lévy, Bernard-Henri. 2006. *American Vertigo: Traveling America in the Footsteps of Tocqueville*. Random House.
Lodge, Rupert C. 2000 [1953]. *Plato's Theory of Art*. London: Routledge and Kegan Paul.
Loesser, Frank. 1961. *How to Succeed in Business Without Really Trying*. Broadway musical.
Luhmann, Niklas. 2012 [1997]. *Theory of Society*. Stanford California: Stanford University Press.
——. 1982. *The Differentiation of Society*. New York: Columbia University Press.
Lukács, Georg. 2010 [1911]. *Soul and Form*. New York: Columbia University Press.
——. 1990 [1919]. "What is Orthodox Marxism?" Pp. 1–2 in *History and Class Consciousness* by Georg Lukács. London: Merlin Press.
——. 1968 [1916]. *La Théorie du roman*. Paris: Denoël.
Macé, Laurence. (ed.). 2010. *Voltaire: Textes Interdits*. Paris: Editions Garnier.
Machiavelli, Niccolò. 2012 [1513–32]. *The Prince*. London: Simon and Brown.
——. 2008 [1517]. *Discourses on the First Decade of Titus Livy*. London: K. Paul.
Makkreel, Rudolf. 2012. "Wilhelm Dilthey." *The Stanford Encyclopedia of Philosophy*. Edited by Edward N. Zalta. http://plato.stanford.edu/archives/sum2012/entries/dilthey/.
Marcuse, Herbert. 2006 [1955]. *Eros and Civilization: a Philosophical Inquiry into Freud*. Boston: Beacon Press.
Marcuse, Herbert. 1991 [1964]. *One Dimensional Man: Studies in the Ideology of Advanced Industrial Society*. Boston: Beacon Press.
Martin-Hagg, Éliane. 2008. "Encore un effort pour être raisonnable." *Magazine Littéraire* 478: 66.
Marx, Karl. 1992a [1845]. "Concerning Feuerbach." Pp. 421–423 in *Karl Marx: Early Writings*. London: Penguin.
——. 1992b [1844]. *Economic and Philosophical Manuscripts*. [First published 1932.] In *Karl Marx: Early Writings*. London: Penguin.
——. 1990 [1867]. *Capital, Volume I*. Introduction by E. Mandel. London: Penguin Books.
—— and Friedrich Engels. 1988 [1845]. *The German Ideology*. Amherst, New York: Prometheus Books.
—— and Friedrich Engels. 1980 [1948]. *The Communist Manifesto*. New York: Penguin Books.
——. 1970 [1859]. *A Contribution to the Critique of Political Economy*. Trans. by S.W. Ryazanskaya, edited by Maurice Dobb. New York: International Publishers.
Mazauric, Claude. (ed.). 1989 [1789–1794]. *Robespierre: écrits*. Paris: Messidor.
McCloskey, Deirdre N. 2010. *Bourgeois Dignity: Why Economics Can't Explain the Modern World*. Chicago: University of Chicago Press.
——. 2006. *The Bourgeois Virtues: Ethics for an Age of Commerce*. Chicago: University of Chicago Press.
Merleau-Ponty, Maurice. 1996 [1945]. *Sens et non-sens*. Paris: Gallimard.
——. 1962 [1945]. *La Phénoménologie de la perception*. London: Routledge.
——. 1942. *Structure of Comportement*. Paris: PUF.
Merton, Robert K. 1968 [1949]. *Social Theory and Social Structure*. [3rd Edition.] New York: The Free Press.
Miller, James. 1994. *The Passion of Michel Foucault*. New York: Anchor Books.
Miller, Judith. 2009 [1970]. Cited in the French weekly magazine, *Le Nouvel Observateur*, 13 February 2009, of an interview by Judith Miller given to another French magazine, *l'Express*, in March 1970.
Mills, Charles W. 2000 [1959]. *The Sociological Imagination*. New York: Oxford University Press.
——. 1971 [1956]. *The Power Elite*. Boston: Beacon Press.

Milton, John. 2010 [1658–1664]. *Paradise Lost.* New York: Signet Classics.

Milza, Pierre. 2008. "Les ambiguïtés assumées du philosophe de Ferney." *Magazine Littéraire* 478: 68.

Mitchell, Jon P. 2007. "A fourth critic of the Enlightenment: Michel de Certeau and the ethnography of subjectivity." *Social Anthropology* 15(1): 89–106.

Montesquieu, Charles de Secondat. 2011 [1748]. *L'esprit des lois.* Paris: Flammarion.

More, Thomas. 1988 [1516]. *Utopia.* London: Penguin Books.

——. 1935 [1515]. *L'ile d'Utopie ou La Meilleur Des Républiques.* Paris: Albin Michel.

Morrison, Toni. 2012. *Home.* New York: Knopf. CBC radio interview: http://www.cbc.ca/q/blog/2012/08/28/best-of-q-toni-morrison/.

——. 2003. "No body of evidence." London: The Times of London, June 3. http://business.timesonline.co.uk/tol/business/law/article1138193.ece.

Moulakis, Athanasios. 2011. "Civic Humanism." *Stanford Encyclopedia of Philosophy.* Winter.

Nicholas, Saul. 2002. "Goethe the Writer and Literary History." Pp. 23–41 in *The Cambridge Companion to Goethe,* edited by Lesley Sharpe. Cambridge: Cambridge University Press.

Nietzsche, Friedrich. 2005a [1888]. *Le Crépuscule des Idoles ou Comment on Philosophe au Marteau.* [*Twilight of the Idols, or, How to Philosophize with a Hammer.*] *Friedrich Nietzsche: Oeuvres.* Paris: Robert Laffont.

——. 2005b [1881]. *Aurore: Réflexions sur les préjugés moraux.* [*The Dawn of Day /and/ Daybreak: Reflections on Moral Prejudices.*] *Friedrich Nietzsche: Oeuvres.* Paris: Robert Laffont.

——. 2000 [1872]. *The Birth of Tragedy.* Oxford: Oxford University Press.

——. 1989 [1886]. *Beyond Good and Evil.* New York: Random House.

O'Brien, John E. 1989. "Organizations as Systems." Presented at the Annual Meeting of the Oregon Academy of Sciences.

Olson, Elder. (ed.). 1965. *Aristotle's "Poetics" and English Literature: A Collection of Critical Essays.* Chicago: University of Chicago Press.

Packard, Vance. 1991 [1957]. *The Hidden Persuaders.* London: Penguin.

—— 1989. *The Ultra Rich: How Much Is Too Much?* Boston: Little Brown.

—— 1977. *The People Shapers.* New York: Bantam Books.

——. 1974 [1964]. *The Naked Society.* New York: Pocket Books.

——. 1973 [1960]. *The Waste Makers.* New York: Pocket Books.

——. 1962. *The Pyramid Climbers.* New York: McGraw-Hill.

——. 1959. *The status seekers; an exploration of class behavior in America and the hidden barriers that affect you, your community, your future.* London: Longmans.

Parsons, Talcott. 1991 [1951]. *The Social System.* New York: Free Press.

—— and Neil J. Smelser. 2002 [1956]. *Economy and Society.* London: Routledge.

—— and Gerald M. Platt. 1973. *The American University.* Boston: Harvard University Press.

Partenie, Catalin. 2011. "Plato's Myths." *The Stanford Encyclopedia of Philosophy* (Fall Edition), edited by Edward N. Zalta. http://plato.stanford.edu/archives/fall2011/entries/plato-myths/.

Polanyi, Michael. 2007 [1952]. *Personal Knowledge: Toward a Post-Critical Philosophy.* Chicago: University of Chicago Press.

Rajchman, John. 2007. "Introduction: Enlightenment Today." In *The Politics of Truth* by Michel Foucault, edited by S. Lotringer. Los Angeles: Semiotext(e).

Rancière, Jacques. 2007 [1995]. *On the Shores of Politics.* London: Verso.

——. 2004. *The Politics of Aesthetics: The Distribution of the Sensible.* London: Continuum.

——. 2002. "The Aesthetic Revolution and its outcomes: Emplotments of Autonomy and Heteronomy." *New Left Review* 14: 133–151.

Rand, Ayn. 1957. *Atlas Shrugged.* New York: Random House.

Rawls, John. 1993. *Political Liberalism.* New York, N.Y.: Columbia University Press.

——. 1971. *Theory of Justice.* Boston: Harvard University Press.

Redman, Ben Ray. 1977 [1949]. *The Portable Voltaire.* New York: Penguin Books.

Reed, T.J. 2002. "Weimar Classicism: Goethe's Alliance with Schiller." Pp. 101–113 in *The Cambridge Companion to Goethe*, edited by Lesley Sharpe. Cambridge: Cambridge University Press.

Rorty, Richard. 2009 [1979]. *Philosophy and the Mirror of Nature*. Princeton: Princeton University Press.

——. 2007 [1989]. *Contingency, Irony, and Solidarity*. New York: Cambridge University Press.

Russell, Bertrand. 2003 [1941]. *Let the People Think*. London: Spokesman.

——. 1950. *Unpopular Essays*. London: George Allen and Unwin.

Saïd, Edward W. 2007. *On Late Style: Music and Literature Against the Grain*. New York: Random House.

Sartre, Jean-Paul. 1945. *L'existentialisme est un humanisme*. [*Existentialism is a Humanism.*] Paris: Nagel.

——. 1944. *Huit Clos suivi de Les Mouches*. [*No Exit, followed by The Flies.*] Paris: Gallimard.

——. 1943. *L'Être et le Néant: essai d'ontologie phénoménologique*. [*Being and Nothingness.*] Paris: Gallimard.

Savater, Fernando. 2008. "La Plaie toujours ouverte du fanatisme." *Magazine Littéraire* 478: 70.

Schiller, Friedrich. 1998 [1793]. *Grâce Et Dignité et autres textes par Friedrich Schiller*. Edited by Nicolas Briand. Paris: Vrin.

——. 1972 [1789]. "The Nature and Value of Universal History." *History and Theory* 11(3): 321–334.

——. 1804. *William Tell*. http://www.gutenberg.org.

——. 1801. *On the Sublime*. http://www.gutenberg.org.

——. 1796. *On Narrative and Reflective Poetry*. http://www.gutenberg.org.

——. 1795. *On the Aesthetic Education of Man in a Series of Letters*. [Gutenberg Public Domain site, includes most major Schiller writings.] http://www.gutenberg.org/files/6798/6798-h/6798-h.htm.

——. 1794. *On the Pathetic*. http://www.gutenberg.org.

——. 1789–1791. *History of the Thirty-Years War*. http://www.gutenberg.org.

——. 1788. *History of the Netherlands*. http://www.gutenberg.org.

——. 1787. *Don Carlos*. http://www.gutenberg.org.

——. 1785. *Ode to Joy*. http://www.gutenberg.org.

——. 1784. *Intrigue and Love*. http://www.gutenberg.org.

——. 1783. *Fiesco: or, the Genoese Conspiracy*. http://www.gutenberg.org.

——. 1781. *The Robbers*. http://www.gutenberg.org.

Schnabel, Johann Gottfried. 1977 [1731]. *L'ile de Felsenbourg*. Paris: Fayard.

Schutz, Alfred. 1997 [1932]. *Phenomenology of the Social World*. Evanston, Ill.: Northwestern University Press.

Scott-Kilvert, Ian. (ed.). 1965. *Plutarch: Makers of Rome*. London: Penguin Books.

Shakespeare, William. 2008 [~1595]. *Richard II*. London: Penguin.

——. 2004 [~1596]. *The Merchant of Venice*. New York: Norton.

Spengler, Oswald. 1926/1928. *The Decline of the West* [V1: "Form and Actuality"; V2: "Perspectives of World History."] New York: Alfred A. Knopf. http://archive.org/details/Decline-Of-The-West-Oswald-Spengler.

Stearns, Peter N. 2008 [1998]. "Why Study History." *The American Historical Association*. http://www.historians.org/pubs/free/WhyStudyHistory.htm.

Stendhal, Marie-Henri Beyle. 1839 and 1841. *La Chartreuse de Parme*. [*Deux Tomes:*] http://gallica.bnf.fr/ark:/12148/bpt6k6900c.

——. 1830. *Le Rouge et le Noir: chronique du XIX siècle*. http://gallica.bnf.fr/ark:/12148/btv1b8623298f.

Stevens, Robert. 2004. "Schiller's *Don Carlos*: the 'light and warmth' of a timeless play." *World Socialist Web Site*. 12 November 2004. http://www.wsws.org/articles/2004/nov2004/schi-n12.shtml.

Stimely, Keith. 1998. "Oswald Spengler: An Introduction to his Life and Ideas." *The Journal for Historical Review*. 17(2): 2ff.

Strobinski, Jean. 1970. *La Relation critique*. Paris: Gallimard.

Sturrock, John. (ed.). 1979. *Structuralism and Since: From Lévi-Strauss to Derrida*. London: Oxford University Press.

Terada, Rei. 2005. "Seeing is Reading." In *Legacies of Paul de Man*, edited by Marc Redfield. A Romantic Circles Praxis Volume, May. http://www.rc.umd.edu/praxis/deman/index.html.

Tilly, Charles. 2007. "Three Visions of History and Theory." *History and Theory* 46(2): 299–307.

Tolstoy, Leo. 2012a [1877]. *Anna Karenina*. New York: Knopf.

——. 2012b [1869]. *War and Peace*. New York: Penguin.

Truzzi, Marcello. 1974. *Verstehen: Subjective Understanding in the Social Sciences*. Boston: Addison-Wesley.

Turner, Victor W. 1974. *Dramas, Fields, and Metaphors: Symbolic Action in Human Society*. Ithaca: Cornell University Press.

——. 1969. *The Ritual Process: Structure and Anti-structure*. Chicago: Aldine.

Vico. 1993 [~1725]. *Oeuvres choisies: memoires, écrits par lui-même, la science nouvelle*. Paris: Gallimard.

Voltaire. 2010 [1717]. "Three Poems: Sur Monsieur Le Duc D'Orléans; Madame de Berri; Regnante Puero." In Laurence Macé (ed.). *Voltaire: Textes Interdits*. Paris: Editions Garnier.

——. 1981 [1752]. *The Portable Voltaire*. Edited by Ben Ray Redman. New York: Viking.

——. 1968a [1731]. *L'Histoire de Charles XII*. Paris: Flammarion.

——. 1968b. *The Complete Works of Voltaire*. Oxford: The Voltaire Foundation.

——. 1900 [1764]. *Philosophical Dictionary*. New York: Carlton House. http://www.gutenberg.org/files/18569/18569-h/18569-h.htm.

——. 1877–1883. *Oeuvres Complètes: Voltaire*. Paris: Garnier. http://fr.wikisource.org/wiki/Livre:Voltaire_-_%C5%92uvres_compl%C3%A8tes_Garnier_tome1.djvu>.

——. 1770. "Épître à l'Auteur du Livre des Trois Imposteurs." University of Chicago Library. http://www.lib.uchicago.edu/efts/VOLTAIRE/restricted/VOLTAIRE.bib.htm.

——. 1761. *Commentaire sur Corneille*. http://www.voltaire.ox.ac.uk/www_vf/ocv/OCV_published_vols_May12.pdf.

——. 1759. *Candide ou l'Optimisme. Nader Web-Library*. http://www.naderlibrary.com/index.htm.

——. 1756a. *Plato's Dream*. http://www.gutenberg.org.

——. 1756b. "Poème sur le désastre de Lisbonne." http://www.gutenberg.org.

——. 1762. *La Pucelle d'Orléans*. http://www.gutenberg.org.

——. 1739. *Siècle de Louis XIV*. http://www.gutenberg.org.

——. 1722–1734 /1894. *Letters Concerning the English Nation*. (*Lettres Philosophiques sur les Anglais*). http://www.gutenberg.org/files/2445/2445-h/2445-h.htm.

Wachowski, Larry and Andy. 1999. *The Matrix: the Film*. Los Angeles: Warner Pictures.

Wallerstein, Immanuel. 1974, 1980, 1989, 2011. *The Modern World System: Four Volumes*. Berkeley: The University of California Press.

Walsh, William H. 1968 [1951]. *An Introduction to the Philosophy of History*. New York: Harper and Row.

Wells, H.G. 1987 [1895]. *The Definitive Time Machine: a Critical Edition*. Edited by Harry M Geduld. Bloomington, Ind.: Indiana University Press.

White, Hayden. 2010. *The Fiction of Narrative: Essays on History, Literature and Theory*. Edited by Robert Doran. Baltimore: Johns Hopkins University Press.

——. 2007. "Guilty of History? The Longue Durée of Paul Ricoeur." *Journal of History and Theory* 46(2): 233–251.

——. 1992. *Historical Emplotment and the Problem of Truth. Probing the Limits of Representation: Nazism and the 'Final Solution'.* Edited by Saul Friedlander. Cambridge: Harvard University Press.

——. 1990 [1987]. *Content of Form*. [Papers from 1979–1985.] Baltimore: Johns Hopkins University Press.

——. 1985 [1978]. *Tropics of Discourse: Essays in Cultural Criticism.* Baltimore: The Johns Hopkins University Press.

——. 1984. "The Question of Narrative in Contemporary Historical Theory." *History and Theory* 23(1): 1–33.

——. 1982. "The Politics of Historical Interpretation: Discipline and De-Sublimation." *Critical Inquiry* 9(1): 113–137.

——. 1980. "The Value of Narrativity in the Representation of Reality." *Critical Inquiry* 7(1): 5–27.

——. 1979. "Michel Foucault." Pp. 81–115 in *Structuralism and Since* by John Sturrock. Oxford: Oxford University Press.

——. 1973. *Metahistory: The Historical Imagination in Nineteenth-Century Europe.* Baltimore: Johns Hopkins University Press.

——. 1972. "The Irrational and the Problem of Historical Knowledge in the Enlightenment." *Studies in Eighteenth-Century Culture:* V 2. *Irrationalism in the Eighteenth Century.* Edited by Harold E. Pagliaro. Cleveland: Case Western Reserve University Press.

——. 1966. "The Burden of History." *History and Theory* 5(2): 111–134.

Wilde, Oscar. 2009 [1890]. *The Picture of Dorian Gray.* http://www.gutenberg.org/ebooks/14192.

——. 1895. *The Importance of Being Earnest: a Trivial Comedy for Serious People.* http://www.gutenberg.org/ebooks/844.

Williams, Raymond. 1981. "English Brecht." London: *London Review of Books* 3(13): 16 July. http://www.lrb.co.uk/v03/n13/raymond-williams/english-brecht.

——. 1968. (ed.). *May Day Manifesto.* Harmondsworth: Penguin.

Wolfe, Katharine. 2006. "From Aesthetics to Politics: Rancière, Kant and Deleuze." *Contemporary Aesthetics* 4.

Wroe, Nicolas. 2002. "High Priest of Lit Crit." London: *The Guardian,* 2 February. http://www.guardian.co.uk/books/2002/feb/02/academicexperts.highereducation.

Žižek, Slavoj. 2012. *Less Than Nothing: Hegel and the Shadow of Dialectical Materialism.* London: Verso.

——. 1996. *The Indivisible Remainder: Essays on Schelling and Related Matters.* London: Verso.

——. 1989. *The Sublime Object of Ideology.* London: Verso.

Zukert, Catherine. 2005. "The Stranger's Political Science vs. Socrates' Political Art." Online *Journal of the International Plato Society* 5. http://www.nd.edu/~plato/plato5issue/contents5.htm.

INDEX